The King's Felons

OXFORD LEGAL HISTORY SERIES

General Editors: Paul Brand, Joshua Getzler, and Daniel Hulsebosch

This series presents original work in legal history from all periods. Contributions to the series analyse diverse legal traditions, including common law; *ius commune*, civilian and canon law; colonial, imperial, and international law; and customary, religious, and non-Western cultures of law. The series embraces methods ranging from doctrinal and juristic analysis through to every variety of historical, social scientific, and philosophical enquiry. A leading purpose of the series is to investigate how legal ideas and practices operated in larger historical contexts. Our authors trace changes in legal thought and practice and the interactions of law with political and constitutional institutions and wider movements in social, economic, cultural, and intellectual life.

The King's Felons

Church, State, and Criminal Confinement in Early Tudor England

MARGARET MCGLYNN

Professor of History, Western University

OXFORD
UNIVERSITY PRESS

OXFORD
UNIVERSITY PRESS

Great Clarendon Street, Oxford, OX2 6DP,
United Kingdom

Oxford University Press is a department of the University of Oxford.
It furthers the University's objective of excellence in research, scholarship,
and education by publishing worldwide. Oxford is a registered trade mark of
Oxford University Press in the UK and in certain other countries

First Edition published in 2023

Published in the United States of America by Oxford University Press
198 Madison Avenue, New York, NY 10016, United States of America

British Library Cataloguing in Publication Data

Data available

Library of Congress Control Number is on file at the Library of Congress

ISBN 978–0–19–288768–9

DOI: 10.1093/oso/9780192887689.001.0001

The prince should avoid every novel idea in so far as he is capable of doing so; for even if conditions are bettered thereby, the very innovation is a stumbling block. The establishment of a state, the unwritten laws of a city, or the old legal code are never changed without great confusion. Therefore, if there is anything of this sort that can be endured, it should not be changed but should either be tolerated or happily diverted to a better function.

Erasmus, *The Education of a Christian Prince*

A mistake the historian can easily make is to assume that a blank in his evidence means that nothing was happening; and when the materials do begin to show something happening he interprets that as a large change, for which he sometimes imagines large intentions.

S.F.C. Milsom, *A Natural History of the Common Law*
(New York: Columbia University Press, 2003), p. 76

Preface

About twenty years ago I learned that Edward Hall gave a series of lectures in the spring of 1540 on *Seint Eglise*. Hall is a well-known Tudor historian, and his career as a lawyer is a standard part of his biography. The fact that he gave these lectures has attracted less attention, and the fact that he chose to deliver them on this topic at a particularly delicate moment in the development of the English Reformation, practically none. Working on Hall's reading prompted me to wonder how common lawyers thought about the Church and their relationship to it in the decades leading up to the Reformation, and that question started me down the path which has led to this book. As historical questions usually do, it has both broadened and narrowed. An edition of a series of readings on topics related to the Church established the places where the lawyers most often encountered the Church professionally and intellectually (for their personal religious beliefs were not the subject of my enquiry), and of those topics sanctuary and benefit of clergy emerged as the most live, controversial, and, frankly, engaging. The picture of them in the historiography was not at all the same as the picture in the readings, and I set out to understand the discrepancy.

This book is the result. It re-frames benefit of clergy and sanctuary as vital elements in a pragmatic move on the part of the English judiciary to reform the administration of criminal justice by providing a consistent and reliable way to punish convicted felons without executing them. It uses legal records and treatises alongside episcopal registers to track actual practices in both the secular and the ecclesiastical systems. It recognizes that the secular and ecclesiastical authorities had their own distinct understandings of the system and how it worked and that for the most part both authorities co-operated effectively and productively. It demonstrates that both contemporary and current discussions have been shaped by the discourses of law, politics, and religion as well as by the important events of the day which drew on those discourses, and all of those have shaped the way the system worked, as well as the way in which we approach it. But at its core it is an analysis of how the recorded experiences of approximately 2,000 men (and a handful of women) allow us to see a lived experience which is quite different from what we would expect from most of those discourses and important events. The specifics of the argument will, I hope, be of interest to historians of both legal practice and legal doctrine as well as to historians of the Reformation. The general approach will be of interest to anyone thinking about how we look at how institutions interact, how they navigate change and the relationship between surviving records and the reality on the ground. But the book as a whole will, I hope, be of interest to anyone who has ever wondered how ordinary people might have navigated a fairly ferocious criminal justice system. Faint as their voices often are at this distance, their resilience, their variety, and their sheer ingenuity never cease to amaze.

Acknowledgements

It is always a pleasure to be able to thank those who have supported the long, slow incubation that every book requires. This book draws on research supported by the Social Sciences and Humanities Research Council of Canada (SSHRC), and I remain grateful for SSHRC's commitment to the support of curiosity-driven research. The research was conducted in a variety of archives and libraries: English medieval historians are blessed, not only by the richness of the records with which we work, but by the enthusiasm and expertise of the archivists and librarians who preserve them and make them available to us. My greatest debt is without doubt to the National Archives in Kew and to Robert Palmer for the Anglo-American Legal Tradition project (http://aalt.law.uh.edu), without which this project would quite simply have been impossible for me. Bob Palmer's and Susanne Brand's dedicated and selfless work have made much possible for many. I am also grateful for the swift and expert help I received from many other archives, both public and private: from the Surrey History Centre, especially Guz Gonzalez; from the Staffordshire Record Office, especially Tim Groom, Rebecca Jackson, and Liz Street; from the Hampshire Record Office; from Dominic Farr at the William Salt Library; from Susan Tomkins, archivist to Lord Montagu of Beaulieu; from Chris Webb at the Borthwick Institute for Archives; from Mathew Payne at the Westminster Abbey Muniments; and from the staff of the Lambeth Palace Library.

I also want to express my appreciation for the colleagues who have debated and discussed criminal justice with me over the last several years and without whose insights, arguments, and much-appreciated references this book would be much poorer, especially Krista Kesselring, Sarah Butler, Paul Cavill, the late Mark Ormrod, and Kit French. Matt Davison spent time thinking about King's Bench rolls and explaining Stats 101 to a historian when he had many more urgent claims on his time, and I am grateful for his expertise and his patience. Tom Green read an early version of the book, and his insightful, probing, and occasionally oblique commentary pushed me to think about what I really wanted to say. Paul Brand provided much-needed moral support at an early crisis point in the development of this project and a keen editorial eye at the end, and I am enormously grateful for both, as well as for his enthusiasm for the project throughout.

As I appreciate the benefits of being in the second half of my career, I find myself reflecting on the influences that brought me to where I am. This book is dedicated to three men whose words and deeds particularly influenced me as a researcher, teacher, and administrator at the beginning of my career: the late Thomas F. Mayer, Richard I. Schneider, and Guy MacLean Rogers.

But as always, my greatest thanks go to Richard, without whom none of this would be possible or fun, and to Niamh and Ardith, who still have only the vaguest idea what I do, but who accept it as a thread that runs through all our lives.

Contents

List of Figures

List of Tables

Abbreviations

Primary Sources

AALT	The Anglo-American Legal Tradition website: http://aalt.law.uh.edu. [image(s) . . .] after TNA KB9 or TNA KB27 references refer to AALT images.
Bracton	*Bracton on the Laws and Customs of England* ed. George Woodbine, trans. Samuel E. Thorne. Cambridge, MA: Belknap Press of Harvard University Press, 1968. 4 vols.
Britton	*Britton: An English Translation and Notes* ed. F.M. Nichols. Washington: J. Byrne & Co, 1901.
Brooke	Robert Brooke, *La Graunde Abridgement*. London: Richard Tottell, 1573. Repr. Clark, New Jersey: The Lawbook Exchange, 2015.
Caryll's Reports	John Caryll, *Reports of Cases by John Caryll* ed. J.H. Baker. 2 vols. Selden Society vol. 115 & 116. London: Selden Society, 1999 & 2000.
CPR	*Calendar of the Patent Rolls Preserved in the Public Record Office: Henry VII*. 2 vols. London: HMSO, 1916. Nendeln, Lichenstein: Kraus Reprint, 1970.
	Calendar of the Patent Rolls Preserved in the Public Record Office: Philip & Mary. 4 vols. London: HMSO, 1937. Nendeln, Lichenstein: Kraus Reprint, 1970.
Fitz	Anthony Fitzherbert, *La Graunde Abridgement*. London: Richard Tottell, 1577. Repr. Clark, New Jersey: The Lawbook Exchange, 2009.
Fleta	*Fleta* ed. H.G. Richardson and G.O. Sayles. SS vols. 72, 89, 99. London: Selden Society, 1953, 1955, 1984.
Lib. Ass.	*Liber Assisarum*
Lords' Journal	*Journal of the House of Lords: Volume 1, 1509–1577*. London, 1802.
LP	*Letters and Papers, Foreign and Domestic, of the Reign of Henry VIII, 1509–1547*. Edited by J.S. Brewer et al. 21 vols. London: Longmans, HMSO, 1862–1932.
Port's Notebook	Sir John Port. *The Notebook of Sir John Port* ed. J.H. Baker. Selden Society vol. 102. London: Selden Society, 1986.
PROME	*Parliament Rolls of Medieval England*, ed. P. Brand, S. Phillips, M. Ormrod, G. Martin, C. Given-Wilson, A. Curry and R. Horrox. Woodbridge, 2005.
Reg. Bothe	*The Register of Charles Bothe, Bishop of Hereford, 1516–1535* ed. Arthur Thomas Bannister. London: Wilson and Phillips, 1921.

Reg. King and Castello	*The Registers of Oliver King, Bp of Bath & Wells 1496–1503 and Hadrian de Castello Bp of Bath & Wells 1503–1518* ed. Henry Maxwell-Lyte. Somerset Record Society vol. liv. Frome & London: Butler & Tanner Ltd, 1939.
Reg. Langton	*The Register of Thomas Langton, Bishop of Salisbury, 1485–93* ed. D.P. Wright. Canterbury and York Society vol. 74. 1985.
Reg. Longland	Register of Bishop John Longland: LAO Episcopal Register XXVI.
Reg. Morton	*The Register of John Morton, Archbishop of Canterbury, 1486–1500*, ed. Christopher Harper-Bill. Canterbury and York Society, vols. 75, 78, 89. Vol. 1: Leeds: Duffield Printers, 1987; vol. 2, Variae Sede Vacante: Woodbridge: Boydell Press, 1991; vol. 3, Norwich Sede Vacante, 1499: Woodbridge: Boydell Press, 2000
Reg. Rotherham	Borthwick Inst. Yorks Abp Reg. 23
Reg. Savage	Borthwick Inst. Yorks Abp Reg. 25
Reg. Warham	Lambeth Palace Library, Register of William Warham. 2 vols.
Reports from Henry VIII	J.H. Baker, *Reports of Cases from the Time of King Henry VIII.* 2 volumes. SS vols. 120 & 121. London: Selden Society, 2003, 2004.
Rights and Liberties	*The Rights and Liberties of the English Church: Readings from the pre-Reformation Inns of Court* ed. Margaret McGlynn, SS vol. 129. London: Selden Society, 2016.
Rot. Parl.	*Rotuli Parliamentorum: ut et Petitiones, et Placita in Parliamento*. 8 vols. London, 1780–1832.
Sanctuarium Dunelmense	*Sanctuarium Dunelmense et Sanctuarium Beverlacense* ed. James Raine. Surtees Society vol. 5. London, 1837.
Spelman's Reports	Sir John Spelman. *The Reports of Sir John Spelman* ed. J.H. Baker. SS vols. 93 & 94. London: Selden Society, 1976, 1977.
SR	*Statutes of the Realm*. 11 vols. London, 1810–1822.
SS	Selden Society
TNA	The National Archives, Kew
YB	Year book

Secondary Sources

Bellamy, *Criminal Law and Society*	John G. Bellamy, *Criminal Law and Society in Late Medieval and Tudor England*. New York: St. Martins, 1984.
Helmholz, *Ius Commune*	R. H. Helmholz, *The Ius Commune in England: Four Studies*. Oxford: Oxford University Press, 2001.
Gabel, *Benefit of Clergy*	Leona C. Gabel, *Benefit of Clergy in England in the Later Middle Ages*. Smith College Studies in History vol. 14. Northampton MA: Smith College, 1929. Repr. New York: Octagon Books, 1969.
Kesselring, *Mercy and Authority*	K.J. Kesselring, *Mercy and Authority in the Tudor State*. Cambridge: Cambridge University Press, 2003.

McSheffrey, *Seeking Sanctuary*	Shannon McSheffrey, *Seeking Sanctuary: Crime, Mercy and Politics in English Courts, 1400–1550.* Oxford: Oxford University Press, 2017.
Pugh, *Imprisonment in Medieval England*	Pugh, Ralph B. *Imprisonment in Medieval England.* Cambridge, Cambridge University Press, 1968.
Thornley, 'Destruction of Sanctuary'	I.D Thornley, 'The Destruction of Sanctuary'. *Tudor Studies Presented to A.F. Pollard* edited by R.W. Seton-Watson, 182–207. London: Longmans Green & Co., 1924.

Introduction

The Big Picture

This book tells a story of failure: the failure of the English criminal justice system to establish imprisonment as a standard punishment for felony in the sixteenth century. Historical failures tend to be relegated to footnotes rather than given the main billing, but this failure is worthy of close examination because for several decades it seemed to be a success. Its emergence, expansion and eventual collapse is not just a historical curiosity, or even a fascinating glimpse into the lived experience of criminal justice, but a window into the process of legal change in the early Tudor period, the transition from medieval to early modern governance, and the dangers of allowing dominant historiographical models to drive our assumptions about historical change.

This story is also largely unknown, for the history of criminal justice in the reigns of the first three Tudors is something of a black hole. The crucial sources, the gaol delivery records, do not survive for this period—having disappeared in the 1460s, they begin to appear again in the 1560s, but do not survive in substantial numbers until the seventeenth century.[1] As a result, we know, and can know, far less about crime and law enforcement in the sixteenth century than in the thirteenth or fourteenth centuries.[2] Without the records of the activities in the counties that we have for the medieval and early modern centuries, discussions of criminal justice in the early sixteenth century tend to focus on the activities of the central government (things like statutes, reports, and pardons) for which records survive, which unavoidably skew our perceptions of what was happening on the ground. There is, however, one largely untapped central source that offers some hope of understanding the system more broadly. The records of the court of King's Bench can serve as a proxy for the kinds of problems that were being raised on circuit, and they allow us to get a fairly good sense of how its judges were approaching criminal law in these years, even if we are left with lots of questions about the scope of the work in the counties. And those records indicate that from the 1490s to the 1530s the judges engaged in a period of active and intensive reform of the criminal justice system, the first stage of which centered on a reform of benefit of clergy while the second and truncated stage began a similar reform of sanctuary.

[1] See chapter 3 below for a full discussion of the criminal justice system.
[2] G.R. Elton, *England, 1200–1640* (Ithaca and London: Cornell University Press, 1969), p. 62.

The King's Felons. Margaret McGlynn, Oxford University Press. © Margaret McGlynn 2023.
DOI: 10.1093/oso/9780192887689.003.0001

This reform drew on centuries of interaction between secular and ecclesiastical authorities, interaction which was mostly co-operative but which was punctuated by periods of productive conflict. By the mid-fifteenth century this had led to the development of a common-law concept of benefit of clergy which was separate from, if mostly compatible with, the ecclesiastical version. When Henry VII set out to restore order after his accession to the throne, this concept, and the ecclesiastical machinery associated with it, was ready and waiting to be exploited. In 1490 parliament passed a statute limiting the use of benefit of clergy for laymen: this probably reflected a desire on the part of its framers to be tough on crime, as statutes tended to. But as it turned out, the statute recognized and solidified the reality of the common law version of benefit of clergy, identifying it explicitly for the first time as a separate entity available to lay felons. The standard assumption is that common lawyers were hostile to benefit of clergy and sought to eradicate it, or at the very least to curtail it, but by the late fifteenth century the opposite was true for the King's Bench judges: they sought to co-opt it. After the passage of the statute they began to extend their authority over ecclesiastical prisons, and thus over the fate of clerks convict after their delivery to the ecclesiastical authorities.[3] Though we don't know the author of this policy, it's tempting to attribute it to John Fyneux, who became chief justice of King's Bench in 1495 and who enunciated the closest thing to a statement of this policy in a year book argument of 1500.[4] As chief justice, he presided over a series of understated but effective changes over the next thirty years which brought the administration of benefit of clergy ever further under secular control. As a result of these changes benefit of clergy became a mechanism for intentionally sending convicted felons to prison rather than to the gallows. Though we don't have the records to provide definitive numbers, the snapshots that survive in King's Bench suggest that by the early sixteenth century about 25 per cent of convicted felons were being imprisoned in ecclesiastical prisons at the behest of the judges, somewhat to the irritation of the ecclesiastical hierarchy who had to absorb this cost in order to maintain their own separate but related privilege.

Through the years in which they were developing this system, as we will see, the judges were willing to work around relevant statutory provisions, largely seeing

[3] Margaret McGlynn, 'Ecclesiastical Prisons and Royal Authority in the Reign of Henry VII', *Journal of Ecclesiastical History* 70.4 (2019), pp. 750–766.

[4] Fyneux presided over a quiet resurgence of King's Bench, pursuing a consistent policy of extending common law jurisdiction wherever possible. See Sir John Baker, *The Men of Court 1440 to 1550: A Prosopography of the Inns of Court and Chancery and the Courts of Law* vol. 1, Selden Society Suppl. Ser. vol. 18 (London: Selden Society, 2012), pp. 722–723; Robert C. Palmer, *Selling the Church: the English Parish in Law, Commerce and Religion 1350–1550*, (Chapel Hill: University of North Carolina Press, 2002), pp. 6, 25–27, 62–66 for a discussion of Fyneux's approach to praemunire, tithes and defamation, which has striking parallels to his approach to benefit of clergy, and Marjorie Blatcher, *The Court of King's Bench 1450–1550: A Study in Self-Help* (London: The Athlone Press, 1978), for an outline of the state of King's Bench in these years. See also Richard M. Wunderli, *London Church Courts and Society on the Eve of the Reformation* (Cambridge, MA: The Medieval Academy of America, 1981), pp. 67–68 for the effect on defamation cases in the London Church courts.

them as options to be exercised rather than rules to be followed. The success of their campaign meant that more men than ever were being imprisoned, however, and the prohibition against repeat claims in the 1490 statute, which had largely been honoured in the breach, came to prominence in the 1520s. A large-enough number of men were being imprisoned for short-enough periods of time that it mattered that they were getting out and re-offending, but the courts were stymied by a lack of information. They could not link the records of men convicted of felonies on different circuits or far apart in time confidently enough to be sure that they were catching repeat offenders. Fyneux responded in 1519 by trying to establish a central repository for the records of all men who claimed benefit of clergy: the assize justices were ordered to return the records of all those who had successfully claimed since the beginning of the reign, and to continue to return such records in the future.[5] This was an overly ambitious plan, and the response from the circuits was dilatory and varied, but even as it failed it established two principles: repeat offenders should not get benefit of clergy, and the justices of King's Bench should have prompt access to circuit records in order to conduct their own business. In the 1520s repeat offenders were much more likely to be denied benefit of clergy than before: the 1490 statute was finally effective once the lawyers established the structures they needed to administer it.

Around the same time, the judges turned their attention to sanctuary, and more precisely to abjuration. Sanctuary remained a regular part of the criminal justice system through this period, though one in which the common law was only peripherally involved: the common lawyers accepted the right of felons to claim sanctuary, and the courts protected those who were drawn from sanctuary against their will or abducted on their abjuration route, while coroners took the confessions of those who chose to abjure. Right into the sixteenth century sanctuaries provided an important place of respite while the consequences of a crime were being negotiated, and a way for felons to choose a self-imposed punishment which was outside the common law but recognized by it. As the judges became increasingly comfortable with their control of the management of benefit of clergy they turned their attention to sanctuary and looked for a way to establish a similar kind of control over this process, bringing it, or some part of it, within the remit of the common law. As with benefit of clergy, there was no desire to eradicate the process, it was simply too useful. Abjuration was a clear point of entry into the bigger issue, and the justices' first foray reflected the same approach they had taken to benefit of clergy: they sought to manage the process rather than the principle. In the 1520s the justices pressured the coroners to return their records of abjurations more regularly, and to distribute abjurers more evenly across the country in order to ensure that no port would receive a disproportionate number of felons. Though the sources for

[5] Margaret McGlynn, 'From Written Record to Bureaucratic Mind: Imagining a Criminal Record', *Past and Present* 250 (2021), pp. 55–86.

sanctuary and abjuration are even more sparse than for benefit of clergy, it seems likely that they wanted to ensure that those who chose to abjure did in fact leave the country, and that they carried out the process in a way that would ensure the least possible disruption along their route and in their port of departure.

By the late 1520s the common lawyers had thus inserted themselves ever more actively into the management of the ecclesiastical side of the administration of criminal justice: they had largely taken control of benefit of clergy and were well on the way to doing the same with sanctuary. And they had achieved this while staying largely under the radar and out of the political fights over both issues. They were generally not interested in conflict with the ecclesiastical authorities, since they could achieve their objectives much more effectively by the slow and steady assertion of their practical authority. The eruption of the Reformation at the end of the decade changed the political calculus, however, and there was no longer any reason to tiptoe around ecclesiastical sensibilities. The Reformation parliament saw a wave of criminal justice statutes: since many of these dealt with benefit of clergy and sanctuary, they have often been seen as part of the reaction against ecclesiastical authority, but in fact they need to be seen in light of the earlier changes. Statutes passed in the 1530s removed benefit of clergy from the most heinous felonies and limited benefit of clergy for those in orders: both were innovative, but they drew on ineffective statutes from the 1510s and on the developments in the courts in the intervening decades. The statutes on sanctuary look even more novel, most notably the statute of 1531 which prohibited abjuration overseas in favour of abjuration to chartered sanctuaries, thus creating a new site for criminal confinement. As with the benefit of clergy statutes, however, while parliament did innovate, that innovation mostly accelerated the efforts of the 1520s to establish control over sanctuary and did so in a way that was largely consistent with the earlier trajectory. The removal of the political need to conciliate the ecclesiastical hierarchy meant that change could become more visible and happen more quickly, but these were at heart criminal justice reforms, not religious ones.

By 1536 the reform process initiated by Fyneux forty years earlier had come a long way: the judges were clearly in control of the ecclesiastical machinery of criminal justice, they had developed a series of rules around the ways in which that machinery could be used to punish a variety of felonies, and they no longer needed to accommodate themselves practically or politically to the will of the ecclesiastical hierarchy. Though the new system was not perfect, the judges could have been forgiven for feeling that the road lay open before them. Instead, the winds of religious change which had thus far propelled them forwards began to blow their house down. The machinery which they had so effectively co-opted was funded and managed on a day-to-day basis by bishops and abbots, and as bishops and abbots lost power and resources the machinery began to crumble. This is most obvious in the dissolution of the monasteries, which also, and involuntarily, caused the dissolution of the chartered sanctuaries, and with them one of the newly-consolidated sites of criminal confinement. The government responded in 1540 by creating secular sanctuaries to serve the same function, demonstrating their investment in the newly-developed model, but the secular sanctuaries had neither the financial nor the cultural capital of their ancient predecessors, and they fizzled. Less obviously, the bishops, who were bleeding resources and who lost the last vestige of the clerical privilege of benefit of clergy in 1540, also lost interest in feeding, housing and managing lay convicts. The government sought to retrieve what it could of the more ambitious programme by reducing their burdens: a series of increasingly inventive pardon statutes over the 1540s made it easier to release felons from prison more quickly and cheaply than the traditional process had done, and a short-lived statute of 1547 allowed bishops to reduce their costs by handing their clerks convict over as slaves. The latter experiment failed quickly, probably because of revulsion at the idea, while the former failed slowly, probably because it undermined one key development in this entire process: it took away the connection between the convicted felon and the crown by automating his release from prison.

The new model of criminal confinement for felons, developed so painstakingly over decades and revealed to the world in the 1530s, crumbled from within over the course of a decade or so and effectively disappeared from the historical record. Nevertheless it was important, for a number of reasons. Firstly, the entire experiment had saved the lives of thousands of men over the course of the sixteenth century while ensuring that they did not go free but were punished with substantial prison sentences, often in chains, in the bishops' prisons. Though the punishment became less harsh as the numbers grew and the resources shrank, Fyneux's experiment demonstrated that it was possible to link the severity of the crime to the severity of the punishment: by the middle of the sixteenth century somewhere around a quarter of convicted felons had been going to prison for their crimes for several decades, and a felony conviction demonstrably did not necessarily lead to the gallows. Secondly, understanding the developments of the first half of the sixteenth century throws a new light on the developments of the second half. Assize records begin to survive again *c.* 1560, and historians interested in the early modern machinery of justice usually begin to pay attention to developments around, or shortly before, that date. This means that they tend to mistake the aftershocks for the earthquake, for the developments of the 1550s to the 1570s are effectively the last tremors of the Henrician changes. The system at the end of the 1540s remained largely unchanged through the end of the century, for, much-reduced as it was, it was the best match between the needs and the available resources. Contemporaries did not recognize this at the time and both Mary's and Elizabeth's parliaments argued over and finally passed some tweaks to benefit of clergy. But their actions make it clear that benefit of clergy and sanctuary were effectively off the table as a focal point of reform, for that model had required a strong and powerful Church as a partner, grudging as it sometimes was. Without that partner the secular state did not have the resources to sustain an extensive system of criminal confinement: when it finally reached a position where it was both able and somewhat willing to commit those resources, several centuries later, the story began anew, with no connections to this early experiment.

Historians do not, for the most part, like dead ends or failed experiments, revealing though they can be of their circumstances. Fortunately, there is a final consequence of the Henrician reforms which had staying power. Though the substance of the experiment crumbled, the process had engaged the Westminster justices in the machinery of local criminal justice in a new and profound way. They had exerted their authority over ecclesiastical prisons, over local records and over coroners in the process of shaping the criminal justice system. A generation of lawyers had been exposed to Fyneux's assumption that the king should exercise direct authority over his felons, many of whom now survived their conviction, and by the middle of the sixteenth century that assumption pervaded the system. This engagement was manifested in a number of Marian and Elizabethan novelties which nonetheless drew heavily on the experiences of the previous decades. Though the Marian parliaments struggled to make any further changes to benefit of clergy, they were more successful in limiting the local power of justices of the peace and ensuring the oversight of justices of gaol delivery. Elizabeth's justices of gaol delivery were given the authority to submit lists of felons recommended for circuit pardons and to release clerks convict immediately after branding or to imprison them for up to a year at their discretion. These changes meant that by 1575 a system which a century earlier had been dominated by local county interests—sheriffs, justices of the peace, juries and ordinaries—was much more closely managed by the justices of gaol delivery. Those justices assumed their right and ability to oversee the justices of the peace, the sentencing process, the prisons and the pardoning process, and they had demonstrated to juries that a conviction for felony served the needs of justice, since a convict who committed a minor felony or who had mitigating circumstances could expect to be convicted and punished without being executed. The Marian and Elizabethan justices thus reaped the benefits of the Henrician experiment in three ways: they inherited a modest but effective and consistent means of mitigating punishment for minor felonies; they inherited a system which made a higher conviction rate acceptable by normalizing non-capital punishment for those felonies, and they inherited a confidence in their own ability and right to manage the local machinery in order to represent royal authority and mercy in the counties.

This argument is not a familiar one; in fact in many ways it is quite counterintuitive. This is mostly because of the frameworks within which benefit of clergy and sanctuary, the core elements of this criminal justice reform, have been understood and studied over the past century or so. The assumption that they are essentially religious institutions has meant that legal historians have not, for the most part, been terribly interested in the nuances of how they worked. Both are indisputably privileges associated with the Church. Benefit of clergy allowed clerics convicted of felony to be transferred to the ecclesiastical system for punishment rather than face hanging under the common law. By the later Middle Ages, for reasons we will examine below, literate laymen were claiming benefit of clergy and thus claiming the same privilege. Sanctuary was much more ancient than benefit of clergy, and it allowed one accused of a crime to find temporary safety within the precinct of a church. By the later Middle Ages, for reasons we will examine below, different churches claimed to offer wildly varying versions of sanctuary, and it had become associated with the process of abjuration, in which a sanctuary man chose to exile himself rather than face the common law punishment for his crime. Benefit of clergy and sanctuary are often assumed to be complementary privileges, with the former being confined to clerics and the latter to laymen.[6] The extension of benefit of clergy to the laity makes any assumptions about complementarity in that sense obviously untenable, and though it was rarer, clerks did also claim sanctuary; furthermore, it was not unusual for a felon to claim both in sequence. Though both privileges were associated with, and to a large extent administered by, the Church, they actually had surprisingly little in common: as we will see, they originated at very different times and places, rested on very different authorities, and followed very different processes.

In much the same way that the assumption of complementarity has served to flatten the differences between benefit of clergy and sanctuary, their categorization as privileges of the Church has meant that legal historians often perceive them as oddly static. A standard description of benefit of clergy, for example, might draw on sources from *Bracton* to Hale without spending much time qualifying which elements were early or late.[7] This is also, in part, a result of the paucity of sources for the later Middle Ages, and of the assumption that the English criminal law did not change much in this period, particularly outside the crimes most associated with the turmoil of the fifteenth century, such as riot and retaining. The law relating to felonies, for example, remained largely unchanged through the fifteenth century: the legal profession in general was far less interested in the criminal law than in the much more lucrative property law, and as a result gave far less time and attention to its development.[8] Legal historians, like their medieval counterparts, have generally been far less interested in criminal law than property law, preferring the intellectual richness of the jurisprudence around property to the paucity of the

[6] I.D. Thornley, 'Sanctuary in Medieval London', *Journal of the British Archaeological Association* 2nd ser. 38 (1932), pp. 305–306.

[7] Bellamy, *Criminal Law and Society*, pp. 115–118, notes the major statutory changes but his general examples slide quietly between periods; Thomas A. Green, 'The Jury and the English Law of Homicide, 1200–1600', *Michigan Law Review* 74 (1976), p. 488 jumps from the fourteenth century to the 1570s.

[8] David Seipp found 800 reports dealing with criminal law in the year books, from a total of 22,318: David J. Seipp, 'Big History and the Hundred Year Test', *Law and History Review* 34.4 (2016), pp. 857, 859; David J. Seipp, 'Crime in the Year Books', in *Law Reporting in Britain*, edited by Chantal Stebbings (London: Hambledon, 1995), pp. 16–17. The numbers in these papers differ slightly, but the point is the same. Seipp also points out that the proportion of reports of criminal cases to civil ones is higher in the fifteenth century than before.

jurisprudence around crime. Baker, in one of the standard introductions to English legal history, concedes that criminal law does have a history, but in spending the last 36 pages of his 536 page volume on it, he accurately represents the level of interest that criminal law tends to inspire in the field. There are two main reasons for this, which he recognizes: in the first place, criminal records are 'rich in details of everyday life', which make them more suitable for social historians than legal historians.[9] In the second place, much more of the record is about process than about principles; indeed Baker spends 20 of his 36 pages on process. And process will be a key element of this study, for the management and manipulation of process is clearly an important element of legal history. Though we have traditionally thought of legal history as examining what lawyers and judges say, there is a real value to examining what they do, and it turns out that what they do over the course of dozens or hundreds of 'ordinary' cases might be quite different from what they say about the extraordinary cases which make it to the reports or the chronicles, or which influence statutes. That too, is surely legal history, though it may be a social history of the law as well as an intellectual one.

Among those legal historians who have delved deeper into benefit of clergy and sanctuary, the latter has generally attracted more attention than the former, largely because it seems to present both a more immediate threat and a more arresting narrative. According to Isobel Thornley, whose work from the 1930s remains seminal, sanctuaries provided safe havens for hardened criminals who could commit their crimes with impunity knowing that they could retreat to safety and then re-emerge to prey once again on the populace.[10] Well-intentioned reformers sought to curtail or remove such sanctuaries, 'but the medieval Church knew how to defend her own, and it was not until the bonds of Rome were broken that the widespread and acknowledged abuses of sanctuary could be brought under due control'.[11] For Thornley, the destruction of sanctuary was both a defeat for Rome and a victory for England, as the ancient practice was 'drawn into the stream of two great movements: the anti-clerical wave which preceded and facilitated the break with Rome, and the Tudor policy – inevitable in the dawning of a modern age – of destroying all jurisdictions which could rival or resist the power of the King'.[12] This narrative was clear, convincing and appealing in its triumphalist nationalism, and for a long time it was largely accepted that 'the hostile attitude of the royal courts towards special sanctuaries in early Tudor times reflected widespread popular opinion'.[13]

If Thornley saw the destruction of sanctuary as part of the Tudor assertion of national and central control over a burgeoning governing and legal system, she was

[9] J.H. Baker, *An Introduction to English Legal History*, 4th ed. (Oxford: Oxford University Press, 2007), p. 500.
[10] Thornley, 'Destruction of Sanctuary', pp. 187, 188–89, 193.
[11] Thornley, 'Destruction of Sanctuary', p. 182.
[12] Thornley, 'Destruction of Sanctuary', p. 200.
[13] J.H. Baker, 'The English Law of Sanctuary', *Ecclesiastical Law Journal* 2 (1990), p. 11.

simply finishing the story told by earlier scholars, who had often accepted sanctuary as a necessary evil in earlier centuries when royal authority was relatively weak.[14] Indeed Thornley closes her account of the destruction of sanctuary with Hallam's much-quoted assertion that

> under a due administration of justice, this privilege would have been simply and constantly mischievous .... But in the rapine and tumult of the Middle Ages, the right of sanctuary might as often be a shield to innocence as an immunity to crime. We can hardly regret, in reflecting on the desolating violence which prevailed, that there should have been some green spots in the wilderness, where the feeble and the persecuted could find refuge.[15]

This belated concession that sanctuary might once have played a useful role in society has in turn become the foundation of more recent work. The anthropological turn of the last decades of the twentieth century shifted the tone of the entire discussion, exploring the penitential, royal, ecclesiastical and local contexts within which sanctuary worked, and seeing it not as a weak substitute for good governance, but as valuable in itself, part of a spectrum of problem-solving mechanisms ranging from violence to arbitration to litigation among which disputants might choose.[16] Though much of this work has focused on earlier centuries, it has influenced studies of early Tudor sanctuary: in Kesselring's study 'abjuration emerges as a cultural artifact that reflected contemporary assumptions about justice and mercy', and she rejects the idea that there was widespread hostility to sanctuary, pointing out that contemporary criticisms were invariably about abuses, rather than the institution itself.[17] McSheffrey's recent study of a series of unusually well-documented cases situates sanctuary firmly in its social and cultural context.[18] These studies have begun to move the discussion of sanctuary away from the assumption of Church/State conflict that Thornley so clearly embodied, and the

[14] N.M. Trenholme, *The Right of Sanctuary in England* (Columbia MO: University of Missouri, 1903), p. 1; J. Charles Cox, *The Sanctuaries and Sanctuary Seekers of Medieval England* (London: George Allen & Sons, 1911), p. 10.

[15] Henry Hallam, *A View of the State of Europe During the Middle Ages* (London, 1818), vol. 2, p. 449 in Thornley, 'Destruction of Sanctuary', p. 207. Also quoted in Karl Shoemaker, *Sanctuary and Crime in the Middle Ages 400–1500* (New York: Fordham University Press, 2011), p. 2.

[16] Barbara H. Rosenwein, *Negotiating Space: Power, Restraint, and Privileges of Immunity in Early Medieval Europe* (London and Ithaca: Cornell University Press, 1999); Paul Hyams, *Rancor and Reconciliation in Medieval England* (London and Ithaca: Cornell University Press, 2003); T.B. Lambert, 'The Evolution of Sanctuary in Medieval England', in *Legalism: Anthropology and History* edited by Paul Dresch and Hannah Skoda (Oxford: Oxford University Press, 2012), pp. 115–144; Shoemaker, *Sanctuary and Crime*; Gervase Rosser, 'Sanctuary and social negotiation in medieval England', in *The Cloister and the World: Essays on Medieval History in Honour of Barbara Harvey*, edited by John Blair and Brian Golding (Oxford: Clarendon Press, 1996), pp. 57–79.

[17] K.J. Kesselring, 'Abjuration and its Demise: The Changing Face of Royal Justice in the Tudor Period', *Canadian Journal of History* 34 (1999), pp. 346, 354.

[18] McSheffrey, *Seeking Sanctuary*.

assumption that this is the only, or the most productive, lens through which to view it.

The scholarship around benefit of clergy is neither as wide nor as deep nor as recent as that around sanctuary. Benefit of clergy has none of the romance or the aura of socially-determined justice which lingers around sanctuary: despite its origins in canon law it is hard to argue that it is anything other than a bureaucratic right, and even its students tend to see it as anything from a moderate to an outrageous abuse. As with sanctuary, the broad outlines of the way in which benefit of clergy functioned have been well known for a long time; the seminal work in the field remains Leona Gabel's *Benefit of Clergy*, published in 1929. It was reissued in 1969, and in her preface to the re-issue Gabel commented that not much had been added to the state of the question in the intervening 40 years.[19] Another 50 years later, we could make much the same statement. Although benefit of clergy shows up regularly in discussions of crime and disorder and of Church/State relations, there has been little new research on the topic itself.[20] This is partly because Gabel did the obvious thing and did it well—she looked at gaol delivery records of the thirteenth and fourteenth centuries to see who claimed benefit of clergy and for what, and she looked at ecclesiastical records to see what happened to criminous clerks when they were handed over to the Church (though in her period, as later, it was difficult to follow any individual offender through the system). It is also partly because the picture of benefit of clergy we have fits quite comfortably into two clear narratives: first, that a corrupt and beleaguered Church, anxious to maintain its rights, provided a revolving door through which criminous clerks could emerge to prey once again on their flock, or second, that a failure in the development of the criminal law left benefit of clergy as a crude mechanism by which the harshness of punishment could be mitigated, though in an unfortunately indiscriminate—and clerical—way.[21]

And it is here that the traditional historiographies of sanctuary and benefit of clergy come together, for in the early Tudor period both of them can easily be understood as, at worst, outdated rights of a corrupt Church, infringements on the sovereignty of the emerging national state, or inappropriate mitigations of punishment outside the common law, and, at best, as outdated vestiges of an older world, awkward remnants that needed to be cleaned away.[22] And both the words

[19] Gabel, *Benefit of Clergy*.

[20] See, for example, John Bellamy, *Crime and Public Order in England in the Later Middle Ages* (Toronto: University of Toronto Press, 1973), pp. 151–155; R.N. Swanson, *Church and Society in Late Medieval England* (Oxford: Basil Blackwell, 1989), pp. 149–153; John A.F. Thomson, *The Early Tudor Church and Society, 1485–1529* (New York: Longman, 1993), pp. 91–97; G.W. Bernard, *The Late Medieval English Church: Vitality and Vulnerability Before the Break with Rome* (New Haven: Yale University Press, 2012).

[21] Gabel, *Benefit of Clergy*, pp. 126–127; C.B. Firth, 'Benefit of Clergy in the Time of Edward IV', *English Historical Review* 32 (1917), p. 175.

[22] William C. Jordan, *From England to France* (Princeton: Princeton University Press, 2015), p. 145.

and deeds of the common lawyers can appear to support those interpretations. Fyneux, for example, seems to have been driven by the principle that anything that could properly be handled within the common law system should be. This does not mean that he or his colleagues were hostile to the ecclesiastical system, however: as loyal sons of the Church they generally shared its values and assumptions.[23] Indeed these shared values and assumptions allowed the common lawyers to build a synergistic relationship between their needs and those of the Church while they simultaneously asserted the claims of an increasingly stable and confident secular power. Much as the concept of Church/State conflict has been questioned and nuanced in recent decades, it maintains a strong hold on our historical imagination, whether because Church/State conflict is intrinsically more interesting than Church/State co-operation, or because a win/lose scenario is always satisfying. But while judges and lawyers were willing to challenge elements of ecclesiastical jurisdiction over these centuries, their challenges were always particular, always within the context of broad acceptance of the Church's authority, and, for most of the period we'll examine, always part of a process of deepening and broadening the authority that both Church and State exerted over the English population. This balance obviously changed decisively once the English Reformation began, but too much of the history of sanctuary and benefit of clergy in this period has been written with the awareness of what would happen after 1529 in mind. I have tried very hard to write this study with the elephant locked firmly outside the room. If we accept that England's governing classes, and the first two Tudors, saw themselves as loyal sons of the Church before *c.* 1529, and examine the evidence from that perspective, the history of sanctuary and benefit of clergy in this period is not a story of Church/State conflict.

Instead, it starts from the key problem faced by an administration which set out with the avowed intention of restoring order, as Henry VII did in 1485: if it effectively administered the law as it stood, large numbers of convictions for felony would result in large numbers of executions, which was hardly conducive to order. For though there was little principled opposition to the death penalty in Tudor England, and though public executions might draw excited crowds, the state had to be judicious in its use of force: the widespread execution of neighbours, friends and family for crimes which seemed relatively trivial would do more to undermine order than to restore or preserve it.[24] Hay points out that the Hanoverian justices were conscious of the need to balance justice and mercy in order to maintain both fear and respect for a legal system that was far more limited in its resources than it

[23] Wunderli, *London Church Courts*, p. 137 makes the same point about Londoners more generally.

[24] Bellamy points out that crimes were committed by all social groups in numbers roughly proportionate to the size of their memberships, and concludes that 'there was less of a gulf between honest men and criminals than in modern society': Bellamy, *Crime and Public Order*, pp. 29–30. He also notes that it could be difficult to find executioners in practice: *Crime and Public Order*, p. 187. See also J.A. Sharpe, *Judicial Punishment in England* (London: Faber and Faber, 1990), pp. 27, 38–39.

wished to appear—how much more was this true for the Tudors, especially the first of the line?[25] Even if Henry, or his advisors, had been willing to gamble on the outcome of higher conviction rates, it's not clear that they could have achieved them; juries were often unwilling to return guilty verdicts on men and women who had clearly committed the crimes for which they were tried when they felt that a sentence of death was not warranted, a phenomenon known as jury nullification.[26] At the same time, the general population seems to have shared the new king's desire for order. At the end of the fifteenth century there was a broad desire for the Church courts to effectively punish unwelcome behaviour and Wunderli argues that frustration with their inability to do so was the cause for a significant decline in the business of those courts.[27] Similarly, McIntosh argues that local courts in market towns and at the county level were increasingly active both in presenting misbehaviour and in passing by-laws to more closely regulate it in the late fifteenth century and through the sixteenth.[28] The desire for order was widely shared through early Tudor society, but the king whose dynasty's survival might depend on achieving it was effectively stuck between the reality of a system with low conviction rates which was heavily reliant on local feeling rather than the technical requirements of the law, and the possibility of a technically more effective system with higher conviction rates which might so outrage local feeling that it provoked serious opposition. Faced with this conundrum, it is apparent that benefit of clergy and sanctuary were neither irrelevant nor inimical to the development of effective criminal justice; quite the contrary. Benefit of clergy, once it was safely under the watchful eye of the justices, provided an effective and cheap way to punish a substantial

[25] Douglas Hay, 'Property, Authority and the Criminal Law', in Douglas Hay, Peter Linebaugh, John G. Rule, E.P. Thompson and Cal Winslow, *Albion's Fatal Tree: Crime and Society in Eighteenth-Century England* (New York: Pantheon Books, 1975), p. 57.

[26] Thomas A. Green, *Verdict According to Conscience: Perspectives on the English Criminal Trial Jury, 1200–1800* (Chicago: University of Chicago Press, 1985), pp. 28–59; Bellamy, *Crime and Public Order*, pp. 29–36; Edward Powell, *Kingship, Law and Society: Criminal Justice in the Reign of Henry V* (Oxford: Clarendon Press, 1989), p. 82. Not every such criminal escaped punishment: rather than finding a thief 'not guilty' the jury might reduce the value of the object he had stolen to the level of petty larceny so that he avoided the death penalty. And the process of standing trial was itself arduous: Green argues, for example, that 'pre-trial incarceration, the strains of standing trial, remand to await pardon, and the forfeiture of goods became de facto sanctions for what a later age called "manslaughter" ': Green, *Verdict According to Conscience*, p. 99. Not all those found guilty were executed: royal pardons could save those who had committed excusable crimes or who were well-connected or lucky.

[27] Richard M. Wunderli, *London Church Courts and Society on the Eve of the Reformation* (Cambridge, MA: The Medieval Academy of America, 1981), pp. 2, 4–5, 61. Wunderli argues that this shift was not ideological, but that litigants thought secular courts were simply more effective, p. 137.

[28] Marjorie K. McIntosh, 'Finding Language for Misconduct: Jurors in Fifteenth-Century Local Courts', in *Bodies and Disciplines: Intersections of Literature and History in Fifteenth-Century England* edited by Barbara A. Hanawalt and David Wallace (Minneapolis: University of Minnesota Press, 1996), pp. 97, 109–110; Marjorie K. McIntosh, *Controlling Misbehaviour in England, 1370–1600* (Cambridge: Cambridge University Press, 1998), pp. 38–39. McIntosh points out that some of this behaviour could have gone to the Church courts, but agrees that secular courts were seen to be more effective.

number of felons while containing the 'number of bodies festooning the gallows'.[29] Once the proper safeguards were in place, the common lawyers intentionally sent a substantial proportion of the men convicted of felony for an extended period of confinement in an episcopal prison as a regular punishment for felony, thus providing a third option: conviction and punishment without execution.[30]

The judges were less interested in sanctuary than in benefit of clergy: though it also relieved pressure on the system, it did not solve any obvious problems for them, and its administration had always been more distant. But as they sought to manage benefit of clergy more closely in the 1510s and 1520s, a weaker version of the same impulse extended to abjuration. It was not central to their concerns, but sanctuary was certainly on their horizons, and when the political and religious context changed radically after 1529 the changes to sanctuary were more obvious than those to benefit of clergy. After 1531 men who would previously have gone abroad went to chartered sanctuaries: those sanctuaries thus became sites of criminal confinement, and sites which could offer mitigation for crimes which were no longer clergiable.

This shift in the norms of punishment for felony did not come about overnight, and indeed it's not clear that anyone, except perhaps Fyneux, saw the logical end of the road that the judges started down in the 1490s. This was an evolutionary process rather than a clear plan to re-shape the criminal justice system, but cumulative, pragmatic and fairly consistent changes over four decades meant that a substantial reform of the criminal justice system emerged. In order to demonstrate this we need to turn to the records which best allow us to see the judges in action in the early Tudor period, the records of King's Bench. Two classes in particular provide insight into the working of benefit of clergy and sanctuary: TNA KB9 includes indictments for felony, inquisitions on the body of homicide victims, coroners' reports and some copies of gaol deliveries among its admittedly miscellaneous contents, and TNA KB27 contains the plea rolls for the court of King's Bench. Only a handful of first-instance cases appeared at King's Bench, but cases were regularly removed there from the counties. These records cannot provide a clear view of how

[29] The phrase comes from Sharpe, *Judicial Punishment*, pp. 38–39. Thomas More's common lawyer seems to support this image, commenting that 'we're hanging [thieves] all over the place . . . I've seen as many as twenty on a single gallows': *Utopia* (Harmondsworth: Penguin, 1965), p. 44. As usual, this can't be taken at face value: Raphael responds by observing that petty larceny isn't bad enough to deserve the death penalty, but petty larceny was not a felony. Though the assize records for this period are patchy, I haven't seen anything to suggest that twenty would be a typical number of convictions, much less executions.

[30] J. M. Beattie, *Crime and the Courts in England 1660–1800* (Princeton: Princeton University Press, 1986), pp. 492–500; Sharpe, *Judicial Punishment*, 25. Kesselring discusses the increased use of imprisonment as a punishment for trespasses, financial crimes and religious or vagabond-related crime, but notes that hanging remained the only recognized punishment for felony: K.J. Kesselring, *Mercy and Authority in the Tudor State* (Cambridge: Cambridge University Press, 2003), p. 25. The Tudors also introduced some barbaric new versions of the death penalty, such as boiling alive, thus reinforcing the distance between the political discourse, which apparently sought tougher capital punishments, and the legal, which sought to find effective mitigations.

the system in the counties worked; most importantly they can't tell us how many men and women were tried and convicted there. But they can give us a pretty good sense of the kinds of things that might happen at gaol delivery, and how they might play out when they got to King's Bench. And they're all we've got. I had no idea how many cases I would find in the King's Bench records in which sanctuary or benefit of clergy might have played a role; the historiography suggested not many. And so I decided to examine all the KB9 and KB27 rolls for the reigns of Henry VII and Henry VIII rather than risk missing something useful by sampling.[31] The rolls in this period are significantly shorter than they would become in the second half of the sixteenth century, so this approach was (just about) feasible.[32] Given the size of the body of source material, and my interest in benefit of clergy and sanctuary, I focused on indictments in which sanctuary was mentioned and cases which came to trial (and usually to verdict) in which sanctuary or benefit of clergy played a role. As anyone who has looked at these sources knows, there are a large number of indictments which never came to trial and a large number of trials which were either not concluded or in which sanctuary or benefit of clergy played no role. I have paid no attention to these, and so this study does not contribute to our knowledge of broader patterns of criminality or the ways in which trial at common law played into wider strategies.[33] I was interested only in the men and women for whom sanctuary or benefit of clergy was part of a strategy to avoid execution.

Though the King's Bench records are the core source for this project, they are not the only one. My interest in this subject was originally piqued by the treatment of benefit of clergy and sanctuary in the readings given at the Inns of Court in these decades. The readers explicated the law with complexity and pragmatism and without any of the outrage, or even hostility, which the secondary sources often imply they were feeling. The same is true of the discussions in the year books and named reports. Though these sources are not easily read for emotion, the relationship between the arguments expressed in the readings and the smaller and more technical reports and those in the high profile cases which have largely shaped our understanding of the law (*Stafford's Case*, *Standish's Case* and *Pauncefote v.Savage*), is revealing.[34] These cases provide material that interested contemporary lawyers enough to write it down and circulate it, but they generally don't tell us why the lawyers were interested, or whether they found the arguments intriguing, convincing or simply puzzling. For the most part the lawyers noted cases which were outside the normal course of events, and this seems like a shaky foundation on which

[31] I also examined KB27 rolls to 1550 to see if cases from the reign of Henry VIII appeared there in later years.

[32] I examined about a third of the KB9 rolls in a series of visits to Kew. The rest of KB9 and all of KB27 were examined via AALT: this took about nine months of full-time work.

[33] J.B. Post, 'Crime in Later Medieval England: Some Historiographical Limitations', *Continuity and Change* 2 (1987), pp. 213–214, 219–221 outlines many of the problems with attempting such tasks with the available material.

[34] These cases are discussed in detail in chapters 5–7.

to build our understanding of how the law worked in practice. Those which circulated over years or generations can be taken as marking points of inflection or change in the law, but it's a risky proposition to treat all reported cases as equal in their own time. This is even more the case when, as often happens, the reported cases reflect only a truncated and often somewhat distorted version of the record. There is no question that the lawyers' discussions in the Inns and the courts shaped how the law functioned, but that process was often more complex than it appears at first glance and needs to be treated with some caution.

Much the same is true of the statutes which are a core but often misleading source for our understanding of benefit of clergy and sanctuary in this period. Statutes are both political and legal documents: they can respond either to a perceived problem in the legal system or to a real problem in the legal system. The preamble to the Act in Restraint of Appeals is the most famous example of a political justification for the legal changes that followed, but many other statutes combine these elements in a less revolutionary form. We often have scant documentary evidence for the genesis of statutes in this period, and with few court records it can be difficult to determine either what a statute was intended to achieve or what, if anything, it actually achieved. To further complicate matters, every statute had to be integrated into all relevant common law, so the actual implications of a new statute might be quite different from those intended by its framers. All of this means that statutes cannot simply be taken at face value and can never be skimmed—the real impact of a new statute is often buried in the lengthy fine print, and we will see that the lawyers' response to statutory change changed considerably over this period.

Finally, bishops' registers are used throughout this book, for they provide the only glimpse at the workings of benefit of clergy from the ecclesiastical perspective. I have examined all the bishops' registers available in print for this period, and a handful of those available only in manuscript: with one glorious exception, benefit of clergy made up such a tiny fraction of the business recorded in the registers that I concluded that a more extensive survey was not worth the time it would take.[35] The bishops were, for the most part, not terribly concerned to note their involvement with clerks convict except at moments of transition or novelty. Like Gabel, I found it almost impossible to connect the registers with the common law records, and so it is the rarest of accidents which allows us to follow a clerk convict from the secular realm into the ecclesiastical one or vice versa. But the examples I found are invaluable, and they remind us that there were two partners in the management of clerks convict, each of whom approached the process with their own expectations, criteria and constraints.

[35] The registers of the archbishops of York are available online at https://archbishopsregisters.york.ac.uk/, while many more are available in microfilm via Harvester Press Microform. The register of the bishop of Lincoln from 1526 to 1543 is unusually rich.

Taken together, these sources reveal an unexpectedly large number of clerks convict in early Tudor England: at least 1200 men claimed clergy in these records between 1485 and 1547.[36] This is only the tip of the iceberg, for most of these are cases which were problematic enough to move from gaol delivery to King's Bench. As we will see, the numbers were not stable: though the sources are mixed and uncertain, there is enough evidence to indicate that they grew through this period, and that about a quarter to a third of those convicted for felony claimed clergy. I also found about 1,100 men (and a handful of women) claiming sanctuary between 1485 and 1547. The numbers for sanctuary are harder to interpret than those for clergy. Sanctuary-seekers could come and go without attracting the attention of the authorities, and so it is much harder to estimate the dark number. The sanctuary numbers fluctuate more than those for benefit of clergy, but they show no real trend up or down for most of the period. This indicates that, if nothing else, sanctuary continued to be a useful tool for those seeking time or distance from the victim of their crime. But if there is no clear pattern among sanctuary-seekers, the numbers of those looking to abjure, to leave the realm in self-imposed exile after confessing their crime, did change substantially in these years, largely in response to government actions.

The arguments presented in this book are drawn from the ground-level experiences of these roughly 2,300 men (and the handful of women), and their hundreds of small, mostly insignificant interactions within the legal system. The individual cases often appear inconsistent, inconclusive and idiosyncratic; individual initiatives often fail or fall short of their goals. There are few direct lines of development and even fewer smoking guns, but that patchwork of individual experiences can be assembled into a coherent and compelling story of change.

This book is divided into three parts. The first part, 'The Foundations' traces the development of each topic through statutes, treatises, year books and readings from the thirteenth century to *c.* 1485. This material provides the intellectual framework within which the common lawyers approached the problems that faced them under the first two Tudors, and which both shaped and limited the options available to them. This part also examines the processes, both secular and

[36] Not every claim of clergy resulted in a delivery, just as not every claim of sanctuary resulted in a restoration. Either, or both, could be used strategically and this was part of their value to the system. It will be clear in the discussion of actual cases where the claims were successful, but most of the tables and charts which look at patterns over a period of years refer to claims rather than actual deliveries, since that gives a better sense of the extent to which these options were used in the criminal justice system. The claims are counted in the jurisdiction within which they were raised if they did not lead to a delivery but counted in the jurisdiction within which they were delivered when this was the outcome. This has the effect of raising the profile of King's Bench deliveries to Westminster and flattening the profile of claims raised but not determined in the counties. This seemed to be a better outcome than artificially inflating the total numbers by counting them twice, or artificially shrinking the importance of either King's Bench or the Westminster Abbey prison. The one place where the relationship between the counties and the centre appears most realistically is in the early years of Henry VIII's reign, particularly between 1509 and 1519, and this is further discussed below, pp. 203–206.

ecclesiastical, within which benefit of clergy and sanctuary operated. This is partly for expediency, to avoid repetition in the discussion of process in later chapters, and the reader familiar with both systems may opt to skip it. But it also makes the point that process determined much of what was possible in both systems: without understanding the processes and the limited flexibility they offered those operating within the system, we will not understand the outcomes. Taken together, common learning and process provided the parameters within which the lawyers had to operate.

The second part, 'Building a Bureaucracy' deals with Henry VII's reign and the first half of his son's. It traces the development of benefit of clergy and sanctuary in parallel, for in these decades they were quite different stories. Each chapter opens with a landmark event—a statute or a prominent case—which has shaped our understanding of the law and re-examines it in the context of contemporary doctrine and practice. It then goes on to examine the issues that the courts were dealing with in the same years in order to provide a more balanced sense of the operation of the system as a whole. These chapters demonstrate the ways in which Henry VII's justices extended their control over benefit of clergy around the turn of the century, and the ways in which they recorded and exerted that control in the early years of his son's reign, as well as the ongoing and effective functioning of sanctuary.

Finally, the third part, 'The Limits of a Quiet Evolution' deals with the effects of the Reformation on this steady and evolutionary process of change. It brings the discussion of benefit of clergy and sanctuary together for the first time, because changes in the law meant that lawyers had begun to see them as complementary, and it traces the acceleration of reform in the 1530s, its collapse in the 1540s and subsequent efforts to secure some elements of the model of criminal confinement which had emerged in these decades. This part of the story spends less time in the courts, because the courts played little role in driving this change, but they had done a good deal to shape the changes that now flowed through parliament.

The absence of smoking guns in this story also means that there is a distinct absence of heroes or villains. The nature of the sources means that we have few names to attach to the changes that happen here: we can assume that Henry VII and Henry VIII largely supported the work the courts were doing, but they were not involved in their day-to-day activities. As chief justice of King's Bench for most of the formative period of this change, Fyneux is a likely driver, but he operated for the most part as an *eminence grise*. Individual lawyers appear by name in the reports, but they rarely win an argument or take a stance that seems to represent an avenue for change—and when they do, they usually don't get very far. The surviving parliamentary records can allow us to know that a given act was controversial, but not why or to whom. And so in some ways this is a story told in the passive voice, where change happens without being caused. But it is very much the nature of the common law system that change cannot be imposed. It can be introduced, but it must then be accepted, primarily by judges and lawyers, but also by sheriffs, bailiffs, coroners, juries, ordinaries and even accused felons. Few of those in the system explicitly objected to or resisted innovation, but all of them had the option, in various circumstances, of ignoring it. Inherent in every legal action was a human interaction, and the human interaction mattered, whether it was Chief Justice Scrope overawing a Westminster monk in King's Bench or being overawed by the archbishop of York at York Castle, a local ordinary telling the assize justices that they were wrong about the ecclesiastical jurisdiction in which they were holding court, or an inexperienced coroner framing a confession to a felony as an indenture. Whether those interactions were right or wrong, they all contributed to the ways in which the law was experienced by justices, officials and felons, as did the perception of the worthiness of the criminal and the horror of the crime. The system is real: it is driven by an understanding of the law derived from custom, statute, treatise, teaching and experience, working within a set of procedures which allow an unruly mass of human interactions to be channeled into an orderly set of problems decided in a limited set of fora before a defined set of people. Common learning and process set boundaries to the system, but within those boundaries men of ingenuity and intelligence found a way in these decades to ensure that a conviction for felony did not always mean a sentence of death, and that felons could be effectively punished without being killed. They established that convicted felons were the king's felons: their survival in greater numbers meant the elaboration of the point that such convicts continued to owe allegiance to the king whose laws they had broken and whose growing bureaucracy made their survival possible nonetheless. Even more remarkable, they did it without drawing attention to the fact that they had done so, and during a period when the political rhetoric around both crime and ecclesiastical authority pointed in the opposite direction. The system that emerged was certainly not perfect; it wasn't particularly fair, and it didn't treat everyone the same—it would have been nothing short of astonishing if it had. But it was reasonably consistent, and it worked reasonably well until the Reformation changes took hold, and the ecclesiastical superstructure on which it had been built began to buckle.

PART I

THE FOUNDATIONS

1
Benefit of Clergy
Common Learning

Benefit of clergy originated in canon law, according to which clerks were exempt from secular jurisdiction and could be tried only by the authority of the Church. Despite the best efforts of Thomas à Becket, this claim was never fully recognized in England: though the clergy continued to argue for the full *privilegium fori* into the fourteenth century, benefit of clergy was not allowed for civil matters, so when it came to issues of rights over land, or debt, clergy took their chances in the secular courts along with everyone else. But the English clergy did gain the privilege of claiming exemption from secular jurisdiction when it came to felonies, crimes for which the punishment was death.[1] Clerks accused of committing felonies were instead handed over to the ecclesiastical authorities for punishment, though there was a good deal of argument across the centuries over when and how that should happen. This chapter traces these arguments from the thirteenth to the fifteenth centuries as they appear and re-appear in statutes, in court cases, and finally in readings at the Inns of Court. It argues that though the secular authorities never challenged the basic right of clerks to be delivered to the ecclesiastical authorities, the need to elaborate the practical processes around delivery gave them the opportunity to develop views on its proper management which would, by the fifteenth century, lead to the emergence of a naturalized version of benefit of clergy in England.

Statutory authority for benefit of clergy came somewhat indirectly: in 1215 chapter one of Magna Carta guaranteed the rights and liberties of the English Church, and benefit of clergy became one of the rights that it was assumed to guarantee.[2] This was a fairly vague foundation, however, and over the course of time it was refined and developed in some important ways. Early statutes accepted that the clerk was outside the jurisdiction of the common law but claimed a role in peripheral matters. In 1267 the statute of Marlborough, for example, made provisions for bailing a clerk accused of a felony, while recognizing that 'he will not answer

[1] High treason was not clergiable, but petty treason, homicide, rape, and theft of an object worth more than 12d were all felony (and more than one theft could be combined to reach this figure).

[2] Margaret McGlynn, 'From Charter to Common Law: The Rights and Liberties of the pre-Reformation Church', in *Religion, Magna Carta and the Rule of Law*, edited by Robin Griffith-Jones and Mark Hill QC (Cambridge: Cambridge University Press, 2015), pp. 53–69.

The King's Felons. Margaret McGlynn, Oxford University Press.
DOI: 10.1093/oso/9780192887689.003.0002

before ... [the king's justices], by reason of a clerk's privilege'.[3] In 1275 Westminster 1, c. 2 provided that 'when a clerk is taken for guilty of felony, and is demanded by the ordinary, he shall be delivered to him according to the privilege of holy Church, on such peril as belongeth to it, after the custom aforetimes used'.[4] The *articuli cleri* of 1315, which dealt with a number of grievances of the clergy, took for granted that 'a clerk ought not to be judged before a temporal judge, nor anything may be done against him that concerneth life or member', and stated that any such clerk who claimed his clergy 'yielding himself to the law of the realm, shall enjoy the privilege of the Church, according to the laudable custom of the realm heretofore used'.[5] Though all of these authorities recognize the rights of the Church, there is a slow shift in their language. The statute of Marlborough states the clerical privilege most strongly, but both Westminster 1 and the *articuli cleri* refer to benefit of clergy as part of the custom of the realm, and the *articuli cleri* implies that the clerk who got benefit of clergy was simultaneously 'yielding himself to the law of the realm'. This suggests that although the privilege was widely recognized, the secular authorities were unwilling to relinquish jurisdiction over criminous clerks completely, and indeed the *articuli cleri* complained that judges were not immediately passing clerks on to the ordinary, but were allowing them to confess to crimes such as theft, robbery, or murder, despite the fact that such clerks 'be not of their court, nor can be judged or condemned before them'.[6] It reiterated that such clerks should be handed over to the ordinary on his demand.[7]

[3] *SR*, I. 25. 52 Hen. III, Stat. Marl. c. 27. This chapter began as clause 24 of the Provisions of Westminster in 1259, which prohibited the fining of sureties for the appearance of men who appeared but pleaded clergy. The argument for amercement was apparently that the sureties had undertaken to ensure that the cleric would 'stand to right' and by pleading clergy he had refused to do so. The argument against it was that the sureties undertook to ensure the appearance, not the plea. See Paul Brand, *Kings, Barons and Justices: The Making and Enforcement of Legislation in Thirteenth-Century England* (Cambridge: Cambridge University Press, 2003), pp. 82–83; Paul Brand, 'The Making of English Thirteenth-century Legislation: Some New Evidence', in *Law in the City: Proceedings of the Seventeenth British Legal History Conference, London, 2005*, edited by Andrew Lewis, Paul Brand, and Paul Mitchell (Dublin: Four Courts Press, 2007), pp. 45–46, 49.

[4] *SR*, I. 28. 3 Edw. I, c. 2. This was simply a statement of the common law and the purpose of the statute was to regulate purgation, discussed below. *Bracton* agreed that a clerk accused, appealed, or indicted should be delivered to the ordinary at once for purgation: *Bracton*, 2, p. 348. The ordinary was the ecclesiastical officer, usually a bishop or his deputy, who had the authority to claim clerks in the secular court. The role and the men who fulfilled it are discussed in greater detail, pp. 76–81.

[5] *SR*, I. 173. 9 Edw. II, c. 15.

[6] *SR*, I. 173. 9 Edw. II, c. 16 [1315–16]. Clerks might also appeal their accomplices: an approver was handed over to the ordinary at the eyre of Northamptonshire in 1329: *The Eyre of Northamptonshire 3–4 Edw. III* vol. 1 ed. Donald W. Sutherland, SS vol. 97 (London: Selden Society, 1983), p. 162; Fitz, *Corone*, 128.

[7] Helmholz argues that 'the years that followed the *Articuli cleri* saw a falling off in the level of complaint on the part of the church' and suggests that the effort to maintain clerical privilege was being quietly abandoned. He notes that the clergy continued to compile *gravamina* and submit them in the following years, but 'in diminished numbers and without repeating the attempts to secure full recognition of the *privilegium fori*' partly, at least, because they were focused on maintaining the criminal privilege: Helmholz, *Ius Commune*, pp. 220–221.

These early statutes demonstrate two points that will be key in understanding how benefit of clergy develops. First, statutes are both legal and political documents: while they change the law, they usually arise in response to a political concern, and are often careful in the way they navigate the politics of the situation. This was never more true than when the situation involved the rights of the Church. Second, there was some ambiguity in the way English law understood benefit of clergy: while none of the statutes challenged the privilege, they all inserted themselves into its implementation, and implementation gave the common law courts lots of room for manoeuvre. Accepting that criminous clerks were to be delivered to the ordinary begged far more questions than it answered: how did the courts know if a particular felon was a clerk? When did they know if he was criminous? When was he to be delivered? Did the common law courts retain any interest in him after delivery? What if he escaped from the ordinary? What if he re-offended? All of these questions had to be answered for the process to work, but all of the answers were complicated, controversial, and continued to change over time.

1. Determining Clergy

To start with the most fundamental question, how did the court know that the man being arraigned before it was a clerk? The simplest method of proof, and the standard one in the thirteenth century, was tonsure and vesture—if you looked like a clerk, you were one. This was also the norm under canon law.[8] But tonsure and vesture were both relatively easy to acquire, especially when the alternative was a trip to the gallows. This method of proof was also complicated by the fact that it was generally accepted that any man who had taken minor or major orders could claim clergy, but taking minor orders did not commit a man to a career in the Church, so he was unlikely to be tonsured or dressed in clerical clothing.[9] Apart from those in the religious orders, clerical garb was not always terribly distinct from secular, since there was as yet no sense of a priestly uniform. How then was the court to deal with a man in ambiguous clothing and with a scruffy coiffure who claimed clergy? In a society where literacy was effectively confined to those who had taken orders, a reading test was one obvious alternative. Such a test appears in a handful of legal records where clerical status was under dispute in the late thirteenth century,

[8] See Helmholz, *Ius Commune*, p. 208.

[9] Gabel argues that the privilege had been limited to those in major orders, but that evidence from the late thirteenth century suggests that it was generally accepted by then that the privilege was open to those in minor orders: Gabel, *Benefit of Clergy*, pp. 62–64. It was generally agreed that women could not claim the privilege, since they could not take orders, but Fitzherbert reports a case where a woman is found guilty and is a clerk and the ordinary demands her 'as a member of the church': Fitz, *Corone*, 461. I have not seen this anywhere else in this period, though of course women claimed clergy in the seventeenth century and later: J. M. Beattie, *Crime and the Courts in England 1660–1800* (Princeton: Princeton University Press, 1986), p. 142.

though it seems to have disappeared as an option in the reign of Edward II.[10] In its earliest appearances, reading was a supplementary test where tonsure and vesture were uncertain, rather than a replacement.[11] This was in accord with the canon law: Boniface VIII had confirmed the point in the decretal *Si judex laicus*, and when a man in lay clothing tried to claim clergy before him, Spigurnel J had the decretal, which was apparently available in the court, read out.[12] Nevertheless, there was apparently some room for negotiation: in 1327, an accused felon claimed clergy on arraignment at King's Bench, and Scrope CJKB answered 'you are dressed in a ray robe … also you do not have a tonsure'.[13] Though this should have been the end of the matter, Scrope went on to ask the man if he had anything to say, and, in a longer version of the case, spoke to him in Latin and then in French, getting no response.[14] A monk arrived from Westminster Abbey to claim the man, and Scrope warned him about the dangers of falsely claiming a clerk. The monk suggested that Scrope should administer the reading test to solve the problem, but Scrope was unwilling to do so, and so the ordinary did not claim him.[15] Though the accused was not successful in claiming clergy, Scrope was willing to explore his knowledge of Latin, and even French, even though he was dressed in secular garb and untonsured. At the same time he was willing to push back against the ordinary, commenting that if the ordinary wished to claim one who was not a clerk, he would lose his temporalities to the king, and his franchise to claim clerks, him, and his successors forever.[16] Here the felon was tested for his knowledge of languages rather than for his reading ability, and Scrope was clearly checking him out in a fairly general way, rather than applying a formalized procedure.

If the respective roles of appearance and literacy in the establishment of clerical status were unclear in the early fourteenth century, it is equally unclear at what stage in the process clergy was claimed. Baker argues that at this period clergy was usually claimed on arraignment, after which an inquest of office was taken to determine if the clerk was guilty.[17] The inquest was less than a full trial, and the accused

[10] Gabel, *Benefit of Clergy*, p. 68.

[11] In a report of a case from the 1293–4 Yorkshire eyre the reading test came first, then the jury said he was in orders, and finally justice checked that he had tonsure: BL MS Additional 31826, f. 208v: Lincoln's Inn MS. Misc. 87, f. 38v. I am grateful to Paul Brand for this reference.

[12] J.H. Baker, 'Some Early Newgate Reports (1315–28)', in *Law Reporting in England*, edited by Chantal Stebbings (London: Hambledon, 1995), p. 49. The decretal stated that clerks arrested without clerical dress or tonsure were not to have the privilege: Sext 5.11.12. See also Helmholz, *Ius Commune*, p. 208.

[13] Fitz, *Corone*, 233. The same case also appears in Fitz, *Corone*, 283. Baker mentions ray cloth as a marker of lay status in 'Early Newgate Reports', p. 50.

[14] The version summarized in YB Trin 9 Edw. IV, p. 28, pl. 41 says that it was the ordinary who spoke to the felon in Latin and French, but Baker cites a manuscript version of the case which has Scrope testing his language skills.

[15] The felon continued to refuse to plead, and Scrope eventually adjudged him to his penance: Baker, 'Early Newgate Reports', p. 51.

[16] Fitz, *Corone*, 233.

[17] *Bracton* explicitly stated that the clerk should be delivered without any inquest: *Bracton*, 2, p. 348.

did not plead and put himself on the jury. This allowed both the Church and the secular authorities to say that the clerk had not been 'tried' under the common law, and so the Church's jurisdiction was intact, but if the accused was found guilty the common law court could pursue any accessories, and had a record of the delivery which could be used to confiscate his chattels.[18] If the accused did not claim clergy on arraignment, he had theoretically accepted the common law's jurisdiction over him and could not later plead clergy. Scrope's encounter with William Dautre in 1328 demonstrates once again that both jurisdiction and literacy could be rather more complicated in real life. Dautre was convicted of felony before Scrope at the gaol delivery at York castle and apparently sentenced to hang. When the ordinary later appeared to claim him, probably during the next circuit, Scrope thought that the sentence had already been carried out, but the ordinary told him that the case had been adjourned. Under the current practice, Dautre had waived his right to claim clergy by submitting to the jury trial, but the next day the archbishop of York came and asked to examine the prisoner.[19] In accordance with the comments he had made the previous year, Scrope warned the archbishop that if Dautre was found not to be a clerk, he risked losing his temporalities, since Dautre had already been convicted. The archbishop answered that he merely wanted an examination to see if the clerk could be claimed, rather than to claim him, and Scrope allowed this. The archbishop then returned, presumably having carried out his examination, and claimed Dautre. Scrope, like Spigurnel, responded by referring to the decretals and pointing out that the claimant had to be dressed and tonsured as a clerk, which Dautre apparently was not. The archbishop retorted that he was wearing only breeches and a shirt, ambiguous attire, but that he was tonsured. Scrope wanted to verify this for himself: the archbishop argued that the examination of the clerk was his right, but Scrope retorted that guarding the Crown's rights was his duty. The prisoner was examined, and was found to be sporting a crisp clean tonsure and, for good measure, to be able to read. Thus though clergy was supposed to be claimed on arraignment, and Scrope specifically protested that it was only available to those in clerical dress, he allowed a reading test after the conviction of a man in secular dress. He reluctantly delivered Dautre to the archbishop, describing him as a confessed felon in lay clothing who refused clergy, while the archbishop received him as a clerk and 'not as a felon, for you are not his judges'.[20] In this stand-off Scrope had flexed his muscles, invoking the authority of both the common and canon laws, but in the end the archbishop got his way. Though the role of the reading test was ambiguous, the timing of the claim was uncertain, and Scrope was clearly jealous of the Crown's authority, he had a much harder time denying the archbishop of

[18] Baker, 'Early Newgate Reports', p. 47; *The Mirror of Justices* ed. W.J. Whittaker, SS vol. 7 (London: Bernard Quaritch, 1895), p. 92; Bellamy, *Criminal Law and Society*, p. 118.

[19] Baker, 'Early Newgate Reports', p. 51.

[20] Baker, 'Some Early Newgate Reports', p. 52.

York at York Castle than a Westminster monk in King's Bench, and this suggests that there was enough uncertainty in the law for the personal interactions to play a part in the final outcome.

Though the question of timing appears at first as a fairly technical issue, it quickly became clear that it was in fact a fight over jurisdiction, and the same was true of the main exception to the claim of clergy, bigamy. In 1274 the second Council of Lyons denied the clerical privilege to bigamists, and in 1276 the statute *de bigamis* provided that any man who had been married twice before the Council could not claim the privilege.[21] The statute meant that the canonical principle was enshrined in English law, but again there was a dispute about its administration. In 1327 the prelates complained that if bigamy was alleged against a clerk that the lay judges would proceed with an inquest, and if it was found by the lay inquest that he had married two women or a widow, 'the justices pronounce against this clerk and by such pretext condemn him to death, even though he is in priest's orders'.[22] The Church's cognizance over bigamy was reiterated in response. This does not seem to have been the end of the matter, as a petition of the clergy in 1344 raised the issue again, and the right of the spiritual court to cognizance over bigamy issues was asserted in *pro clero* in response.[23]

The evidence shows that in the early fourteenth century there were simply no clear rules around claiming clergy: tonsure, vesture, and literacy were the issues generally considered, but their relative weight and role in the process could vary; a bigamist could not claim clergy, but the common law was as yet unwilling to accept the Church's cognizance over the matter. The terms of engagement were being defined, but it is too soon to look for clarity on the outcomes.

2. Engaging with the Ecclesiastical System

Once the felon was accepted as a clerk, however that conclusion was reached, he was handed over to the ordinary for process in the ecclesiastical system. Although, strictly speaking, the procedure in the common law courts was irrelevant in the Church courts, in practice it seems to have carried a fair amount of weight. Helmholz notes that the common law verdict might be read in the canon law as *infamia iuris* and that 'incorrigible' clerics—which could be construed as referring to repeat offenders—lost the *privilegium fori*.[24] The ecclesiastical authorities could re-try a clerk convicted in the secular courts, but the records do not survive

[21] *SR*, I. 43. 4 Edw. I, *Stat. de bigamis* c. 5. It was fairly quickly interpreted to include any clerk who had married a widow: the *Mirror of Justices*, 93, explains this on the grounds of plurality.
[22] PROME, vol. 9, p. 107: Jan 1327.
[23] PROME, vol. 2, p. 152: June 1344; *SR*, I. 302. 18 Edw. III stat. 3 c. 2.
[24] Helmholz, *Ius Commune*, pp. 128, 208.

to indicate whether they actually did so on a regular basis.[25] They did, however, hold clerks in their prisons before they allowed some clerks convict to go forward for purgation.[26] At the purgation a group of clerks—the exact numbers varied, but usually around a dozen—would swear that they believed that the clerk convict was innocent, and he would be restored to good fame and released. The management of purgation was, of course, the key to the actual punishment of a clerk convict, and it was a central concern from at least the time of Westminster 1, which accepted benefit of clergy as part of the common law and went on to admonish the prelates not to allow clerks convict to go free without 'due purgation'. The secular authorities were obviously keen to ensure that a man delivered to the ecclesiastical authorities remained in prison for an appropriate period of time and was released through an appropriate mechanism, but the clerical establishment shared their desire to ensure that clerks convict were properly punished: Archbishop Pecham, for example, had decreed that clerks should not be lightly purged but should have their cases rigorously investigated.[27] Though there are few records of any investigative process, it is clear that the bishops regularly held clerks convict for lengthy periods of time: Gabel points to one John de Hoyville, held from 1317 to 1321 by the bishop of Winchester, and Reginald de Bureford, held for two years by the bishop of Worcester, among others.[28] Though the purgations of clerks convict appear only sporadically in the printed registers of the fourteenth and fifteenth centuries, terms such as these are not unusual.[29]

Not every clerk delivered to the ordinary was eligible for purgation. There was general agreement that clerks attaint were not eligible, but the distinction between clerks attaint and clerks convict is not always consistent. A year book case from 1366 describes a clerk attaint as one who claims clergy after judgement and a clerk convict as one who claims clergy after verdict but before judgement, and this is

[25] Gabel notes that bishops' registers through the fourteenth century generally accept the procedure in the secular court, and she assumes that the inquest which precedes the process of purgation was the clerical trial: *Benefit of Clergy*, pp. 92–95. *Bracton* provides a writ to be sent to the ordinary who refuses to proceed to purgation without a new suit in the ecclesiastical court: *Bracton*, 2, p. 349. Though this may still have been a matter of contention in the first half of the thirteenth century, it appears to have been resolved by the early fourteenth.

[26] For a full discussion of the history, purpose, and process of compurgation see Helmholz, *Ius Commune*, pp. 82–134.

[27] F.M. Powicke and C.R. Cheney ed. *Councils and Synods, with Other Documents Relating to the English Church* (Oxford: Clarendon Press, 1981) vol. II (2), p. 1122.

[28] Gabel, *Benefit of Clergy*, pp. 109–110; Bellamy, *Criminal Law and Society*, p. 123.

[29] Thirteen purgations are recorded in the register of Philip Repingdon, bishop of Lincoln from 1405 to 1419. The shortest period of custody was thirteen months, the longest twenty-four years, with six men going through purgation after two to five years in custody and five after seven to fifteen years: *The Register of Bishop Philip Repingdon 1405–1419* ed. Margaret Archer vol. 1 (Hereford: LRS, 1963), pp. 93–95; vol. 2 (Hereford: LRS, 1963), pp. 243, 248, 268–269, 282–283; vol. 3 (LRS, 1982), pp. 95–97, 170, 227–230, 245, 265–267, 284–285, 288–289. John Catterick, bishop of Coventry and Lichfield from 1415–19, recorded the purgation of only two clerks convict: Alan Rider, a chaplain, was purged after ten years in custody, John Burton, a labourer, after five months: *The Register of John Catterick, Bishop of Coventry and Lichfield 1415–1419* ed. R.N. Swanson, Canterbury & York Society vol. 77 (Woodbridge, Suffolk: Boydell Press, 1990), pp. 28–29.

often the standard distinction.[30] However, as we will see, claiming clergy after trial became standard in the second half of the fourteenth century, and this description reflects that change in practice.[31] Later still, in the fifteenth century, the working distinction between clerks convict and clerks attaint was the way in which they had been convicted rather than the time at which they claimed: clerks attaint had confessed or been outlawed, while clerks convict were found guilty by a jury. In the early fourteenth century, before the jury trial became standard, confession also played a key role in the distinction. In a year book case from 1327 an apprentice of the court asked if an approver who had appealed others of robbery and then claimed clergy could have his purgation afterwards, or if his confession would be prejudicial, upon which it was said 'that the ordinary should not proceed to purgation without consulting the king'.[32] Thus the apprentice understood the approver to be a clerk attaint, who should normally remain in prison. Though the king could extend mercy in this case, there were instances in which he was limited: in 1388 a felon claimed clergy after conviction at the suit of the party and Justice Clopton delivered him to the ordinary, 'and said it was law' that conviction at the suit of the party meant that he should not have purgation.[33] This implies that Clopton saw purgation in the same light as a pardon, an act of clemency which the king could not extend if he had not been the injured party.[34] This adds the nature of the prosecution to the time of the claim and the method of the conviction as possible variables defining clerks convict and clerks attaint. The reporter queried Clopton's statement, however, and I have not seen that argument re-appear elsewhere.[35]

[30] YB Mich 40 Edw. III, pl. 23, p. 42. Fitz, *Corone*, 91.

[31] Baker, 'Some Early Newgate Reports', pp. 47–48.

[32] 'quod ordinarius non debet procedere ad purgationem inconsulto rege': YB Trin 1 Edw. III p. 16, pl. 3. This was shortened by Fitzherbert to 'A man may take his clergy, but he may not go to his purgation *rege inconsulto*'. Fitz, *Corone*, 152.

[33] YB Mich 12 Ric. II (Ames Fdn), p. 40, pl. 5. Fitz, *Corone*, 109. Bellamy, *Criminal Law and Society*, 121.

[34] Kaye argues that by the end of the thirteenth century it was already unusual to pursue an appeal in the teeth of the king's pardon, but there are examples as late as the sixteenth century of a pardoned man being remanded for a year and a day so that the victim could appeal. J.M. Kaye ed., *Placita Corone or La Corone Pledee devant Justices*, SS Suppl. Ser. vol. 4 (London: Selden Society, 1966), p. xxxii.

[35] The distinction between clerks convict and clerks attaint not only determined purgation, it also had implications for the property of the felon. In the early fourteenth century the lands and chattels of a clerk convict and his wife remained in the hands of the sheriff until he was purged: Fitz, *Corone*, 356. The sheriff was to account for them to the exchequer, and when the convict was purged he could sue a writ from chancery to have them returned: Fitz, *Corone*, 356 (eyre of Northampstonshire, 1329); Fitz, *Corone*, 393 (eyre of Kent, 1314–15). If the clerk died in custody his chattels remained in the hands of the king, but his lands were returned to his heirs: Fitz, *Corone*, 365. The shift to claiming clergy after conviction caused confusion around property rights and in the 1366 case which defined clerks convict and clerks attaint, it was noted that if a man takes his clergy after he is found guilty he will forfeit his chattels because he is a clerk attaint and the judgement is entered in the roll that he should be suspended by the neck, but if he takes his clergy before he is attaint he shall forfeit nothing because he is not attaint: YB Mich 40 Edw. III, pl. 23, p. 42. Fitz, *Corone*, 91. This is the lightest interpretation of forfeiture I have seen in the reports, and it seems likely that the reporter was simply wrong when he suggested that a clerk convict would lose nothing, but that his distinction between a clerk attaint and convict was seen as useful.

These cases make it clear that the common lawyers regularly engaged with questions around purgation, even though it could be argued that their interest in a clerk convict was determined when he was delivered to the ordinary. Since an appropriate purgation, properly conducted, was key to the effectiveness of the punishment of clerks convict, it is not surprising that the courts maintained a keen interest in it. In the same way, escapes from the bishops' prisons obviously undermined the whole system, and both the secular and the ecclesiastical authorities took them seriously. According to the *Liber Assisarum*, in 1338 Duket [Marmaduke] Dautre was found guilty before the inquest, but the ordinary refused him because he had previously broken out of the archbishop's prison.[36] By escaping Dautre had demonstrated his contempt for ecclesiastical authority as well as secular: under these circumstances the ordinary was justified in refusing him under canon law as an incorrigible criminal, and the justices all agreed that he should be hanged. This case demonstrates the law operating as it should: Dautre had obviously claimed clergy successfully the first time but had abused the privilege, and on his second conviction both the ecclesiastical and the secular authorities were content to let justice take its course.

Though both the secular and ecclesiastical authorities were in harmony in Dautre's case, in more complex cases there was more room for disagreement. For example, in 1343 a clerk attaint broke out of an ecclesiastical prison and killed two men. On his arraignment in King's Bench he confessed the felony and asked to turn approver. Scot CJKB, with the assent of all the counsel, told him that he could not, because he was outside the law on account of his first attaint. Scot then asked the ordinary if he wanted to claim the felon, whereupon the court remanded the felon to prison so they could be advised.[37] No result is given, but this case suggests that Scot saw the decision to claim the felon, unprepossessing as he was, as the ordinary's, while other members of the court were more hesitant to hand over a repeat and confessed killer. We see this tension between the rights of the ordinary and the desire to punish the felon even more clearly in a 1353 case, when a clerk attaint broke out of the prison of the abbot of Westminster. When he was arrested he simply responded that he was a clerk, to which Shardelow replied with the maxim 'vainly does he who offends against the law seek its help' arguing that because he had done violence to the Church, the ordinary need only refuse him for the hanging to proceed, and citing Dautre's case.[38] The ordinary did indeed reject the felon, but the reporter asked what would have happened if the ordinary had

[36] 12 *Lib Ass* p. 38, pl. 39. The name appears as Dantre in the printed year book. The case also appears in YB Mich 12 Edw. III (Rolls Series) p. 69, pl. 31.

[37] YB Hil. 17 Edw. III, p. 13, pl. 47. Fitz, *Corone*, 109.

[38] Frustra legis auxilium invocat, qui in legem committit. 27 *Lib. Ass*, p. 138, pl. 42. In Fitz, *Corone*, 250, Willoughby uses the same maxim in a case where the clerk convict killed his guard and broke out of the prison. It is possible that this is another version of Dautre's case: it is also dated to 22 Edw. III, but it is in the same run of cases as pleas 254 and 257. Another version of plea 250 appears under 8 Edw. II in Fitz, *Corone*, 419. This also appears in *Spelman's Reports*, vol. 1, p. 63.

instead claimed him and he had been delivered: would this have been a contempt against the bishop?[39] This report suggests that while Dautre's case had established the principle that the ordinary's refusal allowed the justices to go ahead and hang a felon who had offended against the Church's law, it did not mean that the justices could make that decision for the ordinary. Both of these cases demonstrate that if the ordinary was willing to accept the felon, the justices felt obliged to deliver him, though they could potentially punish the ordinary for forcing them to do something contrary to an emerging sense of the right result.

The justices' desire to see Dautre and his ilk punished did not necessarily mean that they were keen to see every felon hanged. In the same year as Dautre's case the *Liber Assisarum* reports that if a clerk is found guilty and the justices know that he is a clerk because he read, but the ordinary refuses to claim him, that he shall not be hanged, as happened with Hugh de Lacy.[40] Brief though it is, this report is quite tricky. The report says that the clerk in this case 'se mit de bien et mal' which it glosses as 's. pled rien culp' indicating that he had gone through a jury trial, rather than the inquest of office which established Dautre's guilt. But the justices knew that he had read, implying that they had allowed the reading test despite having a jury verdict. This suggests that the justices were content to let de Lacy go to the ordinary, but the ordinary was less happy to have him. This may have been part of the reason for the decision that he should not be hanged: having decided to spare de Lacy the noose, presumably the justices were unwilling to allow the ordinary to reverse that decision by his refusal.

Both Dautre's case and Hugh de Lacy's case became standards, appearing not only in the *Liber Assisarum* but in the manuscript year books which were later subsumed in Fitzherbert's *Abridgement*, and they demonstrate that from an early date the courts could take a variety of positions on benefit of clergy, depending on the history of the felon and, presumably, the nature of his crime.[41] Overall, these early fourteenth-century cases show the courts working through the practical implementation of benefit of clergy in a way which generally respects the Church's rights, but which demonstrates that the common lawyers were comfortable testing the boundaries of those rights and working out their own perspectives on how the processes around delivery should work.

[39] 27 *Lib. Ass*, p. 138, pl. 42. Fitzherbert's wording is slightly different, but he makes essentially the same points: *Corone*, 205.

[40] 12 *Lib. Ass.* p. 35, pl. 15. The case also appears in YB Trin 12 Edw. III (Rolls Series) p. 599, though in this case the report is less clear on the reading qualification, suggesting that the justice knows that the felon is a clerk 'par taunt par chaunce qil list apris'. In the *Liber Assisarum* the felon is named as H de Bast, but the Rolls Series has de Lacy, and that is the name which appears in versions of the case in Fitzherbert.

[41] Both cases mutate in their passage through the manuscript year books into the abridgement: see Fitz, *Corone*, 257; 254; 117; 120.

3. The Black Death

The demographic catastrophe of the mid-fourteenth century had real implications for attitudes to benefit of clergy. It is generally accepted that the post-plague clergy were less educated, on average, than those pre-plague. The high clerical death rates meant that there were many vacancies, but with few well-trained men available to fill them: Henry Knighton complained about men whose wives had died in the plague crowding into orders, many of them illiterate, others able to sound out words but not to understand them.[42] Such men were unlikely to go back to school for a number of reasons: they were desperately needed for pastoral work, they were uninclined to do so, and the clerical schools were generally in decline.[43] Post-plague clergy were thus less likely to be comfortably literate than their predecessors, and this almost certainly had implications for claiming clergy: the records talk about the need for a felon to read *ut clericus* in order to establish his claim of clergy, but without ever defining what *ut clericus* means. Whatever it meant in 1348, it would not be at all surprising if it declined in real terms as semi-literate men who had taken orders in the years after the plague found themselves before the courts for felony and the ordinaries fought to ensure that they were delivered.

The effect of this shift in the clerical population, together with the growing confidence of the common lawyers around benefit of clergy, is apparent in contemporary discussions. The *Ordinacio pro clero* of 1351 complains that both secular clerks and monks have been 'drawn and hanged by award of the secular justices, in prejudice of the franchises of holy church and in oppression of the jurisdiction thereof'.[44] Rather than the complete disavowal of temporal jurisdiction clear in the earlier statutes, *pro clero* instead states that both secular and religious clerks 'which shall be from henceforth convict before the secular justices aforesaid' shall be handed over to their ordinary without delay, once demanded.[45] This is a *de facto* recognition of the right of the temporal justices to determine the guilt of such a clerk. In return for the immediate delivery of the clerk, the archbishop of Canterbury, Simon Islip, promised to make an ordinance to ensure that such convict clerks would be 'safely kept and duly punished, so that no clerk shall take courage to offend for default of correction' and he at once issued appropriate instructions to his suffragans.[46] The

[42] Henry Knighton, *Chronicon*, p. 63, quoted in William J. Dohar, *The Black Death and Pastoral Leadership* (Philadelphia: University of Pennsylvania Press, 1995), p. 119.

[43] Dohar, *Black Death*, pp. 121–126.

[44] *SR*, I. 325. 25 Edw. III, stat. 6 c. 4. Baker says that this is an extension to secular clerks, i.e. laymen who could read, rather than seeing it as referring to regular and secular clerks. *Spelman's Reports*, vol. 2, p. 328.

[45] The ordinance specified that clerks could not be held in secular custody with the excuse that further indictments would be forthcoming, suggesting that this was a common evasion: *SR*, I . 326. 25 Edw. III, stat. 6 c. 5.

[46] D. Wilkins ed., *Concilia Magna Britanniae et Hiberniae* (London, 1737), vol. 3, pp. 13–14, printed in part in Gabel, *Benefit of Clergy*, pp. 134–135. According to William Edington's register Islip's mandate meant that clerks convict 'need not punishment, but consolation to help them back to their former life' and provided that they should have bread and water once a day on Wednesdays, Fridays, and Saturdays,

statute also provided that bishops' temporalities were no longer to be seized for any contempts, but an appropriate fine was to be assessed: though no specific mention was made of abuses around benefit of clergy, whether the claiming of suspicious clerks or their escape, there was clearly room for this provision to be applied in that context.[47]

If the statute summarizes the political consensus on benefit of clergy in 1351, a report from the following year summarizes the legal understanding of the main issues in the same period. This case began with an abjuration, but it seems to have turned into a wide-ranging discussion of various methods of mitigating criminal punishment, which the report summarizes into four principles: even if one says that he is not a clerk, he shall have his clergy afterwards; one who committed sacrilege shall have his clergy; if an ordinary claims one who is not a clerk, he shall lose his temporalities; and 'that literacy does not make a clerk, unless he has the tonsure'.[48] The first point clearly descends from de Lacy's case. The second point probably descends from Dautre's, but in the intervening fourteen years it has shifted to allow him clergy, apparently regardless of the desires of the ordinary: though the common lawyers were generally deferential to ecclesiastical authority, there were rumblings of disquiet which tended to err on the side of mercy, rumblings which were apparently quite loud by 1352. The third and fourth points, however, make it clear that the inclination towards mercy was limited only to tonsured clerks, and if the provision to protect the bishops' temporalities in *pro clero* was intended to apply to ambiguous claimants, the message had clearly not been received. The summary given here is thus oddly conservative: it affirms the rights of genuine clergy, but limits the ability of the common lawyers to deliver and of the ordinaries to claim men whose status is more ambiguous. This report and *pro clero* are perfectly compatible, but largely because they effectively talk past each other.

The Black Death also provides the context for a 1376 Commons petition asking the king to drop the exception of bigamy, so that a bigamist 'should have

bread and small beer on Mondays, Tuesdays, and Thursdays, and bread, beer, and vegetables on Sundays. It also notes that there should be an enquiry before purgation. Islip's mandate appears in this register among a series of mandates from the early 1360s: *The Register of William Edington, Bishop of Winchester 1346–1366 part 2* ed. Dom. S.F. Hockey, Hampshire Record Series vol. 8 (Hampshire Record Office, 1987), vol.2: no. 258, p. 35; no. 458, p. 58; Hants RO 21M65/A1/9 pp. 323, 368.

[47] *SR*, I. 326. 25 Edw. III, stat. 6 c. 6. The *gravamina prelatorum* of 1327 had complained that the ordinaries were fined £100 for the escape of a prisoner, while secular wardens were fined only 100s. The king had ordered an investigation, but there was no direct response. *Pro clero* may have been an oblique attempt to accept the £100 fine as a preferable norm to the seizing of temporalities, and that was eventually the outcome: PROME, vol. 9, p. 107: Jan 1327; *Rotuli Parliamentorum Anglie Hactenus inediti*, ed. H.G. Richardson and G.O. Sayles, Camden Society 3rd ser. vol. 51 (London: Royal Historical Society, 1935), p. 107.

[48] The discussion took place in a case before Shardelow at Newgate, 26 *Lib. Ass.* p. 122, pl. 19; Fitz, *Corone*, 191. In the same year Skipwyth said that a man was indicted before him for robbing a chalice and breaking a church, and asked if he should have clergy, and they said yes: 26 *Lib. Ass.* p. 123, pl. 27; Fitz, *Corone*, 193.

the privileges of clerks; that is to say, to go to the bishop's prison, as others do'.[49] The petition argued that because of the plague 'many people of the realm, peers of the land, noblemen and esquires as well as all other manner of people, married widows, some have had two wives and therefore are bigamists and some whose wives are dead refrain from marrying again to avoid being bigamists and therefore live in lechery all their lives'. As is often the case, the logic of the request is not entirely clear: it seems unlikely that large numbers of men who were concerned that re-marriage would inhibit their ability to claim clergy in the event that they committed a felony would be squeamish about living in lechery in the meantime. It seems more likely that the petition was trying to frame a credible context for the request to allow benefit of clergy to bigamous clerks as the number of such men in orders grew in this period. The king said that he would consider the matter further, and the Commons raised the issue again the following year, asking bluntly this time that privilege of clergy should be allowed, notwithstanding bigamy. This time the response was clear: 'Let the law take its established course'.[50] The social turmoil of the post-plague period was not enough to change the exception, presumably because it originated in the canon law, and thus was not within the purview of the common law to change: parliament could change *de bigamis*, but since this built upon the council of Lyons, it was not clear what the impact of such a change would be in practice.

If an influx of older, previously-married, and less-educated men into the priesthood had a fairly predictable effect on benefit of clergy, the more generalized social shocks of the period are likely to have had more diffuse effects: given the demographic impact of the recurring rounds of plague we might expect to see a decline in enthusiasm for execution, and this, combined with the reduced level of literacy among the clergy, is likely to have inclined people to accept the extension of benefit of clergy to the literate laity. Gabel notes, for example, that lay occupations begin to appear regularly for felons claiming clerical status at the end of the fourteenth century, where they had been rare in earlier decades.[51] The desire to remove the exception of bigamy reflects a similar impulse, directed primarily to preserving the clerical labour supply, but with the potential to save other men with valuable skills. At the same time, the social disruptions of the period pushed public opinion in the opposite direction, towards a drive for stricter law and order. Another Commons petitions of 1377 reflects this impulse, asking that 'if any robber or murderer be attainted and convicted to the bishop's prison, defamed as a common murderer or robber, that it shall please the bishops to be better advised upon their purgation than they have lately been, to avoid great injury to the people'.[52] The limitation of

[49] PROME, vol. 2, p. 333: April 1376.
[50] PROME, vol. 3, p. 22: Oct 1377.
[51] Gabel, *Benefit of Clergy*, pp. 76–77.
[52] PROME, vol. 3, p. 23: Oct. 1377.

the request to murderers and robbers points to a concern about violent criminals rather than about benefit of clergy per se, and it is striking that the petition uses language reminiscent of the canon law in its description of the felons.[53] The petition did not generate a statute, but the king responded by charging 'the prelates that they should rather abstain from making such purgations, and especially in respect of common and notorious criminals; and if they do not, the king will ordain some remedy by the advice of the lords'.[54] Though the king did not limit his charge to violent criminals, he shared the concern of the petitioners with 'common and notorious' felons, and thus with widening the scope of the privilege to the undeserving.

Concerns about serious criminal activity are also visible in a statute of 1390 where the Commons argued that pardons were being too readily granted for murder, treason, and rape. They petitioned that pardons should not be available for these crimes, and should only be granted for other felonies on the payment of a stiff fine, starting at £1,000 for archbishops and dukes and working down to 500 marks for an abbot, prior, baron or banneret.[55] Clerks, bachelors, and those of lesser estate were to pay 200 marks and spend a year in prison.[56] Both the petition and the statute were obviously concerned to ensure that those indicted or convicted of crime would pay a substantial penalty, even if they were wealthy and well-connected enough to secure a pardon, but the implication for clerks is interesting: if they claimed benefit of clergy they would be delivered to the ordinary until they could undergo purgation, but if they paid 200 marks for a pardon they would be delivered to the ordinary for a year and then released. Pugh suggests that the statute provided a way out of prison for those clerks who could not otherwise be purged, but it also indicates that a clerk convict would usually expect to remain in prison for a substantial period of time before purgation was available.[57] There is no evidence that the statute was effective, but it suggests that parliament was trying to find innovative ways to ensure both that those who committed violent crimes and those who committed lesser felonies should be appropriately punished, and that the appropriate punishments in the latter case need not involve execution.

The next major statute dealing with benefit of clergy came in 1402, when the provisions of *pro clero* were confirmed by Henry IV. The same statute also provided that since the terms 'insidiatores viarum' and 'depopulatores agrorum' had

[53] Helmholz, *Ius Commune*, p. 128.

[54] PROME, vol. 3, p. 23; Pugh, *Imprisonment in Medieval England*, p. 49.

[55] PROME, vol. 3, p. 268. The Commons requested that if a pardon was granted, any judge before whom it was presented was to find the indictment for the crime, and if the indictment was for murder rather than manslaughter, for example, the pardon was to be void and the party incur the full weight of the common law. See Thomas A. Green, 'The Jury and the English Law of Homicide, 1200–1600', *Michigan Law Review* 74 (1976), pp. 462–472 for more on the statute.

[56] The statute was passed with only minor differences from the petition: *SR*, II. 68. 13 Ric. II, stat. 2, c. 1.

[57] Pugh, *Imprisonment in Medieval England*, p. 41. The statute does not specify that the clerks would be delivered to the ordinary for the year in prison, but this seems the most likely interpretation.

not previously been used in indictments, arraignments, appeals, or impeachments, they should not now be used, though words of similar effect could be used. Nevertheless, the statute continues, any clerk who is the subject of such an indictment or arraignment shall still have the benefit of his clergy when demanded by the ordinary.[58] At first glance this is an obscure provision, but the statute originated from a petition of the archbishop of Canterbury and the clergy, and the phrase 'quod ipsi commones latrones depopulatores agrorum sive incidiatores viarum extiterunt' comes from their petition.[59] The petition asserts that numerous clergy had recently been executed for such crimes on the authority of the secular justices, and characterizes these as part of 'several other attacks against the said ecclesiastical liberties in various other ways, which are increasing more than usual in your realm at present'. This suggests that some secular justices argued that common thieves, pillagers of fields, and nocturnal highway robbers were not eligible for benefit of clergy under the terms of the canon law, and thus should not be delivered. The ecclesiastical authorities were unimpressed with the justices' attempt to interpret and implement canon law, and argued instead that all clerks should be delivered, promising once again to keep any such clerk committed to them safely, and under the terms of a constitution to be made according to the letters of Simon Islip of 1351. They promised that no clerk convict should make any purgation contrary to these constitutions, which would be shown to the king.[60] The statute accepted the clergy's petition for the most part and confirmed the liberties of the Church, including the delivery of clerks convict and the provision for the provincial constitution.[61] This peculiar episode suggests that despite the social upheaval not much had changed in the previous fifty years. But the common lawyers evidently recognized that the canon law could be useful in their quest to limit benefit of clergy, as Spigurnel had done a century earlier. Here we see the unexpected sight of the common lawyers using canon law to limit benefit of clergy, while the ecclesiastical authorities seek a statute to confirm and maintain it.

As this suggests, across the fourteenth century the law on benefit of clergy could be charitably described as confused. In the early part of the century both the ecclesiastical and the secular authorities seem to have agreed that a repeat offender was not a good candidate for mercy, particularly if his second offence was against the Church, and it was accepted that in such circumstances a clerk convict could be executed by the secular authorities. Nevertheless, if the ordinary decided that he did want to claim such an offender, the secular justices seem to have felt obliged to

58 *SR*, II. 132. 4 Hen. IV, c. 2.

59 PROME, vol. 3, p. 494. 'Public thieves' and 'the nocturnal highway robber and pillager of fields' were excepted by canon law from the privilege of sanctuary, not clergy: Helmholz, *Ius Commune*, p. 34.

60 *SR*, II. 133. 4 Hen. IV, c. 3.

61 It did not specify that 'common thieves' should be dropped from indictments. Baker says that the accusation of being a common thief was being dropped by the common law courts by the middle of Edw. III's reign as being too vague: Baker, 'Some Early Newgate Reports', pp. 42–43.

deliver him, though they were inclined to punish the ordinary for forcing such an outcome. Conversely, if they had decided to allow a clerk to be delivered and the ordinary blocked them, the justices were unwilling to hang the clerk, though they had no clear sense of what should happen next. This suggests that while the ecclesiastical authorities were still in the lead on matters relating to benefit of clergy, the common lawyers were starting to develop their own attitudes to the privilege. By the end of the century it is clear that clerks convict were regularly being tried by the secular courts, and that such trials were accepted by the ecclesiastical authorities as long as the clerks were delivered promptly on conviction. The common lawyers were increasingly driving the process in the courts, though they were as likely to justify their actions with reference to canon law as common law, and they continued to protest that the bishops were not meeting their custodial obligations. There are no clear sides here: common lawyers used the canon law when it helped them limit the privilege, and ecclesiastical authorities used statutes when it helped them bolster it. If the statutes give us a reasonably good sense of where the polemic on benefit of clergy stood at any given moment, the arguments made in individual cases, as we would expect, are usually driven by the desire to secure a particular end, and were then reported with little of the context that would allow us to understand the desire or the end.

4. The Reading Test in the Fifteenth Century

In the early fifteenth century there are few statutes or reported cases dealing with benefit of clergy, but a new source appears on the scene, readings from the Inns of Court.[62] Readings were lecture series delivered at each of the four Inns of Court twice a year, in the Lent and Autumn vacations. The readers were prominent lawyers, and the readings were intended to instruct students at the Inns not just what the law was, but how the law worked. Notes from readings circulated around the Inns and were copied and re-copied over generations: this makes them unreliable guides to the state of the law at any given moment, but invaluable insights into the many ways the law could be understood to operate.[63] Readings on Westminster 1 c. 2 are particularly useful for understanding benefit of clergy, and the earliest surviving readings on that statute date from about 1430. Readings on Magna Carta c. 1 also sometimes discuss benefit of clergy, though it was less central to their concerns.[64] The readings are not prescriptive, as statutes are, but they are also not

[62] Bellamy notes that there was little change in the law in this period, and no noteworthy discussions of it: *Criminal Law and Society*, p. 124. This silence is matched by the records: Gabel's numbers show a precipitous decline in the claims of clergy from the reign of Henry V onwards: *Benefit of Clergy*, p. 129.

[63] Margaret McGlynn, 'Idiosyncratic Books and Common Learning: Readings on Statutes at the Inns of Court' in *The Oxford Handbook to English Law and Literature, 1500–1625*, edited by Lorna Hutson (Oxford: Oxford University Press, 2017), pp. 42–46.

[64] *Rights and Liberties*, pp. xv–xvi.

records of conflict, though they often incorporate both statutes and cases. The ways in which they were created and circulated makes them virtual palimpsests, and this quality means that they reflect the ideas of the fourteenth century, and allow us to see how they are shifting in the fifteenth.

By the early fifteenth century the drift of practice meant that clerks were being tried and convicted in the secular courts and 'clergy' was proved by proving literacy. The readings take this as a given, but they give us more insight than the reports into the issues around the reading test. The readers state quite clearly that the ordinary was expected to be present as a matter of course, at least in King's Bench and for gaol delivery, though for other sessions he would be called if necessary. If the ordinary refused to come, he was held in contempt and fined, though at least one reading argued that his contempt was for the *ius ecclesie*.[65] The felon was given a book to read (though it was often a psalter, this was not required) and Kebell's reading emphasizes that the text must be clear, legible, and Latin.[66] Though the ordinary was generally present for the reading test, most of the readings are very clear that the court carried out the test rather than the ordinary, and one explains that this is because the judges are the ones who cause the verdict to be written into the record, and the ordinary is only an officer of the court.[67] An early reading argues that the court may test the felon in the absence of the ordinary, but that if he fails it cannot proceed to execution, but must wait for the ordinary to arrive and give him the option of taking the clerk *sub suo periculo*.[68] This reflects the argument made in 1353, and demonstrates that the principle was still in circulation a century later at the Inns of Court. The same reading concedes that the ordinary may receive a man even if he is not a clerk, but argues that he will lose his temporalities.[69] Here again the ordinary is given some leeway if he is willing to accept the punishment, but the concession suggests that while it was not unusual for an ordinary to claim a laymen, it was not yet seen as routine or broadly acceptable. Kebell's reading, delivered around 1472, states that if the ordinary claims one who is not a clerk he shall not have him, and he shall pay a fine; though this remained a useful orthodoxy, it is unlikely that it represented common practice by this date.[70]

[65] G.O. Sayles, 'A Fifteenth-century Law Reading in English', in *Scripta Diversa* (London: Hambledon Press, 1982), p. 304. The readings do not specify whether the bishop or his officer would be fined, but it was probably the former.

[66] *Rights and Liberties*, p. 25. This is one of the few readings on this topic with a named and distinguished reader: E.W. Ives, *The Common Lawyers of pre-Reformation England* (Cambridge: Cambridge University Press, 1983), pp. 394–417.

[67] *Rights and Liberties*, pp. 2, 25, 155. Gabel says that the commissions from the bishop stated that it was the ordinary who administered the test but that from the reign of Richard II the phrase in the records is 'tradito ei libro per Curiam', whether the ordinary was present or not: *Benefit of Clergy*, pp. 54, 72.

[68] *Rights and Liberties*, p. 2 (before 1430); *Rights and Liberties*, pp. 39, 45 (*c.* 1474).

[69] *Rights and Liberties*, pp. 2, 39. This suggests that the concession of *pro clero* had not entirely banished the older learning.

[70] *Rights and Liberties*, p. 25. Kebell points out that in the reign of Edward II it was judged that if the ordinary claimed a clerk who had not read well enough he would lose the privilege for the future, but he argues that this was not good law, since the privilege was not a franchise, but a right of the Church. Kebell was referring to Scrope's argument in 1327–8, see pp. 23–24.

The readings show that in the first half of the fifteenth century the justices were in charge of the delivery of the reading test, but the ordinary's role in witnessing and in claiming the clerk was still respected. By the second half of the century the discussion in the readings focused more on who set the standard for passing the test. As long as the judges and the ordinary agreed that the felon had (or had not) read *ut clericus* the question of who was in charge was largely moot, but what if the clerk 'does not read well, but spells or reads one word and not another' for example? Two readings say that the decision to take him shall be at the discretion of the ordinary, but another reading says that if the ordinary says that he reads well, but 'other men about seien nay' he will not be delivered.[71] The readings generally confirm the tradition since 1353 which supports the ordinary's right to choose, even if he must be punished for it, but they update the context: in the fourteenth century the ordinaries were exercising that right to claim repeat offenders and clerks found in secular dress, but in the mid-fifteenth century they were trying to claim men who did not pass the reading test. The ordinaries' concern in the post-plague period that they should be able to claim a man who did not read *ut clericus*, but who was nevertheless a clerk, may have provided an easy path for the extension of benefit of clergy to laymen who were likewise marginally literate, and once that pattern was established, it stuck. Though this fits into the argument that benefit of clergy served as a serious loophole in the criminal law, and that churchmen were willing to allow lay criminals to take advantage of it in order to maintain their privileges, the readings betray no significant concern about this problem: some are content simply to deliver the felon, while others point out the penalties that the ordinary should suffer for abusing his privileges.

The readings spend much more time on the other main problem inherited from the fourteenth century: what to do when the ordinary refuses to take a man that the judges have decided is a clerk. Some felt that this represented a much greater challenge to their authority, since 'the examination is for the court and not the ordinary'.[72] The readings work towards finding a solution: the earliest reading argues that if the ordinary refuses a felon who has been judged a clerk the felon has no remedy, but argues that the bishop shall lose his temporalities.[73] This accepts the ordinary's discretion, but it is cold comfort for the felon. By the middle of the fifteenth century most of the readings agree that the court should keep the felon and

[71] *Rights and Liberties*, pp. 16 (mid-fifteenth century), 53 (late fifteenth century); Sayles, 'Fifteenth-century law reading', p. 304. *Rights and Liberties*, p. 74 on Magna Carta says that an unlettered clerk won't get the benefit, but adds that the ordinary may take him at his peril under Westminster 1. There were other possible complications in the literacy test—what if the felon spoke Latin but could not read it? One reader says bluntly that he will not be delivered to the ordinary, but another argues that a blind man who can speak Latin will be delivered, unless he's Italian: *Rights and Liberties*, pp. 7 (*c.* 1450/60), 25 (*c.* 1470). Kebell says a mute man may also have the benefit, though he doesn't specify how it will be tested: *Rights and Liberties*, p. 25.

[72] *Rights and Liberties*, p. 58.

[73] *Rights and Liberties*, p. 2.

compel the ordinary to take him, *in favorem vitae*.[74] This situation played out in real life in 1456, when a felon pleaded clergy before Fortescue at King's Bench. The ordinary, the archdeacon of the abbot of Westminster, came 'and showed him a book, and the felon read well and clearly'.[75] The judges asked the archdeacon if he wished to receive the clerk, and he refused him, saying that he was not a clerk. The judges, however, said that they wished to record that he had read as a clerk, and he was remanded to prison so that the judges could be advised. A new ordinary appeared for Westminster two terms later, and the felon was brought back to court and once again claimed clergy. The new ordinary accepted him as a clerk, and all the judges agreed that this was well within his rights, for 'even if ... [the felon] had failed to read once, and notwithstanding that he had judgement to be hanged, still, in favour of life and the liberties of the Church, if he demanded a book again, notwithstanding that he was below the gallows, and he read, he would still have the benefit of his clergy'. This was a rather peculiar statement on the part of the justices, since the felon had apparently read well the first time—the ordinary did not refuse him for his reading, but more fundamentally on the grounds that he was not a clerk, suggesting that he did not see the reading test as dispositive.[76] Nevertheless the justices wanted to establish the point that if a felon failed to read, was ordered to hang, and then managed to learn to read before execution, that clergy should still be available to him 'in favour of life and the liberties of the Church'.[77] The response of the first ordinary suggests that he did not see this outcome as being greatly in favour of the liberties of the Church, but there is no question that it was greatly in favour of life.[78] This concern with favouring life does not appear in the earlier year books or readings, but it recurs regularly as a phrase from the 1450s onwards, suggesting both that some level of reluctance to execute all felons survived from

[74] *Rights and Liberties*, pp. 16, 38, 155. The ordinary was to be coerced by the imposition of fines, repeated as necessary to achieve the desired end. By the 1530s a reader could argue that if the ordinary refused a clerk without cause, he would 'lose his franchise to challenge clerks and also his temporalities shall be seised into the king's hands': *Rights and Liberties*, p. 157. This seems to refer back to Kebell's rejection of Scrope's 1327 argument, but reach quite a different outcome. See p. 37 n. 70.

[75] YB Trin 34 Hen. VI, p. 49, pl. 16.

[76] Two readings accept that the ordinary may refuse the felon generally—that is, without giving a particular reason—recognizing that the ordinary may have a reason for refusing him that is outside the competence of the secular court, such as bigamy, Lollardy, or excommunication: *Rights and Liberties*, pp. 116, 41. Reading E allows that the ordinary may make such a refusal even if the clerk is a priest. There was no agreement even on this point, however, and another reader argues that even if the ordinary swears to an exception in the spiritual law, such as that the clerk is a bastard or a villein, he shall be compelled to take him: *Rights and Liberties*, p. 16. Kebell notes that if the ordinary refused him generally or specially, and the judges saw that he was a clerk, the ordinary would be fined: *Rights and Liberties*, p. 26.

[77] The readers note that if the felon learns to read in prison, he is to have his clergy, though the gaoler is to be fined for his negligence: Kebell even claims that this is a common inquisition, though I have never seen it: *Rights and Liberties*, p. 24.

[78] The case also falls squarely within the older tradition, for Fortescue's concern was whether the first archdeacon should be fined for refusing to take the clerk even though the court had recorded that he read, and the other judges agreed that he should.

the post-plague years, and that the justices were increasingly comfortable with asserting their understanding of how the system should work.

5. Purgation and Escape

Despite their new desire to favour life, the justices still wanted to see criminals punished. Purgation remained the key to an effective system, and in January 1449 Fortescue presented a case to the exchequer chamber which demonstrates that they were thinking about purgations from a new perspective. A felon convicted and delivered to the ordinary as a clerk attaint was taken on suspicion of another felony and brought before the court. Asked if he were the same person, he confessed that he was.[79] Fortescue's question was whether and how the king should sue process against the ordinary for an escape, since he had allowed the clerk to be purged. All the justices agreed that where one was attaint of felony by his own confession and delivered to the ordinary he should not be allowed to make purgation, and that any such purgation would be considered an escape.[80] This case demonstrates two important changes in the law. The first is the change in the understanding of clerks convict and clerks attaint. In the late fourteenth century the standard division was between those who claimed before and after judgement, though as we saw, there was a good deal of inconsistency in practice. By the mid-fifteenth century the most common argument in the readings was that one attainted by verdict could make purgation whether he claimed clergy before or after judgement, because the jury might have lied and the verdict of twenty-four clerks was more credible than that of twelve laymen.[81] The companion argument was that one who confessed or abjured could not make purgation, since in both cases he confessed his own guilt.[82] The second is the shift in attention from the felon to the bishop: in the fourteenth century when a felon was improperly purged the implication was simply that he would be held without purgation thenceforth. In the fifteenth century the classification of an unwarranted purgation as an escape meant that the bishop could be punished

[79] YB Hil. 27 Hen. VI, p. 7, pl. 4; Fitz, *Corone*, 16; Brooke, *Corone*, 4.

[80] They placed outlawry, abjuration, or approving in the same category. The bulk of the discussion concerned the process against the ordinary. The point was reiterated in a year book case in 1488: YB Mich. 3 Hen. VII, p. 12, pl. 5.

[81] *Rights and Liberties*, p. 35.

[82] *Rights and Liberties*, pp. 86, 58, 35. Reading J also argues that one attainted at the suit of the party would not have purgation, *Rights and Liberties*, p. 58; cf. p. 27. The readings continued to pay attention to the canon law. *Rights and Liberties*, pp. 17–18 notes that the rules about purgation vary between common law and canon law, since under canon law a common thief might not make purgation, but he can under common law, as long as he is not attaint. *Rights and Liberties*, p. 8 argues that one convicted of petty treason or who was a common thief should only have his purgation according to the provincial constitution. Yorke blends both traditions: a clerk convict who confesses may not make purgation, because confession is stronger than verdict, but a clerk attaint shall never make purgation. *Reports from Henry VIII*, vol. 1, p. 91 (Yorke's Notebook).

rather than simply admonished to do better. The readings generally agreed that if a clerk who was delivered to the ordinary to be held without purgation was found at large, this would be considered an escape at the common law and the bishop would be fined £100.[83] Bishops could be, and were, punished for escapes in the fourteenth century, but there is a new emphasis on framing undue purgations in this way from the mid-fifteenth century on.

The justices were not the only ones with purgation on their minds. In February 1449 the Commons presented a petition to parliament which complained that murders, manslaughters, robberies, and other thefts were on the increase because of 'those felons who have been clerks and can read, because of the great boldness of their clergy'.[84] They argued that felons were leaving sums of money with receivers to be sent to them when they were committed to the ordinary, presumably to pay for purgation through bribery, and then returning to their life of crime, and doing the same thing again. The description of the process of evasion is more detailed than in the 1377 Commons petition, and the language more lurid: the Commons claim that 'those persons who have been so robbed, nor their friends, nor the friends of those who have been slain, dare not take it upon them to labour against such felons for fear of death'. This suggests that once again the Commons were most concerned with violent offenders, but their request is more specific than in 1377: they asked that the bishops allow only one purgation, so that a repeat criminal shall be kept in prison, and that any ordinary who does otherwise shall be fined £100, with the money to go to the king's household. As in 1377 the petition did not result in a statute, but where Richard II had widened the scope of the Commons' petition, Henry VI was more evasive. He argued that the matter pertained to the lords spiritual, so the archbishops and bishops should determine a due remedy and that 'the church shall have its freedoms and liberties'.[85] Henry VI was well known as a devout monarch and this, combined with his weakness, is explanation enough for his unwillingness to take on such a touchy issue, but the tone of the Commons petition indicates that the problem was only becoming more politically pressing.

The upheavals of the War of the Roses changed the political calculations and probably contributed to the charter issued by Edward IV in 1462 confirming the liberties, prerogatives, and customs of the Church in which he promised all clerical persons freedom from lay indictments and inquests including those concerning felony, rape, and treason, and provided that if any clerk was arrested on such grounds, he should immediately be delivered to the ordinary.[86] While the charter drew on some traditions of the common law, it was profoundly out of date and likely to generate opposition among the legal profession were it to be used. It was

[83] *Rights and Liberties*, pp. 18, 10, 42, 85.
[84] PROME, vol. 5, pp. 151, 333–334. The answer: le roy s'advisera.
[85] PROME, vol. 5, p. 151.
[86] Wilkins, *Concilia*, pp. 3, 583–584; Bellamy, *Criminal Law and Society*, pp. 126–127.

not supported by any statute, and probably had little, if any, impact on the administration of the law.[87] We have seen previous kings treading carefully in their responses to Commons petitions: they tend to profess respect for the privileges of the Church, even as they exhort them to improve their procedures, and even as their courts steadily establish their own understanding of the law. Edward's charter most likely falls on this continuum, a political concession to a powerful constituency in the search for stability, but one which had little force against the accumulated weight of common law learning.

We can see this in the summer of 1469 when a number of these threads came together in a case before King's Bench. A man had abjured the realm for killing a man and was arrested on his return. He pleaded the king's pardon for the homicide, but since the pardon made no mention of the abjuration, it was disallowed. He then claimed his clergy. The ordinary brought a book 'and the justices opened the book and assigned a verse for him to read, and he did not know how to read well, but one word in one place and another in another place, and he could not read three words together'.[88] The ordinary nevertheless claimed the felon, and the judges warned him to think further on this, for 'if it seems to us that he does not read sufficiently as a clerk, you shall make a large fine and still he shall be hanged, for we are the judges of his reading, for we shall make our record that he reads as a clerk and therefore he shall be delivered to the ordinary'. This is exactly in line with the arguments in the readings, but it caused some elaboration in the court, with one discussant arguing that the ordinary should indeed pay a fine for attempting to claim such a felon, but the man should not be hanged, apparently espousing a moderated version of the classic argument where the ordinary's claim bought a respite for the felon.[89] Billing CJKB pointed out that the man read, but not *ut clericus*, for 'he must read distinctly and clearly'.[90] He remanded the convict to the following Monday, so that the court and the ordinary could be advised. It is not indicated in the report whether the ordinary left the courtroom with the convict, but the discussion continued as Sulyard recalled a case before Fortescue where one claiming his clergy had not read well but 'spelled and put together' the words, but yet had his clergy. Those present recalled that that claimant had confessed the felony and thus was not eligible for purgation, and the same was true for this claimant, since

[87] Bellamy points out that convocations in 1463 and 1471 were still calling for the immediate delivery of clerks in lay prisons, suggesting that the charter was indeed a dead letter. He also speculates that it was an early attempt to separate the rights of clerks in major orders from those in minor orders: *Criminal Law and Society*, pp. 127–128.

[88] YB Trin. 9 Edw. IV, p. 28, pl. 41.

[89] The case seems to have been used as an opportunity to rehearse the accumulated learning on the topic. In the course of the discussion reference was made to most of the major fourteenth-century cases discussed above (pp. 23–30), and to a 1406 case where the ordinary refused a clerk: YB Pas. 7 Hen. IV, p. 41, pl. 6.

[90] il dever lier distincte et aperte.

he had confessed his crime before abjuration.[91] This case confirms two hypotheses about the state of the law, and introduces a third. Firstly, it provides the clear statement that the justices were in control of the reading test. Secondly, it confirms that purgation was not available for a felon who had confessed, and by implication that felons who had been convicted by juries were eligible.[92] Finally, for the first time we explicitly see the lawyers distinguishing between the ability to read, and the ability to read *ut clericus*. The standard for reading *ut clericus* was never defined, but there seems to have been universal agreement that this man did not meet it, and if he were eligible for purgation his claim for clergy might have been denied. The fact that he was ineligible for purgation seems to have influenced the inclination towards mercy, suggesting that the ability to read *ut clericus* could be determined on a sliding scale. The option to deliver the felon to a life sentence in the bishop's prison meant that this confessed, abjured, and partially pardoned homicide might be allowed to claim clergy while being appropriately punished.

Of course for this to be a feasible option the justices had to have some confidence in the security of the bishops' custody, and the case also indicates that such confidence was lacking in some quarters. It was said in the course of the discussion that the bishops allowed all the clerks convict to make their purgation, because they claimed that everything that happened in the common law court was *coram non judice* if the felon was a clerk. This brought the swift response that any such purgation would be an escape, and that if the proceedings before the common law court were *coram non judice*, the bishop would have no warrant for holding the clerk in prison.[93] Though this is a relatively small part of the report overall, it shows how much the law had changed. In the early fourteenth century the role of the common law process in the delivery of clerks was both attenuated and ambiguous: an inquest rather than a trial, it provided a common law record for the delivery of the clerk and the confiscation of his goods, but the ecclesiastical authorities were still arguing that it was unnecessary at best, unwarranted at worst. By the late fourteenth century the inquest had become a trial, and while the ecclesiastical

[91] On the following Monday, the ordinary returned and told the justices that he would take the clerk or not, according to the wishes of the court, and then refused him. There is a counter example from the Newgate gaol delivery in January 1481. Here the clerk read 'well enough' [assets bien], but when Brian asked the ordinary if he wanted to claim him, the ordinary responded, after great deliberation, that he did not read *ut clericus* for divers considerations, and judgement was given that he should be hanged. The reporter was obviously mystified by this outcome, noting that 'the temporal justices have power to determine' and speculating that this felon did not have a tonsure or was a repeat offender, thus demonstrating his familiarity with the historical material. The felon had been arraigned, reprieved, and re-arraigned, so this case seems to have had enough oddities around it that it does not represent normal practice: YB Hil. 21 Edw. IV, p. 21, pl. 1. In 1482 the principle that a felon who read well but was refused by the ordinary should be remanded to prison was agreed by all the justices of Common Pleas and King's Bench, along with the corollary that one who did not read well would be hanged, though there was no mention of the traditional fine for the ordinary who tried to claim: Mich. 22 Edw. Reported in Fitz, *Corone*, 44.

[92] Stated explicitly in YB Pas. 13 Edw. IV, p. 3, pl. 6.

[93] See p. 98 for a later development of this thread.

authorities were not enthusiastic about the change, they largely accepted it as the price of maintaining their privilege. By the mid-fifteenth century the common lawyers were essentially arguing that the bishops could not hold clerks convict without the common law process, thus demonstrating the emergence of a naturalized, secular understanding of benefit of clergy.

The same understanding appears in the readings, which regularly note that the common law and the canon law had different standards and different processes. They recognize, for example, that tonsure was a canonical requirement, quoting the maxim that 'literacy does not make a priest, nor a habit a monk, but the tonsure'.[94] At the same time they point out that the reality was different, for 'if a man who is indicted is a priest and does not have a tonsure, by the rigour of the law he shall be killed notwithstanding that he is a priest and takes his clergy, but ... the custom is otherwise'.[95] This leads them to the natural conclusion that 'the law of England is more favourable to him than is the law of Holy Church, for even if he had neither tonsure or vesture, as a clerk ought to have, still he shall be delivered to the ordinary'.[96] This awareness of a distinction between common and canon law appears even more forcibly in Thomas Kebell's discussion of purgation. The usual tone of secular commentary is that the bishops need to tighten their grip on the clerks in their custody, but Kebell is less concerned with security than with jurisdiction, and he argues that even if the archbishop of Canterbury grants that no-one arrested for petty treason or grand felony should be received to purgation, this is void because 'if all the prelates wish to make a provincial constitution, this shall be void because they cannot change the law of the land'.[97] He is presumably referring to Islip's 1351 constitution and its successor in 1402, both of which appeared at the time as the only way to handle problems with purgation. By *c.* 1470 this prominent common lawyer very clearly saw the purgation of clerks convict as part of 'the law of the land'. It is hard to imagine a clearer statement of the independence of the common law and its freedom to grant a broader privilege of clergy than the canon law.

Helmholz notes this situation with some puzzlement, commenting that 'it is not easy to explain this state of affairs, in which the common law inclined more to the material interests of the church than did the *ius commune*'.[98] The responses of the fifteenth-century ordinaries suggest that they did not see the actions of the common law judges as being in their material interests: though the ecclesiastical authorities were always anxious to maintain their privileges in theory, individual ordinaries

[94] *Rights and Liberties*, pp. 1, 37–38, 49.

[95] *Rights and Liberties*, p. 38. *Rights and Liberties*, p. 1 makes a similar point.

[96] *Rights and Liberties*, p. 74. *Rights and Liberties*, p. 26 agrees and adds clerical vesture. *Rights and Liberties*, p. 38 notes that this has been the case 'since the time before which memory does not run'. *Rights and Liberties*, p. 129 quotes John Hales, reading in Lent 1520, to the effect that the English Church has more privileges than any other Church, because clerks without tonsure may have the benefit.

[97] *Rights and Liberties*, p. 26.

[98] Helmholz, *Ius Commune*, p. 245.

were not nearly as anxious to accept every criminal that the common lawyers had decided was a clerk into their custody. Not only were they being forced to accept men who did not fit the canonical rules for the privilege, they were being forced to accept lay criminals as criminous clerks, with all the potential reputational damage that brought, and to feed, house, and process them, with all the attendant costs. It is not hard to understand why an ordinary might try to reject such a 'clerk': the more intriguing question is why the common lawyers wanted to save him.

2
Sanctuary
Common Learning

Sanctuary does not have the same kind of statutory structure as benefit of clergy, partly because it is much older in both conception and use. Sanctuary cities predate Christianity and in their broad conception fill a need for a place where the law can be suspended while justice and mercy are negotiated. In the Christian era churches became effective sites of sanctuary, for the Church fiercely defended the immunity of its buildings from both violence and secular jurisdiction: a criminal fleeing to a church could be reasonably sure that neither his victim nor the forces of law and order would breach the building to exact revenge or justice, at least in the short term. Though it felt strongly about the protection of the innocent, the Church did not look kindly on sin, however, and sanctuary was usually part of a process rather than an end in itself, though that process changed over the centuries. MacSheffrey points out that Shoemaker, Rosenwein, and Hyams have all

> argued effectively and persuasively that sanctuary was an integral part of an earlier medieval world where wrongdoing was conceptualized as a breach in relationships between people rather than as an offence against a properly constituted authority, such as the king. The response to such wrongdoing was not punishment as deterrence, but instead reconciliation and healing of the social breach—facilitated by the intermediary role of the church and the safe and sacred space of sanctuary.[1]

In this conception if a man stole or killed and was pursued by his victim, the sanctuary served as a respite for the wrongdoer, a place from which he could negotiate an agreed settlement. In later years, as the reach of the common law grew, sanctuary continued to serve as a respite, but also became a place where the wrongdoer could accept the processes of the common law after tempers had cooled and the severity of the crime had been assessed by community members with a less immediate interest in the outcome. If neither reconciliation nor trial were feasible the sanctuary man had two remaining options: he could escape or he could choose to

[1] Shannon McSheffrey, 'Sanctuary and the Legal Topography of Pre-Reformation London', *Law and History Review* 27 (2009), p. 507.

The King's Felons. Margaret McGlynn, Oxford University Press. © Margaret McGlynn 2023.
DOI: 10.1093/oso/9780192887689.003.0003

abjure, to leave the realm and go into voluntary exile. The common law recognized the right of every parish church and churchyard in England to offer a basic right of sanctuary, but over the course of the centuries it also recognized the right of some religious houses to offer an expanded version of the privilege, and this was one of the paths by which the common lawyers came, once again, to develop a naturalized version of sanctuary.

The earliest English material focuses on abjuration as a core element of the claim of sanctuary, but abjuration existed apart from sanctuary. When a criminal abjured, he swore to leave the king's realm, never to return without the explicit permission of the king: in the assize of Clarendon of 1166 those who were acquitted of their crimes could nonetheless be required to abjure within eight days 'if they have been of ill repute and openly and disgracefully spoken of by the testimony of many and that of the lawful men'.[2] Ten years later the assize of Northampton refined the use of abjuration. It provided that only those acquitted of 'murder or some other base felony by the common report of the county and the knights of the country' should abjure, relieving those accused of lesser crimes of this punishment.[3] Those who were convicted of felony were to lose their right hand as well as a foot, and to abjure within forty days. Abjuration thus allowed the punishment of those who had avoided physical mutilation but who were widely agreed to be inimical to good order, as well as adding to the punishment of those who failed the ordeal.

The abolition of the ordeal led to a variety of changes in the common law in the years after 1215, most obviously and importantly the development of the criminal jury trial.[4] But the intensification of governance and the shift to capital punishment for felony in these years also affected the development of sanctuary and abjuration. It became increasingly common for felons who had sought sanctuary to confess their crime to the coroner and to abjure the realm. This allowed them to engage with the common law while avoiding capital punishment. Sanctuary and abjuration thus have a curiously liminal position in the English legal system: sanctuary itself predates the common law and relies very little on it for its validity and operation, but by confessing and abjuring the felon recognized the jurisdiction and authority of the common law, and in return the common law recognized the validity of exile as the punishment chosen by the criminal and supported and protected him against those who would do him harm.

[2] *English Historical Documents 1042–1189* ed. David Douglas and George Greenaway, 2nd ed. (London: Routledge, 1981), vol. 2, pp. 409–410.

[3] *EHD* vol. 2, p. 411. One who passed the ordeal could take his chattels with him.

[4] Thomas A. Green, *Verdict According to Conscience: Perspectives on the English Criminal Trial Jury, 1200–1800* (Chicago: University of Chicago Press, 1985), pp. 50–52; Thomas A. Green, 'The Jury and the English Law of Homicide, 1200–1600', *Michigan Law Review* 74 (1976), pp. 418–422.

1. Early Treatises

None of this was accomplished by statute, and we have little in the way of reported cases so early, but the essential elements of sanctuary and abjuration in the thirteenth century are laid out in *Bracton*, *Britton*, and *Fleta*. None of them goes into detail regarding the origin or purpose of sanctuary, which presumably seemed obvious, but they focus on how to get the criminal out of sanctuary and thus primarily on abjuration. *Bracton*, in the first half of the thirteenth century, assumes that the wrongdoer will confess, and describes how he must select a port from which to leave the country.[5] The time frame for the journey is set for him, and he may not leave the highway (except for necessity or to find shelter), or stay anywhere for two nights in a row. He does not have to confess his crime if he flees after conviction, or is taken with stolen goods. In these cases, *Bracton* argues, he does not have the right to stay in the church for forty days 'as some say' but ought to come forth and submit to the law as soon as the justices or the coroner arrive.[6] If he refuses to leave the sanctuary *Bracton* is adamant that the lay power has no right to drag him out, and hopes instead that the ordinary will do so, 'for sword ought to aid sword'.[7] It recognizes that this is unlikely, since the ordinary will fear irregularity, and so the wrongdoer may, apparently, 'keep himself there for forty days or for a year or two'. The only solution is to refuse him food, so that he will come out voluntarily and head for his port. Once he has reached the port the abjurer must cross 'as soon as he gets a ship and wind'.

Late in the century *Britton* assumes much of *Bracton*'s discussion, and focuses more on the practical details. It notes, for example, that a fugitive who will neither confess his felony nor leave the church will forfeit his chattels, which will be delivered to the township, while his lands will be seized by the king.[8] The refusal to respond is also to be noted in the coroner's roll. By *Britton*'s time the forty day sanctuary was apparently accepted for all fugitives. It notes that if one stays in the sanctuary beyond forty days after the coroner arrives the whole county will be charged with his custody and he will be considered a felon, but *Britton* makes no suggestion that he may be dragged out. It simply notes that after forty days he will be deemed a felon convict, and thus lose the possibility of abjuration or of appealing others. No one may feed a felon after forty days, laymen under forfeiture of life and limb, clerks under pain of banishment.[9] If the fugitive confesses and agrees to abjure, he

[5] *Bracton* makes it clear that he does not have to leave all the king's lands, but just the realm of England, and so argues that the felon may abjure by land if he goes to Scotland. *Bracton*, vol. 2, pp. 382–383. There is no indication that this was a regular practice.

[6] *Bracton* argues that the forty day allowance was a concession only to those who had been cleared by the judgment of water or fire according to the Assize of Clarendon, but who were nonetheless ordered to abjure the realm.

[7] *Bracton*, vol. 2, p. 383.

[8] *Britton*, p. 53. *Britton* notes that the coroner is not obliged to go, even if the fugitive asks for him, but none of the other sources suggests this.

[9] *Britton*, pp. 53–54.

will have the forty days in which to prepare, and will be handed over to the constable of the township, so that he has no opportunity to escape.[10] *Britton* notes that the abjuration will be made at the gate or fence of the churchyard, and both *Bracton* and *Britton* give an abjuror's oath: *Bracton* has the wrongdoer swear to leave the realm and not return without leave from the king or his heirs, while *Britton* prefaces this with the recognition that the abjurer is leaving 'for such an act which I feloniously did, or assented to the doing thereof'.[11] The abjurer was to go on his way with a cross in his hand, 'barefooted, ungirded and bareheaded'. *Bracton* had noted that the abjurer who behaved in any way other than that described would be in peril, but *Britton* reverses this negative statement and guarantees royal protection to the abjuror as long as he remains on the highway.

Fleta dates from around the same time as *Britton*, and for the most part agrees with it.[12] *Fleta* accepts the forty day rule, arguing that the felon cannot be forced out of sanctuary but must be starved out, and that one who refuses to leave voluntarily loses the right to abjure. It adds a few details, noting that the coroner may adjust the time the felon is given to reach his port 'according as the strength or weakness of his body shall require', and describing the abjurer, ungirt, unshod, and bareheaded 'as though he were to be hanged on the gallows'.[13] *Fleta* is also the first to consider what should happen when the felon reached his assigned port: it claims that he was to 'plunge in up to the neck and, having raised the hue, he must remain on the shore until he find passage'. While *Bracton* and *Britton* warned the abjurer not to stray from the road or return without permission, *Fleta* is the first to state explicitly that if he does either 'he may be beheaded with impunity, unless he be arrested, in which case he must be committed to gaol'. Like *Britton*, it suggests that the process is being used to avoid punishment for crimes which are not felonies, such as petty larceny: it points out that those who make false confessions should confess to killing someone whom they 'will afterwards be able to produce alive and well', so that they will be able to sue for a pardon. This suggests that the system was being manipulated by those who had no legitimate claim to sanctuary, but whose crimes caused enough outrage that they were in fear of their life. *Fleta* warns the criminal of the obvious pitfall in this approach, but it does not condone it, warning that the coroner should investigate abjurations and voluntary confessions closely to avoid this kind of manipulation.

These three texts pay little attention to sanctuary, but they agree on the core elements and the key problems of abjuration: what to do if the felon refuses to leave

[10] *Britton*, pp. 53–54. Kesselring notes that the practice of using a constable existed from at least the 1490s, but it is also familiar to the earlier readers, although it was not enshrined in statute until 22 Hen. VIII: K.J. Kesselring 'Abjuration and its Demise: The Changing Face of Royal Justice in the Tudor Period', *Canadian Journal of History* 34 (1999), p. 352. Its actual application was sporadic throughout the later Middle Ages.

[11] *Bracton*, vol. 2, p. 382; *Britton*, p. 54.

[12] *Fleta*, vol. 2, p. 76. It is the first to cite chapter 1 of Magna Carta in support of sanctuary.

[13] *Fleta*, vol. 2, p. 77.

sanctuary, how to protect the abjurer on the road, and what to do if he leaves the road en route to the port, cannot find passage overseas, and/or returns without permission, all of which will continue to vex the system through the next several centuries.[14] Though the core elements remain fairly stable, these texts also show the development of the law over the course of the thirteenth century: *Bracton*'s 'wrongdoer' becomes *Britton*'s and *Fleta*'s felon; the punishments for various infractions during the process are more clearly elaborated; the confession and oath are fleshed out; the Crown's obligation to protect the abjurer who accepts its terms is clearly enunciated; and the possibility that the process might be manipulated to avoid worse punishment is acknowledged. At the same time the ritualistic elements of the process are elaborated, with growing attention to the abjurer's garb and initial plunge into the sea, recognizing the continuing need for atonement and the community's desire to see the wrongdoer appropriately punished.

The fourteenth-century *Mirror of Justices*' account of the process of abjuration generally agrees with *Bracton*, *Britton*, and *Fleta*, though it says that felons who abjure are no longer being allowed to choose their own port of departure, and considers this an abuse.[15] It also implies that the abjurers' travel was controlled, claiming that 'the footpaths that run beside the great roads are forbidden them, and that they cannot use the roads and hospices in the manner of pilgrims', suggesting that the *Mirror*'s author sees abjuration as a kind of penal pilgrimage.[16] Unlike the earlier texts, however, the *Mirror* is equally interested in sanctuary, and in its discussion it blends the provisions of the common law and the canon law, mixing the languages of law and religion as casually. It begins by arguing that one who is 'by habit a thief, robber, murderer, or a wanderer by night, and known and proclaimed as such by the people his pledges or tithingmen' cannot claim sanctuary.[17] This blends the canon law's rejection of sanctuary for 'the public thief' and the 'nocturnal highway robber and pillager of fields' with Clarendon's punishment of those who failed to pass their community's test of probity.[18] The *Mirror* also refuses sanctuary for non-mortal sins, to those who have already been attainted or confessed

[14] The *articuli cleri* of 1315–16 also claim that abjurers are being plucked from the highway and killed by their enemies, and provide for their protection: *SR*, I. 173.

[15] *The Mirror of Justices* ed. W.J. Whittaker, SS vol. 7 (London: Bernard Quaritch, 1895), pp. 157–158. Two manuscripts of Bracton ascribe the innovation (wrongly) to the actions of chief justice Weyland in a 1288 case: *Bracton*, vol. 1, p. 83, n. 2. Weyland himself was assigned to the port of Dover when he abjured in 1290 (and was given specific stages for the journey): TNA JUST 3/87, m. 1 [AALT image 90–91]; Paul Brand, *The Making of the Common Law*, (London: Hambledon Press, 1992), p. 113. *Year Books of the Reign of King Edward the First*: 30 & 31 Edw. I ed. Alfred J. Horwood, Rolls Series (London: Longmans etc., 1863), p. 508 asserts that the abjurer 'should take the port assigned to him by the Coroner, and no other port'. R.F. Hunnisett, *The Medieval Coroner* (Cambridge: Cambridge University Press, 1961), pp. 46–47 suggests that there was a good deal of uncertainty over whether ports should be chosen or assigned throughout the Middle Ages.

[16] *Mirror of Justices*, p. 158. This may also explain why some abjurers did not make it to their assigned ports, if even the rudimentary travel aids available were denied to them.

[17] *Mirror of Justices*, pp. 33–34.

[18] Helmholz, *Ius Commune*, p. 34.

and to those who have committed mortal sin while in sanctuary, and it allows all those so refused to 'be taken, dragged and thrust out of sanctuary, without offence or prejudice to its franchise'.[19] The *Mirror* thus reserves sanctuary for those who have committed a mortal sin outside the sanctuary and who were of good report before committing the sin. Lest there be any doubt on this point, in his abuses of sanctuary the author notes again that 'it is an abuse to suffer thieves and felons, proclaimed and notorious, to be defended by sanctuaries'.[20] The *Mirror* is an idiosyncratic text, but it suggests that while the core practices around abjuration remained quite stable through this period, there was increasing interest among laymen in the question of who could, or should, be able to claim sanctuary.

2. Immunity and Privilege

As long as the sanctuaries remained outside the jurisdiction of the common law the year books paid little attention to the kinds of issues which appear in the treatises, but, as with benefit of clergy, they did pay some attention to the management of sanctuary. One early point of tension was the ability of the secular authorities to guard a sanctuary man. In 1315 *articuli cleri* claimed that those who take sanctuary are guarded so closely that 'they cannot depart from the hallowed ground to empty their belly, and cannot be suffered to have necessaries brought unto them for their living'.[21] It provided that guards should not be in the churchyard while the fugitive is in the church 'except necessity or peril of escape do require so'.[22] This does not seem to have solved the problem, and in Richard II's first parliament the clergy petitioned that sanctuary should be respected, and more particularly that 'within the places covered by such an immunity no guard shall be mounted by the lay power'.[23] The royal response warned those responsible for guarding such fugitives to keep them secure, but to remain outside the sanctuary. There was still room for negotiation over where that boundary lay. In February 1402 John Giffard was arrested and claimed that he was 'dragged out of the ... church [of St. Mary Somerset in London] by some enemies of his in contravention of the liberties of the Church and against the said John's will'.[24] The inquisition held on the matter found that Giffard had left the church to use the common privy, which was a hundred paces from the church, and that he was arrested forty paces from the church on his way back. The

19 *Mirror of Justices*, p. 34. The *Mirror* claims that 'King Henry the Third [sic] at Clarendon granted that they should be protected by the Church for forty days, and he ordered that the townships should guard such fugitives for the whole quarantine, and should inform the coroners'.

20 *Mirror of Justices*, p. 157.

21 *SR*, I. 172. 9 Edw. II, c. 10.

22 *SR*, I. 173.

23 *Rot Parl*. III. 27.

24 *Select Cases in the Court of King's Bench* vol. VII ed. G.O. Sayles, SS vol. 88 (London: Bernard Quaritch, 1971), p. 120.

jurors were asked 'whether or not the aforesaid John Giffard could have excreted elsewhere in some place nearer to the church or its churchyard or sanctuary than the aforesaid privy'. They responded that he could, 'that is to say one, two, three or four paces from the aforesaid churchyard, and he could have done it in many places the same distance round the churchyard or sanctuary'. Leaving aside what this case suggests about the physical environment around the church, it does indicate that both the right of the fugitive to his physical relief and the right of the authorities to guard the sanctuaries against escape were observed. The inquisition implies that if it had been found that Giffard had used the nearest privy he would have been restored to the church, and since he didn't, there is no implication that his arrest was in any way problematic.[25]

These cases were very clear that guards should only be posted when necessary, and that they should keep their distance. As Helmholz points out, under canon law the crucial point was the inviolability of the church buildings.[26] In practical terms, the officers of the law could not (or at least should not) follow a fugitive into the building, and no one could (or should) inflict physical harm on him there. The common law sources clearly accept this principle, both in the recognition that a fugitive could not (or should not) be forcibly removed from sanctuary, and in the practice of abjuration from the gate of the churchyard, where the coroner, even when carrying out a mutually acceptable procedure, remained on the boundary of the Church's jurisdiction. Even when there was general agreement on the principles, however, they could be violated in practice, whether those in hot pursuit of a criminal followed him into a churchyard without recognizing, or caring, that they had passed into hallowed space, or officials grew tired of trying to winkle an offender out after the forty days had passed. Those who respected the immunity of the Church in principle could be frustrated when they experienced a particular abuse, and the *Mirror*'s desire that sanctuary should be allowed only to those of good repute and its willingness to allow those who had committed mortal sin while in sanctuary to be forcibly removed reflect widely held concerns over the abuse of sanctuary by those who really ought to be punished.

As with benefit of clergy, it is important to recognize that the Church shared these concerns. The canonists were unanimous in their support for sanctuary in principle but they had varied and often inconsistent views on how it should work in practice, for it posed a logical problem for them. Though they held firmly to the church's right to physical inviolability and its right to protect the life and limbs of those who found themselves in trouble, they also recognized that criminals should be punished and that the Church should not, even involuntarily, help people sin. As a result, though there was no negotiation on the principle of sanctuary, there

25 Giffard claimed benefit of clergy and was handed over to the ordinary.

26 Helmholz, *Ius Commune*, pp. 25–27. The canon law did not limit the privilege to forty days as the common law did.

was much disagreement on its extent. At one end of the spectrum some canonists excluded from sanctuary all those who had intentionally committed a crime, a view compatible with the approach of the *Mirror*, while at the other end some excluded only 'the public thief, the nocturnal pillager of fields and highway robber'.[27]

The confusion in the canon law was intensified by the confusion associated with the varieties of franchisal jurisdiction in England. Liberties or palatinates could also offer immunity from prosecution. Places like the marcher lordships did not claim rights of sanctuary per se, they were simply places where the king's writ did not run. They had no principled claim, no internal logic, and no system for dealing with fugitives. These sites were not religious, but the sanctuary they offered was the same as the Church's on a practical level: once the offender was in their jurisdiction, the king's justice could not pursue them. Over the course of the later Middle Ages their franchisal rights were whittled away and their ability to offer sanctuary diminished accordingly, with very little protest, but in legal terms they provided a model and an example of how exemption from royal justice might work.

This tangle of principle and practice came together in a handful of major sanctuaries. Durham, for example, was both a palatinate and an important religious centre. Here the right of the felon to avoid royal justice was based on both jurisdictional and ecclesiastical claims, and over the course of time the role of the two was bound to become blurred. Durham was unusually independent, but a version of its immunity arose in a number of other religious houses up and down the country. While they all had sanctuary as religious institutions, some claimed broader rights, usually on the basis of a royal charter, sometimes a forged one. Though the extended rights varied, they were usually some combination of a larger physical precinct, a broader range of crimes, and an indefinite period of immunity. These chartered sanctuaries' rights could be challenged, and they were, but they were invariably defended on the basis of their charters and thus on common rather than canon law grounds. Though the sanctuary which inhered in every church and churchyard in the country remained largely outside the jurisdiction of the common law, the granting of these charters to favoured houses allowed for an expanded common law version of sanctuary and placed the regulation and development of that version in the hands of the courts. But because the charters had originally been granted by devout kings in recognition of the spiritual value of the house, and because the cases were often provoked by the breaking of sanctuary, the arguments which arose in the courts often carried the uncomfortable freight of ecclesiastical privilege and the spectre of Becket. To argue, as Thornley did, that 'the privilege [of sanctuary] was ... purely secular and jurisdictional; but long before the Tudor period opened,

[27] Helmholz, *Ius Commune*, p. 42. Cf. p. 34 where this formulation is applied to those who claimed benefit of clergy.

circumstances had given it a false ecclesiastical colour' is thus to over-simplify the lived experience of medieval sanctuary.[28]

If Durham, in the far north, was the most powerful of the chartered sanctuaries, the abbey of St. Peter in Westminster was the most politically prominent, and also one of the most ample. For both reasons it appeared in early year book cases dealing with both the immunity of the precinct and the breadth of the privilege the Abbey could claim. In 1347 the abbot was accused of having allowed certain clerks attaint to escape from his prison. He denied the escape, and a search of the prison was demanded. Thorp CJKB quickly squashed this option, arguing that 'this is a place outside our jurisdiction'.[29] By 1355 the courts had begun to look more closely at the extent of the Abbey's immunities. In that year the abbot claimed that all those there for debt, account, or any other cause could remain without being prosecuted. He brought his charters to be examined, and though they spoke of fugitives coming 'pro quacunque causa', Shardelow JCP insisted that this was to be understood as referring only to felons, and all the justices agreed.[30] Though this was a blow to the Abbey's broader claims, it is worth noting that the justices accepted their right to provide refuge to felons who came 'for whatever reason' without demur.

Westminster's privileges were further spotlighted in August 1378, when Robert Hawley was killed by the high altar while resisting arrest. Hawley and his friend John Shakell had taken sanctuary in the Abbey after an escape from the Tower, where they were being held for refusing to negotiate a politically desirable ransom.[31] The constable of the Tower was sent after them, and in a botched attempt to arrest them he killed both Hawley and a servant of the Abbey. The Westminster clergy asked parliament for a suitable remedy for the breach of sanctuary, but some of the lords petitioned for an examination of the rights claimed by the Church. The petition claimed that the lords had

> called the justices and other men of law as witness that they well knew, that in the English church no one should or ought to have immunity for debt, trespass or in any other cause whatsoever, still less for crime. And also, that certain doctors of

[28] Thornley, 'Destruction of Sanctuary', pp. 183–184. T. B. Lambert argues that Thornley's conception is backwards in his discussion of the development of sanctuary rights: 'Spiritual Protection and Secular Power: The Evolution of Sanctuary and Legal Privilege in Ripon and Beverley, 900–1300', in *Peace and Protection in the Middle Ages* edited by T.B. Lambert and David Rollason (Durham: Centre for Medieval and Renaissance Studies, 2009), pp. 121–140.

[29] 21 *Lib. Ass.* p. 79, pl. 12. Brooke reports this case and questions Thorp's response, 'car non dicitur que fuit in le santuarie', but this is a later perspective: Brooke, *Sanctuary*, 12.

[30] 29 *Lib. Ass.* p. 164, pl. 34. Brooke adds that 'nota que ceux fuerent claime per charter & non per le pape'. Brooke, *Sanctuary*, 6. Westminster and St Martin le Grand's claims to give sanctuary for debt were extensive and long-lasting, but I will only consider them to the extent that they throw light on their claims to sanctuary for felony. Thornley suggests that these claims were related to the commercial expansion of the fourteenth century, and they do indeed belong in a history of the development of commercial law rather than criminal law: I.D. Thornley, 'Sanctuary in Medieval London', *Journal of the British Archaeological Association* 2nd ser. 38 (1932), p. 302.

[31] Nigel Saul, *Richard II* (New Haven: Yale University Press, 1997), pp. 36–37.

> theology, learned in canon and civil law ... concluded, having thoroughly and fully discussed the matter before the king himself, that in cases of debt, account or trespass, as no one should lose life or limb, so no one ought to have immunity in holy church.[32]

This was an accurate statement of the law, but when the king responded to the petition, though he recognized the problems that sanctuary for debt could cause, he concluded that, out of respect for the Abbey, which held relics of Edward the Confessor as well as the bodies of various of his predecessors, and for the charters of his predecessors, those who could not pay their debts because of 'fortune of the sea, or fire, robbery or other misfortune, without fraud or collusion' should have immunity.[33] This assertion of sanctuary for debtors is clearly one that belongs to the common law, and may be in part a response to the rather hysterical language of the original petition, which claimed that 'neither God, saving his perfection, nor the pope, saving his sanctity, nor any king or prince, could grant such a privilege'.[34] Though the problem of fraudulent debtors would rumble on for centuries, in this episode we see the king support the Abbey's rights against the opposition of the Commons, a pattern which will re-appear in a variety of guises over the next century or so. This is a reminder that, as with benefit of clergy, the jurisdictional issues around sanctuary were political as well as legal, and the political context could influence the outcome in particular high-profile cases without substantially affecting the development of the law.

On occasion, though, a political case was so high-profile that it did manage to change the law. In February 1388 Robert Tresilian CJKB was arrested in Westminster Abbey by the duke of Gloucester in the course of the Merciless parliament.[35] Tresilian was asked if the sanctuary gave immunity to a traitor, and 'he answered steadily that it did, since it was for such offenders in particular

[32] *Rot. Parl.* III, 37. Part of the political fallout of this breach of sanctuary was an attempt to argue that sanctuary was not available in cases of debt, and Wyclif was brought to the parliament at Gloucester to make this argument.

[33] *Rot. Parl.* III, 51. The episode seems to have prompted the composition of a defense of sanctuary by a Westminster monk which survives in Longleat, Wiltshire, Marquess of Bath Collection MS 38, a late-fifteenth-century copy, suggesting its arguments remained relevant: Gervase Rosser, 'Sanctuary and social negotiation in medieval England', in *The Cloister and the World: Essays on Medieval History in Honour of Barbara Harvey* edited by John Blair and Brian Golding (Oxford: Clarendon Press, 1996), p. 71.

[34] *Rot. Parl.* III, 37. The king's masterly obfuscation was followed in the next parliament, held in the spring of 1379, by a statute withdrawing protection from fraudulent debtors: *SR*, II. 12. 2 Ric. II Stat. 2, c. 3. The statute provided that once the creditor had a *capias* on a writ of debt, the sheriff would proclaim at the gate of the sanctuary once a week for five weeks that the debtor or his attorney should appear to answer before the justices. If he did not appear, judgment would be given against him for the default and execution could be made out of the land fraudulently devised.

[35] Tresilian was a staunch supporter of the king and had played a key role both in the suppression of the 1381 revolt and in the judges' response to the ten questions on royal power in August 1387: see Saul, *Richard II*, pp. 75, 78–79, 173–176.

that the privilege had been conferred upon the church of Westminster'.[36] The lords did not accept his answer, and Tresilian was speedily executed. In April of the same year the king sent for Westminster's privileges, and they were read in the presence of the chancellor (Thomas Arundel, archbishop of York), William Wykeham (the bishop of Winchester), and various others. According to the Westminster chronicler, Arundel, brother to one of the chief opponents of the king, thought nothing of having a fugitive removed from sanctuary. The monks argued against him that

> not only should the blood-guilty and those accused of any other offence whatever, together with all their possessions, enjoy the immunity concerned, but others with a bad name, whatever their situation and even though they may be open to the charge of treason against the king, should in sanctuary be awarded the same rights.[37]

This was an astonishingly broad claim, and Wykeham objected at once, arguing that this implied that someone could kill the king in the sanctuary and then stay there in perfect safety: Wykeham was not neutral in this situation, but his intervention once again raised shades of Becket, as well as the concerns of the canonists.[38] The king agreed with the monks, suggesting that all those who were involved in the death of Tresilian were excommunicate.[39] There is no question that the heightened political circumstances influenced the arguments made on both sides: the alliance between the king and the Abbey was further cemented by the abuse both had experienced at the hands of the appellants, while both Arundel and Wykeham were driven more by their political affiliations than by their role as churchmen. But once the crisis was over, the Abbey's position had been reinforced. On 15 May the duke of Gloucester and Sir John Cobham submitted to the abbot of Westminster 'promising to make satisfaction so far as lay in their power', while the Abbey's claim to provide sanctuary for traitors had been successfully staked.[40]

This high-politics case was quickly followed by a test which might have verged on the farcical under other circumstances. On 27 May a clerk who was fighting over a benefice went into sanctuary in Westminster. He had appealed to the chancellor for help regarding his benefice, but Arundel favoured his opponent. While

[36] *The Westminster Chronicle 1381–1394* ed. and trans. L.C. Hector and Barbara Harvey (Oxford: Clarendon Press, 1982), p. 313.

[37] *Westminster Chronicle*, p. 325.

[38] The chronicler, rather than arguing that sacrilege was excepted from sanctuary, makes the charmingly naïve point that 'none of the kings of the past is known to have ended his life that way in a spot so hallowed, and it is not to be supposed that such a thing need happen in the future': *Westminster Chronicle*, p. 325.

[39] The chronicler follows this with a lengthy paean to the king's devotion to the Church and his eagerness to support its rights: *Westminster Chronicle*, p. 327.

[40] *Westminster Chronicle*, p. 333. Since the chronicler does not detail what that satisfaction was, it is likely that it was minimal.

in Westminster the clerk wrote to a friend in Rome, including in his letter, both abuse of the chancellor and gossip 'which touched on matters of state'.[41] He then, unwisely, gave the letter to one who passed it on to the chancellor. The chancellor had the letter read out in parliament, whose members then clamoured to remove the clerk from sanctuary as a traitor. The abbot was sent for and tried to calm matters, but was hard pressed to answer the argument that sanctuary should not save the clerk who had committed his treason while in Westminster: indeed Sir Ralph Basset made the same point as Wykeham regarding a possible assassination of the king.[42] After some discussion the abbot was allowed to guard the clerk until the next parliament, and the whole matter disappeared from view. The echoes of Tresilian's case are more than metaphorical, and the factions on either side were obviously continuing the political fight. The king, unsurprisingly, supported Westminster and its sanctuary once more, and this time the abbot managed not only to claim the theoretical right to protect traitors, but also to keep one alive in the face of opposition from parliament.

While the fights over Westminster focused on the extent of its privilege, other cases in the early fifteenth century revolved around the question of how the privilege, whatever it was, could be proved when challenged. Battle Abbey, for example, had an unusually broad privilege: according to its chronicle, William the Conqueror granted that 'if any thief or homicide or a defendant on any charge, fleeing in fear of death, should take refuge in this church, he must by no means be harmed, but should be released wholly free'.[43] At the very beginning of Henry IV's reign, the new king brought a *quo warranto* against the abbot, and Serjeant Rede, the abbot's counsel, showed the grant of William the Conqueror with allowance in eyre: Hankford JCP and Serjeants Gascoigne and Tyrwhit argued while that the king could not grant the power to another to pardon a felon, because that was his prerogative, where anyone had such a liberty by prescription by force of usage and it had been allowed in eyre, it was good.[44] Broad and idiosyncratic as Battle's claim

[41] *Westminster Chronicle*, p. 337.

[42] *Westminster Chronicle*, p. 341. According to the chronicler the clerk prepared for death and took up a position by the shrine of St. Edward: *Westminster Chronicle*, p. 339.

[43] *The Chronicle of Battle Abbey* ed. and trans. Eleanor Searle (Oxford: Clarendon Press, 1980), pp. 69–71. Searle notes that this claim was based on a forged charter from *c.* 1166–1167. The chronicle also makes the remarkable claim that the abbot could release one condemned for any crime throughout the realm. This is reminiscent of the canonists' suggestion that the sanctity of a priest could represent sanctuary wherever he went, but is a remarkably broad recognition of the principle. I have never seen it claimed in any actual case, but Cox says it was exercised in 1364: J. Charles Cox, *The Sanctuaries and Sanctuary Seekers of Medieval England* (London: George Allen & Sons, 1911), p. 197, citing Mark Antony Lower ed. *The Chronicle of Battle Abbey from 1066 to 1176* (London: J.R. Smith, 1851), p. 204. I have been unable to verify Lower's reference, but cf. also the John of Jerusalem arguments in the late fifteenth century (pp. 167–168).

[44] YB Mich. 1 Hen IV, p. 4, pl. 6. This case has been interpreted to mean that the judges stated that the king could not make any new grants of sanctuary, which is clearly not the case: Thornley, 'Destruction of Sanctuary', p. 197. The relationship between the king's power to grant liberties and their validation through prescription and use constitute a central theme in sanctuary cases through the fifteenth century.

was, it was allowed because it had the right documentation. Beaulieu Abbey in Hampshire was less successful. In the spring of 1429 an attempt to reclaim a villein from London led to a broad discussion of liberties which turned to one of the most notorious sanctuary cases of the period, that of William Waw.[45] Waw was a thief who sought sanctuary at Beaulieu.[46] When his claim was challenged, the abbot came to claim the sanctuary by prescription time out of mind. Serjeant Newton pointed out that it was shown by record that the abbey was founded since the time of memory and so the franchise could not be prescribed, but otherwise it would have been allowed, and with it the claim of the thief.[47]

Both discussions show a growing interest in the documentation on which the privilege rested, and when the villein's case returned to King's Bench the following Michelmas the lawyers took the opportunity to discuss the differences between the documentation required for franchises such as London, Durham, and Westminster, and the implications for their operation. Serjeant Chaunterell pointed out that London had had its customs ratified and confirmed by the king's letters patent and by parliament, unlike Westminster or other chartered sanctuaries, demonstrating that for him, a city and a county palatine were the natural comparators for a sanctuary and introducing the idea that parliament might play a role in validating its rights. At the same time, he recognized the particular privileges of the Church, noting that if someone committed a felony and took sanctuary, the sheriff could not return him to the court for process, even though he was in his bailiwick, because it was against the privilege of the Church. Babington CJCP reinforced the point: he argued that if a felon was removed from the county palatine of Durham and asked to be returned without adding anything else he would be hanged, and the court agreed, 'but of a sanctuary which pertains to God and the Church, such as St. Martin's and Westminster and suchlike, it is otherwise'.[48] As with benefit of clergy, the common lawyers were grappling with the foreign concept of sanctuary, looking for a way to make it fit within their landscape of franchises while recognizing its peculiarities.

[45] R.A. Griffiths, 'William Wawe and his Gang, 1427', *Proceedings of the Hampshire Field Club & Archaeological Society*, 33 (1976), pp. 89–93.

[46] In the vulgate year book the case appears in the context of a writ of *nativo habendo* brought in Buckingham, which led to a writ to the sheriff of London, who answered that London was ancient demesne and had a custom that after a year and a day a villein would not be removed from the city. This prompted an extensive discussion of the nature of London's liberties, and of custom in general, which touched on Chester, Westminster, and St. Martin's.

[47] YB Pas. 7 Hen. VI, p. 33, pl. 27. Newton used this to demonstrate how much stronger London's claims were.

[48] YB Mich. 8 Hen. VI, p. 4, pl. 9. The case is also reported, briefly, in Fitz, *Corone*, 5 and Brooke, *Sanctuary*, 4.

3. Sanctuary and City

Though the lawyers compared a sanctuary to a city when they were grappling with issues of proof, many sanctuaries were inside cities, and as the law governing both was more clearly elaborated, they were more likely to clash. The fiercest conflicts, as well as the best-documented, were in London, where important and powerful sanctuaries were willing to push back against an increasingly assertive civic authority. In 1430 the mayor and sheriffs of London took Henry Ciprian, a canon of Waltham, from the sanctuary at St Martin le Grand, citing a statute of Edward III which would fine the city government if it did not repress disorder.[49] The dean, Thomas Bourchier, immediately appealed to the king, and that seems to have been the end of the matter.[50] The Londoners were not ready to give up, however, and the next dean faced a number of challenges. In 1439 Matthew Philip, an alderman, demanded a tax imposed by the mayor within St. Martin's Lane, denying that it was privileged. The new dean again turned to the king, and the matter seems to have been settled quickly with a dinner. Kempe points out that in the same year the sheriffs of London, Philip Malpas and Robert Largem, were accused of violating the liberties of the White Friars, St. Bartholomew's in Smithfield, and St. Katharine's by the Tower, and suggests that a conscious campaign was being waged against ecclesiastical privileges in the city.[51]

In 1440 the tensions between the sanctuary and the city broke out on a larger scale when a soldier who was being brought to the Guildhall to answer a charge of debt was rescued by four accomplices as he was brought past St. Martin-le-Grand, all of whom took sanctuary in the precinct.[52] The canons, in some panic, wrote to their dean (who was in Cambridge) for help, detailing the events. They related how the sheriffs, the alderman of the ward and the chamberlain of the city quickly arrived to claim back their prisoner and his rescuers, and how the commissary refused to hand him over without the dean's assent. After consulting with the mayor the sheriffs returned to St. Martins to agree that the fugitives should stay there until the canons had had a chance to write to the dean and warning the canons to ensure that they did not escape. There seems to have been a change of heart on the part of the officers, however, for later that day the sheriffs returned again with the under-sheriff and their council, and 'a great multitude of people'.[53] They demanded the

[49] *SR*, I. 346. 28 Edw. III, c. 10.

[50] Alfred John Kempe, *Historical Notices of the Collegiate Church or Royal Free Chapel and Sanctuary of St Martin le Grand*... (London: Longmans, 1825), pp. 113–114 provides the king's writ to the mayor and sheriffs of London instructing them to restore Ciprian to the sanctuary; Cox, *Sanctuaries*, pp. 82–83; McSheffrey, *Seeking Sanctuary*, p. 64.

[51] Kempe, *Historical Notices*, p. 116. Thornley also recognizes that Londoners were generally much more outraged by their 'commercial grievances' against St Martins than by the homicides and thieves who took refuge there: Thornley, 'Destruction of Sanctuary', p. 188.

[52] Kempe, *Historical Notices*, p. 117; Cox, *Sanctuaries*, pp. 83–86. See McSheffrey, *Seeking Sanctuary*, pp. 58–77 for the full context of the dispute.

[53] Kempe, *Historical Notices*, p. 118.

prisoners once more, and once more the commissary refused, saying that 'he in no wise would be irregular ne fal in perjurie for them'.[54] The sheriffs had lost patience by this point, and seized the men, removing them to Newgate in their underclothes and 'chained by the necke and manacled as traytours'.[55] The canons begged their dean to return quickly to deal with the outrage, and warned him that the other tenants of St. Martins 'dreden sore lest they be fecht out with force in the same wise'. Both the sanctuary men and the canons realized that if this seizure stood, the whole sanctuary privilege was undermined.

Dean Caudray was no less concerned and returned to London immediately to ask the sheriffs to return their prisoners. When they refused he complained to the mayor and aldermen, who set up a hearing to be held within five days. The dean, clearly outraged by this chain of events, was unwilling to wait and took his case directly to the king, emphasizing that this was a 'contempt done to God and your hyghnes, whose house it is'.[56] He argued that the city was throwing their full weight into this issue, claiming that the citizens were willing to pay the costs of destroying the sanctuary, whatever they were, and arguing that he could not fight against the power of the city at the common law. The king responded with a letter commanding the return of the prisoners. The Londoners tried to evade the royal command, but succeeded only in infuriating the king and found themselves called to Star Chamber to defend themselves. They argued that if the Church did have any privilege it extended only to cases in which life and limb were in danger, thus demonstrating that their main concern was with immunity for debt. They also argued that the precinct was part of the city. Descending from the general to the specific, they argued that the plea of debt against the soldier was fraudulent, and that the sheriff had seized the prisoners without violence, thus presumably conforming to the canon law on the violation of the peace of the sanctuary.[57] The dean, for his part, insisted that the sanctuary was not limited to felony, that the church had never been part of the city, showed his various charters, and pointed to the statute concerning fraudulent debtors of Edward III to prove that St. Martin's was privileged for treason, felony and debt.[58] He also noted that members of the corporation had taken advantage of the privilege for debt themselves on numerous occasions, a

[54] Kempe, *Historical Notices*, p. 118.

[55] Kempe, *Historical Notices*, p. 118. According to the dean's letter to the king, once in Newgate the men were 'under as many irnes as they mowe bere, and like to be dead hastily, as their frendes sayen': Kempe, p. 119.

[56] Kempe, *Historical Notices*, p. 119.

[57] Kempe, *Historical Notices*, pp. 123–124.

[58] Kempe, *Historical Notices*, pp. 124–127. *SR*, I. 398. 50 Edw. III, c. 6. This is a novel interpretation of the statute, which does mention St. Martin's as a place privileged for debt but makes no mention of felony or treason. Since the city was willing to concede capital crimes, presumably this was all the dean was interested in. The dean also mentioned the peculiar custom that prisoners being charged with treason or felony before the royal justices in St. Martin's gate were kept on the far side of the road lest they make a break for sanctuary.

point that he had already made in his earlier letter to the king.[59] The city responded in some detail, but the two chief justices supported St. Martin's, equating it with Beverley, Westminster, and Glastonbury, and the fugitives were restored.[60] The young Henry VI was an unusually devout monarch, but it is likely that any monarch would have behaved in a similar way. Caudray's emphasis on the royal basis of St. Martin's privileges was canny, but it was also true, and it is likely that the king and his advisors were not unhappy to have the opportunity to push back against the pretensions of the city, demonstrating royal authority while supporting the Church.

Thus by the early fifteenth century the broad outlines of the canon law around sanctuary were widely understood and the principle was widely accepted, but there was skirmishing around the jurisdictional boundaries. As with benefit of clergy, engagement with the practicalities of enforcement and political pressures had led to the development of a separate but related common law version of sanctuary. And as with benefit of clergy, English kings tended to support the Church's rights when they were challenged in a political forum. But unlike with benefit of clergy, the alliance of Crown and Church over sanctuary was often woven into disputes with third parties. In the late fourteenth century Richard's support for Westminster was closely tied to his fights with parliament. In the fifteenth, his successors provided similar support to chartered sanctuaries in the course of their struggles with the growing power of the cities.

The 1440 fight has attracted a lot of attention, partly because it is unusually well-documented, and partly because a political spat of this nature is intrinsically fascinating. It demonstrates many of the main political issues at the heart of sanctuary disputes, and some of the legal ones. But it raised no new legal questions, and while it confirmed St Martin's ability to give sanctuary on a wide range of issues, the fate of a minor debtor was small potatoes in the larger scheme of things. In the growing political turmoil of the mid-fifteenth century, the stakes were somewhat higher, and a series of high-profile men claimed sanctuary in St Martin and Westminster. Their fates demonstrate again that the authorities took sanctuary seriously. In November 1451 Sir William Oldhall, speaker of the parliament, took sanctuary at St. Martin's in anticipation of indictments for treason brought against him by the Lancastrians.[61] In February 1452 some men broke into the sanctuary and succeeded in removing Oldhall to Westminster, but the dean again defended

[59] Kempe, *Historical Notices*, p. 126. McSheffrey points out that Philip Malpas, one of the sheriffs who led the assault, later took sanctuary himself: 'Sanctuary and Legal Topography', p. 510.

[60] Kempe, *Historical Notices*, p. 131. The city's *Letter Books* record that 'because those persons who had plaints against the said prisoners were induced to declare themselves satisfied, the Sheriffs had no further cause for prosecution', *Calendar of Letter-Books of the city of London: K: Henry VI* ed. Reginald R. Sharpe (London: HMSO, 1911), pp. 233–248 'Folios 181–190: Oct 1439 - ' [https://www.british-history.ac.uk/london-letter-books/volk/pp233-248 accessed 6 March 2022].

[61] J.S. Roskell, 'Sir William Oldhall, Speaker in the Parliament of 1450–51', *Nottingham Medieval Studies* 5 (1961), p. 104.

his privileges. Caudray was called before the king and his privileges were examined for three days, and found 'full and sufficient to protect whatever persons who, for what cause soever, criminal or civil, might fly to sanctuary of this nature'.[62] Nine guards were dispatched to ensure that Oldhall did not escape and were directed to ensure that he did not write, speak or do anything out of their presence. This was a clear infringement of the sanctuary rules, and the dean returned to the fray. He succeeded in having the guards removed, the expenses of the proceedings covered, and the offenders confess and pay hefty penances.[63]

Lesser conflicts between St. Martin and the city continued, until finally in 1457 articles were enacted by the king's council for the better government of the sanctuary. Some of the articles were clearly concessions to the city guilds, such as the prohibition of false metal workers and the provisions that all artificers there should observe the same holidays as their London peers.[64] The rest focused on the management of the sanctuary men, and some of them were probably already in operation. They required every fugitive to declare his claim for sanctuary before the dean and be registered and to relinquish all armour and weaponry with the exception of a pointless meat knife. They provided that the gates to the sanctuary should be closed between sunset and sunrise; any sanctuary man who issued forth to commit crimes during curfew was to be confined to prison thereafter, though he did not lose his sanctuary. There was a process for restoring stolen goods; forgers and games of chance were prohibited, and prostitutes were encouraged to leave unless they amended their ways.[65] The articles were thus pragmatic in their understanding of the community while being protective of the privilege, and they reflect both old and new ideas about sanctuary. The provision that 'every erraunt and open theefe, robber, murderer, and felon, notoriously noised by the common fame of the people' had to find sureties during his time in the sanctuary and for three months after he left reflects the same mixture of the provisions of Clarendon and canon law that we saw in the *Mirror of Justices*, while attempting to providing a practical solution for managing that problem.[66]

[62] Kempe, *Historical Notices*, p. 143

[63] Kempe, *Historical Notices*, p. 142. Oldhall used the royal guards to claim that his sanctuary was a prison when he sought the reversal of his outlawry in 1455. Peter Iver Kaufman, 'Henry VII and Sanctuary', *Church History* 53 (1984), p. 474.

[64] Kempe, *Historical Notices*, 150. Shannon McSheffrey, 'Stranger Artisans and the London Sanctuary of St. Martin le Grand in the Reign of Henry VIII', *Journal of Medieval and Early Modern Studies* 43 (2013), pp. 546–551.

[65] The provision regarding stolen goods was responding to a long-standing frustration. In 1425 one J.C. claimed that his servant had fled to the church with stolen goods and the dean responded that 'the privilege of the place is such that if anyone comes to the said sanctuary with goods that he has stolen, etc., if the dean can seize them before the one whose property they were, he will have them', and argued that they were his property. This was essentially a claim of waif on the goods, since J.C. does not appear to have sued the felon for the original theft, but it added to the sense of abuse. YB Hil. 3 Hen. VI, p. 32, pl. 22: Kempe, *Historical Notices*, pp. 147–151.

[66] Kempe, *Historical Notices*, p. 148.

The fights between St Martin and the city of London demonstrate that opposition to sanctuary rights in this period were generally either a pragmatic frustration with disorder or an equally pragmatic desire to assert control over a physical space. There was no concerted opposition to sanctuary in principle or to sanctuary as an ecclesiastical privilege, but there was a steady desire to ensure that sanctuary did not either promote criminal behaviour or undermine the established economic order, concerns which the Church largely shared. When disputes arose, the legal mechanisms for solving them were effectively the same as in any other property dispute: the examination of charters, grants and the history of usage. When the dispute became political, as happened with St Martin's and London, the law did not change, but the defenders of the privilege could heighten their rhetoric by appealing to the king as a defender of the Church. This was not 'false ecclesiastical colour'.[67] The religious nature of the privilege was real, but it was rarely the problem.

4. Sanctuary in the Readings: Elaborating Practice

The discussions of sanctuary among common lawyers in this period reinforce the sense that the rights of the chartered sanctuaries were not really a live issue for them. As with benefit of clergy, there aren't a lot of reported cases in the early fifteenth century, but we do start to get evidence from the readings. Readings on Westminster 1 make occasional mention of sanctuary, but it appears more regularly in readings on Magna Carta c. 1, which guaranteed the rights of the Church, and there are a cluster of readings on that text that date from around the middle of the fifteenth century.[68] The readings spend virtually no time on jurisdictional issues: one reading discusses whether the claimant or the lord of the sanctuary is responsible for proving a disputed claim and cites William Waw's case, but otherwise chartered sanctuaries are conspicuous by their absence.[69] Instead the readings tend to focus on practical details, such as the kinds of crimes for which sanctuary could be claimed. We have seen broad political arguments about whether sanctuary should be available for debt, and moral arguments about whether it should be available for premeditated crime, but the readings get much further into the weeds, arguing, for example, that if a man is indicted for a theft worth only 4d he cannot have sanctuary, because he cannot be hanged for the crime, or that if a man claims sanctuary because he has struck a man and is removed because the man is still alive, he can return to sanctuary if the man later dies.[70]

67 Thornley, 'The Destruction of Sanctuary', p. 184.
68 For details and dates see *Rights and Liberties*, pp. xxvi–xxxii.
69 *Rights and Liberties*, p. 81. See p. 57 for Waw.
70 Statham, *Corone*, 29; *Rights and Liberties*, p. 94.

The readings also consider claims to sanctuary that make it clear that the *Mirror of Justices*' concern about the overall probity of the sanctuary man was long gone in practice and demonstrating why the governors of St Martin were keen to use sureties. One reading claims that if the felon escapes from the sanctuary and kills again, he can claim sanctuary for another forty days, and so on for as long as he can get away with it.[71] If a man kills someone in a church or a church yard he may claim sanctuary: if he kills while he is in sanctuary he will not have the privilege in that church, but the reading is not certain whether he may claim sanctuary for the crime in another church. This is a challenging interpretation of the various arguments made in this area. According to the Church, any killing in a church or churchyard was sacrilege and thus not eligible for sanctuary, but the common-law right here, as in other areas, seems to have been wider and more complex. We saw in the turmoil of 1388 that the example of killing the king in sanctuary and then claiming the privilege was used to highlight the absurdity of enlarging the right.[72] This argument suggests that while that idea was rejected, the next natural question, whether the homicide could then claim sanctuary elsewhere, was in circulation. Though it might seem like a fairly academic question, and probably would have been if the victim was the king, the records make it clear that many sanctuaries were rough places, and the death of a sanctuary man in a brawl was not unusual. It would not be surprising if his killer sought refuge in another local church.[73]

Readings later in the century go into more detail on the process of abjuration than the earlier readings, and again they deal with practical questions. One reading notes that the felon need only admit to having committed a felony when he claims sanctuary, but when the coroner arrives he must swear to the details of the crime.[74] It also comments that if he has trouble with the time and place where it was committed the coroner may help him. Sanctuary men frequently confessed to crimes committed several years in the past, and it is hard to imagine that they all had perfect recollection of their activities. Without these details the confession was incomplete, so it is not unlikely that the coroner would 'help' the felon with his confession, though this does suggest that the coroner would need some level of sympathy for the felon in question. If the felon refused to swear these details to the coroner he could be removed from sanctuary, and even if he later swore, he would not be restored, nor would he be able to abjure.[75] If the felon refused to admit to having committed a felony at all, he could be taken from sanctuary at once.[76]

[71] *Rights and Liberties*, p. 75

[72] See p. 56.

[73] Other readings consider the individual seeking sanctuary rather than the crime. Reading 6 argues that if a heretic is committed to the laity to be executed and flees to a church he will still have sanctuary, for the privilege goes with the place rather than the person: *Rights and Liberties*, p. 94. This is not the standard interpretation, and even the canonists argue that heretics could be excluded, along with excommunicates, Jews and Turks: Helmholz, *Ius Commune*, pp. 49–50.

[74] *Rights and Liberties*, p. 94.

[75] *Rights and Liberties*, pp. 94, 83.

[76] *Rights and Liberties*, p. 83.

There is a good deal of confusion over what should happen to the felon if he refuses to leave after the expiration of the forty days. *Bracton* had reluctantly allowed that the fugitive might stay in sanctuary for forty days or for a year or two, and by the mid-fifteenth century the law on the matter does not seem to have been much clearer.[77] *Bracton* had rejected the option of removing the fugitive by force, and the intervening centuries do not seem to have made that option more palatable. One reading argues that when the forty days are up, the felon may not be removed from sanctuary forcibly, either by the king's men or by the clergy, but that 'in this case the king's officers and those of the town who have charge of him may contain him'. We have seen that guarding a felon in sanctuary was a touchy business, but other readings from this period talk about 'immuring' the felon, which seems to mean imprisoning him within the sanctuary. This appears more often as an idea to be rejected than as one which was actually put into practice.[78] It was more common to argue that after forty days anyone who brought food to the felon would also be considered a felon, thus starving him out, and in the early sixteenth century Fyneux said that the starving was the immuring.[79] One reading considered what would happen if the felon lingered in sanctuary, arguing that if the felon has had his port assigned and tried to stay in sanctuary beyond his forty days, he will be hanged, 'for he has misused his privilege and when he has liberty to go and does not wish to go, then it is his folly'.[80]

These readings give the same basic picture of the abjuration itself as the early treatises: the coroner administered an oath that the felon would leave the country, gave him a cross to carry in his hand, and assigned him a port from which he should leave the country.[81] One reading agrees with *Britton* in saying that the coroner would hand him over to the constable of the next town, who would pass him on to the next constable, and so on until he reached the sea.[82] This sounds like a sensible plan, both to ensure that the abjurer reached his destination, and to protect him along the way, but it is clear that even when abjurers set out in the company of the local constable, they were usually left to their own devices for at least some part of the journey. The readings themselves make this clear: one reading considers what would happen if the abjurer were arrested on his way to the port and then broke out of prison, concluding that he cannot abjure for the prison break, since if he had

[77] Bracton, vol. 2, p. 383. See p. 48.

[78] The English reading says that he will be immured, and no one will give him food and drink: G.O. Sayles, 'A Fifteenth-century Law Reading in English', in *Scripta Diversa* (London: Hambledon Press, 1982), p. 305.

[79] *Rights and Liberties*, p. 130.

[80] *Rights and Liberties*, p. 86

[81] Cox, *Sanctuaries*, pp. 28–30 discusses the length of time that the criminal was allowed to reach his assigned port, which seems to have varied from case to case. He also discusses why coroners seem to have assigned a variety of ports, and not necessarily the closest ones: he gives the examples of felons sent from Norwich to Portsmouth or Southampton, York to Dover, and Lynn to Sandwich, the latter journey to be completed in four days.

[82] *Rights and Liberties*, p. 75.

remained in prison until his status was established he would have been restored to the highway and allowed to continue his journey.[83] This may seem to be placing too much faith in the system, but Statham reports a case for 1443 where an abjurer was arrested for leaving the highway, but argued that he was lost and had sought a constable immediately to put him back on the right route. The argument was accepted, and the abjurer returned to the highway.[84] These arrests would not have happened if the abjurer had been accompanied by a constable, but they demonstrate the kinds of problems an abjurer might face on the road.

The abjurer's problems might not be over when he reached the port. One reading argues that if he goes to the port and cannot find a ship, the constable will bring him back to the church where he claimed sanctuary and he will be assigned a new port. This assumes that the constable has completed the journey with the abjurer and requires considerable self-control on the part of both the constabulary and the fugitive.[85] The alternatives were not palatable, however, for another reading states that if the felon did not take the shortest route to the port, or left the port without taking ship, he could be immediately arraigned on this and killed.[86]

The readings demonstrate that a considerable body of practical knowledge had grown up about sanctuary and abjuration by the middle of the fifteenth century, presumably based on a fairly regular administration of the process. As with benefit of clergy, the readings show no concerns about the ecclesiastical basis of the privilege, and demonstrate both some level of familiarity with the canonical rules and a willingness to depart from them when managing the common law version. The absence of chartered sanctuaries from these discussions suggests again that while such sanctuaries could be political flashpoints, they were in no way central to the common lawyers' understanding of sanctuary, which focused on the regular parish sanctuary and the abjuration which was a likely outcome of such a claim. They also demonstrate that the abjurer was a rather vulnerable figure, likely to face incarceration by the authorities along his route as well as harassment from his victims, and facing an uncertain future whether he managed to secure passage overseas or not.

Political disputes over sanctuary loom largest in the surviving records: the removal of a chief justice from Westminster or the fight between London and St Martin's placed sanctuary at the heart of national and/or local politics and attracted attention then and now. And those stories do tell us something about the development of sanctuary: Westminster Abbey's privilege was not strong enough to save Tresilian, but it worked for Oldhall, and would work again for Elizabeth Woodville

83 *Rights and Liberties*, p. 70.

84 Statham, *Corone*, 27. Fitzherbert reports the same case, contrasting it with the abjurer who left the highway to answer the call of nature, and ended up working as a servant for a year. This lapse in judgment resulted in his sentence being carried out: Fitz, *Corone*, 14.

85 *Rights and Liberties*, p. 86.

86 *Rights and Liberties*, p. 75.

and some of her children.[87] It is clear, however, that this was not the most common use of sanctuary. For the most part sanctuary served as a refuge for those on the wrong side of the law rather than politics, whether they were career criminals or the unlucky, servants who were robbed of their masters' money, one who had stolen out of necessity, or killed in the course of a brawl. Taking sanctuary was not an easy option: the sources make it clear that sanctuaries were rough places, and sanctuary men risked damage to their reputations as well as their bodies. A 1425 Commons petition complained about men 'disloyal, suspicious and not worthy of being believed, hiding in various sanctuaries in the realm, and other caves and hiding places', while in 1472 Robert Bolling, petitioning Edward IV for the full restoration of his rights after being pardoned for treason, used as part of his argument that 'he never took sanctuary, or withdrew himself from your good grace'.[88] Genuine criminals, those who were literally getting away with murder, presumably were more than willing to exchange any reputation they had left for their lives. But for those taking sanctuary for political or economic misfortune, the reputation attached to sanctuary and sanctuary men must have given them some pause for thought.

This sense that sanctuary men had chosen to withdraw from the operation of the common law draws on the much older sense of sanctuary as a means to a private settlement of grievances with which this chapter opened. Sanctuary could still operate in that way, and Rosser has demonstrated how communities could choose to manage sanctuary claims without involving the representatives of the law.[89] But once those officials were involved, sanctuary became a part of the operation of the common law, even if somewhat peripherally. Though abjurers chose to remove themselves from the common law punishment for their crime, by taking their confession coroners effectively put the weight of the common law behind that choice and so the confession and abjuration process needed to be managed. By extending the canonical understanding of sanctuary through charters and grants, English kings constructed a parallel model which the common lawyers then tried to reconfigure within the norms of their increasingly structured system in the late fourteenth and fifteenth centuries. By the mid-fifteenth century there was a common law version of sanctuary, but the discussions over abjuration and jurisdiction did not significantly re-shape the core of what sanctuary was: the majority of the men and women who claimed sanctuary in this period probably achieved their aims with minimal engagement with the officers of the law. Sanctuary was

[87] Elizabeth Woodville 'regestrid hir & such as to hyr belongid as seyntuary ffolkys' at Westminster during the re-adeption, and Edward V was born there. She returned to sanctuary there after Edward IV's death: *The Great Chronicle* ed. A.H. Thomas and I.D. Thornley, (London: G.W. Jones, 1938), pp. 212–213, 230. The experiences of these men and women were so far outside the regular run of affairs, even for a place like Westminster, that they give us little sense either of how sanctuaries generally worked, or of how the law generally considered them, and I will consider them only when the arguments around them either illuminate or develop the law, as would happen in the celebrated case of Humphrey Stafford.

[88] *Rot. Parl.* Vol. 4, p. 291; vol. 6, p. 20.

[89] Rosser, 'Sanctuary and Social Negotiation', pp. 64–70.

thus fundamentally different from benefit of clergy, which originated and operated within its own well-defined legal system before crossing into the common law via statute and being tweaked, poked, and pummelled into a shape that fit the expectations of that system as it grew, and which, by the fifteenth century, required the direct involvement of the common law courts for its operation. Though sanctuary's roots were much older, they were far less firmly planted in the English common law, and that would have important consequences in the Tudor decades.

3

Processes and Records at the End of the Fifteenth Century

The first two chapters of this book outline the common learning on benefit of clergy and sanctuary available to common lawyers at the end of the fifteenth century. As we have seen, their predecessors had defined the big problems in the law over the course of the previous centuries, such as when clergy could be claimed, and the implications of that decision. They had also resolved some of those problems, but some, like the role of the ordinary or the balance between protection and immunity, continued to recur, though the response often changed, subtly or significantly, with the changes in society. In this process of definition and solution, the judges and serjeants of the thirteenth, fourteenth, and fifteenth centuries profoundly shaped the ways in which early Tudor lawyers and judges understood the criminal law. The examples provided in the year books and the readings make it clear that a variety of arguments could be made about any given circumstance, but the reporters and the readers were generally uninterested in the outcome of any particular case or the answer to any particular problem. They were much more concerned with testing which arguments could be made, and they cultivated strict habits of mind about what arguments were acceptable within the logic of the law and how they could be extended, essentially establishing the intellectual toolbox available to lawyers at the end of the fifteenth century.[1]

That intellectual toolbox was accompanied by a procedural toolbox. The common law relied on process to ensure order, and the information required at each step—its format, language, and sometimes even grammar—was strictly prescribed. Though criminal law did not have the technical complexity of property law, its forms and processes were no more flexible, and criminals, juries, and judges had to work within a narrowly defined set of procedures. The technical requirements of those procedures determined the information they gathered and recorded, and thus the information available to us as historians, and this shapes and often limits our ability to see what was really going on. In order to understand both how contemporaries manipulated the system, and how the information they gathered can be used, we need a clear understanding of what the system was and how

[1] Margaret McGlynn, 'Idiosyncratic Books and Common Learning: Readings on Statutes at the Inns of Court', in *The Oxford Handbook to English Law and Literature, 1500–1625*, edited by Lorna Hutson (Oxford: Oxford University Press, 2017), pp. 47, 56–58.

The King's Felons. Margaret McGlynn, Oxford University Press. © Margaret McGlynn 2023.
DOI: 10.1093/oso/9780192887689.003.0004

it worked. This chapter will outline how the criminal justice processes worked, the activities of ecclesiastical officers in the common law courts, the ecclesiastical processes and records around benefit of clergy and purgation, and the rituals of abjuration in the years around 1500. Not only does an understanding of these allow us to better understand the records they generated, it will also be taken for granted in the chapters that follow, so that only irregularities and innovations will be examined.

1. The Prosecution of Felony

Criminal jurisdiction operated, for the most part, at the county level. If the felony was a homicide, the recording process usually began with an inquisition on the view of the body. The inquisition was convened by the coroner, who was charged with the investigation of all unexplained deaths in the county, and attended by the coroner's jury. The inquisition sometimes gave an account of the events leading up to the homicide, such as a fight, which might lay the groundwork for an argument of self-defense or for pre-meditation, depending on the circumstances. It always gave a description of the mortal wounds, including their placement on the body and their depth and width, along with a description of the weapon that caused them and usually the name of the person who wielded the weapon.[2] And the inquisition could note if the killer had fled: in some cases it says nothing more, but in some it indicates specifically that he had fled to sanctuary, and might name the sanctuary.

For felonies where no body was involved the process usually began with an indictment by the grand jury, and for homicides this was often the next stage in the process.[3] The indictment laid out the formal charge against the accused and it had certain standard elements: it had to give the name, the estate, degree or 'mystery', and the place of residence of the accused, and it usually provided the same for the victim; it had to give a precise date and place for the commission of the crime; to be an accusation of felony it had to state that the crime was committed *vi et armis* and to describe any goods stolen, including their value, as well as the circumstances of a burglary, robbery, or homicide.[4] In order to proceed to trial the grand jury had

[2] Sara Butler, *Forensic Medicine and Death Investigation in Medieval England* (New York: Routledge, 2015), pp. 127–128, 137–140.

[3] Prosecution could begin on a private appeal, but few appeals reached verdicts in this period, and so they rarely appear in this discussion.

[4] The *vi et armis* provision was removed by 37 Hen. VIII c. 8: *SR*, III. 995–996. The descriptors were mandated by the statute of additions of 1413, 1 Hen. V, c. 5: *SR*, II. 171. J.M. Beattie notes that in the seventeenth century almost everyone indicted was described as a labourer and suggests that by this period there was enough concern about the failure of indictments on a technicality that 'labourer' became a fictive and acceptable way of filling the statutory requirement: see *Crime and the Courts in England 1660–1800* (Princeton: Princeton University Press, 1986), p. 21, but cf. J.S. Cockburn, 'Trial by the Book? Fact and Theory in the Criminal Process, 1558–1625', in *Legal Records and the Historian*, edited by J.H. Baker (London: Royal Historical Society, 1978), pp. 62–63. In the early Tudor period occupations and status do not seem to be fictive, and there is a good deal of variety and specificity in their

to find the indictment to be a 'true bill', though this did not imply anything about the guilt or innocence of the accused. In the case of a homicide, the details of the indictment generally agree with those of the inquisition on the view of the body, though they were certainly not identical. Anything irrelevant to the laying of the charge might be omitted in the indictment, so, for example, if the accused fled to sanctuary after a homicide but subsequently emerged to go through the normal process of trial, or if the accused had killed a man who was in the process of committing a rape, this information would not appear on the indictment.[5]

Indictments might be taken before justices of the peace or justices of assize and gaol delivery. The majority of the justices of the peace were local men of standing, both magnates and gentry; the *Boke of Justices of Peas* says that they should be 'well dysposed men and lawfull that ben not meyntenours of quarelles'.[6] As this provision implies, there was a real concern that a justice of the peace might use his role to further his own position in his county by supporting allies and acting against rivals. Powell accepts that this happened on a fairly regular basis, but argues both that the crown had little option but to use such men, given the thinness of its own resources, and that including them in the 'circle of government' led them to work increasingly within the judicial system rather than outside it.[7] The local men were joined by two men of law, justices or serjeants from the central courts, who were necessary if the session were to proceed to deliver felons.[8] The sessions of the peace met at least four times a year, in March, July, September, and December, though more sessions could be held if needed, and each session probably lasted two to three days.[9] The justices had a wide remit to deal with law and order, handling issues such as riots, wages, heretics, and fairs and markets, as well as criminal matters.[10]

use. See pp. 118, 210, 265, and 308. The terms burglary, robbery, and murder were not used in the period with any consistency (indeed there is still a lively discussion among historians about the definition and emergence of the concept of murder: see K.J. Kesselring, *Making Murder Public: Homicide in Early Modern England, 1480–1680* (Oxford: Oxford University Press, 2019); J.G. Bellamy, *The Criminal Trial in Later Medieval England* (Toronto: University of Toronto Press, 1998), pp. 57–69; Thomas A. Green, 'The Jury and the English Law of Homicide, 1200–1600', *Michigan Law Review* 74 (1976), pp. 413–499), but I have used them with their modern meanings when speaking descriptively, since the economy of expression outweighs the anachronism.

[5] TNA KB9/434 m. 9 [image 18], TNA KB27/976 m. 9d [image 511]; TNA KB9/960 mm. 80, 83 [not on AALT].

[6] *Boke of Justices of Peas* (London: 1505), Aii, cites 1 Edw. III c. 18. There was also a requirement that the justices must have £20 a year.

[7] Edward Powell, *Kingship, Law and Society: Criminal Justice in the Reign of Henry V* (Oxford: Clarendon Press, 1989), pp. 19–20.

[8] *Boke of Justices of Peas*, Aii, 17 Ric. II ca. ult. The property qualification was waived for the men of law.

[9] *Boke of Justices of Peas*, Aii-iii: the sessions were at the feasts of the annunciation, St Margaret, Michelmas and St Nicholas.

[10] J.R. Lander argues that 'the authority of the justices rested upon a complex, confused amalgam, never precisely defined, of common law, an ever-increasing volume of statutes and the 'charge' delivered to the jurors at quarter sessions': *English Justices of the Peace 1461–1509* (Gloucester, UK: Alan Stroud, 1989), p. 7.

Wide as their remit was, Lander argues that during the late fourteenth and fifteenth centuries the justices of the peace lost their claim to handle felonies, as such serious cases were increasingly referred to the assizes, gaol delivery, and/or King's Bench to be handled by expert lawyers.[11] The commissions of assize and gaol delivery were exclusively made up of justices or serjeants from the central courts who covered six distinct circuits.[12] Justices of assize and gaol delivery could deal with indictments for felony and they generally handled felony trials. Their sessions were less frequent than those of the peace: they usually sat twice a year, in the spring and the late summer. Lander suggests that at any given session they might find thirty or forty prisoners to be dealt with, about half of whom had been indicted before the justices of the peace.[13] Both the sessions of the peace and the assizes were held in a variety of locations around each county. The most common locations in Surrey, for example, were Southwark, Croydon, Guildford, Kingston, and Reigate.[14] The castle of Guildford might be delivered at Croydon, however, or the castle of Lewes at Southwark, and this movement of the sessions around the county required the moving of prisoners, with the attendant costs and risks of flight.[15] Nevertheless, the benefits were seen to outweigh the risks. The sessions were major events in the annual county cycle: the sessions of the peace brought some of the major figures in the country together on a regular basis, while the assizes and gaol delivery added the prestige of the central court justices to the event. Musson notes that the justices tended to stay on the same circuit for some time and points out the value of this continuity for maintaining political connections between the centre and the counties.[16] With the addition of prisoners, appellors, witnesses, lawyers, clerks, and uninterested parties who took advantage of the opportunity to conduct other business or simply to socialize, the sessions represented an economic boom for the towns that hosted them.[17]

[11] Lander, *English Justices of the Peace*, pp. 8, 167.

[12] Mayors joined the assize justices when they sat in towns. The circuits were the Home (Essex, Hertfordshire, Kent, Surrey, Sussex, Middlesex), Midland (Derbyshire, Leicestershire, Lincolnshire, Nottinghamshire, Northamptonshire, Rutland, Warwickshire), Norfolk (Bedfordshire, Buckinghamshire, Cambridgeshire, Huntingdonshire, Norfolk, Suffolk), Northern (Cumberland, Lancashire, Northumberland, Westmorland, Yorkshire), Oxford (Berkshire, Glouctershire, Herefordshire, Oxfordshire, Shropshire, Staffordshire, Worcestershire, and Monmouthshire after *c.* 1542) and Western (Cornwall, Devon, Dorset, Hampshire, Somerset, Wiltshire). See also Powell, *Kingship, Law and Society*, pp. 56–59. Bellamy suggests that the justices of gaol delivery probably did not attend the indicting sessions held simultaneously with the gaol deliveries, but that their inclusion on the commission gave them access to the bills: Bellamy, *Criminal Trial*, p. 111. While only a few records survive with both the indictment and trial record on the same day, it is not unusual to see the justices of gaol delivery listed on the former.

[13] Lander, *English Justices of the Peace*, p. 172. See Margaret McGlynn, 'Trial and Punishment in Early Tudor England' (forthcoming) for numbers and the management of trials.

[14] See Beattie, *Crime and the Courts*, pp. 310–312 for later practice.

[15] TNA KB9/567 m. 11 [image 22]; TNA KB9/454 m. 10 [image 20]. J.S. Cockburn, *A History of English Assizes 1558–1714* (Cambridge: Cambridge University Press, 1972), p. 20.

[16] Anthony Musson, 'Centre and Locality: Perceptions of the Assize Justices in Late Medieval England', in *Law, Governance, and Justice: New Views on Medieval Constitutionalism* edited by Richard W. Kaeuper with the assistance of Paul Dingman and Peter Sposato (Leiden: Brill, 2013), pp. 226–235.

[17] Musson, 'Centre and Locality', pp. 216–217.

With a true bill in hand, whether from a session of the peace or gaol delivery, the accused could be moved forward to trial. The indictment was read out in court, and the accused almost invariably pleaded 'not guilty' and put himself on the country, i.e. asked for a trial by jury.[18] The trial might proceed immediately, or the accused might be remanded while a jury was called. There was no official prosecutor for criminal cases in this period. In earlier centuries there was an expectation that the jury was comprised of men who were familiar with the circumstances of the crime and the criminal, unlike the modern expectation of impartiality. This self-informing jury was effectively a thing of the past by the early Tudor period, declining most likely because of the expansion of judicial business and the mobility of the courts: the jury was likely to come from the locality of the town where the session was held, while the crime could have been committed anywhere in the county.[19] At the same time the investigative justice of the peace authorized by the Marian statutes is not yet evident.[20] In cases which began with an appeal the victim could argue his case, but even in cases which began with an indictment, there is often a figure who argues 'for the king'. In King's Bench this was usually the attorney-general, not surprisingly, and the attorney-general occasionally played the same role on circuit, though usually on his local circuit.[21] But many men argued 'for the king' in the counties as well: most of them were engaged in the legal profession, though at lower levels than the Westminster serjeants and justices. It's not clear how they came to be attached to particular cases, and they usually became involved after conviction rather than during the conduct of the trial, though there are exceptions to this generalization.[22] Though there is little direct information, it is likely that whatever case was assembled was driven by the evidence of the accuser and his witnesses, supplemented by whatever local knowledge was available in or through the jury, and possibly by the engagement of a particularly assiduous local justice of the peace.

[18] For further detail on the process at gaol delivery in the mid-sixteenth century see J.H. Baker, *Oxford History of the Laws of England: vol. 6 1483–1558* (Oxford: Oxford University Press, 2007), vol. 6, pp. 516–519.

[19] Thomas A. Green, *Verdict According to Conscience: Perspectives on the English Criminal Trial Jury, 1200–1800* (Chicago: University of Chicago Press, 1985), pp. 32–35; Powell, *Kingship, Law and Society*, pp. 80–82. Bellamy notes that coroners' juries continued to act as detectives into the sixteenth century, but this was more feasible given the much more local nature of the proceedings, and the impetus provided by homicide: John G. Bellamy, *Strange Inhuman Deaths: Murder in Tudor England* (Westport, Conn, London: Praeger, 2005), p. 13; Bellamy, *Criminal Trial*, pp. 107–108.

[20] Green, 'Jury and the English Law of Homicide', pp. 489–491; J.H. Langbein, *Prosecuting Crime in the Renaissance* (Cambridge, MA: Harvard University Press, 1974), pp. 64–75, 89–95 argues that the justices of the peace were playing a role in the investigation of crime in the early sixteenth century. William B. Robison, 'Murder at Crowhurst: A Case Study in Early Tudor Law', *Criminal Justice History* 9 (1988), pp. 32–41 details the work of Sir John Gaynesford on a murder in his jurisdiction in 1532–1534 and suggests the kind of role such a justice of the peace could play.

[21] James Hobart, for example, appeared 'for the king' at the gaol delivery of Bury St Edmunds in March 1501: TNA KB9/426 m. 71 [images 143–146].

[22] Margaret McGlynn, 'Trial and Punishment'.

Once they were available the jurors were individually sworn, the charges against the accused were read aloud, and evidence for the Crown was presented. We have few sources for actual proceedings in court, and the most evocative source, the *Placita Corone*, is also one of the earliest, dating from early in the reign of Edward I, and designed as an instruction manual rather than a record of practice.[23] This treatise assumes that most felonies began with an appeal, and shows the appellor presenting his narrative of the crime with all the required elements and the appellee responding to the count point by point. Kaye argues that this was probably already becoming unusual, both because this was enormously time-consuming and time was in short supply on circuit, and because counting was a technical proceeding, and there was a limited role for counsel at the assizes.[24] Instead, the judges seem to have taken an increasingly active role in pressing the prisoners to respond to the facts of the case rather than looking to take refuge in technical matters: when Hugh de M, appealed of stealing a mare, asked the judge to allow him counsel, since he was 'an unlettered man ... [who has] scarcely ever made a plea', the judge responded that 'that course would be clearly against the law of the land and against right, for who can tell us more about your doings than you yourself?'[25] When the case was initiated by indictment the justices seem to have played a similar role as the chief questioner of the defendant, and apparently had little compunction about badgering or cajoling him into confessing his crime.[26] The evidence, thin as it is, makes it clear that criminal trials were quick: the lack of legal argument meant that trials focused on the events around the crime, while the lack of witnesses for the defense meant that the defendant could only tell his own version of his story and attack his accuser.

None of the courtroom activity, unfortunately, appears in the official records, which jump from the swearing of the jury to the verdict. If the jury returned a verdict of 'not guilty' the accused went *sine die*, i.e. without a day set for the continuation of the trial. If the jury returned a verdict of guilty, the judge could move to sentencing: in a felony case this was automatically death. Before sentencing, however, the judge asked if the accused had any reason why the court should not proceed to execution, and it was here that claims of clergy or forcible removal from sanctuary were usually made. If a claim for clergy went well the convict could be immediately delivered to the ecclesiastical system, but the prosecution might allege some reason why he was not eligible under the common law, such as a previous conviction or bigamy. Depending on the nature of the claim, the court could

[23] Some reports give a sense of the action in court, see for example *YB 30 & 31 Edw. I* ed. Alfred J. Horwood, Rolls Series (London: Longmans etc., 1863), p. 520.

[24] *Placita Corone or La Corone Pledee devant Justices* ed. J.M. Kaye, SS Suppl. Ser. vol. 4 (London: Selden Society, 1966), pp. xxv, xxvi–xxvii.

[25] *Placita Corone*, p. 17. The justices might also press other participants if they felt that the law had not been appropriately followed and contemporaries might express their frustrations with their bullying: see *YB 30 & 31 Edw.I*, pp. 500–506.

[26] *Placita Corone*, pp. 17–19, 24.

proceed to consider the allegation, but they were more likely to remand the felon in order to gather further information, whether through a search of records or the production of witnesses, and it was not unusual for these kinds of issues to be referred to King's Bench. If the claimant did not pass the reading test he might be sentenced or he might be asked again if there was any other reason why the court should not proceed to execution. If the felon alleged forced removal from sanctuary, again he was usually remanded while information was gathered and again he might find himself before King's Bench.

Once a trial had concluded in the county, the assumption is that the sentence was carried out in short order, though there may have been more delay after trial than we have thought.[27] There was no formal process of appeal to a higher court, but cases did regularly get moved to King's Bench while they were in process, either because an accused felon with influential friends thought that court would be more favourable towards him, or because problems arose during the proceedings in the county that the assize judges were unable or unwilling to resolve.[28] When this happened the King's Bench record includes a transcript of all the processes in the county as well as its own processes, so we can follow the case from its beginning through to its final action. Documentation sent to King's Bench for this purpose survives in TNA KB9, which also contains a large number of coroners' inquisitions. By putting the records together, we can follow some homicide cases from the first record of the view of the body through the indictment, the process at gaol delivery and the final resolution of the case at King's Bench. Sadly, this doesn't happen often, since the pattern of record survival is inconsistent: there are many indictments in the KB9 files with no further process, whether because the victim or the accused died, disappeared, or did not pursue the case. Conversely there are many cases in the KB27 rolls with no supporting documentation in KB9.[29]

There are obvious limitations with the King's Bench records: they contain cases from all over the country, but they do not tell us how many cases appeared in the counties, or what happened with them. By definition, the cases that were moved to Westminster were unusual on some level, and so they do not represent the 'ordinary' case dealt with once and for all on circuit in Devon or Staffordshire. Nor do they tell us anything about the relative frequency with which cases were moved from the counties, or whether the justices at Westminster were more or less lenient there than in their local appearances. But they are all we have, and they do provide some insight into the ordinary procedures as well as the extraordinary problems that might arise, some sense of which counties were more likely to appear in

[27] McGlynn, 'Trial and Punishment'.

[28] Bellamy, *Strange Inhuman Deaths*, p. 31.

[29] For the purposes of this study I have not generally paid much attention to indictments without verdicts: such indictments can provide valuable information on patterns of criminality in various ways, but they don't help us understand criminal punishment.

Westminster, and maybe even why.[30] The King's Bench records also allow us to put together some narratives of complicated criminal lives: some claims of clergy, for example, were challenged on the grounds that the felon had been previously convicted, and (though this is not explicitly stated in the record) had previously claimed clergy. Though such an allegation might be handled on circuit, if the previous conviction was in a different county it was likely to end up in King's Bench, and a lengthy and complicated criminal history might unfold in the Westminster record. The convicted felon might continue with his claim and find himself in the hands of Westminster monks rather than his local bishop, find himself headed for execution, or find himself enmeshed in legal knots that only a pardon could cut through.

2. The Ordinaries and their Records

Such claims of clergy make up a substantial part of the discussion in this volume, and we have already examined their common law history. We also, however, need to consider this process carefully from the ecclesiastical side. Though the records on this side are even thinner than the common law records, the bishops had to maintain the system which brought criminous clerks into their prisons, most crucially the system of ordinaries. All bishops appointed ordinaries to act in their stead in demanding the delivery of clerks convict and clerks attaint from the secular courts.[31] McHardy comments that this was often the first act of business in a new bishop's register, but by the late fifteenth century information about ordinaries has become rather more sporadic: some registers enrolled some commissions but probably not all, while some did not enroll any.[32] The commissions also vary, both from diocese to diocese, and within dioceses. Some of the ordinaries were men of some learning and status: for example, early in his tenure Thomas Langton appointed a canon residentiary of Salisbury, a subdean of Salisbury, and a bachelor of canon law to deliver criminous clerks from secular prisons in the archdeaconries of Somerset and Dorset.[33] This was a fairly wide remit for a well-qualified

[30] The King's Bench records also give us a fairly good insight into the administration of criminal justice in and around the capital: we have more information from the delivery of Newgate and the Marshalsea than any other prison. See pp. 115–117. It is unlikely that the clientele of these prisons, their patterns of criminality, or the responses of their jurors or justices was the same as outside the capital, but they represent a substantial element of the English criminal population at the time.

[31] Strictly speaking the title 'ordinary' belonged to the bishop, but the sources consistently refer to his deputies as ordinaries, and I have adopted this usage. The ordinary was expected to be present in court as a matter of course and usually was, at least for gaol deliveries and assizes where such claims would regularly appear. If he was absent the court would usually, though not invariably, remand the felon.

[32] A.K. McHardy, 'Church Courts and Criminous Clerks in the Later Middle Ages', in *Medieval Ecclesiastical Studies in Honour of Dorothy M. Owen* edited by M.J. Franklin and Christopher Harper-Bill (Woodbridge, Suffolk: Boydell, 1995), p. 167. McHardy is referring to early fourteenth-century registers.

[33] *Reg. Langton*, p. 49, no. 418.

group of men, but later in the same register the vicars of the parish churches of Abingdon, Wantage, Steventon, New Windsor, Reading, and Northmorton, the rectors of the parish churches of Wallingford, and two vicars-choral of St. George's chapel Windsor were commissioned to deliver clerks 'from gaols at New Windsor, Reading, Abingdon, Wantage, Wallingford or elsewhere in Berkshire', and the vicar of Sherborne and two chaplains were commissioned to deliver clerks in the vill of Sherborne and elsewhere in the county of Dorset.[34] This demonstrates that quite a broad range of clerical men might be assigned to this duty, and reminds us that there was a wide range of gaols to cover. The readers noted that ordinaries were expected to be present at King's Bench and gaol deliveries as a matter of course, since they would expect claims on a regular basis, but ordinaries also had to be available for other courts.[35]

Some registers suggest that their bishops saw their role as rather more active than the simple receipt of clerks. In August 1504 Hadrian of Castello, bishop of Bath & Wells, commissioned John Beckham, bachelor in decrees and a canon of his cathedral church, and Sirs John Bushe, vicar of the church of Yeovil and John Chaundeler, rector of the church of St Mary Major Ilchester, to receive clerks released from secular custody, but on the same day he also commissioned the same John Beckham 'to seek out and claim any clerks arrested in the county of Somerset by the king's stewards, constables, bailiffs or other ministers'.[36] He issued a similar set of commissions to seek out and claim clerks in January 1507, but this time they were directed to Bushe and Chaundeler as well as three other vicars and a rector, suggesting that a broader group of ordinaries was being encouraged to be proactive in the claiming of clerks.[37]

There are also hints that the bishops recognized the range of men they might be expected to receive during this period. Though the standard language of the commission instructed the ordinaries to receive 'whatever clerks were arrested or will be arrested and imprisoned ... for whatever crimes or transgressions from whatever justices, stewards, bailiffs, or other minsters of the king have the power to deliver them' a number of commissions in Henry VII's reign authorized the ordinaries to receive 'whatever clerks or clerical men', 'whatever clerks or other clerical men', or 'criminous clerks and other ecclesiastical men and literates'.[38] The fact that a version of this language occurs across a number of dioceses suggests that it was not the peculiarity of a single chancery, but part of a conversation happening among those responsible for the management of these clerks. It is a small but perhaps significant

[34] *Reg. Langton*, p. 91, no. 537; p. 62, no. 457.
[35] *Rights and Liberties*, p. 74.
[36] *Reg. King and Castello*, p. 105 nos. 619, 618.
[37] *Reg. King and Castello*, p. 120–121 nos. 731–733.
[38] TNA KB9/410 m. 54 [image 115] (Lincoln, 20 December 1492); *The Register of Richard Fox, Lord Bishop of Durham, 1494–1501* ed. Marjories Peers Howden, Surtees Society vol.147 (Durham: Andrews & Co., 1932), p. 130 (Durham, 8 April 1500); *Reg. King and Castello*, p. 105 no. 618 (Bath and Wells, not used by King, first used 20 August 1504); *Reg. Langton*, p. 62, no. 457 (Salisbury, 2 June 1487).

point that the Salisbury commission of 1504 which ordered Beckham to seek out criminous clerks did not include other ecclesiastical men in his remit, while the commission on the same day to receive criminous clerks did. Too much should not be made of this, since by 1507 the commission to seek out and claim did include clerks and other ecclesiastical men, but the variety in language is notable, particularly since in the following reign all of these variations disappear, leaving the single term 'clerks'. It is very clear that the bishops did not stop receiving 'literates' in the following reign, so this variation in language is perhaps a response to an expansion in business, along with an explicit recognition that most of these men were not in fact clerics.[39] The bishops may have had a desire to make a quiet point, or to be accurate in describing the authority being conferred on ordinaries, a desire which faded away with the passage of time. It is also possible, however, that the distinctions that the commissions made between clerks, other ecclesiastical men and literates may have reflected distinctions in the way the ecclesiastical system treated these men.[40]

Though the ordinaries were crucial to the operation of the system, only about half of the surviving King's Bench records provide the names of the men who actually received the clerks in court: in some cases the record states simply that he was received by the ordinary of the relevant bishop, in others the name is left blank. A fairly large number of men were commissioned to act as ordinaries, but only a small number appear in the central records. John Bushe, the vicar of Yeovil commissioned by Hadrian de Castello in March 1502, August 1504, and January 1507 does indeed appear as the ordinary at sessions of gaol delivery in Ilchester between August 1502 and January 1506, though none of the other men commissioned in the register appear.[41] John Gobbe, the vicar of All Saints in Sherborne, appears as ordinary in 1509; his predecessor in 1487 had also been commissioned, suggesting that particular benefices might be associated with the role.[42] Effective ordinaries might appear in more than one place: from 1499 to 1506 John Tombrigge, chaplain, appears at the gaol deliveries of Thetford, Norfolk, and Bury St Edmunds, Suffolk, and he appears both for the bishop of Norwich and as the vice-gerent of the archbishop of Canterbury, *sede vacante*.[43]

It was clearly not unusual for a commission to name several men to act as ordinary for a given period of time, and this might appear to be a sensible precaution in case any given ordinary was unable to attend a particular session. However, evidence from Newgate makes it clear that more than one ordinary might be present at any given session, presumably because the business was expected to be more than

[39] See p. 95.

[40] The bishops' registers were more likely to record crimes involving clerics as victims or perpetrators, and clerics may have spent a little longer in prison before purgation: see pp. 106–109.

[41] TNA KB9/442 mm. 32–34 [images 64–68].

[42] *Reg. Langton*, p. 62 no. 457; TNA KB27/995 rex m. 20 [images 226, 227, 210d].

[43] TNA KB27/978 rex mm. 15, 16 [image 181]; TNA KB9/426 m. 71 [image 143].

one man could handle, and suggests that there may have been a chief ordinary, or an ordinary of record, in the eyes of the common law courts. Thomas Smyth, MA, appears to be the dominant figure at Newgate, receiving forty-eight clerks convict between 1505 and 1514, but John Hewet and John Forman are also named as ordinaries in this period.[44] Both Hewet and Smyth were present and claimed clerks in October 1507, while both Forman and Smyth were present and claimed clerks in May and October 1508.[45] Similarly, a decade later a London smith appears on a list of clerks convict delivered to John Godson, ordinary of the bishop of London; in the record of his delivery the ordinary was named as Richard Gatton.[46] It is of course possible that this is a simple slip in the record, and Smyth's earlier dominance may be a trick of the sources: he appears only on lists of Newgate clerks convict, and since none of his charges appeared in the records again, without those lists Thomas Smyth and his MA would have disappeared.[47]

We have the most evidence about the Westminster Abbey ordinaries.[48] In the early years of Henry VII's reign Thomas Flete and John Flete appear most often, Thomas in King's Bench in June 1486, November 1487, October and November 1491, and for the gaol delivery of the Marshalsea in July 1489, and John in both King's Bench and the gaol delivery of the Marshalsea in May 1491.[49] Though we do not have any evidence of them appearing in the same session, this makes it clear that they were commissioned at the same time, and that they might be expected to deal with both a gaol delivery and the regular work of the court on the same day. In the 1490s it becomes common to find the abbot's commission copied into the King's Bench record in full or in summary. The commissions were renewed regularly in November, and normally four monks were commissioned, though the duty seems to have rotated fairly regularly: in November 1497 the abbot commissioned William Brewode, William Borough, Thomas Flete, and Richard Newbery; in November 1498 he named Brewode, Borough, Thomas Ely, and William Mane; in November 1500 the same four; in November 1504 Brewode, Newbery, and

44 TNA KB9/494 mm.101–108 [images 207–233]; TNA KB9/963 m. 8 [not on AALT]; TNA KB9/448 m. 119 [image 239]; TNA KB9/960 mm. 142, 145 [not on AALT].

45 The clerks Hewet and Forman claimed were remanded after objections were raised to their claims of clergy and they later appeared in King's Bench.

46 TNA KB9/477 m. 35d [image 80]; he is also called John Gotson: TNA KB9/493 m. 3 [image 7].

47 See p. 116.

48 Though the ordinaries were usually the local bishops, abbots could also play the role: the abbot of St. Albans was the ordinary in the liberty of St. Alban's. Because he acted as the ordinary for King's Bench and the Marshalsea, the abbot of Westminster probably held as many clerks convict in his gaol as any bishop, except perhaps the bishops of London and Lincoln: see pp. 114–115, 204–206. Criminals operating around the capital might also end up in the hands of the bishop of London, who had responsibility for Newgate, or the bishop of Winchester, who held clerks convicted in Surrey including those operating in Southwark.

49 TNA KB27/898 rex m. 8d [image 289]; TNA KB27/900 rex m. 14d [image 441]; TNA KB27/921 rex m. 2d [image 539]; TNA KB27/921 rex m. 6d [image 545]; TNA KB27/912 rex m. 11d [image 323]: KB27/919 rex mm. 4d, 14 [images 438, 216]. On 27 November 1491 the ordinary is identified only as [blank] Flete, so could have been either one.

Henry Jones, and in October 1506 Brewode, Henry Jones, William Southwell, and Thomas Broun.[50] Not all of these men appear in the King's Bench records, nor do they appear evenly: only Brewode appears in 1496, Borough dominates in 1497–1500, Southwell appears in 1498 but dominates 1505–1508, Ely appears through 1501 and 1502, and Henry Jones appears once in 1503 and Richard Newbery once in 1504. Though their representation in the records may not be proportional to their actual appearances in court, it seems likely that one or two would cycle in and out as the regular ordinaries with another handful with the experience and the obligation to step in as necessary. The duty seems to have been expected of the archdeacon or prior and extended to others.[51]

It's not entirely clear from the records of King's Bench what the duties of the ordinary were: the Newgate sessions indicate that there might be two in court at any one time, suggesting that they were substantial, but the Westminster records indicate that one could cover both the regular session and the gaol delivery. The ordinary was usually present when a convict made a claim of clergy and read to prove his status, but the records make it clear that the court controlled the reading test and the ordinary's role seems simply to have been to request the delivery of the clerk after he had passed it, or, very occasionally, to reject him. By this simple act the ordinary took legal responsibility for the clerk convict, however, and the escape of Hugh Johns in 1505 provides a rare glimpse of this in action. Johns was convicted of felony at the gaol delivery of Northampton on 14 July 1505 and delivered as a clerk convict to John Cokkys, the ordinary for William Smyth, bishop of Lincoln.[52] Cokkys was then obliged to deliver Johns to the bishop's prison at Banbury, about 25 miles from Northampton. He went to Nicholas Gryffyn, the sheriff of Northamptonshire and warden of the prison, and asked Gryffyn to keep Johns overnight, to which request Gryffyn agreed. Cokkys arrived the following day with Thomas Knight and various other servants of the bishop, presumably the guard required to escort Johns to prison, men who most likely would not have attended the gaol delivery itself. When Cokkys requested the transfer of Johns, Gryffyn refused, arguing that Johns was a traitor for clipping and washing coin, and that he wanted to appeal other prisoners, and so he should be examined at King's Bench. The record doesn't indicate whether Cokkys argued with the sheriff, but Gryffyn did warrant the bishop and the ordinary for Johns's custody, and Cokkys left empty-handed. The whole series of events suggests that the sheriff and the ordinary normally had a good working relationship, since Cokkys would presumably not have asked Gryffyn to keep his prisoner otherwise, but that Gryffyn either took advantage of the opportunity to convince Johns to turn approver, or

50 TNA KB27/945 rex m. 7 [image 432]; TNA KB27/949 rex m. 13 [image 528]; TNA KB27/957 rex m. 6 [image 122]; TNA KB27/976 rex m. 6 [image 505]; TNA KB27/981 rex m. 19d [image 276].

51 Thomas Flete is identified as the archdeacon of Westminster in 1491: TNA KB9/389 m. 49 [image 98].

52 TNA KB9/439 m. 6 [image 12].

that Johns decided that this was a more promising avenue for him than the sentence that awaited him in Banbury.[53] The complications of these logistics might also explain why the Westminster monks could apparently cover their court more efficiently, since their transport issues were minimal.

Though the evidence is fragmentary, it suggests that while the range of qualifications associated with the role of ordinary might vary depending on the court they attended, many of the ordinaries were well-educated men of some status, they might be directed by their bishop to be proactive in guarding the rights of clerical men accused of felony, and they might act as ordinaries over a lengthy period of time, often as part of a group of men who had acquired a good deal of experience in the role and developed a working relationship with the common law officers. Given that the gaol delivery judges often remained on their circuits for years, they must have become quite familiar with the local ordinaries. The registers make it clear that the bishops generally commissioned ordinaries on a county basis across their diocese: this was presumably intended to ensure that the ordinaries' load was manageable, but it would also have helped to reduce the confusion caused by the simple fact that the circuits and the dioceses were in no way coincident, and every circuit could expect to deal with the representatives of a variety of bishops. Indeed peculiarities of jurisdiction below the level of the diocese could cause confusion, and one example from the session of the peace for Surrey provides an unusual glimpse of the kind of role an ordinary might carve out. Three men were jointly convicted at Croydon on 13 January 1517 of the theft of Kentish carpets and coverlets. They all claimed clergy, but the ordinary of the bishop of Winchester, within whose diocese Surrey lay, was not present. According to 'one Stacy, clerk' who was present in the court, since the town of Croydon was in the jurisdiction of the archbishop of Canterbury, not the bishop of Winchester, the convicts should not be delivered to the bishop of Winchester in any case.[54] The justices decided to remand the convicts to the next session of the peace at Southwark on 29 January. This should have effectively ended the matter, since Southwark was indisputably in the jurisdiction of the bishop of Winchester, but the court again remanded the men, this time to Reigate in April.[55] Though this might seem like a small administrative bump, the role of 'Stacy, clerk' is intriguing. It seems likely that this was Thomas Stacy, who regularly appeared as ordinary for the bishop of Winchester in Surrey between 1512 and 1520.[56] Stacy seems to have been a useful man, since he also appeared

[53] This seems to have been an accurate calculation, since Johns escaped from Gryffyn's custody on 22 October 1505, just three months later. Gryffyn's warrant does not seem to have carried much weight, for the bishop of Lincoln was indicted for the escape in May 1506. In May 1509 he appeared at King's Bench with a pardon for the escape dated 4 February 1507: TNA KB27/979 rex m. 15 [images 210–211]; TNA KB27/991 rex m. 8 [image 62].

[54] TNA KB9/472 m. 82 [image 158].

[55] In February the trio appeared in King's Bench instead and were delivered to Henry Jones, the ordinary for Westminster Abbey: TNA KB27/1022 rex m. 6 [images 182–183, 150d].

[56] TNA KB9/458 m.105 [image 220], TNA KB9/477 mm. 37, 1 [images 83, 2]; TNA KB9/477 mm. 35, 36, 36d [images 79, 81, 82].

as ordinary for the bishop of Chichester in 1513 and 1514 and as ordinary for the bishop of London in 1515.[57] It is possible that there is some confusion in the records, but it seems likely that a small diocese like Chichester would have been happy to use the services of an experienced man like Stacy, who normally operated just over their border. Stacy was clearly familiar with the processes and presumably with the personnel of gaol deliveries on the Home circuit through the 1510s, and when he spoke up in court in Croydon in January 1517, in the supposed absence of the ordinary of the bishop of Winchester (though he had demonstrably been that ordinary in 1516 and would be again in March 1517) to argue that they were in the jurisdiction of the archbishop of Canterbury, the court would presumably have taken his interjection seriously.[58] Indeed, in a discussion during a reading at around the same time Fyneux suggested that an ordinary could make an argument about the nature of felony as an *amicus curiae*.[59] Though the common law records pay little attention to the ordinaries, and they are often quite literally nameless figures in the administration of the privilege, they were crucial figures in practice, and occasionally raised both procedural and principled issues which stymied the courts.

Once the ordinaries took responsibility for the clerks convict they were theoretically out of the common law courts' jurisdiction, though, as we saw in chapter one, the courts were reluctant to relinquish all interest in them. Nevertheless, in practical terms clerks convict were under the authority of the bishops, who might put them through a canonical trial and, if they were found guilty, punish them according to the canon law. No evidence has surfaced to suggest that bishops in fact went through any such process; they largely accepted the outcome of the common law proceeding, held the convict in their prison, often in chains, for some period of time, and used the process of purgation as both the canonical trial and the record of the convicts' discharge.[60] Only a handful of purgation records survive, usually

[57] TNA KB9/477 m. 35 [image 79], TNA KB9/477 m. 35d [image 80]. The felon in this case is identified as being delivered in Surrey.

[58] It's not entirely clear what lay behind this odd episode. We don't have much evidence of activity at Croydon: apart from the sessions of the peace, it was also a site for the delivery of the castle of Guildford, which happened more regularly at Southwark. When the castle was delivered at Croydon in 1489 Richard Richebele was delivered to the ordinary of the bishop of Winchester without comment, and when it was delivered there in 1544 Miles Sympell was delivered to the ordinary of the archbishop of Canterbury: TNA KB9/1109, no membrane numbers [not on AALT], TNA KB9/560 m. 29 [image 51]. It is possible that growing pressure on the bishops' prisons—with Winchester being one of those under the most pressure, especially when compared to Canterbury—caused the bishop of Winchester to put his foot down in 1517, refusing to accept criminous clerks from a deanery that was not technically part of his jurisdiction, even though it was part of his county: see p. 204. The removal of the case to Southwark could have solved the problem, and the fact that it did not suggests that Foxe, the bishop at the time, was serious in his opposition. Taking the case to King's Bench was one way to solve the issue, and Westminster Abbey absorbed the problem. It's not clear if the point was established in 1517, but the later deliveries demonstrate that by 1544 the bishop of Winchester had been relieved of that responsibility.

[59] *Spelman's Reports*, vol. 1, p. 64. Baker dates the reading to 1511 x 1513.

[60] The bishops did vent some annoyance along the way: the public notice of the purgation of Thomas Wykes and Richard Hebys noted in passing that they had been indicted 'unjustly, falsely and maliciously',

in the bishops' registers.[61] They do, however, give us a fairly clear outline of the procedure that was followed. Bishop Sherborne of Chichester's register, for example, gives the commission for a purgation for John Beverley, a Rye fisherman, who was convicted of killing Peter Sare in Rye in March 1508, and who claimed clergy according to 'the rite vulgarly called clerical privilege, used and observed in the kingdom of England from ancient times'.[62] The commission orders the purgation to be held in the cathedral church on 1 June 1509, and proclaimed in the parish church of Rye on 20, 27, and 29 May, in the market at Rye on 15, 22, and 26 May and in the court at the town of Winchelsea on 19, 22, and 26 May, so that anyone who objected to the purgation could appear. Six vicars, two rectors and four curates served as compurgators for Beverley, who was restored to good fame a little more than a year after Sare's death. This is a model process, and it demonstrates the attention purgation was designed to draw.[63]

Though the records of purgations are scarce, they show a steady march of clerks convict through the doors of the bishops' prisons: on 22 July 1501, for example, five men convicted of burglary, homicide and theft were successfully purged and released from the archbishop of York's prison.[64] This record of success has led to the assumption that purgation was a rubber stamp, and that the bishops regularly moved convicted criminals out of their custody in this way with little concern for their condign punishment or the safety of the community they were returning to. The reality is a bit more complex, however. As Helmholz has pointed out, purgations were meant to succeed, and we would not expect to see the commission issued until the bishop was confident that the clerk convict would pass.[65] In most cases the convict had spent a considerable period of time in custody before the commission

but the other documentation took their conviction as a given and they had apparently been held in chains by the bishop for about two years: *Registrum Ricardi Mayew, Episcopi Herefordensis, 1504–16* ed. Arthur Thomas Bannister, Canterbury and York Society vol. 27 (London: Privately Printed, 1921), p. 70. For more on the conditions in which the clerks were held, see Margaret McGlynn, 'Ecclesiastical Prisons and Royal Authority in the Reign of Henry VII', *Journal of Ecclesiastical History* 70.4 (2019), p. 759.

[61] Early modern scholars have generally been less enthused about editing these registers than their medieval counterparts, so this material is not readily available.

[62] The commission is dated 12 April 1509: West Sussex R.O. Ep.I/1/5, f. 108–108v. According to the *sede vacante* register for Lincoln in 1495 it cost 6s 8d to buy the commission to receive purgation: *Reg. Morton* vol. 2, p. 52. There are eight receipts in the register, but they do not note what the purgation was for. If felons were required to purchase their own commission this was presumably a further barrier to freedom.

[63] A similar process appears in the registers of Bath and Wells in 1515 for the purgation of John Colman; *Reg. King and Castello*, p. 174, no. 108. The length of time between the commission and the purgation varied. In York the purgations were usually between ten days and a month after the commission: see *Reg. Rotherham*, ff. 313, 313v, 314, 314v, 315 all between 1488 and 1491. By the end of the decade Rotherham seems to have been issuing commissions with a much shorter timeframe, but they were prorogued: see f. 316v (commission 11 March 1498 for purgation 15 March, prorogued to 20 March), f. 317 (commission 1 October for purgation 4 October, prorogued to 19 December).

[64] *Reg. Savage* f. 13v. The purgation was certified on 4 September 1501.

[65] Helmholz, *Ius Commune*, p. 244.

and so the key issue in assessing the effectiveness of the bishops as wardens is not the quantity of purgations they allowed, but the time for which they held prisoners before the purgations went ahead.[66] The available evidence also provides some hints, and occasionally clear evidence, of unsuccessful purgations. In some cases purgations were simply postponed, and we might assume some other reason for the delay—perhaps compurgators had not appeared or the whole session had been postponed.[67] In other cases it is clear that a purgation failed. For example, five men were scheduled to be purged by the authority of the archbishop of Canterbury on 3 August 1507.[68] On the day four were successfully purged, while the fifth, James Fulwode, was not.[69] Unusually, we know what happened next: Fulwode came up for purgation again on 7 October 1511, once more as part of a group of clerks convict, and this time he was successful.[70] Fulwode's case makes it clear that the session went ahead, and the failure to purge was particular to him, and presumably to the feeling about his crimes. Thomas Robartes also failed in his purgation, though he remained in prison only six months longer before purging himself successfully.[71] Robartes was originally scheduled for purgation in the bishop's palace at Hereford on 1 June 1492 along with John Robartes, but was postponed successively to 22 June, 28 July, and 25 August before being purged successfully on 3 October.[72] The record of Robartes' purgation raises the intriguing possibility that there were regularly scheduled dates for purgations during which multiple men might be purged, suggesting that this was indeed a regular and ongoing part of the bishops' work. Robartes' failure to purge in June, July, or August could be the result of his own failings or it could be administrative, whether a lack of compurgators, a paucity of other men to be purged, or an unwillingness to gather the commission in the heat of the summer months.

The surviving records of purgation are thus hard to interpret, partly because they are clearly nowhere close to complete: while the ordination of clerks and the movement of benefices appear in all registers, bishops varied a great deal in the other material they chose to include and exclude, and purgations were clearly among the optional extras. The bishops also varied in the format they used. Many

[66] We will examine this in as much detail as is possible below, pp. 106–112, 208.

[67] See, for example, *Reg. Savage*, f.17v where the purgation was postponed from 18 March to 17 April.

[68] *Reg. Warham* 2 f. 420–420v. The orders for the purgations went out in April, earlier than usual for an August ceremony, and they were sent all across the county, to Northfleet, Ryarsh, East Peckham and Canterbury.

[69] Fulwode had killed a clerk in February 1502 and escaped from the archbishop's prison in January 1504: TNA KB9/433 m. 43 [images 85–88]; *Reg. Warham* 2 f. 420–420v. See p. 107.

[70] *Reg. Warham* 2 f. 425. This kind of failure was not new: the bishop of Winchester issued a commission for John de Hoyville's purgation in 1318, but he was not purged until 1321: Gabel, *Benefit of Clergy*, pp. 109–110.

[71] *Registrum Thome Myllyng, Episcopi Herefordensis, 1474–1492* ed. Arthur Thomas Bannister, Canterbury and York Society vol. 26 (London: Privately Printed, 1920), p. 152.

[72] There is no evidence in the sources of any connection between the men other than the dates of their purgations.

registers only include the commission for purgation: this usually includes a summary of the original indictment, so we can see the date and nature of the original crime, though we get no details on the date or place of conviction. Some registers are more thorough, including the various proclamations, a record of the purgation itself, and even a certification of the purgation. For the most part, however, these details do not survive, and I have assumed, unless there is evidence to the contrary, that the purgation was successfully completed. Even the registers which include purgations have only a handful, and often the more thorough the record, the fewer there are—Bishop Sherborne's model purgation record above, for example, is the only one in his register. It is likely that the bishops entered controversial purgations to ensure that there was a record or took particular care to note them when benefit of clergy was in the political spotlight, but that the process was generally both so routine and so peripheral to the bishops' core concerns that it did not seem worth entering every one.[73] These limitations mean that the bishops' registers do not provide as much information as we would like for a process which must have absorbed a good deal of their time and resources, but they nevertheless throw some light on both the time clerks convict spent in episcopal custody and the process through which they left it.

It should be clear by now that both the legal processes and the patterns of recordkeeping mean that our understanding of benefit of clergy will always be limited. The common law and ecclesiastical sources both provide names and at least some information about the men who claimed benefit of clergy, and in some instances they work together to give us a fairly full picture of a particular individual's experience. But often we get only one part of the puzzle; a King's Bench case which makes reference to an earlier crime for which no record survives, or a pardon or a purgation for a clerk convict who does not appear in King's Bench and for whom no indictment survives. Without the gaol delivery records we can see only a fraction of the men who claimed clergy. And the nature and purpose of the material means that even when we have a fairly full suite of documentation, many of the things we would really like to know remain obscure. These records are not interested in context and motivation, so we have no direct information about the motives for a given crime, the judge or jury's assessment of the crime or the criminal, or the reason for any given verdict or sentence. But though we can only see a fraction of this population, that fraction is still a fairly substantial number—around 1,200 men. And though the qualitative evidence for each individual is thin, the patterns that emerge when working through such a large body of cases can provide some insight into the values and assumptions behind the actions.

[73] See pp. 109 and 112 for more on this.

3. Sanctuary and its Records

Similar problems dog the study of claims of sanctuary. I have found records for a similar number of men, around 1,100, but a much smaller proportion of the records come from the common law. More than 500 appear on lists of sanctuary men in Westminster, Beverley, and Durham, and those lists give far less information than the common law sources.[74] Some records of sanctuary appear almost incidentally as part of the regular criminal process, when an inquisition on the view of a body noted that the accused had fled to sanctuary, or a felon, when asked if there was any reason why the court should not proceed to execution, asserted a forcible removal from sanctuary. The only common law records which explicitly and intentionally deal with sanctuary are the records of abjuration, and while the process for indicting, trying, and sentencing felons was within the remit of the common law from start to finish, the same is clearly not true of the process of abjuration. We virtually never know why an individual chose to claim sanctuary and abjure, often long after the commission of the crime to which they confessed. By definition, we have neither indictment nor verdict, so rather than one jury's presentation of the crime and another's response to it, we have the criminal's own version as presented by the coroner, and his self-imposed punishment. The common law did not initiate the proceedings, but it did mandate the coroner's response: he was to attend when requested by the sanctuary man, record the confession, perform the abjuration, and return the abjuration document so the confession would be a matter of record.

Like most common law documents, abjuration records are formulaic, and John Boole's abjuration is a perfectly typical example. The record opens by stating that he claimed sanctuary in the parish church of Westorp in Suffolk on 19 August 1487 'to have the immunity and tuition of holy Church in the said church', and provides his place of origin and status.[75] It relates how Boole called for the coroner, upon which 'I, John Everard, one of the king's coroners in the county of Suffolk' responded the following day. On Everard's arrival the sanctuary man 'voluntarily confessed and acknowledged' his crime, providing the names of his accomplices (of which there were two) along with their origin and status, the date, place, and time of the crime, the name and status of the victim, and a description of the crime.[76] Having recited

[74] See pp. 146, 225, 229, and 278–281 for more on the sanctuary registers.

[75] TNA KB9/375 m. 17 [image 34].

[76] The readers noted that the coroner could 'help' the sanctuary man with his confession if he could not remember the details, but he could also put him under pressure. For example, Robert Myndrym, a London goldsmith, took sanctuary in the parish church of St Martin Otwych in Bradstreet ward on 26 September 1491 and confessed to the London coroner, William Carkeke, that he had broken into a parish church in Lincoln and stolen two silver chalices worth 20s around 30 May 1490 and had killed an unknown man in Northumberland in September the same year. This did not provide the required level of detail, and Carkeke, who had more experience with abjurations than most coroners, pushed for more detail on both the dates and the places of the crimes, but claimed in the record of the abjuration that Myndrym 'did not wish to say anything about this to me etc., but submitted himself to the law'. A writ duly issued from King's Bench on 12 October 1491 and Myndrym appeared in court two days later. He argued that the record was not sufficient in law to make him respond, and the court agreed. He

his confession, the sanctuary man asked to abjure, 'never to return without special license and reconciliation with the said lord king'. The coroner then assigned a port, Ipswich in Boole's case, and he was sent off with a cross in his right hand 'as is law and custom'.

Formulaic though the document is, it sends a number of signals about the process. In the first instance, the common law elements are clear: the information gathered about the felon, the victim and the crime is the same as would be gathered in an indictment, and the coroner is clearly identified as an officer of the king. But the 'immunity and tuition' of the church is also clearly recognized, along with the felon's right to that immunity. The felon's agency is also emphasized. He calls for the coroner, he voluntarily confesses, he chooses to leave the country, and he acknowledges that by doing so he is breaking his relationship with the king. None of this is initiated by the common law or its officers.

The records of abjuration in the reign of Henry VII are quite consistent in the information they give and the way they frame it, but their formulaic nature means that it's not entirely clear if they reflect everything that was actually happening. The confession itself is consistent, but though the records note that the cross is given to the abjurer 'according to law and custom', there is never any discussion of the penitential clothing familiar from the earlier texts.[77] It is not clear if this is because this element of the ceremony has been dropped, or if it simply does not make it into the record. Thomas Bennet's abjuration also suggests that new elements may have been added to the mix. He took sanctuary in a church in Burnham, Bucks, in June 1504 and confessed to Burnham Abbey's coroner, William Duffelde, that he had killed a man and stolen 100s two years earlier and four counties away.[78] Duffelde notes that he led Bennet from the door of the church with a cross in his right hand, and that 'a purse was attached to that cross and in the purse was the bill of his abjuration, and this was done in the presence of John Hill, Richard Aldrich, Richard Wixton, John Gray and many others'. This record is the earliest I've found which makes explicit the coroner's assumption of jurisdiction at the church door, and the earliest to mention a bill of abjuration—presumably a copy of Bennet's confession and

went *sine die*. *Rights and Liberties*, p. 110; TNA KB9/391 m. 79 [image 154], TNA KB27/921 rex m. 2d [image 538].

[77] Kesselring notes that the church provided the 'props that gave the event its sacral character' noting that the abjurer travelled 'bare of head and foot, clothed in a long white robe and carrying a wooden cross' in the dress of a pilgrim or penitent: K.J. Kesselring, 'Abjuration and its demise: The Changing Face of Royal Justice in the Tudor Period', *Canadian Journal of History* 34 (1999), p. 349. Rosser says the white tunic was a symbolic shroud, since the abjurer was dead in law: Gervase Rosser, 'Sanctuary and social negotiation in medieval England', in *The Cloister and the World: Essays on Medieval History in Honour of Barbara Harvey* edited by John Blair and Brian Golding (Oxford: Clarendon Press, 1996), p. 64. Hunnisett argues that by the late thirteenth century abjurers were allowed to wear their own clothes, though they were bare-headed and -footed: R.F. Hunnisett, *The Medieval Coroner* (Cambridge: Cambridge University Press, 1961), p. 48.

[78] TNA KB9/435 m. 3 [image 6].

his assigned port, to be presented to any authority who might challenge his passage.[79] Duffelde's account is also unusual in naming witnesses. They were not necessary for the legal validity of the process, but it is hardly surprising that they were present. The role of the local community was explicit in sanctuary-seeking: they were expected to guard the sanctuary man, and their perceptions of his crime shaped their response. For example, John Pewyk was identified by a commission on escapes, sitting in April 1507, as having taken sanctuary in the parish church of Kempsey in Worchestershire in September 1499.[80] The commission concluded that he had 'remained there for a long time', but escaped for lack of good custody. If the commissioners were correct, this suggests a lengthy period in sanctuary during which Pewyk either negotiated a compromise with his victim, or satisfied the need for atonement, or both, and was then allowed to go free.[81] By definition we can't know how often a sanctuary man either negotiated a compromise or escaped with the support of the local community, but we can assume that the community often played a role in keeping a sanctuary man either contained or protected until the coroner arrived, and that they might have a lively interest in his removal from their church.

The formulaic nature of the documentation can thus obscure a good deal, but the formula was not rigid, and variations on the model appear. For example, in August 1506 Ralph Toker took sanctuary in the churchyard of the parish church of Shoreham in Kent, where, four days later, William Miller came to take his confession.[82] In the record Toker 'publicly and distinctly' made his confession in the first person, opening 'hear this, king's coroner' before going on to admit that on the same day he had broken the close and home of Thomas Polhill and stolen cloth worth 24s. He asked for 'the liberty and tuition of the aforesaid church according to the laws of the realm of the king of England and laudably conceded to the Church of England', thus demonstrating that this coroner perceived sanctuary as a common law right exercised within the remit of the Church.[83] Toker asked to publicly abjure the realm, and the coroner assigned him to the port of Dover 'directly along the common royal ways', once again reinforcing secular jurisdiction. After the abjuration was completed, the coroner 'led Ralph safely from the gate of the said churchyard and set him out on the road to the said town of Dover'. Toker does not seem to have heeded the coroner's injunction, for rather than heading south-east to Dover, a week later he broke into the parish church of Queenborough

79 It's more common to be explicit about the physical boundaries of the sanctuary in the reign of Henry VIII: see p. 240.

80 TNA KB9/445 m. 6d [image 12].

81 The parishioners argued in King's Bench that Pewyk had not claimed sanctuary, but presented a pardon for the escape in November 1509: TNA KB27/990 rex m. 14 [images 209, 188d]; TNA KB27/993 rex m. 10 [images 262–263].

82 For a discussion of Toker's later adventures see p. 168. He is also discussed in McSheffrey, *Seeking Sanctuary*, pp. 83–90.

83 TNA KB9/442 m. 20 [image 41].

on the isle of Sheppey, north-east of Shoreham, and stole church silver worth 28s 8d and 3s in cash. Three days later, on 28 August, he again took sanctuary, this time in the cemetery of the parish church of Higham. The same day another Kentish coroner, John Sharpe, came to take his confession. This record also says that Toker 'publicly, distinctly and clearly' made his confession in the first person, suggesting that this was a local formula, rather than an individual one.[84] Toker confessed his crime and again asked to publicly abjure the realm, and the coroner again assigned him the port of Dover. There is no suggestion anywhere in the record that Sharpe was aware of Toker's previous abjuration, but he seems to have been a less trusting man than his colleague, for his abjuration notes that Ralph was 'safely led from the gate of the aforesaid churchyard and assigned to the constable of the hundred of Shamell to lead to the port'. Once again Toker seems to have quickly lost his way, and on 26 November 1506 writs issued to both coroners to send the records of his abjurations to King's Bench.[85] Toker's records suggest some distinct Kentish practices: both claims of sanctuary were in churchyards rather than churches and both coroners emphasized his agency by presenting his confession in the first person. Both emphasized that it was given publicly and distinctly, implying that there had been an audience present along with the coroner, though the audience was not explicitly presented as witnesses, as in the Bennet case in Buckinghamshire. The appearance of the constable at the second abjuration is particularly interesting. Given that the records are so similar in format, we would expect to see one named if he had been used in the first abjuration. His appearance for the second abjuration suggests that this was a real difference, and raises the question of why. Was Sharpe more concerned about escapes? Was the constable in Higham more available, more pliable or more reliable than the constable in Shoreham? Or, most intriguingly, did Sharpe know about Toker's history in the county, and was a constable more likely to be assigned to a repeat offender? The absence of a constable in the record of an abjuration doesn't prove that one wasn't used, but the fact that they are occasionally, but only very occasionally, mentioned, does suggest that they were not a standard feature of the process. And the fact that Toker did not in fact leave the country explains why that might be—even if the first constable did his duty as expected, it would take a relay team of constables to get an abjurer to his port, and such a system was almost bound to break down.

The abjuration process was remarkably efficient: though the readers indicate that the sanctuary man could remain in place for forty days before the coroner arrived, the surviving abjurations suggest that in fact the coroner tended to respond with some alacrity, usually arriving within a day or two, and the abjurer usually left the same day.[86] It's worth pausing to recognize the human implications of this: a

84 TNA KB9/442 m. 18 [image 37].

85 TNA KB9/442 mm. 17, 19 [images 35, 39].

86 See for example TNA KB9/375 m. 17 [image 34]; TNA KB9/380 m. 23 [image 46]; TNA KB9/1109 last membrane [not on AALT]; TNA KB9/419 m. 5 [image 8]; M. Hemmant ed. *Select Cases in the*

man who woke up expecting a normal day, even if precarious or criminous, could find himself bedding down by the side of the road on his way into legal exile in the evening. The same was theoretically possible for those who went through the full machinery of the common law: there are examples where a crime was committed on the day of an assize and the felon was indicted, tried and sentenced on the same day. In either case the experience must have been overwhelming for even the most hardened criminal. But the criminal justice machinery generally ground rather more slowly than abjuration. And there was a real benefit to a more deliberate pace: as Powell argues, 'considerations of speed and efficiency … had to be balanced against the need to ensure due process and to avoid a miscarriage of justice'.[87] There is no question that the system provides examples of both extremes: for every case that moved from crime to sentencing in one day, there are many more where there is a delay between indictment and trial, where the prisoner was remanded until the jury appeared, remanded again (sometimes several times) when the jury did not appear as ordered, and remanded again after verdict, even without a claim of clergy or other reason given for the delay. In many cases the delay must simply have been the result of circumstances: the accused was not in custody at the time of indictment; the calendar was full at the assize; witnesses were not available to testify; the jury did not appear, or the court found something troubling in the course of the case and 'wished to be advised' before proceeding to sentencing. The speed with which some cases progressed through the system demonstrated that it could be efficient, but there was certainly room for delay, and delay could be either the simple product of circumstance or a useful tactic.[88]

The criminal justice machinery also had many more legal exit points than abjuration. Many men and women who were arrested, appealed and/or indicted did not make it to trial, whether because the accusation was malicious or mistaken, because the defendant and victim reached some compromise, because the victim decided it was too expensive or difficult to pursue the case, because witnesses and/or juries were not available and/or were intimidated, or because the defendant died

Exchequer Chamber vol. II: 1461–1509, SS. vol. 64 (London: Bernard Quaritch, 1948), pp. 55–56. Snede, reading in 1511, suggested that it might take the coroner twenty years to arrive, but this must have been for the sake of argument: *Rights and Liberties*, p. 110. Spelman noted that the sanctuary man could wait for the coroner for forty days, but did not know what would happen if the coroner did not arrive in that time: *Spelman's Reports*, vol. 1, p. 66. I have never seen this arise in practice. It was also agreed that the felon did not have to confess the details of his crime to anyone other than the coroner, though he did have to be explicit that he was claiming sanctuary for felony: YB Mich. 3 Hen. VII, p. 12, pl. 6. I have seen only one instance where sanctuary men explicitly claimed the right to remain in the church for forty days before abjuring, and they escaped from the sanctuary the following day: TNA KB9/438 m. 86 [image 188].

[87] Powell, *Kingship, Law and Society*, p. 75. He is referring specifically to the process of outlawry, but the same principle applied to the general processes of the criminal law.

[88] Powell estimates that the process from indictment to outlawry took between six months to a year, and points out that contemporary petitions complained that it was much too fast: *Kingship, Law and Society*, p. 75.

or disappeared before trial. There is no doubt that some defendants were wrongly acquitted while others were wrongly convicted, whether through political or social pressure, malice, or simple error, but we only rarely have the evidence that allows us to see this.[89] In the absence of the broader context for each crime it can be surprisingly easy to assume either that many convictions or many acquittals were unjust, but the sources simply do not give us the information we need to supply that context for the vast majority of 'ordinary' crimes and criminals, men and women whose crimes were not committed in the context of magnate or gentry politics or who did not challenge the political order in any but the broadest law and order sense. In the vast majority of cases we simply don't know why an indictment appears in the King's Bench files with no further process, why a convicted felon was remanded without sentencing, or why one convict was pardoned while another was not, we just know that it happened. For this reason, and for the sake of consistency, I have chosen to focus primarily on cases which made it through the process to a verdict, and to assume that the verdict was correct, unless there is clear evidence otherwise. Though there is no question that individual sheriffs, juries, and justices of the peace could be corrupt, intimidated, or inefficient, the complaints and concerns about such problems, as well as the working of the system as a whole, suggest that it generally had the support of the population and that it generally worked well, given the norms and constraints of sixteenth-century English society. It did not treat everyone equally, but there was no expectation that it would or that it should.

Indeed, in some ways the criminal justice system was the victim of its own success, as well as a general lack of resources. Its structures were old, familiar, and mostly worked well enough. Problems with law and order could be laid at the feet of the individuals who made up the system—whether criminals, sheriffs, justices, or juries—rather than the system itself, and there was no-one with an incentive to advocate for structural changes, even if there had been consensus on what changes might be beneficial. When Henry VII came to the throne he did not have the political capital or the administrative imagination to look for an overhaul of the criminal justice system, much as he wanted to restore order and ensure that his rule was both effective and seen to be so. His justices clearly did not think that an overhaul was necessary. As we will see in the next chapter, their advice was to ensure that the existing laws were made to work better rather than to introduce new laws, and that was what Henry and his legal establishment set out to do. Working with the common learning developed over the previous two centuries, the machinery available to them, and the occasional but significant new statute, English judges in the early sixteenth century tested what their laws could be made to do and discovered the limits beyond which they would not go. They developed an ad hoc and

[89] Green, *Verdict According to Conscience*, pp. 65–66.

cost-effective system in which felons could be tried, convicted, and effectively punished without necessarily being executed, and they did it by leaning heavily upon the rights of the Church. The next two chapters will explain how, and the four that follow will demonstrate how Henry VIII's justices first built upon the foundation bequeathed to him by his father, and then, after 1529, took advantage of the opportunities presented by the Reformation to consolidate his new system on a secular footing.

PART II
BUILDING A BUREAUCRACY

4

Benefit of Clergy in the Reign of Henry VII

There is little evidence in the early years of Henry VII's reign that he or his justices would significantly change the criminal justice system. Henry was concerned with law and order as part of the process of cementing his claim to the throne, but radical innovation was not a likely path to stability, and the justices were constitutionally inclined to be conservative: in a discussion at Blackfriars before the opening of Henry's first parliament, they agreed that the old statutes on the books, including 'Winchester and Westminster for robberies and felonies' were sufficient, if only they were properly enforced.[1] William Huse CJKB went on to opine that 'the law would never be well-executed until all the lords spiritual and temporal are of one mind for the love and dread that they have of God or of the king, or of both, to execute them effectually'. This, it turns out, was both a succinct and accurate characterization of the strategy for the next several decades.

The problem Henry and his servants faced was not new: how to ensure that those who committed crimes were not only caught and tried, but convicted and punished. While passage through the trial process might serve as punishment enough for some minor felonies, the sight of repeat or heinous felons repeatedly evading punishment was a very concrete reflection of the weakness of the monarchy in general, and of its ineffectiveness in the counties in particular. But the problem was an old one because it was intractable—how could the monarchy enforce its authority in the counties when local powers were unwilling to concede any of their own and/or when the criminal justice system did not offer forms of punishment which met local expectations for condign punishment? The commissions of the peace were one point of entry into the former problem: Lander argues that Henry was unhappy about their constitution and he introduced peers, bishops and lawyers loyal to him to many different county commissions through the 1490s.[2] But useful as they could be politically, unless the justices in the counties had something new to offer, their simple presence was unlikely to solve the latter problem. The beginning of a new approach was marked by a 1490 statute on benefit of clergy. We saw Kebell describe the purgation of clerks convict as part of the law of the land in the 1470s, but it's likely his view was not yet widely held. The 1490 statute shifted perceptions

[1] YB Mich. 1 Hen. VII pl. 3, p. 3.

[2] J.R. Lander, *English Justices of the Peace 1461–1509* (Gloucester, UK: Alan Sutton, 1989), pp. 112–119. Lander argues that the 'extreme intrusion' of foreigners into the commissions ended by 1497, but that Henry continued to introduce both new men in the counties and his trusted servants to commissions throughout his reign: ibid., pp. 128–140.

The King's Felons. Margaret McGlynn, Oxford University Press.
DOI: 10.1093/oso/9780192887689.003.0005

by explicitly separating the lay version of benefit of clergy from the clerical version. Claiming that 'divers persones lettred hath ben the more bold to committe murdre rape robbery thefte and all othre myschevous dedys, bicause they have ben continuelly admitted to the beneffice of the Clergie as ofte as they did offend in any of the premises', it provides that every literate offender who successfully claims clergy is to be branded on the left thumb, and any man thus branded seeking benefit of clergy a second time is to produce a letter or certificate of his orders before being delivered to the ordinary, though he can repeat the process as often as necessary.[3] Not only does this statute recognize the development of a common law version of benefit of clergy in its distinction between 'persones lettred' and clergy, it clearly removes the privilege only from the former, and then only from repeat offenders.[4] It is the first explicit assertion of royal authority over any form of benefit of clergy, and though it did not attempt to change the privilege for clerics, it meant that both legal and political discourse would have to navigate a dual version of the privilege for the next fifty years.[5] Rather than marking the beginning of an attack on benefit of clergy, the statute of 1490 marks the beginning of Henry VII's conscious re-purposing of the clerical right for much more secular purposes. Though the evidence is patchy, it points to a greater engagement with the workings of benefit of clergy on the part of the secular courts after 1490, one which was further intensified and refined after 1495, and which forced the lawyers to think more carefully about how benefit of clergy could be used and how it interacted with other forms of mitigation such as turning approver and claiming sanctuary. Across the reign, claims of clergy on the part of the 'lettred' vastly outnumbered claims made by clerics and they rose in the later part of the reign as lay men of middling status found their way into a penal system managed and funded by the Church, but largely, and increasingly, controlled by the common lawyers.

[3] *SR*, II. 538. 4 Hen. VII c. 13. Polydore Vergil says that the king introduced the statute in council himself, implying that this change in policy came from the very top: Polydore Vergil, *The Anglica Historia of Polydore Vergil, AD 1485–1537* ed. and trans. Denys Hay, Camden Society vol. 74 (London: Royal Historical Society, 1950), pp. 116–117, 130. Cavill implies that this meant no more than that it had been passed by parliament: P.R. Cavill, 'A Perspective on the Church-State Confrontation of 1515: The Passage of 4 Henry VIII, c.2', *Journal of Ecclesiastical History* 63 (2012), p. 660.

[4] The same is true of the statute of 1491 which removed benefit of clergy from soldiers who deserted, and that of 1496 which provided that one James Grame should be executed without benefit of clergy for the premeditated murder of his master, and went on to order that 'if any laie persone hereaftir purpensidly murder their Lord Maister or sovereign immediate, that they hereaftir not be admytted to their clergie'. *SR*, II. 549, 7 Hen. VII c. 1; *SR*, II. 639, 12 Hen. VII c. 7.

[5] I am using the term 'cleric' to refer to men who earned their living through a Church office or whose primary identity was as a religious figure, in distinction to the generic 'clerk', which includes any man who had taken minor orders, but who might well not earn his living or primarily identify as a religious figure, as well as the 'lettred persons' referred to by the statute, who had not taken orders. Though all who had taken orders could claim benefit of clergy for most of this period, the distinction is important in thinking about the place of benefit of clergy in the criminal justice system, and this serves as a useful shorthand for the two groups.

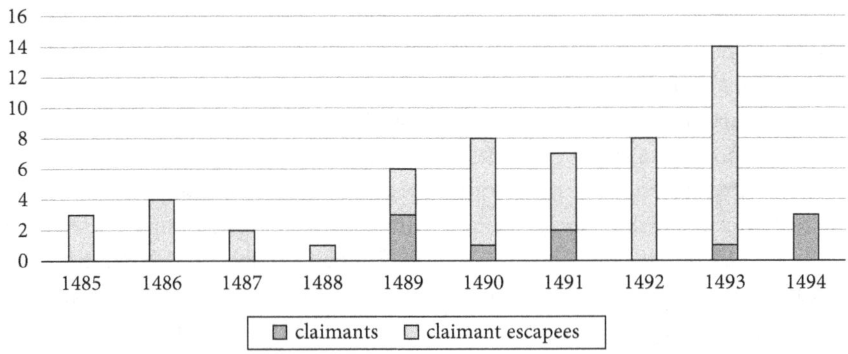

Figure 4.1 Recorded claims of benefit of clergy in King's Bench 1485–1494*

*Data collected from TNA KB27 and KB9 rolls. These are mostly not records of the original claims, but cases in which the claim was presented as part of a later case, usually an escape. Individual cases are discussed below.

1. The 1490 Statute and Episcopal Prisons

Since the 1490 statute marked the beginning of this process of change, it's worth considering both what problem it was trying to solve, and what its logical consequences should have been. Broad though its implications were, at its heart the statute was bureaucratic: it provided a way to indicate to a court that the lay man convicted of felony before it was a repeat offender who had previously been convicted and delivered to the ordinary.[6] This implies that enough men claimed clergy, found their way back into the secular world, and offended again for tracking them to be an issue of concern. The statute did not state what should happen to such a man, though the implication was that one who could produce letters of ordination would be delivered to the ordinary once again, and one who could not would be executed. This fits with a law and order agenda, and in practical terms it means that there should have been a rise in executions for felony after 1490 as those men who would have received benefit of clergy a second or third time went straight to execution. Without the gaol delivery records we can't know if the overall numbers changed, but we would expect to see some reflection of such a change in King's Bench. As fig. 4.1 indicates, though the number of benefit of clergy cases in King's Bench remains low in the first decade of Henry VII's reign there is a distinct increase after about 1490.[7] The actual cases have little to do with the new statute,

[6] See Margaret McGlynn, 'From Written Record to Bureaucratic Mind: Imagining a Criminal Record', *Past and Present* 250 (2021), 57–59 for more on the bureaucratic implications of the statute and the problems of using a brand for this purpose.

[7] The names of fifty-seven men who claimed benefit of clergy in the first decade of Henry VII's reign survive in the records of King's Bench, and only sixteen of them claimed before the passing of the 1490 statute.

however. Instead, the court was overwhelmingly interested in the escapes of clerks convict and particularly in the bishops who were supposed to keep them confined.

The actions against the bishops fall into three phases. In the first, lasting from 1491–1494, the courts focused simply on suits against the bishops for the escape of prisoners in their custody. In 1491, for example, Thomas Langton, bishop of Salisbury, was indicted for the escape of three men from his prison the previous year, but he produced a charter from 1486 which included the privilege to be quit of all escapes and successfully argued to have the case dismissed.[8] John Esteney, the abbot of Westminster, was less fortunate. Indicted for the escape of fourteen clerks convict in 1492, he accepted responsibility for the escape of thirteen and was fined the substantial sum of £1,300.[9] In 1494 the bishop of London was indicted for the escape of twenty prisoners and paid a fine of £1,400.[10]

Escape cases continued to appear in King's Bench in later years, but appealing as the income from fines doubtless was, in two major cases argued between 1495 and 1500 the courts shifted into phase two. Rather than simply penalizing the bishops, they began to investigate the ways in which their responsibilities for the prisons worked. The escape of five men from the bishop of Salisbury's prison during an episcopal vacancy in 1493, and the escape of six men from the bishop of Bath and Wells' prison in 1495 led King's Bench to test the relative responsibility of the previous bishop (Thomas Langton), the archbishop of Canterbury (John Morton) and the dean and chapter of Salisbury in the first instance, and the previous bishop (Richard Fox), the current bishop (Oliver King, who had held the temporalities during the vacancy), and the archbishop of Canterbury (still Morton) in the second.[11] These cases made far less money for the Crown than the earlier escapes

[8] TNA KB9/388 m. 80 [image 160]; TNA KB27/919 rex m. 8 [images 202, 446d]. Langton had appeared in the exchequer in 1488 to answer for the escape of two men from his prison in 1487, and his charter held up there too: *Reg. Langton*, pp. 66–67.

[9] TNA KB9/395 m. 26 [image 52]; TNA KB27/926 rex m. 11 [images 175, 176, 385d, 386d]. *Rights and Liberties* Westminster I c. 3 Reading E says the escape of a clerk convict or attaint will cost the ordinary £100, but Readings B and C reduce the bishop's liability in the case of a clerk convict (pp. 39, 14, 20). Reading G specifies 100 marks for a clerk convict and £100 for a clerk attaint (p. 54). *Rights and Liberties* Magna Carta Reading 5 makes no distinction (p. 85). In practice, by the late fifteenth century, £100 seems to have been the standard amount. The *Boke of Justices of Peas* (London: Pynson, 1505), B i says explicitly that the fine for an escape from a secular prison is 100s and 'yf ony persone convycte and in the pryson of the ordinary' escapes from prison the fine is £100. The abbey probably paid the fine in instalments: a surviving bond from 1494 may be associated with this: Westminster Abbey Muniments 33088. After another escape in 1510, the abbot came with a grant of Edward the Confessor which provided that the abbey should be pardoned all escapes. Since he would presumably have presented such a grant if it were available in 1492, this suggests that it had been constructed in the meantime to avoid another such ruinous fine: TNA KB27/996 rex m. 18 [images 281, 282, 268d, 269d].

[10] TNA KB9/1109 [not numbered, not on AALT]; TNA KB27/930 rex m. 7 [images 176, 177, 374d, 375d, 376d, 178, 179, 377d, 378d, 180, 181, 379d, 380d, 182]. The men escaped the previous year. The bishop was also indicted for the escape of a single prisoner earlier in 1493 but pardoned: TNA KB9/399 m. 20 [image 40]; TNA C66/575 m. 8 (29), *CPR Hen. VII* vol. 1, p. 449.

[11] TNA KB9/402 m. 22 [image 43]; TNA KB27/936 rex m. 7 [images 144, 145, 300d, 301d, 146]; TNA KB27/939 rex m. 4 [images 152, 153, 384d, 385d, 154, 155, 386d, 387d, 388d]; TNA KB27/949 rex m. 16 [images 243, 244, 531d, 532d, 245, 246]: TNA KB9/417 m. 124 [images 249]; TNA KB27/950 rex m. 10 [images 197, 198, 419d, 420d, 421d, 199, 200, 422d]; TNA KB27/952 rex mm 13, 14 [images 208, 209,

had done; Langton paid a £400 fine in the Salisbury case, but the case was dropped against the dean and chapter, and the Bath and Wells case was never resolved. Nevertheless, the pressure placed on the defendants, especially the archbishop of Canterbury, was intense, and in Easter term 1500, in the course of the Bath and Wells case, it was argued for Morton that the custody of clerks convict was part of the temporal responsibility of a bishop.[12] Though the argument could be understood narrowly, and made sense in the context of the individual case, it sounded like a remarkable concession, and later that year the chief justice of King's Bench, John Fyneux, took advantage of it. In a year book discussion he argued that if a clerk convict or attaint is committed to the ordinary, the custody is temporal and not spiritual, because the action, the judge and the authority are temporal and therefore the imprisonment is also.[13] This argument was unlikely to be palatable if generally applied, but it drew on arguments we saw above in the 1469 case and it demonstrates the way in which the common lawyers were ready to move from doctrine to process.[14] Like his king, Fyneux was more interested in practical control than in abstract ideas about jurisdiction, and in the same year book report he effectively claimed that when it came to the custody of clerks convict and clerks attaint the bishops were temporal officers, holding their charges by the king's authority and subject to his commands regarding their management and delivery. He achieved this by arguing that the ordinary would be punished if he allowed a clerk convict or attaint to go on bail or at large or if the clerk's imprisonment was harder or easier than it should be; that if the ordinary refused to allow the clerk to undergo his purgation, the king would send a writ to enforce it, and that the king could pardon the clerk without purgation, all of which proved that the ordinary's custody was temporal.[15]

428d, 429d, 210, 211, 212, 213, 431d, 432d, 214, 215, 433d]. For a full discussion of all these escapes, see Margaret McGlynn, 'Ecclesiastical Prisons and Royal Authority in the Reign of Henry VII', *Journal of Ecclesiastical History*, 70 (2019), pp. 750–766.

[12] TNA KB27/950 rex m. 10 [images 197, 198, 419d, 420d, 421d, 199, 200, 422d].

[13] YB Trin. 15 Hen. VII, p. 9, pl. 8. Brooke, *Corone*, 53. Brooke also makes a brief reference to this at *Corone*, 222.

[14] See p. 43. Fyneux's argument also demonstrates that the interest in escapes was more about control of the system than about money, and this is supported by the evidence from King's Bench after 1500: though clerks convict continued to escape and bishops continued to be indicted, no further fines were imposed. Instead, in most cases the bishops appeared with royal pardons for the escapes, pardons for which they had probably paid a substantial but lesser sum. In typical Henrician style the process, the threat of punishment, and its mitigation were more valuable for asserting royal authority than the simple collection of money. Before the end of the reign, officers of the dioceses of Worcester, Exeter, Coventry, and Lichfield, London, Canterbury, Norwich, Bath and Wells, and Rochester all appeared before King's Bench to answer for clerks convict in their custody: TNA KB27/958 rex m. 2d [images 272, 273]; TNA KB27/965 rex m. 7 [images 270, 271] and TNA KB9/448 m. 38 [image 76]; TNA KB9/431 m. 23 [image 49]; TNA KB9/431 m. 24 [images 51, 52]; TNA KB9/433 m. 43 [images 85-88]; TNA KB9/438 m. 54 [image 119]; TNA KB9/442 m. 33 [image 66]; TNA KB9/442 m. 82 [image 165]. The bishop of Hereford was pardoned for the escape of two men in 1499: *CPR Hen. IV* vol. 2, p. 154. One case was dismissed: TNA KB27/926 rex m. 11 [images 175, 176, 385d, 386d].

[15] YB Trin. 15 Hen. VII, p. 9, pl. 8.

As Fyneux's argument makes clear, purgation remained key to the effectiveness of benefit of clergy as a punishment, and the framing of improper purgations as escapes became phase three of the campaign against the bishops. In 1496 Thomas Hawes appeared in King's Bench charged with an escape: he had confessed to murder and was delivered to the bishop of Lincoln in June 1493, but was purged and released in March 1495, during an episcopal vacancy.[16] As a clerk attaint, Hawes should have remained in prison for life, but the record of his conviction and delivery was ambiguous, and he went *sine die*. Unusually, a commission on escapes returned to Hawes' case in the summer of 1501, and the dean and chapter of Lincoln were indicted for the escape in January 1502.[17] This time around the record of Hawes's conviction was carefully amended to ensure that his status as a clerk attaint was clear, and the responsibility of the dean and chapter for both his custody and his purgation was highlighted. In February 1506 the dean and chapter pleaded not guilty to the escape and presented a warrant from the king discharging them.[18] Around the same time Richard Nykke, bishop of Norwich, was indicted for the escape of five prisoners in February 1505.[19] The bishop's attorney argued that the five men had been duly purged and the King's Bench records give unusually full information on them, including information on their convictions and their crimes. All five were convicted of housebreaking, but their sentences varied quite substantially, with one man spending more than six years in confinement and another less than two years.[20] There were no set rules for how long a clerk convict should be confined and nothing in the indictment indicates that the men could not be purged. Nevertheless Nykke appeared in King's Bench with a pardon for all escapes before 10 March 1506, suggesting that something was perceived to be amiss with the purgations.[21] The lawyers were making good on Kebell's claim that

16 TNA KB9/410 mm. 53, 54 [images 113, 115]; TNA KB27/941 rex m. 8 [images 248, 249, 535d, 536d].

17 TNA KB27/960 rex m. 9 [images 214, 215, 447d].

18 The warrant is dated 3 December 1504 and is in English.

19 TNA KB9/438 m. 54 [image 119]: TNA KB27/977 rex m. 16 [images 231, 232, 225d]. Cavill characterizes the original indictment as 'outrageous' and part of a 'concerted attack by Hobart not only on the bishop, but also on the exercise of ecclesiastical jurisdiction' resulting from a dispute over praemunire cases in the diocese: P.R. Cavill, '"The Enemy of God and His Church": James Hobart, Praemunire, and the Clergy of Norwich Diocese', *The Journal of Legal History* 32.2 (2011), p. 144–145. Hobart was a Justice of the Peace in Norfolk and Suffolk, and Harper-Bill argues that after Morton's death he carried out a 'sustained campaign against ecclesiastical jurisdiction', including *praemunire* proceedings, encouraging charges against clergy at quarter sessions and an attack on Bishop Nykke's probate jurisdiction. *Reg. Morton* pp. 3, 20. Steven Gunn notes that Hobart 'in July 1507 ... with ten years still to live and no compensating promotion, was replaced as attorney general and in November he paid Dudley £533 6s 8d in cash for a pardon of his own', suggesting that Hobart did not come out on top in the battle: *Henry VII's New Men and the Making of Tudor England* (Oxford: Oxford University Press, 2016), p. 286. Cavill agrees with Ives that Hobart's resignation is probably not directly connected with the *praemunire* cases, 'The Enemy of God', p. 147.

20 TNA KB27/978 rex mm. 13–16 [images 176, 177, 160d, 161d; 178, 179, 162d; 180, 181, 163d, 164d; 182, 183, 165d].

21 TNA C66/600 m 17 (7), *CPR Hen. IV* vol. 2, p. 484. The pardon was dated at Westminster on 26 April 1506.

purgation was part of the law of the land, and extending Fyneux's assertion that the king could enforce purgation by demonstrating that he could also restrict it. Oblique as they are, these cases show the common lawyers moving from exhorting the bishops to ensure due purgation to intervening directly when they felt that they had not. As with the escape cases, the bishops got pardons, but pardons cost time and money and were an effective way of reinforcing Henry's authority over men whose own authority he wanted to both maintain and constrain.

While the 1490 statute was aimed at repeat lay claimants, the cases in King's Bench between 1491 and 1506 suggest that the courts were more concerned with finding ways to keep convict clerks in prison once they were there by punishing bishops for lax security and early purgations than they were with denying lay felons benefit of clergy. If the statute made the existence of a common law version of benefit of clergy explicit by setting a statutory floor under the lay privilege, these cases clarified the nature of royal control over the management of that benefit. It's not at all clear if this was the intent of the framers of the statute, or of the justices, in 1490 or if this was an evolutionary process as the cons of potentially destabilizing levels of executions were balanced against the pros of extending a politically unpopular form of mitigation. These cases suggest that when faced with those two options the courts found a *via media*: they pressured the bishops to confine their criminals more securely and thereby created a more acceptable model of mitigation.

Snapshot: The Westminster Escapees

Our focus thus far has been on the bishops rather than the convicts because we usually have little information about the criminal history of the escapees. The thirteen Westminster Abbey escapees of 1492, however, were not only one of the larger groups, but one of the better documented. We know the route six of these men took to their prison, and they give us a good snapshot of the ways in which benefit of clergy was working at the end of the fifteenth century, both before and after the 1490 statute. The first two belong to the older era. Henry Hanshawe went on something of a crime spree in May and June of 1485, stealing a jeweled cross worth £20 belonging to St George's College at Windsor along with three other thefts of silver totaling 26s.[22] He appeared in King's Bench in June 1486 and decided to turn approver. He confessed his crime to the coroner and was given 26, 27, and 29 June to name his appellees. On 26 June he confessed that he and Thomas Wodde attacked a merchant and stole £22 in May 1485; on 27 June he confessed that he and John Waymer stole £30 from the mayor of Chester in July 1485, and on 29 June,

[22] TNA KB9/371 m. 12 [image 23]; TNA KB27/900 rex m. 14 [images 207, 208, 440d, 441d].

saving the most dramatic for last, he confessed that he and John Sarsyn attacked and killed Thomas Malyn in December 1485. When he re-appeared in King's Bench in November 1487 it was determined that the three men he had appealed had already been outlawed that summer. When asked if there was any reason that he should not be executed, he opted to claim clergy and was delivered as a clerk attaint without the possibility of purgation.[23] Richard Fox, a yeoman from Elstree, also began his route to the Abbey by trying to turn approver. On 3 February 1486 he was indicted at gaol delivery in the Marshalsea for three horse-thefts between September 1484 and December 1485.[24] The jury delivered their verdicts on the other cases in the session, but adjourned his until 8 February, and as they were about to deliver their verdict on him, he confessed and turned approver. He was given 9, 10, and 11 February to make his appeals, and he appealed eight men in a trail of criminal activity that stretched from Lancashire and Yorkshire south-east across the country to the capital.[25] When the case returned to King's Bench in June 1486 his appeals were found insufficient because the local sheriffs could not find anyone of the names he gave.[26] He too was asked if there was any reason why he should not be executed and successfully claimed clergy. Fox, however, re-appears in the records after his escape. In February 1493 he was indicted in the Marshalsea for stealing a silver chalice worth 5 marks.[27] Although this indictment notes that he is from Westminster as well as from Elstree, no connection is made with his escape. The second time around Fox decided not to respond to the indictment and a jury was summoned to determine if he was mute by nature or by malice. The jury determined the latter, and he was sentenced to *peine fort et dure*.[28] Hanshawe and Fox were both indicted early in the reign, and few approvers appear in later years. Their decision to turn approver may reflect an older pattern of response to indictment and an ignorance of clergy as a feasible option. Once clergy was readily available, it was much safer than an appeal, even without the possibility of escape.

[23] TNA KB27/900 rex m. 14 [images 207, 208, 440d, 441d].

[24] TNA KB27/898 rex m. 8 [images 129, 130, 286d, 287d].

[25] TNA KB9/369 m. 11 [image 20]. This schedule is unusually compressed: February 12 was Easter Sunday, and the court probably wanted to get the appeals done before the end of the term.

[26] It is tempting to infer that the crimes and criminals were made up in order to buy him some time, but they are unusually specific, and some paint him as a fairly pathetic criminal.

[27] TNA KB27/926 rex m. 15 [images 183, 184, 394d, 395d, 396d, 185].

[28] *Peine fort et dure* was used by the court to pressure an accused felon into entering a plea; under it he was allowed only fetid water on alternate days and moldy bread on the other days while being shackled in his underwear and pressed under weights. By the sixteenth century it appears that he may have been laid on a sharp object intended to break his spine and thus cause death, but this was not the original intention. The apparent benefit of *peine fort et dure* to the accused, in theory, was that if he was not found guilty his goods and lands would not be confiscated and his family was spared the consequences of the verdict. Its value to indigent accused felons is less clear: see Andrea McKenzie, '"This Death Some Strong and Stout Hearted Man Doth Choose": The Practice of Peine Forte et Dure in Seventeenth- and Eighteenth-Century England', *Law and History Review* 23 (2005), p. 279–313. Sara Butler argues that the *peine forte* also reflected a penitential sensibility in the fourteenth-century: *Pain, Penance, and Protest: Peine Forte et Dure in Medieval England* (Cambridge: Cambridge University Press, 2022).

James Wylde represents the next stage in the development of the law, as his career spanned the 1490 statute. He appeared at the gaol delivery of the castle of Cambridge in December 1489, when he was convicted of burglary. Wylde claimed clergy, but the ordinary was not present in court and he was remanded to gaol.[29] He appeared in King's Bench eighteen months later, when he was asked if there was a reason he should not be executed and he claimed clergy again. This time he was branded and delivered, and he remained in custody until the escape in 1492.[30] Wylde too re-appears in the records after his escape. In April 1493 he appeared at the gaol delivery of Newgate as James Childe, charged with burglary.[31] He was found guilty and claimed clergy again, but the brand seems to have done its job. Nicholas Pakenham argued for the king that he had been committed to the abbot of Westminster in May 1491 as James Wylde, and Wylde/Childe was remanded to gaol. The case was removed to King's Bench, and on 26 November 1493 he made the same claim for benefit there. Henry Harman, king's attorney in King's Bench, produced the record from 1491 and argued that because James 'is known and named as a notorious thief through not a small area of the kingdom' he should be executed.[32] Childe protested that he was not the same man as James Wylde, but the jury disagreed and he was sentenced to be hanged. Once again, there is no comment on Wylde having previously escaped from Westminster, but the brand was enough to ensure that he would not have clergy a second time without some scrutiny.

Thus far two out of three of the escapees found themselves before the courts again, and while the escape was not noticed in either record, both men seem to have come to the end of their respective roads within a year of it, and the courts seem to have been happy to move to execution in both cases. There is evidence, however, that the court could be lenient when it saw fit. Robert Rile appeared in King's Bench in November 1491, accused of stealing a number of horses and some cloth worth almost £5 in the course of three thefts the previous month.[33] Rile was found guilty, but even though he had committed multiple thefts, the court seems to have seen some mitigating factor. Rile 'was asked by the court if he was a clerk or not, and he said that he was a clerk and asked for benefit of clergy'. This prompting suggests that if the court thought that a convict should escape the full weight of his conviction, but he did not have the knowledge or the presence of mind to claim clergy, they were quite comfortable nudging him in that direction. This was unusual, but, as we shall see, not unique, and it demonstrates that the courts were comfortable using clergy to moderate punishment when they saw fit to do so. Rile's ignorance may also be of a piece with Hanshawe's and Fox's choice to turn approver

29 TNA KB9/1061 m. 40 [not on AALT].
30 TNA KB27/919 rex m. 4d [image 438d].
31 TNA KB9/399 m. 18 [image 36].
32 TNA KB27/929 rex m. 11 [images 274, 275, 276, 588d].
33 TNA KB27/921 rex m. 6d [image 545d].

rather than claim clergy in the first instance and again suggests that clergy was not yet an obvious option for lay criminals in the years around 1490.

The last two escapees arrived at the Abbey via failed abjurations, demonstrating the interconnection between benefit of clergy and sanctuary, a topic we will examine in greater depth in chapter 5. We have already encountered John Boole's abjuration from Suffolk in August 1487.[34] Boole appeared in King's Bench in November 1487, having been found in the country. When asked if there was any reason why he should not immediately be executed, Boole claimed clergy. He read *ut clericus* and was delivered as a clerk attaint.[35] John Preston also failed to abjure, but in a more spectacular fashion. In March 1490 he took sanctuary in the parish church of All Saints in Bishop's Sutton, Hampshire, and confessed to the coroner that he had killed William Thomas in Yorkshire in May 1489.[36] The coroner assigned him to the port of Poole in Dorset and he left the same day. Three months later he re-appeared, however, having taken sanctuary in the parish church of St Botulph extra Aldgate on 25 June.[37] There he identified himself as John Preston of London, yeoman, alias John Westlake of London, mariner, alias John Preston of Portsmouth, mariner, and he confessed to the coroner that on 15 May 1490 he had killed an unknown man at Hythe, presumably en route to Poole, and once again asked to abjure. William Carkeke, the London coroner, seems to have been unaware of the previous abjuration and he assigned Preston to the port of Ipswich. Perhaps unsurprisingly, Preston was again found in the country early in 1491 and this time a writ issued to bring his record to King's Bench in April. The framing of the case seems to have caused some difficulty, however, and it was brought to the Exchequer Chamber for broader consultation. There, the justices were asked 'whether he should be arraigned on the first or the last abjuration'.[38] They agreed that the second abjuration was void, 'because the first was an attainder, and one cannot be twice abjured for one same cause'. It is not clear from this response if the justices were aware that the second abjuration was for a different crime, though even if they were, it is likely that they still would have considered the second abjuration invalid, since Preston had never received a pardon for either the first crime or the first abjuration. From his plea, it also appears that Preston was not fully aware of the justices' response, for when he finally appeared on 21 October he argued that he did abjure to Poole as required, and that he waited there for a ship for fourteen days, unsuccessfully.[39] He claimed that he then returned to London and there abjured again, though the record does not specify that this abjuration was for a different and later crime. Preston then asked, optimistically, to

[34] TNA KB9/375 m. 17 [image 34]. See p. 86.
[35] TNA KB27/905 rex m. 17d [images 449d, 450d].
[36] TNA KB9/388 m. 29 [image 58].
[37] TNA KB9/388 m. 27 [image 54].
[38] *Spelman's Reports* pl. 3, vol. 1, p. 44.
[39] TNA KB27/921 rex m. 2d [image 539d].

be delivered to the London constables to be allowed to continue his abjuration. Henry Harman, unsurprisingly, objected, and asked that Preston be executed on the first abjuration. The case went back to the Exchequer Chamber, and the response was that Preston should have 'stayed [at the port] until he could obtain a passage, and begged alms there for his living, and therefore his plea was not good'. Spelman notes that after this response Preston 'betook himself to his clergy', but according to the King's Bench record, once again 'the court asked the aforesaid John Preston if he was a clerk or not, and he said he was'. Again, Preston read *ut clericus* and was delivered as a clerk attaint without purgation. Preston's case is remarkable not just for the wide swathe of territory that he managed to cover, but for the ways in which he managed his punishments, and for the ways in which the court responded to him. The Exchequer Chamber case makes it clear that the courts were still working out the implications of the abjuration system and wished to clarify the relationship between the two abjurations, as well as the expectations for an abjurer. In insisting that he should have remained at the port the justices made it possible to go ahead with Preston's execution, and we might expect that a man who had confessed to two separate homicides, one of which was committed while he was abjuring for the other, was not a likely object of mercy. But once again the court offered him the option of benefit of clergy, possibly because they felt that the law around the abjuration was not clear, and possibly because in 1491 they were beginning to consciously use benefit of clergy as a form of mitigated punishment.

The experiences of the Westminster escapees allow us to see the developments in the use of benefit of clergy from a different angle than the cases against the bishops, but they also show us how the courts were using the benefit in increasingly nuanced ways. For Hanshawe and Fox in 1486 an appeal was the natural way to avoid punishment, either because they doubted their ability to read successfully or because benefit of clergy was simply not claimed often enough to seem like an obvious option. Rile had to be prompted by the court to make the claim in 1491, indicating that it was still not obvious, but also that the courts were willing to indicate its availability when they thought it merited. Rile's repeat offence suggests that the court erred in its lenience, but lenience could apparently be merited in a number of ways. The court's decision to offer benefit of clergy to Preston, a man who had both killed and failed to abjure repeatedly, because the law was unclear, suggests that it recognized the problems of adjusting to a new set of norms. At the same time, lest it seem that King's Bench was soft on crime, it's clear that the 1490 statute was immediately put into use, that the courts pursued the histories of those who appeared with the brand, and that notorious criminals were executed, though not all repeat offenders were. The experiences of the Westminster escapees demonstrate that both criminals and courts were exploring the ways in which benefit of clergy could mitigate punishment, alone and in combination with other options such as appeals and sanctuary. None of these options were new, but they were being used in the early 1490s in new ways which forced the courts to think more carefully about how they might work.

2. The Bishops and the Management of Clerks Convict

The activities in King's Bench also registered with the bishops. Across the later Middle Ages, many bishops' registers make no reference to the purgation of clerks convict, and even those that do tend to record only a fraction of the men who must have passed through their hands.[40] Fig. 4.2 reflects the unusual number of records between 1499 and 1502 and suggests that the increased attention to escapes and the formalities of purgation that we see in the King's Bench cases was noticed in episcopal chanceries and spurred an attempt to keep better records, however briefly.

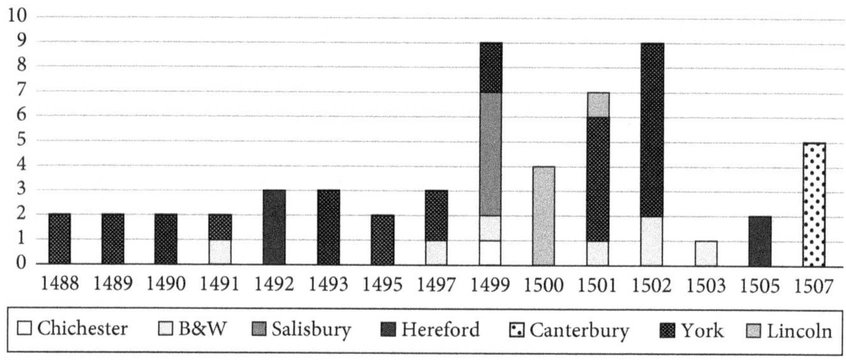

Figure 4.2 Purgations in select bishops' registers 1488–1507*

The Register of Edward Story, Bishop of Chichester, 1478–1503 ed. Janet H. Stevenson (Woodbridge, Suffolk: The Boydell Press for the Canterbury and York Society, 2016), p. 146; *Reg. Rotherham* ff. 313–317; *Reg. Savage* ff. 13v–19; *Reg. King and Castello*, pp. 10, 38, 60–61, 66–68, 82, 145, 147, 151, 154, 174; *Reg. Smith*, ff. 155–156, 165–165v; *Reg. Morton* vol. 2, pp. 14, 160–163; *Reg. Myllyng* 151–152; *Reg. Warham* vol. 2, ff. 420–420v.

Though these numbers are small, just fifty-six over almost twenty years, they give us a rare glimpse at the hidden part of the iceberg: for the most part the men in the registers were purged after a conviction at the local assizes and an uneventful period in the bishop's gaol, unlike the men whose cases ended up in King's Bench.[41] Sadly, the bishops were not bound by the statute of additions, and their records generally give us less information about the clerks convict than the common law records. The bishops also tend not to include information about their convictions,

[40] See above, chapter 3. I am including clerks who were imprisoned under Henry VII but purged early in the reign of Henry VIII in this discussion.

[41] I have been able to find only four of the fifty-six men from the registers in the records of King's Bench, and they were all escapees.

even when they give information about their crimes. Nevertheless, the purgation records give us some answers to two important questions: how long the bishops regularly kept clerks convict in their custody, and whether clerics were treated differently from clerks. They indicate that episcopal confinement was not a slap on the wrist: depending on the crime and the bishop in question, these clerks convict spent from one to ten years in custody, with clerics generally experiencing longer periods of custody than their lay peers.

We know roughly how long fifty-one of the fifty-six men spent in the bishops' custody, and we can break their confinement down by crime.[42] Of the seven who were purged for homicide, three spent nine to ten years in their bishops' custody. Two of these men were in the diocese of York, and the third was James Fulwode, the Canterbury escapee.[43] Fulwode originally came up for purgation after five years and three months, only a little longer than the other four homicides, who were in custody for five years, four years, three years and eight months, and eleven months.[44] Assuming that there were mitigating circumstances (or connections) in the last case, and aggravating circumstances in the first three, this suggests that four to five years might be a typical period of confinement for a straightforward homicide.

Twenty-eight of the purgations were for burglary. In fourteen cases there is no indication that either the perpetrator or the victim were churchmen. Of these John Frank was held the longest, at nine years and five months, but his record notes that his burglary was by night and he was held at York.[45] Three men were held for around five years, but one of those was Thomas Marten, another Canterbury escapee; two were held for three years and six months, but one of these was originally scheduled for purgation after three years; six served two to three years, and two between eleven and fifteen months. This suggests that the standard confinement for burglary by or of a layman was two to three years, though it might be extended as circumstances warranted. In nine burglaries either the perpetrator or the victim was associated with the Church: William Turwyn, whose record included the mysterious statement that he was 'a clerk or reputed as such' stayed in custody for eight years and six months.[46] His crime, breaking into a home with others and stealing money and a chalice belonging to the parishioners, does not seem particularly outrageous, though the suggestion of group activity was always alarming, and his descriptor may suggest other deceptions had contributed to his lengthy confinement.

42 In some cases we have the date of conviction and in others only the date of the crime, so these numbers should be taken as rough guides, though most crimes seem to have moved quickly through the system.

43 See p. 83 above. One was described as committing pre-meditated fratricide: *Reg. Rotherham* f. 313; *Reg. Savage* ff. 13v–14v.

44 *Reg. Rotherham* f. 315v; *Reg. Story*, p. 146; *Reg. Warham* vol. 2 ff. 420–420v; *Reg. Morton* vol. 2, pp. 162–163, no. 557.

45 *Reg. Rotherham* ff. 316v.

46 *Reg. Morton* vol. 2, pp. 161–162, no. 552.

Once again two York prisoners are near the top of the list: John Nevell alias Bery and John Trapp both served eight years for breaking into the home of Thomas Hedon, clerk, at York and stealing clothing and silver worth *c.* £20.[47] Three men were held for three to four years: one of them was a clerk and the other two broke the homes of a chaplain and a vicar. Richard Hebys, a walker from Hereford who was convicted of burgularously breaking the home of Thomas Taylor in May 1504 and stealing four silver spoons worth 10s from the goods of Severus Manus, chaplain, was purged after only one year and five months.[48] Finally, Thomas Mostrop, clerk, and Dom John Browne, also convicted of burglary, spent about sixteen months in custody.[49] Again, though there are a variety of circumstances and only a handful of examples, this suggests that burglary of a cleric or by a cleric might be more harshly punished than a secular burglary, with a confinement of around four years, though the incidental theft from a cleric while stealing from someone else doesn't seem to have had much of an impact on the time in custody.

Five men were purged for stealing from a church. Once again the bishop of York was the toughest: William Setill, a clerk, and Robert Lee both spent eight years and four months in custody for breaking into a chapel and a parish church respectively.[50] John Lamcombe, a chaplain, spent two years and five months in the custody of the bishop of Bath and Wells; William Grene, also a chaplain, almost two years in York, and Philip Owen one year.[51] This is the widest range of confinements, and there is no obvious pattern. It is possible that clerics were held for longer than secular men for similar crimes, though the opposite was true for Dom John Browne; however as a monk or canon he would be returned to the oversight of his superior, who might be expected to keep a closer eye on him in the future. William Boyden served four years and three months for the lesser crime of receiving goods stolen from a church, but like Fulwode he was an escapee: he was convicted by the justices of the peace at Taunton in January 1506 of receiving goods stolen from the church of St Mary Magdalen, escaped from the bishop's prison in August the same year, but was re-captured and then purged in March 1510.[52]

Four men, only one of whom was a clerk, were in custody for some form of robbery or assault. Again, William Markes, a clerk from York, had the longest sentence, spending six years and ten months in custody after attacking Richard Poste and William Watle in the East Riding and stealing 60s and 10s from them respectively.[53] John Saunders' highway robbery cost him one year and ten months

47 *Reg. Savage* ff. 13v–14v.

48 *Registrum Ricardi Mayew, Episcopi Herefordensis, 1504–16* ed. Arthur Thomas Bannister, Canterbury and York Society vol. 27 (London: Privately Printed, 1921), pp. 68–72.

49 *Reg. Savage* ff. 18–19; *Reg. Morton* vol. 2, p. 162, no. 556.

50 *Reg. Rotherham* f. 315v, 316.

51 *Reg. King* pp. 67–68, no. 411; *Reg. Rotherham* f. 315; *Reg. King*, p. 10.

52 *Reg. King* p. 151, no. 942: TNA KB9/442 m. 34 [image 68]. The bishop of Bath and Wells presented a pardon for the escape in February 1508, by which time Boyden was presumably safely back in custody: TNA KB27/986 rex m. 8 [images 162, 163, 142d].

53 *Reg. Rotherham* f. 317.

in Salisbury; Richard Sympson's assault and robbery of a clerk cost one year seven months at Maidstone, and Rees Kynwyn's robbery in the forest of Dean claimed nine months of his life in Hereford.[54] If these periods of custody were typical, the bishops seem to have taken the view that assault was less heinous than the violation of private property, unless the perpetrator was a clerk.[55]

Ten men were purged for theft: seven had stolen horses, cows or sheep, two had stolen silver, and one a purse. Nine of the ten were held in York, and the longest three sentences there again go to clerks: John Herrison was purged after ten years and three months, Christopher Folely after nine years and four months, and Robert Marshall after four years two months.[56] Thomas Snaydon, a clerk from Bath and Wells, served four years six months for the theft of sheep.[57] The other six men, one of whom was also a clerk, served one to three years. Finally, Richard Bower, a York spicer, was held—in York—for two years and nine months after breaking the prison at Beverley.[58]

Though this is only a small glimpse of the bishops' practices, it does suggest that they took their responsibilities as wardens seriously. The men confined in York consistently spent longer in prison than their peers elsewhere, but there were rough norms for the various crimes: four to five years for simple homicide, two to three years for burglary, one to two years for robbery and one to three years for theft. There are outliers, but some longer sentences can be explained by circumstance or behavior, and some shorter sentences were probably mitigated by similar considerations. The bishops, especially in York, were inclined to punish clerics more harshly than the general run of clerks convict, and to punish offences against the persons or the property of the Church more harshly than secular crimes. They were also more likely to note such crimes in their registers: twenty-six of the fifty-six were described as chaplains, priests or clerks, or had assaulted or stolen from clerics or churches. This is a much higher proportion of crimes committed by or against churchmen or churches than we see in the common law records and suggests that the bishops were more likely to record purgations related to crimes which touched on their primary responsibilities.[59]

The records of purgation give us one insight into periods of confinement, though they are restricted both by uncertainty about the timing of the beginning

[54] *Reg. Morton* vol. 2: pp. 161–162, no. 554; *Reg. Warham* vol. 2, f. 420–420v; *Registrum Thome Myllyng, Episcopi Herefordensis, 1474–1492* ed. Arthur Thomas Bannister, Canterbury and York Society vol. 26 (London: Privately Printed, 1920), pp. 151–152.

[55] This is reflected in the later statutes which removed benefit of clergy for thefts from houses where the owners were present: J.G. Bellamy, *The Criminal Trial in Later Medieval England* (Toronto: University of Toronto Press, 1998), pp. 83–85. See chapter 6 and 8 for a discussion of the statutory restrictions in the reign of Henry VIII.

[56] *Reg. Rotherham* ff. 315, 316v–317.

[57] *Reg. King* 147 no. 917.

[58] *Reg. Rotherham* ff. 315v.

[59] Given the somewhat erratic style of the records kept, it's possible that some of the other thirty were also connected to churches or churchmen.

Table 4.1 Periods of confinement before escape, Westminster and London*

Time in custody	Convict	Attaint	Prison
23–26 years	1	1	Westminster
9–12 years	0	3	Westminster
4–8 years	1	6	Westminster 5: London 2
2–3 years	5	1	Westminster 1: London 5
1–2 years	19	0	Westminster 0: London 19
Less than 1 year	11	1	Westminster 2: London 10

*Data collected from TNA KB27 and KB9 rolls.

of the punishment and by the probability that this is not a representative sample. The records of escapes give us another way of looking at periods of confinement. These records are also problematic, since by definition we cannot know how long the escapees should have spent in custody, but their time served can at least suggest some minimums. The escapes from the bishop of London and the abbot of Westminster in table. 4.1 demonstrate that lengthy periods of custody were not unusual. Westminster had many more clerks attaint than London, since men whose cases landed them in King's Bench were more likely to be delivered without purgation. This accounts for the longest period of custody at twenty-six years, but Thomas Thomson, a clerk convict eligible for purgation, remained at the Abbey for almost twenty-three years before he escaped in 1492.[60] These two are clearly outliers, if only because it was unusual to survive so long in prison. The next-longest period of custody is just short of twelve years, with a cluster of three in the nine to twelve year range, all of whom were clerks attaint. There were twice as many in the four to eight year range, most of whom were also clerks attaint and who also should have remained in prison for life. Clerks convict dominate the escapees who fled after fewer than three years, with thirty-one men escaping after less than two years in prison.[61] Although these records can't tell us how long these men should have stayed in prison, we can see one or two men each year being delivered as clerks attaint at Westminster and accumulating in the Abbey over time, another handful of clerks convict staying at least four to eight years in the prison, and a larger number spending one to three years before they escaped.

Even these patchy records make it clear that the total in a prison like Bishop's Stortford could easily reach twenty men, and a year such as 1502, when we know

[60] TNA KB9/395 m. 26 [image 52].

[61] TNA KB9/395 m. 26 [image 52], TNA KB9/1109 [not numbered, not on AALT], TNA KB9/431 m. 24 [images 51–52].

Table 4.2 Periods of confinement before escape, other dioceses*

Time in custody before escape	Bath & Wells	Exeter	Norwich	Salisbury	Canterbury
4-7 years	2	0	2	0	0
2-3 years	4	1	4	3	0
1-2 years	1	1	0	3	4
Less than 1 year	1	7	0	5	2

*Data collected from TNA KB27 and KB9 rolls.

at least twelve men were delivered, might push the prison beyond its capacity and increase the likelihood of an attempted escape, either because conditions became intolerable, or because gaolers were over-stretched, or both.[62] We can't know for sure if the thirteen who escaped from Westminster in 1492, the twenty who escaped from Stortford in 1493 or the sixteen who escaped from the same prison ten years later represented the total population of the prison at that time, but when put in context, it seems likely that they did not.[63] And while the escapes at first glance are demonstrations of the weaknesses in the bishop of London and the abbot of Westminster's security, they conversely demonstrate that they could hold on to substantial numbers of men for lengthy periods of time.

London and Westminster were both unusual in having catchment areas around the capital and enjoying unusually close relationships with the legal establishment. Were the patterns of confinement similar in other dioceses? The answer seems to be yes and no [table 4.2]. There are two obvious differences between Westminster and every other jurisdiction, including London. The first is the much higher number of clerks attaint at Westminster: London had one and Norwich had one, but otherwise all the escapees on record in every other diocese were clerks convict. Westminster was also unusual in the length of time the clerks convict spent there: no diocese had an escapee who had been in custody for longer than seven years. In both cases its role as the ecclesiastical prison for King's Bench and the complicated problems that ended up there probably explains Westminster's distinct profile. But, like the abbot of Westminster, the bishops could also successfully hold clerks convict for extended periods of time, and, as we saw above, some of these men were subsequently recaptured and served more time before they were purged.[64] The fact that

62 TNA KB9/431 m. 24 [images 51–52]: TNA KB27/993 rex m. 10 [images 264, 265, 244d, 245d].

63 TNA KB27/930 rex m. 7 [images 176, 177, 374d, 375d, 376d, 178, 179, 377d, 378d, 180, 181, 379d, 380d, 182].

64 See p. 83.

men who had been in custody for six or seven years were willing to try an escape also suggests that they did not expect to be released soon, or easily.

Taking the surviving records of purgations and escapes together can give us a better sense of the time a clerk convict might expect to spend in a bishop's or abbot's prison. If the registers suggest that four to five years was average for homicide, three to four years was average for burglary, one to two years was average for robbery and one to three years for theft, the evidence from the escapes suggests that those estimates are a little conservative: though the twenty-year terms in Westminster were clearly unusual (and both men had been sent there in the 1460s), up to seven years in custody was not unusual among escapees, and clerks convict who did not escape presumably remained in the prisons for as long or longer. It's possible that the bishops might have been more careful to record purgations that fell short of the norms expected for the crime committed, given the activities of King's Bench in this period, but even taking the norms from the purgations as typical, it's clear that a bishop accepting five to ten criminous clerks a year could find himself with a well-populated gaol in short order.

Perhaps for this reason, the periods of confinement seem to have become shorter over the course of the reign: eleven men of the twenty-one convicted in 1493 or earlier were purged after six to ten years, but no-one convicted after 1495 spent such a long time in prison. Seven of twenty-six convicted after 1495 were purged after four to five years, but that includes five men who all had exacerbating circumstances: one priest, one man who broke into the home of a chaplain, two escapees, and one receiver of goods stolen from a church who also escaped from the bishop's prison. Twelve served two years or less. This shift around 1495 suggests that the term a clerk convict would serve was set at the time that he was received by the bishop, though there is no evidence to indicate whether it was set by the courts or the bishop. It also suggests that something important changed around 1495. As we saw above, this is just about the time that King's Bench moved from simply fining bishops to pressuring them to manage their prisons more carefully, with the presumed intention of keeping clerks convict in custody for longer—so why did the periods of confinement fall?

The obvious answer is that Henry VII and his lawyers were sincere in their desire to improve public order and they were not inherently opposed to benefit of clergy but instead were comfortable elaborating and exploiting a common law version of the privilege for lay criminals. In this narrative, benefit of clergy starts appearing as a more feasible option in the late 1480s and early 1490s for criminals who previously might have become approvers, such as Hanshawe and Fox. By the early 1490s King's Bench even directed somewhat deserving felons who might otherwise have been executed, such as Rile, towards a claim of clergy. If similar attitudes prevailed at gaol delivery, it's likely that the number of claims of clergy grew in these years. The 1490 statute crystalized an already-existing understanding of lay benefit of clergy and provided a practical change which allowed for its more efficient administration, especially necessary if the intention was to use it more widely. At the same time, King's Bench began to fine the bishops and the abbot of Westminster more aggressively for escapes, to signal their expectation that the men being sent to those prisons would be kept securely. The next phase began around 1495, when the courts began pressuring the bishops to manage their prisons more closely at the same time that the periods of confinement set for clerks convict dropped. We have no direct evidence to explain this combination, but it is likely that a confluence of factors came into play. First, Cavill points out that the parliament of 1495 was unique: it was the only parliament of the reign in which the king neither asked for nor received a grant of taxes, but it passed a record twenty-seven statutes, most of them focused on 'corruptions in the commonwealth'.[65] Many dealt with the workings of the legal system.[66] Cavill argues that Henry VII sought to demonstrate the caliber of his government in response to Perkin Warbeck's success, and that may indeed have been the proximate cause, but the message sent and the actions taken in and after 1495 were largely consistent with the messages from the beginning of the reign. By 1495 the young man who had taken the English throne with virtually no experience of government had had ten years to learn about his kingdom, its systems of government, its people and its problems. Warbeck's campaign gave Henry the opportunity he was looking for to intensify his governance in the second half of his reign: not only did the approach to benefit of clergy shift in this year and parliament pass a slew of statutes, this was also the year in which common lawyers turned their attention to the possibilities of *Prerogativa Regis* for the expansion of royal revenue.[67] Second, John Fyneux became chief justice of King's Bench in 1495: Bacon noted that as Henry 'governed his subjects by his laws, so he governed his laws by his lawyers', and we have already seen Fyneux play an important if quiet role in the elaboration of royal oversight over episcopal prisons.[68] Finally, many of

65 P.R. Cavill, 'The Enforcement of the Penal Statutes in the 1490s: some new evidence', *Historical Research* 82 (2009), p. 484.

66 *SR*, II. pp. 569; 570; 573–575; 578; 579–580; 582; 584–585; 588–901. 1 Hen. VII cc. 2, 3, 7, 8, 9, 12, 14, 18, 21, 24, 25, 26: vagabonds and beggars; unlawful assemblies; riots; usury; including north and south Tyndale in the county of Northumberland; suing in forma pauperis; act against sheriffs and undersheriffs; officers of the central courts not to go to war; perjury; untrue verdicts, perjury in officers, returning jurors. Cavill also draws attention to a template for a general pardon associated with the same parliament, arguing that 'the general pardon of past offences ... balanced the strict enforcement of legislation in the future'. Cavill, 'Enforcement of Penal Statutes', p. 487. The pardon was unusual in setting different term limits for the pardon of felony, an innovation that was tried again briefly in the parliaments of Edward VI: Cavill, 'Enforcement of Penal Statutes', pp. 485, 491, see pp. 329–332.

67 Henry's turn to fiscal feudalism was also marked by a statute on uses in 1490 followed by an intensification in practice after 1495: the parallels with benefit of clergy are notable. See Margaret McGlynn, *The Royal Prerogative and the Learning of the Inns of Court* (Cambridge: Cambridge University Press, 2003), pp. 70–73.

68 Francis Bacon, *The History of the Reign of King Henry VII* ed. Jerry Weinberger (Cornell University Press, 1996), 133. Bacon also pointed to 1495 as an important turning point in the reign, see ibid., 131. See Robert C. Palmer, *Selling the Church: The English Parish in Law, Commerce and Religion, 1350–1550* (Chapel Hill: University of North Carolina Press, 2002), pp. 25–26 for Fyneux's role in limiting the reach of Church courts.

the bishops under pressure in the 1490s, men like Morton, Fox and King, were close associates of the king. While their personal connections provided limited protection for them in the courts, they must have been active behind the scenes in both minimizing their personal exposure and navigating the new system as it emerged. As the number of men entering the prisons was rising and the bishops were facing increasing oversight, they probably argued that the periods of confinement would have to fall, given the constraints of the existing system. In the decade that followed this shift Henry and his officials would extend their much-loathed system of bonds and recognizances across the political spectrum as part of this intensification of governance, and churchmen were not exempt. Gunn notes that between 1504 and 1508 Edmund Dudley collected more than £38,000 from English churchmen 'a little over a third of it in cash and the rest in bonds for future payment'.[69] As I have noted elsewhere, the distinction between cash and bonds is crucial: Henry was happy to gather money, but he was more interested in gathering power, and every bond was a financial sword of Damocles suspended over the head of a potential opponent. The courts' approach to the bishops in the late 1490s and early 1500s suggests that a similar approach was being manifested there, though with a slightly different threat. By regularly indicting bishops on escapes and purgations, Henry could not only ensure a more secure system of criminal confinement largely under royal oversight and paid for by the Church, but he could exert the same kind of pressure on the hierarchy that he was exerting on secular lords, thus ensuring that both were 'of one mind for the love and dread that they have of God or of the king, or of both, to execute the [laws] effectually'.

Where, how many and who?

If more felons were being sent to episcopal prisons after 1495, we would expect to see the volume of evidence relating to benefit of clergy increase: fig. 4.3 demonstrates that there is a steady rise in benefit of clergy cases in King's Bench, though as usual we can't be sure how faithful a reflection this is of the activities in the counties.

It is likely that this increase reflects an increase in activity, but it's important to remember that this evidence comes from a number of different sources, all of which are sporadic and may be influenced by specific issues: the dip in 1495-99, for example, probably represents a drop in the number of indictments for escape while the implications of the Salisbury and the Bath and Wells cases before the court in those years were worked out, rather than a real drop in deliveries. It is also important to recognize that the surviving sources are not evenly distributed: both London and Westminster are recorded as receiving clerks in most years, and thus

[69] Steven Gunn, 'Edmund Dudley and the Church', *Journal of Ecclesiastical History* 51 (2000), p. 518.

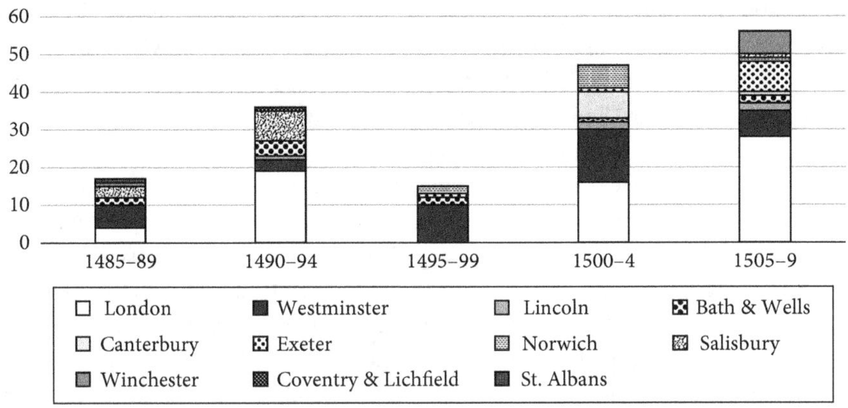

Figure 4.3 Recorded deliveries 1485–1509 by diocese in King's Bench*
*Data collected from TNA KB27 and KB9 rolls.

taking in far more clerks convict and clerks attaint than any other diocese or abbey (fig. 4.4).[70]

In the other dioceses the records of deliveries tend to be sporadic, with greater numbers towards the end of the period. The dominance of Westminster and London is not surprising, both because of the greater population of the capital,

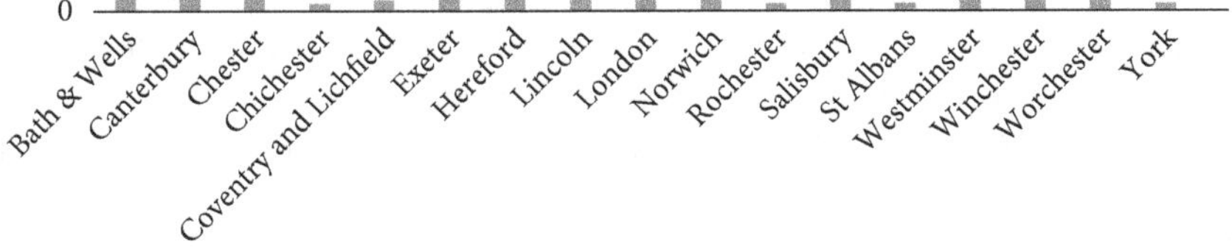

Figure 4.4 Recorded deliveries by diocese in King's Bench 1485–1509 *
*Data collected from TNA KB27 and KB9 rolls.

[70] Ely, Durham, and Carlisle are the only dioceses which do not appear in the King's Bench records for this period. Some men claimed or were alleged to have claimed clergy in more than one diocese and some claimed in one jurisdiction in the county but were subsequently delivered elsewhere, usually Westminster Abbey.

and because the bishop of London was the ordinary for Newgate and the abbot of Westminster was the ordinary for King's Bench, including the Marshalsea. Not only were Newgate and the Marshalsea delivered more regularly than other gaols across the country, but their records were more likely to survive.

With these caveats in mind, is it possible to extrapolate from the surviving records how many men were actually in the custody of the bishops and abbots at any given time? Once again, the records of escapes give us some snapshots. The indictment of the bishop of London for the escape from his prison at Bishop's Stortford in 1503 gives us the dates and places of the original convictions of the escapees: seven were convicted at Newgate on 4 and 13 February and 15 April 1502, and five were convicted at the delivery of the castle of Colchester on 11 April and 21 July 1502.[71] Thus the bishop of London received at least twelve clerks in 1502, though given that most of these deliveries were in the early part of the year, it's likely that the total for the year was higher.

A more complex snapshot of the years 1505–1509 survives in a list of twenty-six clerks convicted at Newgate.[72] Seven men were delivered to the ordinary in 1505 and 1506, two in 1507, four in 1508 and six in 1509; thus between 1505 and 1509 Newgate saw an average of five clerks delivered each year. How does this list affect our picture of the patterns of deliveries there? Between 1505 and 1509 four claims of clergy originating at Newgate were heard in King's Bench; this suggests that for every case problematic enough to go to Westminster, around 6.5 men were delivered at gaol delivery.[73] If this proportion holds reasonably constant for the reign, this would come out to about 180 deliveries of clerks convict at Newgate, or an average of about 7.5 per year, similar to the numbers from 1502, 1505, and 1506, if we assume those are complete. On the other hand, if we assume that the average of five per year for 1505–1509 is representative, this would work out to about 120 deliveries over the reign. Since it seems unlikely that any of these sources are complete, this range of 120–180 men moving into the custody of the bishop of London in these years is an absolute minimum.

Of course the bishop of London received clerks from Essex as well as Newgate, though those deliveries are less-well recorded. Leaving aside the list from 1505–1509, across the reign we have records of twice as many claims of benefit of clergy for Newgate as Essex, though the numbers and proportions vary from year to year [table 4.3].

If we accept the rough calculations for Newgate deliveries above, and if the proportions remain fairly constant between Newgate and Essex, that would suggest

[71] TNA KB9/431 m. 24 [images 51–52]: TNA KB27/993 rex m. 10 [images 264, 265, 244d, 245d]. The July delivery was held at Chelmsford.

[72] This was part of a series of lists compiled around 1518 which will be discussed in more detail in chapter 6: the Newgate return was unusual in dipping back into the later years of Henry VII's reign: TNA KB9/494 mm. 105–108 [images 225–237].

[73] These four cases do not appear on the Newgate list since they were not resolved or delivered there.

Table 4.3 Recorded deliveries to the bishop of London in King's Bench*

	Newgate	Colchester	Colchester @ Chelmsford	Rayley	Halsted	Essex total	Total
Without KB9/494	28	9	3	1	1	14	42
With KB9/494	54	9	3	1	1	14	68

*Data collected from TNA KB27 and KB9 rolls.

another sixty to ninety men moving into the bishop of London's prison from Essex over the reign, for a range of 180–270 or an average of 7.5–11 men a year going to the prison at Bishop's Stortford, at a minimum. Depending on their crimes, as we saw, those men might remain in the prison for anything from one to eight years.

We have no equivalent to the Newgate list for Westminster, which leaves us simply with the records from King's Bench. However, within KB27 there are summaries of the Marshalsea gaol delivery, which give us an idea of how frequently clergy was claimed there. The Marshalsea was usually delivered at least once a year.[74] Across fourteen sessions between 1486 and 1507, twenty-one men were delivered to Westminster Abbey from the Marshalsea, for an average of one per year. The King's Bench rolls indicate that twenty-nine men went to Westminster Abbey from King's Bench over the reign of Henry VII, for a total of fifty, or an average of about two a year. The records of purgations and escapes made it clear that men delivered to the Abbey were likely to remain in custody longer than men delivered to the bishops, so even the delivery of two a year would quickly result in a number in the double digits, as the 1492 escape of thirteen men demonstrates.

Though the overall numbers are not large, the Marshalsea deliveries also give us a rare opportunity to see the rates of conviction in this period. Two hundred and twenty-seven people were indicted across the twenty-five sessions which returned verdicts during the reign, of whom 132 were found not guilty, eight had their indictment dismissed or reduced, and eighty-six were found guilty, for a conviction rate of 38 per cent. Of the eighty-six found guilty, twenty-one claimed

[74] Blatcher argues that the Marshalsea was usually delivered every term, but the justices do not seem to have been as assiduous in the reign of Henry VII as earlier: Marjorie Blatcher, *The Court of King's Bench 1450–1550: A Study in Self-Help* (London: The Athlone Press, 1978), p. 47. In the early years of the reign it was commonly delivered multiple times a year. In the 1490s it seems to have settled into a pattern of Easter and Michelmas deliveries, dropping to just Michelmas in the late 1490s. There was no delivery recorded in 1500, 1503, 1505, 1506, or 1508. Pugh discusses the Marshalsea only as the custodial gaol for prisoners awaiting process at King's Bench, and notes that it was often used by outlaws surrendering in anticipation of pardon but does not mention any gaol deliveries there: Pugh, *Imprisonment in Medieval England*, p. 121. Only two prisoners originally delivered from the Marshalsea, both in 1486, found themselves in King's Bench, and both were part of the 1492 escape. Since the Marshalsea was delivered by the King's Bench judges, we wouldn't expect to see the same process of referral operating here as from Newgate or the county deliveries.

Table 4.4 Occupations of clerks convict*

baker	3	collier	1	groom	5	pouchmaker	1	tanner	2
barber	4	cook	1	haberdasher	2	pointer	1	vintner	1
broderer	1	dyer	3	harper	1	sherman	2	weaver	1
butcher	3	fletcher	1	hosier	1	shoemaker	1	writer	1
brewer	1	fruiterer	2	mariner	1	skinner	1	yremonger	1
capper	3	fuller	4	mason	1	smith	1		
chandler	3	glover	1	mercer	4	spurrier	1		
chapman	1	goldsmith	2	pinner	2	tailor	8		

*Data collected from TNA KB27 and KB9 rolls.

clergy.[75] Though this was not a large number in absolute terms, it meant that almost a quarter of the men who would otherwise have been executed for felony were diverted into custody.

The evidence from King's Bench also makes it clear that the vast majority of the men claiming clergy through the reign were lay. Only eighteen of the 200 claimants (9 per cent) were identified as having clerical occupations: twelve chaplains, one clerk, one monk, three pardoners, and one parish clerk. This is a much smaller percentage than among those recorded as being purged in the bishops' registers.[76] More than half, 109, were identified by status: eleven gentlemen, seventy-seven yeomen, six husbandmen, and fifteen labourers. The remaining seventy-three were a wide cross-section of English society [table 4.4].

These sources make it clear that clerks convict were, for the most part, lay men of middling status whose literacy allowed them to escape the gallows, and who, after 1495, were increasingly directed by the justices into an episcopal system which could generally hold them quite securely for one to four years, depending on their crime and their behavior, before purging them and returning them to their community. This is quite a peculiar development. It's likely that neither the bishops nor their administrators were terribly invested in either the punishment or the rehabilitation of such men, which probably explains their omission from the bishops' registers. Nevertheless, in order to maintain the system for the small number of clerical offenders who needed it, the bishops found themselves managing a substantial machinery for confining perhaps a quarter of the lay men convicted of felony in clerical prisons for lengthy periods of time and taking the blame when

[75] Only fourteen sessions of the twenty-five saw a claim of clergy: though there was a pause between 1486 and 1491, thereafter the claims were fairly steady.

[76] See p. 109 for the records of purgations in the registers.

they escaped. Without the gaol delivery records the most obvious evidence of the system is its occasional failures rather than its regular operation, adding historical insult to administrative and financial injury.

3. New Legal Complications: Bigamy, Repeat Offenders, Pardons

Not only do the recorded numbers of clergy claimants in King's Bench increase in the years after 1500, the complexity of the issues they raise also increases. Though escapes and their consequences continued to appear, King's Bench spent more time on other issues which could affect the claim to clergy, the most important of which was bigamy. As we saw in chapter 1, the exception of bigamy derived from the statute of bigamists, passed in 1276 in response to the Council of Lyons in 1274. The statute stated that the council had excluded all twice-married men from claiming benefit of clergy and provided that all such bigamists, whether their marriages had occurred before or after the council, were to be excluded from the privilege.[77] Over the course of the centuries this fairly straightforward provision had been reinterpreted to mean not only that a man who had legally re-married after the death of his wife could not claim clergy, but that a man who had married a widow as his one and only wife was also excluded, while a man who had married a second wife while his first wife was still living had legally contracted only a single marriage and thus was eligible. Bigamy was thus tricky by definition, but as with most exceptions, it could also be used strategically by both offenders and lawyers and it could be used both to reduce and to intensify punishment. Bigamy cases began to appear regularly in King's Bench after 1498, suggesting that as benefit of clergy was more widely applied to lay offenders after 1495, the courts found themselves grappling more frequently with its implications.

Fifteen of the men who claimed benefit of clergy in Henry VII's reign had bigamy alleged against them. Thomas Acras's experience was typical. He was convicted of burglary at the gaol delivery in Kent in February 1505, and after his claim of clergy it was alleged that his wife Agnes had previously been married and the place of the marriage and the name of her previous husband were provided.[78] Acras was remanded to the next gaol delivery, but his record was delivered to King's Bench in July 1508 and in October he appeared to argue that he was not a bigamist. Since bigamy was an issue for the Church courts, King's Bench sent a writ to the bishop of Lincoln, who responded the following month that Acras was not a bigamist.[79] He duly read, was branded, and was delivered to Westminster. The only point of note

[77] *SR*, i. 43. 4 Edw. I c. 5.

[78] TNA KB27/989 rex m. 21d [images 268, 269].

[79] He noted that Acras had neither married nor carnally known Agnes. This implies that a sexual relationship may have been enough to cause 'bigamy', but I have never seen it alleged in court for anything

in this perfectly ordinary case is that Acras had been in custody for three years and seven months when his case was determined at King's Bench, regardless of how long he then remained in Westminster Abbey's prison.[80]

There were a variety of ways in which a charge of bigamy could be refuted. When it was alleged against David ap Howell in 1498 that he had married a widow, ap Howell denied the marriage.[81] The court sent the matter to the bishop of Coventry and Lichfield and almost two years later, in November 1500, the bishop certified that ap Howell was not a bigamist and he was delivered to the ordinary.[82] When faced with a similar allegation in May 1498 William Rose responded he had indeed married Joan, but that at the time of the marriage she was 'simplex et perantea nemini desponsatur'.[83] Rose was remanded to gaol so that the case could be examined. He did not appear again until November 1508 when his case was brought to King's Bench and the bishop of London certified that he was indeed not a bigamist.[84] Rose then claimed benefit of clergy again and was delivered to Westminster. Since he had apparently spent over ten years in Newgate, it is probable that he went through a fairly quick purgation once he reached the abbot's jurisdiction.

Thomas Whyte has the distinction of facing the allegation of bigamy twice, and each time he defended himself with a different argument. After Whyte's conviction for stealing livestock in July 1505 it was alleged that he had married Benedicta Acton, widow, at Tewkesbury in Gloucestershire.[85] Whyte agreed that he had married Benedicta but claimed that he had previously married Joanna Warren at the parish church of Keynsham in Gloucester, and that she was still alive. A writ was sent to the bishop of Worcester and Whyte was remanded to the next gaol delivery in February 1506 at Ludlow. The bishop appeared, claimed that the time given was too short and asked for 8 March 1507. The case was brought to King's Bench in July 1507 where Whyte appeared with a pardon, two years after his original conviction.[86] On 30 September 1507, just two months later, he was indicted for stealing 1lb of saffron on 26 August and he was convicted at Newgate on 15 October.[87] Once again he claimed clergy, and once again his marriage to Benedicta was cited as an exception. The case was once again moved to King's Bench, and in May 1508

other than a marriage, and the bishops' view of bigamy was somewhat different from the common lawyers', as we will see below.

[80] He was brought to King's Bench in the custody of the marshal, so it's not clear how much of that time he spent in Kent and how much in the Marshalsea. In some cases we have only an allegation of bigamy, e.g. John Orewell, 1490 (TNA KB9/395 m. 32 [image 64]) and John Lacy, 1502 (TNA KB9/430 m. 38 [image 82]).

[81] TNA KB27/950 rex m. 2d [images 404d, 405d, 403d [sic]].

[82] A David ap Howell was pardoned on 7 August 1514, but according to the pardon he was then in the custody of the bishop of Lincoln. *LP*, vol. i, 5309.

[83] TNA KB9/415 m. 17 [image 33].

[84] TNA KB27/989 rex m. 21 [images 298, 299].

[85] TNA KB9/445 m. 14 [images 30, 31].

[86] TNA KB27/984 rex m. 16 [images 228, 229, 211d].

[87] TNA KB9/448 m. 119 [image 239].

Whyte appeared, this time claiming that he had not married Benedicta.[88] Once again a writ went out to the bishop of Worcester, who answered in Michelmas term that they had indeed married and that Whyte was a bigamist.[89]

Nicholas Dolfyn's response to the same allegation was rather unusual. Convicted of stealing cattle in Kent in November 1500, rather than denying the marriage, he claimed that before it he had been a subdeacon at Oxford in the Dominican order.[90] At this the court decided it wished to be advised, and Dolfyn was remanded to gaol. He appeared at Westminster on 27 November, just four days later, where a writ was sent to the bishop of London to enquire whether Dolfyn 'had joined with and married the same Agnes', suggesting that the court had discounted his claim that he was in orders. This case demonstrates that the system could move with speed when it wanted to, though it's not clear why this case was so urgent. Dolfyn's case is also unusual because he seems to have brought a fellow convict along in his wake. Henry Brewster was convicted and claimed clergy along with Dolfyn in Kent, though there is no other apparent connection between the two men: they had different occupations, came from different counties and committed different crimes. No opposition was raised to Brewster's claim to clergy, and when he appeared in King's Bench he read and was delivered to the Abbey: it's not clear why he was brought to Westminster with Dolfyn, since his claim to clergy could easily have been dealt with in Kent.

Simon Estgate and Thomas Bendysh, on the other hand, were joined in crime. Estgate was indicted at the gaol delivery of Bury St Edmunds in March 1501 for having been procured by one John Smalle to commit various felonies, including theft from the parish church of Rattlesden, while Bendysh was indicted as an accessory.[91] Both claimed clergy and read, but James Hobart said that Estgate had previously married Katherine Goneld, widow, while Bendysh had married Joan Balston and then after her death had married Elizabeth Sargeaunt, widow. Writs were sent to the prior of the cathedral church of Norwich *sede vacante*, and to the

[88] TNA KB27/987 rex m. 16d [images 175d, 176d].

[89] Asked if there was any reason why his sentence should not be executed, Whyte then claimed that he had taken sanctuary on 5 October 1508 in the parish church of St. James in Garlykhyne, London and had been removed. This was an unusual claim, both because on 5 October he was officially in the custody of the marshal of the Marshalsea, and because he did not claim to have been removed violently against his will (the standard language) or give the date of his removal or the names of those who did the removing. John Ernley for the king claimed that this was not sufficient in law, and it's hard to argue with that, but the justices apparently did. They convened a meeting of the serjeants and the king's attorney to discuss the case, but finally concluded that Whyte was to be hanged. The fact that Whyte had not committed any violent crime may have contributed to the justices' reluctance to hang him, but many other non-violent offenders did not receive the same consideration. In the King's Bench record from July 1507 Whyte, previously described simply as a gentleman, is identified as clerk of the customs of Bristol, nuper escheator for Shropshire: TNA KB27/984 rex m. 16 [image 211d]. This may account both for his familiarity with the various ways in which he could use the system to delay and reduce his punishment, and the justices' hesitation to execute him.

[90] TNA KB27/957 rex m. 6 [images 121, 122, 254d].

[91] TNA KB9/426 m. 71 [images 143–146].

bishop of London 'sive cuicumque alii eiusdem sedis sive episcopatus ordinario ipso episcopate sive sede de episcopo qualitercunque extunc vacante' to enquire regarding the respective marriages. The language suggests some frustration with getting answers from the ecclesiastical establishment, particularly *sede vacante*. In the meantime, Estgate and Bendysh were remanded to prison. They appeared again in September, when it was noted that neither ecclesiastical authority had responded. Hobart informed the court that the see of Norwich had recently been occupied by Richard Nykke and that, the bishop of London having recently been translated to York, the archbishop of Canterbury was the guardian of London's spiritualities *sede vacante*, and new writs were promptly dispatched to the new authorities. When the court re-convened at Henhowe in February 1502 there was still no information regarding Bendysh's marriage, but Nykke certified that eight or nine years previously Estgate had married Cecelia Baxter, who was still alive in Aylsham, Norfolk, before any pretense of marriage between him and Katherine, so that Simon 'is not in truth a bigamist nor has committed bigamy even if in respect of holy orders by a fiction or interpretation with us he would be deemed a bigamist'.[92] On this response the justices wished to be advised, and the case was called to King's Bench in June 1502, though there was apparently no further proceeding.

Most bigamy cases moved slowly. Thomas Pynchebek, a London yeoman alias stationer, was convicted at Newgate in July 1500 of attacking two men and stealing their goods the previous January.[93] Given his occupation, a plea of clergy was the obvious path, but it was alleged that he had married Alice Goldsmyth, widow, at Reading, and he was remanded to gaol. Though a writ should have issued to the bishop, there is no record of any such process, and Pynchebek next appears in King's Bench in November 1507 with a pardon, having spent almost six and a half years in custody while his marital status was unclear.[94] This could simply have been an example of bureaucratic inefficiency, but William a[tte] Wodde's case suggests that delay could be intentional. A[tte] Wodde was indicted for theft at the gaol delivery at Newgate in December 1505.[95] Both his victims had brought an appeal and the jury convicted him the same day. A[tte] Wodde promptly claimed clergy, but the crown alleged bigamy, though in this case without any details of the alleged marriage. A[tte] Wodde was remanded to Newgate, but no writ was dispatched to enquire regarding the bigamy, presumably because no bishop had been identified in the allegation. He finally appeared in Westminster in July 1509, when he presented a pardon for all crimes before 23 April 1509, one of many to take advantage

92 non est vere bigamus nec vere aliquam bigamiam incurrit licet quo ad sacram ordinum suscepcionem ficte sive interpretacione apud nos subintelligatur bigamus.

93 TNA KB9/431 m. 85 [image 175].

94 TNA KB27/985 rex m. 19 [images 264, 265, 254d]. He may also have returned to a life of crime: a Thomas Pynchebek claimed benefit of clergy at Newgate and was delivered to the bishop of London's custody in February 1509. This Thomas was described as a pardoner, so may be a different man.

95 TNA KB9/451 m. 4 [image 8–9].

of the accession of Henry VIII to clear their record.[96] In a more drawn-out version of the same process, in July 1503 Thomas Hoigge was convicted of murder at the gaol delivery of the castle of Canterbury at Maidstone.[97] Unusually, there is no record of the reading test before the allegation that he had married Elizabeth Basse, widow, at Maidstone. The justices wished to be advised, and Hoigge was remanded to prison until the next gaol delivery. He then bounced back and forth between gaol deliveries at Deptford and Maidstone, with the court continuously wishing to be advised, until February 1507. In November 1508 he finally appeared at Westminster and once again the claim of clergy and objection of bigamy was presented.[98] A writ was finally sent to the archbishop of Canterbury to enquire regarding the marriage but before it arrived Hoigge also took advantage of the general pardon at the beginning of Henry VIII's reign, appearing in November 1509 and going *sine die* six years and three months after his conviction. As with William a[tte] Wodde, Henry VII's death meant that neither the bigamy nor the benefit of clergy were ever established, but given that Pynchebek had had a similar experience, Hoigge and a Woode's experience was not unusual, though they were unusually lucky in their timing.

These cases highlight three important points. First, for a convict to be a bigamist for this purpose, he must have married with the proper ecclesiastical format—the records regularly note that the banns had been properly called three times, for example—and either he or his wife must have been previously married. If this was not a second marriage for one of the parties, he was not a bigamist for the purposes of the criminal law. Second, this was not the church's definition of bigamy for any other purpose. It was standard practice for matters relating to marriage to be referred to the bishops, and so the certification of a marriage was not unusual, but this request, at least by implication, asked the bishop to interpret this act in terms quite different from the canon law. Though there is no direct evidence about the bishops' reaction to this, it is quite common to find them responding with the blanket statement that the convict was not a bigamist, even if they had been asked a more specific question.[99] This often begs the question of whether the convict was not a bigamist in the canonical or criminal senses, and at least opens the possibility that some bishops were unwilling to allow a man to be executed for a marital situation that was perfectly legal in the Church's eyes. If the trial was happening

[96] TNA KB27/992 rex m. 14 [images 168, 169, 153d, 154d]. The pardon was proclaimed on 25 April, three days after Henry's accession, and was unusual in extending the general pardon to treasons, rebellions, murders and felonies, judgements, executions, and outlawries on them, and escapes of prisoners attaint and convict: Paul L. Hughes and James F. Larkin ed. *Tudor Royal Proclamations: The Early Tudors* (New Haven: Yale University Press, 1964), vol. 1, no. 60. See Kesselring, *Mercy and Authority*, pp. 57–60.

[97] TNA KB9/445 m. 63 [image 128].

[98] TNA KB27/989 rex m. 25 [images 306, 307].

[99] The bishops seem to have returned results of non-bigamy more often than bigamy, but one of the few examples to appear in a bishop's register is an unequivocal denial: Mayhew found that 'Meredith ap Howell, layman, is a bigamist and on account of this is stripped of all clerical privileges'. *Reg. Mayhew*, pp. 91–92.

within their jurisdiction they might find themselves with a clerk convict on their hands as a result, but that might be simply the price they paid: since many bigamy cases seem to have ended up in King's Bench, it might generally have been seen as the abbot of Westminster's problem. Finally, the process generally took some time. Estgate and Bendysh's case gives a sense of the frustration that an administration *sede vacante* might cause, but it's clear that well-established episcopal administrations could be equally slow.[100] By the time the response came back to Westminster and the clerk convict was delivered, he might have spent enough time in a county gaol or the Marshalsea that he could be purged with relative speed. On the other hand, the courts could also take their time about sending to the bishops to enquire regarding marital status. Some of these men spent several years in the custody of the secular system before the common law judges moved their cases forward. This could be seen as simple inefficiency, but there are many examples where the process was handled expeditiously. Unintended inefficiency on that scale seems unlikely; it seems rather more likely that all participants in the process saw the exception of bigamy as a strategy to manage a case: if the Crown asserted bigamy they could at worst delay the granting of benefit of clergy and at best avoid it entirely; if the convict argued that he was not a bigamist he could at best ensure his claim to clergy and at worst buy more time to try to get a pardon. If the bishop delayed a response to an enquiry re bigamy, or fudged his answer, he could buy the convict time to get a pardon or hope that the case would get moved to Westminster and out of his jurisdiction.

Repeat Offenders

The ways in which the exception of bigamy worked in practice demonstrate that both convicts and the courts could use the technical elements of the law to achieve a result other than execution or delivery, and the courts seem to have been open to the use of these methods to deliver felons to substantial periods of imprisonment. The same is true of the most obvious innovation of the period, the statute of 1490 which opened the chapter. Though the law stated that those who were simply 'lettred' should only be able to claim clergy once, implying that repeat offenders were to be executed, the courts exercised rather more discretion with the criminals who came before them. Thirteen men who were not in orders are recorded as trying to claim benefit of clergy more than once after the 1490 statute: three were hanged, five were pardoned, one went to *peine fort*, the outcome is unclear in three cases and in one the allegation was found to be untrue. Though each case was

[100] See p. 194 for an example of the delay at Lincoln in the 1520s.

complex, the justices seem to have been most influenced by the convicts' history in making a decision about their treatment.

Thomas Chalkcum, for example, was convicted of burglary in November 1498 and claimed clergy, but James Hobart argued that he had already had benefit of clergy, most likely because of a brand.[101] Hobart did not provide any details of the previous conviction, and Chalkcum was recommitted to the sheriff on pain of £200, an unusually large bond. He disappears from the record until 14 July 1508, when he appeared at King's Bench with a pardon for all felonies before 8 July 1508, having spent nine years and ten months in the custody of the sheriff of Surrey.[102] Similarly, John Donyngton was convicted of horsetheft at the gaol delivery of Newgate in April 1502.[103] Edward Cheseman claimed that he had previously claimed clergy after a conviction at Maidstone and was branded and delivered to the archbishop of Canterbury. Donyngton was remanded to gaol, but in November 1509 he appeared in King's Bench with a pardon after spending seven years and seven months in gaol.[104] Both of these men could, and indeed should, have been executed under the provisions of the statute, but in both cases the courts returned them to prison until they procured pardons.

There is some evidence that the court dealt with repeat claimants separately. John Bere escaped from the Marshalsea along with other prisoners on 14 March 1505 while he was being held on suspicion of felony. The escape was not successful, and he was indicted at Southwark on 18 March and convicted the next day. He claimed clergy, but John Skynner for the king said that he had already had benefit of clergy, though without giving any details of the date and location of his previous conviction, as was usual. The record notes that Bere did not deny his previous conviction but confessed it because it was clear from his brand, and he was remanded to gaol.[105] Bere's case is revealing, because the other escapees, all thirteen of them, were also indicted on the escape at Southwark on 18 March and tried the next day together, but apart from Bere.[106] All the details of the escape are the same, and there is no apparent reason why Bere could not have been tried with the other escapees, apart from his status as a clerk convict. The record of the case was delivered to King's Bench in May 1505, but the case was not pursued until Bere appeared on

[101] TNA KB9/437 m. 40 [image 80].

[102] TNA KB27/988 rex m. 21 [images 199, 200, 167d].

[103] TNA KB9/431 m. 86 [image 177].

[104] TNA KB27/993 rex m. 17 [images 278, 279, 259d, 260d, 280, 281, 261d, 262d, 282]. Cheseman did not give the date of the previous conviction, but he did name the justice before whom Donyngton was convicted. Seven other men were included in the pardon, see pp. 168, 171.

[105] TNA KB9/437 m. 39 [image 78].

[106] TNA KB9/447 m. 30 [images 63, 64]. Of the thirteen, eleven were found guilty, of whom five successfully claimed clergy, and two asserted that they had been violently removed from sanctuary. The clerks convict were branded and delivered, the other four were sentenced to be hanged, and the two sanctuary claimants were remanded to gaol for their claims to be investigated.

23 November 1507 with a pardon after spending two years and ten months in the Marshalsea.[107]

All three of these men were repeat offenders, though none of them seem to be violent. They had already had their first stint in a bishop's or abbot's prison, though we don't know how long they spent there or how they got out. The justices of gaol delivery could have ordered all of them to execution, but instead they returned them to the gaols, apparently indefinitely, and in Chalkcum's case with a strong incentive for the sheriff to ensure that he stayed behind bars. They all remained there for a period comparable to those before purgation until their pardons allowed them to go free. These cases make it clear that a second claim of clergy was worth making, since even if the prosecutor proved the first claim, the court might be lenient.

Though the justices might be flexible in some cases, it is also clear that they had their limits. In May of 1488 and April of 1489 Richard Richebele committed a variety of assaults and thefts, resulting in three separate indictments at an inquisition held at Croydon in June 1489. On 8 July he pleaded not guilty at Southwark and on 14 July he was found guilty by a jury at Kingston and duly delivered to Thomas Parsons, the ordinary of the bishop of Winchester.[108] We don't know how long he remained in the bishop of Winchester's prison, but on 24 October 1493, a little more than four years after his conviction, he escaped from the abbot of Westminster's prison, where he was being held on suspicion of felony. The abbot accepted responsibility for the escape and was fined 100s, making it clear that Richebele was not being held as a clerk convict.[109] Richebele's freedom did not last long: in November 1493 he was indicted on his escape and in January 1494 he appeared in King's Bench to plead not guilty. A jury convicted him on 4 February, and he claimed benefit of clergy, at which point Henry Harman appeared with the story of his previous conviction and argued that because he was a notorious thief he should be hanged.[110] Richebele was not ready to give up and argued that he, who had been convicted of the escape under the name Richard Rychevele, was not the same person. A jury on 6 February promptly returned that he was the same person and Richebele was hanged. In this case the justices decided not to return him to gaol indefinitely: unlike the other three, Richebele's previous crimes were violent, and he had a history of escaping from prison. It is also possible that the King's Bench judges were less lenient than the justices of gaol delivery, but this

[107] TNA KB27/985 rex m. 20 [images 266, 267]. Thomas Pynchebek, the bigamist, was included in the same pardon. In January 1510 one John Bere stole clothing and was convicted at the gaol delivery at East Smithfield in June 1511. The case was removed to Kings Bench and Bere was remanded to prison so the judges could be advised. It's not clear that this is the same John Bere, but if it is that might explain why the judges wanted to think about it. The other five clerks convict disappear into obscurity, but the sanctuary claimants will reappear below (p. 144).

[108] TNA KB9/1109 [not numbered, not on AALT].

[109] TNA KB27/929 rex m. 9d [image 585].

[110] TNA KB27/930 rex m. 10 [images 187, 188, 386d, 387d, 189].

seems less likely than the felon's previous history and the prosecutor's characterization of Richebele as a 'notorious thief'.

Robert Barbour alias Clerk was also executed as a repeat offender. Barbour was convicted at gaol delivery in the Marshalsea in November 1499 of attacking and killing Roland Walker and was delivered to Westminster.[111] He seems to have remained in the abbot's custody for less than a year, however, because in January 1501 he was convicted at Newgate of stealing a horse, other goods and cash from Thomas Hough on 12 November 1500.[112] Edward Cheseman pointed out that he had previously been delivered to Westminster, and Barbour was remanded to the sheriff. The case was removed to King's Bench and in October 1501 Barbour claimed clergy there. Harman pointed to the King's Bench record from two years earlier and he was ordered to be hanged. It was never stated that Barbour had escaped from Westminster, though that seems likely. Even if he had managed to get out of the prison legally, his recidivism did not make him a likely candidate for mercy.[113] Both Richebele and Barbour were violent criminals and proven or likely escapees, and thus the kind of men that the 1490 statute was most likely aimed at.

As with bigamy, however, the argument of a repeat claim could be used as a delaying tactic. William Clerk was convicted at gaol delivery in Newgate on 14 October 1508 of attacking William Bate at the parish of St Martin in the Fields so his life was despaired of and stealing 21d. Clerk read *ut clericus*, but John Mewtes for the king argued that he had previously been convicted of another felony in Michelmas term 1507, though he did not allege that he had had benefit of clergy.[114] Clerk was remanded to Newgate until the next gaol delivery, but on 27 November 1508 he appeared in King's Bench and claimed clergy again. This time the court admitted that there was no previous conviction, and he read, was branded and delivered to the Abbey.[115] It is possible that the fact that Clerk's crime was a violent one contributed to the desire to prevent him from claiming clergy.

Pardons

These repeat offenders demonstrate that one of the purposes of delay, at least from the point of view of the accused, was to create the time to get a pardon, which was, of course, the second-best outcome if an acquittal was unlikely. In this period pardons were clearly being used quite intentionally to end a period of confinement. For example, Henry West, identified as being from Northamptonshire, Warwickshire, Berkshire, and Oxfordshire, seems to have been a habitual criminal.

[111] TNA KB27/953 rex m. 13 [images 233, 234, 499d, 500d].
[112] TNA KB9/423 m. 88 [image 178].
[113] TNA KB27/961 rex m. 9 [images 260, 261].
[114] TNA KB9/960 m. 145 [image not on AALT].
[115] TNA KB27/989 rex m. 12d [images 253d, 254d].

He was indicted before the justices of the peace in April 1489 for breaking into the home of John Gyfford in Berkshire with others, beating him, and stealing household goods, two horses and 60s in cash.[116] This case did not proceed, but in February 1491 West was convicted of a different burglary and horsetheft at gaol delivery in Oxford.[117] On conviction he claimed clergy, but Reginald Pegge argued that West had previously been convicted of certain treasons at Westminster and should be denied. West was remanded to gaol while the matter was investigated, but he appeared in King's Bench in October and November 1496, not to pursue the claim of clergy, but to present pardons for the crimes for which he had been indicted in the one instance and convicted in the other.[118] Assuming he had spent the intervening period in the castle of Oxford, West had spent five years and eight months in custody. Richard Hampton, an Oxfordshire gentleman, committed only one crime, but it was a bad one. In June 1502 he attacked the house of Thomas Bokford in warlike array with about a dozen others when Thomas was in bed around 11pm, burned the door of his room with the intention of burning his house, and stole 60s and goods worth 6s 8d. When he was convicted of the crime at the gaol delivery of Aylesbury in July 1502, he claimed clergy and said that he could not respond without the ordinary.[119] The ordinary, unusually, was not present in court, so Hampton was returned to prison in the custody of the sheriff under pain of £100: this was the usual fine for the escape of a clerk convict, suggesting that the court perceived him as such, even without the test and delivery. Hampton did not pursue the claim of clergy, but in October 1506 he appeared in King's Bench, still in the custody of the sheriff of Buckinghamshire, and presented a pardon.[120] In this case he had spent four years and three months in the Aylesbury gaol: though he had not stolen goods of unusual value, the description of Hampton's warlike array, attack by night while the householder was in bed, and attempted arson likely all contributed to the sentence. In both of these cases the claim of clergy allowed the men to avoid immediate execution, and both were left cooling their heels in the county gaols for periods which were not significantly outside the ranges we have seen for purgations, suggesting that the timing of pardons, like purgations, was not entirely random.

Christopher Ryder's experience supports this and gives us a little more insight into how the machinery of pardoning actually worked for those who had successfully claimed clergy. Ryder, unusually, confessed to killing John Dutton at gaol delivery at the castle of York in March 1506. He successfully claimed benefit of clergy and was delivered. As a clerk attaint, a pardon was Ryder's only way out of

[116] TNA KB27/941 rex m. 4 [images 239, 527d].

[117] TNA KB9/404 m. 4 [image 8].

[118] TNA KB27/941 rex mm. 2, 4 [images 235, 523d, 524d, 239, 527d]. '*Certis prodicionibus*' in this context is most likely petty treason, such as coin clipping, or attacking his master.

[119] TNA KB9/442 m. 110 [images 221, 222].

[120] TNA KB27/981 rex m. 1 [images 264, 265, 244d, 245d].

prison, and on 31 May 1511 George Godman appeared at King's Bench on his behalf, with a pardon dated 20 January. He asked to have Ryder's body delivered from the archbishop's custody, and Ryder duly appeared in court on 1 July 1511, recited the pardon and went *sine die*, having spent five years and almost four months in the episcopal prison.[121] Again, as we saw from the purgations, five years was not an unusual period of confinement for homicide, and while the confession which made him a clerk attaint theoretically committed him to a life sentence, it could presumably be used to argue for remorse and rehabilitation. Ryder may have been part of a relatively new process: according to a year book case from 1505, it was the opinion of all the judges in that year that a clerk convict with a charter of pardon needed a special writ rehearsing the whole matter, and the pardon was to be directed to the ordinary, who then brought the clerk to the justices to have the pardon allowed.[122] This suggests that if the process was not entirely new, the courts were starting to use it more intentionally to release such clerks from prison: there was a new focus on the niceties of procedure and a concern that a clerk should only be pardoned after his ordinary confirmed that he had adequately served his sentence.

This greater attention to process tripped John Hudson up a few years later. Hudson confessed to assaulting a priest and stealing a gown at the gaol delivery in the liberty of St Albans in September 1502 and he was delivered to the abbey as a clerk attaint. Like Ryder, his only route out of the prison was a pardon, and John Williams appeared in King's Bench on his behalf on 8 February 1510.[123] Hudson appeared, as ordered, on 12 February, whereupon he was committed to the Marshalsea.[124] He did not reappear in King's Bench until 21 May, when the pardon was read and he asked to be discharged. The court was not happy with the format of his pardon: rather than discharging him it remanded him to 25 June, but bailed him to the bishop of Chichester and two Surrey yeomen on pain of £40. Hudson reappeared in June, but after being remanded again to November he defaulted, and his sureties were charged. Again, Hudson had served a substantial sentence—more than seven years—before he appeared with a pardon, but the court was not comfortable with letting him go free, and the decision to bail him to the bishop of Chichester as well as the Southwark yeomen suggests that his status as a clerk attaint may have been part of their concern. Hudson must have been enormously frustrated at his continued confinement after he expected to be released in

121 TNA KB27/999 rex m. 8 [images 213, 214].

122 YB Mich. 21 Hen. VII, p. 31, pl. 11. Fyneux took advantage of the discussion to note that a clerk attaint or convict was not outside the common law as an alien was, since his heir inherited his land after his death, and the king's pardon enabled him. Brooke disagreed concerning a clerk attaint, commenting that Fyneux was 'repugnant in luy mesme': *Corone*, 60. Though the year book refers to clerks convict and clerks attaint I have only seen this process being applied to clerks attaint, who had no other way out of confinement. Similar measures would be applied to clerks convict in the reign of Henry VIII, see p. 313.

123 TNA KB27/994 rex m. 17 [images 240, 241, 219d].

124 The Marshalsea often sheltered outlaws anticipating pardons, but this commitment is more unusual. See Pugh, *Imprisonment*, p. 121.

February: his appearance in June suggests a good faith attempt to see the process through, but the further delay to November seems to have been too much for him.

Richard Everard, a Colchester chaplain, also needed a pardon to extricate himself from prison after a conviction for treason. In November 1488 Everard and Robert Wyght alias Everard, a smith from Norwich, allegedly made six pieces of money called Angelettes at Aldeham in Essex. Two weeks later they attacked William Bonie and stole two caskets with £36 in cash and 50s worth of broken silver, presumably to continue their forgery. Bonie appealed them for the robbery, and they were indicted on both offences, the treason and the robbery, at the gaol delivery at Colchester in February 1489.[125] Both men claimed clergy and read but the court pointed out that they could not claim for treason and they pleaded not guilty. After the plea the court remanded them to custody. The Colchester records were sent to King's Bench, but were delivered separately, the forgery on 25 November 1489, nine months after the gaol delivery, and the appeal on 21 June 1490. Both men had been moved to the Marshalsea by June 1491, but they did not appear in King's Bench until 4 July 1494.[126] The court wished to deal with the treason before the appeal, and both men pleaded not guilty again, separately. Juries were called for Michelmas term, but the case was delayed as the juries did not appear. Finally, in January 1496 Richard Everard appeared with a pardon, but Robert Wyght disappeared from the record, most likely having died in prison.[127] By the conclusion of his case Everard had spent at least four years and seven months in the Marshalsea without a verdict, three of those before his case even appeared in King's Bench, and he had been in custody for more than two years before that, some in Colchester and some, presumably, in the Marshalsea. As with the repeat offenders, the courts chose to hold him in prison while giving him the time to find a pardon, possibly because they were reluctant to execute a priest.[128]

All of these cases demonstrate that a wide range of men could acquire pardons; that the pardons were often procured after periods of custody comparable to those served before purgation; that they could be closely scrutinized by the courts, and that they could be the final element of a long and fairly complex strategy to avoid execution. One last case demonstrates that even at the last minute, the presentation of the pardon, strategies could still shift. In January 1509 John Shirborne, a monk of Shirborne, Dorset, was convicted by a commission of stealing gold and silver rings from the abbot in December 1504 and stealing £55 in cash during the abbatial vacancy in January 1505. Two local gentlemen were accused of helping him, knowing that the money and rings were stolen, but they did not appear to stand

[125] TNA KB27/932 rex m. 8 [images 191, 192, 405d, 406d].

[126] Both appear in a list of the prisoners in the Marshalsea on 6 June 1491 preserved in TNA KB27/919 rex m. 11 [image 455d].

[127] *CPR Hen. VII* vol. 2, p. 42.

[128] Some pardons do not appear in King's Bench at all: see *CPR Hen. VII* vol. 2, pp. 42, 273, 466 for the pardon of two clerks convict from Norwich.

trial.[129] Shirborne claimed clergy and was delivered to John Gobbe, the vicar of the parish church of All Saints in Shirborne. In May 1510 John Plimpton appeared in King's Bench on Shirborne's behalf with a pardon, asking to have his body from the hard custody of the bishop, and he was given a date in June. In October, however, Shirborne appeared, still in the custody of the bishop, arguing that his conviction should be re-examined for errors; he alleged both that the commission had not specified that the commissioners had the authority to inquire regarding felonies and murders, and that he was not identified as a monk under the obedience of a named abbot or prior, as was required under the recent statute regarding mysteries.[130] Shirborne was given a day in January 1511 and in the meantime bailed to John Sylston and John Plumpton on pain of £100. Since Plumpton was one of the original accessories, this suggests either that the original theft was part of a power struggle within the monastery under the aging prior, or that the process was being manipulated by local gentlemen, or perhaps both. In any case, Shirborne remained on bail until Easter term when the court agreed that the indictment was in error and restored him to his law. In this case Shirborne had been following a fairly normal pattern of seeking out a pardon to end his period in the abbot's prison, and was quite close to completing that process, when he was presumably advised that this option would void his conviction. Though this particular situation is unusual, it serves as a reminder that for many convicts their strategies might evolve over time, and though they sometimes seem to be more a product of panic than advice, advice was clearly available for some.

4. Conclusion

Though benefit of clergy had been around for a long time before Henry VII became king, the scattered evidence suggests that during his reign it was being used more, and more inventively, than it had been for some time. From the beginning of the reign both the king and the justices committed to restoring order through the better administration of the old statutes: for the most part they stuck to that plan, and benefit of clergy became a key part of the new model they worked out to provide an appropriate and consistent punishment for felony other than execution. In the early years of the reign two key elements of the changes are visible: regular fines for escapes, to ensure that clerks convict would complete their term of confinement, and the 1490 statute, which would help identify criminous clerks if they re-offended. By 1495 the government concluded that increased royal oversight

[129] TNA KB 27/995 rex m. 20 [images 226, 227, 210d].

[130] TNA KB 27/997 rex m. 12 [images 278, 279, 259d, 260d]. There was no such statute in the first parliament of Henry VIII. The addition of 'Estate or Degree, or Mystery' as well as the 'Towns or Hamlets, or Places and Counties, of the which they were, or be, or in which they be or were conversant' to indictments was ordered by 1 Hen. V stat. 1, c. 5: *SR*, II, 171.

over episcopal prisons served its aims better than simple fines, and the ecclesiastical hierarchy accepted that oversight in return for shorter sentences for the felons inhabiting their prisons. A new equilibrium was reached, and for the most part the bishops took their responsibilities as wardens of prisons seriously, keeping a large number of lay men in hard custody for extensive periods of time.

As the reality of lay benefit of clergy was regularly manifested in the courts, both justices and felons explored the options it opened for them, working out the various ways in which the rules and norms around benefit of clergy could be manipulated to avoid, delay, and/or impose punishments other than hanging. The willingness of the courts to allow repeat offenders to claim clergy a second time, without even a hint that they were in orders, suggests that by the end of the century the 1490 statute was seen as giving the courts the option to refuse clergy a second time, but not the obligation to do so. Though any individual case can look inefficient or corrupt, when taken as a group it is apparent that most of the felons who were found guilty and delivered to the ordinary spent some considerable and consistent term in a bishop's prison before they were purged, pardoned or escaped. Most of those who were stymied in their claim, whether because of an allegation of bigamy or a previous conviction, spent a considerable period of time in the Marshalsea or a county gaol before their claim was allowed, they were pardoned, or in a handful of cases, executed. If the Marshalsea deliveries are representative, and about one quarter of those convicted of felony successfully claimed clergy, then about one quarter of those convicted of felony served a prison term, one probably set at the time of their delivery and served in a bishop's prison, but under the authority of the common law, and with the full participation of the justices. A much smaller, but not negligible, number spent extensive terms in the Marshalsea or the county gaols after having claimed clergy, ostensibly waiting for the next stage of their process, but effectively serving time until their delivery or pardon. Though the theory of the common law provided for only two results to a felony trial, execution or freedom, benefit of clergy, and the processes associated with it provided much more room for manoeuver.

5
Sanctuary in the Reign of Henry VII

Sanctuary came to political prominence much earlier and much more dramatically in Henry VII's reign than benefit of clergy did, when a number of those on the losing side took refuge in sanctuary. One, Sir Humphrey Stafford, went to Colchester immediately after the battle of Bosworth. When an act of Henry's first parliament allowed these men to go free, some remained in place, including Stafford.[1] He stayed in sanctuary until the following March, when he left in order to stir up rebellion against the king. The rebellion fizzled and Stafford sought sanctuary again, this time at Culham in Oxfordshire, a property of the abbey of Abingdon. The king was less patient this time, and Stafford was taken from Culham and brought before the justices at Worcester. *Stafford's Case* raised important political issues about the nature of royal authority in the early months of an unstable reign and deserves attention for this reason alone. It is also quite thoroughly reported, and the reports cover many of the key issues associated with sanctuary in this period, so it gives a useful overview of the state of the law at that moment. Stafford's removal from Culham has caused some historians to see the case as marking the beginning of the end of sanctuary in England, but the politics of the case have skewed our understanding of the law. We will begin this chapter with *Stafford's Case*, because we can hardly do otherwise, but having contextualized the case carefully, the rest of the chapter will argue that for less-exalted criminals and less-fraught crimes, sanctuary continued to be a vital and flexible part of the legal system through the end of the century and into the next. Not all sanctuaries were equal, and the chartered sanctuaries, unchartered religious houses, and parish churches could all attract different clienteles and play quite different roles for accused felons. Though the details are often sketchy, in many cases they gave accused felons time to find a way through the legal system which did not end in execution. Some claimants emerged from sanctuary to go through a trial, the results of which could vary widely, while some spent an extended period of time in confinement before presenting a pardon. Some abjured and probably disappeared into the countryside, an outcome that may have been seen as acceptable. Some abjured and eventually secured a pardon. Some abjured and later found themselves once again on the wrong side of the law. There were as many different outcomes to sanctuary claims as there were varieties of sanctuary-seekers, and this was a big part of its value to the system.

[1] 1 Hen. VII c. 6, *SR*, II. 504.

The King's Felons. Margaret McGlynn, Oxford University Press.
DOI: 10.1093/oso/9780192887689.003.0006

1. *Stafford's Case*

When Humphrey Stafford appeared in court in May 1486 his first priority was to prove the ability of Culham to provide sanctuary for treason. At that session the abbot of Abingdon produced a 'letter' of King Coenwulf of Mercia granting Culham to the abbot of Abingdon free of all royal tribute and episcopal authority and giving the abbot jurisdiction over all its inhabitants, and the justices remanded Stafford.[2] He was removed to the tower of London and on 15 June the case was debated in the Exchequer Chamber, although Huse CJKB was absent. Several of the justices argued that since it concerned sanctuary they should consult with the bishops, but Townshend JCP forestalled this move. He argued that the justices should discuss the matter amongst themselves first, and he distinguished between sanctuary and tuition. The latter, he argued, was a common law matter, for

> the king by his letters patent today may grant that any person who enters in such a place and remains there for treason committed against him, that none of his lieges shall take him out, and if they do, that he will be restored if he asks it. Now this proves that there is good tuition without any grant from the pope, or any bishop, and that the pope cannot do anything within this realm. For to pardon treason or to dispense with it pertains solely to the king, and always a place of tuition is a privileged place, and not a sanctuary, but when the pope sanctifies it and dedicates the said place, then it is a sanctuary, and not before, and then the pope can give a sentence of excommunication and other spiritual punishments on those who break it. But I said before that the principle of tuition begins in our law, and the cognizance belongs to us, and so we must see what our law wills in this case, and not remit it to the prelates.[3]

According to the report the other justices thought about this, as well they might. Not only were there no examples of a sanctuary created by the king and later sanctified by the pope, but the prospect of Henry VII making a new grant of sanctuary to one who had committed treason against him seems to have taken them aback. No-one seems to have been willing to directly challenge the king's ability to make such a grant, however, and Sulyard JKB recovered first, arguing that even if the king

[2] YB Trin. 1 Hen. VII, pl. 1, p. 25. The vulgate year book refers to a letter. M. Hemmant ed. *Select Cases in the Exchequer Chamber vol. II: 1461–1509*, SS. vol. 64 (London: Bernard Quaritch, 1948), p. 115 refers to a letter patent. Luckett notes that Abbot Sant of Abingdon was bound to the king in 2,000 marks conditional on the payment of £800 in two instalments on 21 May 1486, and suggests that the abbot may have been suspected of sympathy with the revolt. Dominic Luckett, 'Patronage, Violence and Revolt in the Reign of Henry VII', in *Crown, Government and People in the Fifteenth Century* edited by Rowena Archer (New York: St. Martins' Press, 1995), p. 152. Rosser notes that Sant was close friends with Abbot Estney of Westminster: Gervase Rosser, *Medieval Westminster 1200–1540* (Oxford: Clarendon Press, 1989), p. 213.

[3] YB Trin. 1 Hen. VII, pl. 1, p. 25.

did make such a grant, he could only do so for his own lifetime since his successor could not be bound by such a grant. This argument seems to have reassured the other judges, and they agreed to meet to hear the abbot the next day. This presented a procedural problem: though the case was on its way to King's Bench, it was still formally before the judges in oyer. Hody, the king's attorney, expressed the king's desire to know the justices' opinion, but they were clearly uncomfortable and Huse asked the king the next day not to press for a judicial opinion. The king assented but asked that when Stafford came before them 'the matter should not be delayed for long'.[4]

Stafford appeared in King's Bench four days later, on 20 June.[5] When he was arraigned he pleaded that he had been in sanctuary and asked to be restored. After some argument he was granted counsel and given until 26 June to make his case, apparently to the king's displeasure. When Stafford returned he made a claim based on the letter of Coenwulf, a grant of Pope Leo, a grant of King Edwin, and on continuous use.[6] The court ordered the abbot to come and support the claim, and he appeared on 29 June with his evidence. The charter of Coenwulf, as it turned out, was by an *inspeximus* of Edward III, there was no bull of Pope Leo, the charter of Edwin was signed with a cross but not sealed, and the abbot produced no proof that the privilege had ever been allowed in a court of record. The judges and serjeants debated the case after dinner the following day, and reduced the issue to three points: could the privilege be claimed by prescription, since there was no original charter of Coenwulf? Was it necessary to show allowance of the privilege in eyre? And should the justices give judgment according to the words of the charter? The answers to the first two points were fairly straightforward. The justices agreed that treason so closely touched on the prerogative that it could not be prescribed without the charter, and allowance at the eyre was necessary, though the judges recognized that was an academic point, since none was alleged in this case.[7]

Stafford's fate was effectively sealed with the responses to the first two questions, but the justices spent a good deal of time discussing the words of the charter, apparently taking the opportunity to consider what would become an important question for the future security of sanctuary. Two year book reports survive of the discussion, though they differ slightly in their presentation of the arguments. According to one report, it was agreed that the charter gave the abbot jurisdiction over the inhabitants of Culham but made no mention of fugitives there. There was rather more discussion over the nature of that jurisdiction: some argued that while

[4] la matter ne sera longement delaye: YB Trin. 1 Hen. VII, pl. 1, p. 26.

[5] The year book gives conflicting dates, with Trin. 1 Hen. VII, pl. 1, p. 26 placing his appearance on the Monday, and Pas. 1 Hen. VII, p. 23, pl. 15 putting it on the Tuesday. TNA KB27/900 rex m. 8 [image 189] gives the Tuesday.

[6] The vulgate year book consistently omits references to the pope's grant (Pas. 1 Hen. VII, pl. 15, p. 23), but it is in the exchequer chamber version (*Exchequer Chamber*, p. 118).

[7] They specified that allowance before the justices of gaol delivery was not enough.

the charter gave the abbot jurisdiction generally, it made no mention of treason and that was outside his competence, while others thought the words were broad enough to allow it. The reporter thought that the weight of opinion was in the negative; to illustrate he rehearsed the words of the Westminster charter, which expressly mentioned both fugitives and treason, and he commented that

> there are many abbeys in England which have greater words in their charters from their kings ... in some of them *omnimoda justicia*, and in others *quicquid Regales potestates conferre possint* etc., and still they do not have such franchises, nor any franchises except those which they have used, and which have been allowed in eyre.[8]

In his eyes, at least, the Culham charter did not give the abbot much ammunition.[9] The other year book report argues that the charter gave the abbot the right to do justice but not to exempt those under his jurisdiction from justice.[10]

For practical purposes the outcome of the case was clear, and Humphrey Stafford was hanged, drawn, and quartered. The politics of his situation were simple, but they have affected the ways in which the case has been interpreted from the sixteenth century on. Brooke, for example, drew the sweeping conclusion 'that the pope cannot make a sanctuary in England without the king, because the soil and the people are the king's and their pardon and punishment and suchlike offences pertain to the king, and not the pope'.[11] This, however, is Brooke reading his law backwards from the mid-sixteenth century, and in typical fashion though his comment is obviously based on Townshend's speech, it is not exactly what Townshend said.[12] Townshend's distinction between the royal privilege of tuition and the papal privilege of sanctuary was new and may have been influenced by the incipient distinction between lay and clerical versions of clergy. Though anachronistic, it tried to disentangle rights which had become thoroughly mixed over the course of the previous centuries. Townshend, however, was only referring to treason: he made no attempt to argue against sanctuary per se, and indeed accepted the pope's right to excommunicate those who broke sanctuary. His argument was problematic because in his attempt to boost the king's authority he stated that the king could grant such immunity today, a claim which goes against all the earlier assumptions that grants of sanctuary were from the devout and distant past—hence Sulyard's hasty

[8] YB Trin. 1 Hen. VII, pl. 1, p. 26.

[9] Fitzherbert, *Corone*, 49 and Brooke, *Sanctuary*, 18 abridge this version of the case.

[10] YB Pas. 1 Hen. VII, pl. 15, p. 24. This seems to be the report Brooke used in *Corone*, 128.

[11] Brooke, *Sanctuary*, 15.

[12] See Margaret McGlynn, 'From Magna Carta to the Abridgements: The Naturalization of Benefit of Clergy', in *Challenges to Authority and the Recognition of Rights: From Magna Carta to Modernity* edited by Catharine MacMillan and Charlotte Smith (Cambridge: Cambridge University Press, 2018), pp. 45, 47–48 for a consideration of the ways in which Brooke presents older cases selectively in his abridgement.

assertion that any such grant would only bind the presumably misguided king who made it.[13] Not surprisingly, Townshend's argument appears nowhere in the actual consideration of the Culham sanctuary. It served the purpose of avoiding a conference with the bishops, because it was politically unanswerable, but it was not the common law as it stood.

As a result, the legal implications of *Stafford's Case* are rather less clear than the political. Though Townshend's formulation, like Fyneux's statements on benefit of clergy in 1500, did not reflect common opinion at the time, it does indicate one direction of legal thinking in the early years of the reign, and, together with Brooke's re-interpretation in the following reign, has been influential in our understanding of the case. Elton, for example, argues that King's Bench decided 'that sanctuary was a common-law matter in which the pope could not interfere ... and that the privilege did not cover treasonable offenses', but this is clearly wrong.[14] Even Townshend did not try to remove the pope from sanctuary, and although the justices did agree that the abbot could not prescribe the privilege of protecting traitors, they never claimed that sanctuary for treason was impossible: indeed the reporter implied that Westminster retained such a privilege.[15] Kaufman, on the other hand, argues that the process in *Stafford's Case* was 'deliberate, cautious, and, one might say, conservative'. He points out that at this stage in Henry VII's reign 'fugitives were unwise or extraordinarily naïve to seek sanctuary for high treason', and while the Tudor authorities removed a number of fugitives less prominent than Stafford, Kaufman argues that in each case they were 'rather deferential'.[16] Indeed though Henry VII got personally involved in this case by pressuring the justices to pre-judge the issue, they resisted his pressure, which in any case was quite gentle under the circumstances. As we saw above, and as McSheffrey has recently argued, English kings were traditionally supportive of sanctuary rights, and though Henry was keen to remove the threat that Stafford posed, there is no evidence to suggest that he was opposed to sanctuary in principle.[17]

Rather than ending sanctuary rights, *Stafford's Case* shows the justices struggling to come up with a sustainable standard of proof for sanctuaries, one which fit with their modern requirements, but which also worked within the common law tradition. The earlier cases the lawyers referred to in their discussion turned on

[13] Cf. the Battle Abbey case of 1399 above p. 57.

[14] G.R. Elton, *England under the Tudors* (London: Methuen, 1955), p. 22. He goes on to conclude that the case 'illustrates the Tudor principle of relying on the decisions of the common-law judges, the Tudor readiness to respect the judges' independence, and the Tudor disregard for ancient franchises and immunities'.

[15] In 1493 Littleton's reading claimed that it was impossible to claim a sanctuary for debt, trespass and treason, and any grant purporting to be so wide was void. This demonstrates clearly that in 1493, seven years after *Stafford's Case*, a reader could casually assume ongoing sanctuary for treason. *Spelman's Reports* vol. 2, p. 342.

[16] Peter Iver Kaufman, 'Henry VII and Sanctuary', *Church History* 53 (1984), p. 469.

[17] See pp. 55, 60, and Shannon McSheffrey, *Seeking Sanctuary: Crime, Mercy and Politics in English Courts, 1400–1550* (Oxford: Oxford University Press, 2017), pp. 14–15.

whether sanctuary could be claimed through prescription, and the answer seems to have been no.[18] In two of these cases the weakness was in the documentation, not the principle, and much the same could be said of *Stafford's Case*. It is striking that one reporter contrasts the Culham charter with the Westminster one, and intriguing to wonder what might have happened if Stafford had taken sanctuary in Westminster. It is hard to imagine that Henry VII would have allowed Stafford to go free a second time, but that doesn't mean that he would have dragged him from the best-documented sanctuary in the country. Indeed, the justices may have spent some time thinking about the Westminster charter before their discussion of the Culham one: in a year book report from Hilary 1486 the abbot of Westminster appeared in court to show his privileges, and was advised by the lords spiritual and the justices that it would not be wise to argue his franchises and liberties, but to see that they were well and truly guarded.[19] The overall message is reminiscent of the justices' discussion of law enforcement at Blackfriars in the previous term, but Brooke's version of the case has Townshend declare that franchise or sanctuary can only be granted by the king, without the pope or bishop, and argue that 'only the king can punish treason or pardon it, and not the pope, and it is a privileged place only by the king's grant, and by the spiritual ceremony this is a sanctuary, and they shall be excommunicated who break it'.[20] Brooke seems, again in typical fashion, to have conflated the abbot of Westminster's appearance with *Stafford's Case*, and it is entirely possible that the examination of the abbot's privileges was indeed connected to a discussion of the extent of the sanctuaries' privileges, given the appearance of Westminster material in the reports of *Stafford's Case*.

The evidence presented for Culham's and Westminster's rights in *Stafford's Case* highlights the variations in the rights that individual sanctuaries had and the difficulty of proving those rights, issues that the courts continued to consider carefully. For example, in February 1494 William Toft claimed sanctuary at a possession of St John of Jerusalem at Winkburn, Nottinghamshire, after having killed Humphrey Rollesley. Brought before King's Bench in June 1496, he argued that he had been taken from sanctuary against his will in March 1494 and prayed to be restored, arguing the right of sanctuary by prescription.[21] The case is reported by both John Port and John Caryll, though their versions differ somewhat: Port's discussion

[18] They referred to William Waw, the Westminster case of 2 Edw. IV, and a sanctuary case of St John of Jerusalem temp. Edw IV. For Waw and the Westminster case see p. 57. I have been unable to identify the case of temp. Edw. IV.

[19] YB Hil. 1 Hen VII, pl. 11, p. 10. In the year book the concern was with those who went into sanctuary to defraud their creditors and the abbot was warned that feoffments of goods and lands to their use would not be safe. This problem was remedied by statute shortly after: *SR*, II. 513. 3 Hen. VII c. 4. See also *Rot Parl* VI, 402. A number of such statutes had passed since the *articuli cleri*.

[20] YB Mich. 1 Hen. VII, p. 3, pl. 3. See p. 95. Brooke, *Sanctuary*, 18.

[21] The widow of Humphrey Rollesley, the victim, argued that Toft was not within sanctuary because he was taken from a field called Southgrippe which was not part of the house or its ambit: *Port's Notebook*, p. 35.

picks up on the relative roles of prescription and royal authority in the establishment of a sanctuary from *Stafford's Case*, but goes on to talk more generally about the role of sanctuary in the legal system. According to Port, Huse opened the discussion by pointing out that a claim by prescription would have to be justified by the lord of St. John's, i.e. the prior of the Hospitaller order in England, but that in this case prescription was unnecessary, since 'this privilege has continued for such a long time that it is a common law for this privilege to be allowed. It is likewise concerning the sanctuary of Westminster: it is a common law, by continuance [of time], for that privilege to be allowed'.[22] Having established that Westminster and St John of Jerusalem had their rights under the common law, he went on to argue that sanctuary cannot lie in prescription, for in a sanctuary the party cannot have his remedy, and the king cannot take away the party's protection by his grant, though Huse did concede that 'the king may delay the party for a while, as by a writ of protection'.[23] Huse's conclusion is that 'a sanctuary cannot begin without an act of parliament', which Port queries.[24] Huse seems to be taking his statement that the king cannot take away the party's appeal to its logical conclusion: the only body with the authority to do so is parliament, and so it too must be the only body which can grant sanctuary. Though Port was apparently surprised by the comment, a reader discussing Magna Carta c. 9 in the same period argued that 'I may have a sanctuary by grant of parliament and grant of the pope, but not by prescription nor even by the king's grant'.[25] Rather than returning to the earlier premise that the abbeys could have rights by prescription that kings could no longer grant, Huse and the Magna Carta reader argued that neither would stand. They were either being startlingly anachronistic, since such a level of proof would immediately invalidate all sanctuaries, or obliquely arguing against Townshend's extension of the king's powers in *Stafford's Case*. That the latter is more likely is supported both by the fact that Huse clearly accepted the rights of both Westminster and St John of Jerusalem, and that later readers could argue that a custom is 'something which cannot begin by grant, such as the sanctuary of Westminster'.[26]

Caryll does not include this part of the discussion, possibly because he shared Port's reservations, but both men report Kebell's defence of the king's obligation

[22] *Port's Notebook*, 31. Kebell argued against the procedural point, arguing that claiming prescription where it was not necessary did not invalidate the claim, but Huse shot him down quickly.

[23] *Port's Notebook*, 31.

[24] *Port's Notebook*, 31. Huse argues that the same is true of counties palatine and of grants of the chattels of felons and fugitives. Sulyard had made a similar point in his response to Townshend in *Stafford's Case*, but there it seems to have been prompted by the exigencies of the situation: YB Trin. 1 Hen. VII, pl. 1, p. 25.

[25] J.H. Baker, ed. *John Spelman's Reading on Quo Warranto*, SS vol. 113 (London: Selden Society, 1997), p. 4. Baker dates the anonymous reading to the late fifteenth century. Huse may also have been picking up on the argument made by Chaunterell that London's rights had been confirmed by parliament: YB Mich. 8 Hen. VI, pl. 9, p. 4; Mich. 2 Edw. IV, pl. 21, p. 23. See p. 58.

[26] Baker ed. *Spelman on Quo Warranto*, p. 12.

'to do mercy as well as justice'.[27] Huse argued that the king was bound to do justice, and since sanctuary allowed a felon to escape execution, the only set punishment for his crime, sanctuary was a denial of justice. In response Kebell stated firmly that the king may grant a sanctuary, since in doing so he is not taking away the party's remedy but delaying or moving it.[28] In Port's version Kebell notes that process still lies against a sanctuary man, for 'he shall be outlawed and forfeit his lands and goods: and so the party is not remediless'.[29] Caryll's version is even stronger, for his Kebell adds 'thus nothing [is restrained] of the full punishment except the saving of his life, and his death is no compensation to the party but only a form of revenge'.[30]

Port wraps up his report with Huse's summary of earlier cases: Waw, Huse said, did not get his sanctuary because Beaulieu was founded in the time of King John and yet he prescribed, while Stafford's problem was the language in the charter that gave jurisdiction only over 'all residents'. Huse also noted that when four men were taken from St. Martin le Grand and accused of treason for supporting Perkin Warbeck, three of them did not claim sanctuary, while 'one did pray it and had it'.[31] So much for *Stafford's Case* marking the end of the common law right of sanctuary, or even of sanctuary for treason. From a legal perspective its importance lies in the attention it brought to the standards of proof necessary for a successful claim of sanctuary, and in the exploration of royal authority it engendered. Townshend's version of royal authority was about forty years ahead of its time and alarmed his colleagues enough that it prompted an oblique assertion of the roles of parliament, common law, and custom in containing that authority. But these discussions were happening in the mid-1490s, around the same time that benefit of clergy was also attracting greater attention and as the escapes from bishops' prisons were working their way through the courts. They demonstrate the assertion of royal authority in pursuit of order in a number of contexts, though since it was pursued through the administration of justice rather than through legislative change, it is not terribly apparent. And they make it apparent that while the common lawyers were comfortable with the extension of royal authority over clerical rights through the common law, they were less comfortable with the extension of direct royal authority.

27 *Caryll's Reports*, vol. 1, p. 285. Kebell traces this obligation back to the foundation of Rome: he argues that Romulus set up such a place in the age of justice, therefore the modern prince is even more bound to pity in 'the age of mercy'.

28 *Port's Notebook*, p. 32; *Caryll's Reports*, vol. 1, p. 286.

29 *Port's Notebook*, p. 32.

30 *Caryll's Reports*, vol. 1, p. 286. This also agrees with the canonical notion that sanctuary should protect the fugitive's life, but not exempt him from other punishment for his crime.

31 *Port's Notebook*, p. 32.

2. Religious Houses, Chartered and Unchartered

If Humphrey Stafford's execution tells us very little about the role of sanctuary in the administration of the criminal law in the late fifteenth century, where can we turn for a better picture? There were, in essence, three kinds of sanctuaries in England: chartered sanctuaries in religious houses, non-chartered sanctuaries in religious houses, and parish sanctuaries.[32] Chartered sanctuaries like Westminster and St Martin le Grand have attracted the most scholarly attention, both because they attracted the most political attention at the time and because they were more likely to have a concentrated body of sanctuary men to deal with. The records that survive for them, however, are more likely to be of a-typical cases, such as accounts of controversies with the city of London or of prominent sanctuary-seekers. Though these moments are important and the relative detail they provide is intriguing, they don't help us understand how sanctuaries usually worked within the broader legal system, or how they worked for less-exalted men and women. Registers of sanctuary men survive for Beverley and Durham, the two main chartered sanctuaries in the north: these gives us a much better picture of both the numbers and the crimes they dealt with, but they only provide a snapshot of the men at the moment of entry. The regular sanctuaries, mostly parish churches, but also some religious houses, have far fewer high-profile moments, but they dominate the common law records. Sanctuary-seekers in these churches were expected to abjure the realm, and the processes of claiming and abjuring provided many opportunities for conflict, which can in turn allow us to see how they were supposed to work. As we will see, there are real differences between the ways in which the different kinds of sanctuaries worked, but one key similarity: a claim of sanctuary was rarely an end in itself. Instead, a claim of sanctuary was a strategy to buy time, before, during, or, at worst, after the accused was indicted for felony.

Chartered Sanctuaries: Westminster Abbey and St Martin le Grand

Though Westminster Abbey was certainly the most prominent, well-documented, and powerful sanctuary in the country, and later records indicate that it was large and active, we have common law records for only fifteen men claiming sanctuary there in the reign of Henry VII.[33] Thirteen of the fifteen were alleged homicides who are recorded in the inquisition on the view of a body as having fled to the

[32] Given the complexities of practice, some sanctuaries fell between or across these boundaries, but they are useful basic categories of analysis.
[33] See chapter 8 p. [26] for the traffic through the Westminster sanctuary in the 1530s.

Abbey.[34] Four of the homicides took place within the jurisdiction of the coroner of the liberty of Westminster, John Elryngton.[35] Three more were within the jurisdiction of the London coroner, and in these cases the writs from King's Bench for the inquisitions also survive.[36] There are no further proceedings on any of these cases. The London writs were all issued some time after the crime was committed, suggesting that the court anticipated moving against the alleged felon at some point in the near future, but in the absence of any further detail we can't know if he was in custody at the time the writ was issued or whether the writ was issued in the expectation of his arrest and thus whether the process was frustrated by his escape, death, or continuation in sanctuary.

Without further records of process the inquisition records can be misleading. For example, an inquisition at Barking in Essex in February 1489 found that William and Stephen Burre attacked John Curson on the highway with premeditated malice on 10 February; that Curson died from his wounds, and that the Burres immediately fled from Barking to the sanctuary of St Peter at Westminster.[37] In May 1490 a writ went out from King's Bench to the coroner for the inquisition and on the following day another writ went to the justices of oyer and terminer for the records of any deliveries of the Burres before them.[38] The justices returned a record from the session of the peace at Brentwood in Essex in October 1489 at which the Burres were found not guilty by the jury.[39] It's not clear why this case appeared in King's Bench: perhaps an aggrieved relative wanted to challenge the verdict or perhaps the Burres ended up in London and were arrested on the murder despite having been found not guilty and needed the record to clear themselves. It's also not clear what role sanctuary played in this case. The inquisition implies that the Burres fled intentionally to Westminster, a distance of about 11 miles from Barking, suggesting that they wanted the safest refuge they could find, rather than the nearest. The delay of eight months between the inquisition and the trial suggests that they were indeed out of reach for some period of time, and the implication was that they remained in Westminster until they had some assurance that the trial was likely to go in their favour, at which point they emerged to allow the law to take its course.

Like the Westminster sanctuary men, the majority of those from St Martin le Grand, thirteen of fifteen, were also accused of homicide.[40] Once again they were

[34] Thomas Pytfyn, the least heinous of the Westminster sanctuary-seekers, escaped from the custody of his gaoler in the town of Westminster, presumably en route to King's Bench, suggesting a seizing of the moment. There is no further process on his case: TNA KB9/383 m. 88 [image 179].

[35] TNA KB9/1060 m. 91 [image not on AALT]; TNA KB9/415 m. 79 [image 162]; TNA KB9/424 m. 24 [image 48]; TNA KB9/431 m. 110 [image 226].

[36] TNA KB9/383 mm. 21–22 [images 41–43]; TNA KB9/402 mm. 14–15 [images 27–29]; TNA KB9/1062 mm. 9–10 [image not on AALT].

[37] TNA KB9/382 m. 52 [image 97].

[38] TNA KB9/382 m. 51 [image 95]; KB9/385 m. 20 [image 40]. The writ on 9 May states that John Burre and William Hampton were also indicted on the murder, but they do not appear anywhere else in the records.

[39] TNA KB9/385 m. 21 [image 42].

[40] The other two were Thomas Bovy and Robert Cruse, discussed below, pp. 142, 144.

mostly local: eight inquisitions originated with the London authorities and four were conducted by John Elryngton in Westminster. Only one case proceeded to trial, so, as with Westminster, in most cases we have only the inquisition on the view of the body, with the occasional writ for delivery of the inquisition to King's Bench. The one case which went to trial, however, gives an unusually rich insight into the role sanctuary might play in a homicide. An inquisition on the body of Richard Bery found that his wife, Agnes, traitorously killed him with arsenic in his goblet in March 1503. Thomas Bovy was named as her accessory.[41] This was a particularly heinous crime, not just because the murder of a husband was petty treason, but because poisoning evoked particular horror in this period.[42] But this case also developed in an unusual way. Though the crime was committed on 17 March, the inquisition on the body was not held until 8 July. Inquisitions were usually delayed when the victim took some time to die, but that is unlikely to have been the case here. It seems more likely that Bery and Bovy disposed of the body and bought themselves the time to get to safety. Although the crime was committed in Sevenoaks in Kent, they both took refuge in St Martins, about 24 miles away, but one of the few sanctuaries that could give sanctuary for petty treason. Bovy appeared in King's Bench in January 1504, where he argued that he could not be tried until the case was determined against Bery.[43] The court bailed him to two Sevenoaks yeomen until the following June. Bery did not appear until November 1506, two years later, when she pleaded not guilty and was bailed to Richard Chalkhill of Maidstone and Philip Yoyse of Brasted to appear the following February.[44] A Richard Chalkhill was keeper of the archbishop's prison at Maidstone at this date, so it is possible that she was placed in his custody rather than being set at large.[45] Bery duly appeared in King's Bench in February and argued that the indictment against her was insufficient because it didn't include where and in which county she was when the indictment was taken. The indictment was dismissed, and she went *sine die*, presumably to the relief of Bovy. As in many of these cases, there is no mention of any claim of sanctuary in the indictments and no suggestion by either Bovy or Bery that they had been taken out of sanctuary against their will. Though Bovy apparently gave himself up to the authorities about six months after the inquisition, Bery did not appear for almost three more years, during which time she presumably remained in sanctuary. Again, this suggests that she emerged once she had been assured that the procedure in the courts would end in her favour. This interpretation is supported by the fact that both Bovy and Bery were bailed, which was unusual in cases of petty treason, and both were bailed back to Kent. Bery may have been handed

41 TNA KB9/431 m. 28 [image 28].

42 K.J. Kesselring, 'A draft of the 1531 "Acte for poisoning"', *English Historical Review* 116 (2001), pp. 894–899.

43 TNA KB27/970 rex m. 5 [image 194].

44 TNA KB27/981 rex m. 9d [image 260d].

45 TNA KB27/974 rex m. 6 [image 199].

over to a keeper of the archbishop's gaol, perhaps a compromise between keeping her in the Marshalsea and allowing her the usual freedom of a bailee. And when she appeared in February 1507 her case was dismissed on a technicality that could have been raised and accepted the previous November, or any time since 1503. In the end, Bery seems to have spent about three and a half years in sanctuary and possibly three months in or around the archbishop's gaol before going free on the charge of murdering her husband.[46] Though any individual element of the case could be explained differently, when taken together this suggests a wife driven to poison her husband by some form of abuse, and a community that expected to see her punished for the crime, but not executed.

Agnes Bery's case suggests that while sanctuary could provide an accused felon time to manage their engagement with the common law, the time spent there could also be seen as a form of penal confinement. The very odd resolution to the stories of Thomas Fysher, John Byrde, and Robert Cruse further supports this idea. Fysher was being held in the Marshalsea on suspicion of treason on 14 March 1505 when he abetted a prison break by twelve of his fellow prisoners. The justices of the peace in Southwark found all the gaol-breakers guilty on 18 March 1505 except for John Byrde, who claimed that he had taken sanctuary in the parish church of Lambeth on 15 March.[47] Fysher came before the justices separately, and he too claimed that he had taken sanctuary on the day after the escape, in his case at Westminster. Both men asked to be restored to their respective sanctuaries and were remanded. A writ from King's Bench on 4 February 1508, three years later, ordered the justices of the peace of Surrey to return their records for Fysher and Byrde, and they appeared in King's Bench the following day.[48] Byrde presented a pardon and went *sine die*, while Fysher rehearsed his claim to sanctuary once again. John Ernley, the attorney-general, appeared with a warrant signed by the king which accepted the plea and ordered that 'where as we be moved with mercy and pety in consideracion of the long imprisonment of Robert Crewse and Thomas Fysher, prisoners in our benche for diverse felonies by them committed wherof they be indited and … have pleted that they were taken oute of seyntwarry' the court was to accept the men's pleas and return them to their respective sanctuaries. So who is Robert Crewse? Cruse (as his name appears in his own indictment) was indicted before the justices of the peace for burglary and horsetheft in St Albans. The indictment stated that he had taken sanctuary at St Martin le Grand in July 1502, more than a month after his crime and over 20 miles away. Cruse appeared in King's Bench in October 1507; he claimed that he had remained at St Martins until June 1507 when he was removed from sanctuary against his will and he asked to be restored.[49] Ernley had appeared

46 We saw in chapter 4 p. [30] that four to five years was a fairly typical period of confinement after a claim of benefit of clergy for a homicide.

47 TNA KB9/447 m.30 [image 63]. Five of the eleven successfully claimed benefit of clergy.

48 TNA KB9/447 m. 29 [image 61]; KB27/986 m. 15 [images 159d, 160d].

49 TNA KB27/985 m. 3 [image 227].

then with the very same warrant that later returned Fysher to sanctuary. The obvious question is why, if Ernley had a warrant dated 15 October 1507 ordering the return of Cruse and Fysher to sanctuary, did Fysher remain in custody for a further four months? And why were these three men associated in court? Both Byrde and Fysher had spent just about three years in the Marshalsea waiting for their sanctuary pleas to be adjudicated, but Cruse had been there only four months, so the argument that the king was moved by mercy for their 'long imprisonment' doesn't seem to hold water. Byrde's and Fysher's confinement may nevertheless have had an effect on the king's decision, and the fact that Fysher was being held on suspicion of treason in the first place, rather than felony, may have accounted for his return to sanctuary when Byrde was allowed to go free and for the fact that he was held in the Marshalsea for another four months after Cruse's release. Cruse had not spent nearly as long as the other two men in prison, but according to his own account he had been in sanctuary for almost five years when he was seized and this may have figured as part of the 'long imprisonment'. It is suggestive that though there is no link between Fysher and Cruse in terms of their crimes, their place of origin, their sanctuary, the time they came into custody or the time they appeared in King's Bench, the fact that they were sanctuary men in the Marshalsea was enough to join them in the warrant that returned them to those sanctuaries.

Though this is a relatively small number of cases—and we cannot know what proportion of those who sought sanctuary in Westminster or St Martins they represent—there are clear similarities between the sanctuary-seekers in the two London chartered sanctuaries. The majority in both sanctuaries were accused of homicide. The majority in both sanctuaries committed their crimes in either London or Westminster and of the six who did not, two had committed highway robbery and assault and two were involved in poisoning. This suggests, not surprisingly, that for the worst crimes the strongest sanctuary was preferred, even when it was some distance away. The majority did not come to trial, and where we have nothing beyond the inquisition on the body we have no way of knowing why the case went no further—was the inquisition mistaken in the first place? Did the alleged felon never make it to sanctuary, escape, or remain there indefinitely? Among those who did go to trial, sanctuary was generally not mentioned in the indictment or the King's Bench record, and they were either found not guilty, dismissed on a technicality, or pardoned, though they generally spent some time in confinement before they achieved that result, suggesting that sanctuary could serve as punishment as well as protection. There are only three instances of sanctuary men being taken from the chartered sanctuaries against their will for trial in King's Bench, of whom one was finally pardoned and two were returned to their sanctuaries.

Westminster and St Martins were the most prominent sanctuaries in England, but the very flexibility that made them so appealing, the fact that sanctuary men could remain as long as they wished, and without confession to the coroner, reduces our ability to know what happened in the days and weeks after felons fled to the precincts. They certainly served as places of refuge while misunderstandings were resolved or consequences avoided, often in cases involving heinous crimes. Chaotic as these cases seem, they make it clear that they also served both as a base from which felons could organize a legal defense and as a place of confinement which could be represented as a form of imprisonment and accepted as such by the legal establishment.

Chartered Sanctuaries: Durham and Beverley

Their surviving registers mean we know more about Durham and Beverley than we do about Westminster or St Martins, despite the much higher profile of the London sites. A total of 136 men are recorded in Durham's register and 88 in Beverley's in the course of Henry VII's reign, though as the graph demonstrates, the numbers were by no means even, with Durham's spiking more irregularly than Beverley's (fig. 5.1). We don't know if this reflects changing claims, or if the register was simply not kept regularly, and a single brawl which sent four or five men to sanctuary (as happened in Durham in 1496 and 1505) could shift the numbers markedly.

As we might expect, both sanctuaries were fairly local in their clientele: Durham drew heavily from Durham, Yorkshire, and Northumberland, and Thomas Coke of Bridgewater, Somerset, is the only southerner who seems to have braved the northern sanctuary.[50] Beverley drew most heavily from

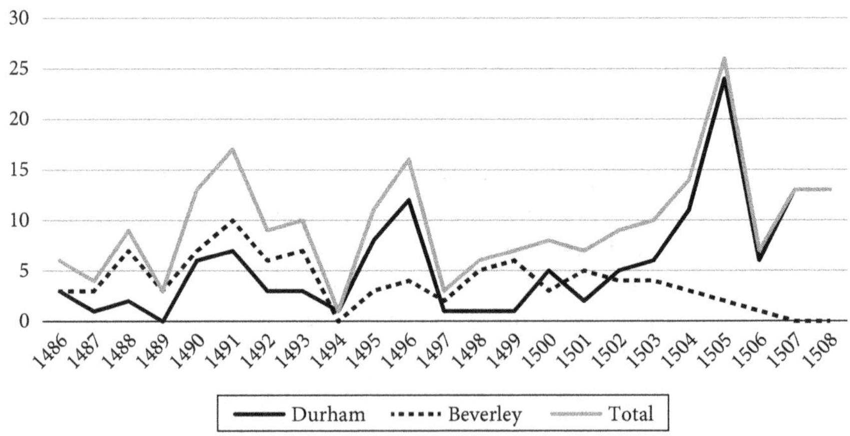

Figure 5.1 Sanctuary claims at Durham and Beverley, 1486–1508*

*Data collected from *Sanctuarium Dunelmense*.

[50] *Sanctuarium Dunelmense*, p. 27.

Yorkshire and Lincolnshire, but its claimants trailed as far south as Leicestershire, Northamptonshire, Cambridgeshire, Essex, London, Surrey, and Devon. It is unlikely that these men had specifically come north to take sanctuary. Tudor criminals were fairly mobile, and it is more likely that southerners who committed crimes in the area would seek the best sanctuary available locally, though this suggests that few southerners made it as far north as Durham, whether for commercial or criminal reasons. In both places the vast majority of the men claiming sanctuary did so for reasons relating to homicide: 122 of 136 at Durham (90 per cent) and 75 of 88 at Beverley (85 per cent).[51] The Durham register gives slightly more information on its claimants than Beverley, and in some cases clarifies that the sanctuary-seekers had killed in self-defense, were present when the mortal blow was struck but did not deliver it, or were afraid of being indicted for a homicide. The fear of indictment appears for the first time in 1496 and appears fairly regularly thereafter, suggesting that the increased attention being paid to law and order had penetrated as far as Durham.[52] But all of these details also suggest that a substantial proportion of sanctuary-seekers at Durham used the cathedral as a place of respite until their role in the homicide could be clarified. Though the registers don't record when the men left sanctuary, we can assume, as with Westminster and St Martin's, that only a small proportion of those seeking shelter either expected to stay for life or actually did so, but we have no way of knowing how long they were likely to remain. None of the men in the Beverley or Durham registers subsequently appear in King's Bench, so if they did leave the sanctuary to reckon with the common law, their cases must have been resolved at the local level.

The evidence, thin as it is, thus suggests that the most prominent chartered sanctuaries in the north and south of the country operated similarly. All seem to have dealt primarily with homicide, or at least were more careful to record the homicides that came their way. In at least some instances their sanctuary men seem to have used them as a haven from which they could negotiate the appropriate punishment for their crimes. But the nature of that negotiation, the relationship between the sanctuary and the common law process, and the outcomes for the sanctuary men who did not emerge to leave a trace in the common law records remain obscure.

[51] At Durham most of the remaining men admitted to felonies, usually theft or burglary, though one was an escapee who had previously abjured and one confessed to rape. At Beverley two men did not specify their crime, three confessed to offences related to coinage and eight to various felonies. One reading on Magna Carta says that Beverley can give sanctuary for homicide but no other felony: *Rights and Liberties*, p. 76.

[52] *Sanctuarium Dunelmense*, pp. 27–28.

Unchartered Religious Houses

Thirty-five men are recorded as claiming sanctuary in religious houses other than Westminster, St Martin le Grand, Durham or Beverley in the reign of Henry VII. In some cases the houses were connected with great monasteries: for example, Culham, the site of Stafford's claim, was a dependency of Abingdon.[53] There is no sense in the records that the connection to the greater house had much, if any, impact on the sanctuary that the dependency could offer, and each seems to have been treated independently for this purpose. Sanctuary-seekers don't seem to have had a preference for any particular order, and we see claims being made at Augustinian, Cistercian, Dominican and Franciscan houses as well as those of St. John of Jerusalem.[54] Unchartered religious houses shared some of the characteristics of the chartered sanctuaries, and though in some ways they functioned in much the same way as parish churches, there were some significant issues which differentiated them from both their more powerful brethren and their secular counterparts.

The most obvious similarity between the unchartered religious houses and the chartered sanctuaries is the high incidence of homicide among those who claimed sanctuary. Of the thirty-five sanctuary seekers recorded at a religious house, twenty-four (69 per cent) were accused of homicide. Though this is substantially lower than the proportion of homicides among the chartered sanctuaries, it is substantially higher than in the parish churches, as we will see below. One, Stafford, was accused of treason, and the absence of any other treason claim among this group reinforces how unusual his claim was, and how unlikely it was to succeed. The rest were accused of various kinds of felony, mostly robbery, burglary, and horsetheft.

If the common lawyers focused on the founding authority of chartered sanctuaries and the range of crimes for which they could give refuge, with religious houses they were generally more interested in the physical limits of the sanctuary. In 1494 Huse and all the justices agreed that a fugitive could not claim sanctuary in the fields around the Clerkenwell house of St. John of Jerusalem, but only in the house itself, or in the 'circuit of the house'.[55] Given the size of many religious

[53] Culham was only a mile south of Abingdon on the other side of the Thames but this put it in Oxfordshire rather than Berkshire.

[54] For examples of Augustinians see: TNA KB9/431 m. 42 [image 89]; TNA KB9/439 m. 16 [image 32]. Cistercians see: TNA KB9/416 m. 59 [image 117]: Dominicans see: TNA KB9/480 m. 31 [image 61]; TNA KB27/976 rex m. 7 [image 240]; TNA KB27/979 rex m. 1d [image 156d]. Franciscans, see: TNA KB9/408 m. 25 [image 52]; TNA KB9/410 m. 90 [image 186]; TNA KB9/975 mm. 127, 125 [images not on AALT]; TNA KB9/521 m. 73 [image 157].

[55] YB Hil. 9 Hen. VII, pl. 15, p. 20. They also added that if a fugitive removed from the house prays to be restored, this is good without any prescription 'because it is incorporated'. This has nothing to do with the case at hand, but the principle recalls the arguments in *Stafford's Case*, indicating that this case still dominated any discussion about sanctuary privileges. This issue had come up before, in 1421, when it was agreed that the fields around St. Johns were not subject to sanctuary but that the houses of the ancient demesne which had a cross on their door were, and Hankford discussed a case when this issue was

complexes and the extent of their landholding, this was an issue of practical concern, one which had arisen in the past, and which would continue to arise.[56] The variety in the types of building available was one source of confusion, but the different opinions of the lawyers and juries also complicated matters. For example, John Clerk alias Grene took sanctuary in St Mary Overy on 11 April 1495 and was removed the same day.[57] He was indicted before the justices of the peace on 30 April and appeared in King's Bench in May 1496, just about a year later, claiming that he had been taken out against his will and asking to be restored.[58] Henry Harman argued that Clerk was at large on that day and was not taken from sanctuary, but the jury responded that he 'took a certain garden within the monastery of St Mary Overy aforesaid, which garden then and now is a holy place annexed to the church of the said monastery and parcel of the churchyard of the said church' and claimed sanctuary there, and that he was removed violently. The jury specified that he did not take sanctuary in the church and was not removed violently thence. This response demonstrates that discussions about the physical extent of the sanctuaries continued to appear in the courts and that juries had their own opinions about what constituted holy space: in this case they were unequivocal that Clerk was not in the church, but equally sure that the garden where he claimed sanctuary was a holy place, with the accompanying displeasure for his unseemly removal. The court wished to be advised and remanded Clerk, but the case did not re-appear.

Popular opinion could interpret sanctuary broadly: in one of the most widely reported cases from 1 Hen. VII, a convicted felon was being brought to execution by the sheriff when the cart of St. John appeared, with its banner. The burial of the bodies of felons was one of the regular duties of the knights of St. John, so their cart was a familiar sight at executions.[59] In this instance, however, the felon grabbed the banner and claimed the privilege of St. John, whereupon 'the rioters of the town and others' rescued the man and brought him to the church.[60] There was some justification in the canon law for their action, since some canonists believed that a priest carrying the host through the streets could function as a sanctuary, and

tried, along with the question of whether the cross was on the door by collusion: see Ralph V. Rogers ed. *Year Books of the Reign of King Henry the Fifth: Year Books 9–10 Henry V* (Wurzburg: Privately Printed, 1948), pl. 25, p. 22.

[56] See pp. 51, 220.

[57] St. Mary Overy was a house of Augustinian canons in Southwark, now Southwark cathedral.

[58] TNA KB27/939 rex m. 9 [image 170].

[59] Gregory O'Malley, *The Knights Hospitaller of the English Langue, 1460–1565* (Oxford: Oxford University Press, 2005), pp. 96–98. Barney Sloane and Gordon Malcolm, *Excavations at the Priory of the Order of the Hospital of St John of Jerusalem, Clerkenwell, London* (London: Museum of London Archaeology Service, 2004), p. 146 notes that in 1502 Elizabeth of York paid the friary clerk of St John 8s for burying felons hanged at Wapping Mill in the churchyard.

[60] YB Hil. 1 Hen. VII, pl. 2, p. 6. The question raised was whether the rescuers had acted feloniously. Huse claimed that a similar case had been argued in the time of Edward IV and that Choke and Billyng had affirmed that this was a felony and there was general agreement. The version of the case in *Exchequer Chamber*, p. 125 makes no mention of the banner, but simply says that the man was rescued.

the logical extension of this could allow any sacred object to operate in this way.[61] Helmholz argues that these possibilities were ultimately rejected by the canonists, but the general population did not necessarily feel the same way.[62] Nevertheless, a mobile sanctuary at an execution site was not conducive to good order, and Brooke notes that the claim was not successful.[63]

Though the 'rioters of the town' are not identified in this case, there is clear evidence that support for sanctuary went beyond the claimants themselves. We would expect to see monks fight to maintain the privileges of their house, but some clergy were clearly ready to take decisive action to support individual claimants. For example, William Johnson was convicted of felony at the gaol delivery of Coventry on 20 February 1490, and ordered to be hanged.[64] The execution was to be carried out on 22 February, but William Glasyer (a Coventry chaplain), Thomas Pylkman (a Coventry yeoman) and others gathered at the place of execution and took Johnson from the custody of the sheriffs. The sheriffs retrieved him, but rather than continuing with the execution they brought him back to the gaol until the sentence could be carried out more securely. This might seem like a rogue operation on the part of Glasyer and Pylkman, but John Hales, the bishop of Coventry and Lichfield, went to the gaol the same day and told Roger Sutton and Richard Chapman, the sheriffs, and John Ryngold, the keeper of the gaol, that they should give Johnson up to him, because he had been taken from sanctuary violently. The sheriffs and keeper refused and Hales anathemized and excommunicated them. With the support of Johnson thus officially sanctioned, the following day Peter Coventry (a Coventry Franciscan), John Draycote, and Lodowick Porter (a gentleman and yeoman of Beaudesert, Staffordshire), and others violently took Johnson from the custody of Ryngold and took him to the cathedral church of St Mary.[65] This all happened on Shrove Tuesday, and it is probably not surprising that the sheriff and his men were not willing to broach the church during Lent. According to the indictment, Johnson remained there for forty days, and on 29 March (the Monday after Passion Sunday, actually thirty-four days later) Draycote and Porter, with others, came and removed him to 'the bochery' in Coventry, with the intention of moving

[61] Cf. p. 57.

[62] Helmholz, *Ius Commune*, p. 29. Gervase Rosser provides English examples of this phenomenon in the twelfth century: 'Sanctuary and social negotiation in medieval England', in *The Cloister and the World: Essays on Medieval History in Honour of Barbara Harvey* edited by John Blair and Brian Golding (Oxford: Clarendon Press, 1996), p. 62.

[63] There was little discussion of the rescued felon. Though the reports give a sense of his desperation, describing how he 'jette ses mains sur le bannier', only Brooke notes the outcome, *Sanctuary*, 8. In 1506 two men in Kent tried to claim sanctuary by seizing the person of a knight of St John, see below pp. 167–168.

[64] TNA KB9/1061 m. 50 [image not on AALT].

[65] The diocese of Coventry and Lichfield was unusual in having a cathedral church associated with both of its main towns: the Coventry church was older than its sibling but destroyed following its dissolution in 1539: *A History of the County of Warwick: Volume 2*, edited by William Page (London: Victoria County History 1908), p. 59. *British History Online*, accessed 3 August 2020, http://www.british-history.ac.uk/vch/warks/vol2.

him back to the church. This implies that Draycote and Porter had continued to support Johnson through the intervening period, and also that there was no intention to suggest that the church was anything other than a normal sanctuary. They knew that the forty-day rule applied and expected the clock to start afresh with Johnson's return. The decision to move him that week rather than to run out both the forty days and Lent is an odd one, but there may have been concerns that Johnson's presence in the church during Holy Week would have been disruptive, though the significance of the season seems to have affected the language of the indictment.

It's not clear what happened to Johnson, Draycote or Porter, but William Glasyer (the chaplain) and Roger Sutton, Richard Chapman, and John Ryngold (the officers) were all pursued by the law. Glasyer appeared in King's Bench in May 1491. He pleaded not guilty and was bailed to two gentlemen, John Horton of Coventry, and William Blayston of Warwick. He appeared at the assize in Coventry on 18 July, where he was found guilty, claimed clergy, and was delivered to the ordinary.[66] Though Glasyer was punished, this was a relatively easy journey through the legal system: he was bailed to his home area, tried quickly at the local assize and delivered to his ordinary rather than being left to languish in the Marshalsea. Sutton, Chapman, and Ryngold also appeared in King's Bench, on 7 July 1491, and they sought to evade the charge of escape in the first instance on a technicality.[67] The jury did not support them and said that they should pay a fine. The court agreed that Sutton and Chapman should pay a fine, but allowed Ryngold to go *sine die*. Sutton and Chapman were fined £100, when the usual fine for the escape of a prisoner was in the region of 5–10s.[68] The harsh treatment of the sheriffs, in contrast to the relatively lenient treatment of the chaplain who apparently led the campaign to free Johnson, suggests that the court saw this as a right mess on the part of the officers, but whether the fine was so large because they lost control of Johnson in the first place, or because they handled the crowd and the bishop so badly, or both, is not evident. This whole chain of events surely stands as an example of how the process was not supposed to work: a standoff between the bishop and the sheriffs over the custody of a sanctuary man on the eve of the holiest season of the year was a public relations disaster.[69]

[66] TNA KB27/919 rex m. 9 [images 204, 205]. John Hales had died the previous September, so the see was vacant.

[67] TNA KB27/920 rex m. 14 [images 227, 228, 486d].

[68] TNA KB27/925 fines [image 197].

[69] Norwich cathedral clergy also actively protected felons from royal officers as well as supporting sanctuary men: in 1506 the prior and three monks attempted to seize an arrested felon from the sheriff: J.C. Tingey, ed. *The Records of the City of Norwich* vol. 2 (London: Jarrold & Sons, 1910), p. 369. In 1464 one Thomas White took sanctuary in the church of St. Mary Incombusta in Norwich, for murder. He refused to abjure after 40 days, so by the advice of William Yelverton a proclamation was made through the city by the coroner that 'no one should give, send, or throw food' to Thomas under penalty of a charge of felony. Though the felon was not in the cathedral, the vicar-general of the bishop, the prior of the cathedral and other ecclesiastical persons came asking leave to spend alms on Thomas, or that he should be delivered to them, and they would provide security. The city recorder was unwilling

A Wallingford monk demonstrated a similar level of commitment to a sanctuary-seeker in his house. An inquisition on the view of the body of John Scolfyld, chaplain, found that Robert Forde killed him in Brightwell with a dagger in his guts on 15 May 1507.[70] It added that Forde fled first to the priory of Wallingford, and then 'to a certain sacred place called Culneham in county Oxford'. The inquisition is dated 16 May, implying that Forde must have moved on from Wallingford the same day or the day after. This is intriguing: Wallingford is about two and a half miles south-east of Brightwell by road, and it is not surprising that Forde might have fled there in a panic after killing Scolfyld. But Culham is about six miles north-west of Brightwell, meaning that Forde retraced his steps to get there, and it is just across the border in Oxfordshire. Why did he change his strategy? An indictment from the session of the peace held at Wallingford on 4 June throws the whole series of events into a different light. It recounts Scolfyld's murder and Forde's flight to Wallingford, where it specifies that he claimed sanctuary. This record adds, however, that he stayed there until 19 May when William Hungerford (a monk of Wallyngford), Thomas Depdale, Thomas Marten, and Richard Morgan, (Wallingford yeomen), Richard Forde (a husbandman from Sotwell and presumably a relation of the accused), Thomas Bedford (a husbandman from Clifton, Oxfordshire), and William Rouland (a laborer from Sotwell), knowing Forde to have killed Scolfyld, brought him along the Thames 'by means of that water to a certain sanctuary and privileged place called Culneham'.[71] These two records taken together raise all sorts of issues. Most obviously, they suggest that someone came to the conclusion that Wallingford was not secure enough as a refuge for Forde, and that Culham was better, either because it was physically more secure, or because he could stay there longer. The choice to move Forde by a circuitous water route rather than the more direct land route, and to move him into a different county and thus into a different jurisdiction, suggests that the immediate concern was with him falling into the hands of the county officers rather than with the range of the sanctuary. The fact that seven men embarked on this adventure with him suggests either that the enterprise was difficult, or that there was a good deal of local support for Forde, or both, and the role of Hungerford, the Wallingford monk, is particularly intriguing. We might have expected him to side with the fallen clerk, and his willingness to go to these lengths for Forde suggests either that Scolfylde was indeed in the wrong in whatever dispute led to his death, or that Hungerford felt an active obligation to ensure the safety of one who had claimed sanctuary in his house, or both. Finally, the dating of the documents is odd. According to the session of the peace Forde

to give them a blank refusal, noting instead that these questions were difficult and ambiguous in law, though in fact their request was clearly outside the law as it stood: Tingey, ed. *The Records of the City of Norwich* vol. 2, p. 96.

[70] TNA KB9/449 m. 46 [image 91].

[71] TNA KB9/452 m.2 [image 4].

did not go to Culham until 19 May, but the inquisition on the body from 16 May already recorded the move. The simplest explanation, and probably the likeliest, is that the inquisition was mis-dated, but it is at least possible that the plan to move to Culham was already known on the 16th, even though it was not executed for another three days.[72]

Johnson's and Forde's cases demonstrate not only that canons and monks might support individual sanctuary claimants in their houses, but that the laity could also express their support for sanctuary men quite vigorously, and we see this again when John Calcott and others broke out of Newgate and took sanctuary in St Sepulchre.[73] Around midnight the keeper of Newgate and about twenty others broke into the church to get them, but Calcott and others in the church 'rang one of the bellis of the said church' so that the inhabitants would come and help them 'by force of whiche then certen prestis beyng a bedde in ther Chaumbers sette in the seid Chirche yarde and various inhabitaunts of the seid parisshe heryng the seid belle rose up of their beddis and came to the seid Chirche to aide those persones then being in the same Chirche'.[74] The priests and neighbours prevented the gaoler and his men from taking the men from sanctuary, but the gaoler brought an action before the sheriff's court of London against three of the parishioners who were also churchwardens, accusing them of breaking Calcott from the prison.

Nothing in the records indicates why these men were willing to go to such lengths to support the sanctuary-seekers: it is entirely possible that Glasyer and Hungerforde and their companions knew Johnson and Forde and supported them personally rather than the institution of sanctuary, but Hales' involvement in the former case indicates that a sanctuary-seeker might expect broad support from churchmen who supported the institution as a whole and not just the privileges of their own house. Similarly, it is unlikely that the priests and parishioners supported the Newgate escapees personally, but they were willing to face both the gaoler in person and the process in the courts in order to support their claim.

It is striking that we have no records of abjurations from religious houses in this period, and all the evidence for these claims comes from inquisitions on the view of bodies or subsequent indictments. It was possible to abjure from a religious house. John Sampyre and Richard Couper claimed sanctuary at St Mary Overy on 22 March 1504 for felonies they had previously committed separately,

[72] A writ issued from King's Bench to the justices of the peace on 13 June 1509 requiring the delivery of the records relating to Robert and Richard Forde, Thomas Bedford and Richard and William Rouland: TNA KB9/452 m.1 [image 2]. Richard Rouland was not mentioned in the original indictment—it may be an error or alias for Richard Morgan. Though there was no further process, this opens the possibility that Robert Forde was still at Culham two years after the crime.

[73] This gaol break took place in either 1495 or 1500. The parish church of St. Sepulchre was right by Newgate; though it was obviously not a religious house, the laity seem to have supported sanctuary claimants in a variety of settings. Having a sanctuary beside a prison might seem like a bad idea, but it was very common. St Katherine's had its fair share of sanctuary traffic from the Tower and St Mary Overy was a quick dash from the Clink.

[74] TNA C1/226/44.

and the following day in the presence of the coroner, the constables, and 'others of the community of the vill and other lieges of the king' they said that they wanted the sanctuary of the church for forty days and would then abjure the realm.[75] In the meantime they 'shrewdly and subtly between themselves schemed how to get themselves at large and to remove themselves from the legitimate order of the law': they escaped the following day. This case demonstrates clearly that the coroners could and did deal with abjurations in religious houses, and that the forty day limit applied, so the complete absence of these records is somewhat surprising.

The unchartered religious houses apparently faced greater pressure than the chartered sanctuaries to defend their boundaries, and they certainly provide more evidence for the active engagement of both clergy and laity in the protection of sanctuary men. Though they were almost as popular with homicides as the chartered sanctuaries, they did not have the ability to mobilize the same kind of political support as houses like Westminster and St Martins, but, partly because of that, they allow us to see the broad base of support that sanctuary enjoyed.

3. Parish Sanctuaries

No individual parish church saw many sanctuary seekers, but we have records of seventy-one men taking sanctuary in parish churches in the reign of Henry VII [table 5.1]. It is probably not surprising that the greatest number of cases come from the London area, with forty-two from Middlesex and sixteen from Surrey, but it is clear that sanctuary was being used all over the country.[76] The felons who claimed

Table 5.1 Recorded sanctuary claims by county 1485–1509*

Berkshire	7	Gloucestershire	1	Middlesex	42	Suffolk	1
Bristol	1	Hampshire	3	Northamptonshire	3	Surrey	16
Buckinghamshire	4	Herefordshire	2	Nottinghamshire	2	Sussex	1
Cambridgeshire	1	Hertfordshire	3	Oxfordshire	3	Warwickshire	2
Derby	1	Huntingdonshire	4	Shropshire	1	Worcestershire	3
Devon	1	Kent	10	Somerset	3	Yorkshire	1
Essex	4	Lincoln	4	Staffordshire	8		

*Data collected from TNA KB27 and KB9 rolls.

[75] TNA KB9/438 m. 86 [image 188].

[76] These numbers are only a small proportion of the likely claimants, but we cannot know how often the coroner was not called or did not return his records: see R.F. Hunnisett, *The Medieval Coroner* (Cambridge: Cambridge University Press, 1961), p. 116; R.F. Hunnisett ed. *Calendar of Nottinghamshire*

clergy in parish churches had quite a different profile from those in either kind of religious house. Of the seventy-one, thirty claimed sanctuary for homicide (42 per cent), thirty-two claimed sanctuary for robbery, burglary, or theft, often horsetheft (45 per cent), and the remainder claimed for assault or undefined felony.[77] We also have a more varied source base and set of outcomes for the parish claimants. For twenty-three of the seventy-one we have the coroner's report of sanctuary followed by abjuration: in most cases we know about the sanctuary and abjuration because the abjurer was subsequently found in the country and appeared at King's Bench to explain why he should not be executed. Fourteen of those twenty-three confessed to killing someone (only one was described as murder), four confessed to assault, three to burglary, and two to horsetheft. For another nineteen we have a trial record in which the accused claimed that he had been forcibly removed from sanctuary and asked to be restored. These men are usually lower on the scale of crime: one was accused of homicide, but he had also previously abjured. Of the remaining eighteen, four were accused of assault and robbery, five of burglary, seven of theft, and two of felony.[78] In both of these situations we generally know a fair amount about both the crime and what happened to the felon afterwards. In fourteen of the seventy-one cases we have the kinds of sources we have already seen for the religious sanctuaries: an inquisition on the view of a body or an indictment for a crime which mentioned that the perpetrator had fled to sanctuary, often with a writ calling the case to King's Bench, but no further process.[79] Eleven of these men were accused of homicide, and the remaining three, two of whom were accused of assault and one of theft, may not actually have taken sanctuary.[80] We know least of all about the ten men who escaped from prison and claimed sanctuary, since these indictments are directed at their wardens and give little information about either the crimes they were accused of committing or their subsequent fate. This section will focus on the abjurers and those removed from sanctuary against their will, both because these are the most typical reasons for process in King's Bench from

Coroners' Inquests 1485–1558, Thoroton Society Record Series vol. 25 (Nottingham: Derry and Sons, 1969), pp. xviii–xix and Carrie Smith, 'Medieval Coroners' Rolls: Legal Fiction or Historical Fact?' in *Courts, Counties and the Capital in the Later Middle Ages* edited by Diana E.S. Dunn (Stroud: Sutton, 1996), pp. 93–115.

[77] Most of these records are abjuration with confessions, but some, mostly those simply described as felonies, are indictments on escapes where the taking of sanctuary for felony is noted but the full confession is not given.

[78] We have less information about escapees, but two were accused of felony and murder, four of felony, one of robbery, one of burglary, and one of horsetheft.

[79] In two of these cases the sanctuaries were identified as being 'in the town of Ripon' and 'in the town of Ryton', one was in 'the franchise of Beaumontrent' and in a fourth the felon seems to have been at the priory of St Augustine's, Bristol, but since the prior was indicted as an accessory it's not clear if he was seeking sanctuary there: TNA KB9/446 m. 86 [image 445]; TNA KB9/446 m. 19 [image 314]; TNA KB9/397 m. 23 [image 46]; TNA KB9/410 m. 31 [image 66].

[80] TNA KB9/386 mm. 25–27 [image 48–51]; TNA KB9/410 m. 31 [image 66].

parish sanctuaries, and because they give the best insight into the ways in which the parish sanctuaries worked.

Abjuration

The surviving failed abjurations suggest that the coroners' first priority was not the simple removal of a confessed felon from the kingdom, for abjurers were not usually sent to the closest or the busiest ports.[81] John Walworth, for example, took sanctuary in the parish church of St Andrew the Apostle in Kingston, Kent in January 1486.[82] There he admitted that he had killed Hugh Peke in Nottingham and asked to abjure. He was assigned to leave from Colchester. This was an odd choice, for Kingston is only about 10 miles from Dover on a fairly direct route, while Colchester is at least 85 miles away, not a major port, and, incidentally, a sanctuary. Perhaps unsurprisingly, Walworth appeared in King's Bench having been found in the country without license. He was asked if there was any reason why he should not be executed, and providing no response, he was ordered to be hanged. Walworth was not alone in this experience. Thomas White took sanctuary at All Saints in Breadstreet ward, London, in March 1486 and confessed to a homicide.[83] He was assigned to abjure from Winchelsea, Sussex, 65 miles away, but appeared in King's Bench in October 1487 and was sentenced to be hanged. Richard Whyte claimed sanctuary for a murder in Newington, Surrey in October 1487 and was also sent to abjure from Winchelsea: Newington was just south of Southwark.[84] He managed to evade detection until 1490, but he too was sentenced to be hanged in May of that year. John Barley senior took sanctuary in his parish church in Enfield, Middlesex on 2 October 1502, having killed Thomas West, chaplain, the same day.[85] The coroner did not appear until 7 October, and Barley abjured the following day, heading for Southampton, about 86 miles away. He appeared in King's Bench in May 1503 and was ordered to be hanged.[86] Thomas Bennet took sanctuary in Burnham, Buckinghamshire in June 1504.[87] There he confessed to robbery and homicide and was assigned to Dover, 97 miles away, rather than the more obvious Portsmouth or Southampton (60 and 61 miles respectively). A writ issued from King's Bench for his abjuration on 20 November, five months after his departure, but unlike the other men he did not appear in court. Why were all of these men sent to relatively distant ports? If the key purpose of abjuration was the efficient removal

[81] This is a change from the thirteenth century when abjurers were sent to the nearest port: *Bracton*, vol. 1, p. 83, n. 2.

[82] TNA KB9/1060 m. 66 [image not on AALT]: TNA KB27/901 rex m. 3d [image 530d].

[83] TNA KB9/375 m. 68 [image 135]: TNA KB27/905 rex m. 8 [image 191].

[84] TNA KB9/385 m. 38 [image 76]: TNA KB27/915 rex m. 5 [image 175].

[85] TNA KB9/429 m. 10 [image 24].

[86] TNA KB27/967 rex m. 4d [image 412d].

[87] TNA KB9/435 m. 3 [image 6].

of a criminal from the country, we would expect to see coroners send them to the nearest port and/or the busiest port. In many cases this would have been London, which, in fact, never appears as a destination for abjuration. So what was actually driving the coroners' choices? There are four likely possibilities. The first is that there was still a penitential sense to the abjuration process: we know that abjurers continued to carry a cross, and while this was of less interest to the common law sources than the facts of the case, this does not mean that we should assume it was unimportant to those participating. It is entirely likely that both coroners and other participants expected the abjurer to travel a reasonable distance as part of their expiation.[88] The second is that coroners were thinking only about the ports with which they were most familiar. If they didn't expect to send abjurers to the nearest port, then any reasonably distant and well-known port might do. The third is that coroners were less concerned with getting abjurers out of the country than out of the county: only one of these abjurers was sent to a port in the county in which they claimed sanctuary, and most were several counties away.[89] We know that in some cases abjurers were accompanied by constables at the beginning of their journey, but as they got further from the sanctuary, their companion was likely to disappear. While this increased the chances that the sanctuary man might disappear en route, that doesn't seem to have been a particular concern: presumably if they managed to blend into a community far from the scene of the crime and did not come to any further official notice, that was a good outcome all around. If they did attract negative attention there was a process in place to deal with the failed abjuration. Finally, the congregation of abjurers in London would undermine all of these expectations: not only would they not undergo the penitential element of the process, but the authorities would fear their disappearance into a concentrated criminal environment instead of a more benign fresh start. Rather than being mutually exclusive, these possibilities are mutually reinforcing and suggest that abjurations could be effective whether the abjurer actually left the country or not.

Not all abjurers managed to melt away, even for a short period, and not all failed abjurations were the fault of the abjurers. James Bell, John Greneway, and Thomas Dawson, all London yeomen, took sanctuary together at the parish church of St James the apostle in Great Gidding, Huntingdonshire, in July 1498 and confessed

[88] Abjurers were always sent to sea ports and the process of crossing the land to reach the port was part of the expiatory process: taking ship in London and sailing downriver may have simply been seen as too easy an option.

[89] Christopher Burton took sanctuary in the parish church of Strode, Kent and confessed to the murder of John Holt in Shropshire. Burton abjured the same day and was sent to Dover, 45 miles distant, but in the same county. He appeared at King's Bench a year later and was asked if there was a reason why he should not be executed, a question to which he 'minime respondit'. Harman asked for execution, but the court remanded Burton to the Marshalsea on pain of £100. It was unusual to remand on a penalty in this circumstance, and no further process was outlined. It is possible that the court intended a custodial sentence: TNA KB9/1109 last membrane [image not on AALT]; TNA KB27/930 rex m. 4 [image 171].

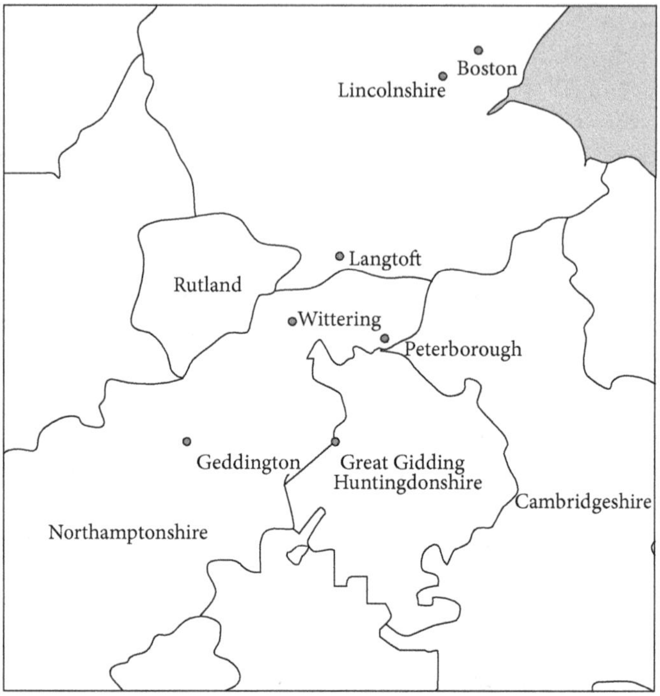

Figure 5.2 The abjuration of Bell, Greneway, and Dawson

to a robbery in April that year at Wittering, Northamptonshire.[90] The geography suggests that they may have been making their way back to London, but if so they were moving at a leisurely pace, having covered about 15 miles in three months, and there is no sense that they were fleeing their crime (fig. 5.2).

They abjured the same day, and all three were assigned to go to Boston, about 45 miles distant. On 20 July 1498, four days and about 23 miles after leaving Great Gidding, the men arrived in Langtoft, where five men took them violently from the custody of the constable and 'other inhabitants then on the highway' and brought them to the gaol of the liberty of the abbot of Peterborough.[91] This is rare evidence of the constable accompanying the abjurers beyond the first stage of their journey, as well as evidence of the passage of abjurers attracting the attention of the wider community. Bell and Dawson seem to have lingered in the abbot's prison for some

[90] TNA KB9/419 m. 5 [image 8]. Bell is also described as a minstrel.

[91] TNA KB27/952 rex m. 16 [images 218, 219]. Grenewey is on the writ calling the record of the abjuration to King's Bench, but he did not appear in court, and it seems likely that he died in (or escaped from) the abbot's custody. The interest of the abbot of Peterborough in the men is never explained, but the manor of Wittering belonged to the abbey: 'Houses of Benedictine monks: The abbey of Peterborough', in *A History of the County of Northampton* vol. 2, edited by R.M. Serjeantson and W.R.D. Adkins (London: Victoria County History, 1906), pp. 83–95. British History Online http://www.british-history.ac.uk/vch/northants/vol2/pp83-95 [accessed 12 March 2022].

months: the record of the abjuration was called to King's Bench in January 1499 and the men themselves appeared in July, when they asked to be restored to the highway to continue their abjuration.[92] Their case was held over to Michelmas, when Hobart accepted the plea and the court ordered them to be returned to the Marshalsea 'and from there delivered by the marshal to the town of Langtoft . . . on the king's road there in the presence of the king's constable of the town so that they may go directly to their aforesaid port according to the abjuration'. Again, efficiency is not the primary concern here: the men were to be brought all the way back to Langtoft so they could be returned to the constable and complete the abjuration as it should originally have been done. Though we have no direct evidence that all went well on the second try, Bell appears one more time: in November 1507 he presented a pardon in King's Bench for all felonies and abjurations before 15 October 1507 and went *sine die* nine and a half years after committing his crime.[93] This suggests something more in line with our expectations of abjuration, that while the felon was overseas his friends or family would work to get him a pardon so that he could return, though his relatively low status is an interesting indication that the process was open to men of a wider social status than we might tend to assume.[94]

Some abjurers were hindered by royal officials. John Whatman took sanctuary at the parish church of St George in Southwark on 16 May 1490, confessed to horsetheft exactly a year earlier and was assigned to Southampton.[95] His record was called to King's Bench in October 1491, and he appeared on 7 November, arguing that he had in fact headed directly to the port, but that on 17 May at Guildford (one day and 30 miles from his point of origin), Thomas Polsted, sub-sheriff of Surrey, and other men had dragged him violently from the highway, put him in the prison of Guildford castle, and provided only bread one day and water the next, a treatment that was usually part of the *peine dure*.[96] Whatman claimed that in order to save his life he had escaped from the prison, but Henry Harman argued that his claim was insufficient in law. The court called the serjeants and attorney general, and they concluded that the plea was insufficient and invalid: the justification for his escape seemed to be accepted, but the court argued that having escaped he

[92] TNA KB9/419 m. 5 [image 6].

[93] TNA KB27/985 rex m. 18d [images 251d–252d]. Dawson disappears from the record after the King's Bench order.

[94] Bell was not an anomaly. John Knapet, a shoemaker alias yeoman of London alias Hertford, took sanctuary in the parish church of All Saints in Hertfordstoke, Essex in April 1507. There he confessed that he, along with Thomas Wodgate, had murdered John Woody on London bridge, stolen 7s 4d and dumped his body in the river. Knapet was assigned to Dover, and subsequently appeared in King's Bench in November 1514 with a pardon for felony, murder and abjuration dated 3 October 1509: TNA KB9/465 m.8 [image 15]; TNA KB27/1013 rex m. 20–20d [images 297, 273d]. He also had a record of the pardon from the close roll dated 8 October 1509. The fact that he did not appear in King's Bench with the pardon for five years suggests that he had been living peacefully for that time, and only appeared when an over-zealous officer or friend of the victim sought to have the punishment for a failed abjuration applied to him.

[95] TNA KB9/391 m. 63 [image 123].

[96] TNA KB9/391 m. 62 [image 121]: TNA KB27/921 rex m. 6 [images 248, 249].

should have returned to his abjuration and headed for Southampton. Since he had not, he was sentenced to be hanged.[97] The report suggests that the court recognized that abjurations could go awry through no fault of the abjurer and was willing to support him, if only he had gone on to abjure.

In other cases the respective responsibility of the abjurer and the officers are more ambiguous. John Marten took sanctuary in the parish church of St Olave in Southwark on 25 January 1489 and confessed to killing William Alwen.[98] He abjured the same day from the church door, headed for Portsmouth. Something appears to have gone wrong from the start, however, for a writ issued from King's Bench for the record of his abjuration the following day.[99] Marten appeared in King's Bench on 14 May, and claimed that the constable of Lambeth and another took him from the highway on 26 January and put him in the Marshalsea. He asked to be restored to the highway to continue his abjuration.[100] Henry Harman claimed that he had in fact left the highway. Marten was remanded until the following summer, and disappears from the record until November 1507, eighteen years later, when he appeared in King's Bench with a pardon.[101] The court was not entirely happy with this development, and consulted with the serjeants and the king's attorney, but in the end it accepted the pardon and Marten went *sine die*. Though we cannot know if Marten had in fact left the route of his own accord, in this case his official abjuration seems to have been replaced with a lengthy custodial sentence.

If the evidence from the religious houses demonstrates that both clergy and laity could be enthusiastic in their support for sanctuary, these cases suggest that abjurers generated less enthusiasm. The concern that abjurers should have protection on their route, whether via a cross or a constable, was justified, and it's clear that both locals and officials were willing to obstruct abjurers in some cases. It's possible that it was generally known that abjurers might seek to start over in an accommodating community on or near their route, and vigilant officials may simply have been seeking to ensure that that did not happen. While the courts were willing to be tough with failed abjurers who appeared before them with no explanation for their continued presence, they were also willing to support those who had been obstructed, either by restoring them to their route, or by ensuring an alternative form of punishment. Of course we can't be sure that the narratives in the documents are accurate, and we have to recognize that while all these scenarios could be true, they could also be used strategically.

[97] Whatman's case is reported in YB Mich. 7 Hen. VII, pl. 11, p. 7.

[98] TNA KB9/380 m. 23 [image 46].

[99] TNA KB9/380 m. 22 [image 44].

[100] TNA KB27/915 rex m. 5d [images 415d, 416d].

[101] TNA KB27/985 rex m. 18 [images 262, 263]. The pardon included five other men and six women, none of whom seem to have been connected otherwise, and has the distinct appearance of a prison-cleaning.

Restoration to Sanctuary

The records also provide numerous complaints from sanctuary men of being removed from sanctuaries against their will. This scenario is just as open to manipulation as the abjurers' assertions of obstruction, for if the allegation could be proved the courts would restore the sanctuary man. Although we don't know what happened to many of these men, we have no record of a conviction for most of them, and this suggests that the claim of having been removed from sanctuary was worth making: even if the claimant was not 'restored' to sanctuary he might be shunted out of the usual process. For example, John Antony was indicted before the justices of gaol delivery at Ilchester in July 1486 for two separate thefts.[102] He claimed that he took sanctuary in the parish church of Bradford in Dorset and asked for the coroner, but that he was removed from the sanctuary against his will, and he asked to be restored. The gaol delivery record is filed in Hilary 1497, and there's no indication of why Antony's case appeared so long after both the crime and the sanctuary, though the patterns evident elsewhere would suggest that he had been held in Ilchester for the intervening eleven years and was brought to King's Bench for his case to be concluded. The fact that he didn't appear suggests that he escaped, or perhaps more likely died, before that could happen. He was not the only one to be left in legal limbo: Richard Crokker took sanctuary in the parish church of St Anne in Aldrichgate on 3 February 1493 but claimed that he was taken out against his will the same day when he appeared for trial in the Marshalsea on 8 November.[103] A jury was called to hear the case in January 1494 but had not appeared by Michelmas 1499, when the case disappears from the record.[104] By the later years of the reign the pattern seems to be better established. After being indicted as part of a gang who committed a burglary on 29 December 1508, Thomas Robynson claimed that he took sanctuary at the church of St Benedict in London on 12 January 1509 but was removed by unknown men the same day.[105] He asked to be restored and was remanded to the next gaol delivery. In August he was remanded again and his record was delivered to King's Bench in February 1510, a year after his first appearance. Robynson himself did not appear until July 1514, when he presented a pardon. He presumably remained in gaol for the intervening 5 years, and it is likely that his original claim to sanctuary shaped the response to a man who had been indicted for taking part in a gang burglary.

Claiming to have been removed from sanctuary offered enough of a benefit that some felons put all their trust in that claim and refused to plead to the crime that

[102] TNA KB9/411 m. 35 [image 70].

[103] TNA KB27/929 rex m. 12 [images 276, 277, 590d, 591d]. He confessed to a burglary.

[104] Crokker's case appears in a collection of cases from King's Bench which survives in the British Library, suggesting that in 1494 there was some novelty to this plea: British Library MS Add 25168 f. 90, pl. 86.

[105] TNA KB27/1012 rex m. 8 [images 189, 190].

they were accused of committing. This should have been dangerous: in the normal course of events, refusing to plead to a felony meant that the accused was subject to *peine forte et dure*, and two cases in Caryll's *Reports* indicate quite clearly that the claim of sanctuary did not change this. In the first, in 1492, John Archer was accused of robbery. He claimed that he had been in sanctuary and had tried to abjure before the coroner but the coroner refused to assign him a port, whereupon he was dragged from sanctuary. He prayed the court to be returned.[106] The court urged Archer to answer more fully, and Fairfax JKB cautioned Archer to 'take good care of yourself, my friend, and think carefully what a great offense it is against God to murder [yourself] voluntarily through obstinacy. For it is more acceptable to God to die according to the form and order of the law. In any case, twelve men will perhaps find you not guilty'.[107] Archer finally pleaded not guilty, but since he had already been convicted of another felony, the whole matter was academic. In Caryll's second case two men indicted for felony at the gaol delivery at Southwark in Lent 1506 claimed that they had been taken from sanctuary and asked to be restored. The judges urged them to plead to the felony, but they refused, even when they were warned that if the jury found against them on the sanctuary, there would be no further inquiry on the felony. The inquest found that they had not been taken from sanctuary, and so the felons were taken as having refused to plead and subjected to *peine forte et dure*.[108] These two cases, fourteen years apart, point to a clear principle, but in practice the courts seem to have been a good deal more patient than the reports suggest. For example, John Moresse and James Gryffon were accused of highway robbery before the justices of gaol delivery at Maidstone in Kent in February 1498.[109] They responded that they had taken sanctuary in the porch of the parish church of Tonbridge and been taken out against their will. They asked to be restored to sanctuary and did not otherwise respond to the felony. The justices wished to be advised and remanded them to gaol on pain of £100 each. The two men appeared at Westminster in June 1505, more than seven years later. The claim of sanctuary was made again, but this time both men also pleaded not guilty. Separate juries were called, but neither appeared until June 1507, at which point both were found not guilty after more than nine years in prison.[110] This could be a profound miscarriage of justice and two innocent men might have lingered in prison for nine years for a crime they did not commit. But it seems more likely that the men used the claim of sanctuary to delay their trial and that the final verdict reflected time served rather than actual innocence.

[106] In an abbreviated version of events, the report says that the coroner certified that the defendant refused to state clearly where the crime took place, thus failing his attempt to abjure.
[107] *Caryll's Reports*, vol. 1, pp. 111–112.
[108] *Caryll's Reports*, vol. 2, p. 469.
[109] TNA KB9/415 m. 80 [image 164].
[110] TNA KB27/976 rex m. 6 [images 238, 239].

Other sanctuary men were more explicit in their rejection of the common law. When Hugh Wenwright was indicted for burglary at the gaol delivery of the castle of Guildford in February 1507, he claimed that he was taken from sanctuary in the parish church of St Michael in Cornhill against his will, asked to be restored, and 'refused the royal laws today'.[111] Explicit as his refusal was, the judges wished to be advised and he was remanded to gaol. He appeared at Westminster a year later, where he was asked if he wished to maintain his plea, but instead pleaded not guilty.[112] Around the same time Edward Bulkeley was indicted at Newgate for theft.[113] Bulkeley claimed that having taken sanctuary in the parish church of Ewell in Surrey he was 'taken out', though he doesn't specify that the taking was against his will, and 'was afterwards at large' until he was re-taken in Holborn. Bulkeley's language was not as strong as Wenwright's: he 'did not wish to respond' to the indictment, but the judges wished to be advised and he was remanded to gaol. These men chose to reject the common law, for it was possible to both claim sanctuary and plead. William Rowland alias Olyver was indicted at the same time as Bulkeley for stealing a pound of saffron worth 10s: he claimed that he had been taken out of the parish church of Bray in Berkshire against his will and asked to be restored, but he also pleaded not guilty.[114] The justices treated him exactly the same as Bulkeley: they wished to be advised and remanded him to gaol. Finally, John Byshop claimed on indictment for theft at the gaol delivery in the Marshalsea on 10 May 1502 that he had been taken from sanctuary against his will, and both asked to be restored and pleaded not guilty.[115] These examples make it clear that even when reported cases point us to something that looks like a clear principle, practice in the courts was a good deal more varied. We don't know if the circumstances attached to these cases were similar and would demonstrate an underlying consistency in the justices' choices, but on the face of it, they seem to have been comfortable making a variety of choices in a variety of situations.

Though these strategies allowed felons to avoid execution often enough to be worth trying, many of the cases have a general air of incoherence, and success seems to have been far from predictable. William Amboler, a clerk from Stony Stratford in Buckinghamshire, gives us a glimpse of a sanctuary man flailing for purchase within the system. He was indicted before the justices of the peace for a homicide committed on 18 May 1499.[116] According to the indictment, Amboler fled the

[111] TNA KB9/445 m. 88 [image 178]. 'set recusat leges regales isto die etc.'.

[112] TNA KB27/986 rex m. 6d [images 137d, 138d]. A jury was called for Easter term, but no verdict is recorded. Wenwright appeared in court again in November 1509, when he presented a pardon: TNA KB27/993 rex m. 17 [images 281, 282]. Seven others were also named in the pardon: see pp. 168, 171.

[113] TNA KB9/446 m. 31 [image 337].

[114] TNA KB9/446 m. 31 [image 337].

[115] TNA KB27/964 rex m. 11 [images 497d, 239]. The jury found against him on both counts in a much more efficient process.

[116] TNA KB27/994 rex m. 15 [image 237].

Figure 5.3 The abjuration of William Amboler

same day to the church of St Giles in Stony Stratford and asked for sanctuary. He remained there for four days, and then left for lack of good custody of the inhabitants, fleeing to St John of Jerusalem where he remained for another two days until he once again fled for lack of good custody.[117] John Smyth of Stony Stratford was indicted for receiving him then, on 24 May, knowing that he had committed the felony, and taking him first to Shenley, and from there to Little Brickhill, Dunstable (Bedfordshire), St Albans, Barnet (Hertfortshire), and Hornsey (Middlesex), suggesting that Amboler returned home after he left St John of Jerusalem, and Smyth quickly moved him back out, escorting him along the route of the A5 directly towards London, with stops in two gaol delivery towns (Little Brickhill and St Albans) and two monastery towns (Dunstable and St Albans) (fig. 5.3). From this itinerary it could be argued that Smyth was trying to get Amboler to the authorities, or to a safer sanctuary, or simply to London along the most major route. The indictment doesn't give any hint as to the men's intentions; it appears in the roll for Hilary 1510 with no further process, suggesting that after Hornsey they managed to disappear for the next eleven years. Though Amboler's and Smyth's strategies are not clear, their path was unusually direct, and if Amboler managed to disappear in London and remain out of sight of the authorities, once again that might count as a victory.

[117] The indictment doesn't specify which house Amboler went to, but the preceptory at Hogshaw was the closest.

This range of outcomes makes it clear that while claims to be restored to sanctuary might not be successful, they were worth a shot. Whether the refusal to plead was as explicit as Wenwright's or as oblique as Bulkeley's, the courts did not rush to impose the *peine fort*: this suggests that Caryll's cases were unusual enough to warrant notice, and that the *peine* was a choice available to the court but not the norm. It's worth noting that eighteen of the nineteen men who asked to be restored to sanctuary were accused of crimes other than homicide, and it may be the case that those who had committed lesser felonies could use this as a path to a lesser punishment, often stewing in prison for several years before being released on a pardon. The evidence here is even more scattered than for benefit of clergy, but these men often spent longer in the county gaols or their sanctuaries than they would have done had they claimed clergy (an option that may not have been open to them), though once again they managed to avoid execution.

4. Sanctuary and Benefit of Clergy

Many of the examples in this chapter have been partial and suggestive due to both the limitations of the sources and sanctuary's common function as a strategy rather than an end in itself. Perhaps fittingly, the most detailed stories we have come from the small group of men who did something technically not allowed under the law: they claimed both sanctuary and benefit of clergy. Their experiences highlight how the individual arguments and strategies discussed above might fit into the development of a complex case, sometimes over several years, and they also demonstrate the remarkable willingness of the courts to consider claims for mitigation in these years.

According to the King's Bench records, George Wolmer, a yeoman from Lingfield, Surrey, claimed sanctuary in St Mary Overy in June 1500 and asked for the coroner, John Couper. He confessed to Couper that in August 1496 he had attacked some unknown men at Farnborough in Kent and stolen 40s, asked to abjure and was assigned to Southampton.[118] Though this reads as a fairly typical abjuration document, in this case we have information which fills some of the gap between 1496 and 1500 and gives us more context for Wolmer's arrival at St. Mary Overy. Under the name George Sawyer of Southwark, Wolmer was indicted by the justices of the peace at Canterbury in April 1499 for a burglary at Codham in May 1498 and for three highway robberies at Otford in August 1498 worth around £5 in weapons, money and fish.[119] In October 1499 Wolmer/Sawyer appeared in King's Bench and claimed that on 21 February 1499 he had taken sanctuary in St Mary Overy and asked for the coroner, but that on the same day he was violently taken

[118] TNA KB9/454 m. 38 [image 76].

[119] TNA KB27/953 rex m. 4 [images 215, 216].

out of sanctuary against his will. He claimed that he was not guilty of the felony and asked to be restored to the sanctuary. Henry Harman argued that Wolmer/Sawyer had not in fact taken sanctuary on 21 February and therefore had not been violently removed. In May 1500 the jury called to settle the question backed up Wolmer/Sawyer's story, and the court ordered him to be taken from the Marshalsea to St Mary Overy and delivered in the presence of the constable who was to guard him there until the coroner came. Since it's unlikely that the constable stood guard for almost two months, there was probably some delay in Wolmer's delivery to the church and his confession on 27 June. This additional information changes our perception of Wolmer's confession and abjuration quite substantially: Wolmer was clearly a regular offender through the late 1490s, but an abjurer was not required to confess all his crimes. The jury accepted his claim to sanctuary and the court respected the jury verdict and returned Wolmer to the church, but with the caveat that the constable should remain with him until the coroner arrived to take his confession and carry out the abjuration. Though the court had followed the law in restoring him to sanctuary, given his lengthy criminal career there was presumably a stronger incentive than usual to monitor his journey to Southampton. This may explain why Wolmer was brought to King's Bench on 4 July 1500, a mere week later, having been found in the country without license. When asked if there was any reason execution should not be carried out, he claimed clergy, read *ut clericus*, was branded and was delivered to Westminster Abbey as a clerk attaint.[120] Given some of the narratives we've seen above, we could speculate that law officers intervened to draw him back to court so quickly, but there is no evidence for this. Once he arrived in King's Bench, and despite his history, the court was lenient, allowing his claim of clergy to result in a life sentence. This should have been the end of Wolmer's story, but there are two more chapters. The patent rolls record a pardon for George Wolmer of Lyngfeld Surrey alias Westminster, yeoman, dated 16 October 1506.[121] This suggests that, like similar men discussed in chapter 4, Wolmer spent about six years in the Abbey for his various crimes compounded by his failed abjuration, and that his sentence was ended by a pardon. Wolmer thus had the chance to reform, but, unsurprisingly, he did not take it. In May 1510, four years after the pardon, he escaped from the custody of the abbot of Westminster, having apparently gone through the cycle, or at least part of it, all over again.[122] Wolmer was clearly a career criminal and both a burglar and a robber, yet he managed to work his way through the system relatively unscathed for upwards of fifteen years.

[120] TNA KB27/956 rex m. 2d [image 779d]; TNA KB27/996 rex m. 18 [images 281, 282, 268d, 269d].

[121] *CPR Hen VII* vol. 2, p. 501.

[122] TNA KB27/996 rex m. 18 [images 281, 282, 268d, 269d]. The abbot appeared with a pardon for his escape dated 10 June 1510, also in *LP*, vol. 1, 1091. The pardon is specific to Wolmer, but it opens with a rehearsal of the grants to the abbey and convent made by Edward the Confessor and other of the king's progenitors and notes Henry VIII's coronation in the abbey and his favour towards it, suggesting that this pardon marked a willingness on the part of the young king to treat such escapes more gently than his father had done.

Though Wolmer demonstrates some of the ways in which the system could be manipulated, he pales beside the ingenuity of Richard Pulham and Ralph Toker. Pulham, a harper from the hundred of Hoo in Kent, attacked and killed John a[tte] Wode in August 1506.[123] He was indicted at the session of the peace in Canterbury on 22 September and pleaded not guilty. The jury was called for the following day, but before it was sworn Pulham claimed that after the court recessed the previous day, he 'took the sanctuary and privilege of the prior and brothers of the hospital of St John of Jerusalem in England by reason of his aforesaid felony and for the tuition and salvation of his life, because he placed his hands on a certain John Rawson, knight, a brother of the hospital . . . and grabbed and held him by his clothes asking the same John . . . for the tuition, sanctuary and privilege of the aforesaid hospital'. Pulham held on to Rawson until he was dragged away against his will, and he asked to be restored to sanctuary. The court ignored Pulham's action and the record notes that despite his claim they continued with the process of swearing the jury, which promptly found Pulham guilty. Pulham then claimed benefit of clergy and Robert Wodeward appeared as ordinary.[124] The justices gave Pulham the book but 'he read nothing nor was at all literate'. John Lucas asked for execution but the justices wished to be advised and remanded Pulham to gaol until the session of the peace at Maidstone in January 1507. Instead, Pulham appeared next in King's Bench on 26 June 1507 where he once again claimed benefit of clergy and the court once again gave him a book. This time he read *ut clericus*, and without further comment the court delivered him to William Southwell of Westminster.

On one level, this is a fairly bizarre case. Pulham's attempt to claim sanctuary seems to reflect the application of the principle that benefit of clergy could be claimed below the gallows to sanctuary: Brooke reports a reading in the time of Henry VII which argued that if a man escaped after sentencing and sought sanctuary he could have it, since his life would be in jeopardy during a long imprisonment, and the rescue of William Johnson above demonstrates a feeling that sanctuary should be available right to the moment of execution.[125] As well as being theoretically innovative, however, Pulham's was a practically challenging claim, since it's not clear what he was trying to achieve. Did he want to be given back to Rawson to be brought to the house? To remain in his custody until he abjured? Though it's possible to speculate on the ways in which Pulham's claim could be argued in the law, it seems likely that his main aim was to cause confusion and to delay

[123] TNA KB27/984 rex m. 4 [images 220, 221]. His victim actually died the following day. McSheffrey, *Seeking Sanctuary*, 83–111 uses this case to elaborate on the Hospitallers' connection to sanctuary.

[124] Wodeward was a weightier figure than many of the ordinaries who filled this role, who were often parish priests or chaplains. Described as 'decretorum doctor', his commission gave him broad authority to hear cases in the diocese, including the authority to purge clerks convict and release them, rather than just the authority to receive them, as most commissions did.

[125] This argument had earlier been made by the canonists, but doesn't seem to have been settled at canon law either. See Helmholz, *Ius Commune*, pp. 32–33. Brooke, *Sanctuary*, 11. The fact that the point was made at a reading may indicate that it was new at this date.

execution. The court, however, saw no validity to the claim at all; unlike other thin claims we've seen it did not even remand him to be advised, it just moved swiftly along. When Pulham performed so very dismally in the reading test, it had the option of moving to execution. This decision would not have been surprising: we've seen that the justices could be lenient with non-violent offences, but Pulham committed homicide, if not murder.[126] Instead the justices chose to shuffle him back to prison and on to Westminster. It is possible that in the intervening nine months Pulham worked hard to learn to read; he certainly had every incentive, and there are other (much earlier) examples of felons learning to read in prison. But if he did, it was because the justices had given him that option, and quite possibly, because they expected that Southwell would take him more readily than Wodeward. They may also have been influenced by Pulham's companion, Ralph Toker.

Unusual as Pulham's strategy was, he did not undertake it alone. In chapter 3 we saw Toker's abjuration from two different Kentish churches in August 1506, but his story did not end there.[127] On 26 November 1506 writs issued to both coroners to send the records of his abjurations to King's Bench, and Toker appeared there on 26 June 1507, the same day as Pulham.[128] The court rehearsed the first abjuration and asked Toker if there was any reason why execution should not be carried out.[129] Toker then claimed that on 22 September 1506 in the castle of Canterbury, he 'seized a certain knight of the order of St John of Jerusalem in England called John Rawson and put his hands corporally on the same John for immunity and tuition of the privilege of St John of Jerusalem in England' until he was removed 'vi et armis' and against his will by certain unknown men.[130] He asked to be restored to the privilege. Though his language is slightly different from Pulham's, the actions and logic are the same, and Rawson was apparently grabbed by both men on the same day. Toker makes no reference to the session of the peace that was the context for this claim, though it seems likely that he had been found in the country, arrested and brought to the castle for the session.[131] Though the court had completely dismissed this claim when Pulham made it, the same claim seems to have caused Toker to be brought to King's Bench, and once there, not only did he advance his claim, but he stated that he did not wish to respond on the previous abjuration but completely rejected it, thus putting all his hopes on the knight of St John. Hobart asked for execution on the previous abjuration, but the court was

126 The inquisition stated that he had killed a[tte] Wode feloniously with a pikestaff to the right side of the head. There was no claim of malice or murder but there were also no obvious mitigating factors such as a fight.

127 See p. 88.

128 TNA KB9/442 m. 17, 19 [images 35, 39].

129 Presumably because it had been established that only the first abjuration was valid: see p. 104.

130 TNA KB27/984 rex m. 12 [images 220, 221].

131 Though there is no indication elsewhere that the two men knew each other, it may not be a coincidence that Pulham was from Hoo and Toker headed to the isolated isle of Sheppey after his first abjuration.

concerned enough about the claim to consult with the serjeants and the king's attorney before concluding that the plea was indeed insufficient in law. Nevertheless, rather than proceeding to execution, the court then asked Toker if he was a clerk or not.[132] Toker responded that he was indeed a clerk, whereupon William Southwell appeared, Toker was given the book, and he read *ut clericus*. Though it now seemed that Toker would follow Pulham to the Abbey, John Hale appeared to argue that Toker had previously been convicted of felony at the session of the peace in Essex (though the specific place was left blank) and had been delivered to the bishop of London as a clerk convict. The court ordered the justices for Essex to return their record to King's Bench by 13 October 1507, and there, for the moment, the case rested. Toker finally re-appeared in King's Bench on 5 November 1509 in the custody of the marshal of the Marshalsea. Both abjurations were rehearsed and he presented a pardon dated 3 October. Like other clergy claimants he benefitted from the pardon on the accession of Henry VIII, but this resolution is as odd as the various other elements of the case, because seven men were covered by the pardon.[133] Toker's case makes it clear again that the justices were far from anxious to execute felons: his first failed abjuration was enough for execution under the law, but he worked his way through a second, a highly imaginative third bid for sanctuary, an offer of benefit of clergy from the court, and an apparent previous claim of clergy, before making his way back onto the street with a pardon three years and three months after his odyssey began. The case also makes it clear that there was a fair amount of confusion about what constituted legitimate sanctuary in the first decade of the century. It is a reasonable assumption that whether or not Pulham and Toker knew each other before their respective crimes, they had discussed possible escape routes while waiting to go before the court—since Toker was the more experienced criminal and abjurer, he seems like a likely candidate for initiating the idea. The brisk dismissal of Pulham's claim in the record suggests that the justices didn't take the idea seriously at first, but the second claim gave them pause and inclined them to send both men to King's Bench for a safer determination.

Though John a[tte] Plough did not demonstrate the ingenuity of Pulham and Toker, he was no less skillful in navigating the system. A[tte] Plough was indicted twice at the gaol delivery of Aylesbury on 6 March 1507. The first indictment was for the theft of a horse on 4 August 1506, and when asked how he wished to plead, a[tte] Plough claimed that on 25 August 1506, while he was being removed from the Breadstreet Compter to Newgate by the serjeants at mace, he escaped and took sanctuary in the Greyfriars for earlier felonies, but the serjeants at mace removed him against his will. He 'refused the laws of the lord king and asked that he be restored to his sanctuary'.[134] A[tte] Plough's second indictment claimed that along

[132] si ipse clericus sit necne.

[133] Including John Donyngton and Thomas David ap Howell, pp. 125, 171.

[134] TNA KB9/444 m. 22 [image 44].

with Hugh Bradbury he broke the close and home of Joan Iwardby at Quainton on 23 July 1506 and stole a horse worth 40s belonging to Elenere Cutlard, widow. A[tte] Plough related the same claim as in the previous indictment, and Bradbury claimed that he too had been taken from sanctuary, in his case from St Martin at Hoddesdon. Bradbury did not give a date for his capture, simply stating that it was during the twenty-second year of Henry VII, but he also 'refused the laws of the lord king and claimed his privilege'.[135] The court pressed them and asked them separately if they wished to respond to the felony, but they both answered that 'they did not nor did either of them wish to respond to the aforesaid felony'.[136] Since they would not respond to the felony, Thomas Pigot asked that both be hanged, an odd request, since the usual punishment for a refusal to plead was *peine fort et dure*.[137]

Both men appeared in King's Bench in May. Bradbury switched his argument, claiming that the house in Hoddesdon was parcel of St Martin le Grand, and that the sanctuary there had the same privileges as in St Martins. In response John Mervyn argued that the abbot of Westminster (who was seised of St Martin le Grand) had no such sanctuary in Hoddesdon, that Bradbury was not taken from sanctuary, and that the house in which he took sanctuary was not a sanctuary. The abbot was given until 6 July to bring his 'charters, writings and muniments for his rights and titles'. He appeared the following Easter term and certified that he had no sanctuary in Hoddesdon, relinquishing any such right. This was a fairly through disavowal, without any of the language of saving possible rights that appears elsewhere, and it suggests that Bradbury had indeed invented the claim or that he was a thoroughly unsavoury character, or both. Bradbury finally pleaded not guilty, and the jury was called for June 1508, though there is no record of a verdict.

When a[tte] Plough in turn appeared in King's Bench he pleaded not guilty. After some delays a jury was called for Michelmas 1508 unless the case was first heard before the justices at the assizes at Aylesbury in July 1508, at which point a[tte] Plough was bailed.[138] He did not appear at Westminster for the Michelmas term, and his pledges appeared to explain that at the Aylesbury assizes he was indicted for breaking the close and home of Joan Iwardby, widow, on 30 July 1506 and stealing a gilded chalice worth 5 marks and a dun horse worth 40s from Elene Cutlard at Little Marlowe.[139] Though the indictment had changed somewhat, a[tte] Plough had not, for he made yet another claim of sanctuary. At the assizes

[135] Caryll reports that his refusal to plead was because the sanctuary was in Hertfordshire, but the record does not mention this and focuses solely on the status of the house: *Caryll's Reports*, vol. 2, p. 553.

[136] TNA KB27/984 rex m. 8 [images 212, 213, 197d].

[137] Without a plea there could be no verdict and without a verdict there could not be a sentence of hanging.

[138] TNA KB27/983 rex m. 18 [images 205, 187d, 188d].

[139] It is not clear if this is a revised version of the indictment in KB9, or if a[tte] Plough had indeed returned to steal from Iwardby and Cutlard again a week later.

> he said that he refused the law and twelve men and also that he is a privileged man, because he says that 14 July 1508 he took the church of St Magnus in London for tuition and salvation for felonies previously committed by the same John. Asked what he wished to say or allege for himself regarding the aforesaid felonies, he said that he wished to say nothing more nor did he wish to relinquish his privilege.

Pigot, predictably, argued that he did not have to respond to this claim and asked that a[tte] Plough 'be adjudged to death'. A[tte] Plough stuck to his claim, but the court agreed with Pigot. Asked, finally, 'if he wished to speak or to respond finally to the premises', a[tte] Plough 'said no, but he said that he was a clerk and asked for benefit of clergy'. Richard Hawardyn, ordinary for the bishop of Lincoln, appeared and a[tte] Plough finally read *ut clericus*, and was branded and delivered. Though the record does not specify, he was presumably only a clerk convict, since through all his machinations he had neither confessed to nor been convicted of a crime. His pledges, however, referred to the record of his conviction at the assize when they asked the justices of King's Bench to accept this as a reason for his non-appearance.

John a[tte] Plough's case shows many of the same characteristics as Pulham and Toker: the attempt to claim sanctuary mid-process, the use of more than one sanctuary, the explicit rejection of the king's law, and the default to benefit of clergy when the claim of sanctuary clearly was not going to work. But the cases also demonstrate an extraordinary willingness on the part of the courts, both local and central, to examine claims of sanctuary carefully, no matter how thin or how novel they were, and not just to allow felons multiple means of avoiding execution, but when necessary to prompt them to new claims, even when the felons were clearly not good men who'd made a single bad choice, but repeat offenders.

The courts' willingness to give accused felons room to navigate also appears in the much simpler case of Thomas David ap Howell, a yeoman from Westminster, who also began his journey through the legal system with a claim to sanctuary. At the gaol delivery of Newgate in May 1508 he claimed that on 20 December 1507 he had taken sanctuary in the cemetery of the hospital of St John of Jerusalem in London, and had been taken out against his will.[140] He asked to be restored and pleaded not guilty to the felony. Thomas Roberts for the king argued that ap Howell was at large on 20 December, and the jury agreed with Roberts. Ap Howell then claimed clergy, the ordinary for the bishop of London appeared, and ap Howell read *ut clericus*. However, John Chauncy claimed that ap Howell had been convicted of a felony and given benefit of clergy in Bristol on 10 August 1504. This was normally the signal for the court to order the justices on the circuit to deliver their record, but in this case 'because the justices did not know if the aforesaid John Chauncy's allegation is true or not' Chauncy was told to bring his record and ap

[140] TNA KB9/960 m. 142 [image not on AALT].

Howell was remanded to gaol until the next gaol delivery in October 1508.[141] It is rare to see the court explicitly question the truth of a statement made on either side, and this suggests that it was deeply skeptical of Chauncy's allegation: although it seems plausible, especially with the specific date given, the court was perhaps suspicious that it was too plausible that a man with a Welsh name had been previously convicted in Bristol. In any case the justices wished to be advised, and in October ap Howell was recommitted to Newgate. The Bristol record does not seem to have been produced, and on 5 November 1509 ap Howell appeared in the custody of the marshal of the Marshalsea to present a pardon—the same pardon as John Donyngton and Ralph Toker.

All six of these men were quite clearly repeat offenders, and between them they had committed homicide, burglary from homes and churches, and highway robbery. They were not obvious candidates for either mitigation or rehabilitation, as Wolmer's career demonstrates. Their claims were often flimsy at best, and in some cases they were testing the relationships between various processes in new ways. This raises intriguing questions about where the claimants got their knowledge of the law: were these simply hail Mary attempts to disrupt the inexorable movement towards execution which sometimes happened to work; did career criminals develop a good enough working knowledge of the law to have a sense for opportunity, or were they getting outside advice? We simply don't have the evidence to answer this, but the record does make it clear that the courts were surprisingly willing to entertain new arguments, many of which seem to have been bumped to King's Bench for further consideration. This suggests that even if we can only see a small proportion of the activity around sanctuary in the King's Bench records, we're seeing much of the innovation and development.

5. Conclusion

We saw in the Durham and Beverley registers that though the numbers claiming sanctuary there fluctuated, there was no clear pattern of either increase or decrease. The same is true of the instances of sanctuary in the common law records (fig. 5.4). The number of men claiming sanctuary in the chartered sanctuaries, religious houses and parish churches fluctuated wildly, and there is no evidence of any pattern other than necessity and proximity. But given the dominance of *Stafford's Case* in the literature this evidence of the widespread use of sanctuary throughout the country and throughout the reign is significant. Sanctuary continued to play its traditional role in providing a breathing space for those who found themselves in

141 TNA KB27/993 rex m. 17 [images 260d, 280, 282].

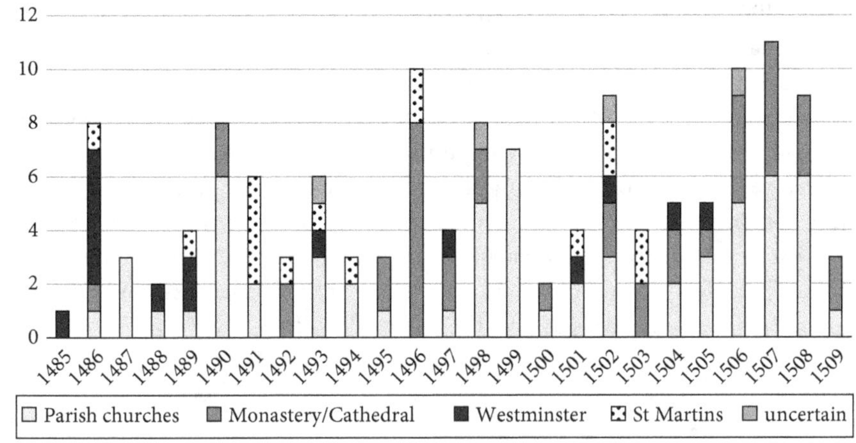

Figure 5.4 Recorded sanctuary claims in the reign of Henry VII by type*
*Data collected from TNA KB27 and KB9 rolls.

a tight spot, whether they could leave freely after a verdict of self-defense or had to organize an acceptable narrative with which to face the legal process.

For these men, and the occasional woman, whether they were in a chartered sanctuary or a parish church, sanctuary was a passing moment, one which might not even register in the official record of their crime, but its fleetness was not a reflection of its importance. Some claimants arrived at the sanctuary in dramatic fashion, like John Hall, who defended himself with his bow to the door and beyond.[142] Many arrived years after the crime they committed, and the immediate impetus for their claim is not obvious. And some clearly took advantage of a moment of opportunity to wrap their arms around the banner of St. John or the person of one of his knights and hope at least to postpone the day of reckoning. And the remarkable thing is that many of them did. Even when a sanctuary claim was not ostensibly successful and the claimant was not restored to his church or to the highway, many were remanded to gaol, delivered to the ordinaries, pardoned, or all three, often after some substantial period of time in a county gaol or the Marshalsea. And though there was clearly a lot of discussion about sanctuary in the courts in this period, there was not a lot of decision-making. Even when the reports point us to something that looks like a principle, that pleading sanctuary rather than pleading to the felony would lead to the *peine fort*, for example, practice paints rather a different picture.

Though the evidence here is less clear than with benefit of clergy, there are at least hints in the new concern with indictments in the North that accused felons in

[142] TNA KB9/419 m. 7 [image 12].

the late 1490s and the early years of the sixteenth century were feeling the pinch of the criminal justice system, and that common lawyers were paying closer attention to the ways in which sanctuary could mitigate criminal punishment, whether alone or as part of a bigger strategy. Kebell was not the only common lawyer who saw the possibility, and the desirability, of punishment without execution. Many of his brethren went to extraordinary lengths to avoid the ultimate punishment without letting convicted felons roam free. Sanctuary added to the options available to accused felons as they tried desperately to escape execution, but it also added to the options available to common lawyers as they determined how to respond, and both sides pushed the boundaries of what the law would allow.

6

Benefit of Clergy 1509–1529

Though benefit of clergy had clearly become part of the legal mainstream in the reign of Henry VII, it remained somewhat controversial in the political realm. The early years of his son's reign saw a tussle for control of both the political narrative and the practical working of the privilege. The historiography of this period is dominated by a statute passed in 1512, which limited the crimes for which clergy could be claimed, and another high-profile case, *Standish's Case*, which supports the argument that benefit of clergy was under siege. As we will see, both tell us a good deal about the political mood in the early years of the new reign, but, as with *Stafford's Case*, they don't tell us much about the regular operation of the courts. They did, however, have an effect on that operation as the justices, led once again by Chief Justice Fyneux, recognized that they needed to respond to the concerns about benefit of clergy reflected in the 1512 statute and in *Standish's Case* by managing the privilege more actively. In the years around 1520 they set out to track criminous clerks more effectively in order to curtail the worst of the traditional abuses of the system: successful claims by repeat offenders, bigamists, and failed abjurers. The courts and the government balanced this strictness, however, by exploring ways to maintain and improve their ability to provide effective mitigation, most notably by the more frequent use of pardons as part of their growing repertoire. Fyneux and his colleagues did not achieve all they set out to do, but by the end of that decade the number of men claiming benefit of clergy had increased, while fewer hardened criminals were using it to avoid execution. Though it may be too grand to hail this as a major reform of the criminal justice system, at the very least it was a good step in the right direction.

1. The 1512 Statute, *Standish's Case*, and the Kyng Burglary

This whole sequence of events began with a statute of 1512 in which benefit of clergy was taken from laymen who committed murder or felony in any church or holy place, or who with malice aforethought robbed or murdered anyone on the highway or in his own house, though it was clearly left in place for those in orders who committed the same crimes. The statute was to last until the next parliament.[1]

[1] *SR*, III. 49. 4 Hen. VIII c. 2. This was the first statute to explicitly remove benefit of clergy from the more heinous felonies, and it would be followed by similar statutes in the later part of the reign: see p. 262.

The King's Felons. Margaret McGlynn, Oxford University Press. © Margaret McGlynn 2023.
DOI: 10.1093/oso/9780192887689.003.0007

Cavill has argued convincingly that some version of the measure was introduced in the parliament of 1510 but did not succeed, and that the passage of the statute in 1512 was contentious.[2] He demonstrates that the bill originally proposed that the restriction should be applied to those in minor orders as well as laymen, that it required the ordinaries to provide proof of ordination by a date set by the court for those claiming exemption, and that it was originally intended to be permanent.[3] When the statute came up for renewal in 1515, the opposition visible only in the editing of the 1512 bill spilled over into the public forum. According to Serjeant John Caryll, our source for these events, on 4 February 1515 the abbot of Winchcomb, Richard Kidderminster, preached a sermon at St. Paul's Cross which claimed that the 1512 act was 'utterly against the law of God and the liberties of Holy Church' and that the makers of the act, both spiritual and temporal, had incurred the censures of the Church.[4] In support of his claim he apparently had a papal decretal which said that clerks in both minor and major orders were exempt from 'temporal punishment for criminal causes before temporal judges' because minor orders were also 'holy'.[5] This suggests that there was a concern that the renewal would not simply extend the 1512 statute, but would return to its original terms. Caryll claims that the Commons asked the king to investigate, and Henry appointed both theologians and canonists to debate the matter at Blackfriars before the justices. Henry Standish, the provincial of the Franciscans, emerged as the most powerful voice arguing on behalf of the statute. He claimed that bringing criminous clerks before the temporal judges, as had customarily been done, was consonant with the law of God, and he responded to the argument that it went against the decretal by pointing out that the decretal had never been received in England, and so was not binding. Standish then bested his opponent, whom Caryll described as 'the principal cause of the schism between the spirituality and the temporalty touching the conventing of clerks before temporal judges, … [who] had taken upon himself to confound all those who held any opinion to the contrary' on scripture.[6] According to Caryll, many of the knights, having heard the arguments, told the bishops that they should cause Abbot Kidderminster to renounce his sermon, but they refused and claimed that they were bound to support him, and there the matter rested.

Thus far the fight seems to have come from Kidderminster, with the bishops supporting him out of clerical solidarity rather than with any real conviction. Standish

[2] P.R. Cavill, 'A Perspective on the Church-State Confrontation of 1515: The Passage of 4 Henry VIII, c. 2', *Journal of Ecclesiastical History* 63 (2012), pp. 661–670.

[3] Cavill, 'Church-State Confrontation of 1515', pp. 664–669.

[4] *Caryll's Reports*, vol. 2, p. 684.

[5] In 1514 Leo X renewed constitutions of Boniface VIII and Clement V which emphasized that the laity did not have authority over the clergy: Bellamy notes that the original decrees had not had much impact, so it's unlikely that Leo's did, but as we've seen, fourteenth-century common lawyers were willing to quote Boniface and it would not be surprising if the constitutions contributed to clerical feelings, even if they were not officially received: see p. 23; Bellamy, *Criminal Law and Society*, pp. 133–134.

[6] Caryll doesn't name Standish's opponent.

was clearly in the right as far as the history of the privilege in England went. If that had been the end of the matter, the statute might have been renewed with little problem. But while this argument was going on, the Hunne case was developing and both clerical morality and clerical prerogatives were suddenly issues of vital concern.[7] While the inquest was sitting which would indict Dr. Horsey, the bishop of London's chancellor, Standish was called before Convocation in Michelmas term and asked, among other points, whether a temporal judge could summon a clerk and whether minor orders were holy orders.[8] Standish, concerned that this was payback for his arguments against Kidderminster and afraid of a conviction for heresy, went to the king. The clergy were quick to disavow any connection between the questions and the earlier debate. They claimed that the questions came from Standish's subsequent lectures at St. Paul's, suggesting that Standish didn't let the matter drop, and they asked the king for his help 'in accordance with his coronation oath, and also in avoidance of the danger of the censures of Holy Church'.[9] The Lords and the justices, having heard about these developments, then asked the king to 'maintain his temporal jurisdiction according to his coronation oath' and the king in turn went to John Veysey, the dean of his chapel, for advice. Veysey advised the king that the English practice 'may well stand with the law of God and the liberties of Holy Church' and the king then called a second meeting at Blackfriars, this one attended by the justices, the king's spiritual and temporal counsel and some members of parliament. Standish was again questioned about his opinions, and answered this time that 'minor orders are in one respect called holy, and in another respect not holy' and that 'the conventing of clerks before a secular judge is not against positive divine law'.[10] The spiritual counsel argued against the second point, but Standish and Veysey rebutted them with some force. The justices listened to both sides and then concluded that all those present in the Convocation which had awarded the citation against Standish were well within the case of *praemunire*.[11] This clear warning seems to have had its intended effect, and the Lords temporal and spiritual, many of the Commons, the justices, and the king's counsel gathered at Baynard's Castle to watch Wolsey kneel before the king and disavow any argument which might smack of *praemunire*. The whole sequence of events seems to have roused the clergy, however, and Wolsey was bold enough to ask that the question be sent to Rome for consideration, to which the king responded that he thought the answers he had heard from Standish and Veysey were good enough. The bishops were not willing to let the matter drop: Warham also asked the king,

[7] For an overview of the Hunne case, see W.R. Cooper, 'Richard Hunne', *Reformation* 1 (1996), pp. 221–251.

[8] *Caryll's Reports*, vol. 2, p. 686.

[9] *Caryll's Reports*, vol. 2, p. 687.

[10] *Caryll's Reports*, vol. 2, p. 688. Standish was questioned on four other points, but these two were most central to the statute and the privilege.

[11] *Caryll's Reports*, vol. 2, p. 690.

on behalf of the clergy, to send the question to Rome, making an oblique reference to Becket, while Fox, now bishop of Winchester, suggested that Standish would not maintain his opinions. This seems to have exasperated the judges, who, at least by Caryll's account, had remained silent throughout the debate. Fyneux pointed out that 'the conventing of clerks had been supported by various holy kings, and many good holy fathers of the Church had been obedient and content with the usage of the law in this point', adding that the bishops had no authority by canon law to deal with felony in any case.[12] The archbishop denied this, but with little force, and Fyneux went on to point out that when a clerk was committed to the ordinary by the temporal judge, 'you have no authority by your law, when he comes to you, to make a determination as to this murder or felony'. This is of a piece with his arguments in 1500 and seems to have been generally accepted by this time.[13] Caryll does not elaborate on the point however, and the king cut short the discussion by decreeing that the law would remain as it stood. The clergy's claims were denied, but the offending statute lapsed.[14]

This fascinating piece of political theatre highlights the long-standing tensions around the jurisdictional boundaries between Church and State. The question of a king's authority over the Church had been the third rail in European politics since the investiture controversy, as the reference to Becket demonstrates, but like most third rails its relationship to practical politics was complex and inconsistent. Most churchmen were ready to defend the independence of the Church in theory, but could differ widely in practice, as Kidderminster and Standish demonstrated. On this specific issue some, like Kidderminster, were set on fighting for the blanket immunity of all clerks, while others clearly felt that it was in the best interest of the Church to do the opposite, emphasizing the distance between major orders and minor to protect clerics from the harm of association with those who were

[12] *Caryll's Reports*, vol. 2, p. 691.

[13] Spelman reports a comment by Brudenell and Coningsby JJ that if one is committed to the ordinary on account of his clergy and breaks the prison, it is felony, for he is committed to him as a felon attaint or convict, and so he is in his keeping for felony: *Spelman's Reports*, vol. 1, p. 66. Coningsby claimed that this was adjudged by all the justices in the time of Henry VII, probably thinking of Fyneux's comment in 1500. Similarly, the abbot of St Albans was indicted for the escape of a prisoner who was convicted and delivered to him as ordinary. The abbot argued that the man was attainted by his own confession, without any indictment or judgement against him, and so he thought he could release him, presumably after purgation, at his own discretion. The justices, however, argued that even if the indictment were insufficient, if the prisoner is committed by judges with sufficient authority, the abbot is charged with him upon peril of forfeiture, 'for it shall not lie in his mouth to annul what they have admitted': *Rpts from the Time of Henry VIII*, 1, pl. 40, p. 56. The prisoner's confession would make him a clerk attaint. Fyneux's distinction between murder and felony is, strictly speaking, tautological, but there was clearly a growing recognition in this period that pre-meditated murder was, or should be, thought of differently from the regular run of felonies: K.J. Kesselring, *Making Murder Public: Homicide in Early Modern England, 1480–1680* (Oxford: Oxford University Press, 2019), pp. 19–32. This is more clearly reflected in the changing weight of felony punishments by the middle of the century, see p. 332.

[14] Standish's case was dismissed from Convocation, and he went on to become bishop of St. Asaph in 1518.

claiming clergy only to avoid punishment for felony and murder.[15] The events at Blackfriars and Baynard's Castle were as much, if not more, about tensions within the clerical establishment as about tensions between the laity and the spirituality. As we saw in chapter 4, even bishops close to the centre of government could find themselves on both sides of this issue, and men like Fox and Warham were trying to square a very thorny circle.

Standish's Case throws a fascinating light on important political issues, but it leaves the regular administration of the law very much in shadow. The King's Bench records indicate that little, if any, attention was paid in the courts to the relationship between major and minor orders, and even less to the nature of the bishops' jurisdiction. It is notable that the justices played virtually no role in the discussions at Blackfriars and Baynard's Castle: the only issue that prompted Fyneux to speak was a practical one concerning felony. The high politics and high drama of *Standish's Case* contribute to a sense that benefit of clergy was in decline in the early years of Henry VIII's reign, but once again, the situation was rather more complicated than that.

Standish's Case had nothing to do with the practical issues that concerned the courts in those years, but the political tensions it reflected had a temporarily chilling effect on the ways in which the law was administered. Surviving returns from the circuits in these years suggest at first glance that the 1512 statute had an immediate impact (fig. 6.1).[16] Although the numbers on a year-by-year and county-by-county basis are quite varied, when taken together there is a clear and sharp decline in the number of clerks convict delivered in 1512. The obvious conclusion is that the statute was successful, but given that it was not passed until the end of 1512 and that the numbers rebound in 1513 and thereafter continue to rise fairly steadily, this doesn't seem like the best conclusion. It's also striking that there is no comparable increase in the deliveries of clerks convict after the statute lapsed in 1515.

A handful of cases in King's Bench and on the circuits suggest an alternative and somewhat counter-intuitive explanation for this pattern; that the discussions surrounding the statute had a greater impact on the use of benefit of clergy than the statute itself, and that neither accused felons nor the justices were entirely certain of the statute's implications. For example, Hugh Boswell was convicted of robbery at the gaol delivery of Northampton in March 1511.[17] He claimed clergy and

[15] Pope Leo's bull of 1516, recognizing that laymen might take minor orders to avoid criminal punishment and ordering that in order to be able to claim immunity they must take minor orders and the order of subdeacon together, or obtain an ecclesiastical benefice, demonstrates that the pope was keenly aware of the political costs of a blanket approach to clerical immunity. The timing suggests that the bull was prompted by *Standish's Case*, but it does not seem to have been implemented. Thomas Rymer, *Foedera, Conventiones, Literae*, (London, 1704–35), vol. 13, pp. 532–533.

[16] We will discuss the circuit returns in more detail below, see pp. 187–190, 203–206.

[17] TNA KB9/462 m. 28 [image 56]. Boswell also alleged that he had left to go to London 6 years earlier, first to Ludgate and then Henry Wiatt.

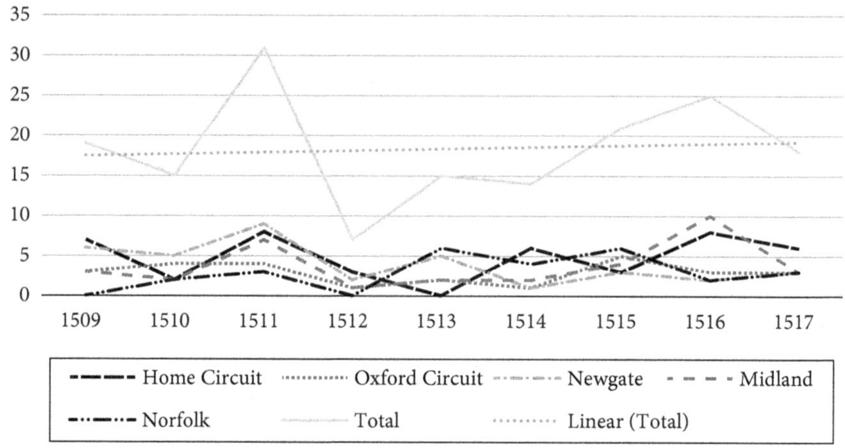

Figure 6.1 Clerks convict and clerks attaint in the circuit records 1509–1517*
*See note 45 for the circuit lists that provide most of this data.

was branded and delivered to the bishop of Lincoln. Two years later, in February 1513, Boswell was convicted at the same gaol delivery of breaking into the parish church of Geddington.[18] When he was asked why execution should not be carried out, he said 'that he is a privileged man in orders in the house of the Carmelites of Alnwick and he took the orders of benet and colet'.[19] If Boswell's claim was accurate he should not have been affected by the 1512 statute, but he was not only looking to be delivered to the same bishop, he was facing the same justices of gaol delivery, Humphrey Conyngesby and Guy Palmes. The court was obviously unconvinced by his claim, and 'on this he was asked if he wished to say more or not: he said that he took the orders of subdeacon and deacon in the diocese of Carlisle'. This suggests that Boswell was aware of the discussions around limiting benefit of clergy in 1512 but not clear on the actual provisions of the statute: he thought that upping his claim to major orders would help him, but also pushed the investigation of the claim to one of the further dioceses of the country to buy the time he needed to come up with other options.[20]

While the justices were certainly better informed on the language of the statute, they seem to have been equally uncertain about its implications, perhaps because it was only valid until the next parliament. This influenced their actions. John Hogges

[18] TNA KB9/462 m. 27 [image 54].

[19] Benet and colet were colloquial terms for the minor order of acolyte, the highest of the four minor orders: see e.g. *Works of John Knox* vol. 1 ed. David Laing (Edinburgh: James Thin, 1895), no. v. https://ccel.org/ccel/knox/works1.viii.html. By the later Middle Ages all the minor orders were usually conferred together.

[20] John Jenour argued that the plea was insufficient, but the court wished to be advised, set 16 July to hear arguments and remanded Boswell to prison. He later appeared at King's Bench and made a lengthy claim to sanctuary. See pp. 217–218.

and Robert Tykhill, for example, were both convicted in the Marshalsea on 2 July 1515: Hogges had been part of a gang of 13 who broke into the house of John Lyons burglarously by night on 22 May, while Tykhill, along with several other men, stole nine horses and a variety of clothing and silver over the course of two thefts in April and May.[21] According to the 1512 statute Hogges should have been ineligible for benefit of clergy unless he was in orders, but Tykhill should have been eligible; neither seems to have had a previous conviction. When they both made their claim, however, rather than denying Hogges and/or looking for evidence of ordination, or delivering Tykhill to Westminster, the court wished to be advised and remanded them to gaol repeatedly, finally allowing both to be delivered in Michelmas 1516.[22] Something similar was happening on the circuits. William Stephenson was indicted in York in March 1514 for breaking into the house of his mistress by night the previous December, and strangling her.[23] Under the 1512 statute Stephenson should not have been eligible for clergy, since there is no mention of him being in orders of any kind. The court hesitated over his claim: though he read *ut clericus* in March 1514, the justices remanded him to gaol until the August gaol delivery, then to March and July 1515 before finally allowing his delivery to the ordinary. No reasons are given for the delays either in King's Bench or on circuit, but it seems likely that the justices did not want to apply the new statute and waited until it lapsed to make a final decision in these cases.

This provides quite a different perspective on the numbers above. The decline in claims of clergy in 1510, probably in response to the discussions around the abortive statute of that year, is followed by a quick rebound in 1511. Claims dipped even more sharply in 1512 as that statute was fought over, and then rebounded through the later part of the decade. Given the cases above, it's likely that the drop in deliveries between 1512 and 1515 reflects a substantial number of putative clerks sitting in county gaols while the justices of gaol delivery waited to see how the statutory change played out. This is supported by the increase in 1515–1516, which reflects the eventual delivery of those men to the ordinaries rather than simply a jump in the number of claims made.

The controversy over limiting benefit of clergy in 1510, 1512, and 1515 demonstrates that while there was an appetite for reform, there was no agreement on what that reform should be. The statute passed and in operation from 1512–1515 looked as though it was reducing access to clergy, but its provisions were irrelevant for all but a small number of those convicted of the worst felonies. The experiences of Hogges and Stephenson demonstrate that even for that small number, the justices might be unwilling to apply the statute while there was the possibility

21 TNA KB27/1016 rex m. 18 [images 231, 232, 214d, 215d].

22 A Robert Tykhill had a subsequent criminal career, though there's no evidence that it was the same person. See p. 284.

23 TNA KB9/969 m. 78 [image not on AALT].

of waiting it out. Thus while the justices were willing to argue for the right of the secular authority to manage benefit of clergy in *Standish's Case*, it is clear that they were not impressed by the remedy produced by parliament, largely because it did not solve the actual problems in the system. To understand these we need to turn from the theatre of Blackfriars and Baynard's Castle to the rather mundane burglary of Henry Kyng's house at Beckenham in Kent in December 1511.

The burglary of Kyng's house was exactly the kind of crime which prompted the 1512 statute. Thomas Wynter alias Wymerton, Richard Layceter alias Hankyn, and John Courteney alias Tanner were all indicted at the delivery of the castle of Canterbury in March 1512 for attacking Kyng and stealing a horse worth 20s, a robe, six silver spoons worth 40s, and 40s in cash.[24] Wynter, a London chaplain, was found guilty and claimed benefit of clergy, but he was remanded to prison without reading. The record of his conviction was delivered to King's Bench on 17 June 1513, and Wynter appeared on 27 June, claimed clergy once again, and was delivered to Westminster Abbey.[25] Layceter and Courteney, both London yeomen, were not convicted at Canterbury, but appeared in King's Bench in May 1512.[26] Courteney was found not guilty on 6 October; Layceter was found guilty on 2 November and claimed clergy, but William Fermour argued that he had previously been delivered to the bishop of London in August 1511 at the gaol delivery of Colchester.[27] Layceter pointed out that the court had no record which demonstrated that he had been convicted as Fermour alleged, so the court promptly sent a writ to the justices of gaol delivery to provide the record and remanded Layceter to gaol. The record appeared quickly and confirmed the alleged delivery.[28] On 22 November the King's Bench judges ordered Layceter to be hanged. Thus far the outcomes for the burglars have been varied but typical: one acquittal, one successful claim of clergy by a chaplain, and one execution of a repeat claimant. There were, however, at least two other men involved in the burglary.

Robert Bulkeley, a London yeoman/gentleman, had been convicted of burglary (of a widow) and highway robbery at the session of the peace in Aylesbury in January 1511, and delivered to the bishop of Lincoln.[29] He had made his way from the prison by the end of the year, when he took part in the burglary of Henry Kyng's home.[30] He was indicted for that burglary in January 1512, two months before Wynter, Laycetur, and Courteney, but when his case came to King's Bench

[24] TNA KB9/462 m. 36 [image 72].

[25] TNA KB27/1008 rex m. 11d [images 187d, 188d].

[26] TNA KB27/1003 rex m. 5d [images 181d, 182d].

[27] He appears on the Home circuit return as having been delivered in autumn 1511: TNA KB9/477 m. 35 [image 79].

[28] TNA KB9/964 m. 94 [image not on AALT]. It also demonstrated that Layceter broke into Henry Kyng's home only four months after his delivery to the bishop of London. It is probable that he escaped rather than being purged quite so quickly; see Joseph Draston p. 189 for another speedy recidivist.

[29] TNA KB9/458 m. 103 [image 216].

[30] TNA KB27/1003 rex m. 15d [images 198d, 199d].

he argued that from the time of his birth he was William Bulkeley, not Robert, and pleaded not guilty. A jury in October 1512 disagreed and found him guilty. Bulkeley then claimed clergy, stating that he had taken orders at Conway in the diocese of St. Asaph. The court sent a writ to the bishop to enquire, returnable at the octave of Hilary. The response finally came in Trinity 1513, when the bishop certified that after a diligent search of his records he could confirm that Bulkeley had not been ordained in his diocese, and that the town of Conway was in fact in the diocese of Bangor. The court wished to be advised, and Bulkeley was remanded to Michelmas term.

This narrative is complicated by the fact that there is a contemporary criminal record for a William Bulkeley, also described as a London gentleman. On 5 December 1511 William apparently broke the home of John Codyngton in Surrey by night, attacked John's wife Agnes and their servants, and stole rings, a woman's kyrtle, silver 'tukkinghokes' and cash.[31] This burglary was only five days before the burglary of Henry Kyng's house in Kent, and it could be argued that Robert/William, having made his way out of the bishop of Lincoln's prison, was looking to put some distance between himself and his earlier crimes. The narratives clash, however, since Robert was indicted for his burglary on 13 January 1512 in Maidstone and then delivered to the Marshalsea, while William was indicted for his on 5 February 1512 in Southwark and convicted on 11 March at the gaol delivery of the castle of Guildford. To add to the confusion, at the gaol delivery at Guildford, John Scott argued that William had been previously convicted at Aylesbury (like Robert), and the record of this conviction was delivered to King's Bench in Easter 1513.[32] Thus in Easter 1513 the King's Bench justices were waiting for the response of the bishop of St. Asaph to Robert/William Bulkeley's claim that he had been ordained, and the appearance of William Bulkeley's earlier Aylesbury conviction presumably added to the confusion and the court's hesitation regarding Robert/William's treatment the following term.

There was at least one more felon associated with the Kyng burglary. Richard Cowdale, a London tailor, was included in Robert Bulkeley's indictment in January 1512, but as with the others, he had a longer history of crime. In July 1502 he was convicted at the delivery of Colchester and delivered to the bishop of London, but he was one of the men who escaped from the prison at Bishop's Stortford on 16 March 1503.[33] Cowdale then disappeared from sight until he re-appeared in the Kyng burglary. He appeared at King's Bench in June 1512, where he argued that on 23 December 1511 he was arrested by Morice Clonne, an official of the Marshalsea, in London and brought via London bridge to 'le Roofe Tavern' in Southwark, where

[31] TNA KB9/458 m. 105 [image 220].

[32] TNA KB9/477 m. 35 [image 79]. This is a very unusual notation in the Home circuit list, which also lists him as a clerk convict delivered from Surrey in March 1512.

[33] TNA KB9/431 m. 24 [images 51, 52]. See p. 116.

Clonne proceeded to drink with other officials. Cowdale took advantage of their distraction to escape through the back door of the tavern and take sanctuary at St Mary Overy. The Marshalsea officials and others then came and tried to take him out, but Cowdale said '"I do not wish to leave, but I wish to claim [*custodire*] the privilege of the church for the safe governance of my life and divers felonies" and then he took a post called le church porche in his arms'.[34] This is a vivid image of Cowdale wrapping himself around the church porch, but it did him little good, as the officials dragged him off to the Marshalsea, and the court decided that his claim for sanctuary was not sufficient in law. As usual the reasons aren't given, so it's not clear whether the porch did not count as safe ground, or whether it was because he had already been arrested. The jury called to try his plea returned its guilty verdict in Easter 1513, and he was sentenced to be hanged.

The Kyng burglary and the men who were convicted for it give us a vivid insight into the problems of studying criminal activity in the early years of Henry VIII's reign and the range of options open to the men who operated in the system.[35] It's not clear how the four men ended up in Kent together: all four were Londoners, and while both Laycetur and Cowdale had previously been convicted at Colchester and delivered to the bishop of London, Cowdale had escaped from the prison long before Laycetur got there. They were obviously quite mobile in the south-eastern part of the country, however, with a joint criminal history which stretched across Buckinghamshire, Hertfordshire, Essex, Kent, and London. Wynter seems to have had no prior record, and so he was quickly convicted in Maidstone, but he was not delivered, presumably because the court was waiting to see what happened with Laycetur and Courteney and possibly other accomplices. The other three had much more chequered pasts: though there is often a temptation to see at least some of these felons as the victims of misfortune, Laycetur, Bulkeley, and Cowdale at best had been serially unfortunate, and when taken together were an unprepossessing crew with a joint history of burglary, highway robbery, and targeting widows. All four moved quite quickly through the system. Indicted in March 1512, Laycetur had pleaded in King's Bench by May and was found guilty in November, while Bulkeley and Cowdale, indicted in January, were both heard in King's Bench by early autumn. While Laycetur was dealt with quite quickly, Bulkeley and Cowdale demonstrated more familiarity with the possibilities in the system, the former claiming ordination to buy some time, while the latter made a last desperate attempt at sanctuary. And as unprepossessing as they were, and as unconvincing

[34] TNA KB27/1004 rex m. 4 [images 220, 198d, 199d]. The words 'le churche porche' are added in a different hand.

[35] Only Bulkeley and Cowdale were indicted together for the crime, so it's not obvious in the sources that it was carried out by such a large group. Laycetur, Courteney and Wynter were all indicted on the same day two months later, but their records were not linked: Wynter's indictment notes that he was accompanied in the crime by 'others not yet captured' but makes no reference to the earlier indictments, suggesting that there may have been more than the four or five men involved: TNA KB9/462 m. 36 [image 72].

as their claims were, the court dealt with each one appropriately before moving steadily, but not hastily, to the sentencing of Laycetur and Cowdale in November 1512 and Easter 1513 respectively, and the delivery of Wynter to Westminster in June 1513, most likely after Bulkeley's fate had been determined.

As a group the men demonstrate why there was a constituency at Westminster pressing for harsher penalties in the years before and after 1512. The burglary of the Kyng household by a sizeable gang was the kind of crime envisaged by the statute, and clergy was central to the burglars' strategies: one of them was a chaplain, one was a repeat claimant, the third tried falsely to claim ordination in a distant diocese and the fourth had previously claimed clergy and probably escaped. But, despite the fact that the crime occurred in 1511 and most of them were convicted before the passage of the act at the end of 1512, only Wynter, a first-time offender, was successful in his claim. Laycetur and Cowdale were both hanged, though Bulkeley's fate remains unclear. In other words, the felons were punished in the same way they would have been after the passage of the statute, and the traditional system worked as it was supposed to in this case.

Though the men who attacked Henry Kyng's home were punished, a cluster of Newgate cases from 1510 and 1511 indicates concerns in those years that other repeat offenders might have been slipping through the cracks. Three men convicted at the Newgate gaol delivery between April 1510 and November 1511 faced the allegation that they had previously been convicted and were thus ineligible to claim clergy. John Cholford was convicted of robbery in April 1510, when a previous conviction at Lichfield in Staffordshire was alleged. Cholford's information was delivered to King's Bench in February 1511, he appeared in June 1512, it was determined in October 1512 that there was no such record, and he was branded and delivered to Westminster.[36] David Bowbank was convicted of burglary in October 1510. His information was delivered in July 1512, Fermour admitted on 19 October that no record of a previous conviction was found, and he too was delivered to the Abbey.[37] William Worsley was convicted of multiple burglaries in July 1511, when it was alleged that he had had benefit in Guildford, Surrey. His information appeared in King's Bench in May 1512, but when he appeared in King's Bench in October the justices of gaol delivery in Surrey said that there was no record of a conviction before them and he was delivered.[38] One man who had used sanctuary before claiming clergy found himself subject to a similar level of scrutiny. Robert Savell alias Favell was indicted for theft on 4 August 1511, but when he came before the justices of gaol delivery at Newgate in November he claimed that he had

[36] TNA KB9/456 m. 43 [images 84, 85]; TNA KB27/1004 rex m. 18 [images 252, 253, 226d, 227d, 254, 255].

[37] TNA KB9/963 m. 12 [image not on AALT]; TNA KB 27/1005 rex m. 2 [images 266, 267, 241d].

[38] TNA KB9/458 m. 22 [image 44]; TNA KB27/1005 rex m. 3 [images 268, 269]. James Marten also had a previous conviction alleged at his Newgate conviction on 23 May 1511, but he did not subsequently appear in King's Bench: TNA KB9/963 m. 8 [image not on AALT].

taken sanctuary at the house of St John of Jerusalem in Clerkenwell on 25 July but that John Grene and others took him out violently against his will. He asked to be restored and pleaded not guilty to the felony. The jury rejected his claim for sanctuary and found him guilty, whereupon Savell claimed clergy. John Chauncy for the king then claimed that he had previously been convicted at Banbury in 1503 and he was remanded to gaol. When the case came to King's Bench, Savell claimed clergy again and the prosecution admitted that no record of a previous conviction had been found. Savell was branded and delivered.[39]

These cases stand out for a number of reasons. It is rare to find an unsubstantiated allegation of a previous conviction, and no other such cluster survives in the records. The fact that they all came from Newgate within a short period of time suggests a problem being considered in that court.[40] There was no hurry to look at the cases: it took eight to ten months for the records to be delivered to King's Bench. As the first, Cholford's case moved particularly slowly: it took fourteen months for him to appear, and he is the only one to be remanded at that stage. Once he re-appeared in June 1512 he was right on track with the others, however, and all of them were delivered on 13 and 19 October and 13 November 1512. The timing is significant, for the bill to limit benefit of clergy had been introduced in the session of parliament which ran from 4 February to 30 March 1512 but was lost when the parliament was prorogued; the new bill appeared in the session which ran from 4 November to 20 December, so the examinations and the deliveries occurred, for the most part, in the break between the sessions.[41] Individually, Cholford could be a prime example of inefficiency and delay, but when taken with the other three men, this looks intentional: it suggests that some of the justices were aware of the concerns about repeat offenders, and were looking for ways to manage it within the court system. Knowing that the 1512 bill was working its way through the system for the second time and unsure of what it might provide, the justices decided to deliver these men to the ordinaries forthwith. Without further details we can't know what prompted the removal of these particular cases to King's Bench, but there are three likely explanations: the allegations of previous convictions were true, but the court could not find the records; the allegations were false, but the Crown wanted to avoid the claim of clergy; or the allegations were false, but the Crown wanted to keep the felons in secular custody for some period of time before delivering them

[39] TNA KB9/963 m. 7 [image not on AALT]; TNA KB27/1005 rex m. 3d [images 243d, 244d, 270]. A Robert Favell had been convicted of theft at the gaol delivery of Newgate in February 1502 and his victim alleged that he had previously had benefit of clergy in Banbury coram Thomas Tremayle. Favell was remanded, but there is no resolution to the case. This suggests that the prosecution may have been right in the allegation and wrong on the date, or that Favell may have been dogged by the rumour of an earlier conviction: TNA KB9/431 m. 87 [image 179].

[40] Robert Porter went through a similar process at the gaol delivery of Cambridge in 1509. He made a weak claim to sanctuary but pleaded not guilty. When he was convicted he attempted to claim clergy, but a previous conviction was alleged. He was remanded but did not appear in King's Bench: TNA KB9/454 m. 58 [image 116].

[41] Cavill, 'Church-State Confrontation', pp. 662–663.

to the ecclesiastical arm, because they continued to have concerns about either security or the terms of confinement.

All this evidence makes it clear that benefit of clergy was under lively discussion in the years around 1512. The outcomes of the Kyng case show that it was working reasonably well in practice, but the Newgate cases show that the justices were paying attention to traditional problems and thinking about ways to solve abuses through better processes. They recognized that the management of benefit of clergy needed some improvement, but their hasty delivery of the Newgate convicts in 1512 and their evasion of the new statute in the following years suggest that they thought that the political scrutiny that parliamentary activity brought was likely to cause unhelpful 'improvements'. So, they set out to find a better way to solve their problems with benefit of clergy, one that they could manage for themselves.

2. Reforming Benefit of Clergy Within the Common Law

Repeat Offenders

The key element in the Newgate cases, and one element in the Kyng burglary, was the ability to track previous convictions. The brand introduced by the 1490 statute made it possible for the court to see that an accused felon had been convicted and delivered, but the brand did not carry any weight by itself and a branded clerk could not automatically be executed on a second conviction. The court had to find the record of the previous conviction and establish that they were dealing with the same man.[42] Without photographs, fingerprints or databases, this must have been challenging. When a felon re-appeared in the same jurisdiction there might have been a good chance of the jury, the county officials, or even the justices recognizing him, but when John Rolle of Hynkley, Leicestershire, was convicted of theft at the delivery of the castle of Bedford on the Norfolk circuit in March 1514, how was he connected to the John Roules of Dodford, Northamptonshire, who had been convicted of horsetheft at the delivery of the castle of Northampton on the Midland circuit in 1509?[43]

In November 1518 Fyneux tried a new approach to deal with this problem. He sent writs to the justices of gaol delivery requiring them to return the names of all those on their circuits who had been convicted of felonies or murders since the

[42] For more on the implications of the 1490 statute and its implementation, see Margaret McGlynn, 'From Written Record to Bureaucratic Mind: Imagining a Criminal Record', *Past and Present* 250 (2021), pp. 58–65. Penal statutes were traditionally interpreted as favourably as possible for the accused, and that may account for the burden of proof on the justices.

[43] TNA KB9/464 mm. 4, 16 [images 8, 32]; TNA KB27/1011 rex m. 10 [images 201–203]. The prosecution at the gaol delivery in Bedford argued only that Rolle had been convicted at Northamptonshire, leaving it to the King's Bench process to provide the complete record.

beginning of the reign and delivered to the ordinaries, along with the indictments of clerks convict and any other records in the hands of the justices. The writ survives for the Oxford, Home, Norfolk and Northern circuits and for Newgate, and it probably went to all of them.[44] The order required the justices to return the information by the octave of Hilary 1519, but in fact the returns trickled in over the following decade, though every circuit but the Western returned something eventually. Over 300 men are listed on the circuit returns as having claimed benefit of clergy between c. 1509 and 1529, and they add substantially to our understanding of the volume of claims and the activities on the circuits as well as in King's Bench. We will return to these matters below, but first we will focus on the Home circuit return, which arrived in King's Bench around March 1520. Fyneux's own circuit, it was the only one to provide the requested indictments and records, and the outcomes of the cases of William Warley, Thomas Mydelton, John Averell, John Richards, and Joseph Draston indicate that Fyneux planned to use this new system to tighten up the use of benefit of clergy by targeting repeat offenders.[45]

William Warley was first convicted of theft in February 1518 at the gaol delivery of Colchester and delivered to Bishop's Stortford as William Waryner.[46] In February 1520 he was convicted at the gaol delivery of the castle of Hertford of breaking into the house of William Baxster, clerk, burglarously and by night, under the name William Hall of Maltby, Yorkshire.[47] His previous conviction and delivery was alleged when he claimed clergy, and Warley was remanded to custody. Thomas Mydelton was also convicted of the burglary from William Baxster, and he likewise claimed clergy.[48] A previous conviction at Southwark was alleged against him, but as with Warley, no record was provided. Both Warley/Waryner/Hall and Mydelton appeared at King's Bench in May 1520, when they claimed clergy again. William Fermour repeated the argument that William Hall was Warley/Waryner and produced the record, and Warley claimed that he was not the same man.[49] A jury in July 1520 disagreed, and he was sentenced to be hanged. Fermour also argued that Mydelton had had benefit of clergy as Thomas Ippeswyche in March 1517 at the gaol delivery of the castle of Guildford at Southwark, and was delivered

[44] TNA KB9/477 mm. 9, 34 [images 25, 77]; TNA KB9/969 m. 83 [image not on AALT]. The Newgate writ is dated 29 November 1518: TNA KB9/494 m. 98 [image 200]. The Norfolk writ is dated 1 June 1524, and both the Newgate and Norfolk returns cover the period to 1524. A change in the format of the Newgate deliveries between 1518 and 1524 suggests that a second round of requests for the information went out in that year: TNA KB9/494 m. 110 [image 240]. A writ for the Midland circuit dated 28 January 1529 asks for the names of clerks convict 'up to now not certified' and that return covers the entire period to 1509–1529, indicating that they did not respond until the third call: TNA KB9/481 m.10 [image 20]. See McGlynn, 'From Written Record', pp. 66–68 for more details.

[45] TNA KB9/477 m. 36 [image 81].

[46] TNA KB9/477 m. 49 [image 107].

[47] TNA KB9/477 m. 55 [image 119].

[48] TNA KB9/477 m. 54 [image 117].

[49] TNA KB27/1035 rex m. 10 [images 170, 171, 146d].

to the bishop of Winchester.[50] Mydelton too claimed that he was not the same man, but a jury on 22 May disagreed and he met the same fate as Warley.[51]

John Averell and John Richards alias Symonds were both delivered to the bishop of London in the autumn of 1518, having been appealed of nocturnal burglary by Geoffrey Thorgood at the delivery of the castle of Colchester in July 1518.[52] However, at the delivery of the Marshalsea in February 1520, Averell and Richards were appealed by William Rogers and Robert Kyng, churchwardens of the parish of St Mary the Virgin of Edwardstone, Suffolk, of maliciously, with premeditation and by night stealing chalices worth over £40 from the church the previous month.[53] When they claimed clergy there was no ordinary, so they were remanded to the prison. They next appeared in King's Bench in May 1520, where they claimed clergy again and John Fitzjames, the attorney-general, pointed to their 1518 conviction and delivery. Averell and Richards argued that they were not the same men, but a jury on 18 May disagreed, and they were sentenced to be hanged.[54]

Finally, Joseph Draston was delivered to the bishop of Lincoln at the delivery of the castle of Hertford in March 1517 after being convicted of burglary.[55] At the delivery at Southwark in February 1518, however, he was convicted of theft as Joseph Drawton.[56] He was claimed by the Winchester ordinary, but Blake for the king argued that he should not have clergy because of his previous conviction. Drawton argued that he was not the same man: he appeared at King's Bench in June 1520 to make that argument, but the jury on 3 July disagreed, and he was sentenced to be hanged.

These cases were very current at the time the Home circuit return was being compiled in February 1520: Warley and Mydleton were convicted for the second time on 9 January 1520 and Averell and Richards on 17 February 1520, though Drawton had been in custody since his second conviction on 15 February 1518. Their cases appeared in King's Bench on 14 and 15 May and 3 July 1520. All five claimed mistaken identity in response to the allegation of a previous conviction, and all five were unsuccessful. They fared much worse than the Newgate convicts in 1510–1511, and it's tempting to conclude that the circuit returns and the accompanying

[50] TNA KB27/1035 rex m. 11 [images 172, 173, 147d].

[51] His indictment as Thomas Ippsewych says that on 4 August 1516 he broke into the house of John Webster at Peckham and stole clothes worth 13s 4d, for which he was indicted at Southwark 20 November 1516, and convicted and delivered to Thomas Stacy 2 March 1517. He appears on the circuit list for that date: TNA KB9/477 mm. 37, 35d [images 83, 80].

[52] TNA KB9/477 mm. 36, 51 [images 81, 111].

[53] TNA KB9/477 m. 53 [image 115]. The indictment specified that the theft had been at East Smithfield in the verge, which brought the case into the jurisdiction of the marshal of the king's household. The records of the court of the verge do not survive for this period: see W.R. Jones, 'The Court of the Verge: The Jurisdiction of the Steward and Marshal of the Household in Later Medieval England', in *Journal of British Studies* 10. 1 (1970), pp. 2, 5–7.

[54] TNA KB27/1035 rex m. 9 [images 168, 169, 143d].

[55] TNA KB9/477 m. 35d [image 80].

[56] TNA KB9/477 m. 2 [image 4]; TNA KB9/477 m. 1 [image 2].

indictments contributed to that outcome, though we have no conclusive proof.[57] What is clear, however, is the response of King's Bench to their situation: unlike in the previous reign, when a number of men demonstrably claimed benefit of clergy twice and were either held in county gaols or returned to the ordinaries, all five were clearly sentenced to be hanged, as the law required.

Not only did indictments appear in King's Bench in 1520 as a result of the writs, but Fyneux also brought cases there from his own circuit. John Rice, William Oxenbregge, John Layland and William Hagg alias Baker alias Tably were all convicted separately of burglary at the delivery of the castle of Canterbury in September 1520.[58] All four claimed clergy and read *ut clericus*. In all four cases objections were raised: it was argued that Rice had been convicted at Worcester in January 1512, that Oxenbregge had been convicted at Newgate in October 1510, that Hagg had been convicted at Newgate in May 1507, and that Layland was a bigamist. In November 1520 Fyneux issued a writ from King's Bench ordering the justices of gaol delivery, in this case himself and John More, to deliver the records.[59] There is no further process on Oxenbregge or Hagg, but both Layland and Rice appeared in King's Bench with pardons in later years.[60]

This desire to tighten up proceedings was also manifested on the spiritual side of the process, and at least one ordinary was also concerned to prevent repeat claims. At the gaol delivery of the castle of Colchester in December 1520, the justices heard indictments of Peter Cropewell alias Payn and Thomas Randall alias Tolly. According to the indictments Cropewell had committed two burglaries and a theft in Essex on 27 and 30 September, in all cases stealing horses. He claimed benefit of clergy and read *ut clericus*, but Richard apRice, the ordinary for the bishop of London, said that he should not have the benefit because he had previously been convicted at Newgate in 8 Henry VIII. The second man, Randall, had broken into the house of Margaret Love, widow, by night on 16 November, tied her up, beaten her, and stolen £13.[61] He claimed that on 17 November he had claimed sanctuary, asked to be restored, and pleaded not guilty to the felony. John Barnabe for the king argued against his claim to sanctuary, and a jury on 12 December agreed and found him guilty. Randall promptly claimed clergy and read *ut clericus*, but Richard apRice, for the second time in a week, argued that he should not be admitted to the benefit because he had previously been convicted at the gaol delivery at Bury

[57] No other circuit submitted a comparable set of indictments with their returns, so it's not clear if Fyneux intended King's Bench to take a more regular role in the adjudication of such cases and the circuit justices objected, or if the labour involved was more than the system could sustain.

[58] TNA KB9/482 mm. 36–39 [images 74, 76, 78, 80].

[59] TNA KB9/482 m. 35 [image 72]. Fyneux was also one of the justices of the peace who had indicted three of the four two days earlier. Oxenbregge had been indicted in February by different justices of the peace.

[60] We will pick up the question of pardons below, pp. 200–203. Layland's pardon appears in TNA KB27/1045 rex m. 10 [images 237, 238, 211d] and Rice in TNA KB27/1047 rex m. 8 [images 189, 190, 191, 192, 193, 194], p. 200.

[61] TNA KB9/481 m. 13 [image 30].

St Edmunds in 11 Henry VIII. It is most unusual to see an ordinary reject a claim for clergy, and apRice is the only one in the records to reject because of a failure on common law grounds, rather than a failure of the reading test.[62] This suggests that the bishop of London may have decided to push back against the secular clerks convict arriving in his gaols, but rather than arguing that they were not clerks, an argument which was largely irrelevant by this point, he turned to the common law for relief.[63]

These cases in King's Bench in 1520 indicate that the court, or at least the chief justice, recognized the broader desire to limit benefit of clergy and indeed may have shared it. But rather than understanding this as an objection to a clerical right, it has to be understood as a desire to more effectively implement the 1490 statute and to ensure that repeat offenders could be tracked and executed. Fyneux clearly realized the importance of this tracking for staying abreast of the problem and the circuit returns were one mechanism for doing this, but the simple return of information was unlikely to change practice. It is probably not a coincidence that all of these cases came from the Home circuit, Fyneux's own, and it is probable that Fyneux brought them to King's Bench with the intention of sending a message about the treatment of repeat offenders. Some notations in the Newgate returns a few years later suggest that he was successful: Robert Sharleston, who claimed clergy in 1523, and Thomas Smart and John Wylson, who both claimed in 1524, each read *ut clericus* 'but was not delivered to the ordinary because he was convicted elsewhere, as it was said'.[64] All of these cases indicate that by 1520 both the courts and the ecclesiastical officials were taking the repeat offender implications of the 1490 statute much more seriously than they had in the previous reign, and such men were more likely to be hanged than to be dispatched to county or ecclesiastical gaols to serve lengthy sentences.

At the same time Fyneux was also pushing the courts' understanding of the reading test. At the delivery of Canterbury in March 1520 Robert Baker was found

[62] In 1517 Richard apRice and Thomas Croxton made the same argument for the king at the gaol delivery of Colchester, where they argued that John Swyrder alias Greneacre of Thorp, horse-harness maker, convicted of stealing 6s 8d worth of goods had previously been convicted at Newgate in July 1511 and that he should 'according to the due form of the law be put in execution'. It is not clear that this was the same Richard apRice, since Henry Marshall appeared in this case as ordinary for the bishop of London. Swyrder appeared in King's Bench in July 1519 and the court found that according to the record among the indictments in Easter 11 Henry VIII his guilt was 'fully apparent' and sentenced him to hang: TNA KB27/1032 rex m. 8 [images 162, 163]. I have not been able to find Swyrder's previous conviction.

[63] Both Cropewell's and Randall's convictions were delivered to King's Bench in November 1522, but neither appeared until 1524. The court noted Randall's conviction at Bury St Edmunds and his delivery to the bishop of Norwich and sentenced him to be hanged: TNA KB27/1052 rex m. 1 [images 142, 143, 113d]. It did not make any reference to Cropewell's previous conviction, but simply asked him if there was any reason he should not be executed. Cropewell had nothing to say, and he too was sentenced to be hanged: TNA KB27/1053 rex m. 10 [images 193, 194].

[64] TNA KB9/494 m. 109 [image 238]. Technically they should not have been on the lists but the Newgate returns tended to be thorough.

guilty of burglary by night and was given the book, 'but because he did not read perfectly or congruously, the aforesaid justices wished to be advised whether the aforesaid Robert should be admitted to the benefit of clergy or delivered to the ordinary or not', and so he was remanded to gaol.[65] This is an unusual record in departing from the language of reading *ut clericus*: although that term had never been defined, and indeed its flexibility seems to have been part of its value, there is no sense that a felon needed to read 'perfectly' in order to claim the benefit. 'Congruously' is a more intriguing term and might have provided a secular equivalent of *ut clericus* if it became the standard. But the fact that the justices were unsure of how to proceed in this circumstance suggests that there were active debates about how the reading test should be used. Baker was not the only claimant to be closely scrutinized. At the same gaol delivery Thomas Smyth and Ralph Fortune were convicted of burglary; they also failed to read 'perfectly and congruously' and were remanded to gaol.[66] This phrasing subsequently disappeared, and there is no evidence that literacy was any more strictly tested than it had previously been, but this moment suggests that the courts were pushing at a variety of the elements of the claim of clergy.

Bigamy

We saw in chapter 4 that bigamy was both an important barrier to the claim of clergy and a part of the process that could be manipulated by the courts, the bishops and the felons: this remains true under Henry VIII. While there are no new issues of law, the documentation suggests that bigamists were slightly harder pressed in these years and gives us a clearer view of how the claims were being administered.[67] When Thomas Jubbes tried to exclude John Vaghan for bigamy at the gaol delivery at Bristol on 15 January 1515, the court agreed to send to the bishop to investigate, but its writ was dated 4 December 1515, almost eleven months later.[68] The writ was not received by the bishop of Bath and Wells until 30 December, though

[65] TNA KB9/477 m. 58 [image 125]. Unusually, the ordinary is not named.

[66] TNA KB9/477 m. 59 [image 126]. Smyth is discussed below p. 200.

[67] In some cases we have only evidence for the assertion of bigamy, or a fairly standard process, similar to what we saw in the last reign: TNA KB9/452 m. 67 [image 135]; TNA KB27/1014 rex m. 9 [images 185, 186, 187, 167d]. William Alye was accused of bigamy at the gaol delivery at Maidstone on 4 August 1511. He denied it, and the record was delivered to King's Bench in July 1512: TNA KB9/963 m. 34 [image not on AALT]. In 1518 he was among a group indicted for imagining and compassing the death of both the king and Wolsey: TNA KB27/1047 rex m. 8 [images 181, 182, 194].

[68] The competence of the bishops to deal with bigamy was generally still assumed in this reign. Port has notes from a reading which add that if someone confesses that he is a bigamist after he has taken his clergy, the justices may not award execution without certification from the ordinary, because 'we cannot have knowledge by our law what *bigamus* is' since it comes from the council of Lyons: *Port's Notebook*, pp. 127–128, pl. 81. Port queries the point, presumably because he thinks that the statute gives the judges competence.

whether this was because of travel time in the midst of winter or some combination of travel and bureaucracy at Wells is not clear. The court demanded a response by 14 January 1516, but the chancery replied on 11 January that the time they had been given was insufficient, which in the circumstances was not unreasonable.[69] Similarly, at the session of the peace in Ludlow on 4 February 1529, Richard Snede, attorney for Princess Mary, alleged that Edward Birmyngham could not have clergy because he was 'a bigamist and twice joined in legitimate marriage and his body was thus handed over to more [than one] and he knew more [than one] woman carnally'.[70] The writ regarding Birmyngham's bigamy was not received by the bishop of Hereford until 11 January 1530, and the response was required for 17 May. Neither of these cases made it to King's Bench, and it is possible that the counties were simply slower than the capital, but if Bath and Wells and Hereford are representative of the usual process, the defense against the allegation of bigamy in the counties could buy an accused felon well over a year in which to try to evade his sentence.[71]

Cases in King's Bench moved a little more expeditiously: when John Lucas alleged bigamy against Richard Annott at the session of the peace in Maidstone on 8 January 1516, he was originally given until the next session on 22 July to prove it. Annott appeared in King's Bench on 5 May, where he denied the bigamy and a writ issued to the bishop of Norwich, to be returned by 6 October: the bishop obliged by 12 November, almost exactly ten months after the conviction. The bishop certified that Annott was a bigamist and he was sentenced to be hanged.[72] Similarly, William Inges claimed that he had not married the widow who was supposedly his wife when he was convicted of murder at Ilchester on 25 August 1522. This was a particularly grisly case, and this, as well as the claim of bigamy, may have attracted the attention of King's Bench. Inges appeared at King's Bench on 27 November 1522 and a writ was dispatched to the bishop to be returned by 22 April 1523; it in fact appeared on 1 July, again just about ten months after the conviction. The bishop certified that Inges was a bigamist and he too was sentenced to be hanged.[73]

[69] *Reg. King and Castello*, p. 179, no. 1112.

[70] *Reg. Bothe*, p. 238. 'idem Edwardus bigamus est et bis matrimonio legitime copulatus et corpus suum sic dimisit in plures ac plures mulieres carnaliter cognovit'. The entry does not give any information on the crime. Snede's reading on Magna Carta c.1 in Lent 1511 included a discussion on benefit of clergy, and he may have felt the need to show off: *Rights and Liberties*, pp. 110, 114–117.

[71] The processes may have been more efficient closer to the capital: when the bishop of Winchester received a writ from the justices of gaol delivery at the castle of Winchester dated 1 July 1529 requiring a response by 19 July, he had his answer dispatched by 17 July: *Registrum Thome Wolsey Cardinalis Ecclesie Wintoniensis administratoris* ed. & transcr. Francis Thomas Madge and Herbert Chitty, Canterbury and York Society vol. 32 (Oxford: Oxford University Press, 1926), p. 14.

[72] TNA KB9/470 m. 23 [image 44], TNA KB27/1019 rex m. 9 [images 153, 154, 127d].

[73] TNA KB27/1045 rex m. 17d [images 220d, 221d, 253]. Along with William Mathewe, William Inges was convicted of murdering John Cotell by the procurement of John's wife Agnes, by strangling him with a linen kerchief and burning his body in an oven at Farley castle. When William was moved to London, he and Agnes were both lodged at the Tower rather than in the Marshalsea.

In most cases we have no sense of what the process of investigating the claims of bigamy entailed, and we saw in chapter 4 that the bishops often seem to have fudged the question of bigamy because of the variance between the two systems of law. In the mid-1520s the bishops become more forthcoming in their responses, and we can get a better sense of why they required five or six months to conduct their enquiries. When Thomas Fyveshelyng was convicted of robbery at Shooter's Hill in Kent in July 1523, it was alleged that he had married Alianora Swyft, a widow, at the parish of St Dunstan in the West in London. A writ was sent to the bishop of London requiring the response by 25 June 1524, and the case was sent to King's Bench. Tunstall's response, dated 20 June 1524, details his diligent inquiries among the inhabitants of St Dunstan's and other neighbouring parishes, all of which led him to conclude that there was no evidence that Fyveshelyng was a bigamist. Though the response from the bishop appeared almost exactly eleven months after the conviction, the court held onto Fyveshelyng for another term, allowing him to be branded and delivered to Westminster Abbey on 6 October.[74]

John Dagnall's case took a good deal longer than the others, but it was also more complex. Dagnall first abjured in March 1526 for burglary and horsetheft, but when he was found in the country and claimed clergy in July 1526, it was alleged that he had married Alice Smewen, widow, in Aylesbury. A writ issued, requiring a response from the bishop by the next gaol delivery, but in November 1527 Dagnall appeared in King's Bench alleging that there was no marriage between him and Alice.[75] King's Bench issued another writ to the bishop of Lincoln, since he had not responded to the first, requiring a response by February 1528. The case was repeatedly continued until January 1529, at which point the court, exasperated, required a response from the bishop by 14 April on pain of the substantial penalty of £100, the usual fine for the escape of a convict clerk. Longland's register indicates that he had received both of the earlier writs, the first on 6 November 1527 and the second on 1 February 1528, but he was evidently unwilling to respond to the court until pressed, and in a certificate dated 19 April 1529, he explained that he had held an inquiry at the prebendal church in Aylesbury, as well as the parish churches of Hardwyke and St Peters in Oxford (neither of which had been specified by the court), which inquiry Dagnall could not attend because of his incarceration.[76] The witnesses apparently testified that Dagnall had indeed married Alice, the widow of Robert Smewen, *in facie ecclesie*, lived with her and produced children. However, the bishop continued, according to Alice's confession and other testimony and documents which the bishop had at the Old Temple in London, long before that

[74] TNA KB9/492 m. 24 [image 49], TNA KB27/1052 rex m. 9 [images 161, 162, 129d]. Fyveshelyng was convicted at gaol delivery of the castle of Canterbury at Rochester.

[75] TNA KB9/502 m. 23 [image 46], TNA KB27/1065 rex m. 9 [images 8902, 8903, 9171d, 9172d, 8904, 8905].

[76] *Reg. Longland*, ff. 158, 168v–169. The record at ff. 168v–169 is the response recorded in King's Bench.

time Dagnall had contracted marriage with Agnes Shelton at Calais, lived with her for two years and produced children. Since Agnes was still alive, Dagnall's second marriage was invalid, and he was not a bigamist. The court again held onto Dagnall until the next term, when they allowed him be delivered to the Abbey as a clerk attaint.[77]

These returns make it clear that in the mid-1520s the bishops were undertaking detailed investigations of the claims of bigamy coming their way, and we can assume that the sources simply allow us to see this more clearly: given that these were literally matters of life and death, it seems probable that the bishops had followed a similar process in the reign of Henry VII.[78] The bishops were, however, rather more forthcoming about their findings in this period. In the five cases where we have results of the investigation, the bishops found fatal bigamy twice, actual bigamy once, and responded that there was no evidence of bigamy in one case, which has a touch of ambiguity. In only one case did a bishop respond emphatically that the felon had not married his alleged wife. This suggests that the exception of bigamy, odd though it looks to modern eyes, was genuine and fatal in many cases.

Although all this evidence indicates that the courts were getting tougher in their handling of bigamists as well as repeat offenders, bigamy could still be used strategically. Four men who had bigamy alleged against them later appeared in King's Bench with a pardon: Francis Wygges, convicted of horsetheft at Newgate in January 1512, presented a pardon at King's Bench on 26 March, before a writ had probably even issued to the relevant bishop.[79] William Shilston, convicted of abetting the theft of cattle in Exeter in March 1518, appeared in King's Bench with a pardon in January 1519, though in his case the writ had issued to investigate his marriage to a widow.[80] John Laylon, convicted of burglary in Kent in September 1520, appeared in King's Bench with a pardon in November 1522, around the time the bishop's writ was due with the certification on his widow.[81] Finally, Richard Swyft, convicted at King's Bench of the murder of John apHarry in November 1527, argued pre-contract in his defense, but also appeared with a pardon in April 1528.[82] A pardon was obviously better than a successful claim of clergy, so these cases don't give much indication whether the claim of bigamy was true or not, but the exception and the process that followed did buy time to organize the pardon;

[77] He was still in custody in 1533, though he is noted as having been in custody for seven years, which includes the entire period since his original abjuration: TNA SP1/238 f. 72, *LP* add vol. 1, p. 295. See p. 284.

[78] It is also worth noting that the appearance of these processes in the bishops' registers is spotty; Tunstall's inquiry for Fyveshelyng does not appear in his, despite the fact that it was obviously a fairly substantial undertaking.

[79] TNA KB 9/458 m.112 [image 234], TNA KB27/1003 rex m. 9 [images 213, 214, 186d].

[80] TNA KB27/1030 rex m. 1 [images 163, 164, 155d, 156d, 165].

[81] TNA KB9/482 m.38 [image 78], TNA KB27/1040 rex m. 16 [images 217, 218, 196d], TNA KB27/1045 rex m. 10 [images 237, 238, 211d].

[82] TNA KB27/1064 rex m. 9d [images 8633d, 8634d, 8480, 8481].

these men got themselves out of prison remarkably quickly, most obviously Swyft, who spent approximately 5 months in the Marshalsea for murder.

In some cases the allegation of bigamy was only one step in a complex dance between the accused and the prosecution. George Grice, described as a gentleman from East Horsley in Surrey, apparently went on a crime spree at Uxbridge in December 1509, stealing a sword and shield worth 10s and £14 in cash from Hector Griffith, another sword, a shield, prayer beads worth 20s and £4 in cash from Gilbert Kyrkby, and a bay horse worth 20 marks—ten times the standard valuation for a horse—and 20s in cash from John Wygson. He was convicted at the gaol delivery at Newgate in April 1510. He read *ut clericus*, but John Chauncey alleged that he had married Agnes Agmondesham, widow, at the church of St George the martyr in Southwark and was thus not eligible. The case came to King's Bench in June, and there Grice did not deny the marriage, but responded that in May 1506 he made a pre-contract with Elizabeth Barton and the banns were legitimately proclaimed twice in the town of Honingham in Norfolk by the vicar there, and so Agnes was not his wife.[83] Grice was remanded to gaol and the case was continued until 9 February 1517, when the court finally declared that the plea was insufficient, and asked if he had any reason why they should not proceed to execution.[84] Grice responded, in English, that he had taken sanctuary in St Magnus's church on 12 February 1517, and asked to be restored. He had presumably escaped from custody in order to effect this misdated claim to sanctuary, and this may be the reason the court had no hesitation in agreeing with John Ernley, attorney-general, that the claim was insufficient in law, and ordering him to be hanged. The extended delay in reaching their conclusion suggests that the court expected Grice to be a good candidate for a pardon: though the descriptor 'gentleman' often needs to be taken with a grain of salt—several clerks convict are described in different indictments as both gentlemen and yeomen, for instance—the nature of his thefts (weapons and an unusually fine horse), suggest that in this case it may be accurate, and there is no suggestion that these thefts were carried out with any violence, other than the standard language of *vi et armis*. The incidents could be pardoned as high-status high jinks, or if that seemed to be letting Grice off too easily, the pre-contract could be accepted to allow for the claim of clergy and some period in the abbot's prison. The fact that Grice presumably escaped from the custody of the Marshalsea to claim sanctuary suggests his growing desperation at the delay, and perhaps the court's concerns about the likelihood of his rehabilitation. Though this is necessarily speculative, it does suggest that not all gentlemen could buy their way out of trouble.

[83] TNA KB9/456 m. 43 [images 84, 85], TNA KB27/1004 rex m. 18 [images 252, 253, 226d].

[84] Two proclamations of the banns without solemnization was not enough to invalidate the subsequent marriage. There is no evidence that the court sent the issue to the bishop to determine, as they should have done.

Failed Abjurers

We saw in chapter 4 that it was not unusual for felons to claim sanctuary and benefit of clergy in sequence, but Grice was in the minority in claiming clergy first: it was more common to claim clergy in the wake of a failed abjuration. For example, Richard Wilson alias Bruer took the parish church of St Mary at Banbury in March 1518 for the theft of 3s 9d that same day. The coroner arrived two days later, when Wilson abjured and was assigned to Southampton.[85] He appeared at the gaol delivery of the castle of Oxford in July 1519, having presumably stayed in the county for the intervening year. He claimed clergy and was delivered to the bishop of Lincoln as a clerk attaint. This sequence of events happened all through the period and all across the country. Thomas Cheselett, a tailor from Mere in Wiltshire, took sanctuary in the Dominican church in Fisherton Anger, Wiltshire in July 1519 and confessed to the theft of fifteen marks and other goods from Alice Kymer, widow, exactly five months earlier. He abjured the same day and was assigned to Poole in Dorset.[86] In March 1520 he appeared at the gaol delivery of Ilchester in Somerset, having apparently headed west towards home, rather than south to the port. There he claimed clergy and was delivered to the bishop of Bath and Wells.[87] These men demonstrate that while an accused felon had a variety of possibilities available to him as he tried to avoid execution, many potential clerks convict preferred a claim of sanctuary with the accompanying abjuration to the claim of clergy with the accompanying imprisonment. Those who abjured avoided all the dangers of a trial, and abjuration obviously provided greater opportunities for quietly disappearing into the countryside. Even those abjurers who did as they were ordered and left the country avoided the dangers of both secular and ecclesiastical prisons, with their shackles, fevers, violence, and possible starvation. Though benefit of clergy is often perceived as an unjustifiably easy alternative to execution, this reminds us that it had its own horrors, and was a clear second choice for many of those who were in a position to choose sanctuary and abjuration first.

It is also worth remembering that, though the examples of Wilson and Cheselett suggest that delivery as a criminous clerk was almost automatic, it was not. Morice Edmund took sanctuary in the cemetery of the parish church of St Mary next to the priory in Hertford in November 1525, and there confessed to a murder committed in Wales almost exactly two years earlier with two accomplices. He abjured the following day, and was assigned to Bishop's Lynn.[88] His record appeared in King's Bench in April 1526, but Edmund himself did not appear until November 1527, when he claimed clergy. The court offered him the book, but most unusually

[85] TNA KB9/495 m. 54 [image 110].

[86] TNA KB9/480 m. 31 [image 61].

[87] TNA KB9/512 m. 36 [image 566]. He was pardoned for the theft on 14 October 1529: the pardon recounts the sanctuary, but not the claim of clergy. *LP* vol. 4.3 6072[13 *recte* 14].

[88] TNA KB9/501/1 m. 89 [image 327].

it recorded that he did not read *ut clericus* and John Fulwell, the ordinary for Westminster, 'thoroughly refused to receive him as a clerk'.[89] He was sentenced to be hanged. Richard Hardyng appeared at King's Bench the same day with an even more convoluted story. He had taken sanctuary at St Dunstan in the West in Farringdon in May 1520 and confessed to two crimes: the killing of an unknown man at Warkworth in Northumberland in May 1517 and the robbery of an unknown man in Westminster four days earlier.[90] He abjured the same day and was assigned to Southampton. In June 1521 he appeared at the gaol delivery of Newgate, but when asked if there was any reason why execution should not be carried out, rather than the standard claim of clergy, Hardying launched into a tale of woe. He claimed that he had abjured as ordered but was captured at Walsingham in northern Norfolk by the bailiff and put in prison in Norwich on suspicion of felony. Since Walsingham is over 100 miles north-east of London, and Southampton about 75 miles south-west of the capital, Hardyng had obviously not followed the standard instruction to take the quickest route to the port, but this caused no comment. He claimed to have been convicted of the alleged felonies in Norfolk, to have claimed clergy and to have been delivered to the ordinary, which, he argued, was the reason he was still in the country. William Paver argued that he did not need to respond to this claim, not surprisingly, but the court wished to be advised and remanded Hardying to the next gaol delivery. He appeared in King's Bench in June 1524, three years later, with the same story. The King's Bench justices decided to investigate and requested a copy of the Norwich record. On 7 July Brudenell and Broke, the justices in question, certified that there was no such record. King's Bench in turn wished to be advised, so Hardyng was remanded again. He did not re-appear until November 1527, and the record this time includes his original abjuration, but not the appearance at Newgate in 1521 or his first run at King's Bench.[91] He now finally claimed clergy and the court offered him the book, but like Morice Edmunde, and on the same day, he did not read *ut clericus*, Fulwell refused to accept him, and he was sentenced to be hanged. Both Edmunde's and Hardyng's pattern of repeated delays are not unusual, but based on earlier examples, we would expect to see them conclude with a pardon rather than a hanging. Both the determination that they did not read *ut clericus* and Fulwell's emphatic refusal are highly unusual and since they both happened on the same day they suggest that something had happened while the men were being held in the Marshalsea to both link them and cause their sentences to be carried out. This was unusual and probably peculiar to the circumstances around these men, but it demonstrates that a successful claim of clergy was never a rubber stamp.

[89] TNA KB27/1065 rex m. 3 [image 8890].

[90] TNA KB27/1052 rex m. 3d [images 117d, 118d].

[91] TNA KB27/1065 rex m. 3d [images 9161d, 9162d].

Even in this increasingly restrictive environment, a small handful of men tried to work their way through a number of these strategies in their campaign for survival. Nicholas Haynes was convicted at the gaol delivery of Newgate in December 1523 of the theft of cloth worth 11s, branded and delivered to the bishop of London.[92] He was released from custody some time before 9 October 1528, when he committed a burglary. He was convicted of that burglary at Maidstone on 30 December under the name George Elyott alias Thomas Taylour of Norfolk and London, but the justices remanded him to custody. He appeared in King's Bench in June 1529, where he claimed clergy.[93] William Fermour introduced his previous conviction at Newgate, but, not surprisingly, Haynes/Elyott/Taylour argued that he was not the same person. On 18 June a jury specified as being from the Westminster area found that he was the same person, but instead of being sentenced, he was remanded again, possibly because of concerns about the origin of the jury. On 12 July, when he was due in court, the marshal appeared to admit that Nicholas had escaped and was ordered to have him back in court at Michelmas. It took another term, but Nicholas finally appeared again in King's Bench in February 1530 and claimed sanctuary. He did not deny the escape, or, in the record at least, his name, declaring

> Be it knowen to your lordshippes all that I Nicholas Heynes toke the churche of Seynt George the vijth daye of Juli for brekyng of the prison for save garde of my lyff whiche was pullyd owte perforce contrari to goddess lawes and the kynges & seynt Thomas of Canterbury and I beseche youe my lords all that I may be restored ayene to my pryvelege and also he seith that his company bare hym owte and too peyer of shakelles apon his legges and that he reportith to his kepars whether he hurt his yernes or natt.

Here Nicholas seems to be suggesting that he was carried out of prison by others (and the shackles on his legs suggest that his keepers were not at fault for his escape) but that once he found himself at large, claiming sanctuary for breaking the prison seemed like his best option. Nicholas knew enough to appeal to the full arsenal of God's laws and the king's and St Thomas in asking to be restored, but he must have known his chances were not good. Fermour argued that his plea was not sufficient in law, and the court agreed and went further. In unusual language it stated that 'because the Court is credibly informed that the material contained in that plea is not true, and also because the said George is known as a notorious thief' he was to be hanged. It is rare for the court to acknowledge openly that a claim made was simply not true, but once again we see the court work through the layers of his defense carefully. Haynes' escape and the fabricated claim of sanctuary seems to have pushed them finally to sentence him.

92 TNA KB9/509 m.152 [image 307].
93 TNA KB27/1072 rex m. 1 [images 1748, 1749, 1976d, 1977d].

The picture of activities in King's Bench is clearly not black and white. Repeat offenders, bigamists and failed abjurers were more likely to be executed than in the previous reign, and there is clear evidence that the courts were being increasingly careful in the ways in which these exceptions were used. There was also some discussion about the nature of the reading test, though there doesn't seem to have been any follow-through on that. This suggests that the common lawyers recognized the concern about misuse of benefit of clergy which prompted parliamentary concerns in the early 1510s and had their own concerns about the way the system worked, though their concerns were not the same as parliament's. At the same time, they were clearly neither hostile to benefit of clergy as a process, nor to the use of exceptions like bigamy as a strategy, as some convicted felons were still able to work their way through bigamy and sanctuary claims in conjunction with their claim of clergy to avoid execution.

Pardons

Most of the men who used these strategies found their way back onto the street via pardons, which appear with greater frequency in these years. Pardons have been widely studied, and as a strategy for avoiding execution they share the same ambiguity as benefit of clergy and sanctuary: while they can be an appropriate source of mitigation for a deserving recipient (and unlike benefit of clergy or sanctuary, direct the gratitude of the recipient towards the beneficent king who provided it), they can also be provided to less- or undeserving recipients, whether through corruption or for political or financial motives. Pardons have mostly been studied on their own terms, however, and there has been no consideration of how they intersected with other forms of mitigation. The King's Bench records make it clear that pardons could serve a useful function that was neither the righteous reprieve of the deserving nor the squalid protection of the well-connected, but which gave the criminal justice system some much-needed flexibility. A pardon could solve problems which were otherwise insoluble, and it could be used in a variety of contexts, individual and institutional.

The latter is apparent in Easter term 1523, when twelve men and one woman appeared in King's Bench to present a joint pardon which necessitated the rehearsal of their crimes.[94] Between them they had committed treason, murders, robberies, burglaries, and thefts, and most of them had claimed benefit of clergy, sanctuary or the belly, but often in ways that were problematic. Some were simple problems. Thomas Smyth did not read perfectly and was remanded to prison.[95] John Rice

[94] TNA KB27/1047 rex m. 8 [image 181, 182, 156d, 157d, 183, 184, 158d, 159d, 185, 186, 160d, 161d, 187, 188, 162d, 163d, 189, 190, 164d, 165d, 191, 192, 166d, 167d, 193, 194].

[95] See p. 191.

was one of the four Canterbury burglars brought to King's Bench by Fyneux after his conviction in 1520, when a previous claim of clergy was alleged against him.[96] Others were more complex. John Gilbert, Walter Facon, and William Alye had been indicted of treason for imagining the death of Henry VIII and Wolsey and pledging support to Richard de la Pole in a Southwark pub in October 1517; William Alye, however, had previously been convicted of robbery at the gaol delivery at Maidstone in August 1511, where bigamy was alleged to his claim of clergy.[97] He was remanded without any writ being sent to the bishop. Henry Michell was convicted of robbery at Eltham in May 1519. He claimed clergy, but was remanded to prison before he could read, possibly because the ordinary was not present. Henry Slithurst, a Wiltshire chaplain, was indicted in July 1516 of breaking into the house of Roger Carpenter by night in March 1516 along with thirteen others with the intention of murdering and despoiling him. He was to be at the session of the peace in October 1516 but did not appear and was finally outlawed in September 1517.

Two of the pardonees had tried sanctuary: Robert Williamson had been indicted for theft at Newgate on 26 January 1511, but claimed that he took sanctuary at St Saviour's church in Southwark on 4 January and was removed against his will. He pleaded not guilty to the crime, but argued that he wanted to acquit himself 'per privilegium ecclesie'. This was a slightly muddled refusal to plead, but it was clearly taken as such by the court, and Williamson was sent to *peine fort et dure* at Newgate. This was supposedly a death sentence, but clearly not in this case. Walter Thompson took sanctuary in the parish church of the Holy Trinity in Coventry in July 1510 for three robberies stretching back to 1508 and covering Warwickshire and Northamptonshire. He abjured and was sent to Sandwich in the company of two sheriffs who were to pass him on to the constable of the next town, but if he did indeed leave the country, he apparently returned without permission.

Three of the group had simply been convicted or indicted for murder: Thomas Halfnoth was convicted of pre-meditated murder at the gaol delivery of Canterbury in February 1511. He presented no ameliorating claim, but the justices remanded him so they could be advised. John Whyghte was convicted of murder on the highway in December 1520 at the gaol delivery of Colchester but remanded to the next gaol delivery. Thomas Tyler was indicted for stabbing Robert Croke in May 1515 while both were prisoners in the Marshalsea—when Croke punched Tyler in the face during a dispute, Tyler responded by stabbing Croke in the chest.

Finally, to round out the picture, Margaret Franke was convicted of burglary at the delivery of the castle of Guildford in July 1518. She claimed the belly and was remanded to be examined by a jury of matrons on 14 March 1519, by which time the issue of her pregnancy would presumably have resolved itself, but she was still in custody in 1523.

[96] See p. 190.

[97] Four others had joined in the treason, and nine more drank to it.

When this motley crew appeared in King's Bench on 18 May, nine were asked why execution should not be carried out, and the three who had been indicted but not yet convicted, Gilbert, Facon, and Tyler, were asked how they wanted to plead. All pointed to the pardon, which absolved them of all treasons, murders, and felonies before 1 January 1523.[98] Group pardons are not common, and they were usually for criminals who were convicted together, or who were connected in some way. There is no obvious thread linking any of these men and woman. While eight of them had been indicted since 1517, the other convictions went back to the early years of the reign. The predominance of cases from Newgate and Southwark may simply reflect the volume of traffic through those courts, but the more unusual prominence of Canterbury cases raises the possibility that again, these were cases which had drawn the particular interest of Fyneux. The clearest link between them is their oddity: though we don't know the reasons in the two murder convictions, something about those cases had prompted the judges to remand the felons to gaol twelve and three years earlier. Those who claimed clergy had been challenged on the grounds of their reading, their marital status and their previous conviction. One sanctuary claimant had effectively refused to plead and the other had returned without leave. Altogether they seem like the accumulation of a dozen years' worth of problem cases in the Marshalsea, and the pardon has the distinct sense of a house-cleaning, though the beneficiaries do not, for the most part, seem particularly worthy. By 1523 Fyneux had been bringing problem cases to King's Bench for several years, and some of these men and women had been in custody for longer. This pardon suggests that their problems were not easily resolved, even with the will of the chief justice behind them.[99] We saw in the reign of Henry VII that a pardon, rather than simply being a means of avoiding punishment, was a way of ending a period of confinement when there was no other mechanism to do so, and that is probably also the case here: these men and women had all been punished for their crimes by lengthy prison terms, and the only way out for them, other than by execution, was by pardon. The growth of pardons in this reign, therefore, is quite

[98] The length and complexity of the record seems to have caused the clerk some confusion. A 'Ralph' appears unexpectedly part-way through Thomas Smyth's indictment: this was Ralph Fortune, who was convicted, claimed clergy and was rejected with Smyth, but who was not included in the pardon; his appearance in the indictment section seems to have been a lapse in concentration on the part of the scribe. Similarly, Thomas Mayford is listed as appearing in May 1523 as one of those who might have had execution, but there is no indictment or conviction given for him. The pardon also includes two other women, Eleanor Spencer of London and Margaret Mathewe of Maidstone, for whom there are no indictments or convictions. The pardon appears in *LP* vol. 3.2 2807[1] but has been mis-calendared as a pardon for gaolers on the escape of prisoners. The original appears in TNA C82/526. The 1523 parliament, which assembled in April, passed a general pardon, but it would not have applied to most of these crimes: *SR*, III. 242–245. 14 & 15 Hen. VIII c. 17. See p. 312 for the parliamentary pardon.

[99] Green notes that 'Doctrinal development in the common-law system depended heavily upon a flow of cases raising problems for which the law had no appropriate answer', but this suggests that sometimes the answer remained unclear: Thomas A. Green, *Verdict According to Conscience: Perspectives on the English Criminal Trial Jury, 1200–1800* (Chicago: University of Chicago Press, 1985), p. 77.

likely a response to the growing number of claims of clergy and the variety of technical problems they posed.

Pardons were not only used to release those who found themselves in legal limbo, they were also used to release clerks attaint from prison, as they had been in the previous reign. On 6 July 1510 Henry VIII pardoned John Williams, a clerk attaint in the custody of the bishop of Hereford, because he was lame, and in 1511 he pardoned a group of four clerks attaint in the custody of the bishop of Norwich.[100] John Gurney was pardoned and released from the custody of the bishop of Lincoln in May 1520, William Glover from the custody of the bishop of Hereford in 1529.[101] Most of these pardons do not appear in the King's Bench records, so we don't know what crimes the clerks attaint had committed or how long they had been in custody, but Richard Fraunceys is an exception. Fraunceys claimed sanctuary in September 1520 in the church of Offord Cluney in Huntingdonshire and confessed to burglary and horsetheft. The coroner assigned him to the port of Lynn in Norfolk. He did not apparently get far, and at the gaol delivery at the castle of Huntingdon in March 1521 he claimed clergy, was branded and was delivered to the bishop of Lincoln as a clerk attaint. He remained in his custody until May 1526, when he appeared at King's Bench. Asked if there was a reason why he should not remain in the custody of the bishop without purgation, he produced a pardon and went *sine die*.[102] The failed abjuration made Frauncеys a clerk attaint, but his original crime was one which, if he had claimed clergy after conviction, would probably have led to a two to three year sentence at most. His release after five years thus recognizes the failed abjuration. Looking more carefully at the crimes and the processes with which they were connected suggests that rather than simply being aberrations or abuses or even manifestations of royal clemency and thus royal authority, pardons were a useful mechanism for dealing with both old and new problems. They were part of the combination of technicalities and processes which allowed some criminals, deserving or otherwise, and well-connected or otherwise, to be punished without being executed: they became increasingly necessary as common lawyers and convicts explored how the processes of mitigation might be expanded and might intersect, but found themselves with no obvious solution for some of the conundrums that their ingenuity produced.

3. The Bishops and the Management of Clerks Convict

As the courts increasingly looked askance at repeat claimants, bigamists and failed abjurers, we would expect to see the overall number of clergy claimants decline in

[100] *LP* vol. 1, 1150, 1569–1572.
[101] *LP* vol. 3.1, 854 [22]. At the same time Atwater was pardoned for all escapes. *Reg. Bothe*, p. 231.
[102] TNA KB9/501/1 m. 137 [image 425], TNA KB27/1059 rex m. 8 [images 175, 143d, 144d].

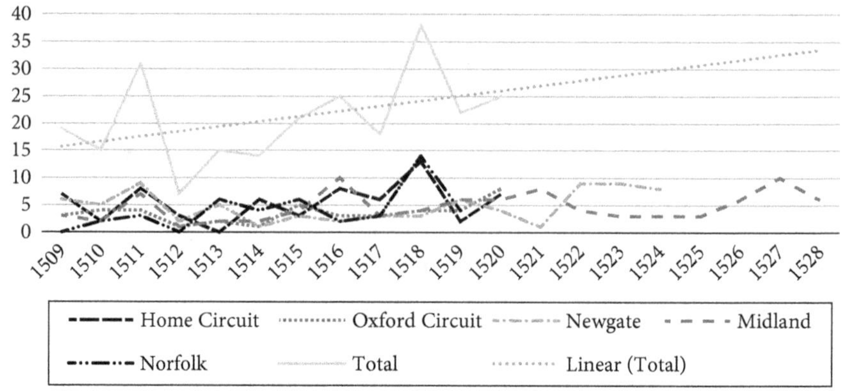

Figure 6.2 Clerks convict and clerks attaint in the circuit records 1509–1520/28*
*See note 45 for the circuit lists that provide most of this data.

this period. However, fig. 6.2 indicates that this did not happen. The circuit returns which Fyneux demanded in 1518 provide us with a much better sense of what was happening across the country than we have for the previous reign: without the circuit returns we would have the records of 162 men claiming benefit of clergy at King's Bench between 1509 and 1529, most of them in the south and east of the country; with the additional 319 men on the circuit returns, we have 481, more evenly spread. The returns make it clear that lay men were regularly delivered to the ordinaries in every diocese, and that the numbers were growing, erratically but steadily, through the first decade of Henry VIII's reign.[103]

While we have approached benefit of clergy from the common law perspective thus far in this chapter, looking at these numbers through the eyes of the bishops helps to fill in the broader picture, both in numbers and practice. The busiest ordinary in this period was the bishop of Lincoln. This is not surprising given the size of his diocese, but it is in sharp contrast to his absence from the records in the previous reign. Adding the bishop of Lincoln's totals from the Oxford, Home, Norfolk and Midland circuits, Atwater received at least eighty men between 1509 and 1520, a number which probably continued to grow in the following years (fig. 6.3).

After the bishop of Lincoln, the bishops of London and Winchester carried the heaviest burden: by 1520 London received at least seventy-seven clerks convict while Winchester came in a fairly distant third with twenty-one.[104] However,

[103] The circuit returns also throw some light on the relationship between the King's Bench numbers and the rest of the iceberg: forty-two of the men who appear on a circuit return also appear in the King's Bench records, suggesting that the King's Bench numbers in these years represent at most about 13 per cent of those delivered on the circuits. Though the numbers are rough, this is fairly close to the suggestion in chapter 4 that 15 per cent of the Newgate clergy cases came to King's Bench. See p. 116.

[104] That number does not include Hampshire, which would have been included in the missing Western circuit return.

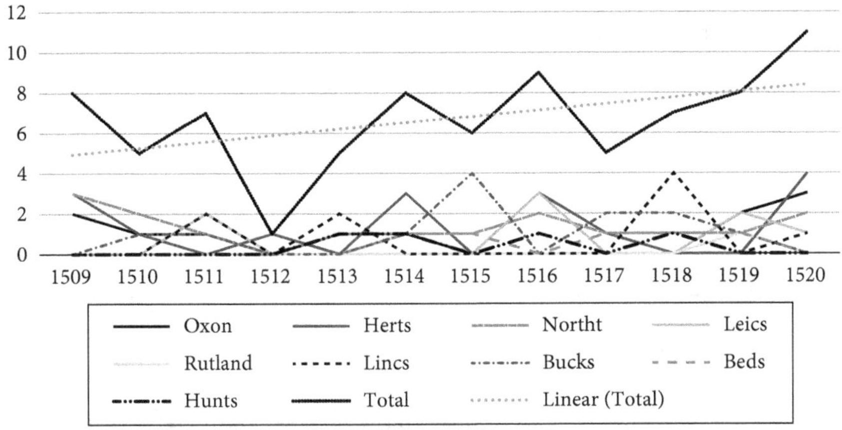

Figure 6.3 Recorded clerks convict and clerks attaint delivered to the bishop of Lincoln 1509–1520*

*See note 45 for the circuit lists that provide most of this data.

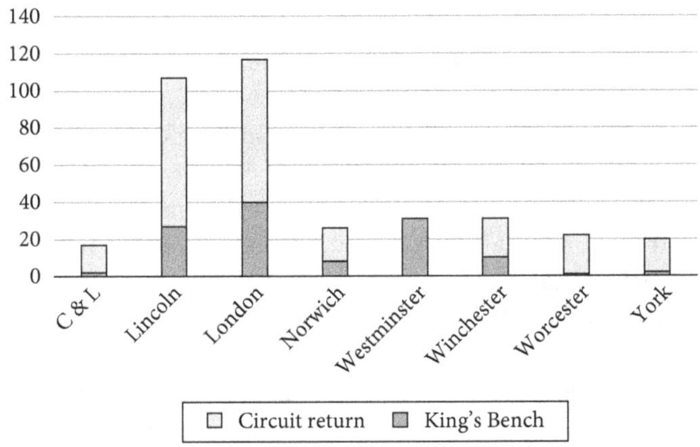

Figure 6.4 Clerks convict and clerks attaint delivered to the bishops in King's Bench and circuit records*

*Data collected from TNA KB27 and KB9 rolls.

comparing the claims which appeared in King's Bench with those from the circuits is instructive (fig. 6.4).[105] Lincoln and London are the heavy hitters in both sets of sources. Westminster Abbey looms large in King's Bench, but obviously does not appear in the circuit returns. But Norwich and Winchester are much busier than

[105] I have only included the busiest dioceses in this chart to avoid clutter. The King's Bench numbers for the other dioceses are: Bath and Wells 11; Canterbury 15; Exeter 6; Hereford 4; Rochester, Salisbury 3; unknown 3; Ely, St. Albans 2; Chichester, St. Davids and Jersey 1.

Table 6.1 Percentage of clerks in the total record and in the KB27 records, by diocese*

	% of total record	% of KB27 record
Lincoln	28	23
London	30	33
Norwich	8	8
Winchester	8	7

*Data collected from TNA KB27 and KB9 rolls.

the King's Bench records would suggest, and Coventry and Lichfield, Worcester, and York, which have virtually no presence in King's Bench, are not far behind.

In fact, Lincoln, London, Winchester, and Norwich each received similar percentages of clerks convict in the combined records and in the plea rolls. [table 6.1] This suggests that a fairly steady proportion of the cases originating in those four dioceses made their way to the central courts: this is not surprising given the relative ease of access and the likelihood of criminals in these dioceses moving around in the ambit of the capital. Conversely, it is not surprising that clerks convict in the north and west were far less likely to appear in King's Bench, and thus in our records.

Looking at the patterns from one other perspective may help us shade in another gap in the record. There are no surviving circuit returns from the Western circuit, and much of the southwest is absent in the other surviving records. There are, however, an unusually large number of purgations in the bishops' registers of Bath and Wells, though they are sporadic. Though the source base differs, there are almost exactly the same number of records of clerks convict extant for Bath and Wells in the period 1509–1529 as for Norwich and Winchester without the circuit returns: six, six and five respectively. Though the numbers are tiny and the sources different, this does at least suggest that Somerset could have had a comparable convict clerk population as the better-documented counties. Taken together, this suggests that the badly documented counties are likely to have done as steady a business in the delivery of clerks convict as the better-documented ones, and with only the spottiest survival of gaol delivery records, municipal and franchisal court records, and purgation records, this may be the best we can say about the patterns in those localities.

The bishops' own records generally continue to be of little help. Describing the six purgations recorded in Bath and Wells under Hadrian de Castello as 'unusually large' hints at the dearth of evidence from the bishops' records for this period. An outstanding exception to this pattern is the register of John Longland, bishop of Lincoln. Although he became bishop in 1521, there are no records related to

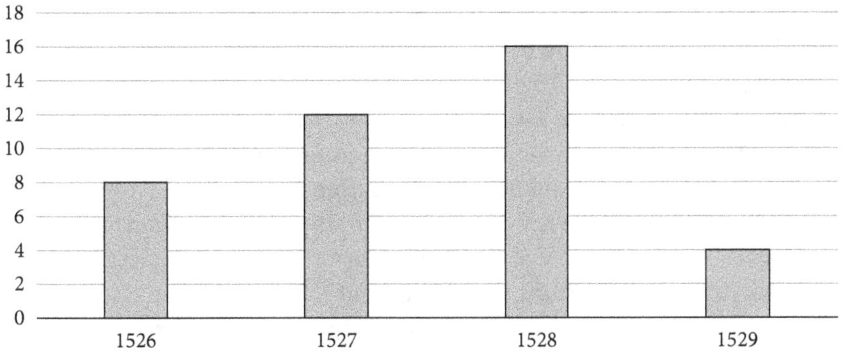

Figure 6.5 Purgations in Longland's *Register* 1526–1529*
**Reg. Longland.*

purgation in his register until 1526, but there are 142 between that date and 1543 when they abruptly cease, four years before the end of his tenure. Many of these fall in the Reformation period and will be discussed in chapter 8, but the forty recorded between 1526 and 1529 allow us to see the business of purgation from the perspective of one of the largest and most important sees in the country (fig. 6.5).[106]

In many ways the register repeats the patterns we saw in the last reign. Purgations were almost invariably held in groups: the commission of 15 February 1526, for example, authorized the purgations of eight men. Only one of the eight was identified as a clerk, and the other seven were the usual kind of mix: a labourer, yeoman, miller, turner, bricklayer, draper, and armorer. Though we have no direct evidence about the purgation ceremonies, one of the men, William Aly, appears again in a commission for purgations issued on 17 January 1527, suggesting that he may have failed the attempt in 1526.[107] Two sets of commissions were recorded in 1527, in January and August, and the twelve men named were a similar mix as before, with only one identified as a clerk.[108] Four sets of commissions appear for 1528, dated 16 May, 3 June, 28 August, and 17 December for a total of sixteen purgations, but there were no clerks in the mix: eight were labourers, one was a yeomen, and the rest were craftsmen.[109] It's not clear from the registers whether the larger number of commissions was the result of the press of business or whether the records were simply being better kept, but the varying dates suggest that there were no set times for purgations and commissions were issued as needed. Only one commission is

[106] In these years the register does not give any information on the place or nature of the crime or the conviction, nor does it record the actual purgation. It does give the names, origin, and status of the convicts.
[107] *Reg. Longland*, f. 111v.
[108] *Reg. Longland*, ff. 111v, 152.
[109] *Reg. Longland*, ff. 153, 161v, 164v.

recorded for 1529, authorizing purgations for four men.[110] Again it's not clear if this is a real decline in activity, but the four were once again fairly typical: one clerk, one butcher and one yeoman with one status not given.

These purgations do raise some new questions, however. In the first place, they are dominated by outsiders. None of the men purged in 1526 was from the diocese of Lincoln: two were from London, three from Berkshire, one from Salisbury (both in the diocese of Salisbury), one from Hampshire and one from Surrey (both Winchester). In 1527 three of the twelve originated within the diocese, with one each from Hertfordshire, Buckinghamshire, and Lincolnshire, but the other nine were again outsiders. The proportions were reversed in 1528, when ten of the sixteen were from the diocese, but in 1529 three of the four, including the clerk, were once again outsiders. Why is this the case? We saw in chapter 4 that the bishops were fairly selective in what they recorded: it's probable that Longland assumed that the mobility that caused these men to commit crimes in his diocese would also cause them to leave after their purgation, and so he was more concerned to have the record of his proceedings for outsiders. The corollary of this, however, is that he expected to be able to produce the same kind of information for local criminals if necessary, and this suggests some ability to track them, presumably through the local clergy.

The second question is prompted by William Ruse. One of the men purged in 1528, he appears on a circuit return, so we know that he was convicted of felony at a gaol delivery in Northamptonshire in the autumn of 1527 and that the commission for his purgation was issued on 3 June 1528, suggesting that he spent less than a year in custody.[111] Ruse's appearance highlights the fact that the rest of the sixteen men seeking purgation that year did not appear on the circuit returns and the men on the returns were not recorded as seeking purgation. Why is this the case? Either the returns were highly defective, or they represent only one stream of clerks convict flowing towards the bishops, and a fairly sluggish stream at that. Most of the circuit returns only cover the years before 1520, and it could be argued that many of the men delivered by that date would have been purged, pardoned, or escaped by the time Longland's register begins to record the commissions in 1526. The Midland circuit return, however, goes up to 1528, and this circuit overlaps the diocese to a considerable degree. The striking lack of convergence between the two sets of records suggests either that the record survival is entirely random, always an alarming idea for a historian, or that the lawyers and the bishops were interested in tracking two quite distinct groups of men whose distinctiveness is not readily visible to us, or both.

Fig. 6.6 indicates the problems with establishing any concrete numbers. The 'returns' in blue are the numbers from the circuit returns: the decline after 1520

[110] *Reg. Longland*, f. 171.

[111] TNA KB9/481 m. 11 [image 23], *Reg. Longland*, f. 153.

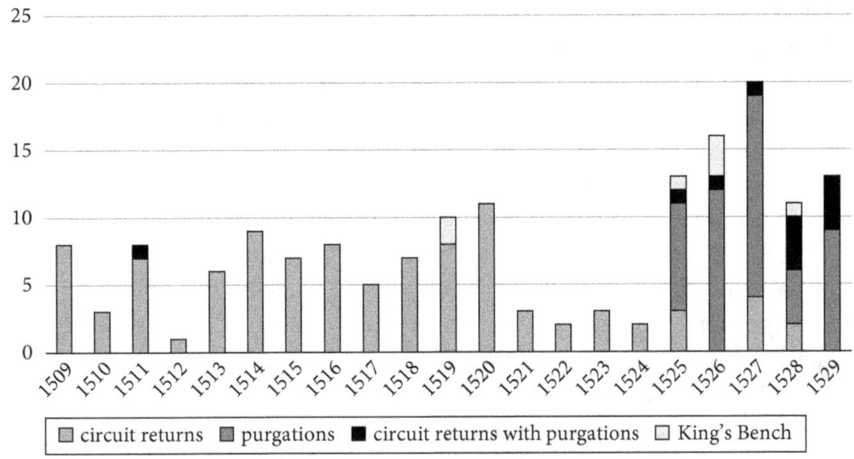

Figure 6.6 Clerks recorded as delivered to and/or purged by the bishops of Lincoln*

*See note 45 for the circuit lists; *Reg. Longland*; other TNA KB27 and KB9 rolls.

reflects the disappearance of information from the Home and other circuits, rather than an actual decline in deliveries. The orange 'purgations' are the commissions from Longland's register.[112] The grey 'returns with purgation' also come from Longland's register, which begins to record the date of the crime for which the clerk was delivered in 1531.[113] Since the clerks were usually convicted fairly quickly, I have used the year of the crime as the year of delivery, though this is almost certainly inaccurate in some cases, and the single grey point in 1511 is a reminder that long-term clerks convict still remained in the prison and could still be purged.[114] The sparse yellow caps are the cases relating to Lincoln which made their way to King's Bench, emphasizing again, and much more emphatically, how rare that was.[115]

Any one of these charting choices is open to argument, and I'm not trying to suggest that these numbers are exact in any way, but to demonstrate two crucial points. The first is that the sources which survive are not only obviously incomplete across the period, they are so rarely mutually reinforcing that it is likely that they

[112] The register does not give the dates of deliveries, but since it was rare for a clerk to be purged within less than a year, I have moved them back by a year in the chart to give a slightly better sense of when those men might have been delivered. They should probably be spread out more over the preceding three to four years, but we don't have clear enough patterns to do this with any confidence. It's worth noting that such a spread could, however, even out the delivery numbers somewhat in 1521–1524.

[113] See p. 269.

[114] George Goldwyn, a Worchester labourer, stole a leather purse containing 2s and an image of Mary in silver worth 6d from John West on 17 March 1511. The commission for his purgation issued on 7 December 1531: *Reg. Longland*, f. 214v. The distribution of grey across the years from 1526 to 1529 supports the argument that the orange 'purgations' should also be more widely distributed.

[115] See p. 203 n. 103. The Lincoln evidence suggests it was far fewer than the 13–15 per cent of cases suggested there.

are not complete for the years they cover. That means that the charted numbers are, as always, a minimum, and probably a fairly conservative minimum. This leads to the second point: if we assume conservatively that the circuits continued to deliver a steady number of men through the 1520s, and that Longland had been purging a similar number of men (who were apparently reaching his prison through other routes) in the years before 1526, then the delivery of fifteen to twenty-five men a year into his hands does not seem unlikely. If the numbers were increasing in the late 1520s, as seems likely, then it may have been as high as twenty-five to thirty-five a year. Though we saw the length of terms drop late in the reign of Henry VII, a good proportion of these men would remain in his prison for multiple years. With this kind of pressure on their resources, it is not surprising that ecclesiastical authorities like Richard apRice joined the secular authorities in the desire to clamp down on repeat or notorious offenders.

This of course raises the question of the number of clerics claiming clergy in this period, and the evidence suggests that there was a slight decline in the number of those in major orders. We have a stated occupation for 469 men, of whom fifty-five were identified with clerical occupations: twenty-four chaplains, twenty-six clerks (of whom five were identified as members of religious orders), three pardoners, one parish clerk, and one rector. Chaplains fell from about 66 per cent of the clerical total in Henry VII's reign to 43 per cent, while the more generic 'clerks' increased.[116] This is a slightly higher percentage of clerics than appeared in the records in the previous reign, about 11.5 per cent of the total compared to 9 per cent, but given the vagaries of record survival, it is strikingly similar. Among those identified as laity there is a similar mixture of stability and change. Again, slightly more than half, 248 of 469, were identified by status: twenty-one gentlemen, 133 yeomen, ten husbandmen and eighty-four labourers. Though the overall percentage identified by status is again quite similar, 53 per cent of the total compared with 54.5 per cent in the previous reign, there is a significant change within the ranks: in the reign of Henry VII 80 per cent of the claimants identified by status were gentlemen or yeomen, but in the first twenty years of Henry VIII's reign that fell to 61 per cent. The Canterbury evidence indicates that it is unlikely that the test was being eased, suggesting that the reading abilities of husbandmen and labourers had improved significantly.[117] The laity identified by occupation in these years were an even wider cross-section of English society than before: in the previous reign thirty-seven occupations were represented, but between 1509 and 1529 there were sixty-nine. Some of the new occupations, such as bookbinder, girdlemaker, hatmaker, horseharness-maker, or gunner, suggest the growing specialization in English society, while others, such as bowyer, carpenter, cooper, miller, or sawyer, suggest that men with traditional skills were increasingly likely to be literate. And

116 See p. 118 for the comparison.

117 See p. 191.

some, such as ploughwright, sadler, and worsted-maker, suggest both. Though the evidence is not conclusive, these are clear indications that benefit of clergy was increasingly available to the lower levels of society, which suggests that these men were literate at some level.

This social shift may account for the surprisingly low number of clerics who actually produced letters of ordination. There was good reason to produce letters of ordination if that was an option, and the sooner the better. Letters of ordination presented at first conviction meant that the convict would not be branded; this might seem to be incentive enough, but it would also mean that the clerk was less likely to be accused as a repeat offender. Clerics did provide letters on occasion: when William Crowe, a chaplain from Norwich, was convicted of nocturnal burglary at the gaol delivery of the castle of Norwich in July 1526 the court noted that since he had letters testifying to his ordination, he 'was not branded with any letter'.[118] But some who could have produced letters did not, perhaps suggesting an optimism about their own future improvement which turned out to be unfounded. William Rogers, a London clerk, got benefit of clergy at Newgate in July 1528, when he was convicted of stealing silver and a rood coat from the parish church.[119] Another London clerk, Henry Sutton, had been convicted at Newgate a few months earlier of stealing a maser, and the two men seem to have become associates in prison.[120] Four years later, in January 1532, they were convicted again before the justices of the peace in Kent, this time of robbery and the theft of a horse, clothing, and a knife, suggesting that not only had they not returned to the straight and narrow, they had moved from crimes of opportunity to a more active criminal career.[121] Rogers appeared at King's Bench in July 1532 and claimed that he was in orders, though he had not made that argument in Newgate. The court asked if he had letters of ordination and gave him until Hilary 1533 to produce them. Unusually, Rogers actually appeared with the letters, and the court remanded him until Easter term, and then until Trinity, when they finally allowed him to be delivered to Westminster.[122] It seems that it should have been an easy decision for a felon to prove his ordination if that were an option, but clerics seem to have been reluctant to do so, and the common lawyers noticed this. According to Yorke's reports, Fitzjames CJKB, Fitzherbert JCP, and Spelman argued that if a priest convicted of a felony who asked for the reading test rather than providing evidence of his orders had a previous conviction alleged against him, and he claimed that he was not the same person or that there was no such record, and a jury found otherwise, he could not then

[118] TNA KB9/511 m. 20 [image 39].
[119] TNA KB9/521 m. 50 [image 107].
[120] TNA KB9/532 m. 54 [image 107].
[121] TNA KB27/1084 rex m. 13 [images 6327, 6328, 6329].
[122] More commonly clerks convict asked to send for letters of ordination as a delaying tactic—we saw this with Hugh Boswell and Robert Bulkeley, who were both careful to send to distant dioceses to wring the most time from the process: see pp. 179, 182. There is no mention in the record of Sutton's fate.

claim clergy based on his orders 'for he has passed his opportunity'.[123] At least one lawyer had doubts about this, wondering if 'it was because, being already convicted of another felony, he ceased to be a priest' and noting that 'one may have his clergy beneath the gallows'.[124] All the evidence in the King's Bench records suggests that the court was willing to allow men who were clearly not priests multiple attempts to avoid execution, and while we can see a clear desire to clean up abuses, there is nothing in the records to suggest that a priest who failed in the claim that he was not the same man, or that the record of his conviction did not exist, would be summarily executed. But the question remains, why was this even an issue? Why would an ordained priest risk the reading test rather than providing evidence of his ordination and claiming his right?

For priests who claimed benefit of clergy the consequences could be long-lasting, even after their purgation. In 1526 Bishop Bothe of Hereford sent a monition to the parishioners of the parish of Stretford in Hereford ordering them to pay their tithes to their rector, since he had purged himself of felony and been released from the bishop's prison.[125] If a beneficed rector, with the support of his bishop, presumably unbranded, and having gone through the rites that were supposed to conclude the process of penitence and reconciliation, was having trouble being accepted in his parish again, how much more difficult must it have been for an unbeneficed cleric? When a priest was convicted of felony, especially one who was not a habitual criminal, it must have been more difficult than it seems to decide between producing letters of ordination in order to avoid branding, thereby highlighting his decline to his bishop and the broader community, or getting by on his reading skills without drawing attention to his status. Given that many of the clerics who appear in the records are described as chaplains, it is likely that some level of financial precariousness contributed to the original crime, and if a cleric had difficulty re-assimilating when he left the prison, it would hardly be surprising if he were to turn to his companions in prison for a different kind of support.

4. Conclusion

Parliament once again attempted to limit the use of benefit of clergy by statute in the early years of a new reign, but its touch was less deft than its predecessor's.

[123] This seems to have been an argument from analogy, for they also argued that if someone had a pardon for a crime, pleaded not guilty and was found guilty, they could not then produce the pardon, 'for when someone has two pleas to plead he must take one of them at his peril; and when he has taken the one he may not have the other'. Yorke's Notebook, *Reports from Henry VIII*, vol. 1, pl. 13, p. 92. Baker dates this to 1526–1536. A similar point is also made at idem. 1, pl. 22, p.95. Idem., pl. 15 p. 93 also notes that if the convict claims to be a priest the justices must first ask for his letters of ordination, and if he does not have them, he shall take the reading test, but this does not seem to have happened in practice.

[124] Yorke's Notebook, *Reports from Henry VIII*, vol. 1, pl. 13, p. 92, note 3.

[125] *Reg. Bothe*, p. 177.

By focusing on recidivism and introducing the new category of 'lettred' Henry VII's parliament managed to pass a useful bureaucratic statute with a minimum of resistance. Henry VIII's, by contrast, passed a statute which achieved little that could not already be done under the law as it stood, which was applied selectively, and which, by seeking to take the benefit away from clerks in minor orders, a category which was largely irrelevant in practice, stirred up resistance among at least some of the clergy. There is no question that the statute had an immediate effect on the number of men delivered as clerks convict, but primarily because the debate around the passage of the bill and the prospect of its renewal or extension in 1515 had a chilling effect on the use of clergy more generally in those years. As the years passed and the statute lapsed that chill faded.

The evidence around the 1512 statute suggests that explicit changes to the law regarding benefit of clergy were likely to result in a political firestorm and a statute of limited utility, and the middle years of the decade demonstrate the justices responding to the desire for reform of the system in a more traditional way—by administering the law as it stood more effectively. There was a clear push to ensure that repeat offenders, bigamists and failed abjurers were hanged rather than delivered to the ordinaries or held in county gaols as they were in previous decades, and there was experimentation with new methods of record-gathering to allow King's Bench to actually access the criminal records needed to make that possible. There were clearly still problems of both information and law, but the prominence of Home circuit cases in King's Bench suggests that Fyneux regularly brought his cases to Westminster for discussion as part of a broader desire to stimulate the development of the criminal law. The fact that the law does not seem to have changed appreciably as a result suggests that the makeshift solutions were working well enough to make any explicit reform unappealing.

Despite the new toughness on the part of the justices, the circuit returns and the bishops' registers indicate that the number of men being delivered to the ordinaries over the later part of the decade and into the 1520s was unsteadily rising, rather than falling. At the same time the social status of claimants was declining. This suggests that while fewer hardened offenders were being allowed to make their way into the hands of the bishops and abbots, their places were being taken by a greater number of men of lower social status who had committed fewer crimes. There is not enough evidence to determine if this was a result of increased literacy or lower standards, but there is clear evidence that those claiming clergy still needed to read at some level, suggesting that the former is more likely. This indicates that while traditional abuses were being rectified, benefit of clergy was becoming available to a broader socio-economic section of the criminal population, though it was, as yet, neither universal nor entirely formulaic.

7
Sanctuary 1509–1529

There was no statute comparable to the 1512 benefit of clergy statute for sanctuary, and indeed parliament remained largely uninterested in sanctuary in the first two decades of Henry VIII's reign. Once again a prominent case, *Pauncefote v. Savage*, which began in the summer of 1516, sets the tone for the discussion, and once again it seems to suggest that sanctuary was, if not defunct, at the very least in decline. There is no question that *Pauncefote v. Savage* was a significant case: it allowed the common lawyers to elaborate and refine some important arguments about papal jurisdiction, the ways in which sanctuary rights could be proved, and the physical limits of sanctuaries, but, as with most such cases, it was not definitive. More importantly, like *Standish's Case*, it does not reflect the activity in either the churches or the courts of the country, where sanctuary continued to be claimed and accepted on a regular basis. Indeed the surviving evidence indicates that abjurations increased in the second half of the 1520s, and that this change was supported, if not driven, by the common lawyers. Though this argument is based on circumstantial evidence, it suggests that as the justices continued to reform and refine their use of benefit of clergy, they began to approach sanctuary in a similar manner for the first time. They moved it from a peripheral but acceptable process to another mitigation for felony housed within the Church which they could nonetheless manage. Their early steps in this direction remained tangential to the working of the privilege itself but provide an important insight into the process by which they came to see benefit of clergy and sanctuary as cognates, each of which had something to offer to the development of a more functional criminal justice system. Small as the steps were, this shift in the 1520s marked a change in attitude on the part of the justices and laid the groundwork for the significant developments of the 1530s.

1. *Pauncefote v. Savage*

In the early years of the reign the common lawyers were still grappling with old and familiar issues. Many of these came to the fore in *Pauncefote v. Savage*, which began not long after the conclusion of *Standish's Case*. Bridget Pauncefote appealed Sir John Savage senior and junior, Sir Anthony Savage, and fourteen others in King's Bench for the murder of her husband on 31 March 1516: John Pauncefote was a Gloucestershire justice of the peace, on his way to the assizes at Cirencester at the time of his murder. In response, Sir John Savage junior claimed that on 10 May he

The King's Felons. Margaret McGlynn, Oxford University Press. © Margaret McGlynn 2023.
DOI: 10.1093/oso/9780192887689.003.0008

had fled to the house of William Hanley in Clerkenwell, which he claimed was a possession of the hospital of St. John of Jerusalem, and thus subject to its rights of sanctuary 'for safeguard of his life there, to remain there for amendment of his life during his lifetime'.[1] He was removed from the house by force on 20 June, the 41st day after taking sanctuary, and taken to the Tower. Savage's lawyers were clearly familiar with the arguments of the last thirty years, and their defense of his claim to sanctuary carefully laid out usage since time immemorial, a bull of Pope Urban III, a letter patent of Henry III (which specifically confirmed the right against prior non-user), a writ of Edward II for allowance sent to Hervey de Stanton, justice in eyre, and restorations of felons taken from possessions of St John of Jerusalem in 3 and 6 Hen. VII and 7 Hen. VIII.[2] Based on the arguments made regarding sanctuary to date, including those in *Stafford's Case*, Savage should have felt fairly confident. Ives points out that his case was clearly a strong one: Savage presented his case in King's Bench in the summer of 1516, but Pauncefote's widow did not respond until Hilary 1517.[3] The case was then adjourned successively until Easter 1518, when the justices finally called the prior of St. John to produce his claim. The prior appeared in Michelmas 1518 but argued that he needed more time to prepare, so the justices again postponed the case until Hilary 1520. In the meantime, a gathering reminiscent of that in *Standish's Case* took place in the Star Chamber on 10 November 1519 where 'many mischiefs were recited which had occurred in times past, and which were increasing from day to day, by reason of the sanctuaries of Westminster and St John's'. The king, Wolsey, various canonists, all the justices, the prior of St. John's and the abbot of Westminster were present 'to consider how remedy and redress might be made'.[4] Why had this case prompted such a gathering?

As we saw with *Stafford's Case*, Westminster Abbey represented the pinnacle of sanctuary rights so it is not surprising to see its abbot appear as part of such a discussion, but the knights of St John appeared regularly in sanctuary claims in these years also, and this history provides important context for *Pauncefote v. Savage*. Apart from the restorations alleged by Savage, fifteen men are recorded in King's Bench as claiming sanctuary in places associated with the order all over the country in these years.[5] The cases cluster in three periods, two before and one after *Pauncefote v. Savage*. In 1510–1511 six men fled to the protection of St. John

[1] *Caryll's Reports* vol. 2, p. 706. The case is discussed in McSheffrey, *Seeking Sanctuary*, pp. 100–103.

[2] *Caryll's Reports* vol. 2, pp. 705–706.

[3] E. W. Ives, 'Crime, Sanctuary and Royal Authority under Henry VIII: The exemplary sufferings of the Savage family', in *On the Laws and Customs of England: Essays in Honor of Samuel E. Thorne* edited by M.S Arnold, T.A Green, S.A Scully, and S.D White (Chapel Hill: University of North Carolina Press, 1981), pp. 296–320. Sir John Sr. was accused of being an accessory before the fact in the murder, but the main thrust of the case against him dealt with the abuse of office.

[4] *Caryll's Reports* vol. 2, p. 710: Ives, 'Crime, Sanctuary', p. 299.

[5] Six of these men were accused of or confessed to murder, and the remainder were burglars and thieves.

in four different locations: an inquisition on the body of John Gray found that John Goldyng claimed the franchise at Horkstow, Lincolnshire, after killing him with a knife to the brain on 2 June; another found that Robert Carre claimed the franchise at Maltby, also in Lincolnshire, after attacking and murdering John Brasebrigge on 1 August. There is no further process associated with these men. William Morfate and Thomas Jones both claimed sanctuary in the lands of the Hospitallers in the town of Gloucester on 5 July: Morfate confessed to burglary and Jones to murder.[6] It is clear from the coroner's report of the confession that Morfate and Jones were not in a church, since they argued that the messuage could provide sanctuary, but the coroner accepted the claim and allowed both to abjure, assigning them to Southampton. Andrew Hardwyn claimed in King's Bench in January 1511 that he had taken sanctuary in a house and messuage in the vill of Botolph Bridge belonging to the Hospitallers on 5 May 1510 and was taken out violently against his will the following day.[7] Ernley did not argue that the sanctuary was not valid; instead the jury was asked whether Hardwyn had in fact been at large on that day, a fairly standard response to the claim of forceful removal.[8] Finally, Robert Savell alias Favell claimed that he had been taken out of 'a certain old house of old tenure of the Hospital of St John of Jerusalem' in Clerkenwell against his will in 1511.[9] Two things are noteworthy about these six cases. First, none of the men claimed sanctuary in a church or churchyard belonging to the order: the two who went to Hospitaller houses at Maltby and Clerkenwell claimed sanctuary based on the franchise or tenure, while the other four all went to lands held by the Knights, but not religious institutions. This demonstrates how broadly the Hospitallers' rights to give sanctuary were understood by claimants. Second, this claim was not challenged in any of these cases: in the four cases where we have more than the simple statement of claim, the abjuration was allowed or it was argued that the claimant had been at large on the stated day, rather than that the location was not a valid sanctuary.

The second cluster of cases is associated with the Hospitaller franchise in Bristol in 1516 and 1517. This story began when John White and John Ball were indicted at the session of the peace in Bristol in May 1516 for stealing clothing while John Johnson and Edward Fowler were indicted at the same session for burglary on 24 April.[10] On the same day, just twelve miles away in Chipping Sodbury, Gloucestershire, White, Johnson and Fowler were also indicted for homicide.[11] The four men appeared at King's Bench on 4 July in the custody of Richard

[6] TNA KB9/455 m. 24 [image 52]; TNA KB9/457 m. 76 [image 147]; TNA KB9/458 m. 80 [image 170]; TNA KB9/458 m. 81 [image 172].

[7] TNA KB27/998 m. rex 12 [image not on AALT].

[8] Hardwyn's crime is not given, and there is no verdict from the jury.

[9] Discussed above, p. 185 as he claimed clergy after the jury found that he was at large.

[10] TNA KB27/1020 rex m. 21 [images 268, 269, 231d, 232d, 270, 271].

[11] TNA KB27/1020 rex m. 22 [images 272, 273, 234d, 235d, 274, 275].

Abyndon and William Vaghan, sheriffs of the town of Bristol. Johnson and Fowler claimed that they had taken sanctuary on 10 April and remained until 29 April, when Abyndon and Vaghan took them out against their will, while White and Ball claimed that they had entered sanctuary on 29 April and been removed the same day. All four asked to be restored and pleaded not guilty to the felonies. In support of their claim to sanctuary, all four provided the same history of the franchise of the Temple Fee in Bristol, starting with Richard Hastings' possession of the house on 10 March 1308, at which time it possessed the liberty to give protection for felony or murder, going on to the dissolution of the Templars and the statute of 1324 which passed the Templar properties to the Hospitallers, and concluding that Thomas Dowcra, the current prior, remained seised of those liberties. Once again, these four were not terribly sympathetic claimants: Johnson and Fowler seem to have claimed sanctuary for the homicide but were indicted for a theft which happened after they were supposedly in sanctuary. The indictment suggests that White did not take sanctuary with them because he was pursuing his own criminal interests, and the arrival of White and Ball in the sanctuary seems to have driven the sheriffs to pull all four out.[12] Ball, White, Johnson and Fowler appeared in King's Bench in the same term that Bridget Pauncefote appealed the Savages, and the coincidence of two such sanctuary cases connected with the Hospitaller houses must have prompted the court to look more closely at the order's rights.[13]

These cases demonstrate both that the Hospitallers continued to offer a generous version of sanctuary to a variety of criminals and that disputes regarding individual claims to that sanctuary were appearing in King's Bench around the same time that *Pauncefote v. Savage* landed. In these years between the end of *Standish's Case* and the first circuit returns, when the better management of benefit of clergy was on the justices' minds, it would not be surprising if they drew connections between the two, and Hugh Boswell's case, which brought claims of clergy and sanctuary together in one ingenious package, may also have inclined them to think about such parallels. We saw the first part of Boswell's story in the last chapter: having successfully claimed clergy for a minor theft in 1511, he was convicted on the charge of burglary from a church at the gaol delivery of Northampton in February 1513. Under the 1512 statute he was ineligible for the standard claim of clergy, so he claimed to be a Carmelite in orders.[14] John Jenour argued that the

12 This kind of tension between a sanctuary and its town was not unusual, and the Dominicans in Bristol had had their conflicts with the town authorities in similar circumstances in the past: TNA C1/31/531, TNA C1/31/532; McSheffrey, *Seeking Sanctuary*, pp. 58–82.

13 Ernley asked to return to court in Michelmas term, but the case was not resumed until Hilary 1518, when he argued that the case was not sufficient in law. The court wished to be advised, and Fowler, Ball and White appeared in Easter 1518: Johnson had presumably died or escaped. The case was once more delayed and it eventually disappears from the record in the summer of 1523. A fifth man, David Jonys, was indicted for horsetheft and burglary at the session of the peace in Bristol in December 1517 and made a similar argument; the chamberlain of Bristol responded that he should not have been admitted because of a previous theft: TNA KB9/476 m. 11 [image 22].

14 See p. 179.

plea was insufficient and the court wished to be advised, set 16 July to hear arguments and remanded Boswell to prison. The case was called to King's Bench on 20 June, the record was delivered on 22 June, and on the same day Boswell appeared and was asked if he wished to maintain the plea he had made in Northampton.[15] Boswell shifted strategies and abandoned his claim to clergy. Asked if there was a reason why execution should not be carried out, he launched into an extensive description of the sanctuary available since time immemorial at the Cluniac house of St Andrew in Northampton, which he claimed offered sanctuary for felonies for the life of the claimant, cleric or layman, 'without having ... any punishment of execution imposed on them by the royal power' but instead 'remaining under the protection of the apostolic see'. He also provided a graphic description of the punishments set out by various popes for those who infringed the liberty, including a comparison with the punishment of Dathan and Abiron. Finally descending to earth, Hugh claimed that on 28 April 1513 he had fled to the priory and 'lived within the seven walls and the cloister of the same monastery or priory in a certain place called the great courte, six feet distant from the west door of the church of the said priory' until he was taken out on 4 May. Boswell asked to be restored to the sanctuary, recognizing that he had neither taken the church or churchyard, nor had he asked for a coroner.

Boswell's argument was clearly framed by someone who was familiar with major issues in the law of sanctuary as it covered the kinds of people who could claim, the physical space occupied by the sanctuary, its legal underpinnings and the protections it offered, but the expansive reliance on papal bulls and the reference to Dathan and Abiron suggests that the claim was not developed by a common lawyer. Port reports that the justices unanimously agreed that sanctuary could not be claimed by prescription without a deed of grant and allowance in eyre, since 'having a sanctuary is the highest thing against the crown that may be'.[16] William Fermour asked for execution, but the court ordered the prior to be present in King's Bench on 29 June with any letters patent, bulls, charters, writings, muniments, or other memorials which might support his title. When Boswell came before the court again they asked him if he wanted to maintain his plea, and this time he said yes, but the prior informed the court that having searched his records he 'at present claimed ... no privilege or sanctuary for the protection of any felons of the lord king coming or fleeing to the said monastery or priory', saving any evidence of sanctuary that might later be found. The prior's brisk but strategic rejection of Boswell's claim suggests that it did not come from the priory, or at least not from the prior's office, leaving the source of his advice unclear. Although all of this seems to be a series of Hail Mary arguments from a repeat felon, the court again wished to be advised, and continued the case to 2 July, then to 6 July. They finally informed

[15] TNA KB27/1008 rex m. 12 [images 198, 199, 189d, 190d, 200]; TNA KB9/462 m. 26 [image 54].

[16] *Port's Notebook*, p. 38.

Boswell that there were no grounds on which he could be restored to the sanctuary and asked him once again if he had anything further to say. He was finally speechless and was ordered to be hanged.

A few years earlier Boswell would probably have been successful in his claim of clergy, though he would have spent some time in a county gaol or episcopal prison before his eventual release. The changes in the early years of the reign meant that as a lay repeat offender clergy was harder to get, hence his imaginative claim to sanctuary. As the justices were contemplating the political opposition to benefit of clergy, the arrival of Boswell's and other sanctuary claims in King's Bench apparently prompted them to use *Pauncefote v. Savage* to think carefully about the limits to sanctuary in the same way they were thinking about the limits to benefit of clergy. Unlike in *Standish's Case*, where the justices seem to have been silent through much of the discussion at Blackfriars and Baynard's Castle, Fyneux took the lead in the Star Chamber discussion.[17] He began with the argument that St. John's had no more privilege than any other parish church in the realm, the standard forty days, which was given by the common law. For anything beyond the common law, he argued, it was necessary to prescribe, but a prescription for sanctuary was 'so much in derogation of justice and against the common weal of the realm that it is not allowable by the law'.[18] Much of the discussion that followed was taken up with the question of how, then, a sanctuary beyond forty days could be proved, using William Waw, Humphrey Stafford, and Hugh Boswell's cases, which Caryll summarizes as follows:

> usage since time immemorial alone, without allowance in the general eyre, will not serve to have sanctuary: as appears from William Wawe's case. And a grant by the king and confirmation by the pope before time of memory, and a confirmation by both of them within time of memory, without usage since time immemorial, will not serve either: as appears from Humphrey Stafford's case. And the pope may not grant sanctuary: as appears from Boswell's case. But a grant from the king and confirmation by the pope before time of memory, and usage since time immemorial, and confirmation by the king within time of memory, will suffice to have the liberty of sanctuary (as I believe) without allowance in eyre, or else it would be hard to maintain any ancient sanctuary in England.[19]

Even with this, Caryll noted 'query nevertheless, because it is difficult'. Indeed, Savage was out of luck by these criteria, since his papal grant from before the time of memory was not preceded by a royal grant.

[17] Caryll's report seems to mix the discussion in Star Chamber in 1519 and the discussion when Savage re-appeared in court in 1520: since both covered much the same points I will treat them together.

[18] *Caryll's Reports* vol. 2, pp. 708, 710.

[19] *Caryll's Reports* vol. 2, p. 709.

The role of the pope in creating a sanctuary was a key part of this discussion, and the report circles back to this issue several times. The lawyers argued that to avoid *praemunire* any good grant of sanctuary must begin with the king, for 'it behoves me ... to begin with the king and to obtain his grant or licence to have a sanctuary ..., and then to have papal bulls of confirmation, and then it is a good and perfect sanctuary'.[20] The canonists and the clergy did not dispute this central premise, but they tried hard to moderate it. They accepted that 'someone who wishes to create a liberty or privilege of sanctuary' must begin with the king, but argued that when a place had been sanctified since ancient times, like a parish church, the pope could extend the sanctuary beyond forty days, an argument which Caryll noted and queried.[21] This argument recognized the confusion between liberties and sanctuaries which was often a key element of their origin and accepted the king's authority over liberties and the sanctuaries therein, while keeping him away from sanctuaries in parish churches and other such anciently sanctified sites. Peter Potkyn, counsel to the prior of St John, further argued that 'awareness and tolerance by kings since time immemorial is equivalent to grants from kings': Caryll notes 'no answer was made to this'.[22] Potkyn, recognizing that many sanctuaries simply did not have the records to meet the standards of proof Fyneux was advancing, was effectively arguing that proof of usage from time immemorial should be enough, an argument that conveniently fit with the Hospitallers' claim, but which would also be crucial for many other houses. The clergy's arguments were certainly more historically aware than the lawyers', as Fyneux scolded 'you have claimed such a privilege in times past, and also various other privileges which the king himself could not grant at the present day by the order of his laws, and therefore cannot have a good beginning, ergo they will not lie in prescription'.[23] Fyneux's statement is striking for its casual limitation of the king's ability to grant sanctuary, an impulse which draws on the 1378 parliamentary petition and which departs from both Townshend's and Huse's points in earlier cases.[24] This is a reminder that though Fyneux was comfortable pushing back on ecclesiastical claims, he invariably argued for the extension of common law jurisdiction rather than royal authority.

If Potkyn's argument was not dignified with a response, the distinction between ancient sanctuaries and new foundations seems to have been more broadly acceptable. Port notes that 'it was agreed by my lord cardinal [Wolsey] and other lords and judges of the king's council that the pope may not make a sanctuary without the king, except in consecrated ground. But he may grant greater privileges or

[20] *Caryll's Reports* vol. 2, p. 710. Some of these arguments also appeared on circuit: as justices of assize in c. 1518 Wood and Rede argued that 'the pope does not have power to make a sanctuary in England for tuition of treason without the assent of the king, as in Westminster, Beaulieu, St. Martin's etc.': *Spelman's Reports* vol. 2, p. 342, n. 1. This echoes Townshend's preliminary argument in *Stafford's Case*, p. 134.

[21] *Caryll's Reports* vol. 2, p. 711.

[22] *Caryll's Reports* vol. 2, p. 710.

[23] *Caryll's Reports* vol. 2, p. 710.

[24] See pp. 54–55, 138.

immunities to a consecrated place than it had before, without the king. If, however, he wishes to enlarge the privilege of a place which is not consecrated, as is said of the privilege of St John's and various places in Westminster, this may not be without the king's consent'.[25] This linked the question of jurisdiction to the old problem of the physical scope of the chartered sanctuaries, a topic which also came up in the discussion. Fyneux argued that it was the opinion of all the justices of England—and of the bishops and clergy—that 'the boundary of every sanctuary shall be understood as the church, cloister, dorter and cemetery, and that this term "ambit" does not extend to their gardens, barns or stables'.[26] Some of the justices found this a little narrow, but when taken with the argument over jurisdiction it allowed for a three-fold approach to sanctuaries: papal founding grants were acceptable for parish churches or other ancient sites, royal founding grants were necessary for recent foundations or liberties, and papal privileges exercised in any large and diverse precinct—such as Westminster or St John's—which fell outside the 'ambit' of the sanctuary as defined by Fyneux had to be confirmed by the king.[27] This was potentially bad news for St. John's, for Savage's claim had made it clear that it could not meet this new standard of proof and might be confined to the basic forty days, but Westminster had nothing to fear from this formulation: the Abbey's grants began with King Edgar and St. Edward, and remained technically unimpeachable.[28] Lest the abbot relax too soon, however, the king intervened to point out that King Edgar and St. Edward had not intended the sanctuary to serve as a home for willful murderers and thieves, and to declare that he meant to 'have this reformed which has been encroached by abuse, and to have the matter brought back to the true intention of the makers thereof in the beginning'.[29] Fyneux hastened to agree with him, noting that 'the law of God and the law of the land are one'. He pointed out that all these grants had been made 'to the praise and glory of God', but that protecting murderers and thieves did not redound to God's praise, thus opening up a new and rather subjective avenue for challenging the privilege.[30]

Having established a set of principles, the report turns to the core of the business at hand, and its conclusions are typically inconclusive. Wolsey suggested that,

[25] *Port's Notebook*, p. 41.

[26] *Caryll's Reports*, vol. 2, p. 707.

[27] Fyneux tried to exclude the pantry and buttery from sanctuary, but the other justices disagreed. The issue was still very much a live one: Caryll notes a case from the Coventry assize in 1520 in which the garden in a Franciscan house was excluded from the sanctuary after some argument. In a reading a few years later Chaloner noted that 'a charnel house, frater, dorter or such places which are occupied with good things shall have the same privilege as the church has ... also a man shall have sanctuary in the steeple and on the church, "for whoever owns it, it is his to the highest or to heaven" ', but that 'a tavern, a shop to sell merchandise, or a bawdy house, and such places which are occupied with sin etc.' cannot offer sanctuary, even if the land is still officially consecrated: *Rights and Liberties*, p. 130.

[28] Cf. *Port's Notebook*, p. 41. Yorke notes the difference in pleading sanctuary at Westminster, because it is 'sufficiently of record before the justices': Yorke's Notebook, *Reports from Henry VIII* vol. 1, pl. 263, p. 191.

[29] *Caryll's Reports* vol. 2, p. 711.

[30] *Caryll's Reports* vol. 2, p. 713.

given the vagueness of the various grants, a commission should be appointed to fix the boundaries of sanctuaries. Dr Veysey, bishop of Exeter and Henry's advisor on *Standish's Case*, argued that under the common law a sanctuary man who committed treason or felony outside the sanctuary would no longer be protected there; though Tunstall and Clerk disagreed with him, all the canonists agreed that any sanctuary man who committed any such crime within the sanctuary would lose his privilege. It was pointed out that the only penalty for breaking the oath taken by Westminster sanctuary men not to commit treason or felony within the sanctuary or outside was a punishment for perjury, which apparently had little deterrent value. Wolsey suggested that the oath should be replaced by a contract to the same effect, which, if broken, would prevent the sanctuary man from re-entering the sanctuary. The abbot of Westminster responded that 'there are express words that 'no one could diminish, infringe or change' the privilege upon pain of excommunication', and there the matter rested.[31]

Pauncefote v. Savage and the other Hospitaller cases had clearly prompted a desire to provide 'remedy and redress' for the abuses of sanctuary, but the key abuses were the old ones, the size of the precincts and re-offending sanctuary men, and the latter problem seems to have been as intractable as ever. Nevertheless, Fyneux clearly took the opportunity of the conference to push the justices to come up with a clear and consistent standard with which to test the claims of chartered sanctuaries, and a clear and consistent definition of their physical extent. Though he pushed hard, the report indicates that some of the justices pushed back, and it's not clear that his arguments were generally accepted, even though they were reported. It is clear that Sir John Savage was out of luck, however, and when he returned to King's Bench in Hilary 1520, presumably informed of the Star Chamber discussion, he dropped his claim to sanctuary and put himself on the king's grace: he presented a pardon in November.[32]

Ives characterizes *Pauncefote v. Savage* as typical of the legal and political environment early in Henry VIII's reign. He compares it to Hunne's case, where 'if ever his authority seemed to be impugned, the king would insist on abject and complete acknowledgement of his regality, but on the practical outcome he was prepared to be lenient'.[33] Ives suggests that 'in the aftermath of Hunne's Case there may have been lawyers in government service willing to probe Church privilege further', but it seems at least as likely that the discussion in *Pauncefote v. Savage* was driven by *Standish's Case* and the arguments about royal authority flowing from it.[34] Though

[31] *Caryll's Reports* vol. 2, p. 713.

[32] Ives, 'Crime, Sanctuary', p. 298. TNA KB27/1037 rex m. 12 [images 214, 215, 188d, 189d, 216, 217, 190d, 191d, 218, 219, 192d, 193d, 220, 221, 194d, 195d, 222, 223, 196d–198d, 224, 225, 199d]; *LP* vol. 3, 1081[27].

[33] Ives, 'Crime, Sanctuary', p. 303.

[34] Ives, 'Crime, Sanctuary', p. 301. Ives claims that the case served its main purpose in bringing the Savages to heel, but even this could be argued: Sir John effectively served a four-year prison sentence for the death of a royal justice and though the financial penalties that went along with the pardon were intended to undermine the family's power, from all the evidence both Sir Johns continued to behave much

they took the lesser role this time around, once again there were churchmen on both sides of the argument, and though it could be seen as a Church/State debate, once again the core of the issue is the practical management of a Church privilege. Indeed Port's report of the discussion concludes that 'even where privileges are granted by the pope and the king, they [the pope and the king] may afterwards interpret and regulate those privileges', and points to a papal bull which allowed the king to place guards on those in sanctuary for treason.[35]

Pauncefote v. Savage did not undermine the privilege of sanctuary in England. Though it gave the justices an opportunity to air their knowledge, and Fyneux a platform to argue for a more modern version of the privilege, it had little immediate impact on the law, much like *Standish's Case*. It is clear that St John of Jerusalem continued to offer sanctuary in locations outside its churches after the Savage case.[36] Two more claims appeared in King's Bench in 1526–1527. An inquisition on the body of Thomas Smyth found that George Tunstall killed Smyth in July 1526, with John Bradley as accessory. While Tunstall fled to Westminster, Bradley sought sanctuary in Clerkenwell.[37] Bradley appeared at King's Bench in May 1527 with a pardon witnessed at Westminster on 12 November 1526.[38] It seems likely that he had remained in the sanctuary at least for the four months before the pardon was granted, well beyond the standard forty days. While the King's Bench record notes his flight to St John of Jerusalem, the sanctuary was not challenged. In a more complex case, Robert Markes was indicted as an accessory to a series of thefts in October 1525, separately indicted for horsetheft committed in November 1525, and tried at the gaol delivery of the castle of Winchester in March 1528.[39] At the gaol delivery he claimed that he had taken sanctuary at the manor of

as they had done before the murder, at least as far as their straitened circumstances would allow: Ives, 'Crime, Sanctuary', pp. 318–319.

[35] *Port's Notebook*, p. 41. A series of papal bulls in 1488, 1493, and 1504 allowed such reforms: D. Wilkins ed., *Concilia Magna Britanniae et Hiberniae*, (London, 1737), vol. 3, pp. 622–623; Thomas Rymer, *Foedera, Conventiones, Literae*, (London, 1704–35), vol. 12, p. 541; vol. 13, p. 104.

[36] There is one other mention of sanctuary associated with St John of Jerusalem in this period: in June 1518 an inquisition on the body of William Fedurston held in East Radclyf, Nottinghamshire, found that Robert Parker had killed him and fled to St John of Jerusalem, though the location was not specified: 'fugam fecit ad quamdam domum que tenetur de priore & fratribus sci Johis de Jerusalem in Anglia & ibm peciit ___ & privilegium predictorum prioris & fratrum'. TNA KB9/969 m. 19 [image not on AALT]. In 1534 the commander of Templecombe abducted a girl and held her in Temple Fee, an area of Bristol that the Hospitallers claimed was exempt from the jurisdiction of the town, and in which the mayor alleged 'the order gave sanctuary to a host of criminals and operated a string of unlawful brewhouses and other unsavoury establishments'. The issue was decided in favour of the corporation and the mayor's officers given the right to serve processes in Temple Fee: Gregory O'Malley, *The Knights Hospitaller of the English Langue, 1460–1565* (Oxford: Oxford University Press, 2005), p. 213 referencing TNA STAC2/6/93; Martha C. Skeeters, *Community and Clergy: Bristol and the Reformation c.1530–c.1570* (Oxford, Clarendon Press, 1993), p. 69.

[37] TNA KB9/501/2 m. 24 [image 490].

[38] TNA KB27/1063 rex m. 3 [images 8066, 8067]. Tunstall was outlawed on 27 May 1527, and this may have prompted the presentation of the pardon: TNA KB27/1075 rex m. 2d [images 4967d, 4968d]. See p. 312.

[39] TNA KB9/504 m. 3 [image 978]; TNA KB9/509 m. 4–4d [images 8–10].

Baddesley in Hampshire on 8 June 1527, but was dragged out against his will on 24 June. He asked to be restored and pleaded not guilty. The language used to describe the sanctuary is the same as that used in 1516 and 1517, claiming that the manor 'is, and from time immemorial has been, a possession of the religious men, the priors and brothers of St John of Jerusalem in England and a privileged house and sanctuary for all that time'.[40] Rather than rejecting the claim, the justice of gaol delivery wished to be advised and Markes was remanded. He appeared at King's Bench a little over a year later, in May 1529, where he presented a pardon in which no mention was made of his claim to sanctuary.[41]

Although the Hospitallers clearly continued to offer sanctuary, the Star Chamber discussion did raise some troubling new concerns about the standards of proof required for sanctuaries, and the Knights tried to remedy the defects in their case for the future. A confirmation of the rights of St John of Jerusalem, now in the Westminster Abbey archives, explicitly notes that the king and his progenitors had known and expressly tolerated their claims to provide sanctuary for 300 years, and confirms the right of any hospital, preceptory, or any house of the order marked with a cross to give refuge for any transgression or crime to anyone who might claim it.[42] The top of the document is missing, the king who is supposedly speaking is never identified, and it is not signed or sealed, but it is filed with documents dating from the 1520s and 1530s, and perfectly answers the objections raised to the Hospitallers' claims in 1519. This suggests that it is a draft of a desired confirmation which never came to fruition. The framer of the document was probably not a lawyer, since the grant refers to transgressions and crimes rather than felony, debt, or treason, and was most likely the prior of the order, Thomas Docwra, who was unusually active in legal business.[43] His closeness to the centre of government and his extensive legal work must have given him reason to believe that such a grant would be approved, even though it apparently was not. This, once again, suggests that while there was growing awareness that the successful defense of such privileges required the ability to meet more modern standards of proof—and the acquisition of new documents when necessary—there was no sense that the privileges themselves were under threat.

As it set new terms for the discussion of sanctuary the Star Chamber discussion also made it clear that the creation of sanctuary rights belonged in the past. While it drew on language about the founding authorities of kings and popes that had

[40] TNA KB9/504 m. 3 [image 978].

[41] TNA KB27/1071 rex m. 6 [images 1319, 1320, 1504d, 1505d, 1321, 1322, 1506d].

[42] Westminster Abbey Muniments 9179.

[43] Though the priors were regularly nominated to commissions of the peace in Middlesex and Essex, Docwra was also on commissions of sewers, walls, and ditches, and gaol delivery, as well as the search for suspicious persons in Islington in 1519 and 1524–1525. He appeared in parliament, council, and star chamber and operated as a diplomat. As O'Malley notes, 'although some of his business was doubtless nominal, there remains the impression that Docwra's workload in the royal service was exceptional': O'Malley, *Knights Hospitaller*, p. 173.

emerged in *Stafford's Case*, it clearly recognized that any argument on that topic was in fact a discussion about forms of proof, rather than about potential future foundations. *Pauncefote v. Savage* was the last major case dealing with broad issues of jurisdiction, not because it marked the end of sanctuary, or the end of chartered sanctuaries, or the end of papal jurisdiction over sanctuary, but because by 1520 there was effective agreement on jurisdiction. Sanctuary rights were unlikely to be extended in this period, and men who claimed questionable sanctuaries for high-profile crimes were unlikely to escape unscathed. But well-established sanctuaries were unlikely to find themselves troubled in the ongoing conduct of their usual affairs.

2. Religious Houses, Chartered and Unchartered

The rest of this chapter will examine what the ongoing conduct of well-established sanctuaries looked like in this period. Our evidence is fuller than for the previous reign: we have about 460 claims of sanctuary between 1509 and 1529. Once again chartered sanctuaries make up the majority of that number, again largely because of the Beverley and Durham registers, which between them account for 203 claims, 95 at Beverley and 108 at Durham.[44] The other chartered sanctuaries are much less well-documented: there are thirty-five recorded claimants from Westminster in the period, but St Martins lags quite far behind with only nine.[45] Fifteen men, as we have seen, are recorded as claiming sanctuary in houses associated with St John of Jerusalem, six in other chartered sanctuaries, and twenty-seven in other religious houses. Two claimed sanctuary in locations they identified as franchises or cities, and eleven appear in other records as having claimed sanctuary, but without the sanctuary being identified. Parish churches again loom larger in the records than in the historiography: though few saw repeat claims, 150 claims of sanctuary in parish churches appear in these years. To put this in context, in Henry VII's reign we have evidence for an average of 5.75 claims of sanctuary in parish churches each year: between 1509 and 1529 we have evidence for an average of thirteen. We can't be sure if we're seeing a rise in claims or a rise in recording, though the evidence suggests more of the latter. But it does seem unlikely that the narrative of decline fueled by *Pauncefote v. Savage* is a reflection of the reality on the ground.

Whether the business in the country's sanctuaries remained steady or grew, it both changed and attracted more attention in these decades. The closer attention to recording demonstrates the greater interest of the authorities in the practical working of sanctuary, but their interest was not, for the most part, hostile. Though

[44] *Sanctuarium Dunelmense*. The registers may not be complete, and the Durham register ends in 1524, so this number is certainly less than the actual total.

[45] The respective numbers from the previous reign were fifteen each.

the changes of this period were often small ones, they served to regularize and streamline the management of sanctuary, bringing it more closely in line with the assumptions of the justices, as well as more closely under their eyes.

Chartered Sanctuaries: Westminster Abbey & St Martin le Grand

Westminster remains the most visible of the chartered sanctuaries through this period. As in the previous reign, homicide dominated the claims, though to a lesser extent: nineteen of thirty five were accused of homicide, while five were accessories (69 per cent compared to 87 per cent). Four men took sanctuary together for burglary, and a fifth claimed sanctuary as their receiver.[46] Two men claimed sanctuary for theft, and for three we have no details. This pattern is similar to the religious houses in the previous reign and suggests that the Westminster sanctuary population was becoming more varied than before.

Up to about 1521 the geographical pattern remains fairly consistent with the previous reign, but in the later 1520s the catchment area seems to have widened. Inquisitions on the body of Richard Algood in 1525 and Robert Poll in 1527 claim that their alleged killers, John Peke of Sutton Valence and Richard Stapull of Allington, both in Kent, were hunted through the neighbouring vills until the coroner got notice that they were in Westminster.[47] Both inquisitions were held by Richard French, and it is possible that both the format and the survival of the records are due to a particularly efficient coroner: French also delivered an inquisition on the body of Thomasine Peny in 1526 which claimed that her killer, Thomas Peny, had fled from Hollingbourne to Westminster.[48] On the other hand, a fourth Kentishman, John Caweston, apparently made the same journey in September 1528 after killing Oliver Burnet in self-defense in Cudham, and his inquisition was returned by Edward Asshe.[49] This cluster of four Kentish killers in four years making a break for Westminster stands out. It is possible that news spread within the locality that this was an effective strategy: Sutton Valence, Allington, and Hollingbourne are only five to seven miles apart, though Cudham is much closer to the Surrey border and also to Westminster. It seems equally likely that this was a more regular occurrence and that these coroners happened to make sure that the

46 TNA KB9/483 m. 17 [image not on AALT]; TNA KB27/1040 rex m. 15 [images 216, 194d, 195d].

47 TNA KB9/499 m. 52 [image 102]; TNA KB9/506/1 m.66 [image 137]. Though the purpose of the notation was presumably to excuse the failure of the hue and cry to secure the men, this is a rare mention of the process of finding out where a fugitive had gone, rather than the simple provision of the information.

48 TNA KB9/973 m. 57 [image not on AALT].

49 TNA KB9/509 m.42 [image 85]. The inquisition was opened on 11 September, the day Burnet died, in Cudham, but it was adjourned to 17 September in Sevenoaks. This is highly unusual, and no reason is given. The inquisition also reports a range of goods and chattels belonging to Caweston in other people's hands, which is also unusual; most inquisitions return that the accused had no lands or chattels. Caweston is described as a labourer.

records survived in these instances. None of the men appear in any other record, so we have no way of knowing if they remained in the sanctuary for some period of time, if they returned to Kent for trial, or if they simply disappeared.

Though the evidence from Henry VII's reign suggested that Westminster and St Martin's functioned in fairly similar ways, the evidence from this period makes them rather more distinct. We have records of far fewer men taking sanctuary in St Martin's in this period but all of them were involved with either murder or treason, and eight of the nine were local. Most of the St Martin's sanctuary men used their time to manage their situation in fairly traditional ways, and their various versions of homicide show a typical range. Robert Pank, a servant of William Holles, serjeant at mace of the city, took sanctuary in the precinct after a failed attempt to arrest Richard Goldsburgh for debt in the Roofe tavern in April 1527.[50] He claimed that Goldsburgh drew a knife on him and he fled, finally killing Goldsburgh in self-defence. Pank, not surprisingly, appeared in King's Bench with a pardon just over a year later, in May 1528.[51] The pardon makes no mention of him taking sanctuary, and it's not clear how much of the intervening period was spent there, but it was dated 13 May, suggesting that Pank took it to be enrolled as soon as he got it, and that he had in fact been in confinement until then. Anthony Mynyon, a London gunner, was a less sympathetic claimant. An inquisition found that he had murdered his wife Katherine in October 1527, stabbing her and producing a wound six fingers and more deep, before fleeing to St Martins.[52] Though nothing in the inquisition laid any groundwork, a writ from King's Bench to the coroner in March 1529 suggested that Anthony had killed Katherine in self-defense, and on 3 May he appeared in King's Bench with a pardon.[53] On the other extreme, William Fermor fled to St Martin's from Staplehurst in Kent, a distance of about forty miles, after he unintentionally stabbed James Kyng 'negligently, casually and by misfortune and against his will'.[54] The inquisition repeats five times, in different terms, that the stabbing was unintentional, but Fermor fled nonetheless and was pursued by the hue and cry until it was known that he was in St Martins. An inquisition on the body of Henry Hawe found that Richard Robbesley, a London yeoman alias staple merchant of Calais, killed him in his home in February 1529 before fleeing to sanctuary.[55] Robbesley appeared in King's Bench in July 1530 to plead not guilty, and was bailed. The jury found him not guilty in November, and asserted that Thomas Methew, a London yeoman, had in fact committed the crime.[56] Once again St Martin's seems to have served its purpose, providing shelter while these

[50] TNA KB9/506/1 m.43 [image 185].
[51] TNA KB27/1067 rex m. 3 [images 9831, 9832, 50d].
[52] TNA KB9/509 m. 153 [image 309].
[53] TNA KB9/509 m. 154 [image 311], TNA KB27/1071 rex m. 1 [images 1310, 1311, 1498d].
[54] TNA KB9/501/1 m.104 [image 357]. It is striking that once again the only non-Londoner in the sanctuary came from Kent, but it may just be coincidence.
[55] TNA KB9/513 m. 61 [image 127].
[56] TNA KB27/1076 rex m. 7 [images 5153, 5154].

men organized a defense or a pardon. There is no question that an apparently innocent man, one who killed by accident, or a London servant on official business all fit the model of the ideal sanctuary man better than the gunner who killed his wife in self-defense, but in all these cases the sanctuary worked as it had in the previous reign, and as we would expect.

Not every St Martin's sanctuary man was, or could present himself as, innocent, and John Cowley represents the other end of the spectrum, and in the process gives us an unusual glimpse into the world of the hardened criminal. Cowley was arrested in November 1515 and confined in the Marshalsea for theft. In March 1516 he apparently expressed heretical opinions in the prison, stating that 'if the prist yn the kynges Benche wold syng masse there he wold howle and that he had lever here a bagpype than a masse songen', and he received the Eucharist that Easter 'being in the same false opinion'. Problematic as his heresy may have been, Cowley really got into trouble the following October, when he and six other London and Southwark yeomen 'intended and desired' the murder of Henry VIII and Wolsey. The inquisition claimed that they asked 'vengeaunce apon the kyng that he wyll not geve a generall pardon and a vengeaunce apon my lorde Cardynall and all the kynges Councell' and went on to promise that 'if ever we may come furth of prison and be att our libertie we wull surely thrust a dagger yn my lord Cardynall orellys kill him with a hand gon'. Cowley was specifically quoted as saying that 'the king is ded & kept secrete yn Wyndesore by meanys of my lorde Cardynall And if ever I myght gete oute of prisone I wold utterly forsake Englond and go beyond the see' and he and others laughed as they said 'lett us fyll the pott apon abone vyage' and 'if I ever may gete furth att my libertie I wyll utterly forsake Englond & goo beyond the see and I know Turnoy so well that I wyll with thre or foure hundreth men fynde the meanys to wynne Tourney from the kynges possession'.[57] Though the inquisition is obviously most concerned with the treasonous implications of what seems to have been a lively drinking session, for our purposes these statements are interesting in what they reveal about the criminal culture: the men involved all seem to have been confined criminals complaining about the lack of a general pardon and expressing their desire to leave the country. The suggestion that they knew Tournai implies that it may have been a regular destination for English criminals. While the whole exchange seems to have been well-lubricated by alcohol and braggadocio, it is a rare glimpse of a criminal confraternity and their experience of the penal system. Facing punishment for treason and/or heresy rather than felony, Cowley escaped from the Marshalsea in January 1518, but rather than making a break for the coast, he took sanctuary in St Martins. He remained there until February, when 'Syr Thomas Lovell knyght and a nother knyght with hym unknowen to me his

[57] TNA KB9/475/2 mm 2d-3 [images 8, 9]. Some of his co-conspirators appear in p. 200 where their records add a conspiracy to support Richard de la Pole's return to England. It is not apparent from that record that the men were in prison at the time they made these statements.

name and many of ther servauntes with them and forsabilly with grete strength & power pullyd me oute of the body of the chirche of Seynt Martyn and so thurgh the Sentory to the towre contrary to Godes peace & the kynges and the right of holy chirch and all the holy canons besekyng youe yn the honour of god that I may be restored to my pryvylege as right requyres according to the lawe of holy Churche'.[58] Cowley appeared at King's Bench on 18 February, where he refused to plead and asked to be restored to sanctuary.[59] John Ernley argued that he should be refused on the grounds that sanctuary was not available for heresy, but he made no mention of the escape or the treason, and there was no suggestion that Cowley should go to the *peine fort* for the refusal to plead. The court wished to be advised, and Cowley was remanded until the following day, but his criminal history and the nature of his crimes made leniency unlikely. When he returned to court he claimed sanctuary once again, and this time the court ordered him to be hanged, disembowelled, his entrails burned, head cut off, body quartered, and the head and quarters to be displayed wherever the king wished, the punishment for treason rather than heresy.[60] Cowley, however, was an unusual claimant, and though he came from a very different milieu than Humphrey Stafford, he learned the same lesson: though some sanctuaries could offer protection for treason, a man who directly threatened the king was unlikely to be able to take advantage of them.

Chartered Sanctuaries: Durham and Beverley

As before, the Durham and Beverley records give us lots of names and crimes, but little sense of the context around the crimes for which their sanctuary men sought refuge. The Durham register ends in 1524, but it enrolled 108 sanctuary men between 1509 and that date. Homicide continues to dominate the register: 88 per cent of the claimants were either the principal or accessory to a murder, a similar percentage as in the previous reign. The sense that the central government was making itself felt in the North continues to grow: the claimants specifying that they feared indictment for their crime that we saw under Henry VII continue, but we also see more men who confess that they were present at a homicide, though they often

[58] Cowley was unusually specific in his description of the sanctuary: he claimed that he 'toke the Seyntory & pryvvelege of Saynt Martyns set & stondyng withyn the citie of London Aldersgate on the northwestsyde of it & Newgate on the southwest syde and saynt Michell yn the querne on the south syde & saynt Leonards on the est syde part passell of the same sentory'. He claims that he was taken out on 11 Feverer, suggesting that he may have been French in origin, though this would also imply a fidelity in the record to the words of the accused that we don't usually expect.

[59] Caryll reports this point but does not give the broader narrative or the outcome: *Caryll's Reports*, vol. 2, p. 694. He identifies the accused as Walter Cowley.

[60] The other conspirators pleaded not guilty on 16 February. Two were found not guilty but the other three were found guilty and received the same punishment as Cowley. There is no verdict recorded for the sixth man.

specify that they did not deliver a mortal blow, suggesting that there was a greater concern that accessories would be indicted and punished than before.[61]

If the crimes for which men claimed sanctuary remained much the same, Durham's geographical pull had grown significantly: it enrolled almost no-one from Durham itself, but it drew heavily from Northumberland, Yorkshire and Lancashire, with a smattering of claimants from further afield: Cheshire, Derby, Lincolnshire, Worcestershire, and even one from Middlesex. The absence of men from Durham is curious: those living in the palatinate were outside the jurisdiction of the common law, but they had used the sanctuary in substantial numbers in the previous reign, suggesting that a change in local administration may have been responsible.

Beverley also remained busy. Between 1509 and 1529 ninety-four men and one woman are recorded at a fairly steady pace: eleven men arrived in 1510 and ten in 1516, but in most years the sanctuary took in three to five claimants.[62] Fifty-six of the claims were for homicide (60 per cent), much fewer than in the previous reign, and most of the rest were for felony, usually unspecified, though in some cases the record notes that the crime was theft, theft, and other causes, felony on a sheep, or theft and debt. Fifty-two of the claimants whose place of origin was specified came from Yorkshire, but Beverley continued to draw claimants from all over the country: fourteen from Lincolnshire and three from Durham, not surprisingly, but also three from London, two each from Worcestershire, Suffolk and Dorset and one from Northumberland, Shropshire, Nottinghamshire, Gloucestershire, Coventry, Essex, Cambridgeshire, Buckinghamshire, Hertfordshire and Devon.[63] This is an even wider range than in the previous reign, and while it's possible that these outsiders had committed crimes in the area, it does at least raise the possibility that some had come to Beverley on purpose.[64]

It's hard to draw conclusions from this scattered evidence, though it is clear that the sanctuaries were still busy and useful. The decline in homicide claims at Westminster and Beverley might suggest that the relative power of those sanctuaries was on the wane: we would need much more conclusive evidence before dethroning Westminster, but the fact that Sir Anthony Savage, one of the defendants in *Pauncefote v. Savage*, took sanctuary at Durham provides pause for thought.[65] The registers suggest that the forces of the criminal justice system were increasingly being felt in the North, but in a cause celebre, distance might still have seemed like an advantage. Even lesser criminals than Savage might have seen an

[61] See, for example, *Sanctuarium Dunelmense*, pp. 59, 60, 79, 80, 83.

[62] Beverley also gave sanctuary for debt, and there were a substantial number of claimants in this category.

[63] The registrar generally did better with local places, and most of the Yorkshire names are fairly clear. Many of the others are much more ambiguous, so I have assumed that the counties are correct.

[64] As we'll see below, pp. 257–259 Beverley was a popular destination in the 1530s too.

[65] *Sanctuarium Dunelmense*, p. 80.

advantage to taking their respite north of the Humber, if time and circumstances allowed.

Other Chartered Sanctuaries

As the clear characteristics that seemed to define the major chartered sanctuaries in the previous reign begin to blur, other chartered sanctuaries begin to appear in the records, though most of them had probably been operating for some time. Inquisitions on the relevant bodies found that William Syncklere and John Taylor alias Akent, for example, fled to Beaulieu after killing Henry Byly on the highway in August 1513; Richard Catenall after killing Edmund Kylgrose in self-defence in December 1514, and Peter Burges after the murder of Richard Sewett in April 1515.[66] None of the men appear in the records again. Catenall and Burgess both committed their crimes within the jurisdiction of Bishop's Waltham, a liberty of the bishop of Winchester about eighteen miles from Beaulieu across Southampton water, the river Test and river Itchen, but Syncklere and Taylor would have travelled about 40 miles from Durweston to reach the abbey; once again we see that though the range of the chartered sanctuaries was primarily local, they could exert a pull for outsiders. And the appearance of four sanctuary-seekers in the space of less than two years suggests that the abbey may have been busier than the King's Bench records indicate.[67]

John Tresanowe's plea also suggests that Beaulieu carried some weight as a sanctuary: an inquisition on the view of the body of William Morgan held in October 1510 in Truro, Cornwall, found that Tresanowe had attacked him with premeditation and killed him before fleeing to sanctuary in St Keverne.[68] St Keverne had come into the possession of Beaulieu in the mid-thirteenth century and the abbey's rights of sanctuary had been extended to the Cornish church.[69] Tresanowe seems to have remained at St Keverne for about a year: he was outlawed in September 1511, and finally appeared at King's Bench with a pardon dated 7 November 1511.[70] We saw in *Stafford's Case* that the rights of a major house did not necessarily extend to its satellites: the extension of Beaulieu's rights to St Keverne would have been acceptable under the terms of the Star Chamber discussion in *Pauncefote v. Savage*, however, though we cannot know how often they were exercised.

[66] TNA KB9/464 m. 61 [image 128]; TNA KB9/966 m. 60 [image not on AALT]; TNA KB9/469 m. 96 [image 192].

[67] See pp. 257, 282, 292–293. Beaulieu's location on the Solent made it an attractive option for criminous travellers, but this doesn't explain why it emerges into the records in these years.

[68] TNA KB9/457 m. 107 [image 209].

[69] Walterus Truron [sic, likely Walter Frere], *Cornish Church Guide* (Truro: Oscar Blackford, 1928), pp. 117–118.

[70] TNA KB27/1002 rex m. 6 [images 200, 201, 185d, 186d, 202].

As a church St Keverne's claims were fairly straightforward, but sanctuary rights also migrated to sites that presented the same kinds of problems as the Hospitaller properties, and they continued to operate in the later years of the decade. An inquisition on the view of the body of Nicholas Fysher in April 1525 found that Leonard Lanstall attacked and killed him and then fled to 'the town of Crake in Yorkshire, parcel of the liberty and sanctuary of St Cuthbert of Durham'.[71] A few years later John Grene fled to Knoll after killing Robert Orgell in February 1528. Knoll is described in the inquisition as 'a liberty town having sanctuary, such that the same John could not be taken or extracted from the same liberty and sanctuary'.[72] Though it is not specified as such, Knowle was a possession of Westminster Abbey, and may have claimed sanctuary status as a result. Local chartered sanctuaries thus continued to perform an important role, but one which generally did not draw the attention of the central government.[73]

Rather than *Pauncefote v. Savage* being a watershed in the campaign against chartered sanctuaries, it is clear that both St John of Jerusalem and other chartered sanctuaries continued much as before in its wake. Their dependencies may also have offered an enhanced form of sanctuary based on the privileges of the mother house, at least to men whose crimes did not seem to challenge the authority of the crown. Any narrative of decline is clearly premature and ignores the substantial evidence provided by the regular and uncontroversial workings of these sanctuaries.

3. Parish Sanctuaries and Abjuration

The discussion in *Pauncefote v. Savage* made it clear that no-one was challenging the rights of parish churches to offer sanctuary, and so we might expect to see them continue to operate much as they had done in the reign of Henry VII. And indeed, we continue to see much more varied claims of sanctuary here than in the religious houses, with about one third of the claimants confessing to homicide of various kinds and one to infanticide while the other two-thirds confessed to theft, burglary, robbery (highway and other) or assault. In general, parish churches continued to see a wider variety of criminals than chartered sanctuaries, and they were clearly the preferred option for non-violent offenders as well as non-homicidal ones. There is, however, a significant change in the patterns of abjuration in this period (fig. 7.1). Both the number and the proportion of recorded abjurers is much higher in the first two decades of Henry VIII's reign than before. Under Henry VII we have the record of seventy-one men claiming sanctuary in parish churches, of

[71] TNA KB9/502 m. 89 [image 183]. There are no further proceedings on this case

[72] TNA KB9/509 m. 156 [image 315].

[73] McSheffrey, *Seeking Sanctuary*, pp. 140–164 details a later case at Knowle which did draw such attention, but mainly because of the individuals involved.

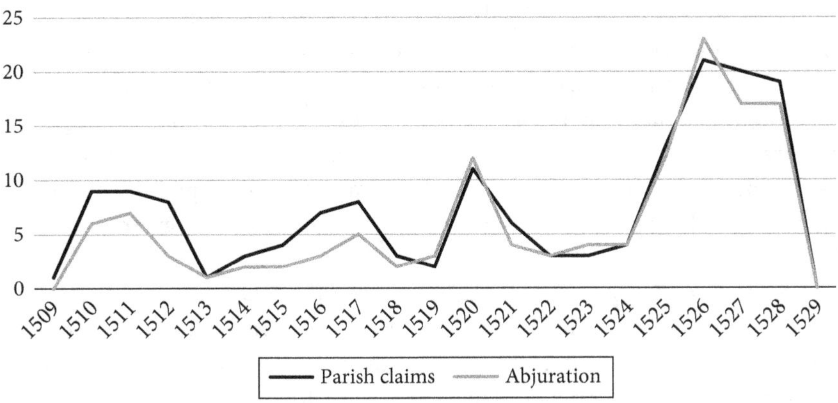

Figure 7.1 Recorded claims of parish sanctuary and abjurations 1509–1529*
*Data collected from TNA KB27 and KB9 rolls.

whom twenty-three (32 per cent) abjured.[74] Between 1509 and 1529 we have records of 150 claims of sanctuary in religious and parish churches of whom 121 (80 per cent) abjured. One hundred and eleven men and one woman abjured from parish churches between 1510 and 1528, and nine men abjured from religious houses.[75] The pattern for abjuration tracks the pattern for sanctuary quite closely, suggesting that a fairly stable proportion of those who claimed sanctuary took this path, though both the number and the proportion of abjurers was higher in the second half of the 1520s than before. Unlike in the reign of Henry VII, where most of the surviving records of abjurations are for men who were later found in the country, in the reign of Henry VIII most seem to have left, or at least not to have been found. Only twelve of the 121 who abjured subsequently appeared in court, either having been found in the country, or with a pardon for their crime and abjuration.

Though the numbers remain low through the early part of the reign, they are fairly steady except for a substantial drop in 1513 and a substantial peak in 1520. The first obvious question is whether this is a change in practice or a change in recording, or both.[76] There is no statutory change or leading case that might account for such an impact, though, as we have seen, the relationship between such

[74] See p. 154.

[75] Though the number for monastic houses is low, there were no such abjurations in the previous reign. There are no recorded abjurations in 1529.

[76] Kesselring notes that the surviving records of abjuration appear in the greatest number in the decade between 1525 and 1535, and speculates that either this rise in the number of abjurations sparked legislation passed in 1529, or that parliament's interest in the matter prompted the coroners to be more diligent in their returns: K.J. Kesslering, 'Abjuration and its Demise: The Changing Face of Royal Justice in the Tudor Period', *Canadian Journal of History* 34 (1999), p. 348. It seems unlikely that a 1529 statute could have prompted the earlier change, though it may well have responded to it. See p. 250 for a discussion of the 1529 statute. Kesselring also provides a clear discussion of the problems of record survival.

events and practice, especially at the local level, is not necessarily direct. Though the numbers quickly drop back to their former levels after 1520, there is a steep and sustained increase in the second half of the 1520s which seems unlikely to be the result simply of a change in recording, or a handful of eager coroners. Though there is no direct evidence in statutes or writs to account for this change, there is some indirect evidence that the increase in numbers was intentional and probably a result of both increased abjuration and better records, and it comes from an unexpected place: the pattern of ports used for abjuration (fig. 7.2).

Dover and Southampton were the most popular ports throughout the period, not surprisingly: between 1509 and 1529 twenty-seven men were sent to leave the country from the former, twenty-five from the latter. Kingston on Hull, Harwich and Bishop's Lynn made up the next rank, with fourteen, thirteen, and twelve abjurers sent their way respectively. Portsmouth and Yarmouth had six each, one ahead of Boston and Rye, while Sandwich, Weymouth, Chester, Poole, Lyme Regis, Newcastle, Ipswich, Plymouth, Chichester, Hastings, and Scarborough saw one to three each. These numbers are not evenly distributed across the period, however. Though the number of abjurers grows sharply in 1525 and after, the numbers going to any individual port don't change substantially. Seven men were directed to Dover in 1527 and five to Kingston on Hull the following year, but those are exceptional: otherwise no port had more than four recorded abjurers in any year, and most had fewer. As the total number of abjurers grew, they were distributed around a larger number of ports: Newcastle, Scarborough, Plymouth, Ipswich, Chichester, and Hastings appear for the first time in 1525, and between then and 1528 nine men were directed their way. The first three ports represent a geographical extension of abjuration ports to the north-east and south-west respectively, while the latter three relieved the burdens in the east and the south.

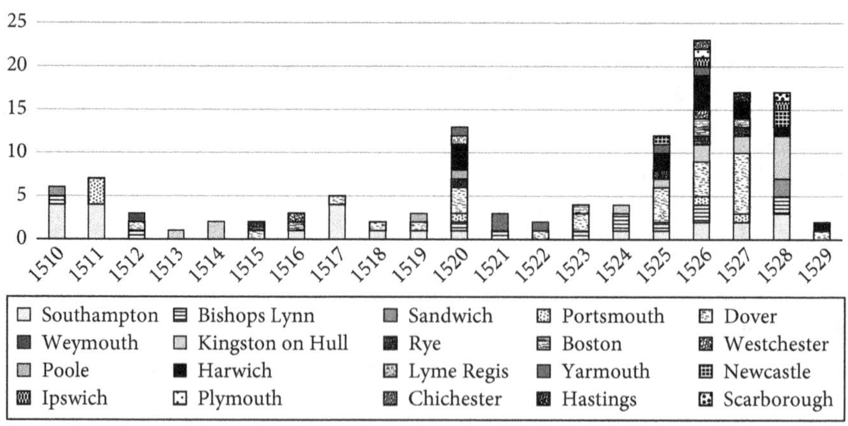

Figure 7.2 Recorded ports of abjuration 1510–1529*

*Data collected from TNA KB27 and KB9 rolls.

To look at the evidence another way, between 1510 and 1519 we see abjurers being sent to between one and three ports in any given year, though the ports might change. In 1520, when the number of abjurers spikes, the number of ports also jumps, to nine, and Harwich, Lyme Regis, and Yarmouth make their first appearance. The numbers drop again for a few years, and so do the number of ports (though Yarmouth continues to appear), until 1526 (thirteen ports), 1527 (eight ports), and 1528 (eight ports). Why did this happen? As the numbers of abjurations grew, it must have seemed unwise to send growing numbers of felons to the same port, whether because they were unlikely to find passage or because they were likely to be troublesome in the port (this is probably also part of the explanation for why no-one ever embarked from London).[77] But if this pattern is intentional it suggests two things: that a substantial proportion of abjurers were expected to make it to their assigned ports, and that the growing numbers were recognized, and probably intended.

Again, there is no direct evidence to explain this, but it is worth keeping in mind that this is the same period in which the justices were trying to track claims of benefit of clergy more closely, and it would hardly be surprising if they also began to pay attention to abjurations and to look for better records of that practice. The most likely venue for the communication of any change in policy on that matter would be the assize sessions, when coroners were expected to turn over their accumulated records and when the justices could pass on instructions about the better recording of abjurations and perhaps their strategic distribution. Such instructions could have been oral, or swiftly disposed of, but the pattern seems too coherent to be the result of chance. As the number of clergy claimants was rising, so was the number of abjurers: as repeat offenders and bigamists were being weeded out and sent for execution, abjurers who might once have disappeared into the countryside were being more systematically distributed around the country and their records more consistently returned to King's Bench lest they should reappear without permission.

This new abjuration model was, like the clergy model, being worked out across these years, and the relative abundance of returns allows us to see both what the justices were trying to achieve, and what the coroners actually did. Though the evidence, as usual, is scattered, it suggests both that there was a strong desire to establish better, clearer procedures, and that the coroners, while generally solid on the principles of what they were to do, were often unschooled on the details. This can often be usefully revealing. For example, though the coroners' records were required to contain certain pieces of information and usually presented them in

[77] Cf. William C. Jordan, *From England to France* (Princeton: Princeton University Press, 2015), pp. 64–78 which develops a complex argument for a system of gathering abjurers at Dover and shipping them en masse to France. If that was in fact happening in the fourteenth century, which seems unlikely for the same reasons, it was certainly not happening in the sixteenth.

the same order, they were not blank forms, and the wording could vary from coroner to coroner.[78] In this period the wording varies more than it had previously done, and in the process sheds some light on the concerns of the coroners as they created the records. For example, after Robert Bromley claimed sanctuary in the parish church of Sutterton in March 1510, he asked for the coroner, Anthony Irby, 'by his own consent without any coercion' and confessed 'that he was a felon of the lord king and said publicly in the presence of the said coroner' that he had killed Richard Taillour.[79] Irby then recorded Bromley's confession in the first person, along with the description of his abjuration. Bromley swore to 'hurry to the port of Bishop's Lynn which had been given to me and that I ought not to depart from the king's highway and I wish to do this as a thief and felon of the lord king and that at the port of Bishop's Lynn I will diligently seek transit and I will only remain there for one tide if I am able to get transit and if I am not able to get transit in such a space I will walk into the sea every day up to my knees and ask for transit and if I do not get transit within forty days I will return to this church as a thief and felon of the king'. Though this is a classic description of abjuration, it had not generally appeared in the records of abjurations in the previous reign and this suggests that Irby wanted to be able to demonstrate that his abjurer had had full and clear instructions, though whether he was uncertain of his own authority or his abjurer's good intentions cannot be known. This is also the earliest record I have found in this period which characterizes an abjurer as a 'felon of the king', in sharp distinction to the earlier texts which characterized him as one outside the law of the realm.[80] This phrase would become more common—we have already seen the prior of St Andrew's in Northampton use it in Hugh Boswell's case in the summer of 1513—and though it is impossible to pinpoint its emergence in this period, it indicates that those engaged with the criminal justice system recognized that the government intended to assert control over all convicted felons, including those who had traditionally removed themselves from the common law system by choosing exile or delivery to the church. Those men were also the king's felons, and his officers and lawyers would determine their fate, including the ways in which they might live as well as die.

This intention to assert control is also evident in the increasing attention paid to getting the abjurer across the country, though the stories that survive demonstrate the gap between the ideal and the reality, as well as the ways in which the

[78] See pp. 86–87 for a discussion of procedures.

[79] TNA KB9/455 m. 25 [image 54].

[80] This language did not appear in the records of Henry VII or earlier in the reign of Henry VIII. An abjuror's oath printed in a collection of oaths among the statutes of uncertain date uses the same language, but it was taken from Rastall's 1557 edition of the statutes: *SR*, I. 250; *A colleccion of all the statutes (from the begynning of Magna Carta vnto the yere of our Lorde, 1557) which were before that yere imprinted And furst a pistle, necessary to be redde by them that shall vse this booke* edited by William Rastell STC/9306 (London, 1557), p. 2. The language may have been older, but at the very least it seems to have re-entered the lexicon of the Tudor lawyers in these years.

abjurers might frame their experience for the authorities. We saw above that it had been possible for some time that a constable might be assigned to accompany an abjurer; though it is impossible to be sure, the evidence suggests that this was not typical. We also saw mention of a 'bill' of abjuration, a document that the abjurer might carry with him as evidence of his status, for the first time in 1504.[81] Both mechanisms for compliance, the human and the bureaucratic, seem to become more common in this period, but both had clear limitations, as Richard Bery's and Jeffrey Jenyns' abjurations demonstrate. Bery took sanctuary in the cemetery of the parish church of Kidbrooke in Kent on 4 April 1512 and two days later confessed that he had stolen a tablecloth, blankets and sheets.[82] Bery claimed the 'liberty and tuition of the said church according to the laudable custom of the English Church' and then 'as the custom is, publicly abjured'. The coroner assigned him to go to Dover, he left from the gate of the cemetery and was delivered to the constable of Blackheath for the next stage of his journey. So far this looks like any other abjuration, but Bery appeared at King's Bench on 21 June, just over two months later, and was asked why he had not completed his abjuration.[83] He claimed that he had been transferred from constable to constable for three days until he reached Boughton-under-Blean, about 45 miles into his 65 mile journey. At that point, on 9 April, Good Friday, the constable left him alone on the highway to wait for the next constable to arrive. Bery claimed he remained in place for three hours until three unknown men came from Canterbury by horse. The dubious benefit of the sanctuary man's garb becomes apparent at this point, for one of the men got down from his horse and (according to Bery) said '"thou errant thefe art thou here I shall slee the with my owen honed" and drowgh his swerde and strake at hym'. Bery fled into the woods for fear of his life, with the men in pursuit, and hid from Friday through the Easter weekend until dawn on Monday, a day late for purposes of maintaining his Paschal narrative. He emerged at Chislehurst, having retraced his steps almost to Kidbrooke, and he asked for food and water.[84] He insisted that he 'carried his cross and purse openly upon him', but he was arrested by one Brograve and brought to the King's Bench prison. When he appeared in King's Bench he 'asked to have his passport again' so that he could return to the road and abjure.[85]

Jeffrey Jenyns's experience demonstrates that even with the proper paperwork and a fairly substantial escort, an abjurer might still be vulnerable. Jenyns was indicted for breaking into the church of St Edmund in New Sarum in October 1527,

[81] See p. 87.

[82] TNA KB9/458 m. 110 [image 230]. Bery's confession is given in the first person, and the items he stole are given in both Latin and English.

[83] TNA KB 27/1004 rex m. 19 [images 256, 257].

[84] Chislehurst is about 5 miles south of Kidbrooke, dominated by the Walsingham family at this point.

[85] Ernley argued that his claim was insufficient, and the court agreed with him when they addressed the case the following Michelmas. However, there was clearly some concern that the process had not gone as smoothly as it should, and the court asked Bery 'if he were a clerk or not'. Bery, demonstrating either a level of honesty or a lack of self-preservation commensurate with sitting alone for three hours

along with two other men, and stealing silver worth well in excess of £200.[86] He apparently escaped capture then, but 'took the degre of Seynt Edithe in the monastery of Wylton' in September 1529.[87] Jenyns did not provide his confession, so it's not clear if the sanctuary was for this crime or another, but he did note that 'the crowner came thyther acordyng to the kynges lawes and ther yn the forseid monasterye the forseid crowner made for me my pasporte uppon the wyche pasporte I was deliveryd from churche to the kynges officers accordyng unto gods lawes & the kynges'. As he was escorted along the highway a group of men from Salisbury seized him and carried him away to the gaol. He appeared before Richard Lyster in January 1530, when he asked to be restored, and named both the four men who were escorting him and the four men who seized him.[88] These cases demonstrate that the 'bill of abjuration' developed fairly quickly into a 'passport', which signaled a properly sanctioned abjuration and apparently carried some weight in the eyes of abjurers.[89]

They also indicate that the use of constables was becoming quite common; though we tend to hear about their presence when the system failed, either because the chain was broken or the constable was outmatched, it is unlikely that coroners would have continued to use them if they did not generally contribute to a positive outcome. Some coroners seem to have thought the use of constables through quite thoroughly, especially in the context of multiple abjurations. On 29 April 1511, for example, Thomas Pleydell took the confessions of John Turnebull, Henry Bewardy, and William and Philip Jonys at the parish church of All Saints at Coleshill in Berkshire: Turnebull confessed to a murder in Southwark earlier

on the highway waiting for a constable to appear, answered that he was not a clerk, and the court sentenced him to be hanged.

[86] TNA KB9/1065 m. 130 [image not on AALT].

[87] TNA KB9/1065 m. 129 [image not on AALT].

[88] TNA KB27/1104 rex m. 8 [images 166, 167, 321d, 322d, 168]. Jenyns appears to have languished in gaol in Salisbury for some time: his records were called to King's Bench in July 1536, when the mayor responded that he had no cause to detain him, but the bishop's bailiff admitted that he had him in custody for various felonies. Jenyns himself finally appeared in King's Bench a year later, on 28 June 1537, with a pardon for all crimes and abjurations before 10 June 1537 and went *sine die*. One of his accomplices in the original theft presented a pardon on 29 November 1529, suggesting that the claim of sanctuary may have done more to complicate the issue than to help it: TNA KB27/1073 rex m. 15 [images 2286, 2287, 2562d]. It's likely that Jenyns had other strikes against him.

[89] Paul Hyams mentions testimonials for twelfth-century abjurers preserved at Edward the Confessor's shrine at Westminster: *Rancor and Reconciliation in Medieval England* (London and Ithaca: Cornell University Press, 2003), p. 135. *SR*, I. 56, 58, 12 Ric. II, cc. 3, 7, 8, in reaffirming the statute of labourers, required servants or labourers travelling to a new master or going on pilgrimage to carry letters patent under a royal seal describing their journey, and also required begging scholars of the universities or returning military captives to provide letters testimonial. This model may build upon those older traditions, or perhaps the safe-conduct, which Lacey notes was common in the late thirteenth century, but faded in the fourteenth: Helen Lacey, 'Protection and Immunity in Later Medieval England,' in *Peace and Protection in the Middle Ages* edited by T.B. Lambert and David Rollason (Durham: Centre for Medieval and Renaissance Studies, 2009), pp. 90–91. Cf. Valentin Groebner, *Who Are You? Identification, Deception, and Surveillance in Early Modern Europe*, trans. Mark Kyburz and John Peck (New York: Zone Books, 2007), pp. 172–174.

that month, Bewardy to a murder in Gravesend in October 1510, and the Jonyses to a murder with a crossbow in Wales in February 1511.[90] The four men had converged on Coleshill from opposite directions, but there is no sense of when or how they joined forces, and Pleydell took separate confessions for the three crimes. No separate date is given for the Jonyses' abjuration, implying that they left for Portsmouth, their assigned port, on 29 April, but Bewardy abjured to Southampton on 1 May and Turnebull to Portsmouth on 2 May. The abjurations were staggered for a practical reason: each one specifies that the felon was delivered to the constable of Coleshill and was to be passed on to the next constable. Thus the constable would have taken the Jonyses to the edge of his jurisdiction on Tuesday, Bewardy on Thursday, and Turnebull on Friday, for a busy week. If the system worked as it should, they would presumably have remained a day or two apart all the way south.

Pleydell's strategy seems to have been primarily driven by the availability of the constable, but it is notable that he chose to allow two of the four to abjure together, while separating the other two. Different coroners made different choices when it came to group claims of sanctuary. When Richard Gybbes took the confessions of Richard Constable alias Waller, William Brygges, Thomas Hoigeson, and Thomas Abromell at the parish church of Cropredy in Oxfordshire in September 1517 he sent the men, who all took sanctuary together and confessed to burglary and assault the previous day, to Southampton together.[91] When Ralph Skrymscher took the confessions of Robert Comforth and William Holred at All Saints church in Cottam, Nottinghamshire in August 1516 he emphatically separated the men: Comforth went to Boston, on the east coast, and Holred westwards to Chester. Comforth confessed to homicide in self-defense in 1512 and horse theft in 1515 and Holred to a burglary in July 1516, but both had broken out of Grantham prison earlier that same day.[92]

The coroners obviously had some discretion in the decision about whether to separate abjurers or leave them together, and Pleydell's decision to separate two and leave the other two together suggests that the decision was made on a case-by-case basis. Though there is never any explanation for the decision, the coroners must have weighed the kinds of circumstances we have seen in operation in numerous cases and recognized that even if they sent their abjurer forth with both a passport and a trustworthy constable, there was no guarantee that later constables would be as trustworthy or that they would reach their destination untroubled by either passers-by or officials. We know that many coroners took the safety of their charges seriously, and the decision to leave some together may have been driven

[90] TNA KB9/459 mm. 64–66 [images 137–141].

[91] TNA KB9/967 m. 35 [image not on AALT].

[92] TNA KB9/1002 mm. 20, 21 [images not on AALT]. Since Grantham is about 35 miles from Cottam, this suggests that there was either another horse theft which went unconfessed, or the dates are not accurate.

by that concern.[93] The treatment of Elizabeth Wallewen, one of the few women to appear in the sanctuary records, points in the same direction. A Gloucester spinster, Wallewen took sanctuary in the parish church of St Mary of Llanthony in March 1511 and confessed that she had killed a male infant before baptism in November 1510.[94] She was assigned to leave the realm from Southampton, but she did not do so alone. Walter Swayne, a yeoman from Newport in Shropshire, had claimed sanctuary in the same church on the same day as Elizabeth. He confessed to a completely different crime, a burglary in March 1510, but he was also assigned to Southampton by William Goldsmith, the Gloucester coroner.[95] On the face of it, this is an odd decision for Goldsmith: infanticide was not a sympathetic crime, and the specification that the child was killed before baptism made it even less so. Although it is possible that Wallewen and Swayne had ended up in the church together on the same day by chance, given the time that had elapsed since their crimes it seems more likely that they took sanctuary together, and that Goldsmith elected to allow them to remain together on the journey to the port, but rather than sending them the 35 miles to Bristol, for example, he sent them the 88 miles to Southampton.[96] In this case it seems likely that he saw Swayne as a possible protector for Wallewen on the journey, and the journey to the distant port continued to serve the penitential function that had long been a part of abjuration. Similarly, though Pleydell separated two of his four abjurers, he allowed the Jonyses to travel together: we could speculate that Pleydell was uncomfortable sending one or both of them—perhaps a father and son, or young brothers—alone on the journey, even with a constable.

Though this might seem to give too much credit to Pleydell, he was clearly thoughtful in his approach to his role. This is apparent not only in his disposition of his abjurers, but in his respect for the physical space of the church. When Pleydell took the confessions of Turnebull, Bewardy and the Jonyses, he was very clear that he went only to the door of the church, where the men came to him to confess; indeed he makes that point three separate times in each document.[97] He was not the only one to pay attention to this detail: when Gybbes took the confessions of the Cropredy four he noted that they confessed in the porch.[98] Not all coroners were so careful: when John Frampton went to take the confession of John Stone at the chapel of St John at Bridport in Dorset in May 1512, by contrast, he cheerfully noted that he had taken Stone out of the chapel, but that Stone claimed the privilege

[93] R.F. Hunnisett, 'The Last Sussex Abjurations', *Sussex Archaeological Collections* 102 (1964), p. 44 quotes an abjuration (no. 11) where the abjuror was to be handed over to the constable 'to lead him from constable to constable to the sanctuary without injury or danger to his life'.

[94] TNA KB9/458 m. 79 [image 168].

[95] TNA KB9/458 m. 83 [image 176].

[96] Busy though it was, Bristol is never assigned: all the abjuration ports, except Chester, faced France.

[97] TNA KB9/459 mm. 64–66 [images 137–141]: Turnebull's and Bewardy's confessions are in the same hand, the Jonyses in a different hand.

[98] TNA KB9/967 m. 35 [image not on AALT].

of the chapel and confessed the crime, whereupon he abjured. The proper sequence of events was not closely observed here, but Frampton seems satisfied that by the end of the day Stone was on his way to Weymouth, his port of choice, and in this case no harm seems to have come to either coroner or abjurer despite the lack of precision in the legal niceties.[99]

In other cases such inexperience cost the sanctuary man dearly. Thomas Parker was found by an inquisition jury in May 1526 to have killed Thomas Otefeld in Clayce Wood in Enderby.[100] The jury noted that Otefeld was hunting deer illegally, and Parker, one of the keepers of the king's deer, 'by vertue of his office came to take the seid Thomas Otefeld and to have delivered hym to the kynges lewetenaunt of the seid chase ther to have ben restrened accordyng to the kynges lawes which the seid Thomas refused to doo and yn no wyse wold submytte hym selfe to the seid Thomas Parker but drewe hys swerd to have slayne and murdered the same Thomas Parker'. Parker fled to the Franciscan house in Leicester, where his abjuration is presented as an indenture in which he was examined and questioned by the coroners.[101] In it he admitted that he had 'strykyn Thomas Otfyld & gaff hym the wound wherof he died & therfor I the seid Thomas Parker clayme & aske this seyntuary for the salvacion of my lyff'. He was sent the following day to the port of Boston in the company of a constable. Parker had an obvious case for a claim of self-defense, and Spelman notes that if a man killed another in self-defense he should not abjure, for by the statute of Gloucester he should have a pardon for the crime, but if he abjures he will be attainted.[102] Though he does not explain why, elsewhere he argues that if a man is convicted and pleads clergy he cannot answer to any previous felonies.[103] If death was the anticipated punishment for felony and thus punishment for one felony automatically took care of the others, when the criminal managed to substitute one of the other possible outcomes, the same logic applied. Thus by abjuring the unlucky Parker was giving up the automatic pardon that would come with a verdict of self-defense, though he could still seek a pardon in the usual way.

Royal officials were not the only inexperienced links in the chain. William Symondson was indicted before the justices of the peace at Chelmsford in Essex in July 1528 for breaking into the house of Richard Riche at Shelley the previous March.[104] Symondson appeared at King's Bench in April 1529 and claimed that the

[99] It's not clear that the chapel could legally provide sanctuary. Chaloner argued that the privilege did not apply to chapels, since they are private, but only to churches 'where every sacrament is ministered': *Rights and Liberties*, p. 3. Kebell and Richard Littleton make similar points in their readings: *Spelman's Reports* vol. 2, p. 335. As with earlier abjurations, the coroner chose distance over convenience: Weymouth was about 20 miles away to the east, while Lyme Regis, a fairly major port, lay only half that distance to the west.

[100] TNA KB9/502 m.146 [image 306].

[101] TNA KB9/502 m.145 [image 304].

[102] *Spelman's Reports*, vol. 1, pp. 67–68.

[103] *Spelman's Reports*, vol. 1, p. 51. Also in *Spelman's Reports*, vol. 1, p. 167; *Reports from Henry VIII*, vol. 1, p 90.

[104] TNA KB27/1071 rex m. 14 [images 1338, 1339, 1520d].

previous October, under the name William Fysher, he had taken sanctuary at the Dominican house at Ilchester in Somerset.[105] The prior accepted him and called for the coroner, who was unable to come because he was in London with the lord chief justice. The prior was apparently both cautious and unfamiliar with the usual processes, for he put Symondson in irons, though Symondson does specify that they were light. Thomas Bloyden, bailliff of Ilchester, John Geffrey, warden of Ilchester gaol, and Thomas Marten of Northeover, along with others, then came and tried to convince him to leave 'through their sweet words'. Failing to convince Symondson, the officers obliged the prior on pain of £50 to keep him there for ten days until they could get advice. With this added incentive Symondson was loaded down with shackles on his legs and an iron chain around his neck, and was kept in the church until 1 November, when Geffrey, Marten, Bloyden, and Bloyden's brother Humphrey came and took him away between midnight and 1am and brought him to the gaol.[106] This suggests that the prior either had no experience of sanctuary, or little support for it, in contrast to the other clergy we have seen actively supporting claims.

Such clerics continued to exist in this reign, however. An inquisition on the view of the body of John Hudson found that John Bewesbery gave him a lethal blow on 30 January and took sanctuary in the collegiate church in Maidstone the same day. Hudson died of the blow on 4 February, and the same day Bewesbery escaped from the church disguised in vestments, with the help of Humphrey Jones of Maidstone, chaplain.[107] Even more dramatically, at the session of the peace in Chichester in April 1521, William Gogan and Simon Saunder were found guilty of burglary and sentenced to be hanged the following day at Broyle Heath.[108] The rope hanging Gogan broke, and he fell to the ground alive. Richard Sutton, the sheriff's deputy, grabbed him and wanted to finish the job, but Richard Inskipp of Chicester, pardoner, John Fesisian of Downeley, physician, Hugh Lassell, Hugh Lykerd, and Humphrey Taylor of Chicester, clerks, and Humphrey Holmes and Benedict Holmes of Chichester, friars, and many others attacked Sutton, took

[105] According to the record he took sanctuary on 39 October [sic].

[106] The court wished to be advised, and Symondson was remanded. He appeared again in Michelmas term 1539 with a pardon.

[107] Bewesbery may have been afraid of being removed from sanctuary while Hudson lingered: Yorke notes that if a man gives one a mortal blow and takes to sanctuary, he can be removed, but if the other dies he will not be restored, since it wasn't a felony at the time. If he had taken sanctuary for a felony other than the murder it would be otherwise, so the wise felon might claim an imaginary felony until his victim died or recovered: *Reports from Henry VIII*, vol. 1, p. 90. Also reported in *Spelman's Reports*, vol. 1, pp. 66–67. This goes against the readings. There is no further process relating to Bewesbery, but Jones, the chaplain, appeared in King's Bench in October 1517. He argued there that the indictment was insufficient because the coroner did not have the authority to enquire regarding murder or accessory on an inquisition on the view of a body, and went *sine die*: TNA KB27/1025 rex m. 1 [images 52, 37d].

[108] TNA KB9/486 m. 10 [image 20]. This case also appears in Hunnisett, 'The Last Sussex Abjurations', p. 40.

Gogan from him, and brought him to the cathedral. This suggests both that a large number of clerics were present at an execution, and that they would not hesitate to step in if they felt that they had an opportunity to do so.[109] Gogan disappears from the record, but his rescuers were indicted at an inquisition at Horsham the following July. Lasselles, Lykerd, and Taylor appeared at King's Bench on 23 January 1522 to plead not guilty, a plea which John Rooper, the attorney-general, accepted according to a warrant from the king.[110] John Fesisian was included in the same warrant, but he did not appear in King's Bench until 4 February 1524 when he likewise pleaded not guilty and the same warrant was accepted.[111] These cases are reminiscent of the cases of William Johnson and Robert Forde in the previous reign, and indicate that the contexts in which sanctuary was claimed and the attitudes of the participants remained quite similar across the decades, even as official attitudes and processes were shifting.[112] Parish churches still saw claims of sanctuary by men (and the occasional woman) accused of a wide variety of felonies on a regular basis, and both local clergy and local laymen were willing to support those claims. Abjurers continued to be rather more likely targets of local aggression, but the evidence suggests that not only were abjurations not under attack from the central authorities, they were part of a more general effort to reform and track the available methods of mitigation.

4. Conclusion

As in the previous reign, despite the prominence of a politically significant case in the early years of the reign, the main developments in sanctuary lie in a different direction. Discussions about the relative role of royal and papal authority were largely laid to rest by *c.* 1520: it was agreed that the pope could not make a sanctuary without the king, but it was also largely agreed that the king could not make one without parliament, and indeed it was generally felt that no-one should want to make one at all. That argument only impinged on the actual working of an existing sanctuary when the crime, or the criminal, were important enough that the normal workings of the law were likely to be set aside in one way or another anyway. For the most part, sanctuaries continued to work in much the same way as they had always done. As in the previous reign, the numbers don't suggest that claims to sanctuary were either rising or falling consistently for most of this period, though there is a clear up-tick in recorded claims of sanctuary in parish churches at the end of the 1520s, mostly because of the up-tick in recorded abjurations (fig. 7.3).

[109] Cf. William Johnson, pp. 150–151.
[110] TNA KB27/1042 rex m. 1 [images 153, 154, 127d].
[111] TNA KB27/1050 rex m. 7 [images 140, 141, 118d].
[112] See p. 152.

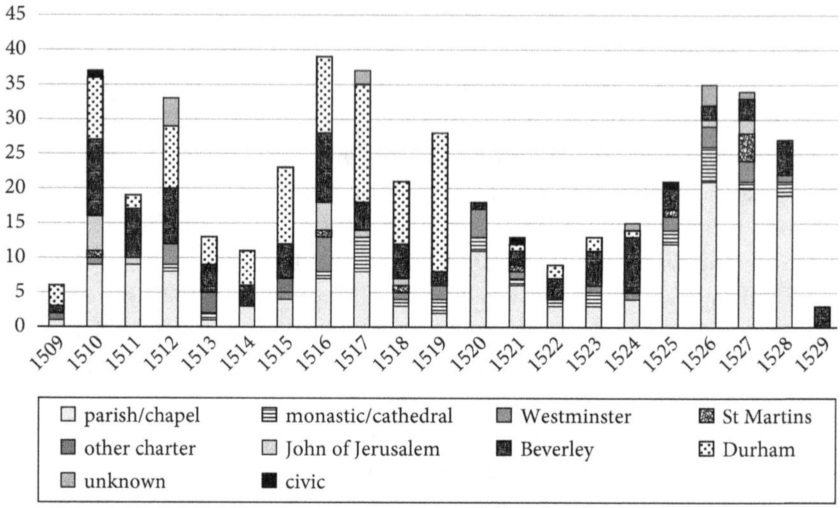

Figure 7.3 All recorded claims of sanctuary 1509–1529 by institution*
*Data collected from TNA KB27 and KB9 rolls; *Sanctuarium Dunelmense*.

The abjuration records from the reign of Henry VII are a model of consistency compared to those from Henry VIII, and it's not clear whether the larger number of records naturally produces more variation, whether more new coroners were encountering abjurations for the first time, or whether experienced coroners were working their way through new situations. Even if the variation is the simple result of more records, that growth suggests greater attention to the procedures and recording of abjurations. The coroners' records in these years tend to give more detailed descriptions of the abjuration, the delivery of the abjurer to a constable, or the instructions to him to hurry to the port, remain on the highway and not return without license. Although these are not technically new instructions, the greater emphasis on them, the higher proportion of abjurers, the efforts to distribute abjurers to a variety of ports, the more regular appearance of constables, and the much smaller number of abjurers who were subsequently found in the country suggest that there was more concern to actually get people out, rather than allowing them to disappear. Though there is no direct evidence for the push behind this, it seems likely that it was connected to the efforts being made to monitor the use of benefit of clergy in the same years and that we are seeing the ongoing effects of the long-term attempt, begun in the early years of Henry VII's reign, to make the existing laws and processes work more effectively. This connection between benefit of clergy and sanctuary is clearly new: though we have seen individuals claiming both under a variety of circumstances for decades, there was little recognition in the legal literature that this was even possible, much less that it was common. Until the second decade of the sixteenth century lawyers maintained the fiction that these were two separate privileges, available to two separate segments of the population. As benefit of clergy became ever more clearly a mitigation of punishment managed by the secular powers in the decades after 1490, however, the benefits of managing sanctuary in a similar fashion must have seemed obvious and quite appealing. The changes made in these decades make it clear that the common lawyers had no desire to eliminate either privilege: they were both far too useful. Theirs was an evolutionary approach, one which allowed both clergy and sanctuary to continue to play their core functions in society while curbing the worst abuses of both, and, all being equal, this pattern could have continued indefinitely. The events of 1529 and beyond ensured that this would not be possible: as the institutions upon which the privileges relied—episcopal prisons and religious houses—careened through a period of previously unimaginable change, the justices found themselves frantically trying to re-shape their fledgling system to match the resources available to them and the political context in which they were operating, with mixed success.

PART III

THE LIMITS OF A QUIET EVOLUTION

8

Sanctuary and Benefit of Clergy 1529–1536

The slow and steady changes of the first three decades of the sixteenth century did not long survive the opening of the Reformation parliament. This was not because that parliament was hostile to sanctuary and benefit of clergy, as has been assumed. Rather, the religious changes which gave that parliament its name changed the political context so substantially that the slow, careful and largely internal processes that had allowed a system of criminal confinement to emerge and develop via bureaucratic change could emerge into the light of day and move more quickly and confidently than had previously been possible. The ecclesiastical hierarchy, absorbed with an existential crisis, had neither the time nor the resources to expend on fighting changes to privileges which, while nominally within their remit, had been increasingly secularized over the previous decades. And while the Reformation parliament clearly earned its adjective, this busiest of early Tudor parliaments had other concerns besides religious change, including law and order. Between 1529 and about 1536 the trajectory visible from late in the reign of Henry VII continued, and in the statutes of that parliament and the activities of the courts we can see three developments which both continued previous practices and built upon them in new ways. First, there was a continuing desire to curtail traditional abuses in the use of benefit of clergy, though both parliament and the courts shifted from focusing on repeat offenders to focusing on heinous crimes. Second, the tentative absorption of sanctuary into the common law system, visible only indirectly through the increased attention paid to coroners' reports and abjuration in the 1520s, became much more explicit and effective. Third, this new model of sanctuary was increasingly coordinated with benefit of clergy as part of a wider system of mitigation and normalized as part of the common law. This chapter will start by examining the changes to sanctuary and benefit of clergy individually, but will highlight the ways in which they were increasingly intertwined, both in practice and in policy. The high-profile and harsh statutory changes with which we are familiar, when taken together with much more low-profile changes in practice, meant that by 1536 the secular authorities were well on their way to solving the problem which had plagued the criminal justice system for centuries: they were finding a way to differentiate between the punishment for a heinous crime like murder and the punishment for a much less severe crime like theft.

The King's Felons. Margaret McGlynn, Oxford University Press.
DOI: 10.1093/oso/9780192887689.003.0009

1. Sanctuary and Statute 1529–1536

As we have seen, the English parliament had paid far less attention to sanctuary than to benefit of clergy through the later Middle Ages, but that began to change in 1529. An act that year made two changes to traditional practices. The first change was the less important. It provided that the felon should take his abjuration at the day and time given to him by the coroner: if he refused to abjure at the time specified by the coroner, he could be taken out of sanctuary and imprisoned, and would have no claim for restoration.[1] This provision meant that the coroner could require a sanctuary man to leave before the conclusion of his standard forty days. As we have seen, there were regular skirmishes over the breadth of the claims of chartered sanctuaries, but there had never been any attempt to argue against the traditional forty days for the regular sanctuaries. Very few abjurers stayed in sanctuary that long; many claimed sanctuary and abjured on the same day, and most went through the process within a few days.[2] While it was unlikely to cause a great deal of change, framing the timing of abjuration as an administrative issue to be determined by the coroner was a subtle way to emphasize the coroner's authority over the process while avoiding any suggestion that customary rights were being infringed. The statute also reinforced the coroner's authority by noting that all mayors, bailiffs, and constables 'shalbe attendaunt at the commaundement of the coroner for due execution therof as they wyll answere at their parels to the King's Highnes for the same'.

The second change mandated by the statute was a good deal less subtle: it required that at the time of abjuration the sanctuary man should be branded on the brawn of the right thumb with an A. This introduction of branding for abjurers paralleled that for clerks convict back in 1490—from now on if an abjurer disappeared from the highway somewhere in the middle of the country he would be physically marked and anyone seeing that mark could arrest him and investigate.[3] Both provisions of the statute increased the role of royal officials in the abjuration process, and the branding brought abjuration more closely in line with benefit of clergy.[4]

[1] *SR*, III. 284. 21 Hen. VIII c. 2.

[2] Though the lawyers had debated how long the sanctuary man could delay calling the coroner and what might happen after forty days if he did not abjure, I have never seen the problem arise in practice.

[3] Loades describes the 1529 branding statute as 'an encroachment by parliament into an area which it had hitherto avoided': D.M. Loades, 'The Sanctuary', in *Westminster Abbey Reformed 1540–1640* edited by C.S. Knighton and Richard Mortimer (Aldershot: Ashgate, 2003), p. 79.

[4] The statute on sanctuary was c. 2, and it was followed by statutes to remedy delays in assizes, to allow lands to be sold in execution of a will without the consent of all the executors, to regulate the fees for probate, to regulate mortuaries, and to punish servants who abscond with their masters' goods: *SR*, III. 284–289. 21 Hen. VIII cc. 3–7. All these statutes dealt with procedural issues which either touched on criminal law or matters previously in the purview of the church, though it framed changes to the latter as administrative rather than principled. The first statute of this parliament was a general pardon: *SR*, III. 283. 21 Hen. VIII c. 1, see p. 312.

We have seen in previous decades that new statutes might be ignored or selectively implemented, but the 1529 statute had an immediate impact, perhaps because it was enforced by coroners rather than justices. Eleven recorded abjurations survive from 1530, and all the coroners' records but one note that the men were branded according to the recent statute. It had long been standard to record the completion of the abjuration ritual 'according to the law and custom of England', and once branding was required it was included in the formula, though its novelty was emphasized. For example, John Frobisher, a Yorkshire coroner, noted in May 1530 that William Multon was 'branded on his right hand with the letter A according to the form of the statute recently produced and provided on this matter ... and the port of Kingston on Hull was assigned to the same William Multon for his departure from the same realm, carrying a cross in his right hand, according to the law and custom of England'.[5] Thus the branding was inserted into the formula in such a way that its parliamentary authority contrasts strikingly with the customary authority of the cross and the rest of the ritual.

Multon's abjuration also demonstrates that Hunnisett was wrong when he argued that after the 1529 statute abjurers were no longer given the cross, and suggested that coroners thought of the one as a substitute for the other 'although its purpose was quite different'.[6] In fact all the coroners' records from 1530 which note the branding also note that the men were given the cross. John Hunt, the Surrey coroner, was clearly aware of the different role each element played. He noted specifically that Stephen Stapulle was branded and handed over to the constable so that he got to Westminster 'without damage and danger to his life, with a wooden cross in his right hand according to the law and custom of England'.[7] The specific material from which the cross was made was never mentioned in earlier records—indeed this is the only such description I've found—and it suggests that Hunt was asserting and maintaining the customary aspects of the ritual even as he accommodated himself to the change. Some coroners innovated beyond the requirements of the statute, adding an oath from the abjurers that they would complete their assigned journey. Though this was less common than branding and the cross, it was not rare and was often combined with the older rituals. In the fifty-nine records of abjuration between 1529 and 1539, three records have the full suite of oath, brand and cross, thirty-one have brand and cross, six have oath and brand, five

[5] TNA KB9/514 m. 110 [image 218]. The language used for branding might also vary: Frobisher said that Multon 'signatus est', while Gregory Waren and John Barnes, Hertfordshire coroners, used 'notatus est': TNA KB9/975 m. 127 [image not on AALT]. The coroners also continued to tweak the language: by 1531 Nicholas Custon noted that John Sawyer was branded according to the statute of 21 Henry VIII: TNA KB9/521 m. 83 [image 177].

[6] R.F. Hunnisett, 'The Last Sussex abjurations: A Postscript', *Sussex Archaeological Collections* 103 (1965), pp. 42–43. In the one example he gives from this period, however, the abjuration of Henry Danby from Chichester cathedral, Danby was given the cross: TNA KB9/519 m. 147, in Hunnisett, 'Last Sussex Abjurations', 48. Danby will be discussed in some detail pp. 275–277.

[7] TNA KB9/517 m. 72 [image 145].

have brand alone, three have cross alone, one has only the oath, and ten make no mention of any of those options. The variations are spread across the period, suggesting that most coroners continued to feel an obligation to both mark and protect, though they varied in the ways they expressed those obligations.

With the obvious exception of branding, the patterns and practices of abjuration in 1530 look very familiar. Coroners continued to send men to a variety of ports: in 1530 three were sent to Dover, two to Kingston on Hull, and one each to Southampton, Portsmouth, Yarmouth, Ipswich, Scarborough and Chester, demonstrating that the ports that had been introduced to the roster in the late 1520s continued to be used.[8] The typical distances travelled also remain consistent: most abjurers were expected to travel between 40 and 70 miles from their sanctuary to their port of abjuration.

Men also continued to abjure for a variety of crimes. Robert Glover, for example, who was assigned a journey of 88 miles, stabbed his pregnant wife in the stomach two days before he claimed sanctuary at the Franciscan house in Ware. The inquisition on her body noted that he did it 'with a greatly diabolical mind, and at the instigation of many demons', and the coroners may have felt that Glover could benefit from the penitential benefits of the longer journey.[9] Three others also abjured for murder. Two abjured for robbery, three for thefts of various kinds, and two for horsetheft.[10] Many of these claims followed the commission of the crime much more quickly than they had in previous years, however: three men took sanctuary within two days and three within twelve to seventeen days.[11] Though the majority of the abjurations don't specify when the coroner arrived, those that do date it within a day or so of the claim.[12] This was fairly typical before the statute, and it seems unlikely that there was any significant change in the other cases.

There does seem to be a drop in the number of abjurations associated with the statute, though the sharpest drop is in 1529, before it was passed, rather than 1530, when it came into effect (fig. 8.1).[13] It would be unwise to assume that this represents a significant change in activity in this year. The survival and delivery of coroners' records was spotty at the best of times, and given that the law changed in 1529 and was to change again in 1531, it would not be surprising if the coroners were slow to keep pace and reluctant to maintain records that might seem to be out of date by the time they were recorded.[14]

[8] The Chester abjuration was the only one from this period which mentioned neither the branding nor the cross: TNA KB9/514 m. 158 [image 315].

[9] TNA KB9/975 m. 125 [image not on AALT]. His abjuration is TNA KB9/975 m. 127 [image not on AALT].

[10] TNA KB9/519 m. 119 [image 241]; TNA KB9/514 mm. 110, 111 [images 218, 220].

[11] Only one, Thomas Dawson, took sanctuary for an old crime: on 24 November he confessed to a theft about seven years earlier: TNA KB27/1081 m. 9d [image 1777d].

[12] TNA KB9/519 m. 147 [image 298]; TNA KB9/519 m. 119 [image 241].

[13] The parliament ran from 3 November to 17 December 1529, and though statutes are dated from the beginning of the session, by the time this one was approved there was a fairly narrow slice of 1529 left in which to apply it.

[14] See p. 154, n.77.

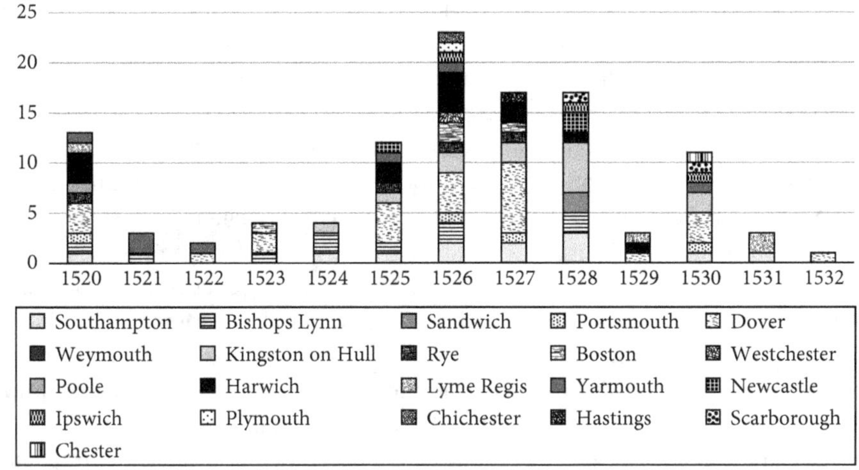

Figure 8.1 Recorded abjurations 1520–1532*

*Data collected mostly from TNA KB9 rolls with some additions from TNA KB27 rolls and State Papers.

Overall, though branding was immediately adopted, the patterns and uses of sanctuary do not seem to have changed significantly in 1530. This is not surprising, and if the statute held the potential for more substantial change we would expect to see it emerge gradually over the next several years. Any such evolutionary change was forestalled by the next session of parliament, which sat from 12 January to 31 March 1531, and whose sanctuary provisions dramatically changed the law only a year after the provisions we have been considering were implemented.[15] In the course of a run of law-and-order statutes, a sanctuary statute inaccurately complained that many abjurers were expert mariners and archers, and that their loss both diminished the martial capacity of England, and boosted that of her enemies.[16] For this reason abjurers were no longer to be sent abroad but were to abjure only their freedom of movement, choosing a sanctuary in which they would remain permanently. This could not be the church in which they originally took refuge, since they still had to go through the process of abjuration, branding and escort by the constable.[17] Any abjurer found outside the sanctuary was to be

[15] This parliament's first foray was fairly tame: it returned to the ill-fated statute of 1512 allowing claims of sanctuary in a foreign county to be tried in the county of the indictment, revived the 1512 act and made it perpetual. The earlier statute had disappeared because of controversy over the benefit of clergy provisions, and the sanctuary provision, which was quite uncontroversial, had been collateral damage.

[16] *SR*, III. 326–332. 22 Hen. VIII cc. 9–12: Acts for poisoning, concerning Egyptians, breaking dykes, punishment of beggars and vagabonds. 22 Hen. VIII c. 13, a statute concerning bakers, brewers, surgeons and scriveners, seems to break the run but it is concerned with clarifying that aliens in these fields were not strangers for the purposes of certain penal statutes.

[17] *SR*, III. 333. 22 Hen. VIII c. 14.

treated as though he had returned from abroad without permission. This change from external to internal abjuration is clearly the biggest innovation of the statute, and we will deal with it in more detail below, but the statute did not end there. It went on to deal with collateral problems caused or exacerbated by the change in abjuration, and a consideration of those collateral matters demonstrates most clearly that this statute was not trying to undermine sanctuaries, but was re-framing them as places of penal confinement and providing some basic principles to ensure that they could function in that role.

The principles enunciated in the statute all drew on past practices, but they generalized those practices in the context of the new penal environment. Thus any sanctuary man who committed petty treason, murder or felony, either inside or outside the sanctuary, was to lose the right to sanctuary anywhere in the country and to be arrested and indicted by the local authorities. If he was found guilty he would be punished as though he had never been in sanctuary, and if acquitted he would be returned to sanctuary. This was intended to deal with one of the constant complaints about sanctuaries, that criminals used them as a base from which to commit crimes. But the statute recognized the possibilities for the abuse of this provision and went on to provide that anyone indicted for a crime committed outside the sanctuary would not be removed from the sanctuary until they were examined by two of the king's council or four justices of the peace. If the sanctuary man convinced the examiners that he had indeed been in the sanctuary when the crime was committed, then he was allowed to remain in the sanctuary, any indictment notwithstanding.[18] This was intended to ensure that any fugitive was not harassed by false indictments or drawn out of a safe environment to one where he or she would be vulnerable to revenge on the part of the victims. The statute also provided that if any former sanctuary man had the king's pardon or was otherwise 'at large and out of Sentuary discharged or purged of that offence or cause' and subsequently committed petty treason, felony or manslaughter 'by chaunce medley and not murder of malyse prepensed' and took sanctuary again, he would be allowed to remain. This provision was framed to include those who had been pardoned or claimed benefit of clergy as well as sanctuary, and it shows some allowance for recidivism, as long as the felon had gone through the proper processes to go free after his first crime, and as long as his second crime was not petty treason or premeditated murder.[19] This demonstrates that the framers of the statute recognized that sanctuary and benefit of clergy were both effectively functioning as prison sentences which were discharged by pardon or purgation, and that anyone who completed their sentence according to the rules was allowed to claim sanctuary again, at least for one of the lesser felonies. The final clause of the statute provided that no-one should be excluded from sanctuary for 'any offence or offences beyng of

[18] *SR*, III. 333–334.
[19] *SR*, III. 334.

any hier nature in the Lawe than the offences and causes specefyed in this Acte be'. Lehmberg took this to mean that abjuration was available for treason, but it seems more likely that it is an obscure reference to the chartered sanctuaries and assures them—by this point effectively Westminster Abbey—that sanctuary for treason would remain intact there.[20] Provisions such as these demonstrate that sanctuary continued to play an important and evolving role in moderating punishment. The statute sought to prevent career criminals from using sanctuary as a base for their crimes, but it was careful to protect those in sanctuary from revenge or harassment, to allow a second bite at the apple for repeat offenders who had previously made their way through the system according to the rules, and to respect the claims of those sanctuaries who could give shelter for treason.

Though the replacement of external with internal abjuration represented a huge change to an ancient system, once again the statute was quickly obeyed, and the three external abjurations which survive from 1531 only serve to demonstrate how quickly they disappeared. In the first, Gabriel Bryghe was sent from Littlington in Bedfordshire to King's Lynn after confessing to burglary, but both his crime and his abjuration took place while parliament was sitting in February.[21] Two men abjured in April after the session ended: George Treynneworth and Robert Turlo claimed sanctuary in the parish church of Northill in Bedfordshire on 12 April and confessed to horsetheft in Hampshire ten days earlier.[22] Treynneworth was assigned to Southampton and Turlo to King's Lynn by Robert Stukeley, the same coroner who presided over the abjuration of Gabriel Bryghe. Stukeley may simply have been late receiving word of the change in the law, but it is possible that he did not like the new system and hoped to squeeze a few more abjurers through the old one while a window remained. If so, he was almost the last gasp of the old model: one more external abjuration is recorded, and it is a bit of a puzzle. According to the record, John Johnson took sanctuary in the parish church of St Margaret in Southwark on 1 April 1532 and confessed to killing William Bishop in Lincolnshire on 17 May 1519.[23] He apparently 'asked for a cross and to abjure the realm' and John Hunt took his confession and assigned him to Dover in the custody of the constables in the usual way. Though this suggests an abjuration a full year after the passage of the statute, the record is filed in Michelmas 1531, and a note scribbled at the bottom complains that the abjuration took place 'at a future time'. Johnson thus presumably took sanctuary the day after the end of the parliamentary session in 1531, perhaps in the hope of abjuring in the nick of time, and Hunt was either unaware of the new law, or unwilling to force Johnson to follow the new rules.[24] A Surrey

[20] Stanford Lehmberg, *The Reformation Parliament, 1529–1536* (Cambridge, Cambridge University Press, 1970), p. 126.

[21] TNA KB9/975 m. 215 [image not on AALT].

[22] TNA KB9/517 m. 146 [image 295].

[23] TNA KB9/517 m. 103 [image 207].

[24] This the same coroner who noted that Stephen Stapulle abjured with a wooden cross in hand: see p. 135.

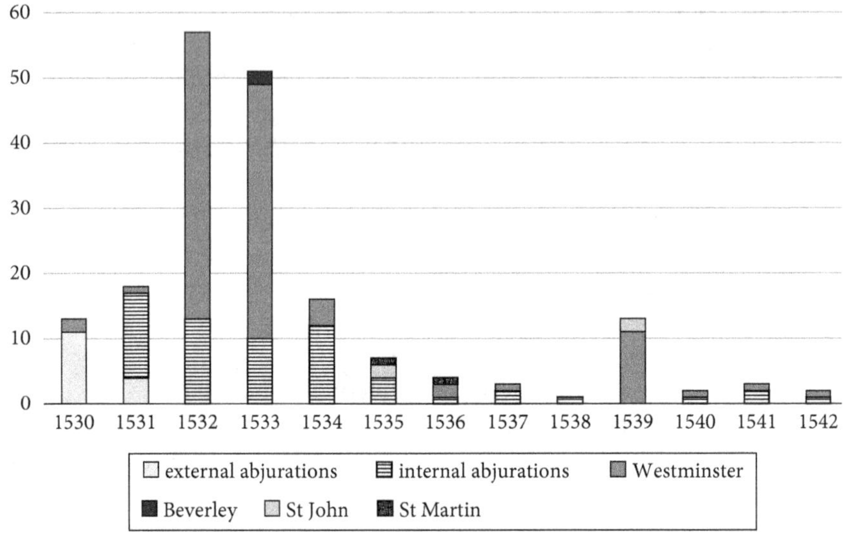

Figure 8.2 Recorded abjurations and claims in chartered sanctuaries 1530–1542*
*Data collected from TNA KB9 rolls.

coroner had even less excuse for ignorance than a Bedfordshire one, however, and the same scribble notes that Hunt was fined 10s. No further external abjurations are recorded (fig. 8.2).

While these coroners allowed external abjurations to trickle on into April, others seem to have adapted to the new regime quickly, though the earliest surviving record of an abjuration under the new statute is a bit of a puzzle and raises questions about the timing and management of the new model. Thomas Horsey, Thomas Harrys, and John Anwick took sanctuary in the parish church of St Peter the Apostle in South Weald, Essex, on 24 February 1531, while parliament was still in session. They confessed to having broken into the home of William Maior, prior of the new hospital of the Virgin Mary extra Bishopsgate, bound Richard Cressall, one of the canons, by the hands and feet, and stolen 20 marks in cash and silver worth another 70s that same day.[25] According to the record the coroner, Edward Broke, did not appear to record their abjuration until 25 May, when the three men chose to go to Beaulieu. This suggests that the first abjuration under the new statute took place almost two months after the end of the parliament, but Thomas Harrys reappeared in King's Bench in February 1533, and the process there throws a different light on his abjuration.[26] Harrys claimed that he reached Beaulieu on 1 March 1531, five days after he claimed sanctuary, and long before the coroner

[25] TNA KB9/517 m. 92 [image 185].
[26] TNA KB27/1086 rex m. 4 [images 141, 142, 299d].

claimed to have taken his abjuration. When he arrived at the abbey the bishop and abbot, Thomas Bangor, would not allow him into the sanctuary but ordered him to leave. Harrys claimed that he set out to return to the church of his abjuration and seek the coroner's advice, but when he got to Winchester 'which is direct and on the same road' on 5 March, four days later, he was seized and put in the Winchester gaol. He appeared at King's Bench in the custody of the warden of Winchester gaol and was asked why he should not be executed on the abjuration since he was found outside the sanctuary without license. He asked to be restored to sanctuary, the court remanded him, and he disappears from the record. The confusion in the dates here muddies our understanding of what was happening: the most likely explanation is that Broke jumped the gun by using the new process before the end of parliament and subsequently post-dated the abjuration to rectify his mistake. If that is indeed what happened, it suggests that he was paying close attention to the deliberations of parliament, and that he liked what he saw. A premature abjuration may also explain the reaction of Thomas Bangor when Harrys appeared at his door: he may have been unaware of the innovation, or hostile to it, and unwilling to accept a sanctuary man under those terms before he was absolutely obliged to do so, a possibility to which we will return below.

This first abjuration under the new model demonstrates that though internal abjuration was a real and substantial change, there was much that was familiar in the processes on the ground. Harrys's declared choice to return to the original sanctuary after he was turned away from Beaulieu parallels the decision of earlier abjurers who had been unable to secure passage abroad. Harrys also clearly recognized that he was supposed to take a direct route both to Beaulieu and back to St Peter's. Finally, the story of being arrested en route is also familiar, and if Harrys's account is true, he was held in Winchester gaol for almost two years before his appearance in King's Bench.

Other elements of this abjuration raise issues which only appear dimly in earlier records, such as the level of choice abjurers could expect regarding their choice of destination. When Horsey, Anwick, and Harrys chose Beaulieu, for example, they were following the language of the statute, which clearly stated that the abjurer was to choose his own sanctuary. The records indicate that the coroners followed this provision, for the most part: thirty two abjurers chose their destination, thirteen were assigned, seven were assigned with their consent and in five cases it was not specified who made the choice (fig. 8.3). Not surprisingly, Beverley was the most popular destination, with fourteen recorded abjurations, and Westminster is not far behind with nine. However, a closer look suggests that the abjurers may have had less choice than the language of the records implies, and that the coroners continued to play an active role in directing them. The popularity of Beaulieu, for example, is unexpected; though it has rarely appeared in our discussion thus far, it attracted ten abjurers.[27] Beaulieu drew many of its abjurers from Sussex, and

[27] St Martin's is at the bottom of the list, with only one abjurer choosing it, and no coroner assigning it.

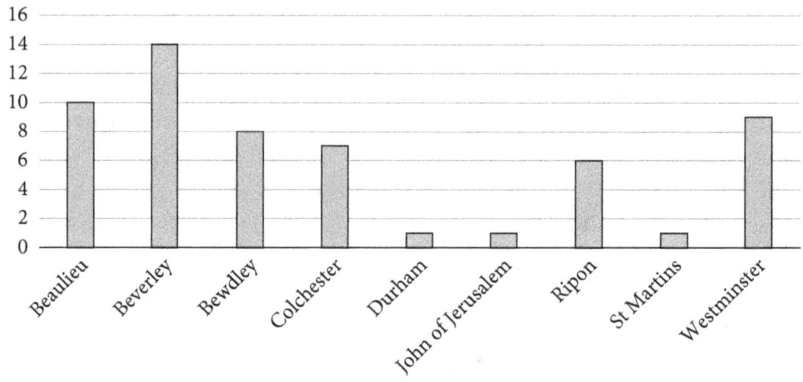

Figure 8.3 Recorded internal abjurations by destination 1531–1539*
*Data collected from TNA KB9 rolls.

the men who made their way along the coast from Chichester or Lancing were travelling a similar distance as those from the decades before. But Beaulieu also drew abjurers from Hastings, South Weald and Cambridge as well as one from the North Riding in Yorkshire, all of whom were covering distances of over 100 miles. Beverley and Westminster also drew from a wide area, and not just in their respective regions. Though two of the Beverley abjurers came from Yorkshire, the rest made their way from as far south as Ware, Northampton and Coventry; similarly, Westminster saw men from Southwark and Woodford, but also from as far afield as Coventry, Spalding, and Forton. As we saw, Beverley was drawing from a wider geographic area in Henry VIII's reign than his father's, but this still seems to be an extension of that range, and the majority of recorded claimants at Westminster had always been local. As with the abjuration ports in the late 1520s, the evidence suggests that the coroners were consciously distributing abjurers around the country, and this is supported by the abjurations to Colchester. St John of Colchester had never been a particularly prominent chartered sanctuary, and this probably explains why no abjurer chose to go there: it doesn't explain why six abjurers were assigned there.[28] The coroners who assigned abjurers to Colchester came from Cambridgeshire, Essex, Kent, Yorkshire, and Bedfordshire, and it seems unlikely that such a diverse group would have gravitated to Colchester without direction from above.[29]

[28] It's not specified whether the seventh abjurer chose or was assigned. The balance between abjurers choosing and coroners assigning is fairly even for the other sanctuaries, none of which show the kind of imbalance we see at Colchester. Cox notes that its privileges were confirmed in 1453, and the physical bounds of the sanctuary were laid out then: J. Charles Cox, *The Sanctuaries and Sanctuary Seekers of Medieval England* (London; George Allen & Sons, 1911), pp. 197–198.

[29] TNA KB9/519 m. 47 [image 94]; TNA KB9/519 m. 83 [image 166]; TNA KB9/527 m. 148 [image 302]; TNA KB9/529 m. 186 [image 371]: TNA KB9/531 m. 92 [image 182]. It is possible that the statute intended the abjurers to choose their sanctuary in the same sense that they had chosen a jury trial.

The direction that abjurers should be able to choose their sanctuary also had implications for another question: could the coroner separate men who abjured together? I suggested in chapter 7 that the coroner made that decision on a case-by-case basis, and that they might balance the desire to protect young or vulnerable abjurers with the desire to ensure that dangerous or habitual offenders were contained. If the coroners remained more active in distributing the abjurers than the statute directed, this suggests that they could continue to exercise a similar kind of discretion in the 1530s. The shift from external to internal abjuration does seem to have changed their calculus, however, and the new pattern is much more clearly connected with the crimes committed by the abjurers than the old one was. The twelve men who claimed sanctuary with someone else and abjured with their companion(s) had, for the most part, committed the more heinous felonies. We have already seen Horsey, Anwick and Harrys choose Beaulieu. John Corrye, Morgan Jones, and William Johnson took sanctuary in St Mary's in Shudy Camps, Cambridgeshire, confessed to having killed an unknown man and stolen his purse the previous day, and were assigned to Colchester.[30] Hugh Ratlif and Peter Massey broke out of Leicester gaol, took sanctuary in the church of St John the Baptist, and asked to go to Beverley.[31] Thomas Savage and John Colynson took sanctuary in the Carmelite church in York, confessed to breaking into the house of William Selby, and were sent to Ripon, with their consent.[32] William Warburton and Robert Maxvile took sanctuary in the church of St Bartholomew of Layston in Hertfordshire, confessed to highway robbery, and asked to go to Beverley.[33] The seven joint claimants who were separated from their companions had, for the most part, committed lesser felonies. Robert Fayere and Richard Stanley are a partial exception: they took sanctuary with the Franciscans in Ware, confessed to multiple burglaries the previous month, and were sent to St John of Jerusalem in Clerkenwell and Beverley, each apparently at his own request.[34] But when John Goodman and Walter Heyte took sanctuary in the parish church of Barrington in Cambridgeshire and confessed to horsetheft, Goodman was assigned to Beverley and Heyte to Colchester, and when Thomas Gadmere, John Russell and John Ploghe took sanctuary in the parish church of Harewood in Yorkshire and confessed to various thefts amounting to a total value of 23s, they were assigned to Colchester, Beaulieu

[30] TNA KB9/519 m. 47 [image 94].

[31] TNA KB9/523 m. 23 [image 42]. The coroner here, Ralph Garsert, seems to have been inexperienced, and the details are a little confused. The men seem to have broken out of the gaol on 19 December 1532, but only taken sanctuary on 13 January 1533.

[32] TNA KB9/529 m. 187 [image 373]; TNA KB9/529 m. 188 [image 375]. Unlike the other group abjurations, these two were recorded separately. Thomas Savage confessed to breaking in on 20 June 1524 and John Colynson on 20 June 1528: both stole 40s of goods, Savage in the form of goods and chattels, Colynson in the form of a bay horse. It's not clear if the difference in dates of the crimes is an error, if both men targeted the unfortunate Selby, or if something more complex was happening.

[33] TNA KB9/533 m. 108 [image 215].

[34] TNA KB9/521 m. 73 [image 157].

and Beverley respectively.[35] Though it seems counter-intuitive, the coroners were more likely to keep those who committed serious crimes together, and to disperse those who committed lesser crimes. This is probably because they were more likely to send those who had committed the more egregious crimes to abjure in the company of an officer—it was a big job to both separate abjurers and accompany them. Those who committed lesser crimes might be sent off in different directions unaccompanied, with the expectation that they would remain separate and the hope that they would reach their destination, but with less concern about that outcome for thieves than for killers and burglars. This suggests that though the coroners were much less likely than the justices to ignore the core provisions of a new statute, they were comfortable bending peripheral elements that seemed to go against the practical execution of its provisions.

If these cases suggest the continuation and adaptation of the patterns of distribution glimpsed in the 1520s, William Orrell's suggests an intensification of the management of abjuration. On 19 September 1532 Orrell, a gentleman of Kingston on Hull, took sanctuary in the church of St Mary the Virgin and confessed to killing John Lownde with malice aforethought at 11am that same day.[36] Stephen Clere and James Johnson, the town coroners, went to the church to take his confession. Like some others we've seen, the confession was framed in the first person, and Orrell described himself as a 'felon of the lord king' and asked to abjure to Westminster. Unusually, however, the confession is followed by another document written by Clere and Johnson, dated 20 September, and addressed to 'all bailiffs, constables, sub-constables and other officials of the . . . king from the town of Kingston on Hull to the town of Westminster'.[37] It did not give the details of Orrell's crime, but explained that he had taken sanctuary in St. Mary's and was abjuring to Westminster, and asked for their assistance in leading him there. This is probably drawing on the reference made in the 1529 statute to the help of such officials in the abjuration process, and it demonstrates again the ways in which the system was developing: the passport of the 1520s, which contained the abjuration record, was now accompanied by a specific request to local officials to ensure that the king's felon completed his journey.

The description of an abjurer as a 'felon of the lord king' had been in circulation for more than twenty years by the time Orrell used it, and I argued above that it indicates a growing sense in those years that all felons remained subjects of the king.[38] Abjuration had traditionally been an effective rejection of the common law, a choice to step outside it in self-imposed exile rather than submitting to its punishment: this is part of the reason why the common law had always had a more

[35] TNA KB9/527 m. 148 [image 302]; TNA KB9/529 m. 186 [image 371].

[36] TNA KB9/529 m. 57 [image 112]. The inquisition on the view of the body is TNA KB9/526 m. 80 [image 160].

[37] TNA KB9/526 m. 79 [image 158].

[38] See p. 235.

tenuous relationship with sanctuary than with benefit of clergy, limited to accepting that choice and recording it. Though the statute makes no direct reference to this, the language of the first abjuration under its provisions, Horsey, Harrys, and Anwick's, clearly recognized that the introduction of internal abjuration significantly changed the relationship between the abjurer and the king: the three men 'freely confessed they were felons of the ... lord king', they asked 'to abjure and be recused from all and singular liberties, possessions, matters and all their free habitations whatsoever within this kingdom of England', and they chose 'never to leave the said sanctuary without license and reconciliation with the lord king according to the form of the recent statute'. Rather than walking away from the common law, these abjurers recognized that they were the king's felons, and rather than leaving the kingdom, they abandoned their liberties and possessions, though, as before, all could be restored through reconciliation with the king. Though this language does not appear in all the 1531 abjurations, it does spread quickly to become the most common form of abjuration for the rest of the decade.[39] The coroners clearly recognized that the provisions of the statute meant that abjuration was now being claimed as part of the common law, and that sanctuary men who chose that option were choosing between two common law options rather than between the common law and exile. The natural corollary was that, in the same way that common law oversight of benefit of clergy had implied that bishops' prisons were under royal authority, common law oversight of abjuration would imply that sanctuaries were under royal authority. None of this is explicit in the statute, but the changes in the language and actions of the coroners suggest that it was recognized as being implicit.

The changes wrought by the statutes of 1529 and 1531 ranged from the bureaucratic to the revolutionary, but, with the obvious exception of internal abjuration, they blend provisions and practices already operating within the common law to provide greater control over abjuration and fashion it into a more rational and efficient system: abjurers were branded to make their status more visible; they were given documentation addressed to officials along the way which would expedite their journey, and they were distributed across the country. When the change to internal abjuration upended the system, these provisions remained in place: the larger watersheds for each sanctuary and the range of sanctuaries that each coroner might assign suggest that their desire to manage and distribute probably intensified as abjurers were required to remain in the country rather than passing through to a port. In return for accepting this royal protection under the common law the abjurer was guaranteed safety within his chosen sanctuary, at least from

[39] One abjuration on 19 May uses the old format: TNA KB9/517 m. 102 [image 205]. There are two recorded abjurations with this language which predate the statute, from May and December 1530. Both are filed in Easter 1532 and may have been re-written in the later language before being entered in the King's Bench records: TNA KB9/519 m. 147 [image 298], TNA KB9/519 m. 119 [image 241], see Henry Danby and James Olyff below, pp. 275–277. For earlier examples of this language see p. 235.

harassment under the common law, a set of structures for the management of disputes within that sanctuary, and the ability to claim sanctuary again in the future if he remained there until released by the approved processes of the law.

2. Benefit of Clergy and Statute 1532–1536

While the 1529 and 1531 parliaments blended old and new practices in a bold first attempt to claim sanctuary for their own, they paid no attention to benefit of clergy. The 1532 parliament was quite a different matter. Benefit of clergy had a much richer statutory history than sanctuary, and this parliament was keenly aware of that history, using the possibilities of the moment to deal with longstanding problems once and for all and to advance a more rational and efficient version of the benefit. Its very first act rehearsed the history of the privilege from Westminster 1 through 4 Hen. IV, and, claiming that the constitutions promised in that statute had never been forthcoming, it promised to deal with the problems caused by the lax administration of the ordinaries by removing benefit of clergy from anyone found guilty of petty treason, willful murder, highway robbery, robbing any church or chapel, robbing anyone in their own dwelling when the owner or his family was present and in fear, or burning dwellings or barns where grain was stored, unless they were in major orders.[40] While suggesting that the problems of the thirteenth and fourteenth centuries had never been resolved, this statute drew on the provisions of the ill-fated 1512 statute and extended it in two ways. First, it extended the crimes for which clergy was not available: for the first time petty treason, willful murder committed anywhere (the 1512 statute referred only to murder in a church, on the highway or in the home), and arson of buildings or barns with grain were defined as non-clergiable crimes. Murder and arson had also been in the list of crimes excepted from the general pardon granted in 1529, however, and this suggests that parliament was drawing on a growing clarity around unmitigatable crimes rather than simply returning to the earlier statute.[41] Second, it expanded the group of people who could not claim clergy: the removal of clergy from those in minor orders, the issue at the heart of the crisis in 1515, was a substantial political change, though in practice the numbers were small.[42] Any clerk in major orders convicted of committing any of these crimes could still claim clergy, but with new restrictions: he was prohibited from making purgation unless he could produce two sureties for his good behaviour who would make recognizances of £40 before the justice of the peace, with the clerk to make one of £20. Any clerk who could

[40] *SR*, III. 362–363. 23 Hen. VIII c. 1. Major orders was defined as subdeacons or above. The statute also applied to accessories. For 4 Hen. IV, c. 2, see p. 34.

[41] *SR*, III. 283. 21 Hen. VIII c. 2. See p. 312.

[42] The statute also clarified a long-standing confusion around accessories.

not provide such recognizances, and any clerk who confessed, who had judgement given against him or who was outlawed was to remain in the ordinary's prison without purgation.[43] These latter categories largely follow the traditional definitions of clerks attaint, and demonstrate that the statute, like the earlier sanctuary statutes, drew heavily on traditional practices, but its new requirement for recognizances for clerks convict highlights once again the assumption that the common lawyers could assert their authority over management of the bishops' prisons.[44] This act was to continue only to the next parliament.[45]

Having opened the session with this broadside, the same parliament turned to a long-standing concern later in the session. It ordained that a clerk breaking the ordinary's prison should be judged a felon, and that any such offender should suffer forfeiture of goods and lands and execution without benefit of clergy or sanctuary, unless he was a subdeacon or above, in which case he was returned to the ordinary to be kept without purgation.[46] Though this statute has curious echoes of the fourteenth-century debates, it also follows naturally from the ongoing efforts to ensure the security of the episcopal prisons by ensuring that any lay escapee could not be returned to custody, but should be executed.[47] Again, clerics maintained their privilege, but the provision against purgation, with no option for recognizances, was designed to ensure that they remained in captivity.

These statutes returned to the concerns of the ill-fated 1512 statute, though the terms differ somewhat, and they clearly sought the execution of laymen convicted of the most heinous crimes rather than the eradication of benefit of clergy per se. They reduced the availability of benefit of clergy to laymen, but they reduced it for very specific kinds of crimes, those which were personally violent and/or which were disruptive to society more broadly, whether by attacking the security of the Crown, of the home, of the highway, or of the food supply. Though the removal of clergy from clerks in minor orders finally ended the argument visible in 1515, the records of the courts make it clear that this was simply not an issue that ever arose in practice. Even after 1532 clerics in major orders could still claim benefit of clergy for all the major felonies and be delivered to the ordinaries, and if they could provide sureties they could be purged, unless they fell under the traditional definitions

43 The inclusion of clerks who had judgement given against them refers to the alternative definition of a clerk attaint as one who claimed clergy after judgement rather than after verdict. See p. 27.

44 The statute also gave the ordinary the option of degrading the clerk 'after the laws of holy church' and then returning him to King's Bench. There the original record would be brought up, the convict given the death penalty and the ordinary discharged of any responsibility for the convict. There is no evidence that this happened in practice.

45 This act denied benefit of clergy only to those found guilty of the offences. In 1534 parliament closed this loophole by adding that those who refused to answer to the charges, who made more than twenty peremptory challenges to the jury, or who were tried outside the county in which the crime was committed, should also lose their clergy. It did not specify that those of the order of subdeacon or above were excepted, but that could be presumed: *SR*, III. 439. 25 Hen. VIII c. 3.

46 Once again the ordinary was given the option of degrading the clerk: *SR*, III. 379. 23 Hen. VIII c. 11.

47 See Dautre above, p. 29.

of clerks attaint. Though these measures were certainly new in the statute book and look quite startling to those not familiar with practice in the courts, they draw quite consciously on the history of the law in their rhetoric, and to some extent in their provisions. Their trajectory is largely consistent with the changes in the previous forty years or so, such as the trend towards the harsher punishment of repeat offenders and the closer administration of the law, though the changed political circumstances certainly allowed for more open and swifter change than had previously been possible.

The King's Bench records suggest that the impact of the 1532 statute was mixed (table 8.1). There are no recorded claims of clergy for petty treason or arson between 1529 and 1536, and these claims are rare in any period, so we'll have to suspend judgment on them. But of the 130 clerks convict whose crimes are identified in this period, twenty-four (18 per cent) claimed for murder, burglary with fear, highway robbery, burglary from churches or chapels, and escapes from bishops' prisons, while a further thirty-seven (28 per cent) claimed for burglary more

Table 8.1 Claims of clergy by crime 1529–1539*

	1529–May 1532	June 1532–1536	1537–1539**
Murder	5	0	0
Burglary (w/fear)	0	5	0
Highway robbery	0	1	0
Burglary (church or chapel)	5	0	0
Escape from bps prison	7	0	1
Homicide	0	0	1
Burglary	10	7	3
Burglary (horsetheft/livestock)	3	7	7
Robbery	1	1	0
Theft (incl pickpocket)	6	8	12
Theft (horsetheft/livestock)	4	7	7
Felony	8	7	1
Accessory	2	3	0
Total	**51**	**47**	**32**

*Data collected from TNA KB 27 and KB9 rolls; *Reg. Bothe*; *Reg. Longland*; Lambeth Palace Library, Register of Thomas Cranmer; Surrey History Centre Loseley MS 961/1.

**The years after 1536 are included for comparison; the three periods are of roughly equal lengths.

generally. Five laymen successfully claimed clergy for murder before May 1532, but none after the passage of the statute: this suggests that it was largely effective. Burglary when the owner or his family were present and in fear was not a separate category before the statute, but five men are recorded as successfully claiming clergy for that crime after June 1532—a crime, to re-iterate, which was defined purely in order to make it unclergiable. The numbers claiming clergy for all kinds of burglary declined slightly (a total of eighteen pre-statute and twenty-nine post-statute), but those claiming for stealing horses and other livestock from closes increased, while those claiming for stealing clothing, silver, money etc. from homes decreased. This suggests that there may indeed have been a greater reluctance to allow clergy for burglary from homes, whether the owner was present or not, and more willingness to allow it for lesser burglaries, but the decisions did not follow the statute precisely. There was one claim of clergy for highway robbery after the statute, but the claimant was a chaplain, and so remained eligible: he was appropriately delivered without purgation.[48] The two areas where the statutory change was most effective, perhaps ironically, is in claims for burglary from churches and escapes from bishop's prisons, both of which largely disappeared after the statute. The evidence indicates that the statute was successful in curbing the use of benefit of clergy for the more heinous felonies, though its effects were not entirely in line with its words when it came to burglary. It was certainly more successful than its predecessor in 1512, and the administrative changes within the common law system had probably done much of the necessary work to make the change more broadly acceptable this time around.

For the sixty-three clerks convict (48 per cent) who claimed clergy for robbery, theft, horsetheft, and generic felony, and who were not included in the statute, we would expect the patterns to remain fairly stable pre- and post-statute, but in fact this was not the case. The number of claims for theft increase substantially, suggesting either that the thieving class was becoming more literate, or that men who might previously have been found guilty of larceny or found not guilty were being convicted of felony and claiming clergy.[49] This brings us, once again, to the social status of clergy claimants (fig. 8.4). In this decade we only have the status markers of 115 of the 145 men who claimed clergy, and only ten of those (9 per cent) were identified as clerics: four chaplains, five clerks and one monk, much the same as we've seen in previous decades. Half of the claimants, fifty-seven of 115, identified themselves by status, which is also a slight drop: most strikingly, there are no gentlemen claiming clergy in this period, and the percentage of yeomen continues to fall, while the percentage of husbandmen rises slightly and the percentage of

[48] TNA KB27/1117 rex m. 6 [images 16–157, 158, 319d]. This was William/Richard Eve—see p. 318.

[49] The numbers for escapes from prison and robbery are too small to tell us much; the disappearance of felony as a descriptive term suggests a growing concern for precision in the definition of crimes.

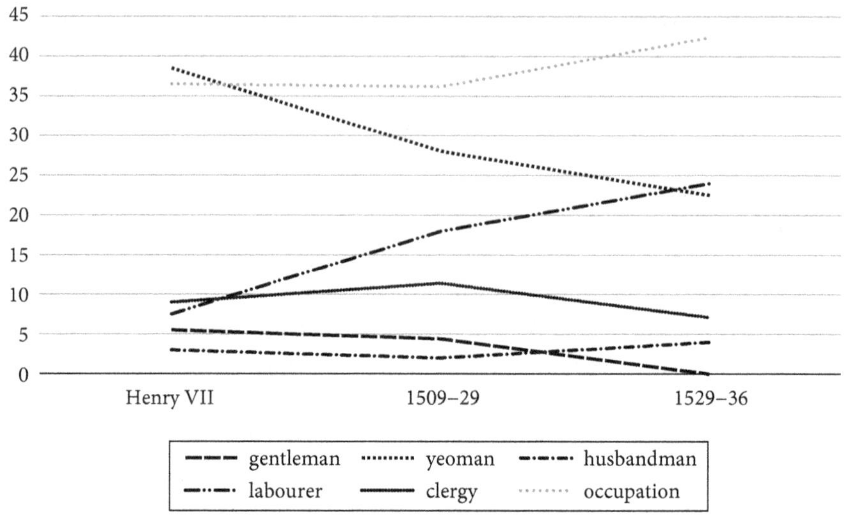

Figure 8.4 Recorded clergy claimants by status (%)*
*Data collected from TNA KB 27 and KB9 rolls.

labourers rises substantially. The remaining forty-eight claimants (42 per cent) are identified by occupation. This is a higher proportion than before, but the twenty-nine occupations provided are a narrower band of English society. Again, the records are so scattered that it's hard to argue that they provide definitive evidence regarding the status of those who claimed clergy, but the impression they give is that both clergy and gentlemen made up a small and shrinking proportion of those who claimed clergy throughout the period, and that the proportion of yeomen, while significantly larger, was also falling steadily. Though status markers are notoriously slippery, it's hard to avoid the sense that the clerks convict of the 1530s were of lower social status than those of the 1490s. Husbandmen, labourers, and craftsmen probably had higher literacy rates in the 1530s than they had had forty years earlier, but it seems unlikely that such improvement accounts for their increased representation among clerks convict. Taken together, the evidence suggests that in the 1530s the number of men who got benefit of clergy for the worst felonies fell, though there were still some exceptions, and a growing proportion of lower-status men claimed clergy for lesser felonies.

This, of course, leads naturally to the question of whether the total number of men claiming clergy was rising or falling in this period: was the 1532 statute an attempt to limit the privilege *tout court* or simply to limit its use for those committing the worst crimes? With the disappearance of murderers, burglars and escapees from the bishops' prisons, did that prison population shrink, or were their places taken by thieves? As usual, we do not have conclusive information, but the Home Circuit records indicate that the numbers remained robust (table 8.2).

Table 8.2 Recorded clerks delivered on the Home Circuit 1531–1537 by county/diocese*

	Surrey/ Winchester	Essex/ London	Herts/ Lincoln	Kent/ Canterbury	Sussex/ Chichester	Total
February 1531	3	1	3	1	0	8
July 1531	0	3	0	0	1	4
February 1532	1	1	1	1	0	4
July 1532	3	1	1	0	0	5
July 1533	0	0	2	0	0	2
February 1534	1	1	2	0	0	4
February 1535	1	0	0	0	0	1
July 1537	4	0	0	3	0	7
Total	13	7	9	5	1	35

*Data collected from TNA KB9/975 m. 148 (image not on AALT), TNA KB9/517 m. 53 (image 108), TNA KB9/519 m. 72 (image 144), TNA KB9/521 m. 72 (image 155), TNA KB9/525 m. 143 (image 289), TNA KB9/527 m. 66 (image 135), TNA KB9/531 m. 70 (image 139), TNA KB9/537 m. 51 (image 101).

Though most of the circuit returns faded away in the mid-1520s, the habit of reporting seems to have continued on this circuit, which returned short lists in February and July 1531, February and July 1532, July 1533, February 1534, February 1535, and July 1537.[50] When compared with the Home Circuit lists from the early years of the reign, the rate of delivery of clerks convict seems to have increased substantially, though as usual the rates of delivery vary over time and by county. Nevertheless, between 1509 and 1520 5.8 clerks per year, on average, are recorded as being delivered to the ordinaries; in the 1530s the average rises to 9.6

[50] TNA KB9/975 m. 148 [image not on AALT], TNA KB9/517 m. 53 [image 108], TNA KB9/519 m. 72 [image 144], TNA KB9/521 m. 72 [image 155], TNA KB9/525 m. 143 [image 289], TNA KB9/527 m. 66 [image 135], TNA KB9/531 m. 70 [image 139], TNA KB9/537 m. 51 [image 101]. It's not clear if this circuit was the only one to report or the only one to survive. The lists are terse, similar in format to those submitted in the 1520s, with simply the name, status and place of origin of the felon along with the county and date on which he was delivered. These lists generally state simply that the felon was delivered to the ordinary without naming the individual or the diocese or giving any information about the crime. On the July 1532 return the justices (Inglefield and Hales) noted that there were no deliveries for Sussex and Kent: since Inglefield and Hales were the justices in 1534 as well, it seems reasonable to conclude that their report then was also complete for the circuit, and that there were no clerks convict in Sussex and Kent in these terms either. On the July 1537 return the justices (Spelman and Baker) noted more specifically that no-one was convicted in Sussex, Essex, or Hertfordshire: TNA KB9/521 m. 72 [image 155], TNA KB9/537 m. 51 [image 101]. The distinction between the 'null' noted in 1532 and the 'nulli fuerunt convicti in hoc circuitu' of 1537 is intriguing. The former suggests simply that no clerks convict were delivered, but says nothing about the relative proportions of clerks convict to secular convicts, or about the conviction rate. The latter seems to say that there were no convicts, secular or clerical, in three of the five counties.

per year (4.8 per circuit), suggesting that the number of clerks convict delivered had roughly doubled. The returns in the 1530s also suggest that both Surrey and Hertford had outstripped Essex as the busiest part of the circuit, though this may well be an accident of source survival. It is clear that the bishops of both Winchester and Lincoln continued to receive a steady stream of clerks convict through these years, and we can assume that with the Newgate deliveries the bishop of London was equally busy. The felons passing through their gates were generally of lower social status and lower criminality than they had been a decade or two earlier, but they were probably no fewer in number.

3. The Bishops and the Management of Clerks Convict

The activity in parliament and King's Bench allows us to see what the government was trying to achieve in these years, but, though they had largely concentrated their political energies elsewhere, the bishops continued to be necessary partners in the administration of benefit of clergy. It is reasonable to assume that the changes in the law would precipitate changes in their practices, but, as we have seen, the bishops might approach benefit of clergy with a different set of concerns and assumptions than their secular colleagues, and their practices indicate how the statutory changes might play out in unexpected ways. Their records are generally thin, evocative rather than probative, but the bishop of Lincoln's register provides an unusually detailed view. We cannot be sure that the patterns in Lincoln are representative of other dioceses, but given the size and placement of the diocese, it's unlikely to be a complete outlier (fig. 8.5).

Between 1526 and 1543 John Longland recorded the purgation of 142 men.[51] This is an extraordinarily large and lengthy record of purgations for an episcopal register: by comparison, the bishops of Hereford recorded only ten men purged and released from the prison of Hereford palace between 1535 and 1539, and this is more than appears in any other contemporary register, as far as I can tell.[52] Longland's register probably does not represent every Lincoln purgation, but it certainly represents a much larger proportion than usual.[53] It confirms

[51] Longland became bishop in 1521.

[52] *Reg. Bothe*, pp. 361, 372, 375, 376, 381, 383. Four purgations were recorded during the tenure of Fox (October 1535–January 1538), three *sede vacante*, and three while Bonner was bishop elect (March-May 1539).

[53] Only six of the men recorded in Longland's register appear in the common law records, five on circuit lists for 1526, 1527, 1533, and 1543, and one in King's Bench. Another fifty-one men were delivered to Lincoln between 1523 (three years before the purgations begin, using a rough estimate of average time served as discussed below) and 1542 according to common law records but do not appear in the bishop's register, for a total of 183 men in the bishop's custody. It's not clear whether Longland didn't purge these men during this period or didn't record the purgations. Given the remarkable lack of overlap between the two sets of records, it's likely that neither the record of purgations nor the common law records are complete. Cf. pp. 206–209.

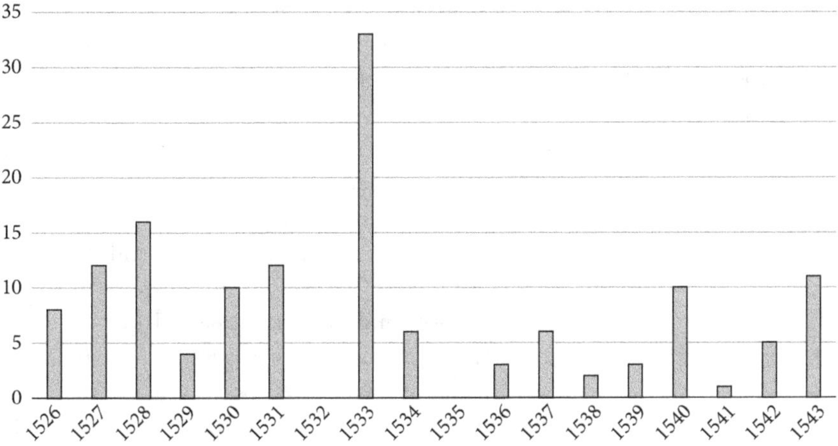

Figure 8.5 Purgations in Longland's *Register* by year, 1526–1543*

*Data collected from *Reg. Longland*, ff. 111v, 117v, 152, 153, 161v, 164v, 171, 187, 205v–207v, 211, 214v, 215, 230v–232, 236–236v, 244v–245, 254–254v, 269, 271, 273v, 277, 280–280v, 287–288, 291–291v, 294v–295, 296v.

that the numbers of clerks convict remained robust in the early 1530s and was probably growing, and it indicates that their terms of confinement became shorter.

The register makes it clear that Longland's approach to recording the purgations of clerks convict changed over the course of his tenure. He did not record purgations in his first five years, but from 1526 to 1530 the register records commissions to receive the purgations of the clerks convict which provide the names and status of the offenders and the prison in which they were held, but give no information about their crimes or convictions. In 1531 the records change: thereafter the register entry includes a description of the crime which is obviously drawn from the indictment, and the date on which the crime was carried out, though it is careful not to include any details of the common law process. The volume of purgations recorded throughout this period indicates that Longland—well-placed, as Henry VIII's confessor, to know what was afoot at court—recognized the value of keeping track of his clerks convict, and though we don't know why he suddenly expanded his recording practices in May 1531, in the interval between the 1531 and 1532 parliament, it's likely that he suspected that the attention paid to clerks convict might intensify in the near future.

The new detail available in the register indicates that the terms for which clerks convict were held became shorter in the 1530s. The registers don't give us all the information we might wish for: without the date of conviction we can only estimate the period of custody, and in the interests of consistency I have counted from the date of the crime rather than trying to guess how long it might have taken to reach conviction.[54] Even this rough calculation is useful, however. Longland's officials purged twelve men in 1531. Of those twelve, one had apparently been in custody for over twenty years for a fairly minor theft and was an outlier from earlier practices.[55] The other eleven illustrate the changes of the 1530s. The sentences served by the first six are fairly similar to the sentences we saw late in the reign of Henry VII, and suggest that practices had not changed substantially since then: one had been in custody for just over six years for a murder; one had served just over three years for a homicide; two served just over three years for burglary and two served twenty-one to twenty-four months for theft.[56] The last five, all convicted in 1530 or 1531, served between nine and twenty-one months for burglary. These were short sentences, and while one or two may have been lucky enough to have their sentence reduced, it seems unlikely that all five would. We noted that in the reign of Henry VII the sentence seems to have been set at the time of conviction, and the same is probably true here. A burglar convicted in 1528 was likely to find himself in the bishop's prison for about three years, but a burglar convicted in 1530 might go free in less than half that time.

The new pattern continues in the following years. There were no purgations in 1532, but 1533 was a bumper year, with thirty-three. Of the thirty-three, one was purged more than five years after his theft, one more than four years after his burglary of a parish church, and one more than three years after his robbery.[57] The other thirty men had all been convicted in 1530 or later, including four men purged for murder between thirty-five and nineteen months after their crimes and two men purged for burglary from two different churches twenty-four and nineteen months after their crimes. Four felons were out of custody less than a year after their crime, three of whom were convicted of burglary and one of assault. The other twenty men, convicted of a range of burglaries, assaults and thefts, were all purged between one and three years after their crimes.[58] In this larger sample the time spent in confinement is once again shorter for those convicted after 1530, for both murder and burglary, and sentences of less than a year become common for the first time.

It seems counter-intuitive to argue that the authorities were easing up on felons in the early 1530s, unless we assume that the statute of 1532 was intended to mask just such a shift. It is rather more likely that the desire to crack down was genuine, but also constrained by circumstance, and the appearance of a new prison in the

[54] While men might claim sanctuary months or years after the crimes they confessed to, the same was not true for indictments, and most men seem to have been indicted within a month or two of their crimes, often within days or weeks. Without a police force, if a criminal was not caught and indicted forthwith the chances he would be caught diminished significantly with time. The occasional delay might account for some of the outliers below, but it is unlikely to significantly affect the overall pattern.

[55] *Reg. Longland* f. 214v.

[56] See p. 109. *Reg. Longland* ff. 205v–206, 206v, 207, 214v, 215.

[57] John White, the thief, seems to have failed his first attempt at purgation: *Reg. Longland* ff. 161v, 230v, 231v.

[58] *Reg. Longland* ff. 207v, 211, 230v, 231, 231v–232, 236–236v, 244v, 245. Some of these commissions are undated, so have been extrapolated from context.

bishop's commissions holds the key to the puzzle. The commissions for purgation specify that thirteen of the men purged in 1533 were held at Banbury, but five were held at Newark. Newark appears for the first time in the commissions in 1531, suggesting that the traditional gaol at Banbury was no longer sufficient to manage the flow of clerks convict: Banbury continues to appear most often thereafter, but Newark remains in the mix. This, together with the shorter sentences imposed after 1530, suggests that the number of men flowing to the bishop's prison had increased, and as a result, the time they could be required to spend there had to fall. This is the same kind of pragmatic response to limited resources that we saw in 1495, but in 1530–1531 it may have been one of the factors that precipitated the 1532 statute and intensified the desire to keep the worst felons out of the bishops' prisons. Thus, as the 1532 statute reduced access to clergy for those convicted of the worst crimes, more of those convicted of the lesser felonies could expect to find themselves confined in the bishops' prisons, but for shorter periods of time. The secular authorities continued to work towards a solution to the lack of differentiation between punishment for murder and for theft, combining high-profile statutory restrictions with low-profile reductions in the length of sentences along with an increase in the number of clerks convict. While we don't have the records to conclusively prove the last element of the strategy, the addition of an extra prison, along with the simple fact that the bishop could release thirty-three men in one year, indicates that he was running a substantial operation.

After 1533 the number of purgations fell, and for the most part they were lower than the numbers in the late 1520s. We have seen before that the bishops tended to be assiduous in their recording in a period of change, but that their attention quickly faded when the law stabilized, and it's likely that this is what is happening here. The fact that Newark continued to appear in the commissions for purgation suggests that the numbers going to Lincoln had probably not declined substantially. Indeed the pattern of sentencing suggests that if anything the opposite was more likely. Of the six men purged in 1534, none had committed their crime before 1532, and four had committed their crime earlier the same year, thus serving between four and eleven months for burglary, theft, and accessory to murder.[59] There were no purgations recorded in 1535, but the three thieves purged in 1536 had all been convicted the previous year and served ten to fourteen months.[60] The six men purged in 1537 had been convicted of burglary in 1535: one served sixteen months, while the other five, who had together broken into the home of William Hamellyngton when he and his servants were present and in fear of their lives, served two years and two months.[61] The longer sentence in this case would seem to reflect the crime, except that this was one of the crimes excepted from benefit

[59] *Reg. Longland* f. 254–254v.
[60] *Reg. Longland* f. 269.
[61] *Reg. Longland* ff. 271, 273v.

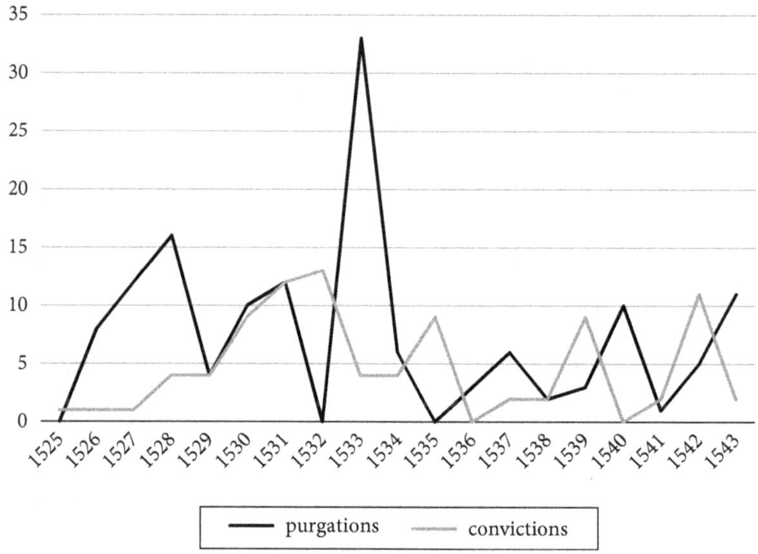

Figure 8.6 Purgations and convictions in Longland's Register 1525–1543*
*See note 57.

of clergy under the 1532 statute, as we saw, so these men should never have been in Longland's prison in the first place. Apart from this aberration, the new pattern holds until 1543, when the recorded purgations end: the two men purged in 1538 committed their crimes in 1537, the three purged in 1539 in 1538 or 1539.[62] Of the twenty-seven men recorded as purged between 1540 and 1543, two men committed their crimes, repeated burglaries in the one case and a single horsetheft in the other, around ten years earlier.[63] One had stolen a horse two years and eight months earlier and one had broken into the home and room of the 'principal and scholars of the Hall called Harteshall' in Oxford and stolen £10 11s 4d thirteen months earlier.[64] But twenty-two were purged less than a year after the commission of their crimes, which ranged from burglary to horsetheft to theft.[65] In fig. 8.6 the chaotic relationship between recorded convictions and recorded purgations in the 1530s settles into a more consistent one-year interval in the early 1540s, suggesting a new equilibrium by that time. Longland's register thus conforms with the evidence from the secular courts that a large and growing proportion of clerks convict

[62] *Reg. Longland* ff. 277, 280–280v.

[63] Henry Tykkysover, crime committed 28 October 1530, purged 21 May 1540; Richard Nytingale, crime committed 27 October 1532, purged 14 April 1543: *Reg. Longland* ff. 288, 296v.

[64] *Reg. Longland* ff. 287, 295.

[65] *Reg. Longland* ff. 287–288, 291, 294v, 295, 296v. One entry was not completed so the time to purgation cannot be calculated: *Reg. Longland* f 291v.

were convicted thieves and burglars rather than murderers, highway robbers or burglars of churches, but also demonstrates that their sentences were considerably shorter than they would have been even a decade earlier.

Not only did the ecclesiastical system hold a substantial number of men securely, more importantly, it held them for free and it fed and clothed them, something the secular system did not do.[66] As we have seen, at least some royal officials were genuinely concerned about the humane treatment of offenders, and the fact that men could and did survive in the bishops' custody for relatively long periods of time made this a particularly attractive model of reform. Of course the system was not actually free: the bishops continued to carry the costs, which were both financial and political. Accounts from the bishop of Winchester's prison from 1530 and the bishop of Coventry and Lichfield's prison at Eccleshall from 1542 give a sense of the former. Both give the same *per diem* of one farthing (.25d) for each man, but the accounts are otherwise quite different. At the bishop of Winchester's prison, for example, the ten men in custody at the end of the year received 14d each as a clothing allowance (dudsilver), and the bishop paid 2s 6d for the funeral of the one man who died in custody.[67] He also paid the warden a salary of £3 10d as well as covering the cost of maintenance—plumbers to fix the gutters, carpenters to fix the doors and windows and a great rope for the trap door, among other items—for a total of £9 11s 10d.[68] The tone of the Eccleshall account is quite different: there is no dudsilver for the six men in this account, but there is a charge of between 4d and 8d for removing the irons from the clerks convict when they were released, as well as a fee of 1d per compurgator.[69] The Eccleshall account also includes payments to the clerk of the assize for Staffordshire, the cost of conveying felons from the court, the cost of attending sessions to receive clerks convict (8 days at 1s a day) and a payment to George Willoughby for representation in King's Bench.[70] The total came out to £7 15s.[71] These accounts suggest that the bishops were taking the security of their prisons quite seriously, and a few pounds for the maintenance of doors, stocks and irons compares favourably to the hundreds of pounds that an escape might

[66] The act for jails of 1532 said that gaols should be in the towns where the assizes and sessions were usually held, both to reduce escapes and to increase the population base for 'relyffe and charyte' for the prisoners, indicating that though the Crown was increasingly concerned with security, there was still no sense that prisoners should be provided for. The statute did note that any taxes left over after the building of the jails should be used as alms for the prisoners, but this seems an unlikely eventuality: *SR*, III. 363, 364. 23 Hen. VIII c. 2.

[67] Sixteen men had been in custody over the course of the year.

[68] Surrey History Centre, Loseley MS 927/3.

[69] Pugh notes that the bishops' prisons might also be the prison for their lay fee and argues that this was the case at Eccleshall. Three of the six prisoners were identified as clerks convict and three simply as convicts, and this might reflect prisoners held under these different circumstances. See Pugh, *Imprisonment in Medieval England*, p. 136. This was also the situation at Wells, where clerks convict and secular prisoners escaped on the same day in 1506: TNA KB9/442 mm. 31, 33 [images 62, 66].

[70] Willoughby read on *Prerogativa Regis*: BL MS Harley 1691, ff. 197–201: Baker, *Men of Court*, vol. 1, p. 1677.

[71] Staffordshire Record Office D(w) 1734 J./1949 mm. 20d–21.

cost, but it is worth remembering that this was mostly money spent on secular convicts, not on clerks.

The financial pressures associated with escapes have been a core part of this story from the beginning: in the 1530s these continued, but there were also political costs. When thirteen prisoners escaped from his prison on 20 February 1534 Longland looked for a pardon for the £1,300 fine.[72] It was duly granted on 10 March and covered the escape of the thirteen prisoners from Banbury, any other clerks convict who had escaped before the date of the pardon, and any fines or amercements associated with the escapes.[73] But there was a trade-off: Longland wrote to Thomas Cromwell on 14 March 1534 that he would give Cromwell's clerk the chantry of Chalgrave, noting both that the chantry was worth £20 a year, and that he had been planning to give it to 'a good MA, a preacher'. In return he asked Cromwell to write to William Fermor 'that I be not indicted for the breach of my prisons, as the king has given me a pardon on such payment as I must make to his grace'.[74] This suggests both that there had been some horse-trading before the pardon was issued, and that the relief from fines given in the pardon was less comprehensive in reality. And this was not an unusual situation: a year later, in April 1535, Anthony Coope wrote to Cromwell to inform him that seven convicts had escaped from the same gaol, and in return for the information asked Cromwell to ask the bishop to lease to him the fee farm of the hundred of Banbury, offering Cromwell £200 to sweeten the deal.[75] It's not clear if the information was worth much to Cromwell, since Longland himself wrote with the news shortly afterwards, blaming 'ill-keepers' and asking for Cromwell's intercession 'that the king may forgive me part of the same and grant days of payment for the rest'.[76] The escape of prisoners continued to represent both a financial and a political liability for the bishops: they could find themselves facing ruinous fines or trading off land and favours in order to reduce the costs to manageable levels.[77] Given the kinds of financial pressures the post-Reformation bishops found themselves under, this situation must have seemed intolerable, especially when the escapees in question were almost certainly laymen rather than clerks. It's not unusual to find the bishops pleading for relief: the bishop of Exeter made the same point a couple of years

[72] It's clear that escapes continued in the 1530s, but the response was much faster than in previous reigns: on 1 January 1532 seven men escaped from the bishop's prison at Wells in Somerset, but an inquisition was held on 7 January, suggesting that official attention to such escapes had tightened significantly, even in the West country: TNA KB9/518 m. 25 [image 50].

[73] *LP* vol. 7, 419 [10]; TNA C66/663 m. 6.

[74] *LP* vol. 7, 322. Writing from Holborn on a Saturday, he asked Cromwell to get the letter to him by the following day, so that he could have it in Oxford when the session met on Tuesday. William Fermour was sheriff of Oxfordshire in 1533–1534: Baker, *Men of Court*, vol. 1, p. 665.

[75] *LP* vol. 10, 1266.

[76] *LP* vol. 10, 1267. Longland was indicted on the escape in July and appeared in King's Bench with the pardon in February 1539: TNA KB9/977 m. 54 [image not on AALT]; TNA KB27/1110 rex m. 9 [images 559, 560, 718d, 719d, 561, 562].

[77] See also *LP* vol. 7, 541.

earlier when asking for 'convenient days of payment for my convicts lately escaped' pointing out that 'though I am in the marches partly at the King's charges, I spare of my revenues little at the year's end'.[78] These men managed prisons full of clerks convict, the vast majority of whom were actually laymen; had greater responsibilities for feeding and clothing them than their secular counterparts; paid substantially larger fines for their escapes than their secular counterparts; and found themselves regularly negotiating for a reduction in those fines, or at least favourable terms of repayment, as the king's other claims on their time and expertise left them short of money.[79]

The changes of the previous four decades meant that by early 1532, as the Reformation parliament was legislating on benefit of clergy, common lawyers had access to a system of imprisonment which held a large number of men, fairly securely, in fairly good conditions, at no cost to the secular authorities. The Lincoln register suggests it had the capacity to absorb more men than it had previously done, but not a great deal more, and only if the authorities were willing to accept shorter periods of confinement for clerks convict. The authorities shifted their priorities in line with both the available resources and the political discourse, sending those guilty of the greater felonies to the gallows, while confining greater numbers of those found guilty of the lesser felonies for increasingly standardized periods of time.

4. Sanctuary and Benefit of Clergy in Practice 1529–1536

Though the statutes of the Reformation parliament clearly drew heavily on well-established practices and understandings of the law, there is no question that they also had radically innovative elements, something that was not a typical feature of the common law. We have seen in previous chapters that the courts were often hesitant in their approach to change, and the common lawyers preferred to let the possibilities for new interpretations of the law unfurl gradually over time. With the newly hectic pace of change both lawyers and felons found themselves forced to work through the problems and possibilities inherent in the new statutes with some dispatch. Evidence from both the courts and the sanctuaries suggest that they could interact in unanticipated ways, but that the courts, not surprisingly, stuck to fairly traditional approaches to working out those problems.

John Spelman reports the experiences of James Olyff and Henry Danby, who both committed crimes in 1530 and both appeared in King's Bench in 1532, and

[78] *LP* vol. 6, 169.

[79] *LP* has numerous remembrances for fines owed or paid by various bishops under these circumstances. In 1531 Longland paid Cromwell £666 13s 4d towards a fine for the escape of prisoners, and the evidence from other bishops' fines indicates that £100 continued to be the standard amount: *LP* vol. 5, 657, 825; TNA E101/421/5.

who, though they are apparently otherwise unconnected, demonstrate that both felons and officials were navigating the shifting rules of those years with some caution. Olyff took sanctuary at the monastery of St Augustine outside the walls of Canterbury in December 1530, along with other men. When the coroner arrived the following day, they confessed that they were 'robbers, thieves and felons of the lord king' having committed burglary in November.[80] They were branded according to the 1529 statute and ordered to abjure from Dover. Olyff appeared at King's Bench in April 1532, and when asked why he should not be executed on the failed abjuration, he claimed that Master Baron John Hales and Bartholomew Bereham, the coroner, had taken him from the church to the king's prison in Canterbury and kept him there for five or six weeks.[81] He was then brought to the Marshalsea and thence before the king's council, which sent him back to the prison and on for abjuration, accompanied by 'several constables'. This process of confinement and examination and his dispatch with multiple constables indicates that the authorities saw Olyff as a much greater danger than the indictment suggests: they certainly did not follow the normal process for abjuration, but the record gives no indication of why he attracted so much attention.[82] Once he was released to abjure, Olyff apparently made it safely to Dover and found a ship, only to be blown back on shore when a storm arose. According to the record the sailors held Olyff responsible for the storm and put him ashore in Kent against his will. When he appeared in King's Bench in April 1532 Olyff asked to be returned to Dover so that he could continue his abjuration, but Fermour demurred for the Crown. In Easter 1533, with the serjeants and the king's attorney present, the court held the plea bad, but went on to ask Olyff 'if he were a clerk or not'. We have seen the court offer this option in the past when it was unwilling to allow the plaintiff's plea but was not comfortable sending him to execution; in this case Olyff's unusual treatment before his abjuration was probably the cause of their unease. Robert Benet, the archdeacon of Westminster, appeared to claim him, and Olyff read *ut clericus*, but the court still hesitated. He was remanded and he returned to court on 16 June with the ordinary. This time the court ordered him to be branded again as a clerk attaint and delivered without purgation.[83]

By itself Olyff's is an unusually detailed and atmospheric narrative of the way an abjuration might play out, but his case does not stand alone. Henry Danby's odyssey began around the same time as Olyff's. He took sanctuary in Chichester cathedral in May 1530 and confessed to the coroners that he had killed an unknown

[80] TNA KB9/519 m. 119 [image 241].

[81] TNA KB27/1083 rex m. 4d, [images 6086d, 6087d, 5935, 5936] printed in *Spelman's Reports*, vol. 2, pp. 277–278. Spelman's report of the case says that he was back in King's Bench because he had been acquitted on a felony at Newgate, but the brand led the court to investigate: *Spelman's Reports*, vol. 1, p. 49, pl. 14.

[82] After Olyff entered his plea in King's Bench Chief Justice Fitzjames told him that he could not amend it afterwards 'because he was of bad fame': *Spelman's Reports*, vol. 1, p. 49, pl. 14.

[83] See p. 316 for the end of Olyff's saga.

Franciscan in Kent and burgled two homes the year before. He was branded and sent to Portsmouth for his abjuration.[84] He appeared in King's Bench in June 1532, and when asked why he should not be executed he too said that he had taken ship as ordered, and a storm had similarly arisen which blew them back to Plymouth. Using almost identical language to Olyff, he claimed that the sailors 'left him on the land and furthermore would not take him back on the ship', but he added that they 'told him that since he was an abjured man they would all fare the worse if they took him back in their company... and they told [him] ... to go seek his fortune'.[85] Unlike Olyff, Danby decided to try his luck under the statute passed the previous year, and he returned to London 'trusting himself there to abjure again to a certain sanctuary in England according to the form of the new statute'. Having reached London, however, Danby was seized and committed to Newgate. He escaped and made his way to Paris Garden, a property of the Knights Hospitaller just across the river, where he claimed sanctuary. He was again unlucky, and a constable from Paris Garden brought him the mile or so to the Marshalsea, whence John Hales brought him to King's Bench. It does not say anywhere in the record that Danby asked to be returned to the port to complete his abjuration, or to be allowed to take sanctuary elsewhere. The court returned to the case at Michelmas, and, having reviewed both the abjuration and the plea 'and they being fully understood by the court here, the lord king's serjeants-at-law and the same king's attorney-general having been called together for this purpose and being present, since it appears to the court here that the plea pleaded above by the said Henry Danby in manner and form aforesaid is insufficient in law and invalid' it ordered Danby to be hanged. The record, as usual, gives no indication of the reasons why they rejected the argument, but Spelman reports that the court felt that he should have stayed 'at his port or in other place or vill next to the sea... and every day proffered himself to pass over the sea'.[86] Spelman also notes that Danby 'was not a clerk' and he links the two cases, adding a quick reference to Olyff's outcome at the end of his report on Danby, even though he had reported Olyff separately only two cases before.

These two cases are puzzling for a number of reasons. It is exceedingly rare to see any evidence that an abjurer had actually taken ship, and we have no other cases where one was blown back on shore and deposited there by the sailors. To have two men abjure in 1530 and appear in King's Bench in 1532 with such similar and unusual stories must raise some suspicion, especially since both seem to have come to the attention of Hales, second baron of the Exchequer.[87] However, it's not

[84] TNA KB9/519 m. 147 [image 298].

[85] TNA KB27/1084 rex m. 7 [images 6308, 6309, 6310, 6507d], printed in *Spelman's Reports*, vol. 2, pp. 278–279.

[86] *Spelman's Reports*, vol. 1, p. 49, pl. 16.

[87] Hales was regularly a justice of gaol delivery in Kent and recorder of the city of Canterbury so his connection with Olyff was fairly straightforward, but it is less clear why Danby was brought to him, unless Hales was connected to the unknown Franciscan Danby confessed to killing. See Baker, *Men of Court*, vol. 1, pp. 802–803 for Hales.

entirely clear where to direct that suspicion. Unless we assume that all abjurers succeeded in disappearing into the countryside, a substantial number of men must have gone through the process of taking ship, and it's not inherently implausible either that some of those ships encountered storms, or that the sailors might have turned against them. In both of these cases the key problem was that the abjurers did not return to their assigned port to try again, a problem that, in its essence, we have seen before. Both men also presented complicating factors: Olyff's treatment before his abjuration suggests that he had a more checkered past than his single conviction reveals, but it also meant that the normal abjuration process had been infringed in his case, and this may have contributed to the court's willingness to offer him clergy as an option. Danby's serial and serious crimes, combined with his serial claims to sanctuary and his escapes, also made him an unlikely candidate for leniency, and it's not clear whether his attempt to jump from the old abjuration regime to the new worked for or against him, though it is rare to see evidence of a sanctuary claimant consciously choosing a strategy. Spelman's note that Danby was not a clerk also suggests that he was not literate, and that this still mattered, no matter how much the system was being re-worked. In both cases we see King's Bench work through the problems in very traditional ways, even as the system was changing around them, and despite their high drama, both Olyff's and Danby's outcomes were very much the same as they would have been before the passing of the new statutes.

Snapshot: Westminster clerks convict and sanctuary men in the 1530s

As usual, we have far less evidence in case reports, or indeed in legal records, of how these changes played out in the sanctuaries. Westminster Abbey remains both the best known and worst understood site of criminal confinement in this period, but lists of sanctuary men in Westminster prepared in June 1532 and 1533, along with a handful of cases, provide a snapshot of how it was operating at this crucial juncture: the complexity of legal and personal relations the sources reveal is instructive.[88] No explanation or context is given with either list, and both include debtors as well as felons, but the timing suggests that the compilations were associated with the 1531 statute, though they were clearly not required by it. The formats of the lists differ. The 1532 list names thirty-one men, of whom twelve are identified as having taken sanctuary for something to do with homicide: John Gonne, for example, was there 'for the dethe of a man in Westminster', while John Hede was in

[88] The former is TNA SP1/70 ff. 133–134, the latter TNA SP1/238 ff. 72–74, also in *LP* add. vol. 1, p. 295.

sanctuary 'upon suspicion for murder' and John Parkyne 'for murder of ij sergeants of London'. The remainder were in sanctuary for felony. Though in most cases no further information was provided, there was some elaboration: John Lovell and William Symson, for example, were both noted as robbing churches, while John ap Howell had stolen hens.[89] In some cases the elaboration throws some light on the crime, or indicates how we might interpret it: Degere Chontwell is identified as an apprentice who conveyed away some of his master's goods, while John ap Howell, the hen-stealer, is identified as 'apoore mane' and Morgan Foulke, in sanctuary for murder, is identified as 'a young mane'. These pieces of information might indicate mitigating circumstances, but others do the opposite: John Huffs was in sanctuary for felony, but it was also noted that 'this mane companythe with suspecte persons' while Simon Hyde's son being 'with suspecte persons resort[ed] to hyme and hys house'. The 1532 list does not indicate how long these men had been in sanctuary, with one exception: John Gonne, listed first, had committed his crime 'almost 20 yers paste'. This list is thus informative, but not consistent in the information it provides. It indicates that there was a substantial number of men in sanctuary at Westminster in the summer of 1532, from a wide variety of social backgrounds. More than one third of them were associated with homicide, and at least one had been there for almost two decades, but he may have been an anomaly.

The second list, a year later, is both longer and more informative, especially when taken in conjunction with the first. Sixty-one men are included, almost twice as many as the year before, of whom only four appeared on the previous list: John Gonne once again heads the list, but John Hede also re-appears, as does Rauf Sampson and John Albone. We don't learn anything new about Gonne (though his crime is more bluntly described as murder) or Hede, but this list notes that Sampson had been in sanctuary for five years and that John Albone, identified only as a goldsmith the previous year, had been in sanctuary for three years for receiving stolen plate. Thirty-seven of the men on this list were in sanctuary for murder, a much higher number and proportion than the year before. This might suggest that Westminster was once again becoming a prime destination for murderers, but a closer examination complicates the picture.

First, the length of time given on the list for each man may conceal a more complicated story. Seven of the murderers on the 1533 list had been in sanctuary for a year or more: Gonne, who was indeed an outlier, Hede, whose time in sanctuary is not provided on either list, but who appears on both, John Parkyne, (about three years), Richard Holter, William Marche and Richard fitz Williams, (two years), and Anthony __rne, who had spent 'on yere and more' in the sanctuary for 'murder in hys own defence'. Parkyne, Holter, Marche, fitz Williams and __rne should thus

[89] Some biographical information was also provided. Fifteen men were identified by their occupation and three by their nationality: two servingmen, 1 baker, 1 vintner, 1 priest, 2 goldsmiths, 1 barber, 1 waterman, 2 cappers, 1 fletcher, 1 tailor, 1 apprentice, and 1 collier; 2 Welshmen and 1 Irishman.

appear on the 1532 list, but none of them do.[90] The first list may simply be incomplete, but they may have been elsewhere, possibly contesting their claim to sanctuary, when that list was compiled. Maurice Bull and Nicholas Roo, for example, were arrested for stealing a miscellaneous array of goods on 20 September 1529, and appeared in King's Bench on 28 May 1530.[91] There they claimed that they had taken sanctuary at Westminster on 21 September and 'were registered and privileged' there until they were taken out of sanctuary against their wills by Thomas Wentworth and others on 21 October. Both denied that they had claimed sanctuary in August or any time before, asked to be restored, and pleaded not guilty to the felony. Christopher Hales countered that both men had taken sanctuary in Westminster on 30 August 1529, but on 20 September they left it with the intention of despoiling the lieges of the lord king. A jury in Hilary 1532 returned that Bull and Roo had indeed taken sanctuary in August and that they were guilty of the felony. Bull and Roo countered that the jury could not say if they were guilty of the felony and asked to be restored. The court wished to be advised, and the following Trinity term concluded that the verdict was indeed insufficient. A new jury in June 1532 side-stepped the whole question of timing and said that they did not enter the sanctuary for felony, and were not registered as felons: Maurice, they said, had entered for debt, and Nicholas 'for a blow called a strype, which was held to be murder'. This might seem to have muddied the waters, but in the event, the serjeants and the court agreed that they should be restored to sanctuary and delivered them to the archdeacon. Both Bull and Roo appear on the 1533 Westminster list as having been in sanctuary for four years for felony.[92] This dates their sojourn from the original claim in August (or September) 1529, with no acknowledgement of the two years, at least, that they spent in the Marshalsea as their case worked its way through King's Bench. Their absence from the 1532 list demonstrates that they were not counted as sanctuary men while their status was under consideration.

Second, while men like Bull and Roo took advantage of the unlimited sanctuary available at Westminster, many had been there for a much shorter period of time. Seven of the thirty-seven murderers spent more than a year in sanctuary, but four had been there for 'about half a year', nine for about a quarter of a year, three for eight-ten weeks, four for one to three weeks, six for two to three days, and three for one day. There is a similar pattern for felony. Of the twenty-two men listed for felony, four were clerks convict or attaint, five had been in sanctuary for three to five years and three for about one year, but four had been there for only three to six months, three for one to two weeks and three for two to four days. It is worth emphasizing that this list is a snapshot of 'of al suche persons ... [as] have taken

[90] Parkyne's flight to sanctuary is noted in the inquisition on a tavern brawl: TNA KB9/517 m. 2 [image 4].

[91] TNA KB27/1075 rex m. 4 [images 4772, 4773, 4970d].

[92] TNA SP1/238 f. 73, *LP* add vol. 1, p. 295.

the privilege and Sanctuarie of holy saynte peter of Westmynster ... wiche nowe be there remanynge & continnenge still' and does not reflect the dozens, if not hundreds, of men who might have claimed sanctuary there since the previous June and departed after a few days, weeks, or months.[93] If this list represents a typical pattern of use, it suggests that around ten to fifteen men a week might claim sanctuary at the Abbey for murder or felony, but most of them would not stay long. Some presumably fled to safety in the aftermath of a brawl and would leave once it became apparent that there were no fatalities. Those who remained for months used the time to negotiate the kinds of relief we saw in previous chapters, by arranging their narratives for the courts, securing a pardon, or evading the law and leaving the sanctuary. Both George Cornwall and John Stoughton, for example, appear on the 1533 list as having been in sanctuary for about a quarter of a year, though they are not listed together and no connection is made between them. Both, however, had been indicted in March for the murder of John Ode alias Wode, Cornwall for having killed him with a pre-meditated blow to the stomach, and Stoughton as accessory.[94] Both records were called to King's Bench in April 1534: though nothing further is heard of Stoughton, Cornwall appeared in King's Bench in November 1537 with a pardon for all murders before 5 May 1534, which notes that he is also pardoned all forfeitures and everything he should have by inheritance.[95]

Third, none of the men who abjured to Westminster according to the King's Bench records appears on this list, suggesting that the men who found their way there by the traditional routes were regarded separately from those who came via internal abjuration. This should remind us that despite the impact of the statutes on our understanding of sanctuary in this decade, the chartered sanctuaries continued to operate as sanctuaries of first resort as well as a destination for parish abjurers. These lists provide the most detailed evidence for this, but there is evidence elsewhere: the King's Bench records provide information on seven men who took sanctuary in Westminster in April 1532 after a fight between Richard Southwell and William Pennington resulted in the death of the latter, on John Symson and Richard Nobyll who both claimed sanctuary there in December 1533 after two separate murders and on Thomas Jones alias ab Adam and John Margettes who claimed in September and October 1534.[96] Similar evidence tells the same story for other chartered sanctuaries, which continued to attract sanctuary claimants: Richard Alyn fled to St. Martin le Grand after killing Richard Rowe in June 1535, and John Webbe after killing Henry Skrevyn in November 1536, while John

[93] TNA SP1/70 f. 133.

[94] TNA KB9/523 m. 105 [image 207].

[95] TNA KB27/1105 rex m. 2 [images 185, 186, 187, 387d].

[96] For Pennington see TNA KB9/520 m. 12 [image 21]; TNA KB27/1087 rex m. 8 [images 134, 135, 261d] and Shannon McSheffrey 'The Slaying of Sir William Pennington: Legal Narrative and the Late Medieval English Archive', Florilegium 28 (2011), pp. 169–203 for a full account of the fight and its context: TNA KB9/527 m. 46 [image 97]; TNA KB9/527 m.75 [image 153]; TNA KB9/531 mm. 73, 55 [images 144, 109].

a[tte] Dayll fled to Beverley after his premeditated murder of William Andersen in October 1530, and in the summer of 1533 Thomas Kuke and William Adamson both claimed sanctuary there after a homicide, though Adamson's was apparently in self-defense.[97]

These two streams of abjurers could pose a substantial problem. I suggested above that Beaulieu may have been a busier sanctuary than the paucity of records related to it suggests. It had certainly attracted attention in 1520, when the attorney-general, John Fitzjames, asked for a *quo warranto* to examine its rights, claiming that on 20 October 1519 and for more than eight years before, the abbey had used the liberty and franchise of a sanctuary for all those living and remaining in the house or manor for high treason against the body of the king as well as other treasons, felonies and murders.[98] The abbey was under scrutiny again in February 1532, when Christopher Hales asked for another *quo warranto*.[99] Though the language of the 1532 document largely repeated that of 1520, it added that sanctuary at Beaulieu was available to persons entering the house and manor as well as those living and remaining there (the addition is actually interlineated). The 1532 request may have been connected to the abjuration of Horsey, Anwick, and Harrys the previous year: if the abbot was turning abjurers sanctioned under the statute away because of over-crowding, the attorney general might have sought to argue that its capacity to accept first-instance sanctuary-seekers should be limited. The Beaulieu *quo warranto* suggests that there was concern about the capacity and the traditional usage of the chartered sanctuaries, and the ways in which this might affect their ability to function in the ways the framers of the 1531 statute wanted. If the abbot of Beaulieu turned internal abjurers away because of concerns about capacity, the abbot of Westminster surely had similar concerns: the Westminster

97 TNA KB9/1065 m. 9 [image not on AALT]. William Leggett was also indicted on Skrevyn's murder, but he was subsequently found not guilty at the assizes in Southwark in February 1537. He was then remanded to prison in case of appeal but bailed until the octave of Hilary 1538: TNA KB9/1065 m. 116 [image not on AALT]: TNA KB27/1101 rex m. 5 [images 135, 277d, 278d]. TNA KB9/975 m. 12 [image not on AALT]; TNA KB9/525 mm. 73, 76 [images 146, 151]. Men also continued to claim sanctuary in parish and monastic churches, though almost all the claims after 1531 are for homicide: TNA KB9/517 m. 90 [image 181], TNA KB9/512 m. 40 [image 574], TNA KB9/514 m. 120 [image 239], TNA KB9/514 m. 73 [image 143], TNA KB9/519 m. 134 [image 270], TNA KB9/524 m. 57 [image 118], TNA KB27/1094 rex m. 2 [images 157, 158, 316d, 317d, 159, 160, 318d], TNA KB9/533 m. 144 [image 287]. Other traditional patterns also continue to appear, though in small numbers. Four men removed from sanctuary asked to be restored, one of whom, William Wade, was successful: TNA KB9/548 m. 194 [image 384]. Wade abjured to Westminster but was later found in the country and claimed clergy: TNA KB27/1116 rex m. 10 [images 208, 209]. The other three disappear from the records without resolution: TNA KB9/520 m. 88 [images 175, 176]; TNA KB27/1101 rex m. 15 [images 156, 157, 158]; TNA KB27/1109 rex m. 14 [images 206, 207]. See also TNA KB9/547 m. 13 [image 27] and TNA KB9/548 mm 188, 189 [images 373, 374]. There is only one case where such a claimant was noted as being hanged, but he had previously claimed clergy and admitted to bigamy when challenged: TNA KB27/1113 rex m. 5 [images 212, 213, 428d].

98 TNA KB9/480 m. 53 [image 105]. The terms of the 1520 request suggest that the *quo warranto* was prompted by a particular case, but I have not been able to find either the precipitant or the results of that inquiry.

99 TNA KB9/518 m. 18 [image 36].

sanctuary was clearly crowded, with an ever-shifting complement of long-term, short-term and potential sanctuary seekers, and permanent or long-term abjurers sanctioned by statute would add significantly to the abbot's responsibilities.

This volatile mix posed problems beyond the simple issue of capacity. A felony case against John Newyngton in December 1534 provides an unusual glimpse into the dynamics within the sanctuary in these years. Newington was indicted for breaking into the house of William Lovell in the sanctuary on 7 November and stealing a purse containing £17.[100] Though the record survives in King's Bench there is no process there, probably because Newyngton turned to Chancery, and not for the first time. A few years earlier Newyngton, a London mercer, had appealed to Thomas More for help, apparently from the same sanctuary. According to the bill, Newyngton had asked Sir William Mote, parish priest of St Margaret's, Westminster, to hold goods worth about £140 to his use while Newyngton was in sanctuary.[101] Newyngton complains that he has little to live on in sanctuary and has asked Mote for the goods, but that Mote refuses to return them. We have no record of the outcome, but this suggests that at the time of his indictment Newyngton had either been in the sanctuary for two to five years and his financial troubles were ongoing, or that he was a habitual sanctuary-seeker. On his second approach to Chancery Newyngton set the scene by claiming that there had been a long-term disagreement between himself and John Parkynson and John Freman, and then provides a narrative of the night in question. Newyngton claims that he and his wife were in bed between 9 and 10pm, when they heard their neighbor, William Lovell, groaning 'in such agony and extremity of sickness ... that they thought he was in peril of his life'.[102] Newyngton went to Lovell's house, where a crowd of people could not wake him 'by drawyng, plukkyng or halyng hym yn veray rude & rygorous maner'. When Lovell did eventually recover, he discovered his purse was missing, and Parkynson and Freman had Newyngton indicted on the theft.

Newyngton's bill provides an unusually immediate glimpse into life in sanctuary, and it is both incoherent and revealing. The 1531 statute had provided that no sanctuary man could be removed to answer an indictment for a crime committed outside the sanctuary without the approval of two of the king's council or four justices of the peace. This crime was committed within the sanctuary, so the statute did not apply, but Newyngton seems to be appealing to its intention, arguing that the sixty men with him in Lovell's house were tenants of the abbot and lived in the sanctuary; they would not accompany him from the sanctuary to testify on his behalf, so he was likely to be 'wrongfully trowbled & falsely dysclaundered'. He also, intriguingly, claims that because Lovell is a 'menyall servant' to the abbot and Parkynson and Freman are his tenants, Newyngton was

[100] TNA KB9/530 m. 21 [image 43].
[101] TNA C1/659/6. The bill is not dated precisely, but More was chancellor from 1529–1532.
[102] TNA C1/861/45.

likely to be 'put falsely and untruely from his clergy' if he were found guilty of the theft. It's not clear from the context who the tenants of the abbot were: the sixty men could simply have been sanctuary men, and if so, this is another indication of the size of that population. But Parkyson and Freman appear to have held some power in the precinct, suggesting that if they were indeed simply sanctuary men, they had acquired some sway over both the rest of the community and the abbot. Newyngton is thus envisaging a situation where he was hauled out of sanctuary on the indictment, found guilty, claimed clergy, and was denied the opportunity to return to the Abbey, albeit with a different status, because of the machinations of Parkynson and Freman.[103] This is another rare glimpse of an accused felon and long-term sanctuary man formulating his strategy, and an even rarer one into the power dynamics that could develop at a long-term sanctuary. Whatever the outcome of Newyngton's case, this reminds us of the practical medium and long-term issues to be faced by the authorities who were seeking to further develop such a system of criminal confinement.

Fourth, though the picture they paint is rather less vivid than Newyngton's, the Westminster lists also throw an unexpected light on benefit of clergy and its relationship to sanctuary. Robert Tykhill appears on the 1533 list, described as a 'clarke convicte attainted for felony & abjured upon the same remanynge in the convicte house vij yere'.[104] Three other men, George Courtney, John Dagnall and William Hull, were described in the same way on the list, though Courtney had been in Westminster for seventeen years, rather than the seven attributed to the other three. Courtney was originally sent to abjure from Kingston on Hull in 1514, but was discovered in the country and claimed clergy at King's Bench in June 1516.[105] Dagnall had originally been sent to abjure from Southampton in March 1526, but claimed clergy after being found in the country, and was eventually delivered to Westminster as a clerk convict in May 1529.[106] Hull was similarly sent to abjure from Dover in November 1527, but was found in the country and delivered as a clerk to Westminster in June 1529.[107] The common language used suggests that Tykhill too had started out as an abjurer, but after being found in the country had ended up in Westminster.[108] This makes sense of the notation that they were held in the convict house, since sanctuary men were not normally confined in this way,

[103] Newyngton asked for a *certiorari* to the justices of the peace of Middlesex to certify the false indictment.

[104] TNA SP1/238 f. 72, *LP* add vol. 1, p. 295.

[105] TNA KB9/467 m. 89 [image not on AALT], TNA KB27/1020 rex m. 9 [image 240].

[106] See p. 194.

[107] TNA KB27/1072 rex m. 5 [images 1755, 1756].

[108] We have no record of an abjuration for Tykhill: he was outlawed in August 1525 and when he appeared at King's Bench in November 1527 he claimed that he was actually John Cotyll alias Arthur. The jury found otherwise, and the court asked Tykhill if he was a clerk or not. He read *ut clericus*, was branded and delivered as a clerk attaint in Easter term 1528: TNA KB27/1065 rex mm. 6, 10 [images 8897, 9167d; 8906, 8907]. He re-appears in 1540, see p. 317.

but it also suggests that their original status as failed abjurers stuck with them, since other clerks convict were not included on the list of sanctuary men. The years in custody provided on the list were clearly only rough approximations: it had been seventeen years since Courtney was delivered, but nineteen since his abjuration, four since Dagnall and Hull were delivered, but seven and six years respectively since their abjurations. The years given match neither the date of their deliveries nor their abjurations consistently, but suggest broader categories of long-term and medium term convicts. Given their confinement, these men did not have the option of slipping away, but they once again testify to the abbot's ability to keep clerks convict in custody for extensive periods of time and demonstrate the system's ability to manage a fairly complex criminal standing. They also make it clear that while individual felons could slip back and forth between statuses, the authorities could maintain a surprisingly clear sense of who was a clerk convict, who was an abjurer, and who was both.

These glimpses into the Westminster sanctuary in the 1530s indicate that the abbot was not only managing the crown jewel of the English penal system, he was also managing a constantly shifting and volatile population. Westminster not only continued to receive its traditional sanctuary claimants, who continued to use the sanctuary in the traditional way, it also had to absorb abjurers who would previously have made their way to ports like Dover and Southampton, and who could be expected to take up residence in the precinct for an extended period of time. It had to manage the relationships between these men, as well as the relationships between the sanctuary men and the other inhabitants of, and visitors to, the precinct. And it had to manage the steady stream of clerks convict who made their way from the Marshalsea and King's Bench to the abbot's prison. While Westminster was unusual in dealing with both sets of felons, and probably unusual in the volume and fluidity of its population, it once again highlights the kinds of issues that lesser houses and prisons up and down the country were facing and the growing complexity of managing this new model of criminal confinement.

5. The Statutes of 1536

By 1536 two distinct sets of changes converged in a new run of statutes. The first was a growing tendency to consider sanctuary and benefit of clergy as naturally connected. As we have seen, this had been manifested in the 1520s and early 1530s by new attempts to manage the abjuration process in ways that had been common with benefit of clergy for several decades, such as the branding of abjurers and the closer oversight of coroners and the abjuration process. In the late 1530s, as new felony statutes were passed, it was reflected in the increasingly common practice of removing benefit of clergy and sanctuary as possible mitigations of punishment for those new felonies. In 1534 parliament made sodomy a felony without benefit of clergy.[109] It also refined the definition of treason and removed sanctuary for the newly defined offences.[110] In 1536 parliament provided that crimes committed on the sea could be tried on land, and removed both benefit of clergy and sanctuary for those thus convicted of robberies, felonies or murders.[111] It made a similar provision for servants who embezzled goods worth more than £2 from their masters.[112] In 1539 the act of six articles provided that those offending under the first article could not claim sanctuary or benefit of clergy and were punished as for treason, while offenders under the other five were also denied sanctuary and punished as felons.[113] Priests who married were declared felons but did not lose benefit of clergy or sanctuary, though priests who maintained concubines were felons on the second offence without benefit of clergy or sanctuary, as were their partners.[114] Excluding those convicted of these crimes from benefit of clergy and sanctuary demonstrates how central they were to the management of the criminal justice system, and their consistent association makes it clear that they were seen, together, as central to the mitigation process.

The second was the growing need to manage the sanctuary inhabitants. The number of long-term sanctuary inhabitants grew in these years and these men either displaced transitory claimants or swelled the existing populations, possibly beyond capacity. Newyngton's case points to the kinds of tensions that might exist within such a population, even at Westminster, which had more experience with a large and semi-permanent sanctuary population than places like Colchester. These new realities probably precipitated a 1536 statute which addressed the behavior of sanctuary men directly.[115] It required them to wear a badge assigned by the governor of the sanctuary, ten inches in diameter, whenever they left 'the House or Mansion wherin they have thir lodging'.[116] Although this statute has been regularly described as part of the Tudor programme of tightening up sanctuary regulation, there has been little consideration of its actual purpose. The preamble to the statute

[109] *SR*, III. 441. 25 Hen. VIII c. 6. The statute was to last until the end of the next parliament.

[110] *SR*, III. 508–509. 26 Hen. VIII c. 13. The succession act in 1536 added further definitions to treason and removed the privilege from those definitions 'any use grant custom prescripcion [or] confirmacion ... to the contrary ... notwithstanding': *SR*, III. 661. 28 Hen. VIII c. 7.

[111] *SR*, III. 533–534. 27 Hen. VIII c. 4. This was extended to apply also to convictions for treason and confederacies in the second session in 1536: *SR*, III. 671. 28 Hen. VIII c. 15.

[112] *SR*, III. 549–550. 27 Hen. VIII c. 17.

[113] *SR*, III. 740–741. 31 Hen. VIII c. 14. Those who refused to confess or receive the sacrament were declared felons on the second offence but the statute does not remove benefit of clergy or sanctuary from these offences.

[114] *SR*, III. 743. The two were not always linked: a proclamation of 1538 removed the privilege of sanctuary for those who killed royal officials carrying out their duties, and, in an early attempt at weapons-control, ordered that anyone who 'shall use in his fight any foin or foins with his sword or other his weapon' in any fray or fight should also lose the privilege: *Tudor Royal Proclamations* vol. 1 ed. Paul L. Hughes and James F. Larkin (New Haven: Yale University Press, 1964), pp. 262–263.

[115] *SR*, III. 551. 27 Hen. VIII c. 19.

[116] *SR*, III. 551. Sanctuary men at Durham wore a gown of black cloth with a yellow cross of St. Cuthbert on the left shoulder: J.T. Fowler, ed. *Rites of Durham* Surtees Society vol. 107 (London: Bernard Quaritch, 1964), p. 42.

draws upon the familiar rhetoric of the sanctuaries as nests of murderers, rapists and thieves, who presumably (though the statute in this case does not explicitly say so) emerge from the sanctuaries to commit their crimes and then return. In this context the badge seems designed to identify a sanctuary man when he left the precinct, but this doesn't make much sense. Any sanctuary man so identified could be immediately arrested, and any criminal intending to murder, rape, or steal and then return to the sanctuary was unlikely to feel compelled to wear his badge while he did so. The more logical reason for the badge was to distinguish the felons from the other, non-criminal, inhabitants of the sanctuary. In her study of St. Martin le Grand, for example, Shannon McSheffrey has estimated that about 82 per cent of the inhabitants of the sanctuary area were foreign artisans taking advantage of the freedom from the city guilds within the liberty, rather than criminals taking advantage of the sanctuary jurisdiction.[117] Though such artisans clearly benefitted economically from the situation, the ongoing possibility of being taken for a felon must have weighed on these men, and a distinguishing badge would have reassured both them and outsiders passing through and doing business in the sanctuary. Any sanctuary man found in the sanctuary without his badge could be arrested by any of the king's subjects and removed to the nearest gaol.

The other provisions of the statute are more clearly directed to controlling the behavior of the felons. They are not to carry any weapons but meat knives, and those only at meal times.[118] A curfew was imposed from sunset to sunrise with a sliding scale of punishment: two days in the sanctuary prison for the first offence, six days for the second, and loss of sanctuary for the third, though for such a forfeiture the matter had to be proved before the lord chancellor, demonstrating again that the loss of sanctuary was taken very seriously. The final clause of the statute gives the governor of the sanctuary the authority to determine debts or trespasses worth less than 40s between the sanctuary men, or between them and the other inhabitants of the sanctuary. This was a practical provision, and one that already existed at Westminster. It is notable though, given that these Tudor statutes are often discussed in terms of the destruction of franchises.[119] As with the 1531 statute on internal abjuration, this statute is building a more coherent and carefully elaborated law to govern the management of the chartered sanctuaries for the future.

There was one more statutory flourish in 1536. Though the Reformation parliament ended its marathon sitting on 14 April 1536 and the political classes departed

117 Shannon McSheffrey, 'Stranger Artisans and the London Sanctuary of St. Martin le Grand in the Reign of Henry VIII', *Journal of Medieval and Early Modern Studies* 43 (2013), p. 551.

118 This was similar to the fifteenth-century regulations at St Martin-le-Grand, see p. 62.

119 Lehmberg comments of this statute that 'it is perhaps surprising that sanctuaries were not abolished altogether, considering the complaints against them' but in his discussion of the 1540 statute, which he says 'regulates rather than abolishes' he speculates that 'this milder approach was dictated by the Commons, for we know that they re-wrote the original proposal'. Lehmberg, *Reformation Parliament*, p. 230, Stanford Lehmberg, *The Later Parliaments of Henry VIII, 1536–1547* (Cambridge: Cambridge University Press, 1977), p. 100.

with the expectation that they would have some time to work through the mountain of legislation they had passed, parliament reconvened unexpectedly on 8 June and its first act dealt with sanctuary and benefit of clergy. At first glance the statute is not especially significant, and, as Lehmberg suggests, looks simply like a confirmation statute to extend the legislation so recently passed.[120] It rehearses the 1531 act which introduced internal abjuration, the 1532 act which limited benefit of clergy, the 1534 act which closed the loophole around standing mute and the act which made sodomy a non-clergiable felony, and extends them to the end of the next parliament.[121] However, the slender records from the Lords suggest that parliament may have been considering making substantial changes to sanctuary and benefit of clergy. A bill dealing with sanctuary is described as 'for the limitation of privileged places to those who have perpetrated homicide', while two bills on benefit of clergy are described as 'for robbery and homicide perpetrated by privileged men', and 'that those who perpetrate felony, homicide, or similar crimes shall be deprived of benefit of clergy'.[122] Eustace Chapuys, the well-connected ambassador of Charles V, noted in February that proposals had been submitted 'to deprive the bishops of their tribunals and jurisdiction and to subject all churchmen to temporal courts'.[123] Lehmberg suggests that this might mean that there was a proposal to remove everything but probate and matrimony from the Church courts, but it seems more likely that it was a proposal to end benefit of clergy.[124] If these titles accurately describe the proposed bills, they would have substantially curtailed the use of both sanctuary and benefit of clergy, potentially making the former available only for homicide and the latter either not available at all, or more likely, only for lesser felonies such as theft. These proposed bills did not pass the house, but even the eventual title of the statute, 'An act that felons abjuring for petty treason, murder or felony shall not be admitted to the benefit of their clergy' suggests that quite a different act was proposed, one which would break the growing connection between sanctuary and benefit of clergy by allowing felons access to one or the other, but not both.[125] In the event, the more generous and combined system was preferred, for the most part, and the lumping together of these four acts makes it clear that benefit of clergy and sanctuary had become entwined in the eyes of parliament as part of a system for mitigating punishment.

There is one substantial novelty in this statute, though it reads almost as an afterthought, and it demonstrates that one element of the proposals to tighten up on

[120] Lehmberg, *Later Parliaments*, p. 18.

[121] *SR*, III. 651–652. 28 Hen. VIII c. 1.

[122] *Journal of the House of Lords vol. 1, 1509–1577* (London: His Majesty's Stationery Office 1767–1830), pp. 87–88. 17 June 1536.

[123] *LP* vol. 10, 308

[124] Lehmberg, *Reformation Parliament*, p. 223. Lehmberg notes that there is no evidence for his suggestion.

[125] The title of the act in the calendar is similar: 'An Act that abjurors in certain cases shall not have clergy'. *SR*, III. xxvii.

benefit of clergy did gain traction: it applied the provisions of the earlier acts to clergy in major orders, until the end of the next parliament. Thus after 1536 benefit of clergy was no longer available to clerics who committed petty treason, willfully committed murder, robbed a church, robbed someone in their own home or on the highway, committed arson or abetted any such crime. This is the first time that parliament passed a statute which limited benefit of clergy for those in major orders, and the profound lack of reaction to the change reflects both the resources available to the hierarchy for fighting such a change and the effective irrelevance of the issue by that point, given the small number of men affected.

6. Conclusion

By the end of 1536 the secular authorities could be forgiven for congratulating themselves for having cleaned up traditional abuses in benefit of clergy: having largely eliminated the claims of repeat offenders in previous decades, they had removed the right of laymen to claim clergy for heinous felonies in 1532 and in 1536 had, apparently without significant opposition, imposed the same limitation on clerics. The operation of benefit of clergy had been effectively under the control of the justices since the beginning of the century, but the statutes of the Reformation parliament make it clear that by the mid-1530s it was publicly under the control of the secular authorities: though they modified that control, the statutes did not establish it. The sudden appearance of these statutes and their limitation of benefit of clergy have caused historians to assume that parliament's intention or desire was to eradicate it, but the activities in the courts and in Longland's register make it clear that the statutes have to be understood as one element in a more complex plan to use benefit of clergy as an appropriate punishment for lesser felonies rather than an inappropriate mitigation for greater ones.

In the same decade the secular authorities made giant strides in asserting their authority over sanctuary: indeed the change there was much faster and much more explicit, partly because it had so much further to go. From the introduction of the brand to the assertion of statutory control over benefit of clergy had taken forty years; with sanctuary it took two. The accelerated pace of change reflects not only an increasingly active and confident parliament, but a clearer sense of what the management of ecclesiastical prisons and sanctuaries could offer to the criminal justice system. Absorbing sanctuary into the system allowed it to perform its traditional function as a safety valve in a new way: those who were no longer eligible for benefit of clergy continued to have this option for mitigation, but they exercised it in a process carried out under the watchful eye of the justices and within the boundaries of the realm. A lot of new law had to be tested in the crucible of the courts, but Fyneux's vision had come close to being achieved, if not in any way that he could have imagined.

9

Sanctuary and Benefit of Clergy after 1537

The system in place at the end of 1536 was not perfect, but it was reasonably consistent and coherent. Sanctuary and benefit of clergy had been drawn together in a structure that was clearly under royal control, and between them they provided a graduated mitigation for most felonies. With the end of external abjuration, the chartered sanctuaries could provide lifelong confinement for those who confessed to a variety of felonies. All else being equal, it is not unreasonable to assume that such sanctuaries might expect to find themselves receiving a larger number of murderers, burglars, highway robbers, or arsonists, since those crimes were no longer eligible for benefit of clergy: the legislation of 1536 which meant that the sanctuaries were more closely managed than ever before could allow them to become a relatively high-security site of confinement. Literate felons who committed mid-level and lesser felonies such as homicide, robbery, and theft might face either the dangers of abjuration and indefinite confinement in these sanctuaries or the rigours of confinement in a bishop's prison for a year or two, while illiterates still had only sanctuary to rely upon. And those who prevailed upon the sympathies of the jury, whether because of the pettiness of their crime or the misery of their circumstances, might still hope for jury nullification and punishment only by a passage through the trial process. While constructing this system, the statutes on benefit of clergy had drawn heavily on common law practices and doctrines even while they innovated. This was less true for the statutes on sanctuary, but they had rather less to draw on. And we might expect that while the pace of change would slow, the courts or parliament would continue to tweak this model by periodically revising eligibility, refining crimes, or tightening security.

All else did not remain equal, however, for reasons that were entirely outside the control of the common lawyers. For while criminal justice reform rode the wave of religious reform successfully through the early 1530s, it crashed painfully in the last years of the decade. The first and most obvious problem was that as the dissolution of the monasteries got underway the chartered sanctuaries began to disappear along with them. The second and more slowly emerging threat was the shrinking resources of the ecclesiastical hierarchy. Over the previous four decades the justices had developed a new model of criminal confinement, sometimes in the face of ecclesiastical opposition, which confidently, if unthinkingly, assumed that the resources of the institutional church would be available to fund and manage it. In the 1530s the opposition disappeared, but so did the resources. Without any compensating secular resources devoted to the problem—for that was never an

The King's Felons. Margaret McGlynn, Oxford University Press. © Margaret McGlynn 2023.
DOI: 10.1093/oso/9780192887689.003.0010

option—the common lawyers increasingly found themselves responding on the fly to religious changes which undermined criminal justice practices in ways that were often not intended or foreseen. They were forced not only to improvise, but to improvise quickly. If the story of the five decades from 1490 to *c.* 1536 is of the creation of a secular system of criminal confinement housed, funded, and managed by the ecclesiastical authorities, the story of the two decades from 1537 to *c.* 1553 is of the swift collapse of that system as religious changes removed the institutional foundations on which it had been built. The justices clearly wanted to preserve some part of the system they had worked so hard to build, and pardons, which have thus far been a minor if necessary part of the system, move to the centre of the story, for, properly used, they could both relieve some of the pressure on the ecclesiastical system, and maintain the connection between the king and the felon. The justices struggled to find that balance, however, and by the time of Edward VI's accession in 1547 the potentially complex and nuanced system of the 1530s had declined into a system of brief imprisonments for minor felons. Under Protector Somerset there were innovative and somewhat extreme attempts to create a leaner and more efficient system, but they filled the requirements neither of justice nor mercy and seem to have been abandoned after his fall. As a result, by the end of Edward's reign the options for the punishment of felons were much diminished, and his sisters inherited a pale shadow of the structure in operation when their father's matrimonial adventures began.

1. Sanctuary: The Dissolution of the Monasteries and Statutes, 1529–1540

The story of decline most obviously begins with the changes to sanctuary in the late 1530s. The relatively abundant abjuration records which allowed us to trace changing practices through the 1520s and 1530s largely disappear in 1535–1536 (fig. 9.1).[1] We once again find ourselves in the position of having only documents which survive because of their use in later processes. This slender source base does suggest that the patterns continued as before: in 1535, for example, we see two men taking sanctuary together at Buntingford Herts, confessing to highway robbery, and abjuring to Beverley; one woman taking sanctuary at a priory at Barnwell, Cambridgeshire, confessing to housebreaking and abjuring to Westminster, and one man taking sanctuary at the monastery of St Mary in Coventry and also abjuring to Westminster.[2]

[1] There were no substantial changes in the law in these years, but this may be the reason for the decline: it's possible that as the law stabilized, officials became less concerned about maintaining records. It's also possible that as abjurers carried their documents with them the responsibility for preserving such records may have shifted from the coroners to the sanctuaries.

[2] TNA KB9/531 m. 95 [image 188]; TNA KB9/533 m. 108 [image 215]; TNA KB9/533 m. 140 [image 279].

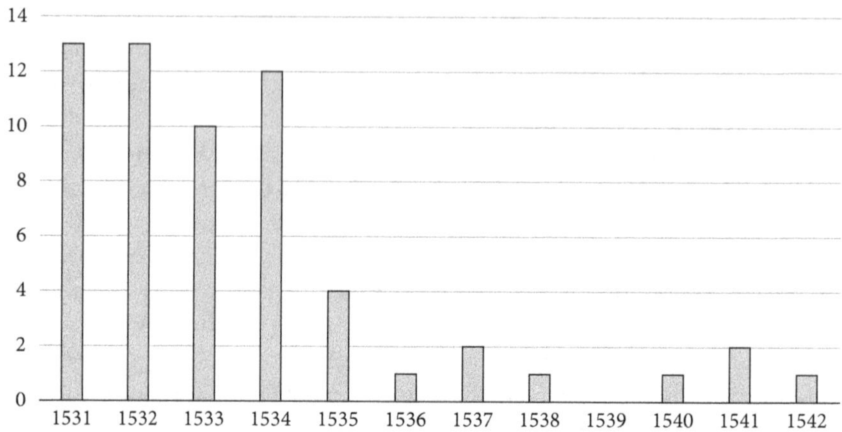

Figure 9.1 Recorded internal abjurations 1531–1542*
*Data collected from TNA KB9 rolls.

Though these sources indicate that abjurations could and did continue under the new model at the end of the decade, the dissolution of the monasteries which began in 1536 and ended in 1540 irretrievably changed the context within which they were happening. If the monastery which housed a chartered sanctuary was dissolved and the lands sold on, what happened to the sanctuary men? We saw in chapter 8 that Beaulieu was both a long-standing and quietly busy sanctuary: when it was dissolved in 1538 there were thirty-two sanctuary men in residence there, along with their wives and children. On 3 April 1538 the commissioners for the dissolution wrote to Cromwell to ask what to do with them. In their letter they are explicit that some of the sanctuary men are there for murder and felony, as well as for debt, and they claim, in language similar to that used for the monks, that 'many of them [are] aged some very secke'.[3] The letter emphasizes that the men had 'wyves and children and dwelling howses and ground wherby they lyve with their famylies'.[4] Though the commissioners were not explicit about the plans for the sanctuary men, they told Cromwell that when the men were told of the king's plans,

[3] Letter transcribed in W.H. St. John Hope and Harold Brakspear, 'The Cistercian Abbey of Beaulieu in the County of Southampton', *The Archaeological Journal* 63 (1906), p. 176; *LP* vol. 13.1, 668.

[4] A rural abbey like Beaulieu provided a very different set of options to Westminster, and the image of sanctuary men integrated into the community that we see here is quite different from the kinds of glimpses that we've had of Westminster. While it's entirely possible that the harmony of the situation is over-stated for political purposes, there is likely some truth to the image, and it may also help to explain why places like Beverley and Beaulieu appealed to so many abjurers: for the genuinely penitent or unlucky, especially men who were used to a rural environment, it may have been a much more appealing prospect than the rough and tumble of the London sanctuaries. This may also explain why Abbot Bangor turned Harrys away in 1531—if he had established a certain equilibrium with his sanctuary population, the prospect of men arriving there at the coroners' behest from all around the country was presumably quite alarming: see p. 256.

'they have verye lamentable declared that if they be nowe send to other saynturyes not onlie they but their wyves and children also shall be utterly undon'. This suggests that the sanctuary men were to be sent on to one of the sanctuaries that remained open, in much the same way that monks from smaller houses were moved to larger houses in the early days of the dissolution. The scheme was no more welcome to the sanctuary men than it was to the monks, and they asked to be allowed to remain at Beaulieu, though they accepted that no others would be admitted. The commissioners supported the sanctuary men in their plea, and concurred with their assessment, asking Cromwell for his instructions.

If Cromwell responded the letter does not survive, but two weeks later, on 16 April, Thomas Stevens, the late abbot of Beaulieu, wrote to Thomas Wriothesley, who had been granted the abbey.[5] Stevens moderated the earlier request, asking Wriothesley to allow those who were in the sanctuary for debt to remain, assuring him that they had always been 'in ther behavyor very honest men' and warning him that if they were expelled the houses in which they lived would not be rented.[6] The following day John Crayford, a sub-commissioner for the dissolution, also wrote to ask Wriothesley for his compassion for the debtors. He painted their potential misery with an even heavier brush, and claimed that they 'must be compelled to begg and failing of foode in a sanctuary of smale compasse must other ... ther bodyes and slender goods in goyng abrode or dey for hungar'.[7] The implication is that the new sanctuary would be smaller than Beaulieu, and would not allow the men to maintain themselves economically. Crayford is also explicit that his request for clemency is only for the debtors, since 'the morderers and felons woll incontinently and without any further sute as hopeles men depart', presumably to another chartered sanctuary: as confessed felons they were due rather less consideration than the debtors who might be expected to become productive members of society once again in due course. Finally, Crayford asked Wriothesley to ask the king for license to maintain the debtors and their families 'not by virtue of thold Sanctuary ther but be new protection under the kings greate seale'. Thus in Crayford's mind the obvious alternative to sending the men on to another sanctuary was to create a secular sanctuary in Beaulieu with the king's license, purely for debtors who could be self-sustaining.[8]

Whether it originated at Beaulieu or elsewhere, there is evidence that the idea of a secular sanctuary was circulating the following year in Westminster, of all places. On 31 January 1539 John Maynwaryng alias Maneryng and four other men claimed sanctuary in Westminster for their various parts in the pre-meditated

[5] *LP* vol. 13.1, 1519[67] dated 29 July 1538.
[6] Hope and Brakspear, 'Beaulieu', p. 176: *LP* vol. 13.1, 792.
[7] Hope and Brakspear, 'Beaulieu', p. 177: *LP* vol. 13.1, 796.
[8] These requests seem to have been allowed and the Beaulieu men stayed in peace: *LP* vol. 13.1, 877.

murder of Richard Cholmeley in St Paul's churchyard.[9] When Maynwaryng appeared in King's Bench a few months later, he claimed that he

> came yn to the kynges pryvyledge at Westminster and there desyryd of Master Webbe the kynges pryvylege that ys graunted to Westminster there for the safegard of hym and that he myght have his name regestred there; wher upon Master Webbe grauntyd yt me the kynges pryvyledge there accordyng to my request & apon that gave me on othe accordyng to the pryvyledge there.[10]

Maynwarying goes on to complain that he was removed from the sanctuary against his will by Cromwell's command and he asked to be returned to 'have the advauntage of the pryvyledge thereof accordyng to the kynges graunt there to the monastery of Westminster'.[11] Though Maynwaryng is explicit that he was at the Abbey, he is emphatic in his reiterations that the sanctuary he claimed relied on 'the king's privilege': this might simply refer to the royal origins of Westminster's privilege, but at the very least it is a new emphasis on that royal authority. The fact that this sanctuary was managed by Master Webbe rather than the abbot or archdeacon suggests that there had in fact been a change of jurisdiction rather than simply of diction, though Master Webbe did keep the same kind of register as the chartered sanctuaries had typically done.

On 1 November 1539, later that same year, Anthony Spencer also claimed sanctuary in Westminster, having killed John Morres with pre-meditated malice and stolen £17. Spencer, however, equally explicitly came to the town of Westminster, asking William Webbe, an officer there, for the privilege 'propter tuicionem et salvo custodia vite sue', and reporting that Webbe had given it to him in as full a manner 'as the lord king and his council had granted it'.[12] When he appeared before the justices at Croydon in July 1540 he claimed that he too was extracted from the sanctuary against his will by Cromwell, and asked to be restored. He was repeatedly remanded to custody until he appeared in King's Bench in May 1544. Spencer repeated his claim to sanctuary, arguing that Webbe, the 'legitimate governor and

[9] TNA KB9/541 mm. 85, 86 [images 165, 166]. Cholmeley died on 9 February. Robert Jones confessed to having delivered the mortal blow while the others abetted. They all claimed that Ralph Maynwaring of Swanley procured the murder.

[10] TNA KB9/541 m. 85 [image 165]. The other four all said that they had not been taken from sanctuary against their will but had emerged at the lord privy seal's command, trusting that they would keep their privilege. Their pleas were found insufficient and all four were ordered to be hanged. Ralph Maynwarying was found not guilty of procuring the crime: TNA KB27/1112 rex m. 9 [images 142, 143, 284d, 285d, 144].

[11] See McSheffrey, *Seeking Sanctuary*, pp. 166–170 for a discussion of this case. See William B. Robison, 'Murder at Crowhurst: A Case Study in Early Tudor Law', *Criminal Justice History* 9 (1988), pp. 47–49 and Shannon McSheffrey, 'The Slaying of Sir William Pennington: Legal Narrative and the Late Medieval English Archive', *Florilegium* 28 (2011), pp. 177–187 for Cromwell's involvement in the management of other individual cases.

[12] TNA KB9/550 m. 40 [image 74].

registrar of the aforesaid sanctuary, accepted the aforesaid Anthony to the privilege of the sanctuary'.[13] Whorwood, the attorney-general, accepted that Spencer was removed from sanctuary against his will, but argued that he was guilty of murder and asked for a jury. In response, the court and the king's serjeants together agreed 'that the aforesaid Anthony Spencer should be restored to the said sanctuary at Westminster and he should have the immunity of that sanctuary for the tuition and salvation of his life in as ample manner and form as it extends'. Webbe, once again described as the governor and registrar of the sanctuary, returned to King's Bench to ask for Spencer, and he was duly restored.[14] It seems unlikely that there were two separate sanctuaries at Westminster in 1539, both presided over by Webbe, but it does seem clear that Webbe had taken over the wardenship of the sanctuary and that both his role and his jurisdiction were perceived as being royal, whether he was operating within the Abbey or the town. This is early evidence that the king was extending his authority over the sanctuaries in the same way that he had extended his authority over the episcopal prisons, and these cases represent another intermediate step in the transition from chartered to secular sanctuary, not in this case generated by the dissolution and regranting of the institution to a secular lord, but by the direct application of royal authority.

It was in this context that the crowning sanctuary act of Henry VIII's reign was passed in the summer of 1540. The bill was introduced in the Lords on 3 June as 'the bill to abrogate sanctuaries', read again on 5 June, and read and unanimously approved on 7 June.[15] The following day it was sent to the Commons as 'the bill to abolish sanctuaries'.[16] We don't know what happened in the Commons, but on 23 July, the penultimate day of the session, a new bill came back to the Lords. It was quickly read and passed on the same day.[17] This act seems to be quite different from the bill that went to the lower house. Its preamble lays out clearly the king's desire to find a middle path: he wished neither to allow sanctuaries to encourage lawlessness, nor, despite the titles of the Lords' bills and Cromwell's oft-cited desire to accomplish the 'utter destruction of sanctuaries', to abolish the practice entirely.[18] Instead, the act lays out a two-pronged plan. All chartered sanctuaries

[13] TNA KB27/1131 rex m. 6. [images 216, 422d].

[14] Westminster continued to be a busy sanctuary and at least five other men claimed sanctuary there in the course of 1539: John Caryon alias Caron for the death of John de Ordonia, a Spanish merchant in TNA KB9/544 m. 157 [image 316], TNA KB9/548 m. 160 [image 321], TNA KB27/1113 rex m. 6 [images 214, 215, 429d, 430] and William Ryder for the death of Ralph Holcroft at St Paul's along with John Dawn, John Lord and Richard Hokwell as accessories in TNA KB9/545 m. 88 [image 168]. These men did not specify if they were claiming in the Abbey or the town.

[15] It was passed as 'Concerning sanctuaries', in *Journal of the House of Lords vol. 1, 1509–1577* (London: His Majesty's Stationery Office, 1767–1830), pp. 140–142. 3 & 7 June 1540.

[16] *Lords' Journal*, p. 143. 8 June 1540.

[17] *Lords' Journal*, pp. 160–161. 23 July 1540.

[18] *LP* vol. 10, 254. J. Charles Cox, *The Sanctuaries and Sanctuary Seekers of Medieval England* (London: George Allen & Sons, 1911), p. 326 says that Cromwell in 1540 was looking for a 'determynatyon of the sanctuaries', which he interprets as 'that the religious element should be entirely blotted out from the idea and practice of special sanctuary'.

were to be 'utterly extinguished adnulled voide and of none effect', but they were to be replaced by eight secular sanctuaries in Wells, Westminster, Manchester, Northampton, Norwich, York, Derby, and Launceston.[19] No reason is given for the choice of these towns, but it is probably no accident that, with the exception of Manchester, they were regular stops on the assize circuits. The new sanctuaries would continue to offer respite for all felonies except murder, rape, highway robbery, burglary which threatened the life of the householder, arson of houses or barns with corn, and sacrilege: these were mostly the same crimes for which benefit of clergy had been removed from laymen and those in minor orders in 1532.[20] This meant that after 1540 there were no mitigations available for these crimes, but illiterate men who committed the lesser felonies could still seek sanctuary for their crime, while literates still had the choice between sanctuary and benefit of clergy. This statute not only brought sanctuary and benefit of clergy closer together in the definition of the crimes to which they applied, but by locating the secular sanctuaries in gaol delivery towns it began the process of amalgamating their administration. Their location provided the geographical coverage necessary, but their role in the legal system ensured that they would be visited by justices of assize and gaol delivery on a regular basis. The abjuration records bound for Westminster were already handed over at the assizes, so the justices were familiar with the system: they could keep an eye on the functioning of the new model and manage the new provisions for both trying and protecting sanctuary men.[21]

The 1540 statute was careful to order the chancellor to appoint commissions to establish the physical boundaries of the new sanctuaries and to limit the number of felonious inhabitants to a maximum of twenty. If an abjurer arrived at a sanctuary to find it full, the statute laid out in great detail how he was to be moved to another sanctuary until space was found for him, provisions which probably drew on the coroners' experience of assigning abjurers to both ports and chartered sanctuaries since the 1520s. There was no provision for every sanctuary to be full, implying that legislators did not expect there to be more than 160 sanctuary men in the country under these new rules. This is substantially fewer than the estimates of 1,000 for the country given by Trenholme and accepted by Cox; we saw in chapter 8 that there were at least sixty men in sanctuary at Westminster in 1532, not including internal abjurers.[22] We have already seen that overcrowding posed a problem for internal abjurers to Beaulieu, and it's not clear whether the framers of the statute had no real sense of the number of felons in sanctuary, or whether they expected the limitations placed on sanctuary to reduce the demand for the privilege. It is perhaps

[19] *SR*, III. 756–757. 32 Hen. VIII c. 12.

[20] *SR*, III. 757. The earlier statute did not except rape: *SR*, III. 362.

[21] Carrie Smith, 'Medieval Coroners' Rolls: Legal Fiction or Historical Fact?' in *Courts, Counties and the Capital in the Later Middle Ages* ed. Diana E.S. Dunn (Stroud: Sutton, 1996), pp. 96–97.

[22] N.M. Trenholme, *The Right of Sanctuary in England* (Columbia MO: University of Missouri, 1903), p. 70; Cox, *Sanctuaries*, p. 33.

most likely that they did not have a detailed understanding of the workings of the system, but twenty seemed like a nice round number—large enough to sound realistic, but not so large as to be threatening.

All the regular sanctuaries in parish churches and cemeteries were to remain, though with the same restrictions regarding eligible crimes as the secular sanctuaries. This suggests that parliament was willing to allow the parish sanctuaries to continue to play their traditional role as breathing spaces for those committing lesser felonies, but increasingly expected murderers, rapists, arsonists, burglars, and robbers to surrender themselves to the common law forthwith.[23] The act ended with a grandfathering clause; nothing in it was to affect those already in sanctuary, which was to 'stand for them in like force and effect neither better nor worse than it was before the making of this acte'.[24] Kesselring comments that this statute meant that 'those already in the old church sanctuaries were largely out of luck', but this seems unlikely.[25] Those who claimed sanctuary in parish churches could still abjure, though their destinations had changed, while those in the chartered sanctuaries could, and probably did, remain quietly in place as long as the sanctuary continued to exist.

Both its passage through parliament and its preamble have provided an easy narrative for this statute: Cromwell set out to abolish sanctuaries and the same conservative faction which produced the act of six articles stymied him. According to this narrative the eight secular sanctuaries were a novel and hasty compromise in the Commons.[26] This explanation, however, does not quite align with the facts. First, the statutes of the 1530s had established a system which required the existence of chartered sanctuaries: closing them down would end the option of internal abjuration, and however they felt about the dissolution of the monasteries, the members of the lower house may have been unwilling to see abjuration end as the indirect result of a different process. Second, the 1538 correspondence on the Beaulieu sanctuary men and the 1539 abjurations make it clear that secular sanctuaries operating under royal authority existed in theory as early as 1538, and in reality by 1539. Though parliament had passed startling religious changes in these years, it tended to be somewhat more conservative on criminal matters: even innovations which look radical had often been tried in practice in some way before

[23] The parish sanctuaries continued to function through this period: Thomas Tykenor took sanctuary in the parish church in Rowsparre, Surrey on 6 April 1539 (Easter Sunday) and asked for the coroner so he could confess the malicious killing of George Smyther five days earlier. The following day, he claims, a group of thirty men took him from the church, and he asked to be restored. The case was called to King's Bench in the summer of 1540, but no process survives: TNA KB9/547 m.13 [image 27].

[24] *SR*, III. 758.

[25] K.J. Kesselring, *Mercy and Authority in the Tudor State* (Cambridge: Cambridge University Press, 2003), p. 50.

[26] G.R. Elton, *Reform and Renewal: Thomas Cromwell and the Common Weal* (Cambridge: Cambridge University Press, 1973), p. 138. Elton, not surprisingly, attributes both the change in direction and the flaws in the new plan to the removal of Cromwell's hand. Stanford Lehmberg, *The Later Parliaments of Henry VIII, 1536–1547* (Cambridge: Cambridge University Press, 1977), p. 100 relies on Elton.

appearing in the statute book, and the same is clearly true of the secular sanctuaries. They were not hastily created as part of the negotiations in 1540, though they were probably brought to the foreground by them. They were, in fact, a logical development: internal abjuration effectively assumed royal authority over sanctuary, and once the religious houses began disappearing royal sanctuaries were the obvious replacement. There is no question that the 1540 statute was a compromise, but it was a compromise which gave both sides something: those on the side of religious reform could see their cause advanced and comfort themselves with the idea that the days of the religious sanctuaries were numbered. Conservatives could comfort themselves with the idea that the surviving religious sanctuaries were protected for the time being and might be more fully restored once the political winds changed. Looking at the distribution of the secular sanctuaries and the major chartered sanctuaries on the map, it is hard to avoid the suspicion that some, at least, expected both to survive (fig. 9.2).

Like the introduction of internal abjuration, the establishment of the secular sanctuaries was a substantial innovation, but unlike internal abjuration, it does not seem to have been a successful one. Westminster was the only chartered sanctuary listed among the secular sanctuaries, and, as we saw, the language around it was ambiguous in the late 1530s. It remained ambiguous after the statute. In November 1540 Leonard Mallhome fled to 'the king's sanctuary at Westminster'.[27] In March 1541 Robert Whitfeld alias Johnson fled 'to the sanctuary at Westminster'.[28] And in April 1542, Thomas Sybbell fled to the 'sanctuary and privilege of the church of St Peter of Westminster'.[29] It is probable that the king's sanctuary and the church were the same: the conflation visible in 1539 may have continued. But Sybbell's case makes it clear that by 1542, two years after the chartered sanctuaries had been ordered to stop taking new claimants, men were still running to the privilege of the church at Westminster for protection for homicide and receiving it. It is possible that the Abbey was no longer functioning as a chartered sanctuary, that it was simply providing the same kind of protection as any parish church, but given its prominence that seems unlikely.[30]

[27] TNA KB9/978 m. 36 [image not on AALT]. Though his surname suggests otherwise, the inquisition frames the death as the result of a mutual quarrel. Mallhome, identified as a yeoman, also is described as having a fairly large number of possessions, including 'a base blowenghorne' and a silver cross.

[28] TNA KB9/550 m. 17 [image 31], TNA KB27/1125 rex m. 7 [images 318, 319, 632d]. Whitfeld argued at King's Bench that the indictment was insufficient because it did not identify him according to the correct forms, and went *sine die*.

[29] TNA KB9/551 m. 31 [image 61], TNA KB27/1124/1 rex m. 6 [images 186, 187, 371d]. Sybbell appeared at King's Bench in July 1542 and was remanded to the Marshalsea. He re-appeared in November 1542 with a pardon and went *sine die*.

[30] D.M. Loades, 'The Sanctuary', in *Westminster Abbey Reformed 1540–1640* edited by C.S. Knighton and Richard Mortimer (Aldershot: Ashgate, 2003), p. 80, argues that in 1540, when the property was transferred to the dean and chapter, 'the sanctuary itself, and presumably its existing occupants, were transferred with it'. This might explain the ambiguity over chartered vs. secular, but it does not explain the ways in which the king's authority operated in the precinct.

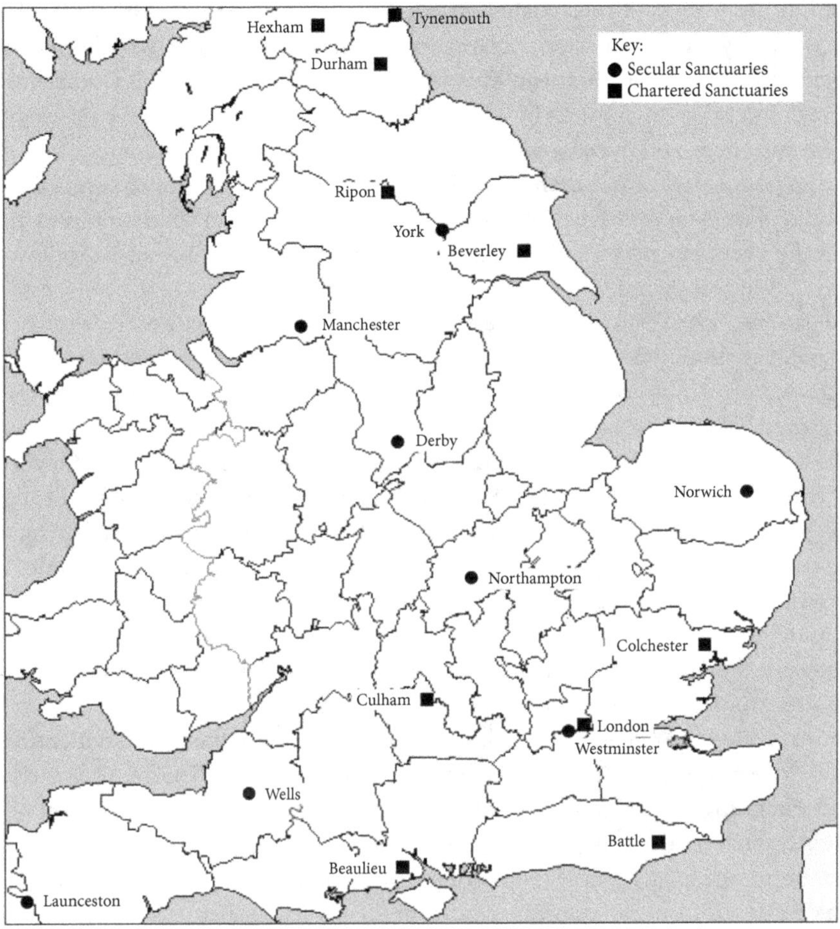

Figure 9.2 Chartered sanctuaries and secular sanctuaries

The operations of the other seven secular sanctuaries are also obscure. Manchester was named as one of the eight locations in 1540, but it was replaced by Chester in 1542.[31] The statute which accomplished the change laid out the various problems associated with admitting a felonious population into the town, from the need for widespread credit in a cloth-making town to the need to be able to leave cloth unguarded outside as it was processed. It also pointed to the absence of town walls which could keep the abjurers somewhat contained, particularly at night, and the lack of a mayor, sheriff, bailiffs, or gaol to deal with the crimes committed by them. Though no details are given, the statute implies that the arrival of sanctuary

[31] *SR*, III. 850–851. 33 Hen. VIII c. 15.

men in the town had precipitated all these ills and provides for the removal of all sanctuary men to Chester, accompanied by the constables of Manchester and twenty inhabitants of the town. This implies that Manchester had a substantial population of sanctuary men by 1542, but there is no further evidence relating to them anywhere, and the language of the statute may have been framed to ward off such a population rather than to deal with an existing one. Chester seems like a good replacement for Manchester—it had been an occasional abjuration port and had the necessary personnel, though like Manchester it was not an assize town. The statute recognized that Chester might not be willing to assume Manchester's obligations, however, and it allowed the king to remove the sanctuary elsewhere by proclamation. On 30 May 1542 he moved it to Stafford, on the grounds that Chester's proximity to the march of Wales made it too easy for sanctuary men to escape.[32] Stafford was a gaol delivery town and thus fit the pattern better than Manchester or Chester, but again there is no evidence of sanctuary men in Stafford.

There is some evidence that other cities named in the statute followed through on the requirement to detail the boundaries of their secular sanctuaries. Two maps of sanctuary cities from around this date survive in the National Archives, one for Norwich and one for York, though both are in bad condition.[33] In the Norwich map the market cross is clearly visible, with St Peter Mancroft to its right and St Stephen's church well above it (the map is oriented to the south). A blue line extending around a cluster of houses north and slightly to the east of the church is drawn around St Stephen's. Though the north boundary of the area is not entirely clear, it seems to be marked by Abraham's Hall, later an inn on the Haymarket, thus enclosing an area roughly bounded by William Booth St, Haymarket and Brigg St on a modern map. The map of York is in much worse condition, and is even more schematic, but it too has a precinct marked out, this time in red ink, which extends from St Sampson's church in the top left corner to St. Helen's in the bottom right and encloses an area roughly bounded by Stonegate, Low Petergate, Church St and Davygate on a modern map. Three things are striking about these maps. The first is the simple fact that they exist: the statute called for the establishment of clear boundaries for the new sanctuaries to ensure that they should not have the same kinds of uncertain boundaries as the old, and some cities, at least, obeyed the statute. The second is the size of the precincts they enclose: given that the new secular sanctuaries were intended to hold only twenty people who would have limited economic opportunities, both demarcate fairly substantial areas of the city. The third is the nature of the space they delimit: when given the opportunity to create a new 'secular' sanctuary, both Norwich and York understood that

[32] Paul L Hughes and James F. Larkin ed. *Tudor Royal Proclamations vol. 1: The Early Tudors* (New Haven: Yale University Press, 1964), pp. 311–313.

[33] TNA MPI1/221; TNA MPB1/49/1 and TNA MPB1/49/2. The Norwich map is briefly discussed in P.D.A Harvey, *Maps in Tudor England* (London: The Public Record Office and The British Library, 1993), pp. 68–69.

as a precinct intrinsically connected to a church or two. It could be argued that the sanctuary men needed access to the ministrations of the Church, perhaps more than most, and thus it was the provision of a practical service; or that both cities were so liberally sprinkled with churches that any sizeable precinct would inevitably contain a church or two, but there is no question that the size and structure of these sanctuaries is strikingly similar to that of Westminster or St Martin le Grand, the two chartered sanctuaries whose physical precincts we understand most clearly. This suggests that the secular sanctuaries were expected to have the same kind of mixed population as the chartered sanctuaries, despite the concerns of the Beaulieu men. The provisions of the 1540 statute support this: the governors of the secular sanctuaries were to perform a roll-call daily, and any felon who did not appear for three days in a row lost his privilege, as did anyone who committed another felony.[34] Realistically, this would only be a concern if the sanctuary men were part of a large and mixed population, though once again, as in 1531 and 1536, the sanctuary men had some leeway before they were expelled from sanctuary.

Though this kind of conservatism in the understanding of both the population and the space of the new sanctuaries is not surprising, when combined with the radical innovation of the statute it must have been tremendously confusing. How would the general population understand and accept that Beverley, for example, could no longer offer long-term refuge to new claimants, but that an area of the city of York which enclosed two parish churches and had never had any such right could now offer that refuge because of a new statute? This was expecting a lot: it was one thing to ask people to trust their lives to a system which had been in place for centuries and was backed by the authority of the Church, but quite another to place the same trust in a handful of new institutions created by parliament and backed only by the authority of statute, particularly in a period when statutes were beginning to change quickly.

Perhaps for these reasons, there is virtually no evidence for the functioning of the new secular sanctuaries. There are exactly four surviving abjurations in the King's Bench material after 1540. In the first, William Crippes abjured from the parish church of Bledlowe in Buckinghamshire in June 1541 after confessing to the theft of a horse worth 20s.[35] He was assigned to the 'liberty of the city of Norwich' with his consent and sent on his way with a cross in his hand. In the second, Robert Mere abjured from the parish church of Barrington in Cambridgeshire on 5 October 1541, also following a horsetheft.[36] Mere was assigned 'the privilege and liberty of the city of Westminster which he chose', branded with an A and given a cross. Both men thus went through the traditional process, and though they went to secular sanctuaries they were given the cross, whether from bureaucratic inertia,

[34] *SR*, III. 757. 32 Hen. VIII c. 12.
[35] TNA KB9/550 m. 52 [image 98].
[36] TNA KB9/979 m. 171 [image not on AALT].

because the cross had simply come to signify protection for the abjurer, or because the ceremony itself was still perceived as essentially religious.

In the third abjuration William Arthur left the cemetery of the parish church of Culmington in June 1542 after breaking a close and stealing a horse.[37] Arthur's record is unusual in providing some detail about his process. He apparently 'did not wish to go out of the same [church] to the peace of the lord king but claimed the same privilege for tuition of his life'. After his confession he abjured according to the form of the statute and chose the sanctuary and privilege of the town of Wells. Arthur was clearly hesitant to trust his safety to the new statute, and this may account for the unusual form of his document: rather than the usual report from the coroner, Arthur's abjuration is in the form of an indenture signed by both men. This is not unique, but we have only seen one other abjuration in this form, which does suggest that the agreement between the two men provided a level of reassurance which was apparently missing from the statutory provisions.[38] In the fourth abjuration Cuthbert Rud abjured from his parish church of St Michael in Stainsmore after committing murder in July 1542: the record does not specify his destination, but York would have been most likely.[39]

After 1542 sanctuary for felony simply disappears from King's Bench: not only are there no further records of abjurations to the secular sanctuaries or anywhere else, there are no further records of flights to sanctuary in inquisitions on the view of a body and no requests for felons to be restored to sanctuaries from which they had been improperly removed. This is remarkably odd. Though the 1540 statute has often been described as abolishing sanctuary, in fact it left the common law privilege of sanctuary for forty days in parish churches intact, though it limited the crimes for which it could be claimed; it allowed those who had previously established themselves in a chartered sanctuary to remain in place, and it introduced new secular sanctuaries to replace them for the future. Under these provisions most of the patterns we have seen repeated through the century could have continued largely unchanged: sanctuary could still function, quite legally, as a breathing space for those fleeing a crime; sanctuary men could still protest their illegal removal and ask to be restored; and the affairs and interactions of the sanctuary populations could still need regulation. If these things happened, they have left no record. This is not only odd by itself, it stands in stark contrast to the blossoming of records related to benefit of clergy in the 1540s: it can't be argued that the justices were not interested in the criminal law and its administration. I argued above that the intention in establishing the secular sanctuaries in gaol delivery towns was to ensure that the circuit justices could deal with problems in the sanctuaries during their

[37] TNA KB9/554 m. 90 [image 182].

[38] See p. 241.

[39] TNA KB9/552 m. 130 [image 264]. The record was delivered to Christopher Jenney et al. at the castle of Appleby, Westmorland on 16 August 1542.

visits: the justices were clearly there, but either there was no-one to manage, or the law had become so clearly elaborated and so routine that no record of the process has survived. Neither seems entirely likely, but we have to recognize that if there was not a catastrophic decline in the use of sanctuary, it went so far underground that it effectively disappeared.

2. Benefit of Clergy: Statutes, Records, and Pardons 1540–1547

The changes to benefit of clergy in the 1540 parliament were far less dramatic than those to sanctuary, though they were significant. In a structure reminiscent of the 1536 act, a continuation act confirmed the novelties of the previous decade and made them perpetual, while providing that everyone in major orders who claimed his clergy should also be branded, as laymen were, and should thereafter be treated as laymen were.[40] Without fanfare this act ended the aberration begun in 1490 when the lay and clerical versions of the privilege were first separated and brought them back together. This time, however, clerics found themselves reduced to the layman's privilege: while 'benefit of clergy' would survive for centuries, the complete disjunction between title and reality began in 1540.

There was only one more relevant statute in Henry VIII's reign and once again the provision regarding benefit of clergy reads as an afterthought, though once again it was quite significant. The body of the statute, passed in 1545, recognized that the phrase 'vi et armis', an allegation of force that brought a case that would otherwise belong to a lesser jurisdiction into the king's court, was often fictitious, and provided that as of Christmas 1545 no indictment could be voided because it was missing.[41] To this legislation, which quietly but confidently assumed the supremacy of the king's courts, was attached a quick proviso that anyone who stole any kind of horse and was found guilty, confessed, or refused to plead was no longer to have benefit of clergy but should 'suffer death in suche maner and forme as they shulde have if they were noe Clerkes'. This was in many ways a departure from all the previous statutes: horse thieves did not generally threaten violence to their victims, nor did they verge on sacrilege or raise the fears associated with arson or the destruction of grain. By 1545, however, horse thieves made up about 30% of the men who claimed clergy and this provision substantially reduced the number of men eligible for mitigation.

[40] *SR*, III. 749. 32 Hen. VIII c. 3. The act confirms 22 Hen. VIII c. 14 §6, 23 Hen. VIII c. 1, 25 Hen. VIII c. 3, 25 Hen. VIII c. 6 and 28 Hen. VIII c. 1. Bellamy suggests that those in major orders were no longer eligible for purgation after this statute: *Criminal Law and Society*, p. 145. This seems unlikely, but there is not much evidence either way.

[41] *SR*, III. 996. 37 Hen. VIII c. 8.

As the restrictions on claims of clergy multiplied, it became increasingly important to be able to track the men who were successful in their claim. We saw how common lawyers recognized this in the 1520s and attempted to find a workable system to connect the assize convictions at the national level. Their attempts seem to fade away in the 1530s, but there is some evidence that they continued to be concerned about this problem, though that evidence is indirect. In a pardon statute of 1523, the 'embesylyng and raysyng of records' appears for the first time among the excepted crimes.[42] It reappears in the 1529 and 1540 pardons, and an extension to the 'rasyngs, enterlynyngs, embeselynge and withdrawinge of any recorde in any of the king's courts' in the 1544 pardon demonstrates that there was an ongoing and indirect concern about record-keeping.[43] A statute passed in 1543 for the first time directly tackled the problem that this presented for the management of benefit of clergy.[44] The statute betrays some uncertainty in its composition. It complains both that records of previous convictions before justices of the peace, justices of gaol delivery and justices of oyer and terminer were not readily available to the justices of King's Bench or other justices, and that there was no sure place to which the justices could turn to acquire such records, blaming the problem squarely on 'the negligence of the clerke of the Crowne, Clerkes of Peace, Clerkes of Assize and suche other as have had the Ordre rule keaping and governaunce of the same Recordes'. As we have seen, this meant that it was difficult to either prove or disprove a previous conviction, and so the statute provided that the said clerks should, from the following Pentecost, 'certifie a transcript brieflie and in a fewe words conteyning the tenour and effecte of everye suche indytement owtlawrye conviccion and Clerke atteincted before them so to be hadde made or pronounced' specifying that the record should include the name, surname and addition of each convict and details of the felony, along with its date and the date and place of conviction, all of which was to be returned to King's Bench within forty days if the felon was convicted during term time and within twenty days of the beginning of the next term if not. The format was essentially the same as that adopted in the 1518 circuit returns and suggests that the framers of the statute saw that model as the best balance of information and efficiency. The clerks were also to deliver a copy of the record to the ordinary to whom the felon was delivered, and the ordinaries were to pay 12d for every such record, a provision perhaps intended to defray some of the costs to the common law side. The weight of the law rested squarely on the clerks, who were to be fined 40s for every record which was not certified and copied to the ordinary in the manner described, half of which fine was to go to the king, and the other half

42 *SR*, III. 244. 14 & 15 Hen. VIII c. 17. This had been a long-standing concern, expressed as early as *Fleta*, p. 64.

43 *SR*, III. 982. 35 Hen. VIII c. 18.

44 *SR*, III. 912–913. 34 & 35 Hen. VIII c. 14. Some of this description is taken from Margaret McGlynn, 'From Written Record to Bureaucratic Mind: Imagining a Criminal Record', *Past and Present* 250 (2021), pp. 75–76.

Table 9.1 Recorded convictions at gaol delivery, summer 1543*

Circuit	Attainted	Benefit	Remanded	Total
Home	6	5	0	11
Midland	21	4	0	25
Western	16	10	5	31
Oxford	1	2	1	4
Norfolk	11	2	1	14
Total	55	23	7	85

*Data collected from TNA KB9/556 mm. 3–10, 74, 75, 77, 136–136d (images 4–17, 142, 146, 262–263).

to the one who would sue. Similarly, the clerk of the Crown in King's Bench was to receive the record without charging for the service on penalty of 40s for every certificate refused. The statute further provided that if others named in the indictment were not convicted they were to be omitted from the transcript, that the transcript was to be as effectual for legal purposes as the original, and that the clerk of the Crown in King's Bench was to respond to requests for such records from the justices of the peace 'incontinentlie without delaie', again on pain of 40s.[45] This was an ambitious plan, and thus one which was probably doomed from the start. There is no evidence, for example, that the ordinaries sought, or were willing to pay for, a copy of the record. The burden placed on the clerks was quite substantial, as the fines suggest, and it is clear that the Crown was unwilling to pay for their extra labour, though it was willing to benefit from any default. Nevertheless, some such scheme had to be attempted if the system were to work effectively, and it seems that the clerks gave it their best shot, at least in 1543.

For the summer sessions of that year we have a fairly full set of returns from the circuits, with only the Northern missing.[46] Table 9.1 provides the combined numbers across this circuit. Although we cannot extrapolate the conviction rate

[45] A final proviso excepted the clerks in the counties of Wales, Chester, Lancaster, and Durham. Some returns seem to have excluded those found guilty who did not claim clergy as well as those found not guilty. This can cause confusion as well as adding information. For example, Robert Turnor, yeoman, was convicted at the gaol delivery of Aylesbury in March 1544 of entering the king's park by night to hunt with Richard Marshe, a falconer: TNA KB9/564 mm. 79–80 [images 152–154]. They were apparently procured to do so by Robert Hawkes, a gentleman who provided them with greyhounds and a crossbow and who was found not guilty. Marshe was found guilty and sentenced to death but pardoned in February 1546: TNA KB27/1137 rex m. 12 [images 221, 222, 423d, 424d, 425d, 223]. Turnor claimed clergy at the gaol delivery, but the record of his indictment returned to King's Bench not only omitted Hawkes and Marshe but says that he was delivered in July: TNA KB9/560 m. 183 [image 352].

[46] The lists vary in format, suggesting that the different circuits were experimenting with their understanding of the statute and that there was no template for the returns.

Table 9.2 Recorded convictions at gaol delivery, spring 1544*

Circuit	Attainted	Benefit	Remanded	Total
Home	8	0	0	8
Midland	25	1	0	26
Western	15	10	12	37
Norfolk	0	7	0	7
Total	**48**	**18**	12	**78**

*Data collected from TNA KB9/558 mm. 101–106, 193–193d (images 198–216, 390–391); There are no surviving returns for this Oxford or Northern circuit.

without information for those found not guilty, these returns give us another snapshot of the punishments meted out to those convicted.

On these circuits 65 per cent of those convicted were hanged and 27 per cent claimed benefit of clergy, with 8 per cent being remanded, either because their case presented some kind of legal problem, or because they hoped to get a pardon, or both. The returns for the spring 1544 circuit are fairly similar (table 9.2).

Altogether 62 per cent of those convicted on this circuit were sentenced to hang, with 23 per cent claiming benefit of clergy.[47] Two circuits aren't enough to allow us to establish any pattern, but the numbers here indicate that the proportion of convicted felons claiming clergy remains surprisingly consistent across the entire period. In the reign of Henry VII about 24 per cent of those convicted in the Marshalsea successfully claimed clergy; we have no comparable snapshot early in the reign of Henry VIII, but the evidence from the 1530s suggests that the number of claims doubled, which makes it unlikely that the proportion was falling. This suggests that through all the changes in both the politics and the law around benefit of clergy, a mitigation rate of around 25 per cent and an execution rate of around 60 per cent remained broadly acceptable. This is much higher than the percentage of executions given by Hay for the eighteenth century, and indicates that he was right to refer to 'the severities of the Tudors', but it also indicates that the Tudor governing classes performed the same kinds of instinctive calculations about the need to balance severity and mitigation as their Hanoverian successors.[48] Though the Tudors started with a lower percentage of convictions, diverting 25 per cent of those convicted from the gallows to another form of punishment provided another

[47] The drop in both categories resulted from the fact that 14 per cent were remanded after conviction, all of them on the Western circuit.

[48] Douglas Hay, 'Property, Authority and the Criminal Law', in *Albion's Fatal Tree: Crime and Society in Eighteenth-Century England* edited by Douglas Hay, Peter Linebaugh, John G. Rule, E.P. Thompson, and Cal Winslow (New York: Pantheon Books, 1975), p. 57.

Table 9.3 Recorded claims of clergy at gaol delivery, 1543–1546*

Circuit	Summer 1543	Spring 1544	Summer 1544	Spring 1545	Summer 1545	Spring 1546	Summer 1546	Total
Home	5	1	4	2	9	–	3	24
Midland	4	1	3	5	3	2	–	18
Western	10	10	7	3	12	6	4	52
Oxford	2	–	1	1	2	3	2	11
Norfolk	2	7	2	–	5	4	3	23
Northern	–	–	1	–	–	–	4	5
Total	23	19	18	11	31	15	16	133

*Data collected from TNA KB9/560 mm. 29, 87, 92, 168–168d, 183 (images 51, 163, 173, 322–323, 352); TNA KB9/562 mm. 4, 12, 46, 47 (images 8, 24, 92, 94); TNA KB9/563 mm. 55–55d, 150, 202, 225–225d, 235 (images 101, 102, 284, 385, 428–432, 451); TNA KB9/565 mm. 11, 113, 114–114d (images 22, 224, 226, 227); TNA KB9/567 mm. 12, 72, 92, 123, 142 (images 22, 144, 145, 188, 252, 290, 291). There is also a return for Newgate from the summer of 1545: TNA KB9/565 m. 1 (image 2).

level of protection from popular discontent, while also providing a real punishment for felons.

The demands of the new system seem to have worn away the enthusiasm of the clerks by the summer of 1544, and after this date the returns provide only the names of those who were delivered to the ordinaries, without the other convictions. They do continue to be returned regularly until the summer of 1546: with the exception of the Northern circuit, which provided only brief and sporadic returns, and the Western circuit, which is complete, the other circuits missed only one session. Table 9.3 gives a sense of the ongoing claims of clergy. What does it tell us?

Although the information about other convictions drops away, the numbers claiming benefit remain fairly steady—there is both a low and a high in 1545, but the average per session is about nineteen, with about thirty-eight men per year making their way to the bishops' prisons.[49] These numbers also suggest that while benefit of clergy was a valuable mitigation of punishment, it did not undermine the common law: if a steady 25–30 per cent of those convicted claimed clergy, for the 133 men reprieved here another 310–400 were hanged.

[49] The Western circuit, for reasons that are not at all clear, provides more clerks convict in almost every session. The 1543–1544 records show that the circuit hanged as many as it delivered, suggesting that if the pattern holds across the period the south-west produced a large proportion of the country's convicts but allowed clergy more often than other circuits. It's not clear why this should be so: though the circuit was large it was not populous, and it has usually been assumed that its western-most extremities in particular felt the weight of central government only lightly and periodically: Hans Kleineke, 'Poachers and Gamekeepers: Four Fifteenth-century West Country Criminals', in *Outlaws in Medieval and Early Modern England: Crime, Government and Society, c.1066–c.1600* edited by John C. Appleby and Paul Dalton (Farnham: Ashgate, 2009), pp. 129–147.

Crimes and Criminals

Incomplete as the circuit records are, once again they provide valuable information about both the criminals who claimed benefit of clergy and the crimes for which they claimed it. Taking these together with other King's Bench records and episcopal records, we can find 253 men claiming clergy between 1537 and 1548.[50] Of those 253, we have occupations for 235. Ninety-eight men identified themselves by their occupation: twenty of them were tailors (by far the largest single occupation), ten were butchers, eight were weavers, six shoemakers, and four carpenters, but the other fifty came from thirty-six different occupations. There are only two clerks and one gentleman, and 57 per cent are identified by status: forty-two yeomen (18 per cent), eighteen husbandmen (8 per cent) and seventy-two labourers (31 per cent).[51]

It is clear from fig. 9.3 that the decline in the social status of clergy claimants apparent in the 1530s continued in the 1540s, as husbandmen, labourers, and craftsmen made up a growing proportion of claimants, while yeomen declined substantially and gentlemen and clerks effectively disappeared.

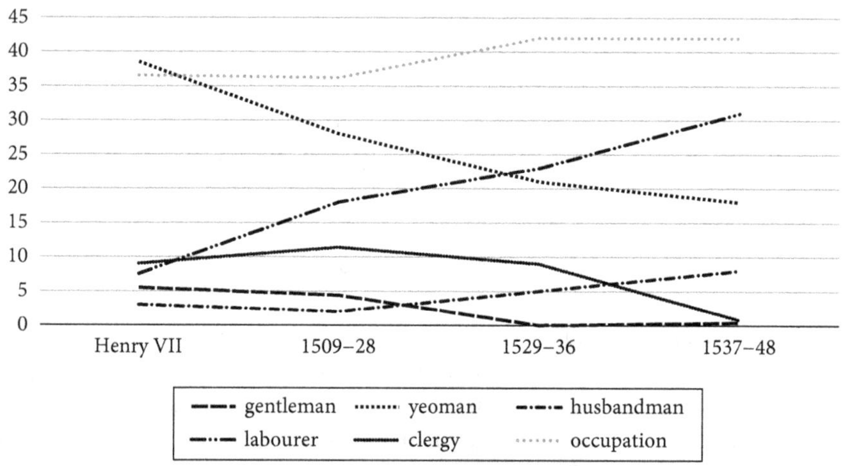

Figure 9.3 Recorded clergy claimants by status (%)*
*Data collected from TNA KB27 and KB9 rolls; *Register of Thomas Cranmer*; *Reg. Longland*.

[50] Some of these are purgation or escape records, so the date at which the men claimed clergy has been estimated.

[51] Some of these men identify themselves by more than one label: two labourers also identified as a brewer or yeoman, one yeoman also identified as a barbersurgeon and one forester identified as a yeoman.

Table 9.4 Crimes for which clerks convict were delivered 1537–1546*

Clergiable crimes		Non clergiable crimes	
accessory to theft	1	accessory	3
burglary	42	arson	2
homicide	2	burglary with fear	1
robbery	1	burglary from church	1
theft	99	escape from bishop's prison	1
felony	1	murder	4
Horsetheft (before 1545)	61	Horsetheft (after 1545)	6
Total	**207**		**18**

*Data collected from TNA KB27 and KB9 rolls; *Register of Thomas Cranmer; Reg. Longland.*

The crimes for which clergy was claimed also continued to change in this period (table 9.4). Claims for violent crimes declined substantially, with only two claims for homicide and one for robbery, even though such crimes remained technically clergiable.[52] Most of the claims are for theft of some kind, including burglary which was not specified as inducing fear.[53] The statutes passed in the 1530s clearly had an enormous impact on the crimes for which benefit of clergy could be claimed, but, as before, men still claimed and got clergy for crimes which had been excepted, implying that the justices still exercised some discretion. Clergy was supposedly not available to accessories to all the prohibited crimes: of the three who appear in these records, two were accessories to highway robbery, and one received silver stolen from Westminster cathedral.[54] One man successfully claimed clergy though the indictment clearly stated that he broke into the house of John Good and attacked his male servants who were in fear of their life, and one claimed clergy after being convicted of stealing two chalices belonging to the parish church of Bensted while he, and they, were in Westminster.[55] In some of these cases it's possible to see why the courts might have been willing to bend the law: we don't have the details on the accessories, but accessories came in a variety of shapes and sizes; the fact that the servants in the burglary indictment were specified as male rather than female probably worked to reduce the level of fear that should have been induced; after his conviction and claim the chalice-stealer was remanded and subsequently went *sine*

[52] One of the homicide claimants was indicted for murder, but the jury found that Hugh Jones killed Hugh Havard by misfortune and not from premeditated malice. Jones was later pardoned: TNA KB27/1143 rex m. 1 [images 171, 172, 343d, 344d].

[53] In three cases the burglary was specified as occurring by night.

[54] TNA KB27/1125 rex m. 5 [images 313, 314, 628d, 629d]; TNA KB27/1137 rex m. 7d [images 407d, 408d, 409d].

[55] TNA KB9/567 m. 72 [image 144]; TNA KB9/563 m. 52 [image 96].

die on a technicality, and the six who got clergy for horsetheft were all in 1546, and may simply reflect a slow acceptance of that change. The three murders are harder to explain: all specify murder in the indictment and there is nothing to indicate why these men were allowed to claim.

The most intriguing cases are the arsonists. Arson became non-clergiable in 1532 and appeared as an exception in the pardon statutes of 1529, 1534, and 1544. It is a rare crime in this period, and one unlikely to provoke much sympathy. Nevertheless, two men convicted of arson successfully claimed clergy. Richard Materfaco and Henry Spaldyng were both convicted on the Western circuit in 1546, Materfaco on 24 March, and Spaldyng on 26 July.[56] Materfaco's indictment claims that he entered the home of William More in the middle of the night and burned it with pre-meditated malice, as well as stealing a variety of cloth worth £14. It could be argued that the theft was pre-meditated and the arson accidental, which might explain the exercise of discretion for Materfaco. Spaldyng's indictment, however, leaves little room for such an interpretation. It states that 'with a lighted match which he carried and held in his hand, with malice aforethought and at the instigation of the devil, he feloniously and voluntarily lit a fire and with the same fire then and there voluntarily and feloniously burned the house and with that fire feloniously and voluntarily totally consumed the house', language which leaves little room to doubt Spaldyng's motives. But both men were delivered to the ordinary.

The successful claims for non-clergiable crimes are a fairly small number, about 8% of the recorded total, and they demonstrate that parliament had been effective in restricting benefit of clergy to the lesser felonies: for the most part men who committed murder, aggravated burglary or robbery, or horsetheft, faced the gallows. In the late fifteenth and early sixteenth century these crimes had made up the majority of the claims, and it is perhaps not surprising that as the more complex crimes disappeared, the more complicated exceptions mostly disappeared with them. There are, for example, only two allegations of bigamy among the King's Bench records in this period, and there is only one case where the claimant failed the reading test.[57] The cases of previous conviction virtually disappear: at Northampton in 1545, when a convict asked for clergy 'the clerk of assize said that he was previously a clerk convict at Warwick, and showed the record of his conviction and delivery'.[58] It was doubtless easier to keep track of convictions on the

[56] TNA KB9/565 m. 114 [image 226], TNA KB9/567 m. 142 [image 290].

[57] Thomas Bocher was pardoned when his case got lost in geographical limbo: see p. 321. Robert Byde was remanded without further process: TNA KB9/556 m. 6 [image 10]. William Bednell, a London yeoman, was convicted of horsetheft in the West Riding of Yorkshire on 30 July 1543 and read, but not *ut clericus*: TNA KB9/556 m. 77 [image 146]. He was remanded to the next gaol delivery so the justices could be advised.

[58] It was alleged at the gaol delivery in Exeter in March 1544 that Henry Hayne could not claim clergy because of a previous conviction, but the record is extraordinarily confused: TNA KB9/558 mm. 104, 105 [images 207, 208, 212]. Haynes was indicted for committing two crimes on 20 February 1544, one in Cornwall and one in Devon, and apparently tried at the gaol delivery of both Launceston and Exeter, the former on 24 March and the latter on 20 March 1544. It is possible that Haynes had been tried by

same circuit, but the fact that the clerk of the assize had the record to hand, along with the general absence of the allegation in King's Bench, suggests that the various experiments with record-keeping had been fairly successful and recidivists were unlikely to try to reclaim. These cases demonstrate that these exceptions were still available, but both lawyers and claimants were less likely to go down these paths for thieves who would be released in a year or two than they had been for murderers, homicides, burglars or robbers who were facing the possibility of execution or extended periods in prison. By the 1540s these men were effectively outside the system, and benefit of clergy was operating as a fairly streamlined process for imprisoning lower-status men for lower-impact crimes.

Pardons and Purgations

The evidence makes it clear that by the early 1540s benefit of clergy claimants were a much more homogenous group than at the beginning of the century. This made it much easier to standardize their terms of confinement, as we saw in the last chapter. It also raised the possibility that there might be a more streamlined way to release them from prison, and in the 1530s the common lawyers began to look more closely at the ways in which pardons might be used for that purpose. As we have seen, clerks convict and clerks attaint were pardoned regularly across this period, especially in situations where they could not otherwise be released from confinement, but through the reign of Henry VII and most of the reign of Henry VIII these pardons were individual, sought and granted on a case-by-case basis. General pardons did exist, but they were rare and usually applied only to a limited number of crimes. Henry VIII's accession pardon was unusually generous in applying to all felonies, as part of his campaign to mollify those smarting under his father's exactions and to cement the Tudor dynasty.[59] It does not refer, implicitly or explicitly, to clerks convict and clerks attaint, but we saw that a handful of men whose claims were stuck in the courts in 1509 took advantage of it, thus demonstrating that such men were eligible in practice.[60] We also saw a group of men in the Marshalsea in 1516 complaining about the lack of a general pardon, suggesting both that there was some level of expectation that such pardons might appear on a regular basis, and that pardons factored into criminals' expectations about their passage through the justice system.[61]

the justices on circuit at both places and the return mixes up the dates. *Reports from Henry VIII*, vol. 2, p. 469. The prisoner said he was not the same person, the jury found that he was.

59 *Tudor Royal Proclamations* vol. 1, pp. 81–83.

60 See p. 122.

61 See p. 228.

Pardons have been well-studied as a manifestation of royal mercy, the authority such mercy implied, and the ways in which such authority was understood and experienced by the broader society, but less attention has been paid to the details of how pardons actually worked in practice and how they fit into the machinery of the criminal justice system. It is assumed that general pardons applied, for the most part, to those who had not yet been indicted and/or convicted of felony, and the Marshalsea men fit into that pattern, but pardons could also apply to those who had been convicted. Though execution often followed sentencing quite quickly, there were numerous exceptions to this pattern. Convicts could be remanded for lengthy periods without explanation: the justices might have been unhappy with something in the conduct of the case, or they may have had reason to expect an individual pardon. Most obviously, as we have seen, putative clerks convict could contest allegations of bigamy or previous conviction. And of course there were those who had been delivered to the ecclesiastical system. It could be argued that questions of jurisdiction would preclude general pardons from applying to clerks convict or attaint: having been delivered to the bishop, they were no longer in the common law system. Fyneux's arguments in 1500 implied, however, that such clerks remained under royal jurisdiction, and thus if the king wanted such a pardon to apply, he could make it so. There is evidence for an early move in this direction when Christopher Bainbridge, the archbishop of York, ordered a general purgation of his clerks convict in September 1509, most likely as a parallel to the general pardon.[62] At the beginning of the reign, then, there is evidence that both putative clerks convict tied up in procedural exceptions and clerks convict who had been delivered to an episcopal prison could benefit from a general pardon.

After 1509 this potential lay dormant for some time. The general pardons of the early decades of Henry VIII's reign were much more restricted than the accession pardon. No text survives for the pardon of 1514, but the 1515 pardon specifically excepted murders, robberies, and felonies under the common law, and the 1523 pardon excepted murder and all felonies except manslaughter and the taking of less than 20s.[63] The 1529 statute elaborated on the crimes, but they remained much the same in essence: prepensed and voluntary murder, robbery of churches, robberies upon men's person, felonies and robberies by the common law, felonious taking above 20s, felonious burning of houses, and carnal ravishing of women were all excepted.[64] The list demonstrates that felonies were being more carefully

[62] Borthwick Institute, Yorks Abp Reg 26, f. 74v. The commission noted that if there were objectors to the purgations the convicts should be returned to the prisons, which was standard procedure, so Bainbridge did intend to maintain the canonical process, even if the men in question would be released far sooner than normal.

[63] *SR*, III. 203. 7 Hen. VIII c. 11; *SR*, III. 242. 14 & 15 Hen. VIII c. 17. Kesselring argues that 'over time and in an uneven fashion, the general pardons tended to remit the punishments for fewer and fewer offenses', but after 1509 the pardon statutes were fairly consistent until they extended pardon to manslaughter and thefts under 20s in 1523: Kesselring, *Mercy and Authority*, p. 63.

[64] *SR*, III. 283. 21 Hen. VIII c. 1.

defined, but the result was the same: pardons were only available for those who had committed homicide and fairly minor thefts. At least one sanctuary man claimed the pardon, and the definition of his crime was crucial. George Tunstall took sanctuary in Westminster in July 1526 and was outlawed in May 1527 before appearing in King's Bench in May 1530.[65] Tunstall recited his claim of sanctuary in St Peter's, pointed to the parliamentary pardon and argued that though he had been indicted for murder, the death of Thomas Smyth, his victim, was because of a quarrel between them and was neither voluntary nor from malice, and so he should not be excepted from the pardon. Christopher Hales agreed that the jurors of Middlesex accepted that the death was the result of a quarrel, and so the court allowed the pardon for the outlawry and the murder, and Tunstall went *sine die*. This is the only example I've found of a sanctuary man claiming a parliamentary pardon, and it suggests that the framing of the crime could matter a great deal. Sanctuary men who had committed murder or other serious felonies were likely to be stuck there, but those whose crimes were ambiguous, or who could convince a jury that they had served an appropriate period of confinement, might use the pardon as a strategy to legally exit their punishment. Tunstall's experience also suggests that sanctuary men who had committed pardonable crimes were free to leave the precinct immediately, and, as so often with sanctuary, we have no idea how many might have taken advantage of this opportunity, or whether this had been common practice with earlier pardons. The next general pardon, which appeared in 1534, specifically excepted clerks convict and clerks attaint for the first time, though it did not mention sanctuary men, and it excepted a similar list of crimes.[66]

While the parliamentary pardons were not generally fruitful for clerks convict in these decades, the records of King's Bench suggest that the court began to pay more attention to traditional pardons in the mid-1530s. A handful of cases in these years provide a significant link between the traditional practice of releasing clerks attaint through pardons and the issues of jurisdiction raised by the changes of the early 1530s. Thomas Cheselett, who appeared in King's Bench in May 1530, represents the traditional model. Cheselett abjured in July 1519, claimed clergy at the gaol delivery of Ilchester in March 1520, and presented a pardon for all crimes before 13 November 1529.[67] Cheselett thus spent over ten years in the bishop of Bath and Wells' custody, but his final release was fairly straightforward: the pardon rehearses his original theft, sanctuary and abjuration, but makes no mention of the claim of clergy. By 1534, when William Smyth came to the attention of King's Bench, the court was paying closer attention to both the process and the content of pardons.

[65] TNA KB27/1075 rex m. 2d [images 4967d, 4968d]. We saw Tunstall's claim of sanctuary above, p. 223.

[66] *SR*, III. 515. 26 Hen. VIII c. 18. Benefit of clergy still applied to many more crimes than general pardons and though the latter was doubtless much to be preferred, it was far less likely to be an option.

[67] See p. 197. TNA KB27/1075 rex m. 6 [images 4776, 4777, 4973d, 4974d]. The pardon also appears in *LP* vol. 4.3, 6072[13], dated 12 November 1529.

One Chalsunt appeared on 10 June with a pardon for all crimes committed by Smyth and the court ordered Smyth to appear in King's Bench on 7 July 1534.[68] Much like Cheselett, Smyth had been delivered to the archbishop of Canterbury after a failed abjuration, but, unlike Cheselett, his path to freedom was littered with bureaucratic obstacles. In the first instance, although Smyth appeared on time, his record did not. Rather than delivering him to the marshal of the Marshalsea, the court ordered him to be remanded to the archbishop, for 'if the prisoner were to be awarded to the marshal, and the [arch]bishop discharged, then perhaps afterwards the pardon might be disallowed, and then it would be a great question how the prisoner could be delivered back to the [arch]bishop'.[69] The court may have been particularly careful in this case because they knew that in fact the pardon would be disallowed. Spelman notes that the pardon was for the felony, judgement, and execution, but not imprisonment in the archbishop's prison. Though this was exactly the same as Cheselett's pardon just four years earlier, Spelman thought it was backwards, for 'the felony and everything dependent thereon are determined by the commission to the ordinary, and nothing remains except the imprisonment in the ordinary's prison'.[70] Rather than sending Smyth back to prison, however, the court urged him to sue for a better pardon, which he did. The fact that the case appears twice in Spelman's collection suggests that it attracted a good deal of attention, and the argument indicates two important points. In the first place, the court was clearly not trying to prevent Smyth from going free, which suggests a genuine desire to clarify the issues surrounding his—and presumably others'—pardons, probably because pardons for this kind of crime were becoming more common. In the second place, the shift in the pardons from focusing on the crime to focusing on the custody indicates the growing assumption of integration between the secular system and the ecclesiastical system.

The pardons of two Westminster clerks attaint, George Courtney and William Hull, make this integration even more explicit. Courtney abjured in April 1514 and claimed clergy at King's Bench in June 1516.[71] On 23 October 1533 William a[tte] Lee appeared in King's Bench on his behalf with a pardon for all crimes before 16 October 1533, stating that Courtney 'remains in the king's prison in the hard custody of William, now abbot of the monastery of Westminster' and asking for a writ to bring him to King's Bench.[72] Hull abjured in 1527 and claimed clergy at King's Bench in June 1529. William a[tte] Lee appeared on his behalf with a pardon on 27 January 1534, again noting that he was in the king's prison in the hard custody of

[68] TNA KB9/527 m. 59 [image 122], TNA KB27/1092 rex m. 17 [images 188, 189, 387d, 388d, 190].

[69] *Spelman's Reports*, vol. 1, p. 52.

[70] *Spelman's Reports*, vol. 1, p. 169.

[71] TNA KB9/467 m. 89 [image not on AALT]; TNA KB27/1020 rex m. 9 [image 240].

[72] TNA KB27/1089 rex m. 1 [images 217, 218, 463d, 464d, 219]. The pardon appears in *LP* vol. 6, 1383[13] dated 16 Oct 1533. Courtney appeared on 27 October and went *sine die* nineteen years and six months after his abjuration.

the abbot.[73] It is a significant change in language to characterize the Abbey prison as the king's, while recognizing William Benson's authority over it. This was not peculiar to Westminster. Nicholas Dery, a clerk from Rochester, was one of the rare criminals in this period to confess to his crime.[74] He was delivered to the ordinary for Canterbury as a clerk attaint on 9 January 1526, with the unusual and explicit notation in the record that the sheriff was relieved of his custody. In February 1534 one Petyte appeared in King's Bench on his behalf, stating that Nicholas 'remains in the king's prison in the hard custody of Thomas . . . of Canterbury', indicating that the new language applied to episcopal prisons as well as the Abbey.[75] By late 1533 the extension of royal authority over episcopal prisons was clearly complete, even though, as William Smyth's pardon makes clear, the usual technical boundaries between jurisdictions remained in place. This shift did, however, make it easier to activate the option, which had for so long remained dormant, of making parliamentary pardons applicable in the ecclesiastical system.

This change came quickly after 1540. The parliament of that year passed a general pardon for all offences before 1 July 1540: the only felonies excepted were murder and robberies from churches.[76] Though the pardon did not draw attention to clerks convict or attaint, for the first time it was quickly used by them, and ten men presented themselves at King's Bench looking to be released under its provisions, six of them in November 1540. All of them demonstrate how the parliamentary pardon could be used in the context of the ecclesiastical system to expedite a fairly traditional process, but they also demonstrate the variety of ways in which punishments and mitigations could be blended to achieve an appropriate result.

The first two men appeared on 3 November, both with long and complicated criminal histories. John Davy, a chaplain from Hemel Hempstead, had been indicted for two crimes in October 1524: a burglary of goods worth 21s in October 1522, and, more seriously, the treasonous washing and clipping of 10 gross of silver in July 1524. Davy was convicted at the castle of Hertford in April 1525, but remanded to gaol.[77] He should, of course, have been executed, since benefit of clergy was not available for treason, but as one of the few actual clerics convicted, the

[73] TNA SP1/238 f. 72; TNA KB27/1072 rex m. 5 [images 1755, 1756]; TNA KB27/1090 rex m. 15 [images 155, 156, 319d, 320d, 157]. Hull appeared on 11 February and went *sine die* four and a half years after his delivery.

[74] TNA KB9/526 m. 39 [image 77]: he broke the close of Edward Pratt and stole £5 in gold on 28 December 1525.

[75] TNA KB27/1090 rex m. 11 [images 149, 150, 314d, 315d]. Henry Cheyny also pleaded a pardon via the bishop of Winchester on 26 April 1536: TNA KB9/977 m. 4 [image not on AALT]: TNA KB27/1100 rex m. 11 (images 180, 181, 357d, 358d]. At the end of the record Cheyny averred that he was the same person who had committed the crimes and Fermour accepted this for the king, suggesting that there could be such confusion at the end of a sentence as well as at the beginning.

[76] *SR*, III. 809–812. 32 Hen. VIII c. 49.

[77] TNA KB27/1100 rex m. 7 [images 170, 171, 349d, 350d, 351d].

prospect of his execution must have caused the justices some disquiet. The record of his conviction was delivered to King's Bench in October 1526, eighteen months after his conviction, but Davy himself did not appear in court until July 1536. It's not clear whether he was confined in Hertford or the Marshalsea for the intervening decade, but when he appeared he argued that the indictment for treason was insufficient, because it did not specify that the coins he clipped were sterling money of the realm of England, and so the charge should be dismissed. The court agreed, and he went *sine die* on that offence. Having removed the charge of treason, Davy then claimed clergy and specified that he was in orders. He read *ut clericus*, but the court asked for his letters of ordination. Davy responded that he did indeed have letters, but not on him—he seems to be virtually patting his pockets as he answers. He was given until November 1536 to produce the letters, but he did not return to court until October 1539, when he 'relinquishes the claim to the letters of ordination aforesaid and asks to be allowed general benefit of clergy'. Denis Dalyance, the ordinary for Westminster, once again requested him, and the court agreed that he should be delivered as a clerk convict, fourteen and a half years after his conviction. Davy had done well from his original description as a chaplain, which appears to have convinced both the gaol delivery and King's Bench justices not to execute him, even though in the final instance he could not produce evidence that he actually was in orders. But while reluctant to execute him, the justices had no compunction about punishing him with a lengthy term of imprisonment before they dropped the charge of treason, and then pushing him to provide letters of ordination before finally allowing his delivery. Davy was then one of the first clerks convict to use the 1540 parliamentary pardon: he once again appeared in King's Bench, this time in the custody of William Webbe, warden of the king's gaol of Westminster.[78] The record of Davy's pardon specifies that his crimes were not among those excepted in the statute, and that he was a liege subject of the king, born in [blank] in county [blank].[79] After this long and complex journey through the legal system, Davy went *sine die* fifteen years and seven months after his conviction.

The second clerk convict to be pardoned on 3 November 1540 had spent less time in the system, but his career was no less checkered. We have already examined James Olyff's failed attempt at abjuration in 1530 and his successful claim of clergy in 1533.[80] He too appeared in King's Bench in the custody of Webbe (here described as warden of the king's gaol 'called the convict house within the king's

[78] This is presumably the same William Webbe who was managing the Westminster sanctuary in 1539: either he had moved to a different branch of the system by 1540 or, more likely, the management of the sanctuary and the prison had been combined.

[79] The relationship between the statute and the resulting document is intriguing: the statute grants the pardon to all the king's subjects, specifying that this meant the inhabitants of England, Wales, Jersey, Guernsey, Berwick, and Calais, as the 1534 pardon had done. No earlier pardons pick up on this language of nationality and allegiance, but it is standard in the pardons entered in the King's Bench rolls in the early 1540s, and reinforces once again the felon's relationship with the king: *SR*, III. 809.

[80] See p. 275.

palace of Westminster'), cited the statute, noted his allegiance and went free almost ten years after his abjuration, and more than seven after his delivery as a clerk attaint.[81]

The next man to appear in King's Bench was Robert Tykhill, one of the clerks attaint on the 1533 Westminster sanctuary list.[82] Tykhill had been outlawed in August 1525 and delivered to Westminster in January 1528. He appeared in King's Bench on 17 November 1540, once again in the custody of Webbe, and went through the same process, going free fifteen years after his outlawry and twelve years after his delivery. Tykhill was followed on 19 November by John Pares, a surgeon from Horningsheath in Suffolk who had been convicted at the gaol delivery of Bury St Edmunds in July 1534 of escaping from gaol by night. Pares had pleaded guilty, unusually, and was delivered without purgation. He appeared in the custody of the bishop of Norwich, and the language of his entry differs: he does not note the place of his birth, but states simply that 'he is a subject of the now lord king and was born within this kingdom of England'.[83] Anthony Johnson appeared in King's Bench on 22 November, also in Webbe's custody. Johnson had been convicted of stealing 14s from John Hawson in the great hall at Whitehall on 25 June 1539, the same day as the theft, and had a much shorter passage through the legal system.[84] Though their journeys were mostly long and complicated, once they got to King's Bench these five men all went through a fairly typical process, simply substituting the parliamentary pardon for individual pardons.

The experiences of Davy, Olyff, Tykhill, Pares, and Johnson demonstrate that there were still a fair number of clerks attaint lingering in the system, and the parliamentary pardon provided a cheaper and more efficient process than individual pardons for getting them out of prison after a condign and often lengthy period of confinement.[85] But, like many experiments, when placed in the context of the broader machinery the parliamentary pardon seems to have had some unintended consequences. We do not know in much detail how the pardon process was initiated. Kesslring notes that after 1515 general pardons provided that the beneficiaries did not need to obtain an individual copy of the pardon, but if they had to plead it in court they paid 12d to the clerk to have it enrolled.[86] This meant that those who had committed a crime but had not yet been indicted could no longer be charged, while those whose cases were pending before the court or who had been convicted and remanded could plead the pardon and walk away once it was entered. But what happened to those who had successfully claimed clergy? Without any explicit

[81] TNA KB27/1083 rex m. 4d (images 6086d, 6087d, 5935, 5936].

[82] TNA KB27/1065 rex mm. 6, 10 [images 8897, 9167d: 8906, 8907]. See p. 284.

[83] TNA KB27/1117 rex m. 1 [images 144, 145].

[84] TNA KB27/1112 rex m. 1 [image 126].

[85] Kesselring notes that husbandmen and labourers made up only about 14 per cent of those who received a special pardon, despite being a much larger proportion of the population: parliamentary pardons could close this gap: Kesselring, *Mercy and Authority*, p. 77.

[86] Kesselring, *Mercy and Authority*, p. 61.

provision for them in the statute, clerks convict and clerks attaint must have been heavily dependent on the bishops' response to the statute. If the bishop was willing to accept the pardon and let them go, they could simply walk free, with no recorded process. If the bishop had concerns about the applicability of the pardon or if he simply wanted to avoid the risk of a later indictment for escape, he might bring the clerk before the court himself to ensure that the pardon was accepted and recorded. But if the bishop was not willing to accept the general pardon, the clerk convict could presumably sue to have it recognized, and this is probably the context for the process surrounding the last man to claim the parliamentary pardon in November 1540, Richard Eve.

Richard Eve's pardon became intertwined with those of two other men, Thomas Stathom and William Michyll. Eve, a chaplain, was convicted at the gaol delivery of Colchester in July 1532 of attacking Thomasine Kekewyche on the highway and stealing a scarlet cloak worth 20s. Under the 1532 statute highway robbery was no longer clergiable for laymen, but as a chaplain Eve was still eligible, though without purgation unless he could provide recognizances for his good behavior. Eve apparently could not provide such recognizances, and he was delivered to the ordinary for London without purgation.[87] On 17 November 1540 a writ issued from King's Bench to Edmund Bonner, bishop of London, ordering him to send the reason why Eve, Stathom and Michyll were detained 'in our prison under your custody'. The bishop responded that Stathom and Mychyll had been attainted of felony in Newgate, Eve in Chelmsford, and that they were delivered into the convict house of the bishop's prison at Stortford to be punished for their misdeeds, where they remained in irons as clerks convict.[88] On receipt of this response, indeed the following day, a writ issued to the justices of gaol delivery for Newgate and for Essex, asking for their records. Eve appeared at King's Bench on 29 November, pleaded the parliamentary pardon and went free, eight years after his conviction. Stathom and Mychell's process took a little longer. Both men were failed abjurers: Stathom had confessed to assault and theft when he took sanctuary at St Sepulchre in Farringdon in June 1525 and abjured to Dover.[89] He appeared at Newgate in October 1525 and claimed clergy. Mychell had confessed to two burglaries when he took sanctuary at St Katherine Christchurch in Aldgate in September 1533 and, in accordance with the changes in the law in 1531, abjured to St Martin le Grand.[90] He appeared at Newgate in April 1537 and also claimed clergy.[91] The Newgate justices were a little slower than the Essex justices in returning their records, but Stathom and Mychell

[87] TNA KB27/1117 rex m. 6 [images 157, 158, 319d].

[88] TNA KB27/1118 rex m. 1 [images 114, 115, 225d, 226d]—the text says 'in quondam domum ibidem vocat le convyct house' and after he took over he found them held 'ferro mancipatos ut clericos attinctos'.

[89] TNA KB9/549 m. 58 [image 116].

[90] TNA KB9/549 m. 57 [image 114].

[91] TNA KB27/1118 rex mm. 1, 2 [images 114, 115, 225d, 226d; 116, 117, 227d, 228d, 118].

appeared in King's Bench to claim the pardon on 26 January 1541. By the time they walked free, Stathom had been in custody for fifteen years and three months, and Mychell for at least three years and nine months, though he probably spent time in sanctuary at St Martin le Grand. Eve, Stathom, and Mychell's crimes were widely separated in time and different in kind, and their pardon provides the only obvious reason why they were joined in the King's Bench writ. Though Bonner, King's Bench and the assize justices all moved the pardons along quite quickly, suggesting that in these cases the authorities were reasonably comfortable with the outcome, this suggests that they were testing the possible uses of the new statute.

This testing probably explains the appearance of a second and distinctly different round of pardon claimants in King's Bench in 1541–1542. John Clerke of Deptford, gentleman, appeared in February 1541. Clerke was convicted of breaking the close of Thomas German and stealing two 'stoned horses' in July 1539.[92] He was delivered to the archbishop of Canterbury in February 1540, just a few months before the passage of the pardon statute. Richard Harryson and Henry Larne appeared in February 1542. Both had been convicted at the gaol delivery in Ilchester in July 1539: Harryson of strangling Elizabeth Harryson in May 1538, Larne of burglary in March 1539.[93] Both were delivered to the ordinary, and both went free two and a half years after their conviction on very different crimes. These three cases raise two quite distinct questions. First, all these men were clerks convict, eligible for purgation, so why pardon them? The answer to this is obvious: a parliamentary pardon was surer and more discreet than a purgation. The second question is a bit trickier: all three crimes pre-dated 1 July 1540, so under the terms of the pardon Clerke, Harryson and Larne should have been able to walk free by November 1540, as Anthony Johnson had done. Why then did they stay in prison for an extra three to fourteen months? The most likely reason is that the bishops, or the courts, or both, generally did not wish to allow clerks convict who had not served some reasonable period of confinement to go free: there was no expiration date on the pardon, so while it could be pleaded at any time, it did not have to be used at the first opportunity. From being a solution to the very specific problem of releasing clerks attaint, parliamentary pardons could be adapted to solve the much bigger chore of releasing clerks convict while allowing the authorities to retain a good deal of control over their use.

The bishop of Lincoln's register once again provides a useful perspective on this change. We saw in chapter 8 that over the 1530s the bishop of Lincoln was generally holding his clerks convict for shorter periods of confinement, which settled at

[92] i.e. stallions. It's fairly common to note when the horses stolen were geldings, but this is the only time I've seen this description. TNA KB9/549 m. 32 [image 64]: TNA KB27/1118 rex m. 3 [images 119, 120].

[93] TNA KB9/978 m. 24 [image not on AALT]: Harryson was indicted on 24 May 1538 and no reason is given why it took a year to bring him to trial. TNA KB9/978 m. 25 [image not on AALT].

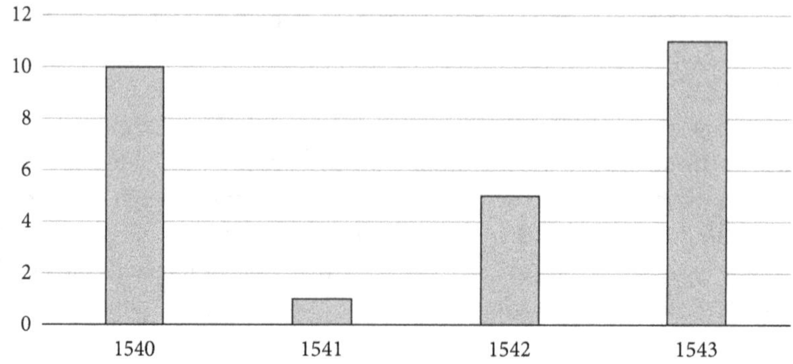

Figure 9.4 Purgations in Longland's *Register* 1540–1543*
**Reg. Longland*, ff 287–288, 291–291v, 294v–295, 296v.

about a year in the early 1540s. It's likely that purgations had become an increasingly unrealistic method of releasing such men. Purgations were time and resource intensive: as long as they served an important role in reconciling convicts to their communities the commitment of resources was justified, but as the number of men needing purgation increased, and the severity of their crimes and the depth of bishops' resources decreased, the cost/benefit analysis must have shifted. Parliamentary pardons could perform much the same task, much more efficiently.

The effect of the pardon statute on purgations in Lincoln is clear in fig. 9.4: the ten purgations in 1540 was the highest number in any one year since 1533, but the number plummets in 1541. It is likely that as those eligible for the pardon—those who had committed their crime before July 1540—took advantage of it, the number of purgations naturally fell, and indeed the bishop's prison seems to have emptied out in these years. Purgations return to more typical levels in 1542 and 1543 because the men purged in those years had all committed their crimes five to thirteen months earlier, i.e. after the date of eligibility in the statute.[94] The parliamentary pardon thus made it easier for the bishops to move long-term clerks attaint out of the prisons, and, whether intentionally or incidentally, also helped clean out short-term clerks convict. Even when bishops had concerns about the release of individual convicts, like Eve, Stathom, and Mychell, they were presumably happy enough to relieve themselves of the burdens of feeding, clothing and purging large numbers of lay thieves, especially after a decade in which their

[94] Canonical purgations did continue to be an option in these years: they are recorded not only in the bishop of Lincoln's register, but also in the archbishop of Canterbury's in 1542, 1543, and 1551: *Reg. Cranmer*, f. 427–428v. The register is recording a genuine process, not just a formula: in March 1546 Henry Holbeach, the bishop of Rochester, wrote to Cranmer regarding the purgation of John Frende, who had been convicted of breaking the close of Thomas Thomas and stealing eighteen pregnant sheep and twenty-one wethers worth a combined £6 on 20 June 1545. When the bishop sent the usual notices of purgation to the parish church and area a large crowd gathered and protested the purgation, and Holbeach was unsure whether to proceed or not: *Reg. Cranmer*, f. 24.

obligations to the criminal justice system seemed to be growing while their income was shrinking. After 1541 new clerks convict continued to be delivered to the ordinaries and purged by them, but with fewer clerks attaint and long-term clerks convict, the burden on the system was less than it had been. This sounds like a simple story of growing efficiency, but there are two obvious drawbacks to it. The first is the possibility for abuse inherent in such a generous pardon, and the second is the loss of the benefits conferred by purgation: though it was costly and presumably stressful, it did allow the convict to be restored to good fame through a traditional process.

Perhaps for these reasons, the next general pardon was substantially less generous: whether the 1540 statute had served its purpose in relieving the pressure on the system or whether it was abused, or both, the framers of the 1544 statute clearly wanted to keep much closer control of convicts.[95] An interesting mix of the new and the traditional, it effectively incorporated the exceptions to benefit of clergy as defined in 1532 and in the new felony statutes, and it allowed pardons for thefts under 40s, rather than the 20s typical until the 1530s.[96] It thus recognized the ways in which mitigation was limited in other parts of the criminal justice system, and brought pardons back into line. The statute does not specify whether clerks convict or attaint were eligible for the pardon, but a single case in the King's Bench records demonstrates that they were, and that it was used in a very traditional way. Thomas Bocher was convicted of breaking the close and home of John Martyn at the castle of Lewes in July 1541.[97] When he claimed clergy it was asserted that he had married Maud Holywell, widow, in July 1534 at the parish church of Tukefeld in Sussex. Bocher denied the assertion, and he was remanded to gaol while the issue was forwarded to the bishop. A year later, in July 1542, Richard Sampson, the bishop of Chichester, returned that there was no place or parish called Tukefeld in his diocese, so he couldn't enquire, and Thomas was remanded again.[98] He returned to court in August 1543 to be remanded again, without explanation, until finally in May 1544 he appeared at King's Bench to claim the parliamentary pardon.[99] Thomas's crime postdated the earlier pardon, and the response to the claim of bigamy seems to have left him in limbo, since it could neither be confirmed, so that he could be executed, or refuted, so that he could be delivered. Even though burglary was among the crimes specifically excepted from the pardon, the court seems to have turned a blind eye, since once again a pardon was effectively the only way

[95] *SR*, III. 981–983. 35 Hen. VIII c. 18.

[96] Crimes before 14 January 1544 were pardoned. Those in the Tower or elsewhere between 14 January and 16 March 1543 for heresy or high treason were also excepted from the pardon. This was an innovation, in the timing as well as the provision, but it would become more common later in the 1540s.

[97] TNA KB9/558 m. 137 [image 277].

[98] Tukefeld was likely an error for Uckfield, introduced at some point in the court proceedings. I am grateful to Paul Brand for this suggestion and many other placename clarifications.

[99] TNA KB27/1131 rex m. 7 (images 217–219, 424d, 425d].

forward for Bocher, and a parliamentary pardon was cheaper and simpler than an individual one.[100]

Throughout the early Tudor period pardons had been a useful way to deal with problem cases and to end periods of confinement, as well as a way to show mercy, but traditional pardons were expensive and often slow. As sentences became shorter and the numbers in the bishops' prisons increased, it's not surprising to see some experimentation with general pardons, either to achieve a one-time relief for over-crowded prisons, or to provide an ongoing system for regular releases. The surviving records of purgations demonstrate that the bishops could continue to use traditional methods to release clerks convict in challenging cases, but the parliamentary pardons gave them a quick and easy way to deal with the mass of ordinary clerks convict. The King's Bench records suggest that the courts were willing to show a fair amount of flexibility in the ways in which they used pardons, as long as the flexibility was at their discretion. The 1540 pardon, however, raised the spectre of clerks convicts returning to the streets without purgation after a year or less in custody, with limited options for oversight. This does not seem to have been the intended aim, and the 1544 pardon retrenched, combining the restrictions of earlier pardons with the convenience of the parliamentary process.

By the end of the reign of Henry VIII sanctuary and benefit of clergy remained available to mitigate punishment, but their range was increasingly circumscribed. Though the establishment of secular sanctuaries in 1540 was intended to continue the regime established in 1536, it seems to have failed spectacularly. The only secular sanctuary for which there is more than a hint of evidence is Westminster, and that was most likely because of its long history, and perhaps because of its ongoing ability to offer sanctuary for debt. Parish sanctuaries could still offer a breathing space, but the overall decline in the status of the major sanctuaries, along with broader fights over doctrine and the control of sacred space, are likely to have made them less appealing too. They certainly became far less visible.

Benefit of clergy, on the other hand, became increasingly regulated and systematized. Though the 1512 statute was largely ineffective, the pardon statutes through the 1520s indicate that a consensus was emerging on unmitigable crimes, and the 1532 benefit of clergy statute added arson of dwellings or barns where grain was stored to murder, burglary in a church, highway robbery, and burglary in a household with fear, while horsetheft joined the list in 1545. The shorter periods of confinement established for the lesser felonies in the late 1530s continued in the last years of the reign, and both King's Bench and parliament experimented with more efficient ways to get clerks convict and clerks attaint out of prison: purgation must have seemed like an increasingly cumbersome way to release clerks convicted

[100] Though they are rare, individual pardons do continue to appear: TNA KB27/1121 rex m. 10 [images 267, 268, 527d, 528d].

of crimes which had less need for social reconciliation. The pardon statute of 1540 went too far, however, and the normal processes of purgation seem to have continued through the later 1540s, though it would not be surprising if the purgation of a thief who had spent six months in custody was more perfunctory than the purgation of a homicide who had been in the bishop's custody for seven years or a burglar who had been in custody for three years had been.

The application of these limitations to those in minor orders in 1532 and those in major orders in 1536 and 1540 was an important political change. Though, as we have seen, clerics were a small proportion of claimants through this entire period, the eradication of their separate version of benefit of clergy meant that the ecclesiastical hierarchy had less reason than ever before to engage with the criminal justice system. Indeed 1540 was a watershed year for them: in that year the last monasteries were closed, clerical benefit of clergy was finally aligned with the lay version, and parliamentary pardons became available to clerks convict and clerks attaint. The Church was no longer integral to the system of criminal confinement, though bishops continued to manage much of the process for some time.

The changes in practice were equally important, if more varied. The statutes passed in the Reformation parliament and after clearly had a more immediate impact on practice than statutes had had in previous decades, but the impact was not always consistent. The small number of recorded claims for homicide and robbery in the 1540s, for example, suggests either that men were not claiming or were not being allowed clergy for violent crimes, even though such claims were legal, or that such claims were routinely processed at gaol delivery without provoking the kinds of issues that might bring them to King's Bench. The claims for murder, arson and burglary indicate that the justices retained some level of discretion, even as the statutes became increasingly directive. Where we have been able to see the proportion of convicts who claimed clergy, it has remained surprisingly steady in the 25 per cent range from the 1490s to the 1540s, even as the total number of clergy claimants seems to have risen. But the men who were making the claim changed, as did their experience: in the early years of Henry VIII's reign benefit of clergy was used by relatively affluent and educated homicides, burglars, and robbers, some of whom may have felt some shame in its use. They spent a prolonged period of time in the bishops' prisons and emerged via a purgation process designed to restore them to society, whether it accomplished that goal or not. By the end of the reign benefit of clergy was primarily the preserve of poorer thieves who might spend less than a year in custody and be rehabilitated as well by a parliamentary pardon as by purgation. It's impossible to know if these were men who would previously have been hanged for their felony or men who would previously have been found guilty of larceny or acquitted, but it is clear that by the end of the reign benefit of clergy was being used, for the most part, to imprison lower-class lay convicts for non-violent felonies. The corollary was that more-affluent men with more resources, who might also be expected to know better, were required to either expend their resources in seeking a pardon or to suffer the penalties of the law, while lower-class or illiterate men convicted of violent felonies were more likely to go to the gallows.

3. Sanctuary and Benefit of Clergy in the Reign of Edward VI

The much-reduced system in place at Henry VIII's death was quite sustainable, but like his father, though for different reasons, when Edward VI came to the throne in 1547 he set out to conciliate. The first parliament of his reign recognized explicitly that some statutes passed under Henry VIII had been harsh: it noted that believing that 'sharper lawes as a harder bridle shoulde be made to staye those men and factors that might ellse be occacion cause and aucthors of further inconvenience', Henry VIII's parliaments had made 'certaine lawes and Statutes which might seme and appere to men of exterior realms and many of the Kinges Majesties Subgectes verie streighte sore extreme and terrible'.[101] Arguing that those measures were appropriate to the time, it went on to equate Edward's reign to calm weather following a tempest, and to provide for the relaxation of some of those measures. Though the language was conciliatory and the statute repealed important Henrician acts regarding treason and religion, the 'repeal act' was less generous when it came to criminal law.[102] It repealed all new felonies created during Henry VIII's reign, but with a couple of exceptions: acts against counterfeiting and servants stealing their masters' goods were confirmed, and poisoning was deemed murder. In effect this meant that crimes like sodomy, which were rarely prosecuted, were repealed. The statute then went on to elaborate the limits to benefit of clergy and sanctuary, linking them as they had been linked in 1540. The core provisions are familiar, but they were re-worked slightly. Benefit of clergy and sanctuary were to be unavailable for willful murder, robbing any church or chapel, and highway robbery, but the statute extended these categories to include willful poisoning and robbery near the highway, though the distance was not specified. Breaking into a house when anyone in the house was put in fear was clarified: the crime was the same by day or night and whoever was in the house—it no longer had to be the householder, his family, or servants. Horse thieves remained unclergiable but became ineligible for sanctuary for the first time. For every other felony, sanctuary and benefit of clergy were to be available in the same way as they had been at the beginning of Henry VIII's reign. The statute thus effectively provided that arsonists, rapists, and

[101] *SR*, IV. 18. 1 Edw. VI c. 12.

[102] See W.K. Jordan, *Edward VI: The Young King*, (Cambridge MA: Harvard University Press, 1968), pp. 172–174; M.L. Bush, *The Government Policy of Protector Somerset* (Montreal: McGill-Queen's University Press, 1975), pp. 131–132.

robbers could once again claim sanctuary and benefit of clergy, though as usual this doesn't necessarily mean that they did.[103]

The implications of the repeals act for sanctuary are unclear. The scattered evidence that we have suggests that parish sanctuaries continued to be used through all the more high-profile changes, and this statute could simply be recognizing that fact and continuing the process of bringing their mitigating functions more clearly into line with the rules for benefit of clergy. But what happened to the chartered and secular sanctuaries? It's reasonable to assume that the statute removed the whole structure of internal abjuration, and external abjuration seems to have been restored in theory, though there is little evidence for it in practice.[104] Some of the religious houses dissolved in the late 1530s were re-constituted, and the 1540 statute which erected the secular sanctuaries had specifically allowed the chartered sanctuaries to continue to function, though it prohibited them from taking new claimants. For those still in operation—most obviously Westminster, where the relationship between the chartered sanctuary and the secular sanctuary is ambiguous, but also places like Beverley and Durham—this statute may have provided a new lease on life or may simply have provided authorization for their ongoing work. The Beverley register of sanctuary men, for example, ended in 1540, presumably because of the statute of that year. It added new names between August 1548 and 1549, however.[105] This suggests that in the north, at least, sanctuaries remained both viable and popular.[106] At the same time it is clear that sanctuary did not, by any stretch of the imagination, return to its position at the beginning of Henry VIII's reign. Removing the sanctuaries from their sacred locations removed something of the essence of the privilege, and the peculiar hybrid of sacred and secular control of the late Middle Ages was crucial to the social and cultural function of the sanctuaries. Once parliament started nipping and tucking at the rules of sanctuary, their cultural capital was damaged—they needed to be seen as absolute, unchanging, if people were to trust their lives to them. A privilege which relied on

[103] It also repealed all new treason laws, returning the law to the provision of the statute of 25 Edward III; repealed a number of statutes relating to religion, going back as far as 1 Ric. II but focusing on Henrician statutes; and ordered that royal proclamations should no longer have the same force as statutes. Bush mis-interprets the implications of the sanctuary and benefit of clergy provisions, given his understanding of previous practice: Bush, *The Government Policy of Protector Somerset*, pp. 132–133.

[104] William Rastell, *A Collection in English, of the statutes now in force* STC 221:01 (London, 1594), 2a provides a form of confession and abjuration which refers to the abjurer as a felon of King Edward. Abjuration also appears as a form of punishment in later statutes, such as 35 Eliz I. c. 2, which provided for abjuration in the case of those who did not attend their parish churches: *SR*, IV. 844. Thornley, 'The Destruction of Sanctuary', p. 204, esp. n. 116 is uncharacteristically uncertain about the implications of the statute.

[105] Cox, *Sanctuaries*, pp. 147–149. Thornley says these are burgesses, not sanctuary men, but she is assuming that sanctuaries had been eradicated. There is another pause until 1553 when names once again are recorded until 1557, with a total of 210 claimants in these two periods.

[106] Evidence for St Martin's is scarce, but in 1558 viewers of the city of London described land in Bell Alley as 'privileged and sanctuary ground'. Janet Loengard ed. *London Viewers and Their Certificates, 1508–1558: Certificates of the Sworn Viewers of the City of London* London Record Society Publications vol. 26 (London Record Society, 1989), p. 146.

the whims of Henry VIII was rather less secure than one which rested on a thousand years of the Church's practices and it seems that desperate men and women found other ways to avoid their fate—a striking indication that the criminal justice system did not just work from the top down, that it required some level of buy-in from all participants.

The implications of the repeals act for benefit of clergy are clearer, partly because benefit of clergy had a much clearer statutory tradition, and partly because the act contained two provisions which were completely new. First, it provided that parliamentary peers who could not read were eligible to claim clergy once for any felony except willful murder. They were not to be branded or to suffer forfeiture, and they were eligible for purgation. Since the statute provided elsewhere that parliamentary peers were only to be tried by their peers, as had previously been done in cases of treason, this ensured that any peer who was indicted could claim clergy without seeing the inside of a courtroom, and could be swiftly purged, if his peers so wished. Given the decline in social status associated with benefit of clergy, this seems designed to ensure that peers could keep the desirable mitigation without having to suffer the social stigma associated with it. Second, the statute ended the exception of bigamy, allowing any man who had married multiple single women or widows to claim clergy, though as we have seen, this had become largely irrelevant in practice.[107]

Though it is the most obvious, the repeals act was not the only statute in this session which had implications for benefit of clergy. And if the repeals act set out to establish a kinder, gentler tone for the reign, the statute on vagabonds headed in the opposite direction. It declared that anyone who was unemployed for more than three days was to offer his services in return for 'meat and drynke'.[108] If anyone thus unemployed refused such an offer, or, having taken it, ran away, he was to be taken as a vagabond: his master was to take him to the justices of the peace to offer proof of the circumstances, and once proved, the vagabond was to be branded on the chest with a V. He would then become the master's slave for a period of two years, during which time he would be fed only bread and water, or 'small drink and such refuse of meat as [the master] shall think meet', and his master could 'cause the said slave to work by beating, chaining or otherwise in such work and labour how vyle so ever it be as he shall put him unto'. If the slave were to run away within the two years and remain absent for fourteen days or more, the master could pursue him and punish him by beating; if he were detained by another the master could bring an action of trespass before the justices of the peace to recover the slave, damages of £10, and costs, as well as having the slave branded on the forehead or the cheek with an S, and a judgement that he would

107 A proclamation in April 1548 also clarified the definition of bigamy: *Tudor Royal Proclamations* vol. 1, pp. 421–423.

108 *SR*, iv. 5. 1 Edw. VI c. 3.

be a slave forever. If he ran away a second time, such a slave would be condemned and executed as a felon. Though this introduction of personal slavery to England is framed as a solution to a social and moral evil, it was also linked with criminal justice. The second part of the statute provided that any clerk convict might find someone who would be bound in the sum of £20 to two sureties to hold the clerk as his slave for a year, with the same regulations that applied to vagabonds (with the exception of the branding on the chest).[109] The ordinary who delivered his clerk convict to such a master was thereby discharged of all obligations. If the clerk convict could not find anyone to take him as a slave, he was allowed to make his purgation in the usual way after a year. Clerks attaint, who were not eligible for purgation, could go through a similar process but would remain as a slave for a period of five years. This is a remarkable provision. It builds on past practices in the way we have seen repeatedly: the 1532 statute had banned clerks in major orders from purgation unless they could find sureties who would be bound for £20, while the clerk was to be bound for £40. But the conversion of this safeguard to personal slavery is the final proof, if proof were needed, that by 1547 clerks convict were assumed to be of low social status. The term of one year comports with the shorter sentences apparent in the purgations and pardons since the late 1530s, but the explicit recognition of the ordinary's discharge suggests that even this lighter regime of sentencing was stretching the bishops' resources, and using clerks convict as free labour in this way both relieved the cost of their confinement and made them more useful citizens. The rather counter-intuitive provision that men who could not find masters to take them as slaves could nonetheless be purged as usual after a year implies that such slavery, with bread and water and vile labour would still be preferable to confinement in the bishops' prisons—thus the new scheme was a win for all parties.[110]

This statute did not last long. It was repealed in 1549, when the statute of 22 Hen. VIII concerning vagabonds was revived and clerks convict were not mentioned.[111] Davies argues that it was never enforced, and this may be true for vagabonds, but Cranmer's register makes it clear that it was enforced at least twice for clerks

[109] Three bills on vagabonds were read on 30 November and they were committed to Shelley and Marvin, justices, and Mulleneux and Saunders, serjeants at law: *Lords' Journal*, p. 302. 30 November 1547. Three days later a bill on vagabonds appeared again and was committed to the same men: p. 303. A bill for vagabonds appears again on 6 December and was concluded on December 8: pp. 304–305. There is no mention of clerks convict anywhere in the *Journal*. It appears in the *Commons' Journal* on 10 December as the Bill for Vagabonds and Slaves: *Journal of the House of Commons: Volume 1, 1547–1629* (London: HMSO, 1802), p. 2. 10 December 1547. It passed there on 19 December 1547: p. 3. Another bill 'for the punishment of Vagabonds' appears in the Lords on 20 December 1547: pp. 310–311.

[110] C.S.L. Davies assumes that such clerks would find 'a compliant and wealthy friend' with whom to spend the year, but the social profile of clerks convict demonstrates that this is unlikely to have been feasible for most: 'Slavery and Protector Somerset; the Vagrancy Act of 1547', *The Economic History Review* NS 19.3 (1966), p. 534.

[111] *SR*, IV. 115. 3 & 4 Edw. VI c. 16.

convict.[112] On 7 November 1548, George Wiggam, a husbandman from Wickemeir in Norfolk, came to William Cole, Archbishop Cranmer's chancellor in London, to ask for the body of George Gower, a Southwark cooper.[113] Wiggam provided Cole with a copy of Gower's conviction and a letter from the archbishop which noted that two men convicted at Croydon 'do nowe remayne in prysonne in the kinges benche at my charge' and ordered the recipient to 'directe forthe a commission for the delivery of the saide two convictes according to thordre of the lawe'.[114] Wiggam also provided a copy of the obligation in which Nicholas Hacker, fisherman, and Richard Croke, merchant tailor of London, were bound in £20 to ensure that 'the within boundene George Wiggam to whome the sayde George Gower is delyvered as a slave do retayne the sayde George Gowre as his slave and do kepe his person so convicted for the space of one yeare nowe next following, that he shall not goo abrode and at large accordinge to the teanor, purpose, forme and effecte of thacte of parliament made in the cession of parliament holden at Westminster in the first yeare of the reigne [of Edward VI] in that behalf stablysshed and provided'. The second man delivered at the session, Robert Cookeson, a London tailor, was also handed over to a new master, Thomas Pate, a merchant tailor.[115] Cookeson's delivery to tailors could be interpreted as a delivery to friends or colleagues who would ease his passage through the year, or it could be that a skilled slave would be of most value to a master in the same trade. The connection between Gower and his master is harder to see: a cooper would also be a useful slave, but why would a Norfolk husbandman and fisherman claim a Southwark felon? It is tempting to see a prodigal son story playing out, but there is no evidence either way.

There are no other deliveries of convict slaves in Cranmer's register, but it's not unusual to see a novelty recorded once and then dropped: if the men were laymen convicted at gaol delivery and held in King's Bench, their connection to the bishop was purely financial. The register carefully notes all the paperwork connected with Gower's delivery, but by the time they got to Cookeson only the bond is given in any detail, and it would not be surprising if any subsequent deliveries did not make it into the register. It is unlikely that large numbers of clerks convict became slaves during the short life of this statute, but the simple fact that any did is quite remarkable. Cranmer's transactional approach to these men emphasizes again the distance between the archbishop and the criminals whose management he was responsible for without any compensating benefit. Not only were these men not clerics, they passed from King's Bench into the hands of their masters without going through

[112] Davies, 'Slavery and Protector Somerset', p. 545. Jordan, *Edward VI*, pp. 177–178 discusses the statute without mentioning its application to clerks convict and also asserts that it was never enforced.

[113] Gower broke the home of Peter Richards in April 1548 and stole £32. He was convicted at the gaol delivery of the castle of Croydon on 19 September: Lambeth Palace Library, *Reg. Cranmer*, f. 430. The record notes that Croydon was the archbishop's peculiar jurisdiction; see p. 81.

[114] The archbishop's letter was dated 5 November 1548.

[115] *Reg. Cranmer*, f. 431. No details are provided for his crime. His sureties were Thomas More, another merchant tailor, and Robert Graves, a tailor.

his prison or his purgation: the archbishop had become entirely incidental to the process.

Pardons in Statute

Though the statute for vagabonds demonstrates that clerks convict could be treated harshly in these years, the traditional methods of release from confinement, including pardons, continued to be available. Protector Somerset was quite comfortable taking on the royal prerogative of pardon and Edward VI's accession pardon was fairly traditional: two men appeared in King's Bench in the summer of 1547 with his pardon for all felonies committed before the beginning of the reign.[116] But the protector, or the men around him, were clearly familiar with the language and the direction of the experimental 1540 statute: Edward VI's first parliament turned again to that model, but took it a little further. The statute passed at the end of the first session on 23 December 1547 opened by pardoning a wide range of crimes, including all felonies and robberies committed before 25 December 1547.[117] The novelty came in the exceptions: murder was excepted *tout court*, but the pardon could be claimed for some crimes which were not clergiable, such as highway robbery, burglary, and horsetheft, as well as crimes which were clergiable, such as clipping coins, arson, ravishment of women, and robbery, if the crime had been committed before 27 January 1547 (coin clipping) or 1 August 1547 (everything else).[118]

Pardon statutes have not generally inspired close reading: the combination of their bulk and their formula means that it's easy to overlook any actual change in them, but this use of dates to separate crimes is a real innovation. Previous general pardons applied to crimes committed before a set date which usually fell sometime during the parliamentary session in which it was passed. This statute carefully delineated two separate time frames within the year before the statute, thus effectively dividing felonies into four tiers. Tier one, willful murder, was not mitigable; tier two, greater felonies such as highway robbery, were not eligible for benefit of clergy, but those charged or convicted could be pardoned under the terms of the statute. Tier three, mid-range felonies such as manslaughter and robbery, were eligible for clergy but were not claimed very often: those who had committed their crimes before August and had probably been indicted, perhaps convicted and remanded,

[116] TNA KB27/1143 rex m. 1 [images 171, 172, 343d, 344d]; TNA KB27/1142 rex m. 6 [images 205, 206, 423d, 424d].

[117] The pardon was passed in the Commons on 22 December 1547 and in the Lords on 23 December: *Commons' Journal*, p. 4; *Lords' Journal*, p. 312. *SR*, IV. 33–35. 1 Edw. VI c. 15.

[118] The statute also returned to a novelty from the 1544 pardon, providing that anyone who was a prisoner in the Tower of London after 2 December 1547 was ineligible. The previous pardon specified that this applied to those in the Tower for heresy or high treason, and it is likely that the intention was the same here. This assumes that those prisoners were best pardoned individually, if at all.

maybe even delivered, by the time the statute passed could claim the pardon, while those who had committed their crimes more recently, and thus were less likely to have gone through the legal system, could not. Tier four was the lowest felonies, effectively theft: those who had committed this felony had easiest access to benefit of clergy, but under the statute were also eligible for immediate pardon, and thus could avoid process through the courts entirely. Once again parliament seems to have been trying to make the processes around punishment more systematic and more efficient by letting thieves go free and letting some mid-level felons off with something like time served.

If we assume that the framers of the statute expected it to operate as previous general pardons had done, then the provisions of the pardon would take some time to swing into action and there might be some means by which the bishops or the courts could slow the process down. Many of those in prison would be released without any record of the process, but with the passage of time a new group of felons who had committed their crimes after the prescribed dates would fill their cells. Only one claim for this pardon appears on the King's Bench rolls, and it fits those expectations. Roger Landesdell was convicted at Newgate of breaking into the home of the chancellor, Thomas Wriothesley, and stealing black satin worth £8 in May 1546.[119] In February 1548 he appeared at King's Bench in the custody of the bishop of London to claim the pardon.[120] His crime had been committed well before 1 August 1547, and though he broke the chancellor's home, it seems to have been categorized as a theft rather than a burglary, suggesting either that there was no violence involved, or that no-one was home, or both. A man who was stupid enough or unlucky enough to burgle the chancellor's house might seem like an unlikely object of mercy, and either his victim or the ambiguity of his crime may have caused his case to come before King's Bench. When it did, the pardon was applied and he went *sine die*.

This first parliamentary pardon of the reign was unusual in the time limits it set on the application of the pardon, but it was also succeeded unusually quickly by a second general pardon. In Henry VIII's reign general pardons appeared every four to eight years, with five or six years as the most common gap.[121] Edward's subjects waited only fifteen months for their next general pardon, passed in the second session of his first parliament on 14 March 1549.[122] This pardon was similar in some ways to the first, most notably in its use of dates to separate crimes, but it also tinkered with the processes the previous statute had established. This general pardon

[119] TNA KB9/565 m. 1 [image 2].

[120] TNA KB27/1145 m. 3d [images 381d, 382d]. The record specifically notes that on December 1547 he was not a prisoner in the Tower.

[121] The pardons were in 1509, 1514 (no surviving text), 1515, 1523, 1529, 1534, 1540, and 1544.

[122] The pardon was introduced in the Lords on 8 March, read for the second time 9 March 1549 and passed on 13 March: it moved to the Commons the same day and was passed there on 14 March: *Lords' Journal*, pp. 350–353, *Commons' Journal*, pp. 10–11. Pardons often passed three readings at once: this lengthy passage suggests that it was controversial. *SR*, iv. 95–98. 2 & 3 Edw. VI c. 39.

applied to all offences committed before 14 March 1548, a full year before the passage of the statute: this must mean that the statute was intended to apply to those who had already been convicted. This pardon also differs from the 1547 act by specifically including clerks convict and clerks attaint. This could be taken to imply that previous pardons had not applied to them, but, as we saw, it had certainly been used by them. It is more likely that the intention was to clarify the situation and to ensure that clerks attaint and convict could plead the pardon, as they had pleaded both general and individual pardons in the past.[123] As well as being directed more clearly at those convicted rather than just suspected or accused of felonies, this pardon also re-calibrated the levels of felony. It brought highway robbery and burglaries of homes back into the top tier of unmitigable crimes along with murder and burglaries of churches. In practice this meant that those who had committed mid-tier felonies, i.e. had forged or clipped coins between 27 January 1547 and 13 March 1548 or committed manslaughter, robbery, arson, or ravishment between 1 August 1547 and 13 March 1548, could go free after March 1549; this could apply to those who had never been indicted or convicted, but it could also allow those who had been convicted and either remanded or delivered to the ordinary to go free after twelve to twenty-five months in custody. Finally, the statute once again allowed those who had committed minor felonies to be pardoned forthwith.[124] Most of these mid-tier felonies were clergiable, and the pardon statute again demonstrates the emergence of agreement over the calibration of crimes, but it also shows how this agreement allowed for greater consistency in punishment and the more effective alignment of mitigation and pardon.

The third session of this parliament opened in November 1549 and ended in late January 1550. The general pardon, passed on 25 January 1550 in the wake of the 1549 rebellions, included rebellions, insurrections and unlawful assemblies among the crimes it pardoned, along with the typical felonies and robberies committed before 20 January 1549.[125] The framework was similar to the previous year's pardon, but this statute was even more lenient. For the first time prepensed murder, burglary, highway robbery, and theft from churches or chapels were only excepted if they had been committed since Michelmas, i.e. in the previous four

[123] This statute also added to the provisions in the 1547 statute by excepting all prisoners in the Tower or the Fleet between 1 February and 14 March 1548: we associate the Tower with political prisoners, and the Fleet with debtors, but earlier in the century the Fleet had also been used for prisoners of war and state prisoners, and that may be the reason for its inclusion: Pugh, *Imprisonment in Medieval England*, p. 117.

[124] There is one further novelty: this pardon specified that it applied to traitors and felons who fled overseas before 1 March 1548 if they returned before 25 December 1549. This seems to appeal to an older tradition of abjuration combined with the concerns with nationality and allegiance expressed in more recent general pardons: a desire to bring 'the king's felons' who were the notional 'expert mariners and archers' of Henry VIII's statute, home.

[125] *SR*, IV. 125–128. 3 & 4 Edw. VI c. 24. This was the last act of the session, which began 4 November 1549 and ran to 1 February 1550.

months.[126] The mid-level felonies, counterfeiting, manslaughter, robbery, ravishment, and horsetheft, were not excepted from the pardon, so those charged or convicted of those crimes could go free along with thieves.[127] And, once again, clerks convict were included. The details here are different from the year before: the time periods within which the greater felonies were excepted was significantly shorter and clerks convict were included without clerks attaint, though it's not clear if that distinction was becoming less important by this point, or if there were simply fewer clerks attaint remaining in the prisons.

There was no general pardon in the final session of this parliament, but Edward VI's last parliament, sitting in the spring of 1553, also closed with a general pardon.[128] While its format looks similar to the earlier pardons, it returns to a much more traditional model. Passed on 29 March, it pardoned crimes committed before 1 February 1553, and the greater felonies (prepensed murder, counterfeiting, burglaries in houses, robberies in churches, robberies on the person, and rape and carnal ravishment of women) are excepted without specifying any date.[129] This meant that such crimes committed since Michelmas 1549, the date set by the last parliament, were once again unpardonable. The 1553 pardon marks the end of a period of experimentation which allows us to see the areas of agreement and disagreement around mitigation. Four felonies remained consistently pardonable through these experiments: homicide, arson, theft and horsetheft. The first three were also clergiable, suggesting that there was general agreement across the system about mitigable crimes, with the exception of horsetheft, which always seems like the oddest restriction of benefit of clergy. Murder remained consistently unmitigable, with the single exception of the 1549 pardon, but the mid-range felonies, which remained unclergiable, alternated between being pardonable with time restrictions and unpardonable in the four Edwardian general pardons (table 9.5). This could represent a tussle among law makers about the weight of those crimes, or it could demonstrate a desire to ensure that the men committing those crimes stayed in custody for a fairly consistent period of time: given the careful attention the framers of the statutes paid to dates, I would incline towards the latter. The general pardons of 1547 to 1549 worked out a structure within which felons convicted of lesser felonies could be pardoned on a fairly regular schedule

[126] Arson committed since Michelmas was also excepted: arson was not excluded at all in the previous pardon, so this may have been a topic of disagreement.

[127] Once again, prisoners in the Tower and the Fleet were a point of concern: those present on 26 January 1549 were excepted, unless they had stolen less than 20s, or their theft was on a highway, in a house at night, or in a church or chapel. This suggests that prisoners held in those prisons for regular felonies had been barred from the pardon against the intention of the statute. It also indicates a clear distinction between breaking into houses and breaking into houses at night.

[128] *SR*, IV. 193–198. 7 Edw. VI c. 14. The pardon was passed in the Lords on 29 March 1553 and read in the Commons the same day: *Lords' Journal*, pp. 441–442; *Commons' Journal*, p. 26. On 31 March the bill was read again in the Lords, with a request that 'certain words might be amended therein': *Lords' Journal*, pp. 444–445.

[129] Robberies on the person replaced highway robbery, and presumably encompassed it.

Table 9.5 Clergiable crimes in statute 1547–1553*

	Clergiable after Repeals Act 1547	**Sanctuary after Repeals Act 1547**	**Pardon 23 Dec 1547**	**Pardon 14 March 1549 [incl/clerks convict]**	**Pardon 25 January 1550 [incl/clerks convict]**	**Pardon 29 March 1553**
All crimes			before 25 Dec 1547	before 14 Mar 1548	before 20 Jan 1549	before 1 Feb 1553
Except:						
Willful murder	✖	✖	✖	✖	✔ before 29 September 1549	✖
Robbing church or chapel	✖	✖	✔ before 1 Aug 1547	✖	✔ before 29 September 1549	✖
Highway robbery	✖	✖	✔ before 1 Aug 1547	✖	✔ before 29 September 1549	
Burglary in fear	✖	✖	✔ before 1 Aug 1547	✖	✔ before 29 September 1549	✖
Horsetheft	✖	✖	✔ before 1 Aug 1547	✔	✔	✔
Coin clipping/ forgery	✖	✖	✔ before 27 Jan 1547	✔	✔	✖
Homicide	✔	✔	✔ before 1 Aug 1547	✔	✔	✔
Arson	✔	✔	✔ before 1 Aug 1547	✔	✔ before 29 September 1549	✔
Rape/ ravishment	✔	✔	✔ before 1 Aug 1547	✔	✔	✖
Robbery	✔	✔	✔ before 1 Aug 1547	✔	✔	✖
Theft	✔	✔	✔	✔	✔	✔

* *SR*, iv. 18. 1 Edw. VI c. 12; *SR*, iv. 33–35. 1 Edw. VI c. 15; *SR*, iv. 95–98. 2 & 3 Edw. VI c. 39; *SR*, iv. 125–128. 3 & 4 Edw. VI c. 24; *SR*, iv. 193–198. 7 Edw. VI c. 14.

and felons convicted of greater offences could be pardoned equally regularly, but with some time spent in confinement. One innovation in the otherwise traditional 1553 pardon also supports this argument: prisoners in the King's Bench or the Marshalsea were excepted, suggesting a new focus on ensuring that felons went through a trial before being pardoned.

This period of experimentation came to an end with the 1553 statute: like its 1544 predecessor, it restores the longer gap between pardons and is unwilling to pardon the greater felonies. Though it becomes visible in 1553, this change of direction probably dates from 1551–1552. On the previous pattern we would expect to see a pardon statute in the parliament which met in the spring of 1552, but none was forthcoming: the reappearance of purgations in Cranmer's register in 1551 may reflect his understanding of the return to traditional methods of releasing clerks convict.[130] The fairly tortuous progress of relevant bills through parliament in 1552 also suggests some conflict among law-makers over the direction of policy: though there was no pardon statute, there was a good deal of discussion of criminal justice. On 23 January, the first day of the session, a bill 'for the Making of Prisons, and Punishment of Vagabonds' was introduced, but it received no further readings.[131] Though the title implies that the prisons in question were intended for the vagabonds, we have seen vagabonds and clerks convict linked in these years. This bill may have been the product of a recognition that if any of the criminal justice innovations of the past several decades were to be preserved, the secular authorities would have to take on some of the structural work previously carried out by the ecclesiastical authorities, most obviously the building and maintaining of prisons.[132] Both the language and the content of many of the statutes proposed and passed over the first half of the century, however, make it clear that parliament largely still saw benefit of clergy as an abuse to be remedied and was either ignorant of the ways in which common law practice had co-opted it, or unconvinced of their value, and so it is likely that a bill which proposed to replace ecclesiastical prisons with an equivalent secular version would not gain much traction.

Indeed, rather than continuing to innovate, this parliament returned to a traditional inclination to limit benefit of clergy. A week after the prison bill disappeared,

[130] See p. 320, n. 94. Given the timing it's likely that Somerset's fall changed the direction of government policy in this area as in others, though there is no direct evidence of his involvement with these changes.

[131] *Commons' Journal*, p. 16.

[132] The founding of Bridewell in 1553 may have been connected to this: John Howes, writing in Elizabeth's reign, claimed that 'all the theves which shoulde be acquytted eyther by theire booke or by proclamacion … shoulde all be broughte to the house of labour and there kept vntyll they mighte be better provided for'. 'A Familiar and Frendely Discourse Dialogue Wyse Setting Forthe the Fyrste Order and Manner of the Erreccions of the Hospitalles Christes, Bridewell and St. Thomas the Apostle' [etc.] (London, 1582) in *Tudor Economic Documents*, ed. R.H. Tawney and Eileen Power (London: Longmans, Green & Co., 1924), vol. 3, p. 417. I am grateful to Paul Cavill for this reference. It is worth noting that thieves acquitted by their books were discussed here in the context of beggars and vagabonds, as in the 1547 Act.

on 30 January, a new bill appeared in the Commons which probably tried to further restrict the crimes for which clergy could be claimed.[133] It passed through the Commons fairly quickly, but on 20 February it was read for a fourth time in the Lords, and there it seems to have died.[134] A statute regarding benefit of clergy was passed in this parliament, but it was a new act which appeared for the first time in the Lords on 21 March as a bill 'That no man, robbing any house, tent, or booth, to have the benefit of clergy'.[135] This too has a slightly muddled process, but was apparently read in the Commons on 1 and 8 April.[136] The bill that was passed seems to have been read in the Commons on 11 April, though it was still titled 'the bills to take away clergy in divers felonies' and on 12 April there was a first reading for yet another bill 'touching the taking away of the benefit of the clergy from certain offenders' in the Lords, though any further progress was halted by the dissolution of parliament on 15 April.[137] Without further information on the debates our reading can only be speculative, but the *Journal* suggests that the Lords argued strenuously over the bill to limit benefit of clergy and some section of the house introduced a competing bill which resolved a long-standing debate over the nature of burglary and which, by broadening that definition, limited benefit of clergy somewhat, but which was significantly narrower than the original bill. In 1552 benefit of clergy was obviously still in play: one group sought to constrain it further, another group sought to refine it, but the parameters of the argument were largely familiar.

It is clear that the pardon statutes of 1547–1550 represent an innovative attempt to preserve a version of the model of imprisonment for felony which had emerged by the end of the previous reign. They follow the earlier trajectory of declining sentences, allowing thieves to go free with something between time served and a year or so of confinement, and those convicted of mid-range felonies to go free after periods of incarceration more typical of those served for theft in the previous reign. More surprisingly, they open the door to pardoning convicted murderers. This growing leniency may have been a cause of the opposition to this innovation which seems to have emerged after Somerset's fall, or the opposition may have been driven by the impersonal nature of the process: individual pardons, after all, even when they were ending a sentence, allowed both for the individual manifestation of royal clemency and for the application of judicial and episcopal discretion.

[133] It was read a second time and ingrossed on 3 February and read a third time on 5 February: *Commons' Journal*, p. 17. The bill was promptly picked up in the Lords and had its third reading on 11 February as the bill 'for the taking away of the clergy from certain offenders'. The Lords' process was a little muddled, and later the same day the bill was read again, 'with request, that certain words, which were amiss there, and lacked for the making of the sentence perfect, might be amended and put in'. Three bills were sent to the Commons on 11 February, possibly including this one: *Lords' Journal*, p. 401.

[134] *Lords' Journal*, pp. 403–404.

[135] *Lords' Journal*, p. 414.

[136] Oddly, the bill for taking clergy from certain offenders was read again in the Lords on 30 and 31 March.

[137] *Commons' Journal*, pp. 21, 22, 23; *Lords' Journal*, pp. 417–418, 424–425.

While pardons by definition extended mercy to those who did not deserve it, there were clearly categories of the more-deserving—the young, the remorseful, the poor and women.[138] Both individual pardons and the general pardons of the early 1540s allowed secular and ecclesiastical authorities to exert some level of control over the access convicted felons had to such pardons and ideally to reap the reward of gratitude such a grant was intended to inspire. The parliamentary pardons of the later 1540s, by contrast, flattened distinctions between deserving and undeserving convicts and removed the objects of mercy from any immediate connection with the source of their benefaction. There is no question that such pardons were more efficient, but as we have noted before, efficiency was not necessarily the most important consideration in the criminal justice system.

4. Conclusion

This chapter has concluded with an analysis of statutory pardons in the late 1540s and early 1550s, not just because those pardons are important in understanding the ongoing desire to use imprisonment as a standardized form of punishment under increasingly challenging circumstances, but because the core source material for this study, the King's Bench plea rolls, largely disappears. This is not the same kind of disappearance as the gaol delivery rolls: the King's Bench rolls survive for these years, indeed they grow in bulk, but the records of the Crown side of the court shrink, and they contain nothing on sanctuary or benefit of clergy after 1542. This is probably because sanctuary and benefit of clergy had been so thoroughly worked over in parliament in these years that there was little for King's Bench to grapple with, and when problems did appear on circuit they were likely to be referred to parliament for solution rather than to King's Bench. For example, when it became apparent that the language in the repeals act of 1547 was ambiguous, a statute was hastily passed the following year to clarify that those who stole a single horse were just as ineligible for benefit of clergy as those who stole more.[139] The statute must have been tested on circuit, but in this case the disjunction between the intention and the language was clear, and in an era where the language of statutes was increasingly directive, a revised statute was probably the only option. The 1552 statute on burglary discussed above also demonstrates parliament intervening where the courts might previously have reached consensus. As we have seen, the definition of burglary was in flux through this period: an earlier focus on breaking into the house by night gradually gave way to a focus on the inhabitants of the house and the fear they experienced as part of the crime. We've seen a case in King's Bench

[138] Kesselring, *Mercy and Authority*, pp. 77–82, argues that women were less likely to receive an individual pardon than men, but after 1559 the focus shifted to poor felons, especially poor women.
[139] *SR*, IV. 74. 2 & 3 Edw. VI c. 33.

which seemed to assume that male servants might be expected to feel less fear than female, and the statutes as framed had allowed such room for interpretation. The 1552 statute rehearses the 1532 and 1540 statutes and clarifies that in future one who is convicted of a burglary where the owner, his wife, his children or his servants were in any part of the house or the precinct, asleep or awake, or anyone who steals from a booth or a tent at a fair or market while the owner et al. are present, shall not be eligible for benefit of clergy. Not only does this remove the kind of judicial discretion which had been common in the early years of the century, it expands the understanding of burglary to contain all the previous elements: one who broke into a house by night and terrified the inhabitants would get the same punishment as one who broke into a storehouse by day while the family were in another part of the precinct and unaware of the act until they discovered goods or money missing. As parliament steadily put this kind of stamp on the law, reducing the number of crimes for which clergy was available and reducing the discretion available in managing those crimes, there was simply less for King's Bench to do.

The years from 1537 to 1553 represent a sharp break with the preceding decades, as a steady and fairly consistent process of criminal justice reform was undermined by the fallout from religious reform. Core elements of the earlier changes survived: the worst abuses of benefit of clergy, for example, had been tamed. But the potential for further development inherent in the system of the 1530s was lost. While the experiments of Edward VI's reign make it clear that the appetite and the opportunity for innovation was still there, it proved impossible find a model which aligned legal needs, financial resources, and political realities in the ways the earlier reforms had done. By the end of Edward VI's reign sanctuary and benefit of clergy were in much the same state as they were at the end of his father's. The former was probably still in operation, but much reduced and off the record. The latter was the preserve of poor men—men in the same sphere as vagabonds—who committed minor felonies. Men of this kind doubtless continued to make claims of clergy on circuit, successfully, but the Church no longer had any vested interest in them, and the common lawyers no longer had much room for manoeuver, and so they fade away into records that no longer survive.

10
Epilogue

The ability to maintain order was a crucial marker of effective kingship throughout the later Middle Ages, and it was of great practical importance to a dynasty founded on usurpation. From the moment of Henry VII's accession to the throne he looked for ways to establish his authority in the counties: this was both a practical and a political necessity as he brought over-mighty subjects under control and disposed of a succession of pretenders. Though the fear of deposition faded somewhat, it was replaced by the more amorphous disruptions caused by the upsets of the early sixteenth century. As social relations were strained by economic dislocation, social mobility, and religious difference, maintaining order without inflaming tensions became ever more difficult and ever more necessary. The common lawyers went about their business with little direct reference to the social realities within which they were operating, but the criminal justice reforms they accomplished had their origin in the intensification of government driven by Henry VII and their conclusion in the religious changes driven by his son. Throughout they were profoundly shaped by the traditions of thought and practice handed down through the profession.

The principles Fyneux expressed in 1500 were brought to fruition by Cromwell far more thoroughly than the chief justice could have imagined and in a context he did not live to see. Fyneux sought to establish the proper relationship, within the common law, between an assertive modern monarch and the Church to which he owed religious loyalty and with which he could work in partnership. Cromwell sought to establish royal authority over the Church and was comfortable using the common law as a tool to achieve that end. Along the way the ecclesiastical hierarchy lost not only the independent control of their criminal justice institutions, but any reason to be invested in the outcomes. After 1540 they were increasingly distanced from their system: with the end of the specifically clerical version of benefit of clergy there was no longer any incentive for the bishops to support the prisons in order to sustain their own privilege, and as the monasteries were dissolved the chartered sanctuaries mostly dissolved along with them. Though the bishops continued to hold clerks convict in their prisons and the secular sanctuaries were often attached to churches, the connection was much looser than it had ever been.

The legal story told here represents a real change in the management of criminal justice. Though it is easy to be skeptical about the rehabilitation of clerks convict in any period, there is no doubt that early in the reign of Henry VII the bishops kept

The King's Felons. Margaret McGlynn, Oxford University Press. © Margaret McGlynn 2023.
DOI: 10.1093/oso/9780192887689.003.0011

men who had been convicted of a wide variety of felonies in custody for extended periods of time, thus saving them from execution while ensuring that they endured a fairly harsh punishment. By the second half of the reign the time convicts spent in confinement was falling while their numbers were rising. The justices had found a way to solve the age-old problem of balancing the severity of the crime and the severity of the punishment: both judges and juries were more comfortable convicting felons knowing that they might face imprisonment rather than execution, but the static resources available within the system meant that the rise in the number of clerks convict had to be balanced by a drop in the number of years they served. The balance reached after about 1495 was a good one, and the patterns of incarceration remained fairly stable for the next thirty-five years, though the number of felons rose.

The political story is rather more complex, and there is a clear tension throughout the period between the 'tough on crime' lobby who wished to tighten up on the punishment of felons and those who recognized that such an approach would be counter-productive. Parliament was dominated by the former, and parliamentary attempts to reduce access to benefit of clergy were rarely informed by actual practices or problems in the courts before the 1530s. The justices mostly stayed out of skirmishes between MPs who sought to limit benefit of clergy and the ecclesiastical authorities who supported it on principle.[1] They also tended to ignore or work around parliamentary restrictions, focusing instead on refining the system they were building in the counties to confine, manage and track clerks convict and to distribute abjurers. The upheavals of the Reformation threw these established patterns into turmoil, and as the ecclesiastical hierarchy lost both power and resources they were less able to withstand the pressures of those who wished to be tough on crime, reinforced as they were by those who wished to be tough on the clergy. The changed political circumstances meant that the pace of change picked up and the discourse around it changed somewhat, but for a decade or so the criminal law remained conservative to the extent that the new statutes drew on past practices and the trajectory remained fairly consistent with the patterns established in the first decades of the century. The common lawyers took clearer ownership of the running of the ecclesiastical prison system, they brought sanctuary under closer secular control and they began to apply the same limitations to those in minor and major orders as they had previously applied to lay criminals. By the late 1530s the slow steady change seemed to be bearing fruit in a model of criminal confinement that was largely under secular control (though ecclesiastically funded) and reasonably graduated, standardized and consistent. It was only after 1540 that the logic of

[1] Though we have virtually no evidence for the drivers behind these patterns, it is tempting to see the parliamentary push for harshness as reflecting the concerns of the county powers with local criminality, given the proportion of justices of the peace among the members of parliament (MPs), and the judicial inclination to find sources of mitigation as reflecting the concerns of the central powers with maintaining order in the broader sense.

the Reformation changes, political, financial and ideological, began to bear heavily upon it. After a decade of increasingly innovative experiments sanctuary disappeared and benefit of clergy emerged as a stripped-down method for incarcerating lower-level felons for short periods of time: the other possibilities of the system were so far out of reach that they were, and have remained, forgotten.

This is a fairly demoralizing conclusion to such a fertile period of experimentation, but the processes that Fyneux drove had important consequences. Most obviously, thousands of men avoided the gallows by claiming clergy between 1490 and 1540, and many thousands more in the succeeding centuries. We have long known that benefit of clergy served as a form of mitigation, but recognizing the scale on which it was used and understanding that those lives were saved as part of an intentional process of criminal justice reform, means understanding that not only were some reprieved, but others were punished for their crimes when they might previously have gone free.[2] For several decades around the turn of the sixteenth century the justices intentionally sent convicted felons to prison, and they forced this convict population on the ecclesiastical hierarchy rather than the other way around. They may also have forced this change on other elements of the governing classes, given their attitude to parliament's approach to benefit of clergy. In the reign of Henry VII and early in the reign of his son the justices were clearly happy to work around parliament when they saw fit, and it's likely that Fyneux was largely responsible for the relatively consistent approach King's Bench took to criminal punishment during his tenure. His death in 1525, followed by the growing confidence and range of parliament in the 1530s and after, meant that the justices had less discretion. It's impossible to tell from the surviving records if Fyneux's approach was supported by common lawyers more broadly: as we saw in *Standish's Case*, it is dangerous to assume that all the clergy fell on the same side of any putative Church/State divide, and it is equally dangerous to assume that common lawyers agreed over either policy or practice. Still, though individual lawyers may have had qualms in individual cases, and definitive decisions were hard to come by, the overall movement of the law was clear.

Nevertheless, looking at the reports of individual cases in the context of the activities in the courts is a salutary reminder that every argument in every case was specific to that case. While any argument might have been worth noting and pondering for a practicing lawyer, we should not rush to take it as a statement of what the law was: at best it represents a statement of what one lawyer hoped the law might be for that particular client at that particular moment. The constrained inventiveness of the profession meant that there was always a variety of ideas available for expansion and development, but only time and circumstance would determine which threads of the tapestry would dominate the pattern as it

[2] A small proportion of them presumably would have been held in confinement for longer had the late fifteenth century model continued.

developed. Townshend's argument in the run-up to *Stafford's Case* may have reflected ideas circulating in the profession in the 1480s or it may have been a blatant ploy to curry favour, for example: without the events of the 1530s to throw it into relief, would it have attracted any scholarly attention? The politically prominent cases, like the statutes, are seductive in their availability, but they are only one element of the story, and without the records of practice are as likely to push us to the wrong conclusions as the right ones.

Having shifted our perspective, we should also re-consider how we understand developments in the following decades against the backdrop of this collapse of the Henrician reforms in the 1540s. Edward's sisters, and their parliaments, continued to tinker with the criminal justice system they inherited. The records of the 1555 parliament demonstrate that sanctuary and benefit of clergy were not dead letters, and their role and range exercised this and the next parliament. On 25 October a bill to take benefit of clergy from accessories to murder was introduced in the Commons, and it was read again the following day, the same day that a bill 'touching abjurations' appeared in the Lords.[3] While the latter promptly disappeared, the former was read and ingrossed in the Commons on 31 October as the bill to remove clergy and sanctuary from accessories to murder or felony, a substantial expansion of the original title.[4] The inclusion of sanctuary in the bill may simply be a throwback to the inclination of the 1530s and 1540s to think of sanctuary and benefit of clergy as complementary, or it may be a concession to those who supported the abjuration bill. It does suggest, however, that sanctuary was less defunct than we tend to assume. Indeed the newly restored abbot and convent of Westminster went in procession on 6 December 1555, during this sitting of parliament, and in the procession were 'all the santuary men with crosse keys apon their garments, and after whent iij for murder'.[5] Brief as the entry is, it confirms that Westminster continued to offer sanctuary for felony, including murder, and that the sanctuary men continued to wear the kinds of badges required under the 1536 statute, indicating that some parts of the Henrician processes remained active.

Although the abjuration bill disappeared, the accessories bill continued to work its way through parliament. It was read for a third time in the Commons on 2 November, though it had been refined to apply to 'procurers in murder and felonies': it appeared in the Lords on 5 November under the same title and was sent

[3] *Commons Journal*, p. 42; *Lords Journal*, p. 494.

[4] *Commons Journal*, p. 43.

[5] J.G. Nichols ed. *The Diary of Henry Machyn* Camden Soc. Vol. 42 (London: Camden Society, 1848), p. 121. J. Charles Cox, *The Sanctuaries and Sanctuary Seekers of Medieval England* (London; George Allen & Sons, 1911), pp. 75–77 also gives various examples of people going into sanctuary in the later 1550s from Mary's *Acts of the Privy Council*. Loades notes that the abbey had only been restored on 18 November and argues that the sanctuary men were probably there before the restoration, since it is unlikely that they could have been assembled so quickly: D.M. Loades, 'The Sanctuary' in *Westminster Abbey Reformed 1540–1640* edited by C.S. Knighton and Richard Mortimer (Aldershot: Ashgate, 2003), p. 83.

to committee the following day.[6] The change in title suggests that bill was related to the case of Benedict Smythe and Gilles Rufford, which appeared in the Commons on 18 November, the same day as a new bill 'for a more grievous Punishment for Murder'.[7] According to Rufford's wife, Smythe had first maliciously appealed her husband for robbery, and then had him falsely indicted. Rufford was acquitted by the jury on the indictment and Smythe was nonsuited on the appeal; Rufford sued successfully for damages of £100, whereupon Smythe successfully procured his murder. Smythe and the main witnesses to the case were brought before the Commons on 22 November and examined. Two men confessed to the actual murder and pointed to Smythe as the procurer; after their removal from the House Smythe confessed. This was a dramatic event, and led to a most unusual statute which provided that if Smythe were convicted he would not be allowed benefit of clergy.[8] The House seems to have decided to focus on this single outrageous case however, and though the bills to remove benefit of clergy and sanctuary from procurers of murders and felonies (after Smythe's hearing called the 'bill to punish procurers of murder') and the bill for a more grievous punishment for murder were read again at the end of the month, neither passed.

Though parliament did not meet again until early 1558 it picked up on the problem with accessories immediately. This time it focused on the particular problem of procurement from the beginning, suggesting that Smythe was a single example of a larger problem. It tried a new tack, and on 24 January a bill was introduced into the Lords 'that Hirers, Commanders, and Counsellors, to any wilful Murders, Robberies, etc. ... be adjudged principal Offenders'. This attempt to turn accessories into principals did not garner support, and the following day the bill returned to a more traditional format as it sought to remove benefit of clergy from such accessories. Even in this format the bill provoked fairly extensive discussion as it was ingrossed twice before passing on 31 January.[9] It was read in the Commons the same day, suggesting some urgency, but it was as controversial there as it had been in the Lords. On 3 February it was argued that a new bill should be made, and that bill was read on 8, 9, and 10 February before being returned to the Lords, where it passed on 15 February.[10] The bill that passed was short and to the point: it removed benefit of clergy from anyone who hired or counselled anyone to commit petty treason, murder, robbery, highway robbery, or arson of houses or barns.[11] These crimes had been non-clergiable under Henry VIII—accessories were clear beneficiaries of the Edwardian repeals act—and so this statute once again left

[6] *Commons Journal*, p. 43; *Lords Journal*, pp. 497–498.

[7] *Commons Journal*, p. 44.

[8] *SR*, IV. 292–293. 2 & 3 Philip & Mary c. 17.

[9] *Lords Journal*, pp. 515–518.

[10] *Commons Journal*, p. 48; *Lords Journal*, p. 524.

[11] *SR*, IV. 322. 4 & 5 Philip & Mary c. 4. The bill also provided that peers indicted of such offences should be tried by peers: the *Lords Journal* notes that when the new bill came back from the Commons the original bill returned with it, and this may have been the focus of their concern.

accessories before the fact without clergy. This was not an innovative statute, and procurers of felony were not a sympathetic class of criminals, so it is striking how hard parliament found it to pass this statute, and how focused the final act was.

While the accessories bill was making its rocky way through the Commons, the House was also considering the fate of sanctuaries. On 8 February, the same day as the first reading of the accessories bill, a 'bill touching sanctuaries' was introduced. It was read again on 9 February, but replaced on 11 February by a new bill addressing 'what churches shall be reputed for sanctuaries'.[12] This seems to have been intended to clarify the implications of Edward VI's repeal act for sanctuaries by finally abolishing all chartered sanctuaries and, while recognizing the traditional sanctuary rights of parish churches and churchyards, prohibiting abjuration from them.[13] It was noted that 'abjuration could neither be made into the parts beyond the seas, the same being forbidden by the statute [of Henry VIII], nor into any sanctuary within the realm, where none was indeed, though at Westminster by usurpation and permission it had of late been used'.[14] Westminster Abbey, as usual, represented the most visible and politically important version of sanctuary available: since sanctuary men were apparently living there under the noses of the MPs the abbot was allowed to address parliament 'to show by what warrant he held Sanctuary at Westminster'.

Though the *Commons Journal* notes that Abbot Feckenham was appointed to come with his counsel, he arrived the following day 'only with one monk attending on him, bearing two old muniments: the one whereof was the charter of sanctuary granted to the house of Westminster by King Edward the Saint; the other a confirmation of the same charter, with a censure, by curse, upon the breaches thereof, made at request of the said King Edward by the Pope John'.[15] Thus armed, Abbot Feckenham's speech opened with the assumption that parliament could not possibly mean to abolish all sanctuaries, 'for that were too much injurious, considering that sanctuaries and places of refuge are, and always have been, used and inviolably maintained, not only in every country throughout Christendom, but also among the Jews, yea and among the Turks and infidels'.[16] His purpose was to demonstrate why Westminster should be among those sanctuaries chosen to continue. He proceeded with a history of the sanctuary from its foundation 1400 years earlier by King Lucius to its end 'at the time of the late schism' and its restoration under Philip and Mary.[17] Much as Dean Caudray had a century earlier, he made

[12] *Commons Journal*, pp. 48–49.

[13] Arthur Penrhyn Stanley, *Historical Memorials of Westminster Abbey* (London: John Murray, 1868), p. 610.

[14] Stanley, *Historical Memorials*, p. 610.

[15] *Commons Journal*, p. 49; Stanley, *Historical Memorials*, p. 610. At the end of his speech Feckenham noted that the survival of these documents was a miracle, as one of Pole's servants found a child playing with them in the street.

[16] Stanley, *Historical Memorials*, p. 611.

[17] Stanley, *Historical Memorials*, pp. 611–613.

an appeal to parliament's self-interest, warning them 'to have in consideration the profit and commodities that you have received thereby . . . queens, princes, dukes, earls, barons, knights and all sorts have been preserved by sanctuary, so as all degrees of you owe thankful consideration to sanctuary; for by sanctuary your lives, bodies, and goods have been preserved'.[18] He concluded by referring to Mary's restoration of the Abbey's privileges, and asked to be allowed to return to parliament again with counsel and any further documents he could find. The House agreed and Feckenham returned three days later 'with Mr. Plowden and Doctor Storye of his counsel, alleging his old grants of kings for the sanctuary and also the Queen's grant'.[19] The House appointed a committee to examine the grants, but in the three weeks before the end of the session the committee did not report and the sanctuaries bill disappeared.

This parliament indicates that though there was still an appetite in some quarters to further limit benefit of clergy and sanctuary, both institutions were still functioning and had fairly strong support. Loades dismisses Feckenham's speech as 'an exercise in selective amnesia' and argues that parliament would 'have known that his memory of recent events was seriously defective', but given that those men were intimately familiar with Westminster and its environs, it seems more likely that Feckenham was representing a living tradition.[20] The whole episode suggests that enough parliamentarians recognized the value of sanctuary, tenuous and ambiguous as it was in the middle of the century, to be unwilling to stamp it out entirely. Similarly, the attempts to further limit benefit of clergy, attempts which would simply restore a Henrician limitation, and which were made manifest in parliament in the singularly unattractive person of Benedict Smythe, needed two sessions and a great deal of discussion to pass. The rollercoaster ride of the 1530s and 1540s was indeed over: the model of the late 1540s, diminished as it was, best fit the available resources and the needs of the criminal justice system.

Instead of investing much time or energy on that front, the government seems to have turned most of its attention to the administration of criminal justice in the counties. Mary shared some of her grandfather's concerns with stability in the localities: though her early parliaments, largely absorbed with political and religious matters, spent little time on criminal justice, her first parliament did pass a statute forbidding sheriffs from acting as justices of the peace while in that office. This was aimed at curbing an obvious abuse of power in the counties, and was the first of a number of such statutes in her reign.[21] Her third parliament, which opened in November 1554, linked this political concern with a standard part of

[18] Stanley, *Historical Memorials*, p. 615.

[19] *Commons Journal*, p. 49. The focus on royal foundation grants rather than papal reflects the final and complete victory of the arguments of the 1520s, even under this Catholic queen: see pp. 219–220.

[20] Loades, 'Sanctuary', pp. 83, 87. Cf. his point about the continuity of sanctuary men above n. 5.

[21] *SR*, IV. 207. 1 Mary c. 8.

the legal process, bailing prisoners accused of felony.[22] Since 1487 such prisoners could not be bailed by a single justice of the peace; the decision required the consent of at least two justices, one of whom must be of the quorum.[23] According to the 1554 preamble, however, individual justices had been avoiding the provision by accusing offenders of suspicion of felony and bailing them on that charge, as a result of which they had 'often tymes by sinister labour and meanes sett at large the greatest and notablest Offenders'. A bill to curb the abuse was introduced in the Lords on 21 November 1554 and moved steadily through its readings, passing on 6 December.[24] It appeared in the Commons the following day, but its passage there was much rockier: the original bill seems to have been jettisoned in favour of a new version which went to committee twice. This version provided that two justices (who must both be physically present) would be required to bail anyone accused of felony or suspicion of felony; that before bailing him they would examine the prisoner and 'them that bringes him' on the circumstances of the crime 'or asmuche therof as shalbee material to prove the felonye', and that they would certify a written copy of the examination as well as the bail at the next gaol delivery. The new bill was finally passed in the Commons on 14 January 1555, returned to the Lords the same day and passed at the last possible moment, on 15 January, the day before parliament was dissolved.[25] As Langbein notes, this was an extraordinary level of debate, and he concludes that the Commons was greatly exercised by a bill which might significantly affect the 'power adjustments between the rulers of the realm and the "rulers of the county"', since a large proportion of Tudor MPs had been, were, or would be justices of the peace.[26] Though we don't know what the original bill contained, the statute clearly intended the certified examination of the accused and his accuser to serve as a check on the discretion of the justices of the peace: the act remained very much in the spirit of its 1487 predecessor, but the solution it adopted drew on developments in the recording and management of the criminal justice system in the decades since.

Parliament returned to this issue in its next session, which opened on 21 October 1555. A bill 'that Justices of Peace shall take Examination of Suspects of Manslaughter and Felony' was introduced in the Commons on 4 November and passed five days later with none of the wrangling associated with its predecessor.[27]

22 *SR*, IV. 259. 1 & 2 Philip & Mary c. 13.

23 *SR*, II. 512–513. 3 Hen. VII c. 4.

24 *Lords Journal*, pp. 468, 474.

25 *Commons Journal*, pp. 39, 40, 41; *Lords Journal*, pp. 488–489.

26 John H. Langbein, *Prosecuting Crime in the Renaissance* (Cambridge, MA: Harvard University Press, 1974), p. 58.

27 *Commons Journal*, p. 43. There was some administrative confusion. On 7 November another bill appeared in the Commons dealing with the bailing of prisoners accused of manslaughter or felony: the following day these two were combined into a single bill 'for bailment and examination of prisoners'. The reference to bail was dropped in the final title of the bill. Langbein argues that the confusion was at least partly because the draftsman drew heavily on the language of the January act: *Prosecuting Crime*, p. 38.

It moved equally smoothly through the Lords between 12 and 18 November.[28] This act, which was much shorter than its predecessor, rehearsed the earlier statute and provided that justices of the peace should conduct a similar examination and provide the same certification when committing an accused felon to prison as when bailing him, since such examination 'is as necessarie or reither more, then where suche Prysoner shalbee let to Bayle or Mayneprice'.[29] Langbein argues that with this provision 'the figure of the investigating magistrate had stumbled into the common law', but it is probably more accurate to say that he had stumbled into the statute book, for the statute does rather less than has been attributed to it.[30] Both its language and its passage through parliament suggest that this statute, like the 1548 statute on horsetheft, was covering a loophole: if the justices of the peace could corruptly bail those who should be imprisoned, they could equally corruptly imprison those who should be bailed—a decision that could have far worse consequences for the accused, as the statute recognized—and in both cases the record of the examination would allow the gaol delivery judges to determine if the justices had shown fear or favour. The suggestion that these statutes created either an inquisitorial process or an investigatory magistracy is also undermined by Robison's demonstration that in the early 1530s, more than twenty years earlier, a conscientious but ordinary justice of the peace carried out an extensive investigation into a murder within his jurisdiction, complete with examinations and depositions.[31] Bellamy notes that in 1554 'common judicial practice was now being given proper sanction by means of statute', and this is true, but more importantly the requirement that these documents be certified before the justices of gaol delivery provided statutory sanction for those justices' oversight of the local process.[32]

[28] *Lords Journal*, pp. 500, 502.

[29] *SR*, IV. 286. 2 & 3 Philip & Mary c. 10.

[30] Langbein, *Prosecuting Crime*, p. 62. Powell assumes that the main thrust of the statute is the justice's binding over of the accuser to give evidence at trial and the prosecutorial role that implies: Edward Powell, 'Jury Trial at Gaol Delivery in the Late Middle Ages: The Midland Circuit, 1400–1429', in *Twelve Good Men and True: The Criminal Jury Trial in England, 1200–1800* edited by J.S Cockburn and T.A. Green (Princeton: Princeton University Press, 1988), p. 107, but cf. J.S. Cockburn, 'Trial by the Book? Fact and Theory in the Criminal Process, 1558–1625' in *Legal Records and the Historian* edited by J.H. Baker (London: Royal Historical Society, 1978), pp. 69–71; he argues that the justices themselves often failed to appear at the trials of those they had bound or bailed, but the accused were convicted in their absence.

[31] William B. Robison, 'Murder at Crowhurst: A Case Study in Early Tudor Law', *Criminal Justice History* 9 (1988), pp. 31–62.

[32] Bellamy, *Criminal Law and Society*, p. 41. There was one further attempt to manage the justices of the peace in this parliament: on 30 October a bill was introduced in the Commons that 'no Man's Servants, wearing their Cloths, shall be Justices of Peace, but the King's and Queen's'. By the following day the title had been amended so that the reference to livery and to the king had been dropped, but the bill moved forwards. It was read and engrossed in the Commons on 7 November (with the reference to the king restored) and read again on 12 November with the more neutral title 'The Bill, what Persons shall be Justices of Peace'. When it appeared in the Lords the following day it had been reframed to provide 'That divers Persons shall not be Justices of Peace' and it was read three more times under that title before being rejected on 18 November. *Commons Journal*, pp. 43–44; *Lords Journal*, pp. 500–502.

The Marian statutes on the justices of the peace reflect the same kinds of problems that Henry VII faced, but besides dealing with the county power structures by stacking the commissions of the peace, Mary had the option, and the capacity, to take on the problem more directly, and this is the less-obvious consequence of the experiments with benefit of clergy and sanctuary. The centuries-old struggle to ensure that justices of the peace were representatives of central government rather than local power was advanced by tools developed in the last few decades, not only the obvious expansion in the use of statutes under her father, but also the habits of oversight and reporting by the justices of gaol delivery under both her father and her grandfather reflected in the two 1555 statutes on the justices of the peace.

At the same time, Mary also built upon the use of pardons by her father's and her brother's governments. She had issued the customary pardon at her coronation, one which was as broad as might be expected for a queen whose road to the throne was as rocky as hers. It pardoned all treasons and felonies, but though no crimes were specifically excepted, 'any offense or offenses . . . of which any evidence is now before our bench or Court of Exchequer' was.[33] Edward's pardons had increasingly assumed that the felon needed to complete the trial process, but this was the first general pardon which explicitly prevented claimants from walking away from the process in the courts. And after that first traditional pardon, Mary did not issue any further parliamentary pardons during her reign, perhaps conscious of the indiscriminate nature of parliamentary mercy, and keen to reap the rewards of the mercy she could offer directly. Instead, in August 1554 her Privy Council instructed all the justices of assize to stay the execution of all prisoners on the circuits 'whose offences are not with in the compasse of treason, burgularie, rape, robbing of churches, robbing by the heigh waye, [or] willful murder', the typical crimes excepted from the pardon statutes.[34] In February 1555, eighty-six men and women were pardoned under those terms, followed by another twenty-four in July.[35] Though we can't be sure that these were the felons whose executions were stayed it seems probable that they were: they represented all six circuits and the numbers are comparable with those convicted on the circuits in the previous decade [table 10.1]. Like her predecessors, Mary was looking for a regular way to release those guilty of lesser felonies, but she wanted to keep the pardoning process under tighter control than parliamentary pardons allowed: asking the justices to stay executions and, presumably, to return lists of the names of the condemned and their crimes, allowed her to strike a balance between the impersonality and randomness of the

33 Paul L. Hughes and James F. Larkin ed. *Tudor Royal Proclamations vol. II: The Later Tudors* (New Haven: Yale University Press, 1969), p. 15.

34 *Acts of the Privy Council of England Volume 5, 1554–1556* ed. John Roche Dasent (London: Her Majesty's Stationary Office, 1892), pp. 67–68.

35 *CPR Philip & Mary* vol. 2, pp. 39–41; 44–45. In June 1555 the privy council ordered the keeper of the King's Bench prison to bring a list of his condemned prisoners and the reasons why they had not been executed, probably as part of the same process: *APC* vol. 5, pp. 144–145.

Table 10.1 Recorded convictions 1543, 1544; pardons 1555*

Circuit	Convicted Summer 1543	Convicted Spring 1544	Pardoned Feb 1555	Pardoned July 1555
Home	12	8	15	-
Midland	25	26	30	1
Western	32	40	1	22
Oxford	4	-	25	-
Norfolk	14	7	3	-
Northern	-	-	2	-
Other**	-	-	10	1
Total	**87**	**81**	**86**	**24**

*Data collected from TNA KB9/556 mm. 3, 3d, 5, 6–10, 71, 74, 75, 136d; KB9/558 mm. 103–105, 106, 193, 193d; *CPR Philip & Mary* vol. 2, pp. 39–41; 44–45.

**London 2; Wales 8; Bristol 1

parliamentary pardon and the cost and complexity of the individual pardon.[36] These pardons were granted in the months between the first statute on the justices of the peace and the second in 1555, and it seems clear that both were part of the same process of asserting royal control over local justice.

Elizabeth continued to tweak the model in small but important ways. Her circuit pardons picked up on Mary's 1555 pardon but again streamlined the process. After 1559 the circuit justices submitted lists of those condemned at the sessions who they thought should be pardoned based on their character and the nature of the offence.[37] This meant that individual offenders were no longer faced with the daunting prospect of navigating the pardon system, but the justices could exercise discretion in the granting of pardons, and, equally importantly, could represent royal mercy far more effectively than a faceless statute. Kesselring notes that there were often more than a hundred pardons a year, again roughly in line with the Marian numbers with a slight increase.[38]

Elizabeth's parliaments also continued to tweak the use of benefit of clergy. In 1566 parliament removed it from pickpockets and cutpurses: the 1553 pardon statute had excepted robbery from the person, and, like the accessories statute of

[36] Mary did continue to issue individual pardons through this period. Apart from those connected to the rebellion, they were mostly for excepted crimes such as burglary or robbery, or for outlawry: e.g. *CPR P&M* vol. 2, pp. 53, 72, 76, 87–88; 89, 98, 102–103, 113, 140, 149, 150.

[37] K.J. Kesselring, *Mercy and Authority in the Tudor State* (Cambridge: Cambridge University Press, 2003), p. 80.

[38] Kesselring, *Mercy and Authority*, pp. 80–81. She calculates that 1,730 individuals got a circuit pardon in Elizabeth's reign.

1558, this brought benefit of clergy back into line with a consistent sense of which crimes were mitigable.[39] The 1566 statute assumes that clerks convict were being delivered to the ordinary and purged in the traditional way, but this was soon to end. A statute of 1575 removed benefit of clergy for rape or burglary, again returning to the norms of the 1553 pardon statute, but it also provided that anyone who successfully claimed clergy could be released after branding, rather than being delivered to the ordinary. The justices who allowed the claim of clergy could, however, choose to send the clerk convict to prison for a period of up to a year, at their discretion.[40] As we saw, periods of confinement for clerks convict had already fallen to somewhere in the range of a year or two by the late 1530s, and the pardons of the 1540s had allowed those convicted of the lesser felonies, whether clerks or not, to go free with little or no confinement. This statute allowed the justices to manage that process on the ground, in much the same way that they were managing the pardon process.

Conclusion

Lander argued that in Henry VII's reign 'at best administration and justice were conducted in an atmosphere of imprecision. The entire system creaked under the disadvantage of a lack of exact knowledge'.[41] A century later, though error, inefficiency and simple malice had surely not been driven from the system, it was much more precise and exact in a variety of ways. First, developing the processes of mitigation had encouraged the better definition of crimes. As long as every felony was punishable by execution, there was little incentive to define crimes precisely: even earlier versions of benefit of clergy, which assumed the limited literacy of the laity, had done little to change this. The elaboration of a more nuanced model of punishment, however, had the incidental effect of allowing a more nuanced definition of felony. The intentional expansion of benefit of clergy, the steady exercise of judicial discretion in court, the arguments over statutory attempts to limit benefit of clergy, and the pardon statutes all forced the legal community to grapple with the various elements of various crimes and to rank them. They did not reach complete agreement—arson and rape, for example, did not settle into a consistent position—but crimes like murder, burglary, highway robbery and pickpocketing were much more clearly defined and differentiated in 1575 than they had been a century earlier.

Second, while pardons had been a core prerogative of royal justice for centuries, they became a key element of the criminal justice system in this period. Pardons

[39] *SR*, IV. 488. 8 Eliz c. 4.
[40] *SR*, IV. 617–618. 18 Eliz. c. 7.
[41] J.R. Lander, *English Justices of the Peace 1461–1509* (Gloucester, UK: Alan Sutton, 1989), p. 173.

have been well-studied: we understand their political value, whether explicitly in the pardon of rebellion or the conversion of rebels or criminals into soldiers, or implicitly through a consideration of the implications of royal mercy for royal authority and the subjects' allegiance.[42] Far less attention has been paid to their operation within the criminal justice system, and none to the ways in which they interacted with other forms of mitigation. It is clear that in the early sixteenth century they provided a practical way to solve logical and procedural problems in other forms of mitigation which were otherwise insoluble, and thus became a means for ending terms of imprisonment on a case-by-case basis. This ad hoc solution was systematized and scaled up on an experimental basis in the 1540s, and while the more innovative elements of the experiments were not entirely successful, they did cement the value of pardons as part of the criminal justice machinery and point towards the emergence of the circuit pardons.

Third, the evolution of benefit of clergy made it possible to think about punishments for felony in a new way. Our understanding of benefit of clergy has been enormously hampered by the survival of the name while the substance changed so very dramatically. In the late fifteenth century a distinctly secular version of benefit of clergy already existed, but it was deeply intertwined with the clerical version. The 1490 statute liberated it from its sibling and it began a period of independent development. By 1540 it had been so thoroughly filtered through common law practice and statute that nothing of its ecclesiastical origins remained except its name and its exercise in ecclesiastical prisons, albeit prisons firmly in the hand of the king. This change could never have been brought about in one fell swoop, or over a short period of time—the attempt to change sanctuary bears witness to the need for deep foundations and slow adaptation. But having made the transition from seeing benefit of clergy as a useful mitigation of punishment for a fairly random selection of felons, to a beneficial mitigation for a more carefully considered group of felons, to an appropriate punishment for a circumscribed group of felons, the common lawyers could go on to imagine other ways in which felons and felonies could be punished, from the inclusion of women in benefit of clergy to the introduction of transportation and the eventual re-introduction of imprisonment. There is no direct line from the ecclesiastical confinement of the early Tudor period to the secular imprisonment of the eighteenth century, but the capacity to imagine and implement intentional and consistent non-capital punishment opened the path for later developments.

Finally, as a result of all these changes, the central court justices had a much firmer grasp on the criminal justice system. Their assertion of control over ecclesiastical prisons was something of a Pyrrhic victory, but it was a victory nonetheless.

[42] Naomi Hurnard, *The King's Pardon for Homicide before A.D. 1307* (Oxford: Clarendon Press, 1969), Kesselring, *Mercy and Authority*, Helen Lacey, *The Royal Pardon: Access to Mercy in Fourteenth-Century England* Woodbridge: York Medieval Press, 2009.

From the time of Henry VII the Westminster judges steadily worked to extend their authority over episcopal prisons and chartered sanctuaries, to direct the work of the coroners in bringing abjurers and eventually sanctuaries into the remit of the common law, and to ensure that the records generated by gaol deliveries should be available to them as and when needed. In the mid fifteenth century the common law judges played a relatively limited role in the criminal justice process: for the most part the justices of the peace managed the indictment, bailing and imprisoning of the accused; the judge presided over the trial but the jury might nullify and the ordinary might demand his clerks, to do with as he saw fit; the judge sentenced but the king might pardon. By the mid sixteenth century the judges oversaw the justices of the peace, the prisons and a standardized pardon process. They lost almost every fight the first time around, but they won most of them in the end: in the process they expanded the sense of what the system could and should do and demonstrated that the justices could, and probably should, assert effective control over the workings of criminal justice in the counties. Though the struggle between county power and central power was by no means over, central power had taken a big step forward.

This was partly possible because central mercy had also taken a big step forward. Though the spottiness of the records and the variety of approaches taken by historians make it hard to provide a smooth graph of the change, it is widely agreed that conviction rates for felony went up over the late Middle Ages and into the early modern period. From a low of somewhere around 15–20 per cent in the early fourteenth century they rose to somewhere around 35 per cent in the late fifteenth and early sixteenth century and up to around 55 per cent by the mid to late sixteenth century.[43] At the same time, the proportion of those executed for felony dropped, from around 76 per cent of those convicted in the reign of Henry VII to about 65 per cent of those convicted in the 1540s, to 40 per cent in the late sixteenth century.[44] As more were convicted, fewer were executed—or perhaps as fewer were executed, more were convicted.[45] We saw a new emphasis in the mid-century pardon statutes on the need to go through the trial process before reprieve: taken together this suggests that, true to the spirit of Henry VII, there was an increasing emphasis on ensuring that all involved recognized and experienced the authority

[43] J. G. Bellamy, *The Criminal Trial in Later Medieval England* (Toronto: University of Toronto Press, 1998), pp. 93–97; B. W. McLane, 'Juror Attitudes towards Local Disorder: The Evidence of the 1328 Lincolnshire Trailbaston Proceedings' in *Twelve Good Men and True: The Criminal Jury Trial in England, 1200–1800* edited by J.S. Cockburn and Thomas A. Green (Princeton: Princeton UP, 1988), pp. 54–55, 58; Barbara Hanawalt, *Crime and Conflict in English Communities, 1300–1348* (Cambridge MA: Harvard University Press, 1979), pp. 58–59; Powell, 'Jury Trial at Gaol Delivery,' pp. 100–103; J.S. Cockburn, ed. *Calendar of Assize Records: Home Circuit Indictments Elizabeth I and James I* (London: HMSO, 1985), pp. 175–181.

[44] See pp. 117, 307; Cockburn, ed. *Calendar of Assize Records*, 175–181. I have not been able to find statistics that would allow me to work out the equivalents for the earlier period.

[45] See Ian Archer, *Pursuit of Stability: Social Relations in Elizabethan London* (Cambridge: Cambridge University Press, 1991), p. 248.

of the courts, but this was balanced by agreement on all sides that, having recognized that authority, a substantial number of those convicted could be reprieved.[46]

Cockburn argues that in the mid-1580s a growth in the numbers in the system led to a 'mini-revolution' in criminal trials with the introduction of a form of plea-bargaining in felony cases and a renewed strictness in the administration of the reading test for benefit of clergy. He recognizes that this development 'fell short of a wholesale rationalization of trial and sentencing procedures. But in so far as the changes appear to have been initiated and co-ordinated by a central intelligence ... they may, perhaps mark something of a watershed in criminal administration.'[47] Both the problem and the tactics sound familiar, and it is entirely possible that the 1580s saw a new surge in convictions and/or mitigations of the kind we saw forcing a reduction in the lengths of sentences in 1495, 1530, and perhaps the 1540s. But rather than being a watershed, these actions in the late sixteenth century were simply the last trickle of the flood of judicial innovation from the decades before 1540.

The changes after that date were mostly attempts to rescue some elements of a complex system which assumed that the ecclesiastical hierarchy and the justices were partners in a process which had been developed and refined over centuries, and in which criminals, lawyers, justices and clerics shared common assumptions about punishment, mitigation, and reconciliation. As those shared assumptions weakened, along with the institutions that supported and reflected them, the structures of criminal confinement which rested on them could not be sustained in any robust way. But two core mechanisms emerged from the vicissitudes and the experiments of the 1540s: benefit of clergy as the primary means of reprieving minor felons with some level of literacy, and pardons as the primary means of releasing them, and other minor felons, from their prisons. Together, benefit of clergy and circuit pardons became stable sources of mitigation for minor crimes and pitiable criminals, and, perhaps ironically, were part of the reason for the growth in conviction rates in the later sixteenth century. As it became apparent that convictions for felony did not automatically lead to execution it must have become easier to convict: justice was served by passing felons through the gauntlet of the courts, while mercy could be demonstrated by directing an appropriate proportion of the appropriate kind away from the gallows. Both were clearly dependent on the queen and on the justices of her courts.

[46] Assessments of the use of capital punishment in this period vary widely. Kesselring argues that the Tudor state 'used massive amounts of physical force': *Mercy and Authority*, p. 15, while Andy Wood points to the routine deployment of both capital and corporal violence 'in the physical, symbolic and ritual assertion of [the state's] authority': 'The Deep Roots of Albion's Fatal Tree: The Tudor State and the Monopoly of Violence', *History* 99 (2014), p. 406. Wood provides Hindle's estimate that 75,000 felons were hanged in England between 1530 and 1630: this seems high based on the numbers here. These qualitative judgements are hard to assess: for one opposed to capital punishment, any number of executions is too many, but there is no question that the state consistently executed far fewer felons than it was legally entitled to.

[47] Cockburn, 'Trial by the Book?', p. 78.

Bibliography

Primary Sources

Manuscript:

The National Archives

KB8
KB9
KB27
E36/2
E36/141
E101/421/5
C66 C146/7243
C82
C1
E101/42/5 E315/24
E101/61/88

MPB 1/49 (York)
MPC 1/64 (Southwark)
MPI 1/221 (Norwich)

SP1
SP2/N
SP2/O
STAC 2/29/198
STAC 2/31/150
STAC 2/20/26
STAC 2/20/100
STAC 2/24/299

Borthwick Institute

Abp Reg. 23: Thomas Rotherham.
https://archbishopsregisters.york.ac.uk/browse/registers?register_id=c247dt49c
Abp Reg. 25: Thomas Savage
https://archbishopsregisters.york.ac.uk/browse/registers?register_id=41687j72p
Abp Reg 26: Christopher Bainbridge
https://archbishopsregisters.york.ac.uk/browse/registers?register_id=fj236343m
Abp Reg 27: Thomas Wolsey
https://archbishopsregisters.york.ac.uk/browse/registers?register_id=wh246t141

British Library

BL Egerton 2104.A f.220
BL Lansdowne MS 24 ff. 206–7
MS Add 10106 f.34b
MS Add 25168

Hampshire RO

21M65/A1/9 Bishop William Edington's register

Lambeth Palace Library

Register of William Warham
Register of Thomas Cranmer
CM IV/197 Daniel Wyght, Clink

Norwich Record Office

NCR Case 9f/6
NCR Case 9g/9
NCR Case 9g/10
NCR Case 9g/11
NCR Case 9i/1

Staffordshire Record Office:

D(w)1734 J/1948 m.8
D(w)1734 J./1949 mm. 20d-21
D(w)1734 J./2032

Surrey History Centre

Loseley MS 927/3
Loseley MS 961/1-16
Loseley MS 962/1
Loseley MS 962/2

Westminster Abbey

WAM 33088
WAM 37456–7
WAM 64905–64913
WAM 9179

West Sussex Record Office

Ep.I/1/5: Robert Sherborne's register

Lincoln

Register of Bishop William Smith: LAO Episcopal Register XXIV
Register of Bishop John Longland: LAO Episcopal Register XXVI

Print

Archer, Margaret ed. *The Register of Bishop Philip Repingdon 1405–1419*. Vol. 1 & 2 Hereford: Lincoln Record Society, 1963; vol.3 Lincoln Record Society, 1982.

Bacon, Francis. *The History of the Reign of King Henry VII* ed. Jerry Weinberger. Ithaca: Cornell University Press, 1996.

Barker, Eric E. ed. *The Register of Thomas Rotherham, Archbishop of York, 1480–1500, vol. 1*. Canterbury and York Society vol. 69. Torquay: The Devonshire Press, 1976.

Bannister, Arthur Thomas ed. *Registrum Ricardi Mayew, Episcopi Herefordensis, 1504–16*. Canterbury and York Society vol. 27. London: Privately Printed, 1921.

Bannister, Arthur Thomas ed. *The Register of Charles Bothe, Bishop of Hereford, 1516–1535*. London: Wilson and Phillips, 1921.

Bannister, Arthur Thomas ed. *Registrum Thome Myllyng, Episcopi Herefordensis, 1474–1492*. Canterbury and York Society vol. 26. London: Privately Printed, 1920.

Calendar of the Close Rolls Preserved in the Public Record Office: Henry VII. Vol. 2 London: HMSO, 1963.

Chisolm-Batten, Edmund ed. *The Register of Richard Fox while Bishop of Bath and Wells, A.D. 1492–1494*. London: Privately printed, 1889.

Chitty, Herbert transcr. & ed. *Registra Stephani Gardiner et Johannis Poynet Episcoporum Wintoniensium*. Canterbury and York Society vol. 37. Oxford: Oxford University Press, 1930.

Church Authority and Power in Medieval and Early Modern Britain: The Episcopal Registers. Harvester Press, 1983–87. Microform.

Cockburn, J.S. ed. *Calendar of Assize Records: Home Circuit Indictments Elizabeth I and James I: Introduction*. London: HMSO, 1985.

Dasent, John Roche ed. *Acts of the Privy Council of England Volume 5, 1554–1556*. London: Her Majesty's Stationary Office, 1892.

Douglas, David and George Greenaway ed. *English Historical Documents 1042–1189*. 2nd ed. London: Routledge, 1981.

Du Boulay, F.R.H. ed. *Registrum Thome Bourgchier, Cantuariensis Archiepiscopi, 1454–86*. Canterbury and York Society vol. 54. Oxford: Oxford University Press, 1957.

Fitzherbert, Antony (attributed). *Boke of Justices of Peas*. London: Pynson, 1505. STC (2nd ed.) 14862.

Fowler, J.T. ed. *Rites of Durham*. Surtees Society vol. 107. London: Bernard Quaritch, 1964.

Hector, L.C. and Barbara Harvey ed. and trans. *The Westminster Chronicle 1381–1394*. Oxford: Clarendon Press, 1982.

Hemmant, M. ed. *Select Cases in the Exchequer Chamber vol. 2: 1461–1509*. SS vol. 64. London: Bernard Quaritch, 1948.

Hinde, Gladys ed. *The Registers of Cuthbert Tunstall, Bishop of Durham 1530–59 and James Pilkington, Bishop of Durham 1561-76*. Surtees Society vol. 161. Durham and London: Privately Printed, 1952.

Hockey, Dom. S.F. ed. *The Register of William Edington, Bishop of Winchester 1346–1366* part 2. Hampshire Record Series vol. 8 Hampshire Record Office, 1987.

Horn, Joyce M. ed. *The Register of Robert Hallum, Bishop of Salisbury 1407–17*. Canterbury & York Society vol. 72. Torquay: The Devonshire Press, 1982.

Horwood, Alfred J. ed. *YB 30 & 31 Edw. I*. Rolls Series. London: Longmans etc., 1863.

Howden, Marjories Peers ed. *The Register of Richard Fox, Lord Bishop of Durham, 1494–1501*. Surtees Society vol.147. Durham: Andrews & Co., 1932.

Hughes, Paul L. and James F. Larkin ed. *Tudor Royal Proclamations vol. II: The Later Tudors*. New Haven: Yale University Press, 1969.

Hughes, Paul L. and James F. Larkin ed. *Tudor Royal Proclamations vol. I: The Early Tudors*. New Haven: Yale University Press, 1964.

Hunnisett, R.F. ed. *Sussex Coroners' Inquests 1485–1558*. Sussex Record Society vol. 74. Lewes, 1985.

Hunnisett, R.F. ed. *Calendar of Nottinghamshire Coroners' Inquests 1485–1558*. Thoroton Society Record Series vol. 25. Nottingham: Derry and Sons, 1969.

Journal of the House of Commons: Volume 1, 1547–1629. London: HMSO, 1802.

Kaye, J.M. ed. *Placita Corone or La Corone Pledee devant Justices*. Selden Society Supplementary Series vol. 4. London: Selden Society, 1966.

Knighton, C.S. ed. *Acts of the Dean and Chapter of Westminster 1543–1609*. Part Two: 1560–1609. Woodbridge, Suffolk: Boydell Press, 1999.

Knighton, C.S. *Acts of the Dean and Chapter of Westminster 1543–1609, Part One: The First Collegiate Church 1543–1556*. Woodbridge, Suffolk: Boydell Press, 1997.

Loengard, Janet ed. *London Viewers and Their Certificates, 1508–1558: Certificates of the Sworn Viewers of the City of London*. London Record Society Publications vol. 26. London: London Record Society, 1989.

Lower, Mark Antony ed. *The Chronicle of Battle Abbey from 1066 to 1176*. London: J.R. Smith, 1851.

Madge, Francis Thomas and Herbert Chitty ed. & transcr. *Registrum Thome Wolsey Cardinalis Ecclesie Wintoniensis administratoris*. Canterbury and York Society vol. 32. Oxford: Oxford University Press, 1926.

Maxwell-Lyte, Henry ed. *The Registers of Thomas Wolsey, Bishop of Bath and Wells 1518–1523, John Clerke, Bishop of Bath and Wells 1523–1541, William Knight Bishop of Bath and Wells 1541–1547 and Gilbert Bourne Bishop of Bath and Wells 1554–1559*. Somerset Record Society vol. 55. Frome: Butler and Tanner, 1940.

Maxwell-Lyte, Henry ed. *The Registers of Robert Stillington Bishop of Bath & Wells 1466–1491*. Somerset Record Society vol. 52. 1937

McGlynn, Margaret ed. *The Rights and Liberties of the English Church: Readings from the pre-Reformation Inns of Court*. SS vol. 129. London: Selden Society, 2016.

Nichols, J.G. ed. *The Diary of Henry Machyn*. Camden Soc. Vol. 42. London: Camden Society, 1848.

Powicke, F.M. and C.R. Cheney ed. *Councils and Synods, with Other Documents Relating to the English Church*. 2 vols. in 4. Oxford: Clarendon Press, 1964–81.

Rastell, William. *A Collection in English, of the statutes now in force*. London, 1594. STC 221:01.

Richardson, H.G. and G.O. Sayles ed. *Rotuli Parliamentorum Anglie Hactenus inediti*. Camden Society 3rd ser. vol. 51. London: Royal Historical Society, 1935.

Rotuli Parliamentorum: ut et Petitiones, et Placita in Parliamento. 8 vols. London, 1780–1832.

Rymer, Thomas ed. *Foedera, Conventiones, Literae . . .*, 20 vols. London: 1704–1735.

Sayles, G.O. ed. 'A Fifteenth-century Law Reading in English.' *Scripta Diversa*, 301–312. London: Hambledon Press, 1982.

Sayles, G.O. ed. *Select Cases in the Court of King's Bench* vol. VII, SS vol. 88. London: Bernard Quaritch, 1971.

Searle, Eleanor ed. and trans. *The Chronicle of Battle Abbey*. Oxford: Clarendon Press, 1980.

Sharpe, Reginald R. ed. *Calendar of Letter-Books of the city of London: K: Henry VI*. London: HMSO, 1911. [https://www.british-history.ac.uk/london-letter-books/volk accessed March 6, 2022].

Sneyd, Charlotte Augusta trans. *A Relation, or Rather a True Account, of the Island of England . . . about the Year 1500*. Camden Society vol. 37. London: John Bowyer Nichols & Son, 1847.

Spelman, Sir John. *John Spelman's Reading on Quo Warranto* ed. J.H. Baker. SS vol. 113. London: Selden Society, 1997.

Statham, Nicholas. *Statham's Abridgement of the Law* trans. Margaret Center Klingelsmith. Repr. Clark, New Jersey, The lawbook Exchange, 2009.

Staunford, William. *Les Plees del Coron*. London: Richard Tottell, 1557. Repr. Clark, New Jersey: The Lawbook Exchange, 2006.

Stevenson, Janet H. ed. *The Register of Edward Story, Bishop of Chichester, 1478–1503*. Woodbridge, Suffolk: The Boydell Press for the Canterbury and York Society, 2016.

Stubbs, William ed. *Chronicles of the Reigns of Edward I and Edward II vol. 1: Annales Londinienses and Annales Paulini*. London: HMSO, 1882, Kraus Repr. 1965.

Sutherland, Donald W. ed. *The Eyre of Northamptonshire 3–4 Edw. III* vol. 1, SS vol. 97. London: Selden Society, 1983.

Swanson, R.N. ed. *The Register of John Catterick, Bishop of Coventry and Lichfield 1415–1419*. Canterbury & York Society vol. 77. Woodbridge, Suffolk: Boydell Press, 1990.

Tawney, R.H. and Eileen Power ed. *Tudor Economic Documents* vol. III. London: Longmans, Green and Co., 1924.

Thomas, A.H. and I.D. Thornley ed. *The Great Chronicle of London*. London: G.W. Jones, 1938.

Thomas of Marlborough. *History of the Abbey of Evesham* ed. Jane Sayers and Leslie Watkiss. Oxford: Clarendon Press, 2003.

Tingey, J.C. ed. *The Records of the City of Norwich* vol. 2. London: Jarrold & Sons, 1910.

Vergil, Polydore. *The Anglica Historia of Polydore Vergil, AD 1485–1537* ed. and trans. Denys Hay. Camden Society vol. 74. London: Royal Historical Society, 1950.

Wilkins, David ed. *Concilia Magnae Britanniae et Hiberniae*. 4 vols. London, 1737.

Whittaker, W.J. ed. *The Mirror of Justices* SS vol. 7. London: Bernard Quaritch, 1895.

Wright, David ed. *The Register of John Blyth, Bishop of Salisbury, 1493–1499*. Chippenham: Wiltshire Record Society, 2015.

Secondary Sources

Archer, Ian. *Pursuit of Stability: Social Relations in Elizabethan London*. Cambridge: Cambridge University Press, 1991.

Aston, Margaret. *Thomas Arundel: A Study of Church Life in the Reign of Richard II*. Oxford: Clarendon Press, 1967.

Baker, John H. *The Men of Court 1440 to 1550: A Prosopography of the Inns of Court and Chancery and the Courts of Law*. 2 vols. SS Suppl. Ser. vol. 18. London: Selden Society, 2012.

Baker, John H. *An Introduction to English Legal History*, 4th ed. Oxford: Oxford University Press, 2007.

Baker, John H. *Oxford History of the Laws of England: vol. 6 1483–1558*. Oxford: Oxford University Press, 2007.

Baker, John H. 'Benefit of Clergy in England and its Secularization 1450–1550.' *'Ins Wasser geworfen und Ozeane durchquert': Festschrift für Knut Wolfgang Nörr* ed. Mario Ascheri, 27–38. Köln: Böhlau, 2003.

Baker, John H. 'Some Early Newgate Reports (1315–28).' *Law Reporting in England* ed. Chantal Stebbings, 35–53. London: Hambledon, 1995.

Baker, John H. 'The English Law of Sanctuary.' *Ecclesiastical Law Journal* 2 (1990): 8–13.

Bates, J. C. 'Edward Leche - a recidivist criminous clerk.' *Nottingham Medieval Studies* 30 (1986): 97–100.

Bedford, W.K.R. and Richard Holbeche. *The Order of the Hospital of St. John of Jerusalem*. London: F.E. Robinson and Co., 1902.

Beattie, J. M. *Crime and the Courts in England 1660–1800*. Princeton: Princeton University Press, 1986.

Bellamy, John G. *Strange Inhuman Deaths: Murder in Tudor England*. Westport, Conn, London: Praeger, 2005.

Bellamy, John G. *The Criminal Trial in Later Medieval England*. Toronto: University of Toronto Press, 1998.

Bellamy, John G. *Crime and Public Order in England in the Later Middle Ages*. Toronto: University of Toronto Press, 1973.

Bernard, G.W. *The Late Medieval English Church: Vitality and Vulnerability Before the Break with Rome*. New Haven: Yale University Press, 2012.

Bevan, Amanda. 'The Henrician Assizes and the Reformation.' *The Political Context of Law: Proceedings of the Seventh British Legal History Conference* ed. Richard Eales and David Sullivan, 61–76. London: Hambledon Press, 1987.

Blatcher, Marjorie. *The Court of King's Bench 1450–1550: A Study in Self-Help*. London: The Athlone Press, 1978.

Bowker, Margaret. *The Henrician Reformation: The Diocese of Lincoln under John Longland 1521–1547*. Cambridge: Cambridge University Press, 1981.

Brand, Paul. 'The Making of English Thirteenth-century Legislation: Some New Evidence.' *Law in the City: Proceedings of the Seventeenth British Legal History Conference, London, 2005* ed. Andrew Lewis, Paul Brand, and Paul Mitchell, 42–53. Dublin: Four Courts Press, 2007.

Brand, Paul. *Kings, Barons and Justices: The Making and Enforcement of Legislation in Thirteenth-Century England*. Cambridge: Cambridge University Press, 2003.

Brand, Paul. *The Making of the Common Law*. London: Hambledon Press, 1992.

Brayshay, Mark. *Land Travel and Communications in Tudor and Stuart England: Achieving a Joined-up Realm*. Liverpool: Liverpool University Press, 2014.

Britnell, Richard ed. *Pragmatic Literacy, East and West 1200–1330*. Woodbridge: Boydell, 1997.

Burrow, Colin 'Tudor Sanctuaries.' *Essays in Criticism* 41 (1991): 51–61.

Bush, M.L. *The Government Policy of Protector Somerset*. Montreal: McGill-Queen's University Press, 1975.

Butler, Sara M. *Pain, Penance, and Protest: Peine Forte et Dure in Medieval England*. Cambridge: Cambridge University Press, 2022.

Butler, Sara M. *Forensic Medicine and Death Investigation in Medieval England*. New York: Routledge, 2015.

Camargo, Martin. 'If You Can't Join Them, Beat Them: or, When Grammar Met Business Writing (in Fifteenth-Century Oxford).' *Letter-Writing Manuals and Instruction from Antiquity to the Present* ed. Carol Poster and Linda Mitchell, 67–87. Columbia: University of South Carolina Press, 2007.

Cannon, Debbie. 'London Pride: Citizenship and the Fourteenth-Century Custumals of the City of London. *Learning and Literacy in Late Medieval England and Abroad* ed. Sarah Rees Jones, 179–198. Utrecht Studies in Mediaeval Literacy, 3. Turnhout: Brepols, 2003.

Cavill, P.R. 'Polydore Vergil and the first English Parliament.' *Writing the History of Parliament in Tudor and Early Stuart England* ed. Paul Cavill and Alexandra Gajda, 37–59. Manchester: Manchester University Press, 2018.

Cavill, P.R. 'Preaching on Magna Carta at the End of the Fifteenth Century: John Alcock's Sermon at Paul's Cross.' *The Fifteenth Century* XV: Writing, Records and Rhetoric ed. Linda Clark, 169–189. Woodbridge: Boydell, 2017.

Cavill, P.R. 'A Perspective on the Church-State Confrontation of 1515: The Passage of 4 Henry VIII, c.2.' *Journal of Ecclesiastical History* 63 (2012): 655–670.

Cavill, P.R. '"The Enemy of God and His Church": James Hobart, Praemunire, and the Clergy of Norwich Diocese.' *The Journal of Legal History* 32.2 (2011): 127–150.

Cavill, P.R. 'The Enforcement of the Penal Statutes in the 1490s: some new evidence.' *Historical Research* 82 (2009), 484.

Cheney, Christopher Robert. 'The Punishment of Felonous Clerks.' *English Historical Review* 51 (1936): 215–236.

Cockburn, J.S. and Thomas A. Green ed. *Twelve Good Men and True: The Criminal Jury Trial in England, 1200–1800*. Princeton: Princeton UP, 1988.

Cockburn, J.S. 'Trial by the Book? Fact and Theory in the Criminal Process, 1558–1625.' *Legal Records and the Historian* ed. J.H. Baker, 60–79. London: Royal Historical Society, 1978.

Cockburn, J.S. *A History of English Assizes 1558–1714*. Cambridge: Cambridge University Press, 1972.

Cooper, W.R. 'Richard Hunne'. *Reformation* 1 (1996): 221–251.

Cox, J. Charles, *The Sanctuaries and Sanctuary Seekers of Medieval England*. London: George Allen & Sons, 1911.

Cullum, P. H. 'Learning to be a man, learning to be a priest in late medieval England.' *Learning and Literacy in Late Medieval England and Abroad* ed. Sarah Rees Jones, 135–153. Utrecht Studies in Mediaval Literacy, 3. Turnhout: Brepols, 2003.

Davies, C.S.L. 'Slavery and Protector Somerset; the Vagrancy Act of 1547.' *The Economic History Review* n.s. 19.3 (1966): 533–549.

Deller, William S. 'The Texture of Literacy in the Testimonies of late-medieval English Proof-of-age jurors.' *Journal of Medieval History* 38:2 (2012): 207–224.

Dodd, Gwilym. 'The Spread of English in the Records of Central Government, 1400–1430.' *Vernacularity in England and Wales c. 1300–1550* ed. Elisabeth Salter and Helen Wicker, 225–266. Utrecht Studies in Medieval Literacy, 17. Turnhout: Brepols, 2011.

Dohar, William J. *The Black Death and Pastoral Leadership*. Philadelphia: University of Pennsylvania Press, 1995.

Draper, G.M. 'Writing English, French and Latin in the Fifteenth Century: A Regional Perspective.' *Conflicts, Consequences and the Crown in the Late Middle Ages* ed. Linda Clark, 21–35. Woodbridge: Boyell Press, 2007.

Elton, G.R. *Reform and Renewal: Thomas Cromwell and the Common Weal*. Cambridge: Cambridge University Press, 1973.

Elton, G.R. *England, 1200–1640*. Ithaca and London: Cornell University Press, 1969.

Elton, G.R. *England under the Tudors*. London: Methuen, 1955.

Emden, A.B. *A Biographical Register of the University of Cambridge to 1500*. Cambridge: Cambridge University Press, 1963.

Everett, Michael. *The Rise of Thomas Cromwell: Power and Politics in the Reign of Henry VII*. New Haven: Yale University Press, 2015.

Ewen, Lorna. 'Debtors, Imprisonment and the privilege of Girth.' *Perspectives in Scottish Social History* ed. Leah Leneman, 53–68. Aberdeen: Aberdeen University Press, 1988.

Firth, C.B. 'Benefit of Clergy in the Time of Edward IV.' *E.H.R.* 32 (1917): 175–191.

Fleming, P. 'Sanctuary and Authority in pre-Reformation Bristol.' In *Historic Churches and Church life in Bristol: Essays in Memory of Elizabeth Ralph 1911–2000* ed. Joseph Harold Bettey, 73–84. Gloucester: Bristol and Gloucestershire Archaeological Society, 2001.

Fleming, P. 'Conflict and Urban Government in Later Medieval England: St Augustine's Abbey and Bristol.' *Urban History* 27 (2000): 339–342.

Foster, Andrew. 'Bishops, Church and State, c.1530–1646.' In *The Oxford History of Anglicanism, vol. 1: Reformation and identity c. 1520–1662* ed. Anthony Milton, 84–102. Oxford: Oxford University Press, 2017.

Freeman, Jessica. 'And he abjured the realm of England, never to return.' *Freedom of Movement in the Middle Ages: Proceedings of the 2003 Harlaxton Symposium* ed. Peregrine Horden, 287–304. Harlaxton Medieval Studies, 15. Donington: Shaun Tyas, 2007.

Gee, Stacey. 'Parochial Libraries in Pre-Reformation England.' *Learning and Literacy in Late Medieval England and Abroad* ed. Sarah Rees Jones, 199–222. Utrecht Studies in Press, 1969. Mediaval Literacy, 3. Turnhout: Brepols, 2003.

Gorski, Richard. 'Justices and Injustice? England's Local Officials in the Later Middle Ages.' *Outlaws in medieval and early modern England: crime, government and society, c.1066–c.1600* ed. John C. Appleby and Paul Dalton, 55–74. Farnham: Ashgate, 2009.

Green, Thomas A. *Verdict According to Conscience: Perspectives on the English Criminal Trial Jury, 1200–1800*. Chicago: University of Chicago Press, 1985.

Green, Thomas A. 'The Jury and the English Law of Homicide, 1200–1600.' *Michigan Law Review* 74 (1976): 413–499.

Gregory-Abbott, Candace. 'Sacred Outlaws: Outlawry and the Medieval Church.' *Outlaws in medieval and early modern England: crime, government and society, c.1066–c.1600* ed. John C. Appleby and Paul Dalton, 75–89. Farnham: Ashgate, 2009.

Griffiths, Ralph Alan. 'William Wawe and his gang, 1427'. *Proceedings of the Hampshire Field Club & Archaeological Society* 33 (1976): 89–93.

Groebner, Valentin. *Who Are You? Identification, Deception, and Surveillance in Early Modern Europe*, trans. Mark Kyburz and John Peck. New York: Zone Books, 2007.

Gunn, Steven. *Henry VII's New Men and the Making of Tudor England*. Oxford: Oxford University Press, 2016.

Gunn, Steven. 'Edmund Dudley and the Church.' *Journal of Ecclesiastical History* 51 (2000): 509–526.

Guth, DeLloyd. 'Introduction: Formulary and Literacy as keys to unlocking late-medieval law.' *Écrit et Pouvoir dans les Chancelleries Médiévales: Espace Français, Espace Anglais* ed. Kouky Fianu and deLloyd J. Guth, 1–12. Louvain-la-Neuve: Fédération Internationale des Instituts d'Études Médiévales, 1997.

Hall, David. 'The Sanctuary of St. Cuthbert.' *St. Cuthbert, his Cult and his Community to AD 1200* ed. Gerald Bonner, David Rollason, and Clare Stancliffe, 425–436. Woodbridge: Boydell, 1989.

Hallam, Henry. *A View of the State of Europe during the Middle Ages*. 2 vols. London, 1818.

Hanawalt, Barbara. *Crime and Conflict in English Communities, 1300–1348*. Cambridge MA: Harvard University Press, 1979.

Hanawalt, Barbara. 'The Female Felon in Fourteenth-Century England.' *Viator* 5 (1974): 253–268.

Hart, Rev. A. Tindal. 'Part II: The Reformation and its Aftermath 1474–1660.' *A House of Kings: The Official History of Westminster Abbey* ed. Edward Carpenter, 87–175. New York: The John Day Company, 1966.

Harvey, Barbara. *The Obedientiaries of Westminster Abbey and their Financial Records c. 1275–1540*. Woodbridge, Suffolk: Boydell, 2002.

Harvey, Barbara. *Living and Dying in England 1100–1540: The Monastic Experience*. Oxford: Clarendon Press, 1993.

Harvey, P.D.A. *Maps in Tudor England*. London: The Public Record Office and The British Library, 1993.

Hayes, Rosemary C.E. "Ancient Indictments' for the North of England, 1461–1509.' *The North of England in the Age of Richard III* ed. A.J. Pollard, 19–45. New York: St. Martins, 1996.

Hay, Douglas. 'Property, Authority and the Criminal Law.' *Albion's Fatal Tree: Crime and Society in Eighteenth-Century England* ed. Douglas Hay et al., 17–63. New York: Pantheon Books, 1975.

Hay, Douglas. 'The Criminal Prosecution in England and its Historians.' *The Modern Law Review* 47.1 (1984): 1–29.

Heal, Felicity. 'The Tudors and Church Lands: Economic Problems of the Bishopric of Ely during the Sixteenth Century.' *Economic History Review* 26.2 (1973): 198–217.

Heal, Felicity. *Of Prelates and Princes: A Study of the Economic and Social Position of the Tudor Episcopate*. Cambridge: Cambridge University Press, 1980.

Heath, Peter. *The English Parish Clergy on the Eve of the Reformation*. Toronto: University of Toronto Press, 1969.

Helmholz, R. H. 'The Ius Commune and Sanctuary for Insolvent Debtors in England.' *Panta rei: studi dedicati a Manlio Bellomi* ed. Orazio Condorelli. 5 vols. (Roma: Il Cigno, 2004), Vol. 2, 581–593.

Helmholz, R. H. 'Canon Law and the English Common Law.' *Canon Law and the Law of England*, 1–19. London: Hambledon, 1987.

Herrup, Cynthia. 'Negotiating Grace.' *Politics, Religion and Popularity in Early Stuart Britain* ed. Thomas Cogswell, Richard Cust, and Peter Lake, 124–140. Cambridge: Cambridge University Press, 2002.

Honeybourne, Marjorie Blanche. 'The Sanctuary Boundaries and Environs of Westminster Abbey and the college of St Martin le Grand.' *Journal of the British Archaeological Association*, 2nd ser., 38 (1932): 316–333.

Hope, W.H. St. John and Harold Brakspear. 'The Cistercian Abbey of Beaulieu in the County of Southampton.' *The Archaeological Journal* 63 (1906): 129–186.

Houlbrooke, Ralph. 'Refoundation and Reformation, 1538–1628.' *Norwich Cathedral: Church, City and Diocese 1096–1996* ed. Ian Atherton et al., 507–539. London: Hambledon, 1996.

Houlbrooke, Ralph. 'The Decline of Ecclesiastical Jurisdiction under the Tudors.' *Continuity and Change: Personnel and Administration of the Church of England 1500–1642* ed. Rosemary O'Day and Felicity Heal, 239–257. Leicester, 1976.

Hunnisett, R.F. 'The Last Sussex Abjurations: A Postscript.' *Sussex Archaeological Collections* 103 (1965): 49–52.

Hunnisett, R.F. 'The Last Sussex Abjurations.' *Sussex Archaeological Collections* 102 (1964): 39–51

Hunnisett, R.F. *The Medieval Coroner*. Cambridge: Cambridge University Press, 1961.

Hunt, William. *The Somerset Diocese, Bath and Wells*. London: SPCK, 1885.

Hurnard, Naomi. *The King's Pardon for Homicide before A.D. 1307*. Oxford: Clarendon Press, 1969.

Hyams, Paul. *Rancor and Reconciliation in Medieval England*. London and Ithaca: Cornell University Press, 2003.

Ives, E.W. *The Common Lawyers of pre-Reformation England*. Cambridge: Cambridge University Press, 1983.

Ives, E.W. 'Crime, Sanctuary and Royal Authority under Henry VIII: The Exemplary Sufferings of the Savage Family.' *On the Laws and Customs of England* ed. Morris S. Arnold et al., 296–320. Chapel Hill: University of North Carolina Press, 1981.

Johnson, Tom. *Law in Common: Legal Cultures in Late-Medieval England*. Oxford: Oxford University Press, 2020.

Jones, Sarah Rees. 'Civic Literacy in Later Medieval England.' In *Writing and the Administration of Medieval Towns* (Medieval Urban Literacy I) ed. Marco Mostert and Anna Adamska, 219–230. Turnhout: Brepols, 2014.

Jones, William R. 'Sanctuary, Exile, and Law: The Fugitive and Public Authority in Medieval England and Modern America.' *Essays on English Law and the American Experience* ed. William R. Jones et al., 19–41. College Station: Texas A&M University Press, 1994.

Jones, William R. 'The Court of the Verge: The Jurisdiction of the Steward and Marshal of the Household in Later Medieval England.' *Journal of British Studies* 10. 1 (1970): 1–29.

Jordan, William C. *From England to France.* Princeton: Princeton University Press, 2015.

Jordan, William C. 'A Fresh Look at Medieval Sanctuary.' *Law and the Illicit in Medieval Europe*, ed. Ruth Mazo Karras, Joel Kaye, and E. Ann Matter, 17–32. Philadelphia: U Pennsylvania Press, 2008.

Jordan, W.K. *Edward VI: The Young King.* Cambridge MA: Harvard University Press, 1968.

Kaufman, Peter Iver. *The 'Polytyque Churche': Religion and Early Tudor Political Culture, 1485–1516.* Macon GA: Mercer University Press, 1986.

Kaufman, Peter Iver. 'Henry VII and Sanctuary.' *Church History* 53 (1984): 465–476.

Kempe, Alfred John. *Historical Notices of the Collegiate Church or Royal Free Chapel and Sanctuary of St Martin le Grand: also, observations on the different kinds of sanctuary formerly recognised by the Common Law.* London: Longmans, 1825.

Kesselring, K.J. *Making Murder Public: Homicide in Early Modern England, 1480–1680.* Oxford: Oxford University Press, 2019.

Kesselring, K.J. 'Bodies of Evidence: Sex and Murder (or Gender and Homicide) in early Modern England, c.1500–1680.' *Gender & History* 27 (2015): 245–262.

Kesselring, K.J. 'A draft of the 1531 'Acte for poisoning'.' *English Historical Review* 116 (2001): 894–899.

Kesselring, K.J. 'Abjuration and its Demise: The Changing Face of Royal Justice in the Tudor Period.' *Canadian Journal of History* 34 (1999): 345–358.

King, E.J. *The Grand Priory of the Order of the Hospital of St. John of Jerusalem in England.* London: Fleetway Press, 1924.

Kleineke, Hans. 'Poachers and Gamekeepers: Four Fifteenth-century West Country Criminals. *Outlaws in Medieval and Early Modern England: Crime, Government and Society, c.1066–c.1600* ed. John C. Appleby and Paul Dalton, 129–147. Farnham: Ashgate, 2009.

Lacey, Helen. *The Royal Pardon: Access to Mercy in Fourteenth-Century England.* Woodbridge: York Medieval Press, 2009.

Lambert, T.B. 'The Evolution of Sanctuary in Medieval England.' *Legalism: Anthropology and History* ed. Paul Dresch and Hannah Skoda, 115–144. Oxford: Oxford University Press, 2012.

Lander, J. R. *English Justices of the Peace 1461–1509.* Gloucester, UK: Alan Sutton, 1989.

Langbein, John H. *Prosecuting Crime in the Renaissance.* Cambridge, MA: Harvard University Press, 1974.

Leach, Doreen. 'The Turners of Medieval London' *Medieval Prosopography* 28 (2013) 105–136.

Lehmberg, Stanford. *The Later Parliaments of Henry VIII, 1536–1547.* Cambridge: Cambridge University Press, 1977.

Lehmberg, Stanford. 'Parliamentary attainder in the reign of Henry VIII.' *Historical Journal* 18:4 (1975): 675–702.

Lehmberg, Stanford. *The Reformation Parliament, 1529–1536.* Cambridge, Cambridge University Press, 1970.

Lindenbaum, Sheila. ' Literate Londoners and Liturgical Change: Sarum Books in City Parishes after 1414.' *London and the Kingdom: Essays in Honour of Caroline M. Barron* ed. Matthew Davies and Andrew Prescott, 384–399. Harlaxton Medieval Studies, 16. Donington: Shaun Tyas, 2008.

Loades, D.M. 'The Sanctuary'. *Westminster Abbey Reformed 1540–1640* ed. C.S. Knighton and Richard Mortimer, 75–93. Aldershot: Ashgate, 2003.

Dominic Luckett. 'Patronage, Violence and Revolt in the Reign of Henry VII.' *Crown, Government and People in the Fifteenth Century* ed. Rowena Archer, 145–160. New York: St. Martins' Press, 1995.

McAleer, John Philip. 'The North Portal of Durham Cathedral and the Problem of 'Sanctuary' in Medieval Britain.' *Antiquaries Journal*, 81 (2001): 195–258.

McGlynn, Margaret. 'From Written Record to Bureaucratic Mind: Imagining a Criminal Record.' *Past and Present* 250 (2021): 55–86.

McGlynn, Margaret. 'Ecclesiastical Prisons and Royal Authority in the Reign of Henry VII.' *Journal of Ecclesiastical History* 70.4 (2019): 750–766.

McGlynn, Margaret. 'From Magna Carta to the Abridgements: The Naturalization of Benefit of Clergy.' *Challenges to Authority and the Recognition of Rights: From Magna Carta to Modernity* ed. Catharine MacMillan and Charlotte Smith, 37–54. Cambridge: Cambridge University Press, 2018.

McGlynn, Margaret. 'Idiosyncratic Books and Common Learning: Readings on Statutes at the Inns of Court.' *The Oxford Handbook to English Law and Literature, 1500–1625*, ed. Lorna Hutson, 41–60. Oxford: Oxford University Press, 2017.

McGlynn, Margaret. 'From Charter to Common Law: The Rights and Liberties of the pre-Reformation Church.' *Religion, Magna Carta and the Rule of Law* ed. Robin Griffith-Jones and Mark Hill QC, 53–69. Cambridge: Cambridge University Press, 2015.

McGlynn, Margaret. *The Royal Prerogative and the Learning of the Inns of Court*. Cambridge Studies in English Legal History. Cambridge: Cambridge University Press, 2003.

McHardy, A.K. 'Church Courts and Criminous Clerks in the Later Middle Ages.' *Medieval Ecclesiastical Studies in Honour of Dorothy M. Owen* ed. M.J. Franklin and Christopher Harper-Bill, 165–183. Woodbridge, Suffolk: Boydell, 1995.

McIntosh, Marjorie K. *Controlling Misbehaviour in England, 1370–1600*. Cambridge: Cambridge University Press, 1998.

McIntosh, Marjorie K. 'Finding Language for Misconduct: Jurors in Fifteenth-Century Local Courts.' *Bodies and Disciplines: Intersections of Literature and History in Fifteenth-Century England* ed. Barbara A. Hanawalt and David Wallace, 87–122. Minneapolis: University of Minnesota Press, 1996.

McKenzie, Andrea. "This Death Some Strong and Stout Hearted Man Doth Choose': The Practice of Peine Forte et Dure in Seventeenth- and Eighteenth-Century England.' *Law and History Review* 23 (2005): 279–313.

McLane, B. W. 'Juror Attitudes towards Local Disorder: The Evidence of the 1328 Lincolnshire Trailbaston Proceedings.' *Twelve Good Men and True: The Criminal Jury Trial in England, 1200–1800* ed. J.S. Cockburn and Thomas A. Green, 36–64. Princeton: Princeton UP, 1988.

McLaren, Mary Rose. 'Reading, Writing and Recording. Literacy and the London Chronicles in the Fifteenth Century.' *London and the Kingdom: Essays in Honour of Caroline M. Barron* ed. Matthew Davies and Andrew Prescott, 346–365. Harlaxton Medieval Studies, 16. Donington: Shaun Tyas, 2008.

McSheffrey, Shannon. 'Stranger Artisans and the London Sanctuary of St. Martin le Grand in the Reign of Henry VIII.' *Journal of Medieval and Early Modern Studies* 43 (2013): 545–571.

McSheffrey, Shannon. 'The Slaying of Sir William Pennington: Legal Narrative and the Late Medieval English Archive,' *Florilegium* 28 (2011): 169–203.

McSheffrey, Shannon. 'Sanctuary and the Legal Topography of Pre-Reformation London.' *Law and History Review* 27 (2009): 483–514.

Merritt, J.F. *The Social World of Early Modern Westminster: Abbey, Court and Community 1525–1640*. New York: Manchester University Press, 2005.

Molekamp, Femke: 'Popular reading and writing.' *The Ashgate research companion to popular culture in early modern England*; ed. Andrew Hadfield, Matthew Dimmock and Abigail Shinn, 59–74. Farnham: Ashgate, 2014.

Moran Cruz, Jo Ann Hoeppner. *The Growth of English Schooling, 1340–1548: Learning, Literacy, and Laicization in Pre-Reformation York Diocese*. Princeton: Princeton University Press, 1985.

Moreton, Charles. 'The 'Diary' of a Late Fifteenth-Century Lawyer.' In *Estrangement, Enterprise and Education in Fifteenth-Century England* ed. Sharon D. Michalove and A. Compton Reeves, 27–45. The Fifteenth-Century Series no. 5. Stroud, Gloucestershire: Sutton, 1998.

Mortimer, Richard. *Guide to the Muniments of Westminster Abbey*. Woodbridge, Suffolk: Boydell, 2012.

Musson, Anthony. 'Centre and Locality: Perceptions of the Assize Justices in Late Medieval England.' *Law, Governance, and Justice: New Views on Medieval Constitutionalism* ed. Richard W. Kaeuper with the assistance of Paul Dingman and Peter Sposato, 211–241. Medieval law and its practice, 14. Leiden: Brill, 2013.

Neville, Cynthia. 'The Courts of the Prior and the Bishop of Durham in the Later Middle Ages.' *History* 85 (2000): 216–231.

Neville, Cynthia. 'Common Knowledge of the Common Law in Later Medieval England.' *Canadian Journal of History* 29 (1994): 461–478.

Neville, Cynthia. 'Gaol Delivery in the Border Counties, 1439–1459: Some Preliminary Observations.' *Northern History* 19 (1983): 45–60.

O'Malley, Gregory. *The Knights Hospitaller of the English Langue, 1460–1565*. Oxford: Oxford University Press, 2005.

Page, William ed. *A History of the County of Warwick* vol. 2. London: Victoria County History 1908.

Palmer, Robert C. *Selling the Church: The English Parish in Law, Commerce and Religion, 1350–1550*. Chapel Hill: University of North Carolina Press, 2002.

Parkes, M.B. 'The Literacy of the Laity.' *Scribes, Scripts and Readers: Studies in the Communication, Presentation and Dissemination of Medieval Texts*, 275–297. London: Hambledon, 1991..

Post, J.B. 'Crime in Later Medieval England: Some Historiographical Limitations.' *Continuity and Change* 2 (1987): 211–224.

Post, J.B. 'Local Jurisdictions and Judgment of Death in Later Medieval England.' *Criminal Justice History* 4 (1983): 1–21.

Postles, David. 'Country *Clerici* and the Composition of English Twelfth- and Thirteenth-Century Private Charters.' *Charters and the Use of the Written Word in Medieval Society* ed. Karl Heidecker, 27–42. Turnhout: Brepols, 2000.

Powell, Edward. *Kingship, Law and Society: Criminal Justice in the Reign of Henry V*. Oxford: Clarendon Press, 1989.

Powell, Edward. 'Jury Trial at Gaol Delivery in the Late Middle Ages: The Midland Circuit, 1400–1429.' *Twelve Good Men and True: The Criminal Trial Jury in England, 1200–1800* ed. Thomas A. Green and J.S. Cockburn, 78–116. Princeton: Princeton University Press, 1988.

Powell, Edward. 'The Administration of Criminal Justice in Late-Medieval England: Peace Sessions and Assizes.' *The Political Context of Law: Proceedings of the Seventh British Legal History Conference* ed. Richard Eales and David Sullivan, 49–57. London: Hambledon Press, 1987.

Powell, Edward. 'The King's Bench in Shropshire and Staffordshire in 1414.' *Law, Litigants and the Legal Profession* ed. E.W Ives and A.H Manchester, 94–103. London: Royal Historical Society, 1983.

Pugh, Ralph B. 'The Duration of Criminal Trials in Medieval England.' *Law, Litigants and the Legal Profession* ed. E.W Ives and A.H Manchester, 104–115. London: Royal Historical Society, 1983.

Pugh, Ralph B. 'The Knights Hospitallers of England as Undertakers.' *Speculum* 56 (1981): 566–574.

Reynolds, Susan. 'Magna Carta 1297 and the legal use of literacy.' *Historical Research*, 62 (1989), 233–244.

Richardson, Malcolm. *Middle-Class Writing in Late Medieval London.* London: Routledge, 2010.

Robison, William B. 'Murder at Crowhurst: A Case Study in Early Tudor Law.' *Criminal Justice History* 9 (1988): 31–62.

Rosenwein, Barbara H. *Negotiating Space: Power, Restraint, and Privileges of Immunity in Early Medieval Europe*. London and Ithaca: Cornell University Press, 1999.

Roskell, J.S. 'Sir William Oldhall, Speaker in the Parliament of 1450–51.' *Nottingham Medieval Studies* 5 (1961): 87–112.

Rosser, Gervase. 'Sanctuary and social negotiation in medieval England.' In *The Cloister and the World: Essays on Medieval History in Honour of Barbara Harvey* ed. John Blair and Brian Golding, 57–79. Oxford: Clarendon Press, 1996.

Rosser, Gervase. *Medieval Westminster 1200–1540*. Oxford: Clarendon Press, 1989.

Samaha, Joel B. 'Hanging for Felony: The Rule of Law in Elizabethan Colchester.' *The Historical Journal* 21 (1978): 763–782.

Seipp, David J. 'Big History and the Hundred Year Test.' *Law and History Review* 34.4 (2016), 857–871.

Seipp, David J. 'Crime in the Year Books.' *Law Reporting in England* ed. Chantal Stebbings, 15–34. London: Hambledon, 1995.

Serjeantson, R.M and W.R.D Adkins ed. *A History of the County of Northampton* vol. 2. London: Victoria County History, 1906.

Shagan, Ethan. *Popular Politics and the English Reformation*. Cambridge: Cambridge University Press, 2003.

Shapiro, Barbara J. *A Culture of Fact: England 1550–1720*. Ithaca: Cornell University Press, 2000.

Sharpe, J.A. *Judicial Punishment in England*. London: Faber and Faber, 1990.

Shepard, Alexandra. *Accounting for Oneself: Worth, Status, and the Social Order in Early Modern England*. Oxford: Oxford University Press, 2015.

Shoemaker, Karl. *Sanctuary and Crime in the Middle Ages 400–1500*. New York: Fordham University Press, 2011.

Skeeters, Martha C. *Community and Clergy: Bristol and the Reformation c.1530–c.1570*. Oxford, Clarendon Press, 1993.

Sloane, Barney and Gordon Malcolm, *Excavations at the priory of the Order of the Hospital of St John of Jerusalem, Clerkenwell, London*. London: Museum of London Archaeology Service, 2004.

Smith, Carrie. 'Medieval Coroners' Rolls: Legal Fiction or Historical Fact?' *Courts, Counties and the Capital in the Later Middle Ages* ed. Diana E.S. Dunn, 93–115. Stroud: Sutton, 1996.

Stanley, Arthur Penhryn. *Historical Memorials of Westminster Abbey*. London: John Murray, 1868.

Storey, R.L. 'Malicious Indictments of Clergy in the Fifteenth Century.' *Medieval Ecclesiastical Studies in Honour of Dorothy M. Owen* ed. M.J. Franklin and Christopher Harper-Bill, 221–240. Woodbridge, Suffolk: Boydell, 1995.

Storey, R.L. 'Clergy and Common Law in the Reign of Henry IV.' *Medieval Legal Records Edited in Memory of C.A.F. Meekings*, ed. R.F. Hunnisett and J.B. Post, 347–351. London: HMSO, 1978.

Summerson, H.R.T. 'The Early Development of the Peine Forte et Dure.' *Law, Litigants and the Legal Profession* ed. E.W Ives and A.H Manchester, 116–125. London: Royal Historical Society, 1983.

Swanson, R.N. 'Profits, priests and people.' *The Parish in Late Medieval England* ed. Clive Burgess and Eamon Duffy, 146–159. Harlaxton Medieval Studies, 14. Donnington: Shaun Tyas, 2006.

Swanson, R.N. 'Problems of the Priesthood in pre-Reformation England.' *English Historical Review* 105 (1990): 845–869.

Swanson, R.N. *Church and Society in Late Medieval England*. Oxford: Basil Blackwell, 1989.

Tanner, Norman. 'The Cathedral and the City.' *Norwich Cathedral: Church, City and Diocese 1096–1996* ed. Ian Atherton et al., 255–280. London: Hambledon, 1996.

Thiery, Daniel. *Polluting the Sacred: Violence, Faith and the 'Civilizing' of Parishioners in Late Medieval England*. Later Medieval Europe, vol. 3. Leiden and Boston: Brill, 2009.

Thomson, John A.F. *The Early Tudor Church and Society, 1485–1529*. New York: Longman, 1993.

Thornley, I.D. 'Sanctuary in Medieval London.' *Journal of the British Archaeological Association* 2nd ser. 38 (1932): 293–315.

Trenholme, N.M. *The Right of Sanctuary in England*. Columbia MO: University of Missouri, 1903.

Truelove, Alison. 'Literacy.' *Gentry Culture in Late Medieval England* ed. Raluca Radulescu and Alison Truelove, 84–99. Manchester: Manchester University Press, 2005.

Truron, Walterus [sic], *Cornish Church Guide*. Truro: Oscar Blackford, 1928.

Uribe-Uran, Victor M. '"*Iglesia me Llamo*": Church Asylum and the Law in Spain and Colonial Spanish America.' *Comparative Studies in Society and History* 49.2 (2007): 446–472.

Westlake, H.F. *Westminster Abbey: The Church, Convent, Cathedral and College of St. Peter, Westminster* vol. 2. London: Philip Allan & Co., 1923.

Wood, Andy. 'The Deep Roots of Albion's Fatal Tree: The Tudor State and the Monopoly of Violence.' *History* 99 (2014): 403–417.

Wunderli, Richard M. *London Church Courts and Society on the Eve of the Reformation*. Cambridge, MA: The Medieval Academy of America, 1981.

Index

For the benefit of digital users, indexed terms that span two pages (e.g., 52–53) may, on occasion, appear on only one of those pages.

The manufacturer's authorised representative in the EU for product safety is Oxford University Press España S.A. of el Parque Empresarial San Fernando de Henares, Avenida de Castilla, 2 – 28830 Madrid (www.oup.es/en or product.safety@oup.com). OUP España S.A. also acts as importer into Spain of products made by the manufacturer.

www.ingramcontent.com/pod-product-compliance
Lightning Source LLC
LaVergne TN
LVHW011906200926
848484LV00002B/547

* 9 7 8 0 1 9 2 8 8 7 6 8 9 *